HANDBOOK OF HIV AND SOCIAL WORK

Principles, Practice, and Populations

EDITED BY

Cynthia Cannon Poindexter

WILEY

John Wiley & Sons, Inc.

Library of Congress Cataloging-in-Publication Data:

Handbook of HIV and social work : principles, practice, and populations / edited by Cynthia Cannon Poindexter.
   p.; cm.
  Includes bibliographical references and index.
  ISBN 978-0-470-26093-7 (pbk. : alk. paper)
    1. AIDS (Disease)–Social aspects. 2. Social service. I. Poindexter, Cynthia Cannon, 1954-
  [DNLM: 1. HIV Infections–psychology. 2. Counseling–methods. 3. Social Work–methods. WC 503.7
H2365 2010]
  MRA643.75.H36 2010
  362.196′9792—dc22

2009034008

Printed in the United States of America

10 9 8 7 6 5 4 3 2 1

HANDBOOK OF HIV AND SOCIAL WORK

To all the people living with HIV who have taught us all so much about living.

Contents

Foreword   Vincent J. Lynch   xi

Preface   xiii

About the Editor   xvii

About the Contributors   xix

Part One: HIV Basics and Social Work Principles   01

Chapter 1   **HIV History, Illness, Transmission, and Treatment**   03
Ryan M. Kull

Chapter 2   **Underlying Principles of Helping in the HIV Field**   31
Hugo Kamya

Chapter 3   **Cultural Competence and HIV**   41
Manoj Pardasani, Claudia Lucia Moreno, and Nicholas Robertson Forge

Chapter 4   **The Human Rights Framework Applied to HIV Services and Policy**   59
Cynthia Cannon Poindexter

Part Two: Social Work Practice   75

Chapter 5   **HIV-Related Case Management**   77
Douglas M. Brooks

Chapter 6   **HIV-Related Crisis Intervention and Counseling**   89
Michael P. Melendez

Chapter 7   **HIV Social Work Roles, Tasks, and Challenges in Health Care Settings**   103
Brian Giddens

Chapter 8   **HIV-Related Group Work and Family Support**   **123**
Patricia A. Stewart and Valerie Dixson-Anderson

Chapter 9   **Administration of HIV Services: Program
Development, Management, and Fund Development 143**
Dana B. Marlowe

Chapter 10   **HIV-Related Community Organizing
and Grassroots Advocacy**   **159**
Larry M. Gant

Chapter 11   **HIV-Related Political and Legislative Intervention**   **173**
Gary Bailey

Chapter 12   **HIV Prevention Innovations and Challenges**   **183**
Peter A. Newman

Part Three: Specific Vulnerable Populations   197

Chapter 13   **Women and HIV in the U.S.: From Invisible to
Self-Determined**   **199**
Sally Mason

Chapter 14   **HIV Prevention and Services for Gay, Bisexual,
and Other Men Who Have Sex with Men: Now
is Still the Time**   **211**
David J. Brennan and Winston Husbands

Chapter 15   **The Impact of HIV on Children and Adolescents**   **231**
Lori Wiener and Susan Taylor-Brown

Chapter 16   **HIV-Infected and HIV-Affected Midlife and Older
Persons**   **253**
Charles A. Emlet

Chapter 17   **HIV and Black and African American Communities
in the Twenty-first Century**   **271**
*Darrell P. Wheeler, Bernadette R. Hadden, Michael Lewis,
Laurens G. Van Sluytman, and Tyrone M. Parchment*

Chapter 18   **Latinos and HIV: A Framework to Develop
Evidence-Based Strategies**   **291**
Vincent Guilamo-Ramos, Alida Bouris, and Susan M. Gallego

Chapter 19 **HIV-Affected Caregivers** 311

Helen Land

Chapter 20 **Afterword: Looking Back, Looking Forward**
in HIV Social Work 327

Cynthia Cannon Poindexter and Nathan L. Linsk

Author Index 333
Subject Index 347

Foreword

Throughout the history of the HIV pandemic in the United States, a vast number of professionally trained social workers have provided critical psychosocial care to those infected or affected. However, there have been few HIV and AIDS textbooks, handbooks, or other published works that have been written *by* and *for* social workers. It has been a decade since the last such published contribution was released. Clearly, such a volume is long overdue. Many of us who authored or edited earlier social work HIV and AIDS volumes have either retired from our professional work or are close to retirement age. Other HIV social workers need to build on our earlier contributions. Now is the time to pass the baton to a new cadre of men and women who can advance the HIV knowledge base for social work practice, policy, education, and research.

Cynthia Cannon Poindexter has taken that baton and given us a remarkable edited volume that contains much information on HIV that every professional social worker needs to know in order to practice competently in today's complex world. Certainly, for the social worker committed to HIV social work practice as a specialty area, this volume is a must-have for one's professional library. I believe it will be the leading text that guides our work in this country for at least the next 5 to 10 years.

This important book is crisply organized and begins with four chapters that outline the basics of the disease and their relationship to social work practice (Part 1). We then are presented with a rich set of chapters that address the important and diverse HIV-related roles and tasks in which social work is involved in HIV service delivery (Part 2). The book concludes with several chapters that address very specific service delivery needs and practice approaches in working with those most vulnerable to HIV disease (Part 3).

In my role as founder and chair of the Annual National Conference on Social Work and HIV (in its twenty-second year as I write) I witness each year the hunger that our colleagues from across the country have for continuing education offerings that are produced *by* and *for* HIV social workers. Our extensive and diverse conference presentations each year fill that need to some degree, but they are not enough. Such offerings need to be augmented by various published works such as this one that will keep us informed and current about the ever-changing aspects of HIV practice today. This important book will help a great deal in addressing many of those unmet social work continuing education needs now and for the next several years of the pandemic. It will also provide inspiration for some of our younger colleagues to add to our knowledge base by writing other important contributions in the not too distant future. Many of the chapter contributors are longtime friends and social work colleagues who, like me, have worked in HIV since the early years of the pandemic. Others have more recently entered the field. All have in common the same degree of passion and commitment to this important work. This handbook builds a critical intergenerational bridge by linking tomorrow's leaders in HIV social work practice, policy, education, and research with those mentors who are rich with many years of practice wisdom. I commend the editor and all chapter authors for this much-needed and excellent addition to our HIV social work knowledge base.

Vincent J. Lynch, MSW, PhD
Boston College Graduate School of Social Work

Preface

This handbook on HIV-related social services is intended for social work and human services practitioners, managers, advocates, and students. We hope it is also useful for HIV-infected and HIV-affected persons. The chapter authors, all of whom have been involved in the HIV field for years as advocates, educators, case managers, counselors, or administrators, hope that their contributions will address the current realities of the HIV pandemic in North America almost 30 years after the disease was identified.

It is a shock for old-timers in the HIV field to meet young adults—as students, coworkers, friends, and neighbors—who have *never known* a world without HIV. We realize with disbelief that HIV is no longer the new disease that once captured the world's attention and became a focal point for the public's fears and prejudices. What happened to that "new emergency" we jumped to address? It seems to have grown old with us and to have become routine. Even though HIV has been around long enough to seem commonplace, we still know without a doubt that it cannot be taken for granted; it cannot be ignored. Even though HIV is becoming integrated into mainstream health and social service organizations, we know that the response to it cannot be like the response to any-thing else. HIV is not exactly like any other physical condition or social problem. The HIV pandemic is unlike any other health phenomenon in recorded history. Science has known of no other infectious, life-threatening, blood-borne, and sexually transmitted dis-ease that destroys the body's immune system, whose symptoms remain hidden for years, and that keeps the host alive long enough to spread the agent far and wide. Social science has not recently dealt with a disease as hidden, highly stigmatized, and full of religious, political, societal, economic, behavioral, or cultural barriers to ameliorating it. HIV calls for responses and skills that are HIV-specific. This handbook strives to begin to address those issues. Now that it is clear that the pandemic will be with us for many decades to come, what should the service, prevention, and advocacy responses be in light of what we now know?

We have seen two different HIV pandemics in the developed world. During the first 15 years or so, before the advent of combination antiretroviral therapy, the social serv-ice and social action response was to an extreme emergency. Everyone operated in crisis mode, needing to create systems and practice models quickly, yet still hoping that a vac-cine and a cure would be soon developed. In the earliest years, most efforts were made by small community-based advocacy organizations run by people directly affected by HIV and their allies. In the second 15 years of the pandemic, the medical progress made in a relatively short period of time in developed countries has been amazing: Death rates from HIV have plummeted. Advancements in treatment have shifted the required serv-ice and advocacy responses away from crisis intervention to a more traditional long-term approach.

Still, over the past decade some new challenges have appeared. One challenge has been that a social service system originally developed to address acute needs, crises, and death has struggled to adapt rapidly enough to the realities of today's pandemic, which comprises an ever-growing number of people who are living longer and longer with more and more chronic conditions. As Peter Piot, the former head of UNAIDS, has stated, we must shift "from crisis management to sustained strategic response" if we are to address the pandemic in its third decade (2006, p. 526). A second challenge has been that the availability of, competition for, and reliance on federal and state funding has led many HIV organizations to become more bureaucratic and less aligned with the infected and affected communities. Third, early prevention strategies were based on the reality that most people with HIV did not live long, and thus they focused on short-term changes in individual behavior to disrupt further spread of the virus in the hope that a vaccine or cure would be around the corner. We were therefore not prepared to offer realistic, alternative safer sex messages when advances in medical treatment led to a much longer life expectancy and everyone with HIV realized they were expected to modify their sexual and injecting behavior for decades. Fourth, we are challenged by a popular view that HIV is now manageable and "no big deal" due in large part to pharmaceutical advertisements that foster the myth of a cure. These realities, along with media silence, public and political apathy, and educational failure, have created a recipe for continued disaster.

In a changing HIV landscape, some things do appear constant: HIV stigma still keeps people from getting tested and disclosing their HIV status to each other; universal access to treatment still seems a distant dream; it is clear that there will probably be no cure; the federal government still refuses to fund syringe exchange programs; developing a vaccine seems to be impossible; and our efforts toward prevention have fallen alarmingly short. Even though the amount of attention given to HIV may convince some that the problem is under control, that is far from true: More people are living with HIV now than ever before; 25% of those who are infected in the United States do not know that they have HIV; and 45% of those newly diagnosed with HIV have tested positive so late in their disease process that they progress to AIDS within three years of their HIV diagnosis.

The book is structured in three sections, which parallel the subtitle: *Principles, Practices, and Populations*. The first section—on *principles*—lays the groundwork necessary to understand all HIV services, advocacy, and prevention. Chapter 1 is an overview of the disease: history, transmission, disease process and progression, testing, medication and side effects, and adherence support. Chapter 2 outlines the perspectives—such as human rights, social justice, and empowerment—that are the foundations to successfully working with HIV-infected and HIV-affected persons and communities. Chapter 3 addresses a skill that should permeate all of the others: cultural competence. Chapter 4 suggests how HIV social work would be different in the United States if the human rights framework were applied more universally.

The second section focuses on social work *practices* and how they are used in the HIV field. Experienced practitioners and experts were asked to write what they would like other practitioners to know about their methods. Chapters 5 through 8 address case management, crisis intervention and counseling, social work in medical settings, and group work and family support. Chapters 9 through 12 address the practice methods of program development and management, community organizing and grassroots advocacy, political and legislative interventions, and HIV prevention.

The third section highlights some of those *populations* that have been particularly vulnerable to HIV. The retrovirus cannot differentiate between humans, but humans certainly can and have differentiated between each other, and those disparities have caused much despair. We acknowledge that there is overlap: An individual can be a member of several groups, and vulnerable groups have many experiences in common. Even though it is problematic to separate people in this way, it is done purely for educational purposes. Chapters 13 through 19 highlight the particular vulnerabilities of women, men who have sex with men, children and adolescents, midlife and older persons, people of African descent, and people of Latin descent. The final special population is HIV-affected caregivers.

Each of the aforementioned chapters includes vignettes by HIV-infected or HIV-affected persons who have written about their experiences in regard to the topic on which the chapter is focused. In this way, we include the voices of those who are living with the reality of HIV so that the reader is not hearing only from those of us in agencies or in academia.

Finally, the Afterword looks backward and forward, reflecting on the major lessons brought forward by the book's contributors and calls attention to what practitioners might expect. Turning to face the future of the pandemic, what do we need to hope, what do we need to fear, what do we need to learn, and what do we need to do?

Several notes about the book's scope are required. First, this book has an unabashed social work perspective. I am a social worker and invited only other social workers to be first authors of each chapter. Most of the coauthors are social workers as well. We made efforts not to drown the reader in professional jargon and to stay connected to HIV-infected persons and their communities, but we must acknowledge that these chapters are written by authors with a particular philosophy, experience, and worldview. There has not been a handbook or textbook specifically for social workers in the HIV field for almost a decade, and given that the pandemic has changed dramatically during that time, the chapter authors were tasked with updating the practice wisdom in the social work field. Second, we chose to focus on HIV practice and policy in the United States. HIV is international, but this book strives to address the need for a handbook in the United States, and one book cannot cover the globe. Third, although we address many types of people who are hit hard by HIV, there are still many vulnerable populations to which we did not have the space to devote a chapter (such as sex workers, injectors, persons with chronic mental illness, and men and women in the criminal justice system).

ACKNOWLEDGMENTS

The HIV field is one of the few where the original services and advocacy responses were invented by those who were most affected and most vulnerable. We all owe a tremendous debt to persons with HIV who patiently showed us what they needed us to do as we stood in solidarity with them. Michael Shernoff, an HIV-infected New York social worker, published an editorial in *Social Work* in 1990 saying that AIDS would touch the professional lives of almost every social worker, that social work skills and values were well suited to HIV work, but that there was still much for us to do. I remember being both stunned and overjoyed as I read his comments (when I was a community-based advocate and case manager), because the main journal of my profession was finally acknowledging HIV. Michael died on June 17, 2008, of pancreatic cancer; although he was too ill to accept my repeated invitations to write a chapter or vignette, he knew that I was going to acknowledge our gratitude to him as one of the first to write about HIV and social work practice. He is one of countless pioneering HIV-infected teachers, supervisors, activists, service recipients, and mentors who taught us what we know. For this reason, many of the chapter authors have acknowledged a colleague or friend who is living with HIV or who died from AIDS.

I end with several personal notes. First, it was my honor and privilege to work with these distinguished longtime HIV advocates and practitioners who contributed chapters, to be the one to stitch together the quilt pieces woven by these accomplished colleagues. Obviously, the book would not have been possible without each and every one of them. They all wrote because of dedication and love, and they have my deep appreciation. Second, I could not have made it through the arduous editing and publishing process without the stellar John Wiley & Sons team: Peggy Alexander, Rachel Livsey, Kara Borbely, and Sweta Gupta. Third, it was never my idea to edit a social work and HIV anthology; that was always the brainchild and heart-child of Lisa Gebo, my colleague and friend, who urged me to do this for a decade before she accepted a job at John Wiley & Sons and convinced me to sign a contract after she went there. Although she could not work on this project due to being seriously ill, I felt her spirit shepherding me all the way. Fourth, I must acknowledge my own HIV mentor, Bill Edens Jr., who recruited me into the HIV field in 1987, convinced me that I was needed and could do the work, and generously and brilliantly taught me everything I know about HIV work: case management, crisis intervention, prevention, community organizing, professional education, volunteer training, group work, committee work, fund-raising, supervision, management, and legislative advocacy. He was a social worker in every way but name and training. He died of AIDS in 1993, and I still miss his humor and wisdom. Finally, I dedicate the book to my father, Ralph Alston Cannon, from whom I got my interests in scholarship, writing, teaching, and social justice. Although he did not live to see this book come into being, it is nonetheless an extension of his legacy.

REFERENCES

Piot, P. (2006). AIDS: From crisis management to sustained strategic response. *Lancet, 368,* 526–530.

Shernoff, M. (1990). Why every social worker should be challenged by AIDS. *Social Work, 35*(1), 5–8.

About the Editor

Cynthia Cannon Poindexter, MSW, PhD, is Associate Professor at the Fordham University Graduate School of Social Service in New York, where she teaches HIV practice, HIV policy, management, supervision, and human rights. Dr. Poindexter has been in the HIV field since 1987, when she began volunteering with the Palmetto AIDS Life Support Services (PALSS), the first AIDS Service Organization in South Carolina, as a crisis line volunteer, volunteer buddy, grant writer, and trainer. She went on to become the first social worker employed by that agency, becoming statewide Program Director and then Assistant Director. She has consulted with seven local and state HIV service programs in Boston and Chicago. She has been a trainer for the South Carolina AIDS Training Network, the Midwest AIDS Training and Education Center, the New England AIDS Education and Training Center, the NASW HIV Spectrum Project, the Massachusetts Department of Public Health HIV Division, and the HIV/AIDS Service Administration of New York City. She received a bachelor's degree from Duke University, an MSW from the University of South Carolina, and a PhD from the Jane Addams College of Social Work at the University of Illinois at Chicago.

About the Contributors

Gary Bailey, MSW, is Associate Professor at Simmons College School of Social Work, Boston, Massachusetts. He received an MSW from Boston University School of Social Work in 1979. He received an Advocacy Award from the Multicultural AIDS Coalition in 1997, the Congressman Gerry Studd's Visibility Award in 1996 from the Fenway Community Health Center in Boston, and the Bayard Rustin Spirit Award in 1999 from the AIDS Action Committee of Massachusetts. Bailey was named Social Worker of the Year by both the National and Massachusetts NASW in 1998. He has been in the HIV field for more than 20 years.

Alida Bouris, MSW, PhD is Assistant Professor at the University of Chicago School of Social Service Administration. She has 15 years of experience in the HIV prevention field. Her research interests are in family-based interventions to prevent sexually transmitted infections, HIV infection, and pregnancies among Latino adolescents and young adults. She received a BA in Women's Studies from the University of California at Berkeley and MSW and PhD degrees from the Columbia University School of Social Work. She has published scholarly articles on parental influences on Latino adolescent risk behavior, including youth involvement in alcohol, tobacco, and sexual risk behaviors.

David J. Brennan, MSW, PhD, is Assistant Professor at the Factor-Inwentash Faculty of Social Work, University of Toronto. He has been in the HIV field since 1983 when he volunteered on the AIDS Action Hotline in Boston, Massachusetts. His research focuses on HIV among gay and bisexual men, particularly the effect of childhood sexual abuse, optimistic beliefs about treatment, and body image on risk. He received his bachelor's degree, MSW, and PhD from Boston College. In 2006, Brennan was the recipient of the Boston College Graduate Student Research Excellence award for the work on his dissertation.

Douglas M. Brooks, MSW, is Vice President for Health Services at the Justice Resource Institute in Boston, Massachusetts. He began volunteering in HIV work in 1983 and began paid work in 1992 with the Provincetown AIDS Support Group. He consults with South Africa's Eastern Cape Province Department of Health. He received an MSW from Boston University in 1999. He is a recipient of the Bayard Rustin Award and the Stonewall Award for his leadership in the LGBT community in Boston and of the Hubie Jones Award for Urban Social Work from the Boston University School of Social Work Alumni Association. He has recently been appointed to the Presidential Advisory Council on HIV/AIDS.

Valerie Dixson-Anderson, MSW, is a parent and child specialist with the Health Federation of Philadelphia's Home Visitation Program. She is also a co-facilitator for an HIV support group for women for the past seven years. Her group work experience began in 1995 when she facilitated support groups with a variety of agencies throughout the Philadelphia area, working with adult women and teenage girls, providing educational support, parenting skills, and wellness services. Dixson-Anderson received an MSW from the University of Pittsburgh. She incorporates poetry as a therapeutic tool to foster personal growth, to allow for self-expression, and to promote healing.

Charles A. Emlet, MSW, PhD, is Associate Professor of Social Work at the University of Washington, Tacoma, and affiliate faculty member at the University of Washington Center for AIDS Research. He entered the HIV field in 1986 when he initiated an AIDS home care project and AIDS Medicaid waiver program in Solano County, California. Emlet received an MSW from California State University, Fresno, and a PhD from the Mandel School of Applied Social Sciences at Case Western Reserve University. In 2004 he received the University of Washington Tacoma's Distinguished Research Award for his work on aging and HIV.

Nicholas Robertson Forge, MA, MSW, is a Professional Associate in the Social Work Department at Mercy College in Dobbs Ferry, New York. He received an MA in sociology from Florida Atlantic University, an MSW from Georgia State University, and is currently a PhD candidate at Fordham University Graduate School of Social Service. His MSW field placement was with persons with HIV at a large public hospital. His research interest is HIV stigma. He is on the steering committee of the New York City NASW LGBT Committee. He is a trainer for the New York City HIV/AIDS Services Administration.

Susan M. Gallego, MSSW, is Mental Health/Substance Abuse Rural Border and HIV Programs Coordinator with the Texas Department of State Health Services. She has been in the HIV field for more than 20 years, serving as Director of Client Services at the San Francisco AIDS Foundation and Director of Client Services for AIDS Services of Austin. She is a Certified Master Trainer for the National Institute of Drug Abuse and has served as cochair of the advisory board of NASW's HIV/AIDS Social Work Training Project. Her master's degree is from the University of Texas at Austin School of Social Work.

Larry M. Gant, MSW, MA, PhD, is Professor at University of Michigan School of Social Work. He has been in the HIV field for more than 20 years. His research concerns HIV-affected children, HIV risk among Latinos and African Americans, and HIV treatment. He has received research support from the Kellogg Foundation, Blue Cross/Blue Shield, Centers for Disease Control, Microsoft, and the National Institutes for Drug Abuse. He received a master's degree in psychology, an MSW, and PhD in social work and social psychology from the University of Michigan. He served on the Advisory Committee of NASW's HIV/AIDS Spectrum Training Project.

Brian Giddens, MSW, is Associate Director of Social Work and Care Coordination for the University of Washington Medical Center and Clinical Associate Professor with the University of Washington School of Social Work, where he teaches courses integrating organizational practice, leadership, ethics, and health care. Previously he was Director of Services for the Northwest AIDS Foundation in Seattle and on the Advisory Committee of the NASW HIV/AIDS Spectrum Project. He received an MSW from the University of Washington. In 2004 he was named a DHHS Primary Health Care Policy Fellow and NASW Social Worker of the Year by the Washington State Chapter.

Vincent Guilamo-Ramos, MSW, PhD, is Associate Professor at the Columbia University School of Social Work and a licensed clinical social worker. His research on HIV prevention is funded by the National Institutes of Health and the Centers for Disease Control and Prevention. He has been working in the HIV field for 20 years. He was a national trainer and Advisory Committee member for the NASW's HIV/AIDS Spectrum Project. He received an MS in Nonprofit Management and Public Policy and an MSW from New York University and a PhD in Social Welfare from the State University of New York at Albany.

Bernadette R. Hadden, MSW, PhD, is Assistant Professor in the MSW program at the Hunter College School of Social Work, New York and in the PhD social welfare program at the Graduate Center of the City University of New York. She has been conducting research on HIV risk and prevention for the past 20 years. She received a BSW from the University of the Western Cape in South Africa, a master's degree in philosophy from the Columbia University Graduate School of Arts and Sciences, and MSW and PhD degrees from the Columbia University School of Social Work.

Winston Husbands, PhD, is Director of Research and Program Development at the AIDS Committee of Toronto. He entered the HIV field in the early 1990s as a volunteer with the Black Coalition for AIDS Prevention in Toronto. He joined the AIDS Committee of Toronto in 2001. He has been cochair and Director of the African and Caribbean Council on HIV/AIDS in Ontario. His bachelor's and master's degrees are from the University of the West Indies (Kingston, Jamaica), and his doctorate is from the University of Western Ontario (Canada). He taught at the University of Zambia and Ryerson University in Toronto.

Hugo Kamya, MSW, PhD, is Professor at Simmons College of Social Work. For the past 20 years, he has worked in the HIV field and has been committed to serving HIV-affected children and families. A native of Uganda, he has for many years returned there to do research on child-headed and granny-headed families. Kamya received an MSW from Boston College, a Master of Divinity from Harvard University, and a doctorate in psychology from Boston University. In 2003, the American Family Therapy Academy recognized his work with an award for Distinguished Contribution to Social and Economic Justice.

Ryan M. Kull, MSW, provides psychotherapy services in private practice with an emphasis on working with gay men or those infected with HIV. He is also an Adjunct Instructor at Fordham University Graduate School of Social Service, provides training to caseworkers at New York City's HIV and AIDS Services Administration, and is a full-time doctoral student at New York University Silver School of Social Work. He served as a codirector at Columbia University's Gay Health Advocacy Project for six years and served as a prevention expert for The Body.com, a web site that provides information on HIV.

Helen Land, MSW, PhD, is Associate Professor at the School of Social Work at the University of Southern California, Los Angeles. She has been in the HIV field since 1986; she has volunteered in facilitating support groups for HIV caregivers and has educated volunteers and social workers about suicide prevention and depression associated with HIV. She has published two books on HIV and has written about coping in HIV caregivers. She received an MSW at Syracuse University and a PhD at the University of Pittsburgh School of Social Work. She has received the Hutto Patterson Award for excellence in teaching and research.

Michael Lewis, MSSW, PhD, is an Associate Professor at the Hunter College School of Social Work. He has degrees in psychology from Western Maryland College (BA), the Columbia University School of Social Work (MSSW), and the Graduate Center of the City University of New York (PhD in sociology). Lewis teaches courses in social policy and the economics of social policy, and his research interests are primarily in the areas of income distribution and quantitative methods. He is new to the HIV field.

Nathan L. Linsk, MA, PhD, is Professor at the Jane Addams College of Social Work at the University of Illinois at Chicago. In 1988 he established and continues to be Principal Investigator for the seven-state Midwest AIDS Training and Education Center. He is Co-Principal Investigator for the Great Lakes Addictions Technology Transfer Center. Linsk has shared leadership for establishing the first MSW and PhD social work education programs in Ethiopia. He was an African AIDS Regional Research Fulbright Fellow in Ethiopia in 2006. Linsk is founding coeditor of the *Journal of HIV/AIDS and Social Services*.

Vincent J. Lynch, MSW, PhD, is Director of Continuing Education, Boston College Graduate School of Social Work. In 1988, he founded the Annual National Conference on Social Work and HIV/AIDS, which he continues to chair. He has edited four books on Social Work and HIV/AIDS. His awards include the Council on Social Work Education's "Distinguished Recent Contributions to Social Work Education Award" (1998), the Harlem Life Community AIDS Center's "Harlem Life Award" (1998), and the Massachusetts National Association of Social Workers' "Greatest Contribution to Social Work Education Award" (2001). Lynch has obtained more than $1 million in grants for social work AIDS education projects.

Dana B. Marlowe, MSW, PhD, is an Assistant Clinical Professor at the Fordham University Graduate School of Social Services in New York, where she teaches Generalist Practice, Social Justice, and Social Policy. She began working in the HIV field in 1989 as a volunteer buddy. She has worked for a Hospital Pediatric AIDS Program and a community-based AIDS Service Organization. She served on Ryan White Title I and II Steering Committees. She is a trainer for the New York City HIV/AIDS Services Administration. She received an MSW at the State University of New York at Buffalo School of Social Work.

Sally Mason, MSW, PhD, is Associate Professor of Clinical Social Work at the Institute for Juvenile Research, University of Illinois at Chicago, where she is Director of Social Work Training and researcher and clinician in the Division of Child and Adolescent Psychiatry. She began working with people with HIV in 1987 at the Howard Brown Memorial Clinic in Chicago. She established one of the first custody planning programs for HIV-positive parents in the United States. She received an MSW from Loyola University and a PhD at the Jane Addams College of Social Work at the University of Illinois at Chicago.

Michael P. Melendez, MSW, PhD, is Professor and Chair of the Clinical Practice Sequence at Simmons College School of Social Work in Boston, Massachusetts. He has been in the HIV field since 1983, volunteering for four AIDS Service Organizations in Boston. He received an MSW from Boston University and a doctorate from the Mandel School of Applied Social Sciences, Case Western Reserve University. He is the recipient of the 1998 Elizabeth Ramos AIDS Activist Award from the Latino

Health Institute and the 2003 AIDS Action Spirit Award of the AIDS Action Committee in Boston.

Claudia Lucia Moreno, MSW, PhD, is Associate Professor at the Fordham University Graduate School of Social Service in New York, teaching HIV policy and practice. She received an MSW from Rutgers and a PhD from Ohio State University. She has consulted with several national HIV programs, funded by organizations such as the American Psychological Association and the Centers for Disease Control, to address HIV risk for Latinas. She was the Principle Investigator of a pilot study at the Columbia University Center for Intervention & Prevention Research on HIV and Drug Abuse on Cultural Adaptation of HIV interventions with high-risk couples.

Peter A. Newman, MSW, MA, PhD, is Associate Professor at the Faculty of Social Work, University of Toronto. He conducts HIV prevention research in Canada, India, South Africa, Thailand, and the United States. He entered the HIV field 25 years ago as a volunteer at the AIDS Action Committee in Boston. He received an MSW from Hunter College School of Social Work in New York and a PhD from the University of Michigan. He received the Early Researcher Award from the Ontario Ministry of Research and Innovation in 2007 for his cutting-edge work on the social dimensions of HIV vaccine development.

Tyrone M. Parchment, MSW, is the Black Male Initiative Program Coordinator at John Jay College of Criminal Justice, which intends to increase, encourage, and support the inclusion and educational success of underrepresented groups in higher education, particularly Black males. He is a Research Assistant for Darrell P. Wheeler, PhD, at Hunter College School of Social Work. Parchment is new to the HIV field. He is engaged in initiatives to encourage diversity and undo structural racism. He received a BA in sociology from Hunter College in 2006 and an MSW with honors from Hunter College School of Social Work in 2008.

Manoj Pardasani, MSW, PhD, is Associate Professor at the Fordham University Graduate School of Social Service in New York, where he teaches management and social work practice. From 2001 to 2004 he directed a residential program for dually diagnosed HIV-positive individuals. His HIV-related research, presentations, and writing concern prevention among sex workers in India and African American gay men in the United States, homelessness, and cultural competence. He received an MSW and a PhD from the Wurzweiler School of Social Work at Yeshiva University. In 2004 he was named Outstanding Researcher of the Year by the National Council on Aging.

Patricia A. Stewart, MSS, is a Site Director for Behavioral Health at the Family Practice and Counseling Network, an affiliate of Resources for Human Development in Philadelphia, Pennsylvania. She is also in private practice. She has been involved in work with people living with HIV since the early 1990s. Stewart received a Master of Social Service degree from Bryn Mawr College Graduate School of Social Work and Social Research. For her work in the field of HIV, she has twice received commendations from the National Association of Black Social Workers for outstanding contributions to the African American community.

Susan Taylor-Brown, MSW, PhD, is Clinical Professor of Pediatrics at the University of Rochester Medical School, incorporating HIV concerns into teaching and research.

She has been working with HIV-affected families since 1986, when she became involved in efforts to address the needs of HIV-affected children. Throughout her academic career, she has drawn attention to the unmet needs of HIV-affected families. She received an MSW from Catholic University of America and MPH and PhD degrees from the University of Pittsburgh. She created and for 12 years directed the Family Unity Retreat, a four-day retreat for HIV-affected families.

Laurens G. Van Sluytman, MA, MSW, is a licensed therapist and Project Director of the Community Response Study, an NIH research study of crystal methamphetamine use and interventions among men who have sex with men (MSM) in New York City. He received an MA from New York University and an MSW from Columbia University and is a doctoral candidate at the Hunter College School of Social Work. His research focuses on identifying and exploring network risk and resiliency among Black men who have sex with men. He was the project coordinator of a CDC study investigating HIV risk behaviors among Black MSM in New York City.

Darrell P. Wheeler, MSW, MPH, PhD, is Associate Professor and Associate Dean for Research at Hunter College School of Social Work (HCSSW). For the past 20 years, Wheeler's research and publication interests focus on identification and exploration of individual and communal resiliency in HIV prevention and intervention through strength-based approaches. Under his direction, HCSSW, in partnership with other U.S. and Nigerian organizations, has been selected by American International Health Alliance's HIV/AIDS Twinning Center Program to assist in developing and strengthening the capacity of Nigerian institutional services provided to Nigerian children orphaned or made vulnerable by HIV.

Lori Wiener, MSW, PhD, is Coordinator of the Pediatric Psychosocial Support and Research Program at the National Cancer Institute. She has been working in the field of HIV since 1982. She entered the National Institutes of Health in 1986 to help the National Cancer Institute incorporate pediatric HIV disease into its pediatric oncology program. Wiener has published several unique therapeutic workbooks—including *This is My World,* for children living with life-threatening diseases, and *Brothers and Sisters Together,* for siblings. Wiener received master's and PhD degrees in social work from New York University.

PART ONE

HIV BASICS AND SOCIAL WORK PRINCIPLES

Chapter One

HIV HISTORY, ILLNESS, TRANSMISSION, AND TREATMENT

Ryan M. Kull

INTRODUCTION

HIV disease—a condition caused by infection with the human immunodeficiency virus—is a complex, incurable illness that can lead to a life-threatening condition called *Acquired Immune Deficiency Syndrome* (AIDS). Since the first documented AIDS-related deaths in 1981, HIV disease has grown into a global epidemic—known as a *pandemic*—that profoundly affects individuals and their interpersonal relationships throughout the human life cycle. In addition to being a serious biological disease, HIV creates social, political, and economic problems that highlight international injustices. HIV disease brings global attention to homophobia, oppression of women, racism, poverty, and health care disparities.

Early in the pandemic, it was clear that people could reduce HIV transmission if they had access to the tools to do so, such as condoms, clean needles, and reproductive care. Advances in medication treatments have made HIV disease more manageable and much less deadly, but millions of people worldwide still do not have access to adequate medical care and treatment. A person with access to skilled HIV care in New York City might perceive and experience HIV disease quite differently than a working-class single mother in the rural southern United States. Epidemiological data illuminate how HIV disease disproportionately affects marginalized people throughout the world: Women, African Americans, Latinos, those in poverty, sex workers, injecting drug users, and men who have sex with men. While advances have been made in the medical treatment of HIV, social and political actions have fallen behind.

Health care and social service professionals can have a powerful impact on the effects of HIV. Basic knowledge about the science of HIV disease—how it is transmitted, prevented, and treated, as well as its sociopolitical history—is an important foundation for any human services practitioner. This chapter provides basic historical, epidemiological, biological, immunological, medical, and prevention information so that social service providers can be prepared to provide information and support to persons with HIV and those at risk for HIV infection. Some information found in this chapter is knowledge that will remain relatively stable over time (for example, information about biology, transmission, and history). Facts about treatment, prevention, and epidemiology change more frequently, and those working in HIV services should monitor these changes regularly.

Acknowledgments: I thank Laura Pinsky, Peter Staley, and Dr. Paul Bushkuhl for their expertise on the medical and prevention aspects of HIV and AIDS, and Michael Clemens for feedback on a draft of the chapter. I am also grateful to Chris for providing his perspective on living with HIV.

THE EMERGENCE OF HIV IN THE UNITED STATES

The First 20 Years

From June to August 1981, the Centers for Disease Control and Prevention (CDC) published three reports documenting two rare conditions—a form of cancer called *Kaposi's sarcoma* (KS) and a pulmonary condition called *Pneumocystis carinii pneumonia* (PCP)—in previously healthy men living in New York and California (CDC, 1981a, 1981b, 1981c). Of the 108 documented cases, 95 percent were 25 to 49 years of age and 43 of the men had died. The mysterious link between these rare fatal illnesses and the subjects' histories of same-gender sexual behavior confounded public health investigators. Because physicians treating these cases associated the illness with men who identified as gay, names like *gay-related immunodeficiency disease* (GRID) and *gay cancer* were assigned to the condition. The CDC—a branch of the government public health service that monitors and intervenes in existing and emerging diseases—sent researchers to investigate the possible causes of this emerging public health crisis. Through months of extensive interviews, medical examinations, and analyses of social networks, researchers speculated that the mysterious illness was likely caused by an infectious microorganism transmitted between people through sexual contact.

Gay men were not the only population being affected by this newly discovered disease. In the first half of 1982, the CDC had documented cases among people with hemophilia, injection drug users, heterosexuals, babies, and Haitians. Because the disease was no longer considered to be limited to gay men, and because it was transmitted not only through sex but also blood contact, the CDC identified the illness more broadly as *acquired immune deficiency syndrome,* or AIDS (Harris et al., 1983).

In 1983, a French virologist Dr. Luc Montagnier and his research team at the Pasteur Institute isolated HIV, the virus that causes AIDS. By mid-1985 this pivotal discovery led to the development of an antibody test which could detect HIV in the blood supply and human infection well before an AIDS diagnosis. The HIV antibody test remains the gold standard for diagnosing HIV infection to this day.

In the absence of a clear scientific understanding of AIDS, the disease readily became a metaphor for the "immoral" behavior of gay men and drug users. The pandemic's emergence during Ronald Reagan's presidency, backed by social and religious conservatives, resulted in a lack of federal governmental attention to the public health emergency. President Reagan did not make any reference in his speeches to AIDS until 1987, six years after the first reports of a fatal infectious disease. That same year, Republican senator Jesse Helms introduced a bill that refused federal funding to groups that "promote" homosexuality in their education and literature, creating a significant barrier to public funding of gay-related AIDS organizations (Levine, Nardi, & Gagnon, 1997).

Gay communities in New York City and San Francisco, responding to political and social inaction, organized grassroots political action and community advocacy groups such as AIDS Coalition to Unleash Power (ACT UP), Gay Men's Health Crisis (GMHC), and AIDS Project Los Angeles (APLA). ACT UP's primary mission was to bring attention to the absence of a public health response to the AIDS crisis; the slogan "Silence = Death" (see Figure 1.1), accompanied by a pink triangle that the Nazis used to identify homosexuals, became a symbol of AIDS activism. The coalition sponsored highly effective, nonviolent demonstrations at locations deemed critical to combating the public health response and institutionalized homophobia (a 1990 demonstration at the National Institutes of Health is a good example of their tactics). Over several years, ACT UP uncovered inherent disparities in U.S. health care delivery, not just for gay men living with HIV, but also for women and people of color, and broadened their message to "health

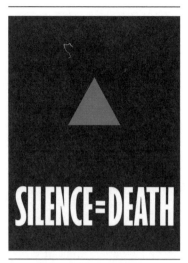

Figure 1.1   Silence = Death
Source: Silence = Death Project (1986).

care is a right." ACT UP is credited for significant changes in the ways pharmaceutical companies and the FDA research and approve medications through the clinical trial process, as well as bringing national attention to the AIDS crisis and discrimination.

AIDS gained greater media attention when public figures affected by HIV entered the spotlight, leading to widespread awareness, controversy, and fear. Rock Hudson, a prominent Hollywood star who was a leading man in romantic roles, began showing signs of illness and deterioration and publicly announced in 1985 that he had AIDS. He died shortly thereafter. Some describe this as "giving AIDS a face," which simultaneously signified a pivotal moment in gay and lesbian recognition. Never had such a prominent Hollywood icon openly and publicly acknowledged being gay, and AIDS awareness spurred a powerful gay and lesbian movement. Olympic medalist Greg Louganis and basketball star Magic Johnson are two professional athletes whose HIV status created controversy in the sports world, and both have become public advocates for HIV awareness and prevention.

In 1984, Ryan White, a 13-year-old Indiana boy with hemophilia, was diagnosed with AIDS. Ryan's diagnosis drew national attention due to the stigma he experienced in his public school. Initially the superintendent barred Ryan from attending school, and after that was reversed, a group of parents sued to keep him out. Despite the confirmation of his right to attend school by the courts, the daily verbal and emotional assaults that he experienced forced him and his family to move to another community and school. After Ryan White's death in 1990, Congress passed the Ryan White Comprehensive AIDS Resources Emergency (CARE) Act, the first legislative initiative to provide comprehensive care funds for people with AIDS (PWAs). The act provided emergency relief grants to cities with more than 2,000 AIDS cases to provide care for people with AIDS and funding for prevention and intervention for at risk groups. In 2006, the CARE Act was renamed the Ryan White HIV/AIDS Treatment Modernization Act, which placed greater emphasis on funding medical care–related programs and services. In fiscal year 2008, $2.1 billion of federal funds were allocated toward the Ryan White HIV/AIDS program.

The number of HIV infections and deaths peaked in the 1990s. This was partly attributed to the introduction of a 1993 revised case definition for AIDS that not only measured the disease through clinical manifestations (that is, symptoms or opportunistic illnesses), but also through the measurement of cells critical to immune function, called CD4, or T cells (Castro, Ward, & Slutsker, 1992). Levels of the CD4 marker helped determine disease progression. A CD4 count below 200 signified an infected person's acute risk for AIDS-related illnesses and death. The revision also shifted AIDS diagnoses among women by including cervical cancer and other diseases specific to HIV-infected women in the new criteria (Castro et al., 1992). Case definition revisions influenced important changes in U.S. HIV-related health policies during the 1990s.

The Clinton administration, taking office in 1992, made notable advances in HIV funding, increasing allocations to the CARE act by 200 percent, targeting funds to research, prevention, and housing. President Clinton also developed the Office of AIDS Research, responsible for overseeing efficient allocation of HIV research funds, and passed an AIDS disaster bill that provided up to $4 billion for research.

A highly significant HIV-related development was the introduction of uniquely effective medication treatments. A 1996 cover story for the *New York Times Magazine* titled "When Plagues End" (Sullivan, 1996, November 10) captured a powerful, though misguided, optimism for an imminent HIV cure. Dr. David Ho, a principal researcher at the Aaron Diamond AIDS Research Center was *Time* magazine's 1996 Man of the Year for his role in developing a promising new drug class called *protease inhibitors* and a highly effective HIV-inhibiting triple-drug treatment (called "combination therapy"). New technologies developed to measure HIV levels in blood led to Ho's discovery that HIV was never, in fact, latent; rather, billions of HIV particles were being produced daily, slowly wearing down the immune system. Presumably, medications that inhibited HIV replication in blood would prevent the onset of AIDS.

Use of these new medication combination regimens (popularly known as drug cocktails) controlled HIV replication in infected people, often reducing the virus to undetectable levels. People with usually life-threatening AIDS-related illnesses were recovering at unprecedented rates, AIDS diagnoses began to plummet, and hospitals burdened by the number of HIV cases witnessed significant reductions of AIDS cases and deaths. A phenomenon called the *Lazarus syndrome* referred to people with AIDS who, expecting to die soon, living on disability, and having taken cash payments for insurance policies, suddenly found themselves leaving their sickbeds and returning to life. Hopes that these medications could eradicate HIV—essentially a cure for AIDS—were high, but continued attempts to do so have so far failed.

EPIDEMIOLOGY: STATISTICS AND POPULATIONS IN THE TWENTY-FIRST CENTURY

In 2006—the last year for data collection by the CDC—the estimated number of AIDS-related deaths was 14,627, and the total number of people who have died of AIDS since the beginning of the pandemic reached 565,927 (CDC, 2006). Approximately 56,300 people in the United States became newly infected with HIV in 2006 (Hall et al., 2008). Research suggests that the number of new HIV infections per year peaked in the 1990s and has remained stable since the year 2000. Men who have sex with men (MSM) of all races comprise the majority of these new annual infections (53%), followed by heterosexual transmission (31%), injection drug users (IDU) (12%), and both MSM and IDU (4%). At the end of 2003, it was estimated that 1.1 million people were living with HIV infection (Glynn & Rhodes, 2005). Approximately a quarter of those HIV-infected do not know that they have HIV, and recent research suggests that the number of people living with HIV has been significantly underestimated (Hall et al., 2008).

Rates of infection among young men who have sex with men in the United States continue to rise. In the five years between 2001 and 2006, researchers observed an 8.6%

increase in new HIV infections among MSM, and a 33% increase among MSM under 30 years of age (CDC, 2008). Men who have sex with men represent the only group that experienced an increase in HIV or AIDS diagnoses during this time. More alarming are statistics showing disparities in race and HIV transmission among youth: During 2006, more than 90 percent of newly infected MSM under 20 years of age identified as African American or Latino. HIV and AIDS disproportionately affect people of color in all categories. African Americans experienced approximately 45% of new HIV infections from 2001 to 2006: African Americans and Latinos had infection rates 7 and 3 times the rate of Whites, respectively (Hall et al., 2008).

Women represented 27% of AIDS diagnoses in 2000, compared to 8% in 1985, and HIV incidence has remained stable since it peaked in the late 1980s. African American women are disproportionately affected by HIV or AIDS: Those older than 13 represent 66% of AIDS cases among women and the majority of new HIV infections, while representing 12% of all women in the general population. All women are primarily infected through heterosexual sex. Black men and women have the highest mortality rates.

The global HIV pandemic is staggering. UNAIDS (2008) estimated that at the end of 2007 there were 33 million people living with HIV worldwide, a dramatic increase from the estimated 8 million reported in 1990. Following are other significant statistics about the pandemic:

- Approximately 67% of people living with HIV reside in sub-Saharan Africa.
- More than 2.5 million adults and children were infected with HIV in 2007.
- More than 25 million people have died from AIDS since 1981.
- There are approximately 11 million children orphaned by HIV in Africa.
- People under age 25 account for almost half of all new infections.
- Women represent half of all HIV infections.
- 31% of people in low- and middle-income countries who need antiretroviral treatment, receive it. Children are one-third as likely to have access to these life-saving drugs.
- Less than 40% of people under age 15 know basic information about HIV.

BIOLOGICAL ASPECTS OF HIV

HIV is a retrovirus. Retroviruses, like other viruses, require a host to survive, but they differ in how they replicate and function. HIV, using an enzyme called *reverse transcriptase,* converts viral RNA into DNA, which is then integrated into the genetic coding of certain human immune cells crucial for the body's defense against illness. (This reverse action is where *retro* viruses get their name.) HIV's ability to encode itself in immune cells makes HIV treatment challenging and eradication of the virus virtually impossible. Viral suppression or elimination while simultaneously preserving the immune system is a formidable task; medications have shown much success in suppressing viral replication, but not in complete eradication of HIV. Vaccine development has presented an even greater challenge, with little prospect of a successful HIV vaccine on the horizon.

There are two genetic types, HIV-1 and HIV-2, which are essentially the same virus, transmitted and causing illness in similar ways. The vast majority of infections in the world are caused by HIV-1. HIV-2 is more common in Western Africa. There is some evidence that HIV-2 may not be as easily transmitted as HIV-1, and the time from infection to illness is longer (CDC, 2007). Differences between the two types of HIV have greater implications for detection (a specific test exists to detect antibodies to HIV-2) and treatment. Current antiviral medications are developed to treat HIV-1 subtypes, and less is known about effective antiviral treatment for HIV-2 infection.

HIV and the Immune System

HIV targets an infected person's immune system. The immune system is a complex system of specialized organs, tissues, cells, and proteins whose primary task is to defend the body against infection, illness, and death. The immune system relies on White blood cells called *leukocytes* to perform central functions of immunity: identifying foreign substances in the body, initiating an immune response, and destroying or inhibiting that substance's function. Among the many different types of White blood cells, a particular category called *lymphocytes* is critical in understanding how HIV disease works.

Two types of lymphocytes, B and T lymphocytes, are generated in a person's bone marrow, later mature in bone marrow and lymphoid tissue (such as the lymph nodes, thymus, and spleen), respectively, and circulate throughout the body in blood and lymphatic fluids. B cells, upon encountering a foreign substance in the body, generate *antibodies* that bind to receptors on that substance, marking it for attack by other cells of the immune system. T cells are responsible for cell-mediated immunity: That is, they identify "self" cells in the body that have been infected and alert the immune system to attack and destroy those cells. One subtype of T cell—commonly referred to as a CD4 cell or a *helper cell*—helps orchestrate an immune response when it identifies an *antigen* (a marker identifying a foreign substance). Using a protein on its surface called CD4, the helper cell binds to the antigen and activates certain immune responses to begin their attack. (Figure 1.2 shows a representation of the HIV life cycle.)

HIV essentially hijacks a person's immune system to reproduce copies of itself. After HIV is transmitted, HIV seeks out the CD4 molecules. Given the abundance of this molecule on helper cells, HIV attaches to this cell, inserts its genetic coding, integrates itself in the cell's DNA, and changes that cell's function into an HIV "factory." Eventually this process wears down and destroys the CD4 cell, while generating thousands of new copies of HIV from one single cell. Without a sufficient number of CD4 cells, a person's immune system cannot orchestrate an adequate response against pathogens, resulting in severe vulnerability to certain forms of cancer and viral, bacterial, parasitic, and fungal infections that normally do not affect people with healthy immune systems. These conditions are known as *opportunistic infections and cancers* that comprise the condition called AIDS.

Course of HIV Disease

Without anti-HIV medication (called antiretrovirals), the number of years from infection to AIDS ranges from 7.7 to 11 (Babiker, Darby, De Angelis, Ewart, & Porter, 2000). A small number of HIV-infected persons (less than 5 percent) can be described as *long-term nonprogressors*—those who naturally mount an effective immune response against HIV, demonstrating significant viral suppression and elevated CD4 counts without treatment for longer than 10 years. When a person has less than 200 CD4 cells (people with normally functioning immune systems have anywhere from 500 to 1,800 CD4 cell counts), or if a person has an AIDS-defining opportunistic infection, that person meets the criteria for an AIDS diagnosis.

The course of HIV disease can be divided into four major categories: primary or acute infection, asymptomatic, symptomatic, and AIDS. There is not a single test that can be used to diagnose a person with AIDS; rather, a combination of diagnostic procedures is used to determine an AIDS diagnosis.

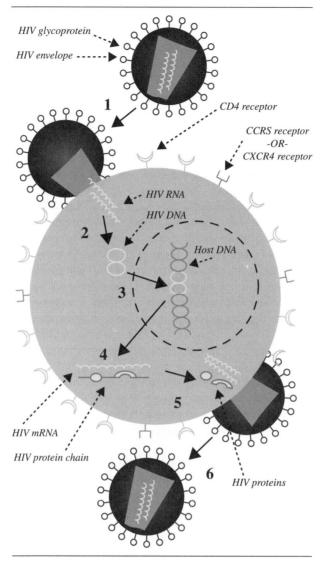

Figure 1.2   Stages of HIV life cycle
Source: http://aidsinfo.nih.gov/contentfiles/HIVLifeCycle_FS_en.pdf

Progression of HIV disease is determined through clinical manifestations of HIV-related symptoms and illnesses and through routine blood tests to monitor diagnostic markers, like CD4 counts and levels of virus in the blood (viral load). The CDC defines the progression from one disease stage to another by (1) measuring CD4 counts and/or (2) diagnosis of medical symptoms.

The stages are not rigid and exist on a continuum; they serve as a map for understanding disease progression, for deciding when to think about particular treatment interventions, for collecting data for epidemiological studies, and for the provision of certain entitlements.

Primary or Acute Infection

When a person is infected with HIV, the retrovirus travels to nearby lymph nodes where it begins replicating and infecting CD4 cells over the course of two to three days. HIV levels peak within weeks of infection (25 days on average). It is estimated that 87% of people who are at this stage of infection will develop a set of symptoms described as *acute retroviral syndrome* (ARS), or primary HIV infection. A cardinal symptom of ARS is a high fever, generally accompanied by a number of other symptoms, including joint and muscle pain, fatigue, swollen lymph glands, and a rash on the trunk of the body. This transient condition has symptoms similar to those of influenza or mononucleosis and lasts an average of 14 days. Identifying the acute period is critical, because at that stage people are simultaneously highly infectious and unlikely to be aware of their HIV status. Some practitioners advocate for antiretroviral medication treatment during this period, as it might provide long-term advantages to the immune system. Health care professionals aware of a person's risk for HIV infection and of the symptoms involved in primary infection can play an important role in early treatment intervention and the prevention of transmission to others.

As the immune system identifies and targets HIV, antibody production begins. This process is called *seroconversion, at which point* a person is considered antibody-positive or HIV-positive (more on testing positive later). The time between the transmission of HIV and the production of antibodies that can be detected by standard antibody tests is called the *window period* (see section on testing). Even though HIV does attack and eventually weaken a person's immune system, the body does mount an immune response, and following the acute phase, HIV levels are generally reduced to low, and sometimes undetectable, levels. The level of virus in a person's blood at the end of the acute phase is identified as the *viral set point.*

Asymptomatic

For many years it was believed that HIV remained inactive or dormant in a person's body for a number of years until an unknown factor activated the virus, thus beginning replication and compromising the immune system. It is now clear that HIV remains active throughout the course of infection, slowly wearing away a person's immune system for an average of 10 years without resulting in any overt symptoms. An HIV-infected person in this stage has a 500 or greater CD4 count and has no or few HIV-related or AIDS-related symptoms.

HIV Symptomatic

During this period, a person has a range of 200 to 499 CD4 cells and may begin to manifest certain symptoms that do not qualify as AIDS-defined illnesses. This period can be critical in initiating certain medical treatments to address symptoms, as well as anticipating prophylactic treatment to prevent the onset of an opportunistic infection. If antiviral treatment has not been initiated, it is likely to be recommended and/or initiated if CD4 counts drop below 350. Some conditions that may present during this period are thrush of the mouth, throat, or vagina (candidiasis), diarrhea, shingles, and peripheral neuropathy (pain and tingling sensations in extremities).

Late-Stage Disease: AIDS

HIV-infected persons are identified as having AIDS when they have CD4 counts below 200 and/or they have two or more AIDS-related opportunistic infections or cancer. Antiretroviral treatment is prescribed during this period. For classification purposes, even if a person experiences remission of opportunistic infections and returns to a CD4 count above 200, that person is still classified as having AIDS. When a person's CD4 count drops below 200, physicians will likely offer to begin prophylactic treatments to prevent the onset of certain opportunistic infections, such as Pneumocystis carinii (PCP) or mycobacterium avium complex (MAC).

The multiple conditions that can affect a person who has HIV in every area of the body—brain, eyes, mouth and throat, lungs, gastrointestinal system, skin, and extremities—signifies the profound impact that HIV has on immune function. Approximately 33 conditions have been identified as being AIDS-related. The symptoms, conditions, and treatments are diverse and complex.

HIV TESTING

Diagnosing HIV infection is a critical tool in both prevention and treatment. People who know that they are HIV-infected are less likely to engage in high-risk behavior and more likely to seek treatment (MacKellar et al., 2005; Marks, Crepaz, Senterfitt, & Janssen, 2005). One study estimated that if all people in the United States became aware of their HIV status, unprotected anal and vaginal sex could decrease by 57% and yearly HIV incidence attributed to sex could be reduced by 31% (Marks, Crepaz, & Janssen, 2006).

The usual method for diagnosing HIV infection is an HIV antibody test. Testing technologies have changed and improved since the identification of HIV and methods used to detect infection. Antibodies produced in response to HIV, like most other antibodies that are generated, persist in a person's body throughout his or her life. For this reason, when a person is infected with HIV, that person is often characterized as being "HIV-positive," which refers to the fact that a person has shown the presence of antibodies to the virus. While tests exist (PCR or viral load tests) for detecting HIV in the body, antibody tests are technically less demanding, are more cost efficient, and have higher accuracy.

The process of antibody testing is supposed to begin with a pretest interview by a trained counselor. The purpose of the session is to discuss risk factors, explain the testing process, assess risk for HIV infection, and get informed consent to perform the test. Following the interview, fluid is collected for testing. Blood is standard, while oral fluid tests have been increasing in popularity. Oral fluid tests are cost efficient, do not require a phlebotomist, and are easier to administer in venues other than hospitals and clinics. Once fluid is collected, an enzyme immunoassay (EIA) test is performed. The EIA sacrifices *specificity* for *sensitivity*: For this reason, a negative result outside of the window period is highly accurate, and no further testing is necessary. If an EIA comes back positive, a test that is less sensitive but more specific, the Western blot test, is used to confirm the presence or absence of HIV antibodies. The Western blot test is highly accurate. In some cases, an indeterminate result might occur, where the test cannot be interpreted as either positive or negative; this most often occurs when someone is tested during the process of seroconversion.

Standard tests involve drawing a small amount of blood that will be tested for antibodies in a lab. Tests that use oral fluid (sometimes called saliva tests) are less invasive. Oral tests are subjected to the same testing process as blood. The FDA has also approved rapid tests: A significant barrier to HIV testing is associated with the psychological stress people experience between specimen collection and receiving their results, which is one week to ten days. Rapid tests produce results within an hour (if the result is negative), can be obtained in clinics, labs, and doctor's offices, and have similar accuracy to other methods. A disadvantage is that the test is similar to the EIA; while a negative result is accurate, a positive result requires an additional test, like the Western blot, to confirm results.

Since there is delay between infection with HIV and antibody production, called the *window period,* it is important that antibody tests are performed after the window period has ended. Most people develop a detectable level of antibodies within a few weeks of infection (within 25 days, on average). With rare exceptions, HIV-infected people will have a detectable level of antibodies by three months, and a test performed at this point is usually considered accurate. To allow room for error, the CDC suggests that six months elapse before a test is considered accurate; it is reasonable for people with high-risk exposures to wait six months for testing, or be retested after a negative result at three months.

HIV-1 and HIV-2 are the only known types of HIV in the world, and two tests exist to detect the different types. Since HIV-1 accounts for the vast majority of infections worldwide, HIV-1 tests are typically used. HIV-1 antibody tests will detect the antibodies for HIV-1 with greater than 99% accuracy and will detect HIV-2 antibodies about 70% of the time. HIV-2 antibody tests should be used in cases where people have had high-risk exposures in endemic areas (West African countries). A combination HIV-1/HIV-2 test is used to test the U.S. blood supply and in many national labs.

HIV TRANSMISSION

Armed with accurate information about the dynamics of HIV transmission, social service and health professionals will be equipped to educate people in preventing the spread of HIV infection and reducing unrealistic fears of infection. Concerns about HIV infection can be psychologically and interpersonally debilitating, and many people are understandably anxious about their risk for HIV infection. Education about the basics of transmission can calm people's fears and help them feel in greater control of their health.

Communicating accurately about HIV transmission requires the language of odds and probability. Claiming that HIV can never be transmitted in a particular situation is inaccurate; scientists cannot claim that HIV cannot be transmitted in a particular situation with 100% certainty. What needs to be emphasized is the *probability* of transmission in any given circumstance. It is theoretically possible that an airplane will crash the next time you fly; the probability that it will crash in any given flight is about 250,000 in 1. Since the odds are extremely low, and assuming a vacation is very important to you, you might take a *calculated risk* and fly regardless of the small dangers involved. People make similar decisions when engaging in sexual activity.

Unique and bizarre situations arise that scientists cannot predict; discussion about transmission does not account for extremely rare circumstances. The CDC has been monitoring the ways that HIV is transmitted since the beginning of the pandemic, and epidemiological data strongly establishes how HIV is and is not transmitted:

- Unproducted vaginal or anal sexual intercourse
- Oral sex (rarely)
- Blood contact: primarily sharing syringes or needles for injection drug use, and much less frequently through occupational exposures and blood transfusions
- Mother-to-infant transmission: in the uterus, during vaginal delivery, or through breast-feeding

Reported transmission is also broken down into population categories that imply routes of transmission: men who have sex with men (MSM), injection drug users (IDU), MSM who also use injection drugs, and heterosexuals. (See Table 1.1.) The CDC annually monitors cases of HIV infections and AIDS diagnoses.

A phenomenon called the *masking effect* influences the accuracy of identifying transmission routes. When a person engages in more than one sexual behavior (for example, oral and vaginal sex) with partners, researchers cannot firmly establish the route of

Table 1.1.   HIV Transmission Estimates Involving Sex and Injection Drug Use in the United States

	2006 Incidence	Incidence per Year (2003–2006)
MSM	20,100	31,200
IDU	4,900	5,900
MSM/IDU	1,400	1,600
Heterosexual	13,100	16,400

Source: JAMA, August 6, 2008

transmission and therefore attribute transmission to the higher-risk category (in this case, vaginal sex). If HIV was in fact transmitted through oral sex, this is *masked* in the documentation. Research studies that control for these variables (for example, studies that look at people who engage *only* in oral sex) better establish the odds of transmission through a particular behavior, since people often engage in more than one type of sex with their partners.

How HIV Is Transmitted

A person can become infected with HIV when certain fluids containing HIV come into direct contact with a person's mucous membranes or bloodstream. Mucous membranes are tissue that line cavities in the body: Those that are implicated in HIV transmission line the mouth and throat, rectum, urethra, and vagina. Damage to the mucous membranes or the existence of any inflammation or lesions (such as due to sexually transmitted infections) increases the risk for infection. Mucous membranes in certain areas of the body are more susceptible to transmission than others: Rectal mucous membranes are more prone to damage during sex and also contain higher numbers of cells that HIV targets.

Coming into contact with concentrated HIV-infected fluids (blood, semen, vaginal or cervical secretions) does not inevitably mean that infection will occur. Intact skin is an effective barrier against HIV, so where contact occurs is significant. Many variables that can and cannot be observed determine the likelihood of transmission during any exposure: (1) the type of fluid, (2) the concentration of HIV in that fluid, (3) the type and location of exposure, (4) the presence of sexually transmitted infections, and (5) the immune response of the exposed person all influence the likelihood of infection.

Introduction of HIV-infected blood into one's bloodstream poses the greatest risk for transmission, since it contains the highest concentration of HIV in people who are infected (Levy, 1998). Other body fluids that usually contain enough concentration of HIV to cause transmission include semen, cervical and vaginal secretions, and breast milk. HIV can be isolated in pre-ejaculatory fluid in much smaller concentrations. HIV can also be isolated in other areas of the body, such as cerebrospinal fluid, but risk of transmission from other fluids is generally a concern only for health care and first response workers. HIV can be infrequently isolated, in trace amounts, in an HIV-infected person's saliva and tears, but there is no evidence that people get infected through contact with these fluids. HIV has not been found in sweat.

Sexual Transmission

Approximately two-thirds of all cases of HIV infections worldwide are attributed to sexual transmission, particularly anal or vaginal sex without condoms. When describing sexual transmission, partners can be identified as *insertive* or *receptive*. The insertive partner refers to the person who is inserting his penis into another person's mouth, vagina, or anus. The receptive person is the one whose vagina, anus, or mouth is in contact with the penis. The receptive partner, regardless of gender, is considered to be at significantly greater risk for infection than the insertive partner when having sex without condoms if ejaculation occurs inside the body. Epidemiology has revealed a high variability in the insertive partner's risk around the world; insertive partners in the United States are at much lower risk for infection compared to men in other regions of the world, for reasons that are not fully known (Padian, Shiboski, Glass, & Vittinghoff, 1997). One explanation is that in any population with a high prevalence of sexually transmitted infections (STIs), the incidence of HIV transmission through sex seems to be much higher (Fleming, 1999). Research also demonstrates that uncircumcised men are at greater risk for HIV infection than circumcised ones (Auvert et al., 2001). The lining of the foreskin in uncircumcised men has been found to contain cells vulnerable to HIV infection; in circumcised men, transmission could occur only through a much smaller area, the urethra. African countries where circumcision practices are highly dependent on cultural and religious practices show that those that do practice circumcision have much lower rates of transmission to the male than in those communities where it is not practiced (Auvert et al., 2001; Auvert et al., 2005; Williams et al., 2006).

Research demonstrates that a person is 18 to 43 times more likely to transmit HIV to a partner during the acute phase compared to the asymptomatic phase of HIV infection (Pinkerton, 2007). When someone is initially infected, there are fluctuating high levels of HIV in that person's body. A person usually does not know that he or she is infected during this period because standard HIV tests may not detect infection in the early weeks of infection.

Controversy persists regarding transmission through oral sex. Since many people engage in oral sex under the assumption that it is safer than anal and vaginal sex, it is important to ascertain the probability of transmission. Transmission risk through receptive oral sex (meaning those who are performing oral sex on another person, potentially getting fluids in their mouth) is low compared to the risks associated with vaginal and anal sex without condoms. When comparing the different kinds of oral sex people engage in (fellatio, cunnilingus, and analingus), receptive fellatio carries the most risk, while there is little to no evidence that people have been infected with HIV while performing cunnilingus or analingus. A small number of cases have been attributed to oral-vaginal contact and one case of oral-anal contact, and the presence of blood in those cases potentially increased that risk. Studies examining the risk for transmission during fellatio have been most effectively studied among men who have sex with men, due to the capacity to control for other variables of transmission.

Characteristics of the oral cavity that reduce the likelihood of HIV transmission include a thicker mucous membrane, fewer cells that are targeted by HIV, and certain proteins in saliva that inhibit HIV's function and infectivity (Campo, 2006). Additionally, antibodies against HIV have been detected in HIV-infected people, reducing the likelihood that HIV will be transmitted to another person through saliva. An oral cavity that is healthy—no tears, lesions, STIs, or oral disease—is an excellent barrier against infections by bacteria and viruses, including HIV.

A systematic review of the existing studies that examine oral sex risk concluded that there is insufficient data to determine the precise probability of transmission, but confirmed that the risk is extremely low (Baggaley, White, & Boily, 2008). A study identifying 102 men having sex with men who had recently seroconverted suggested that eight of them (7.8 percent) were probably infected through oral sex (Dillon et al., 2000). The presence of oral ulcers, contact with ejaculate or pre-ejaculate, and frequent exposures were associated with some of these infections. This study estimated the route of transmission for only a small group of recently infected people and does not suggest the probability of transmission through oral sex in the general population. Another study of heterosexual couples of mixed HIV status that engaged only in oral sex resulted in no cases of HIV transmission (del Romero et al., 2002). An additional study of men having sex with men who engaged only in receptive oral sex with partners of known and unknown HIV status resulted in no transmissions (Page-Shafer et al., 2002). In order to more accurately determine oral transmission risk, larger and costlier studies need to be conducted.

Blood Transmission

Transmission through contact with blood occurs mostly when people share injection equipment: needles or syringes. Sharing injection needles or syringes accounts for approximately one-third of all HIV cases in the United States, although the incidence of HIV infection in this category has decreased by 80 percent since the beginning of the pandemic (Hall et al., 2008). It is likely that increased education and access to needle-exchange and syringe-exchange programs has had an impact on transmission in this category.

HIV transmission to health care workers exposed in the health care setting, called *occupational exposure*, is very rare. As of December 2001, only 57 reports of infections through occupational exposure have been reported (CDC, 2003). Six people who were infected (seemingly accidentally) by their HIV-infected dentist during surgery received much attention in the 1980s, but this is the only reported incident of provider-to-patient transmission (Rom, 1997).

The United States has one of the safest blood supplies in the world. Through the end of 2001, approximately 14,262 AIDS diagnoses were attributed to blood transfusion, with the vast majority of infections occurring before 1985 (CDC, 2003). The introduction of antibody screening in 1985 increased the safety of the blood supply, and in 1996, p24 antigen tests were included in the screening method, which reduces the window period by about a week. The risk of receiving a blood transfusion containing HIV is 1 in 676,000.

Vertical/Perinatal Transmission

An HIV-infected mother can transmit HIV to her infant at three different stages, all described as vertical or perinatal transmission: gestation (in the uterus), labor and vaginal delivery, and breast-feeding. Vaginal delivery poses the greatest risk of transmission to the infant due to increased exposure to maternal fluids. Without medical interventions, such as anti-HIV treatment to the mother and/or newborn or cesarean delivery, an HIV-infected mother has a 25 to 30% chance of transmitting HIV to her infant (CDC, 2008a). In the United States, medical interventions have reduced the rate of transmission to less than 2%, with a 95% reduction in AIDS cases due to vertical transmission since 1992. In 2006, only 115 children diagnosed with HIV or AIDS were infected perinatally, with 92% of all pediatric cases being associated with this route of transmission.

While the rates of vertical transmission have radically declined in the Unites States, education about prevention of perinatal transmission is still necessary and screening for HIV among pregnant women has become more widespread. From 2001 to 2004, approximately 7% of documented HIV-infected women were unaware of their status at time of delivery. The CDC has recommended *universal voluntary routine* screening for all pregnant women, with counseling and consent, and the availability of rapid tests increases the feasibility of testing pregnant women during labor.

During the first months of an infant's life, he or she carries maternal antibodies, so an infant will be HIV-positive by standard antibody tests (if the mother is HIV-infected) regardless of the presence of HIV in his or her body. Maternal antibodies are eventually replaced by the infant's own antibodies, but antibody tests can have false positives up to 18 months after birth. Tests that detect HIV itself are more accurate in determining the HIV status of a newborn when used repeatedly in the first six months after birth.

No Evidence for Other Transmission Routes

Numerous studies have examined the possibility of transmission through the major routes of transmission. The following are examples of ways that HIV is *not* transmitted:

- *Casual contact.* Several epidemiological studies early in the pandemic examined households where those who were uninfected had daily contact with an HIV-infected family member, and no cases of transmission through casual contact were detected (Fischl et al., 1987; Friedland et al., 1986; Lusher et al., 1991) through activities such as sharing kitchen utensils or bathroom facilities or kissing.
- *Inanimate objects.* HIV is fragile when exposed to the environment outside the human body. HIV requires a host—a living human cell—to survive. Laboratory studies have allowed fluids that contain high concentrations of HIV to dry and have found that infectiousness is reduced significantly within several hours (by about 95 percent). These studies do not replicate real-life situations, and there is no documented evidence that someone has been infected through contact with inanimate objects (http://www.cdc.gov/HIV/resources/qa/qa35.htm).
- *Accidental injury with injection needles outside of health care settings.* Since the beginning of the pandemic, anecdotes of people being exposed to HIV through accidental injury by a needle (for example, in a movie theater) have not been verified.
- *Insects.* There is no evidence that HIV is transmitted by insects, such as mosquitoes or ticks. In areas where there is a high prevalence of HIV infection and large populations of insects, there have been no documented cases of transmission through this route. Insects inject their own saliva as a lubricant to assist feeding (malaria and yellow fever are transmitted through insect saliva). They do not inject their own or a previously bitten person's blood. Also, HIV does not survive or reproduce in insects; HIV does not survive long enough outside of its host to be spread by the insect's mouth area; and insects also do not generally feed on two people in immediate succession.

TREATMENT

The development of effective medication regimens that radically reduce HIV-associated illness and death alters psychological and social perceptions of HIV disease. For people who have access to anti-HIV medication and expert medical care, HIV has largely become a manageable, chronic disease instead of a fatal one. Unfortunately, disparities in access to quality medication and treatment illuminate the complicated interplay of socioeconomic class, oppression, political and economic ideologies, and health care delivery. In 2007, approximately 31% of people in low- or middle-income countries in need of anti-HIV medication received it (WHO, 2007). While these numbers are unacceptably low—less than a third of those who need medications are getting them—there have been notable advancements in providing access to treatment in the twenty-first century, and international public health initiatives are gaining greater attention and funding.

Medications used to treat an HIV-infected person can be broken down into five categories:

1. Those that suppress HIV replication, called *antiretrovirals* (ARVs), *antiretroviral treatment* (ART), or *highly active antiretroviral treatment* (HAART)
2. Those that treat or prevent opportunistic infections (such as antibiotics)
3. Those that treat or manage HIV symptoms
4. Those that treat or manage the side effects of other medications
5. Psychotropic medication for psychiatric symptoms related to HIV infection

In addition, some HIV-infected people choose to use supplements, such as vitamins, herbal and homeopathic preparations, and alternative treatments such as massage, Reiki, and acupuncture. However, given the lack of rigorous research and regulatory control over their production, alternative treatments need to be used with caution and under the guidance of a medical professional. People with HIV often take a number of different medications, and potentially harmful interaction between different substances needs to be closely monitored by a medical professional. This section focuses primarily on antiretroviral treatment (ART or ARVs).

Antiretroviral Treatment

The development of and access to a new class of antiretrovirals called *protease inhibitors* in the mid-1990s marked a turning point in HIV treatment. Protease inhibitors, used in combination with other classes of medications, reduced HIV to undetectable levels in many HIV-infected persons, resulting in decreasing mortality rates and AIDS diagnoses (see Figure 1.3). While protease inhibitors represent just one class

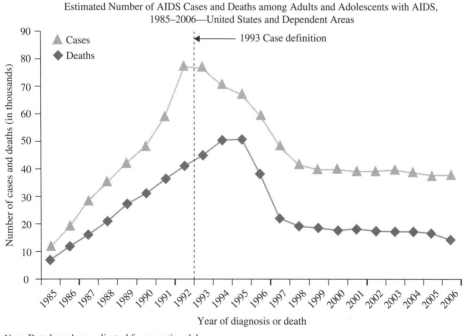

Note. Data have been adjusted for reporting delays.

Figure 1.3   Impact of Combination Therapy
Source: http://www.cdc.gov/HIV/topics/surveillance/resources/slides/epidemiology/slides/EPI-AIDS_1.pdf

of medications that are now used to treat HIV disease, their development and success gave medicine a sophisticated understanding of how to medically intervene in HIV disease progression.

There are now more than 30 FDA-approved HIV antiretroviral medications. The largest groups of anti-HIV medications that are prescribed can be broken down into three classes: nucleoside/nucleotide reverse transcriptase inhibitors (NRTIs, or "nukes"), non-nucleoside reverse transcriptase inhibitors (NNRTIs, or "non-nukes"), and protease inhibitors (PIs). There are three other classes of medication—entry inhibitors, integrase inhibitors, and maturation inhibitors—which are newer medications that are less frequently used or are still considered experimental. The classes are named in reference to where they act in *inhibiting* the life cycle of HIV in a CD4 cell. By disrupting certain HIV replication processes—fusion and entry into the cell, reversing HIV RNA into DNA, integrating itself into the cell's DNA, and assembling new replications of HIV—ART can attack HIV's Achilles' heel: its need to use CD4 cells to produce replications of itself.

Antiretroviral treatments are always prescribed in certain combinations—called *combination therapy*—most often using three drugs from two different classes of medication. Treatment with only one particular drug, called *monotherapy,* is likely to fail by encouraging a drug-resistant mutation of HIV to develop. Prescribing different types and classes of medications attacks the virus at different stages of its life cycle, reducing its capacity to develop resistance against the drugs. Consistent suppression of HIV replication is crucial, since the development of drug-resistant strains of HIV can render a particular medication treatment ineffective. Drug-resistant HIV strains can also be transmitted to another person, in whom the same medications would likely be ineffective, which is a public health concern.

The primary aim of ART is to reduce and maintain HIV at undetectable levels. Undetectable *does not mean that there is no HIV!* Even if HIV is not detected by standard viral load tests, that does not mean that HIV is not present in a person's blood or body. The virus can be present in amounts too small to be detected by current tests, in a CD4 cell, or in areas of the body called *reservoirs* (for example, in semen or cervical fluid or lymphoid tissue). While there is strong evidence that a person who has undetectable HIV levels in his or her blood has a much lower chance of transmitting HIV than someone who has a detectable level, that person on treatment is still infected and can still transmit the virus to another person. Given the impossibility of knowing the amount of HIV present in a person's body at any given time, experts are reluctant to say that HIV-infected people on ART cannot transmit HIV to a partner.

Anti-HIV treatment has dramatically reduced rates of mother-to-infant transmission in the United States and other countries where adequate medical treatment exists. Without medication, an HIV-infected mother has a 20% to 30% chance of transmitting HIV to her infant. Administration of anti-HIV medication during pregnancy and/or delivery, performing cesarean sections in women with high viral loads, and providing medication to newborns has reduced the rate of vertical transmission to less than 2% (Cooper et al., 2002). Another study demonstrated 90% effectiveness in preventing HIV transmission to infants among a cohort (European Collaborative Study, 2005). These reductions reflect statistics in areas where there is access to adequate prenatal and HIV care. Mother-to-child HIV transmission accounts for the vast majority of the estimated 700,000 new annual HIV infections in children worldwide. These data emphasize how education, treatment, and increased access to prenatal care in resource-challenged areas can dramatically reduce HIV transmission to infants.

The Challenges of Taking HIV Medication: Side Effects

Medications to fight HIV could be considered blunt instruments; they effectively debilitate HIV, but in the process can also produce unwanted and unintended side effects in the people who take them. As people live longer with HIV, and as the field sees people living longer on ART, greater understanding is developing about the long-term effects on HIV-infected persons, leading to efforts to fine-tune medications.

Side effects that people on HIV treatment experience should always be taken seriously. If short-term side effects can be managed and tolerated until they subside, that is preferable to changing an already effective treatment. If side effects are too difficult to manage, alternative treatment regimens should be explored with the physician. Intolerable side effects that a person experiences can lead to not taking the medicine correctly or stopping treatment altogether, and effective ongoing communication and interaction with caregivers can help prevent this.

The cause of physical and psychological symptoms can be difficult, and sometimes impossible, to accurately identify. While certain side effects are relatively easy to identify and diagnose, others can be attributed to multiple factors: for example, lifestyle, unidentified illness, and nutrition. If the initiation of a particular antiretroviral medication coincides with the development of depressive symptoms, the task of identifying the cause of symptoms can be daunting. One antiretroviral, called Sustiva, has been reported to result in depressive symptoms in some people. However, it is not unusual for a person who is struggling with being HIV-infected and having to take medication to experience depression. Determining what is causing a symptom in a person taking ART is an inexact science that requires thorough biopsychosocial assessment, different levels of intervention, and the willingness of caretakers to take concerns seriously and to be flexible, and sometimes creative, in their approaches to treatment. A thorough assessment of a person's way of life and psychological status can also illuminate factors that can contribute to, and possibly improve, side effects of medication.

Most people can tolerate short-term side effects to continue their medication regimen; rarely are side effects severe enough to merit changing a medication regimen, but all adverse reactions should be taken seriously. The most common short-term side effects are gastrointestinal symptoms (diarrhea, nausea, vomiting), headache, rash, fatigue, dry mouth, and psychological symptoms (depression, anxiety, and nightmares). As people live longer with HIV on antiretroviral treatments, long-term side effects are only recently being observed and studied. Longer-term health problems could be associated with the anti-HIV medications themselves, the dynamics of HIV infection, older age, or unidentified risk factors. Some of the long-term side effects associated to ART are:

- Fat redistribution. Lipodystrophy is an abnormal distribution of fat (lipids) in the body. Lipohypertrophy refers to abnormal fat accumulation, usually seen in the abdomen, breasts, or upper back. Fat loss (lipoatrophy) usually occurs in the face, arms, legs, and buttocks. These symptoms may be associated with other metabolic abnormalities and often result in distressing psychological reactions. Some treatments that replace or remove fat in affected areas exist.
- Higher levels of cholesterol and triglycerides, which are associated with increased risk for heart attack, stroke, and pancreatitis.
- Diabetes as a result of increased glucose and insulin levels.
- Bone loss and weakening of bones (osteoporosis and osteopenia).
- Liver and kidney damage.

Certain medications are implicated in the risks of the development of some of these long-term side effects, and understanding the risks associated with particular medications, as well as thorough assessments of other health factors, nutrition, and lifestyle, can all have an impact on these conditions.

Medication Adherence

A critical determinant of successful antiretroviral treatment—and a considerable challenge for many people taking ART—is adherence (sticking to) to medication regimens. When antiretrovirals are not taken in accordance with how they are prescribed, HIV can mutate and develop *resistance* to that medication, possibly resulting in *cross-resistance*—a resistance to other drugs in a particular class of medication—leading to failure in that particular treatment. Adherence to regimens can be particularly difficult when there are multiple drugs that need to be taken multiple times every day, sometimes with particular dietary restrictions, dosage, and timing requirements. Advancements in drug formulations have greatly reduced the amount of pills that a person may need to take; medications continue to be developed that combine different drugs within and across classes into one dose.

Research suggests that poor adherence is a widespread problem (Murphy et al., 2001; Nieuwkerk et al., 2001), though few long-term studies exist. It is believed that 95% adherence is needed for the best results, or the person with HIV risks increased viral replication and development of drug-resistant virus (Paterson et al., 2000). However, there is evidence that levels of adherence needed to achieve sufficient viral suppression is dependent on the class of medication taken. One study demonstrates that regimens of protease inhibitors require greater adherence (greater than 95%) than NNRTI regimens (greater than 54%), a significant finding since protease inhibitors are commonly prescribed in treatment regimens (Bangsberg, 2006). While more research needs to be conducted on medication-taking behaviors among HIV-infected populations, the importance of adhering as closely as possible to a medication regimen is vital to treatment success.

Researchers and clinicians study and observe varying psychosocial factors that predict medication adherence, such as socioeconomic status, race, gender, psychiatric conditions and cognitive functioning, family and social support networks, attitudes toward treatment, physician-patient relationships and rapport, and the complexity of treatment regimens (Ammassari et al., 2002; Stone et al., 2001; van Servellen, Chang, Garcia, & Lombardi, 2002). While research studies have attempted to identify personality traits, behaviors, and environmental conditions that contribute to suboptimal medication adherence, providers should be cautious about drawing premature conclusions about a person's likelihood to adhere to medication. Individual readiness to begin medication, recognizing potential barriers to adherence, effective provider-client communication, and ongoing monitoring and assessment are all critical in supporting medication adherence. It can be difficult for service providers who are not on complicated medication regimens to understand why a person would risk his or her health by not taking medications correctly, and active empathic engagement with persons with HIV is a vital tool to support adherence.

When to Start Treatment

Since the development of effective antiretroviral treatment, debates have persisted about when to treat a person who is infected with HIV. With the advent of protease inhibitors and combination therapies, a "hit early, hit hard" approach was endorsed, with the hope that early, intensive treatment would offer the possibility of viral eradication. When the hope for eradication was never realized, physicians and researchers began to think more critically about when was the most effective time to initiate treatment. The debates have been vigorous, involving an intersection of different principles, ethics, and values, along with a lack of thorough enough understanding of the mechanics of antiretroviral treatment and disease progression.

From a medical standpoint, researchers have conflicted opinions about whether early intervention actually demonstrates long-term advantages for survival rates and viral suppression, though the tide seems to be turning, with the support of important research, toward suggesting earlier medication interventions. Dr. Anthony Fauci, a central figure in the study of anti-HIV medication research, recently suggested that early intervention has the promise of a "functional cure" of HIV. The arguments against treating early involve starting someone on medication that cannot be stopped once started, that causes long-term physical side effects, that puts financial and psychological burdens on the person with HIV, and that raises the risk of developing resistance to the medication due to difficulties involved in long-term adherence. Ethically, one should be treated only when benefits outweigh costs. Given the long-term side effects of long-term treatment, the person with HIV and his or her physician must weigh these decisions carefully.

The U.S. Department of Health and Human Services has set, and continues to revise, guidelines on when a person should begin ART. (See Table 1.2.) Physicians, as well as HIV-infected persons and those who provide services to them, need to stay abreast of these changing guidelines.

HIV has a tendency to mutate quite rapidly, creating slightly different variations of itself, which has resulted in a genetic diversity of HIV that can present challenges to treatment. Given the number of different medications and mutations of HIV that are resistant to particular medications, choosing a good treatment regimen requires specialized medical testing

Table 1.2   Indications for initiating ART therapy

Clinical Condition and/or CD4 Count	Recommendations
• History of AIDS-defining illness (**AI**) • CD4 count <200 cells/mm^3 (**AI**) • CD4 count 200–350 cells/mm^3 (**AII**) • Pregnant women* (**AI**) • Persons with HIV-associated nephropathy (**AI**) • Persons coinfected with hepatitis B virus (HBV), when HBV treatment is indicated (Treatment with fully suppressive antiviral drugs active against both HIV and HBV is recommended.) (**BIII**)	Antiretroviral therapy should be initiated.
• Patients with CD4 count >350 cells/mm^3 who do not meet any of the specific conditions listed above	The optimal time to initiate therapy in asymptomatic patients with CD4 count >350 cells/mm^3 is not well defined. Patient scenarios and comorbidities should be taken into consideration. (See box below and text regarding risks and benefits of therapy in patients with CD4 count >350 cells/mm^3).

Source: http://www.aidsinfo.nih.gov/Guidelines/GuidelineDetail.aspx?MenuItem=Guidelines&Search=Off&GuidelineID=7&ClassID=1

and expertise. Laboratory analysis (called *genotyping* and *phenotyping*) of the specific characteristics of HIV with which a person is infected can anticipate medications the virus might be resistant to, which drugs will more likely work, and at what dosage and combinations. Resistance testing is recommended for all HIV-infected people, especially for those newly infected (even if they don't plan on starting treatment), before a medication regimen is decided upon, and those for whom medication regimens fail or are not working well.

Similar to diabetics who need to closely monitor and manage glucose levels, people with HIV need to closely monitor viral levels and CD4 counts to determine how effective a particular drug regimen is and to prevent disease progression. Drug-resistant mutations of HIV are most commonly attributed to poor medication adherence, problems with how the medication is absorbed into the bloodstream, and adverse drug interactions. When medications fail to suppress HIV replication sufficiently, HIV-infected persons need to make informed decisions with their doctors about changing treatment regimens.

HIV PREVENTION

In the absence of effective medical interventions to prevent HIV transmission and cure infection, educational and behavioral interventions have been the cornerstone of HIV prevention since the early years of the pandemic. Assuming that people cannot take the steps to promote and protect their health unless they have an understanding of the risks involved in engaging in certain behaviors, a central piece of HIV prevention has been educating people about how HIV is transmitted, how to prevent transmission of the virus, and how to get tested. With the advent of effective anti-HIV treatments, cultural attitudes have changed in accordance with access to the medications. Prevention experts express concern that, especially among populations that are at significant risk for HIV infection, people have become complacent about HIV transmission and safer sex and drug behavior. Recent research on continued high rates of HIV transmission among certain populations suggests that prevention efforts are not effective enough and need to be closely examined and revised.

Early in the pandemic, when scientists began to realize that HIV was an infectious agent that could be transmitted through *behaviors* like sex and sharing syringes, there were ideological debates about funding prevention efforts toward those who engaged in risky behavior. The "Just Say No to Drugs" campaign of the Reagan administration was in vogue, and in many ways the message was applied to sex: Abstinence is the best way to prevent HIV infection. Conservatives did not want to support and fund explicit messages about condom use and needle sharing to prevent HIV transmission for fear of appearing to condone promiscuous or drug-using behavior. Implicit in this position was a fundamental rejection of homosexuality, drug use, and any behavior that was deemed deviant. Prevention advocates urged that preventing the spread of a fatal disease took precedence over moral messages.

Safer sex education began in the private sector. The initial strategies started by community organizers in the gay community involved disseminating explicit information about HIV transmission and distributing condoms throughout community venues. Materials that were unapologetic about using frank and culturally appropriate language to describe the realities of sexual behavior and HIV transmission were considered to be more effective than information that was euphemistic or omitted information that might be "offensive." Attitudes toward sex in the United States made transparent and accurate transmission of information difficult.

HIV prevention efforts through federal government funding in the United States have been fueled primarily by politically conservative and religious principles, focused primarily on abstinence-based education. Federal funding to schools has been strictly pro-hibitive of comprehensive sex education to students, restricting funds to abstinence-only education models. A meta-analysis of the existing empirical research on the effectiveness of abstinence-only programs in the United States found that the programs showed no con-sistent beneficial effect on HIV infection rates, the incidence of sexual behaviors, including sexual initiation, unprotected or frequency of vaginal sex, amount of partners, or condom use (Underhill, Operario, & Montgomery, 2007).

Federal funding of needle-exchange or syringe-exchange programs—services where people can exchange used needles for new ones or have access to clean needles without a prescription—has also proven controversial, because opponents argue that it will increase or condone illegal drug use. Injection drug users share needles due to limited access to clean needles, and not supplying them with clean needles perpetuates the HIV pandemic. Since cleaning needles requires knowledge about the process, access to supplies, and careful atten-tion after each use, programs that provide clean needles to users increase the odds that they will not need to share needles. In 1992, Connecticut decriminalized possession of syringes or needles without a prescription, which made them available for sale through pharmacies for nonmedical use. The amount of needles or syringes purchased for nonmedical use increased significantly (Valleroy et al., 1995). New Haven, Connecticut, also implemented legal needle-exchange programs in 1990. Studies demonstrated that this intervention decreased the incidence and prevalence of HIV among injectors in the area and increased referrals to drug treatment programs (Heimer, Kaplan, Khoshnood, Jariwala, & Cadman, 1993; Vlahov & Junge, 1998). Despite the evidence, the United States has steadfastly refused, on ideological grounds, to federally fund needle-exchange and clean-needle programs.

A harm-reduction model of prevention presumes that complete abstinence from risk-taking behavior is unrealistic for many people and that there are ways to reduce harm when taking risks. Methadone maintenance programs are based on the harm-reduction model; a less harmful drug, methadone, is administered in a controlled fashion for heroin addicts to prevent the more harmful effects of illegal heroin use. The harm-reduction approach respects the reality of the person's psychological preparedness for change, emphasizes the importance of avoiding judgment of people's behaviors, and places the value of individual and collective health over moral and ideological arguments.

When condoms are used correctly for anal and vaginal sex, they are very effective in preventing the transmission of HIV and many other STIs. Male condoms are latex, poly-urethane, or animal membrane sheaths that are placed on an erect penis to prevent the recep-tive partner in vaginal or anal sex from coming into contact with semen or pre-ejaculate. While animal-membrane condoms are effective as birth control, they should never be used to prevent HIV transmission because they contain pores that HIV can pass through, while latex and polyurethane condoms have pores smaller than the virus. Water- or oil-based lubri-cants can be used with polyurethane condoms, while one should exclusively use water-based lubricant with latex condoms. Nonoxynol-9, a spermicide that is in some lubricants, should not be used for disease prevention, as allergic reactions and irritation to the substance have been shown to increase the risk for HIV transmission when exposed, and spermicides do not kill retroviruses.

Since the data show that condoms should be used for vaginal and anal sex consistently, we need to educate people how to use condoms correctly. The CDC has set forth the following guidelines for using male condoms:

- Use a new condom for each act of intercourse.
- Put on the condom as soon as erection occurs and before any sexual contact (vagi-nal, anal, or oral).

- Hold the tip of the condom and unroll it onto the erect penis, leaving space at the tip of the condom, yet ensuring that no air is trapped in the condom's tip.
- Adequate lubrication is important, but use only water-based lubricants, such as glycerin or lubricating jellies (which can be purchased at any pharmacy). Oil-based lubricants, such as petroleum jelly, cold cream, hand lotion, or baby oil, can weaken the condom.
- Do not use lubricants with nonoxynol-9 (a chemical that inhibits sperm from causing pregnancy) for HIV prevention, as it can cause an allergic reaction that increases a person's risk for HIV infection.
- Withdraw from the partner immediately after ejaculation, holding the condom firmly to keep it from slipping off.

The FDA approved a female condom in 1993. Statistics reflecting increasing rates of HIV infection among women through heterosexual sex raised concerns about their ability to negotiate condom use with their partners. The female condom is a polyurethane pouch with two rings on each end, and one opening. A removable flexible ring at the closed end is inserted into the vagina, and the ring on the opened end stays outside the vulva, which prevents it from slipping or bunching up. The fact that women can wear the condom for up to eight hours prior to sex, or use it if their partner refuses to wear a condom, empowers them to have more control during sex. Female condoms are more expensive than male condoms and can be difficult to use and negotiate, so it is still widely unavailable around the world. Female condoms can be used for anal intercourse as well, whether the insertive partner is male or female.

CONDOM EFFECTIVENESS

There is some confusion about the research on condom effectiveness, due to both the methodological complexity of this research, misinterpretation of findings, and ideological debates. Theoretically, a condom should be 100 percent effective in preventing the transmission of HIV based on laboratory studies, since HIV cannot permeate condoms (Carey et al., 1992). Epidemiologic studies have demonstrated that condoms are highly effective in preventing the transmission of HIV, as well as preventing the transmission of certain STIs—such as chlamydia, gonorrhea, and trichomoniasis (Weller & Davis, 2003). It has been incorrectly presumed that condoms do not work because they do not prevent the transmission of all STIs 100% of the time; some STIs, like herpes, syphilis, and genital warts (HPV), are transmitted by lesions on the skin that may not be shielded by the condom. Reviews of existing literature show that condoms are effective in preventing HIV transmission 80 to 95% of the time, with considerable limitations in some of the research to account for correctness of use (Pinkerton & Abramson, 1997; Weller & Davis, 2003). In a longitudinal four-year study of mixed-HIV-status couples, all 124 couples who used condoms every time prevented transmission of HIV, while 12 partners of 121 couples who did not consistently use condoms became infected (De Vincenzi, 1994). Other studies of serodiscordant couples where consistent versus inconsistent use was closely examined yielded similar results (Allen et al., 1992; Guimarães, Muñoz, Boschi-Pinto, & Castilho, 1995; Laurian, Peynet, & Verroust, 1989; Nicolosi, Leite, Musicco, Arici, et al., 1994; Saracco et al., 1993).

Studies conducted about condom failure among sexual partners have shown widely different rates, with most failures resulting from incorrect use and not with the condom itself. Condom breakage during intercourse is estimated to be anywhere from 1 to 8%. One study of couples using condoms over a period of time showed that 62% of them experienced no condom failure (meaning breakage or slippage), 29% had one to three failures, and 9% had four or more failures. Most studies show that higher rates of condom failure happen among a small percent of the general population (some have estimated as low as 4 to 6%), depending on aspects of condom use like technical skill, experience using condoms, prior episodes of breakage, condom fit, and amount of lubrication. Commercial sex workers, presumably due to their experience in using condoms, have demonstrated the lowest condom breakage or slippage rates.

Medical Approaches to Prevention

Two interventions use existing antiretroviral treatments to attempt to prevent HIV infection prior to exposure and immediately after exposure. Postexposure prophylaxis (meaning prevention), or PEP, was first conceived in health care settings following occupational exposures to HIV-infected blood among health care workers. Theoretically, if anti-HIV medication is used shortly after exposure, long-term infection could be prevented. The effectiveness of PEP in nonoccupational exposures has not been studied. One study did demonstrate a 81% reduction in HIV infection among health care workers treated with PEP compared to those who remained untreated following an occupational exposure (Cardo et al., 1997). PEP has subsequently become available to the general public, usually through clinics or emergency rooms, for sexual exposures that present a high-risk for transmission. For example, it has been routine to offer PEP to victims of sexual assault when there is the possibility of transmission, or among serodiscordant (one is HIV-positive and one is HIV-negative) couples when there is an incident that poses significant risk for infection.

In order for PEP to be effective, treatment needs to be initiated within 32 hours of exposure, and some suggest that administration within 12 hours is optimal. Beginning PEP has several complications. First, access to medication in the short time period following exposure is unrealistic for most people. Also, a person has to commit to taking medication daily for about one month; these medications are typically not covered by health insurance for PEP, so it can be expensive, and adherence to the medication can be complicated by side effects and adverse psychological reactions.

PrEP, or preexposure prophylaxis, is a more recent area of investigation, and works on the same principles as PEP, except medication is administered to an HIV-negative person *prior* to being exposed to HIV. PrEP can be especially useful for women around the world who experience cultural barriers to negotiating condom use, active injection drug users, or men who have sex with men engaging in unprotected intercourse. Animal studies among nonhuman primates have demonstrated that administration of PrEP to an uninfected animal resulted in zero transmissions when repeatedly exposed to the primate equivalent of HIV, called *simian immunodeficiency virus* (SIV), compared to an untreated control group that resulted in significant levels of infection (Garcia-Lerma et al., 2006). While human research trials in Africa are under way, there is no evidence that PrEP will be effective in humans.

Microbicides are creams or gels that are applied inside the rectum or vagina to protect against HIV and other STI transmission. Research on microbicides was initiated and designed to provide more control to people, especially women, in preventing HIV transmission when condom use is sporadic or unavailable. There are many experimental microbicides that have shown effectiveness in animal studies, but human studies have been unsuccessful so far, and more need to be conducted to determine the effectiveness of microbicides.

Ultimately, a vaccine would be the most effective way to prevent transmission, and potentially eradicate HIV transmission around the world. Vaccines work by stimulating antibody production against a particular pathogen before someone is exposed to it, providing resistance to infection when exposed in the future. Vaccine trials to date have been limited due to ethical and programmatic difficulties, and none of the vaccine trials have yielded successful results. The high genetic variability of HIV and its capacity to mutate and evolve at a rapid pace makes the development of an effective vaccine against all strains of HIV a formidable task.

Personal Perspective

Living with HIV, by Chris

I tested HIV-positive on October 28, 1992. I was an active alcoholic and cocaine addict at the time, and my life was already a train wreck. The HIV diagnosis just felt like the final nail in the coffin. My HIV diagnosis co-occurred with a case of Hepatitis A. I continued to drink and do drugs throughout this time.

In 1992, being HIV-positive was still very much a death sentence. I was in show business in New York City, and many people in my world were getting sick and dying. The first time I got blood work done, my CD4 count was 424. AZT was the only approved treatment, and it wasn't thought of as being great. They said it might prolong your life for a little while. I took it briefly in 1993, but it made me dizzy and nauseated and I soon gave up. So from the end of 1992 through the beginning of 1995, I just kind of waited to get sick.

In February of 1995, I heard about a new drug called Epivir (3TC) that was shown to be effective in combination with AZT. I went on it right away, and three months later my CD4 count had doubled from 267 (the lowest it's ever been) to 545. I also got sober in July of that year, and know that that helped strengthen my immune system as well.

In December of 1995, I was prescribed Invirase, one of the first protease inhibitors, to add to my regimen. I was one of the very first people on combination therapy, called "the triple cocktail." Over the next nine years my CD4-cells went up and stayed up (at one time topping 1,500) while my viral load was most often undetectable. When it wasn't, my doctor changed my medication. And yet I still felt that my life was only really being increased in three-month increments, from doctor's appointment to doctor's appointment. I kind of waited for what I thought would be the inevitable fall. Side effects could be bad too: rash, nausea, kidney stones, and stomach problems. Some I was able to deal with. Some of the medications I simply couldn't take. Lypodystrophy also occurred. I lost fat in my face and gained it in the back of my neck.

In August of 2004, after almost nine years of antiviral therapy, I wanted a break. I was tired of Sustiva and the resulting horrible dreams that often woke me up feeling terrified. I had done so well for so long; I wanted to see how I could do without medication. And I must admit I sort of wanted to see if the virus would "still be there" untreated.

Under the supervision of an HIV specialist, at first my treatment vacation was quite liberating. It was a relief not to have to take pills anymore. At first my counts remained stable. Then over the course of the next 19 months, my T cells slowly decreased while my viral load slowly increased. It became increasingly demoralizing. I was reminded that I "still had it."

In March of 2006, with my T cells back down to 426 and my viral load at about 10,000, my doctors advised that I resume antiretroviral treatment and I agreed. The vacation was over and that was okay. Since then I've been on a very good combination of Reyataz and Truvada (three pills a day) that I've tolerated quite well. My counts are great, and I have other options should this "cocktail" lose its efficacy. Thankfully, the fat deposits on my neck—known as lypodystrophy—have been surgically removed and the areas of my face that have lost fat—lypoatrophy—have been filled in with a treatment called Sculptra.

It's only been in the past couple of years that I've really come to believe that I'm not going to die from HIV. Sixteen years after my diagnosis, I remain grateful and pretty astounded that my story has played out as it has.

CONCLUSIONS

The HIV pandemic continues to have a profound impact on people around the world, and it is crucial that social workers and other professionals in the human services are prepared to meet the needs of those confronted with the disease. While people in the helping professions are not required to be medical experts on HIV, being aware of the basics of HIV disease can have a significant impact among individuals and communities affected by HIV and AIDS. Armed with basic knowledge about transmission, treatment, policy, and prevention, we can listen intelligently and compassionately to people with HIV and their caregivers, provide support in seeking treatment and adhering to medication, reduce barriers to safer sex or access to clean needles and syringes, and reduce people's anxieties about the risks associated with HIV disease.

REFERENCES

Allen, S., Tice, J., Van de Perre, P., Serufilira, A., Hudes, E., Nsengumuremyi, F., et al. (1992). Effect of serotesting with counselling on condom use and seroconversion among HIV discordant couples in Africa. *British Medical Journal, 304*(6842), 1605–1609.

Ammassari, A., Trotta, M. P., Murri, R., Castelli, F., Narciso, P., Noto, P., et al. (2002). Correlates and predictors of adherence to highly active antiretroviral therapy: Overview of published literature. *Journal of Acquired Immune Deficiency Syndromes, 31*(Suppl. 315), S123–S127.

Auvert, B., Buvé, A., Lagarde, E., Kahindo, M., Chege, J., Rutenberg, N., et al. (2001). Male circumcision and HIV infection in four cities in sub-Saharan Africa. *AIDS, 15,* S31–S40.

Auvert, B., Taljaard, D., Lagarde, E., Sobngwi-Tambekou, J., Sitta, R., & Puren, A. (2005). Randomized, controlled intervention trial of male circumcision for reduction of HIV infection risk: The ANRS 1265 Trial. *PLoS Medicine, 2*(11), 1112–1121.

Babiker, A., Darby, S. C., De Angelis, D., Ewart, D., & Porter, K. (2000). Time from HIV-1 sero-conversion to AIDS and death before widespread use of highly active antiretroviral therapy: A collaborative reanalysis. *Lancet, 355,* 1131–1137.

Baggaley, R. F., White, R. G., & Boily, M.-C. (2008). Systematic review of orogenital HIV-1 transmission probabilities. *International Journal of Epidemiology, 37*(6), 1255–1266.

Campo, J., Perea, M. A., del Romero, J., Cano, J., Hernando, V., & Bascones, A. (2006). Oral transmission of HIV, reality or fiction? An update. *Oral Diseases, 12*(3), 219–228.

Carey, R. F., Herman, W. A., Retta, S. M., Rinaldi, J. E., Herman, B. A., & Athey, T. W. (1992). Effectiveness of latex condoms as a barrier to human immunodeficiency virus-sized particles under conditions of simulated use. *Sexually Transmitted Diseases, 19*(4), 230–234.

Castro, K. G., Ward, J. W., & Slutsker, L. (1992). 1993 revised classification system for HIV infection and expanded surveillance case definition for AIDS among adolescents and adults. Centers for Disease Control and Prevention: *Morbidity and Mortality Weekly Report MMWR, 41,* 961–962.

Centers for Disease Control and Prevention. (1981a). Follow-up on Kaposi's sarcoma and Pneumocystis pneumonia. *Morbidity and Mortality Weekly, 30*(33), 409–410.

Centers for Disease Control and Prevention. (1981b). Kaposi's sarcoma and Pneumocystis pneumonia among homosexual men—New York and California. *Morbidity and Mortality Weekly,* 30, 305–308.

Centers for Disease Control and Prevention. (1981c). Pneumocystis pneumonia—Los Angeles. *Morbidity and Mortality Weekly,* 30, 250–252.

Centers for Disease Control and Prevention. (2003). Preventing occupational HIV transmission to health care workers. Retrieved March 31, 2009, from http://www.cdc.gov/HIV/resources/Factsheets/hcwprev.htm

Centers for Disease Control and Prevention. (2006). *HIV/AIDS Surveillance Report, Volume 18.* Atlanta: Department of Health and Human Services, Centers for Disease Control and Prevention. Retrieved March 31, 2009, from http://www.cdc.gov/HIV/topics/surveillance/resources/reports/2006report/default.htm

Centers for Disease Control and Prevention. (2008). Trends in HIV/AIDS diagnoses among men who have sex with men—33 States, 2001–2006. *Morbidity and Mortality Weekly, 57*(25), 681–686.

Cooper, E. R., Charurat, M., Mofenson, L., Hanson, I. C., Pitt, J., Diaz, C., et al. (2002). Combination antiretroviral strategies for the treatment of pregnant HIV-1-infected women and prevention of perinatal HIV-1 transmission. *Journal of Acquired Immune Deficiency Syndromes, 29*(5), 484–494.

del Romero, J., Marincovich, B., Castilla, J., García, S., Campo, J., Hernando, V., et al. (2002). Evaluating the risk of HIV transmission through unprotected orogenital sex. *AIDS, 16*(9), 1296–1297.

De Vincenzi, I. (1994). A longitudinal study of human immunodeficiency virus transmission by heterosexual partners. *New England Journal of Medicine, 331*(6). 341–346.

Dillon, B., Hecht, F. M., Swanson, M., Goupil-Sormany, I., Grant, R. M., Chesney, M. A., et al. (2000, January 30). Primary HIV infections associated with oral transmission. Paper presented at the 7th Conference on Retroviruses and Opportunistic Infections.

Fischl, M. A., Dickinson, G. M., Scott, G. B., Klimas, N., Fletcher, M. A., & Parks, W. (1987). Evaluation of heterosexual partners, children, and household contacts of adults with AIDS. *JAMA, 257*(5), 640–644.

Fleming, D. T. (1999). From epidemiological synergy to public health policy and practice: the contribution of other sexually transmitted diseases to sexual transmission of HIV infection. *Sexually Transmitted Infections, 75*(1), 3–17.

Friedland, G. H., Saltzman, B. R., Rogers, M. F., Kahl, P. A., Lesser, M. L., Mayers, M. M., et al. (1986). Lack of transmission of HTLV-III/LAV infection to household contacts of patients with AIDS or AIDS-related complex with oral candidiasis. *New England Journal of Medicine, 314*(6), 344–349.

Garcia-Lerma, J., Otten, R., Qari, S., Jackson, E., Luo, W., & Monsour, M. (2006). Prevention of rectal SHIV transmission in macaques by tenofovir/FTC combination. *PLoS Med 5*(2), e28. doi:10.1371/journal.pmed.0050028, 0291–0299.

Glynn, M., & Rhodes, P. (2005, June 12). Estimated HIV prevalence in the United States at the end of 2003. Paper presented at the National HIV Prevention Conference, Atlanta, GA.

Guimarães, M. D. C., Muñoz, A., Boschi-Pinto, C., & Castilho, E. A. (1995). HIV infection among female partners of seropositive men in Brazil. *American Journal of Epidemiology, 142*(5), 538–547.

Hall, H. I., Song, R., Rhodes, P., Prejean, J., An, Q., Lee, L. M., et al. (2008). Estimation of HIV incidence in the United States. *JAMA, 300*(5), 520–529.

Harris, C., Small, C. B., Klein, R. S., Friedland, G. H., Moll, B., Emeson, E. E., et al. (1983). Immunodeficiency in female sexual partners of men with the acquired immunodeficiency syndrome. *New England Journal of Medicine, 308*(20), 1181–1184.

Heimer, R., Kaplan, E. H., Khoshnood, K., Jariwala, B., & Cadman, E. C. (1993). Needle exchange decreases the prevalence of HIV-1 proviral DNA in returned syringes in New Haven, Connecticut. *American Journal of Medicine, 95*(2), 214–220.

Laurian, Y., Peynet, J., & Verroust, F. (1989). HIV infection in sexual partners of HIV-seropositive patients with hemophilia. *New England Journal of Medicine, 320*(3), 183.

Levine, M. P., Nardi, P. M., & Gagnon, J. H. (1997). *In changing times: Gay men and lesbians encounter HIV/AIDS.* Chicago: University of Chicago Press.

Levy, J. A. (1998). *HIV and the Pathogenesis of AIDS.* Washington, DC: ASM Press.

Lusher, J. M., Operskalski, E. A., Aledort, L. M., Dietrich, S. L., Gjerset, G. F., Hilgartner, M. W., et al. (1991). Risk of human immunodeficiency virus type 1 infection among sexual and nonsexual household contacts of persons with congenital clotting disorders. *Pediatrics, 88*(2), 242–249.

MacKellar, D. A., Valleroy, L. A., Secura, G. M., Behel, S., Bingham, T., Celentano, D. D., et al. (2005). Unrecognized HIV infection, risk behaviors, and perceptions of risk among young men who have sex with men: Opportunities for advancing HIV prevention in the third decade of HIV/AIDS. *Journal of Acquired Immune Deficiency Syndromes, 38*(5), 603–614.

Marks, G., Crepaz, N., & Janssen, R. S. (2006). Estimating sexual transmission of HIV from persons aware and unaware that they are infected with the virus in the USA. *AIDS, 20*(10), 1447–1450.

Marks, G., Crepaz, N., Senterfitt, J. W., & Janssen, R. S. (2005). Meta-analysis of high-risk sexual behavior in persons aware and unaware they are infected with HIV in the United States: Implications for HIV prevention programs. *Journal of Acquired Immune Deficiency Syndromes, 39*(4), 446–453.

Murphy, E. L., Collier, A. C., Kalish, L. A., Assmann, S. F., Para, M. F., Flanigan, T. P., et al. (2001). Highly active antiretroviral therapy decreases mortality and morbidity in patients with advanced HIV disease. *Annals of Internal Medicine, 135*(1), 17–26.

Nicolosi, A., Leite, M. L. C., Musicco, M., Arici, C., Gavazzeni, G., & Lazzarin, A. (1994). For the Italian Study Group on HIV Heterosexual Transmission. The efficiency of male-to-female and female-to-male sexual transmission of the human immunodeficiency virus: A study of 730 stable couples. *Epidemiology, 5*(6), 570–575.

Nieuwkerk, P. T., Sprangers, M. A. G., Burger, D. M., Hoetelmans, R. M. W., Hugen, P. W. H., Danner, S. A., et al. (2001). Limited patient adherence to highly active antiretroviral therapy for HIV-1 infection in an observational cohort study. *Archives of Internal Medicine, 161*(16), 1962–1968.

Padian, N. S., Shiboski, S. C., Glass, S. O., & Vittinghoff, E. (1997). Heterosexual transmission of human immunodeficiency virus (HIV) in northern California: Results from a ten-year study. *American Journal of Epidemiology, 146*(4), 350–357.

Page-Shafer, K., Shiboski, C. H., Osmond, D. H., Dilley, J., McFarland, W., Shiboski, S. C., et al. (2002). Risk of HIV infection attributable to oral sex among men who have sex with men and in the population of men who have sex with men. *AIDS, 16*(17), 2350–2352.

Paterson, D. L., Swindells, S., Mohr, J., Brester, M., Vergis, E. N., Squier, C., et al. (2000). Adherence to protease inhibitor therapy and outcomes in patients with HIV infection. *Annals of Internal Medicine, 133*(1), 21–30.

Pinkerton, S. D. (2007). Probability of HIV transmission during acute infection in Rakai, Uganda. *AIDS and Behavior, 12*(5), 677–684.

Pinkerton, S. D., & Abramson, P. R. (1997). Effectiveness of condoms in preventing HIV transmission. *Social Science & Medicine, 44*(9), 1303–1312.

Saracco, A., Musicco, M., Nicolosi, A., Angarano, G., Arici, C., Gavazzeni, G., et al. (1993). Man-to-woman sexual transmission of HIV: Longitudinal study of 343 steady partners of infected men. *Journal of Acquired Immune Deficiency Syndromes, 6*(5), 497–502.

Stone, V. E., Hogan, J. W., Schuman, P., Rompalo, A. M., Howard, A. A., Korkontzelou, C., et al. (2001). Antiretroviral regimen complexity, self-reported adherence, and HIV patients' understanding of their regimens: Survey of women in the HER study. *Journal of Acquired Immune Deficiency Syndromes, 28*(2), 124–131.

Sullivan, A. (1996, November 10). When plagues end: Notes on the twilight of an epidemic. *New York Times Magazine*, pp. 52–62, 76–57, 84.

Underhill, K., Operario, D., & Montgomery, P. (2007). Abstinence-only programs for HIV infection prevention in high-income countries (Review). *Cochrane Database of Systematic Reviews, 4*. Article CD005421. DOI: 10.1002/14651858.CD005421.pub2. Retrieved April 7, 2009.

Valleroy, L. A., Weinstein, B., Jones, T. S., Groseclose, S. L., Rolfs, R. T., & Kassler, W. J. (1995). Impact of increased legal access to needles and syringes on community pharmacies' needle and syringe sales—Connecticut, 1992–1993. *Journal of Acquired Immune Deficiency Syndromes and Human Retrovirology, 10*(1), 73–81.

van Servellen, G., Chang, B., Garcia, L., & Lombardi, E. (2002). Individual and system level factors associated with treatment nonadherence in human immunodeficiency virus-infected men and women. *AIDS Patient Care and STDs, 16*(6), 269–281.

Vlahov, D., & Junge, B. (1998, June). The role of needle exchange programs in HIV prevention. *Public Health Reports, 113,* 75–80.

Weller, S., & Davis, K. (2002). Condom effectiveness in reducing heterosexual HIV transmission. *Cochrane Database of Systematic Reviews, 1,* Article CD003255. DOI: 10.1002/14651858. CD003255. Retrieved April 7, 2009, from http://mrw.interscience.wiley.com/cochrane/clsysrev/articles/CD003255/frame.html

Williams, B. G., Lloyd-Smith, J. O., Gouws, E., Hankins, C., Getz, W. M., Hargrove, J., et al. (2006). The potential impact of male circumcision on HIV in sub-Saharan Africa. *PLoS Med, 3*(7), e262. Retrieved April 7, 2009, from http://www.plosmedicine.org/article/info:doi/10.1371/journal.pmed.0030262

Chapter Two

UNDERLYING PRINCIPLES OF HELPING IN THE HIV FIELD

Hugo Kamya

The HIV pandemic has created major challenges for people in the helping fields. Although the rewards are many, helping professionals are cast into an arena where their values and sensibilities are constantly challenged. These challenges include the increased incidence of HIV in communities of color, causing these groups to be HIV-infected and affected in disproportionate rates, and complacency around the dangers of HIV disease, caused partially by treatment advances among some groups. All in all, a lot remains to be done to ensure that people living with HIV are well served to meet the variety of challenges that confront them.

Determining who is in need and what kind of help they need continues to puzzle many helpers. The challenges of serving people living with HIV touch the core of the helping professions and the principles that guide helping. These principles are rooted in the care of the other, the stranger, and those who are disadvantaged. Attention to these principles evokes age-old debates of those deserving of help and those undeserving of help. Reid (1995) defines *social welfare*—society's methods of taking care of the most vulnerable—as "an idea . . . of a decent society that provides opportunities for work and human meaning, provides reasonable security from want and assault, promotes fairness and evaluation based on individual merit, and is economically productive and stable." Social welfare, then, refers to a full range of activities that seek to improve the social problems that affect people's lives. HIV is a major social problem that has affected the fabric of society while challenging helpers' commitment and response to human rights and social justice values.

At the core of the development of social welfare institutions (organizations and agencies, both privately and publicly sponsored) within the helping professions is the value system within which these institutions occur. The value system includes assumptions, convictions, and beliefs about the way people should be and the principles that should govern their self-understanding. The social welfare system in the United States has always been in a state of flux, from the time that the country adopted the English Elizabethan Poor Law through the Colonial period, the settlement house movement, to the New Deal, the Social Security era, the Great Society programs, and recent welfare reforms, into the twenty-first century. This welfare system provides the context within which attitudes to caring for all people, including people living with HIV, must be seen.

The English Elizabethan Poor Law established categories of assistance, underscoring the aged, the chronically ill, people with disabilities, and orphaned children as "worthy" and deserving of assistance. Assistance was given to the worthy in almshouses by those who were physically able. For the United States, the Elizabethan Poor Law established, among

Acknowledgments: I dedicate this chapter to my brother, Henry, who loved so much in the face of so much tragedy. May his life continue to be an inspiration for others.

other things, clear governmental responsibility for those in need. But underlying this responsibility was a concern that focused on managing the poor because the poor were considered to be "at fault" for their poverty.

Early Europeans brought with them to the United States a religious tradition that held charity at the core of its existence. The care for the stranger pervaded the needs of the poor. Questions such as these abounded: "Who is my neighbor?" "What does it mean to take care of our own?" These questions seemed to be rooted in biblical and other scriptural texts. There were also anthropological dimensions to the welfare of or care for the stranger. "Is the human nature redeemable? Do we expect to reform those we care for or aid? If not, then why help them?" At the core of some of these questions was the expectation that those we aid will become like those who aid them. Religion therefore provided emotional foundations and a long rootedness of caring in the human experience.

The settlement house movement was created, among others, by Jane Addams, who sought to integrate immigrants into a new society. For Addams (1909/1910), "a society that calls itself democratic must make possible the participation of all of its members; the wealthy have no monopoly on political wisdom or social ethics . . . peaceful dialogue across the lines of class, ethnicity, and gender would have to replace conflict, brute force, and repression if American democracy was to survive urban industrialization" (p. 2). Addams further opposed the Social Darwinian principle of survival of the fittest, thus acknowledging individual achievements and the influences of culture and environment.

More recently, there has been greater attention to power imbalances as part of the Great Society and the vast array of unmet needs within the socially oppressive structures. Throughout all of this, social workers have been guided by key values. Understanding these values is central to grasping the heart and soul of the helping fields. It is especially even more compelling when these principles are juxtaposed against the urgent needs that affect people living with HIV.

The preamble of the National Association of Social Workers (NASW) *Code of Ethics* is unambiguous when it states that "the primary mission of the social work profession is to enhance human well-being and help meet the basic human needs of all people with particular attention to the needs and empowerment of people who are vulnerable, oppressed, and living in poverty" (NASW, 1999, p. 1). The core values embraced by the helping professions include social justice, dignity and worth of a person, importance of human relationships, human rights, cultural competence, empowerment, strengths perspective, social transformation, compassion, hope and witness, and an ethic of care. These values and skills are here discussed in the context of HIV.

SOCIAL JUSTICE

Social work as a helping profession brought with it the strongest tradition of commitment to social justice concerns. The field sought to promote charitable giving for the poor, community organizing, and trade union organizing (Reisch & Andrews, 2002; Specht & Courtney, 2000). Although government efforts sought to crush the social justice spirit of social workers, the commitment to social justice was the glue to social work. Writing about the 1960s, Gil (1998) says:

> A social justice orientation re-emerged among social workers, under the influence of civil rights, peace, and feminist movements. Social workers became involved in community organizing in antipoverty and Model Cities programs, and in the Welfare Rights movement. These unconventional practice experiences led to a renewal of a radical critique of capitalist society and culture (p. 84).

The NASW *Code of Ethics* is laden with major ethical principles, all of which are based on social work values. Social justice is a central social work value. The principle underlying this social work value of social justice is the charge that social workers challenge social and economic injustice. To challenge social and economic injustice, helping professionals must address the injustice committed against people because of race, gender, age, disability, sexual orientation, and class. By extension, these injustices have come to include all forms of oppression, including various vulnerable groups such as children, families, immigrants, and people with mental illness. Clearly enshrined in this charge are people living with HIV. As one reads the *Code of Ethics,* one quickly realizes the evolution of language from "worthy poor and unworthy poor," those "at fault," to clearly "everyone in need." In short, the invitation is to "cease any discrimination" of any individual, group, or community. But the principle underlying this value is to invite all helping professionals to "promote sensitivity to and knowledge about oppression and cultural and ethnic diversity." In a way, there is no greater call than attending to people living with HIV—without any discrimination, first and foremost, but more important, attending to knowing more about their cultural, social, economic, and physical circumstances so that they are well served.

DIGNITY AND WORTH OF THE PERSON

Helping professionals are committed to the dignity, worth, and value of all human beings regardless of social class, race, color, creed, gender, sexual orientation, or age. The NASW *Code of Ethics* clearly states that social workers must "respect the inherent dignity and worth of the person." For the person or persons living with HIV, helping professionals must respect and be mindful of the individual's or community's unique differences. Such unique differences must take into account one's ability for self-determination. For people living with HIV, the debilitating effects of the illness not only compromise their physical health and well-being, but also their ability to self-determine. Social workers are called to reach out to the marginalized members of society, not least of them the people living with HIV.

THE IMPORTANCE OF HUMAN RELATIONSHIPS

Social workers strive to build relationships between and among people. Central to the building of relationships is the recognition that human beings need such relationships to survive and to enhance their well-being. People living with HIV are often at a disadvantage, because the challenges of living with HIV often rupture the very relationships they need to have. HIV often cuts them off from others and, more important, from themselves. Social workers ought to be mindful of the paradox that people living with HIV have to endure. Attending to developing healthy human relationships means attending to all aspects that affect people living with HIV, including social, cultural, psychological, occupational, and economic well-being, among others.

HUMAN RIGHTS

To understand the social worker's response to people living with HIV, one cannot ignore the stance of social justice in the larger context of human rights. Indeed, many writers on social justice seek to conceptualize social justice as a human rights construct

(Caputo, 2001; George, 1999; Stainton, 2002; Reichert, 2003). The Universal Declaration of Human Rights of the United Nations clearly spells out the international community's responsibility toward all human beings. It underscores the rights due to every human being. Right from Article 1, the Declaration addresses the dignity and rights of all human beings. Fundamental protections and rights that must be applied to all human beings reverberate throughout the declaration. All these rights are grounded in the fact that they are universal and all who work for social justice must ensure the protection of these rights. It is imperative, then, that any response to people living with HIV must take into consideration the rights and protections enshrined in the Universal Declaration of Human Rights.

Today, many people living with HIV are subject to many forms of discrimination, including unfair practices like exclusion from opportunities for gainful employment, housing discrimination, lack of access to services, denial of freedom of movement, lack of privacy, lack of equal protection of the law, and in some cases assaults or inhumane treatment. Perhaps one of the greatest challenges for social workers and those in other helping professions is advocating for people living with HIV in the face of overt and covert discrimination.

A human rights stance compels social workers and those in other helping professions to advocate for change. Providers in the helping field must be social activists. Social activism has no greater imperative than for people living with HIV. Such activism invites providers and helping professionals to challenge the status quo. Justice refers to the fair and equitable allocation of burdens, resources, and opportunities in society (Miller, 1999). Helping professionals facilitate wellness for people living with HIV in three areas: the personal, the relational, and the collective. At the center of wellness is power, capacity, and opportunity. Social workers must facilitate all of these for people living with HIV.

As stewards of the profession's values, social workers must protect the rights of others. These rights include access to health care, due process rights, institutional rights, treatment rights, and civil liberties. The protection of these rights for people living with HIV includes preservation of the community as a whole. It is important that social workers strive to preserve the community's survival.

CULTURAL COMPETENCE

Every human is shaped in both conscious and unconscious ways by his or her multiple layers of culture, which is a way of making sense of the world through norms, values, belief systems, codes, rituals, traditions, myths, and communication. In social work, where diversity is commonplace, addressing culture is key.

Cultural competence is an important component of effective ethical social work, because the historical roots and the belief system of an individual and family affects how a difficult situation is defined, whether and how an issue is presented, whether and how help is sought, and what solutions are considered (Pinderhughes, 1989). Culturally competent practice includes knowledge of cultures, values about the inherent worth of cultures and the right to have a culture, and practice skills for building relationships and problem solving with persons in other cultures (Cross, Bazron, Dennis & Isaacs, 1989). Individuals and organizations must constantly strive for increasing levels of competence with knowledge, values, and skills and not fall into the traps of complacency, apathy, or stereotyping. Humility, respect, and constant learning are vital skills in this process (Cross, Bazron, Dennis & Isaacs, 1989).

EMPOWERMENT

Social workers and other helping professionals ought to engage in practices that invite participatory engagement toward empowerment. Paulo Freire (1970) and the Latin American experience can offer an important backdrop to participatory engagement. The work of Freire provides a model for critical reflection and action in the struggle for social transformation. Rappaport (1987) defines *empowerment* as "a process, a mechanism by which people, organizations, and communities gain mastery over their affairs, and involve themselves in the democratic processes of their communities and employing institutions" (p. 122). Social workers and helping professions must assist people living with HIV to see themselves not as objects passively being acted on, but rather as subjects actively living out their lives. Participatory engagement toward self-empowerment values people living with HIV as subjects with critical skills essential for influencing the institutions that have control over their lives.

Freire (1973) proposed developing a sense of critical consciousness, which, for him, equaled liberation. Helping professionals must develop this critical consciousness, which is a dialectical process that involves helping individuals name the multiple conditions of life, identifying limits imposed on them, and taking action toward change. When helping professionals act from a stance of critical consciousness, they open up individual groups and communities to questioning historical and social conditions with the goal of transformation. Helping professionals must continually examine power structures and conditions that continue to oppress and subjugate people Attention to participatory planning between providers and consumers is crucial, as is the equal sharing of responsibilities between and among all groups. The HIV field has always espoused the value and practice of empowerment and participation of people with HIV in service development, planning, provision, monitoring, and evaluation (Dearing, Larson, Randall, & Pope, 1998; Poindexter & Lane, 2003; UNAIDS/UNIFEM, 2008).

STRENGTHS PERSPECTIVE

Helpers must acknowledge the richness and strengths that each and every person and culture brings to each situation. Such attention to strengths underscores the capacities, talents, possibilities, resources, and visions that all human beings bring with them. As a field, social work values a strengths perspective because it enhances an individual's and a community's empowerment and capacity to overcome problems and adversities. In the context of HIV, a strengths perspective seeks to view those living with HIV as people with capacities rather than people with deficiencies. A strengths perspective opens up professionals and people living with HIV to imagine new futures and new possibilities. The strengths perspective is about writing new stories in people's lives and communities; it is about providing hope in the face of hopelessness, despair, and doubt. Such a viewpoint opens individuals and communities to become agents of change, no longer objects being acted upon but subjects with a dignity that values their lives and their potential (Freire, 1973; Chazin, Kaplan, & Terio, 2000; Rappaport, 1987).

INVITATION TO SOCIAL TRANSFORMATION

What then must the role of social workers and those in the helping professions be in the HIV field? What is today's charge that echoes the history of the helping tradition? How do social work and other helping professions remain true to the values and principles that have grounded their missions? How can social work and other helping professions antici-pate the challenges of tomorrow? These are but a few perplexing and vexing questions to which there are no easy answers. And this may be one of the best things for the profes-sion. It points to further exploration and invites all those in the helping professions to keep asking new questions. It is an invitation to engage in practices of accountability and curiosity. The history of the helping tradition has emerged from a place that had all the answers to a place that now values the indigenous or local knowledge of the people who are being "helped" (White & Epston, 1990).

To further the dignity and worth of the individual, group, or community living with HIV, helping professionals must engage in accountable practices. Being accountable must take into account the people living with HIV and the oppressive structures that surround them. The helping professions must be suspicious of our own abilities and of society's maneuvers (Schüssler-Fiorenza, 1984). People living with HIV have been betrayed by the very societal systems and structures that they have relied on. Unchecked or unques-tioned, these structures can be harmful. Helping professionals should be curious and ask questions. Asking questions and allowing people living with HIV to keep asking ques-tions widens new areas of inquiry toward social transformation. Freire (1973) called this a "problem-posing" approach in which learning becomes a mutual process of discovery. Others have written about this as a movement from one voice to many voices in which multiple ideas emerge (Morson & Emerson, 1990; Kamya & Trimble, 2002).

INVITATION TO COMPASSION

The origin of the word *compassion* is the Latin *cum-passiere,* which means to "suffer with." To "suffer with" suggests entering into a victim position. More appropriately, this refers to "being with" or "one with." Helping as a profession invites us to "be with" people living with HIV. HIV creates a deep sense of isolation that helping professionals must attend to. "Being with" means entering into passion with those alienated by others. To enter into this experience means opening ourselves to loving those who suffer oppression and alienation.

INVITATION TO HOPE AND WITNESS

Helping principles also invite us to enter into a spirit of hope and witness. As helpers we are called to hold hope in the face of despair and doubt. People living with HIV are threatened with a loss of hope. Society exacerbates their sense of alienation. The unpredictable course of illness often shatters any sense of hope. Social workers can provide the hope for people living with HIV in a variety of ways, including listening to their stories and the complexities of those stories. Social workers also challenge the dominant stories that often oppress and marginalize other stories. In doing this, social workers bear witness to these stories. They give credence to yet other stories and allow people living with HIV find their voice in this complex marketplace of ideas. In this case, as Weingarten (2000) states, we are always witnesses. But as witnesses, we must also embrace certain risks. Weingarten writes:

> First, there is the risk that attends grasping—even for a second—the experience of another. Then, there is the risk of staying with the other, extending the moment of perception until another reality circulates conterminously with one's own. Finally, there is the risk of attempting to share what one has learned from a perspective that is at once own and another's (2000, pp. 393).

Weingarten further illustrates these risks as occurring in one of four positions. As witnesses, we can position ourselves as aware and empowered, as aware and disempowered, as unaware and empowered, and finally as unaware and disempowered. While these witness positions can shift over time, each witness position has consequences for the individual, family, community, and society (2000, p. 398).

Witnessing is listening to people's stories, hearing them tell and retell these stories, and allowing them to build and rebuild plots and subplots to these stories. Michael White has described witnessing a "thickening" of stories (Epston & White, 1992). As a helping profession, we are called to be witnesses. Witnesses agitate and advocate on behalf of others. No greater story needs more witnessing than the story of HIV and/or AIDS.

ETHIC OF CARE

These underlying principles of helping can be best understood if seen as part of an ethic of care. Some people have described this ethic of care as a "relational stance" (Madsen, 2007), an "emotional posture" (Griffith & Griffith, 1992), or a "way of being in relationship with our fellow human beings, including how we think about them, talk with, act with, and respond to them" (Anderson, 1997, p. 94). The ethic of care concerns the way helping professionals position themselves as allies, culturally curious and always seeking collaboration, partnerships, and engaging in accountable practices even, and especially, in the absence of codes. An ethic of care presupposes no rules or codes to be followed. An ethic of care concerns being human with all other humans and acting in humane ways. Such humane ways pay respect to all human beings regardless of their social condition. An ethic of care encompasses attention to all aspects of human life, not just those that do no harm, but also those that enhance well-being. The challenge for the helping fields is to live these principles of helping grounded by an ethic of care.

Personal Perspective

Anabel's Story

My father died when I was only 12. My mother died shortly thereafter. They both died of HIV. I remember how sad I felt at that time. The world looked darker than I could imagine. I was afraid that no one would care for me because I too had contracted HIV. I have never felt so sad. Medications have helped. Now at 22, I am glad to have social workers fighting for my existence. I am glad to know that someone cares. It is nice to hear myself being addressed by my name. Sometimes I forget that I live with HIV because I have a name.

CONCLUSIONS

The helping profession leans on a very rich tradition of rights and values as it reaches out to serve all people. No clearer is the call to service than the charge to reach out to people living with HIV. Such a call rests on the foundational values of the helping professions.

The values, embedded in the tradition of charity and care, are a commitment to social justice, service, the importance of human relationships, human rights, empowerment, and the strengths perspective. These values compel helping professionals to pursue a critical agenda for all persons, including people living with HIV. Such a commitment propels helping professionals to work for social transformation, compassion, hope, and witness as part of the ethic of care.

REFERENCES

Addams, J. (1909/1910). *Twenty years at Hull-House.* Edited and with an introduction by V. B. Brown. Boston: Bedford/St. Martin's Press.

Anderson, H. (1997). *Conversation, language, and possibilities.* New York: Basic Books.

Caputo, R. K. (2001). Multiculturalism and social justice in the United States: An attempt to reconcile the irreconcilable with a pragmatic liberal framework. *Race, Gender and Class, 8*(1), 161–182.

Chazin, R., Kaplan, S., & Terio, S. (2000). The strengths perspective in brief treatment with culturally diverse clients. *Crisis Intervention, 6*(1), 41–50.

Cross, T., Bazron, B., Dennis, K., & Isaacs, M. (1989). *Towards a culturally competent system of care: A monograph on effective services for minority children who are severely emotionally disturbed: Volume I,* Washington, DC: Georgetown University.

Dearing, J. W., Larson, S., Randall, L. M., & Pope, R. (1998). Local reinvention of the CDC HIV prevention community planning initiative. *Journal of Community Health, 23*(2), 113–126.

Epston, D., & White, M. (1992). Consulting our consultants: The documentation of alternative knowledges. In D. Epston & M. White (Eds.), *Experience and contradictions, narrative and imagination: Situated papers of David Epston and Michael White, 1989–1991.* Adelaide: Dulwich Centre Publications.

Freire, P. (1970). *Pedagogy of the oppressed.* New York: Seabury.

Freire, P. (1973). *Education for critical consciousness.* New York: Continuum.

George, J. (1999). Conceptual meddle, practical dilemma: Human rights, social development and social and social work education. *International Social Work, 42,* 14–26.

Gil, D. G. (1998). *Confronting injustice and oppression.* New York: Columbia University Press.

Griffith, J. L., & Griffith, M. E. (1992). Owning one's own epistemological stance in therapy. *Dulwich Center Newsletter, 1,* 5–11.

Kamya, H., & Trimble, D. (2002). Response to injury: Toward ethical construction of the other. *Journal of Systemic Therapies, 2*(3), 19–29.

Madsen, W. (2007). *Collaborative therapy with multi-stressed families.* New York: Guilford Press.

Miller, D. (1999). *Principles of social justice.* Cambridge, MA: Harvard University Press.

Morson, G. S., & Emerson, C. (1990). *Mikhail Bakhtin: Creation of a prosaics.* Stanford, CA: Stanford University Press.

National Association of Social Workers [NASW] (1999). *Code of Ethics.* Washington, DC: National Association of Social Workers. Retrieved from http://www.socialworkers.org/pubs/code/default.asp

Pinderhughes, E. (1989). *Understanding race, ethnicity and power: The key to efficacy in clinical practice.* New York: Free Press.

Poindexter, C. C., & Lane, T. S. (2003). Choices and voices: Participation of people with HIV on Ryan White Title II Consumer Advisory Boards. *Health & Social Work, 28*(3), 196–205.

Rappaport, J. (1987). Terms of empowerment/exemplars of prevention: Toward a theory for community psychology. *American Journal of Community Psychology, 15*(2), 121–145.

Reid, P. N. (1995). *Encyclopedia of social work* (19th ed. Vol. 3, pp. 2206–2225). Washington, DC: NASW Press.

Reisch, M., & Andrews, J. (2002). *The road not taken: A history of radical social work in the United States.* New York: Brunner-Routledge.

Reichert, E. (2003). *Social work and human rights: A foundation for policy and practice.* New York: Columbia University Press.

Schüssler-Fiorenza, E. (1984). *Bread not stone: The challenge of a feminist biblical interpretation.* Boston: Beacon Press.

Specht, H., & Courtney, M. E. (2000). *Unfaithful angels: How social work has abandoned its mission.* New York: Free Press.

Stainton, T. (2002). Taking rights structurally: Disability rights and social work response to direct payments. *British Journal of Social Work, 32,* 751–763.

UNAIDS/UNIFEM. (2004). Equal sharing of responsibilities between women and men, including care giving in the context of HIV/AIDS. New York.

Weingarten, K. (2000). Witnessing, wonder, and hope. *Family Process, 39*(4), 389–402.

White, M., & Epston, D. (1990). *Narrative means to therapeutic ends.* Adelaide, Australia: Dulwich Centre Publications.

Chapter Three

CULTURAL COMPETENCE AND HIV

Manoj Pardasani, Claudia Lucia Moreno, and Nicholas Robertson Forge

---

INTRODUCTION

Due to the rapidly changing demographic characteristics of HIV and the increasing complexity of implementing effective interventions, the need for culturally competent practitioners has never been more critical. Cultural competence is an imperative practice element that every practitioner and student should possess to ensure effective service design, implementation, practice, and evaluation.

Culture has been identified as a key factor in the social work helping process (Lum, 2003). Culture is an integrated pattern of human behavior and symbolic structures that give our lives meaning and significance. Culture refers to the way of life, a worldview, and includes codes in language, religion, rituals, norms of behaviors, belief systems, and values. Culture is shaped by multiple factors that interact in a complex, dynamic interplay and is affected by education, race, ethnicity, nationality, region, religion, gender, income, sexual orientation, and environmental or situational context. These factors are sociocultural factors that shape our values, form our belief systems, influence our definition of family, and motivate our behaviors (Betancourt, Green, & Carrillo, 2002). Overall, culture encompasses behavioral patterns, intergenerational transmission, and specific group life experiences (Lum, 2003).

DEFINITION OF CULTURAL COMPETENCE

Culture is an essential component in the helping process because it is embedded in how the problem is defined and manifested, the individual seeking help, the help provider, and the treatment options (Pinderhughes, 1989). Cultural competence is a cornerstone of effective ethical practice. Cultural competence is a set of behaviors, attitudes, and policies that come together in a system—such as a family, agency, or among professionals—that enables that system to work effectively in cross-cultural situations. Cultural competence is not a destination but a journey, one in which practitioners recognize their internal biases

---

Acknowledgments: The authors dedicate this chapter to all Latina women living with HIV who have inspired us, and to Anthony Gillespie, who has taught us the meaning of selflessness, untiring advocacy, and true compassion.

and how they distort their own worldview, as well as begin to incorporate the worldview of others.

Individuals and organizations may be at various levels of awareness, knowledge, and skills along the cultural competence continuum, and this may affect their effectiveness in reaching out to diverse individuals, couples, families, and groups (Cross, Bazron, Dennis, & Isaacs, 1989). Therefore, cultural competence within the context of HIV work is a process of sustained learning and growth that requires the humility to acknowledge that it will be impossible to know about all the cultures with which one will have contact. Nevertheless, the practitioner develops a deep respect for other cultures, is willing to learn about other cultures, is ready to engage people's different worldviews, and is willing to use appropriate engagement skills and to tailor and adapt interventions for culturally diverse individuals and groups (Cross, Bazron, Dennis, & Isaacs, 1989).

THE SIGNIFICANCE OF CULTURAL COMPETENCE IN HIV PREVENTION AND TREATMENT

While the biological risk of HIV infection is equal for all segments of the population, certain groups are at higher risk than others due to social and economic factors:

- Although men make up three-quarters (75%) of people living with HIV, women are the fastest-growing segment of the HIV-positive population.
- Nearly half (50%) of all individuals now living with HIV are men who have sex with men (MSM).
- While only 13% of all men are reported to have contracted HIV through heterosexual contact, over 72% of women were reportedly infected through high-risk heterosexual contact.
- Nearly one in five adults (19%) was infected with HIV through injection drug use (IDU).
- While African Americans make up only 12% of the U.S. population, 46% (510,100) of all individuals living with HIV are African American. Prevalence rates for African American men are 6 times higher, and women 18 times higher, than their Caucasian counterparts.
- While Latinos and Latinas make up 13% of the U.S. population, they account for nearly 18% (194,000) of persons living with HIV (CDC, 2008).

The surveillance reports identify heterosexual women (especially African American women and Latinas), African Americans, Latinos, men who have sex with men (MSM), and injection drug users (IDU) as at significantly higher risk for contracting HIV than the general population. All of these groups either represent a disenfranchised and/or an oppressed minority group. Poverty and lack of access characterize the life experiences of many African American and Latino individuals (Boone, Mayberry, Betancourt, Coggins, & Yancey, 2006; Rowe, 2007). Although women make up nearly half of the general population and have made tremendous social and economic strides in the United States, there still exists a significant inequity in terms of resource sharing, access, and empowerment compared to their male counterparts. Many women simply lack the power of decision making in heterosexual relationships within the context of a traditional patriarchal society. Another group of women that are deemed at high risk are sex workers (Pardasani, 2005a; Rowe, 2007). Three of the high-risk groups— MSM, sex workers, and IDUs—are engaged in behaviors that may be deemed immoral or deviant by other members of society. Furthermore, injection drug use and commercial sex work are illegal activities that can yield criminal penalties and incarceration if conducted openly. Societal discrimination, rejection, fear of value-laden condemnation, and, potentially, even physical harm have pushed many members of these vulnerable groups further into the shadows, whereby help-seeking behaviors may be discouraged (Rowe, 2007; Taylor-Brown, Garcia, & Kingson, 2001; Vinh-Thomas, Bunch, & Card, 2003).

The complex and dynamic interplay of discrimination, stigma, shame, poverty, powerlessness, cultural norms, dominant moral values, and social inequities has a significant and profound impact on the lives of individuals and groups (Bowleg, 2004; Boone et al., 2006; Rowe, 2007; Taylor-Brown, Garcia, & Kingson, 2001). These life experiences are bound to influence self-esteem, self-perceptions of efficacy, individual decision making, access to information, openness to education, and vital care, as well as the motivation to seek help (Hunt, 2005; Meleis, 1999; Vinh-Thomas, Bunch, & Card, 2003). Care providers (health care, social services, community prevention) must take into account the life experiences and concerns of the members of these vulnerable and high-risk groups in order to effectively reach out and serve them. Incorporating the influence of cultural experiences, personal worldviews, and the impact of stigma, discrimination, and inequity into the treatment or prevention model is an integral component of effective practice (Kitzinger & Barbour, 1999; Meleis, 1999; Pardasani, 2005b). Thus, cultural competence is critical in HIV outreach, prevention, and treatment (CDC, 2008; Meleis, 1999; Poindexter, Lane, & Boyer, 2002).

CULTURAL COMPETENCE AND HIV: A LITERATURE REVIEW

A review of literature on cultural competence in the HIV field revealed three major areas of focus: definitions and models of cultural competence, descriptions of vulnerable contexts and groups, and discussions of successful models of prevention or interventions. Following are our findings in these categories.

Defining the Concept of Cultural Competence and Developing Universal Models of Culturally Competent Social Services and Health Care

Many researchers have conceptualized cultural competence within the HIV service field either by identifying the skills critical to such an approach or by arguing for the need for culturally relevant models of treatment, prevention, or harm reduction. Meleis (1999) identified the necessity for developing an explanatory system that seeks to value diversity and promotes the utilization of that explanatory system to understand a person's worldview as essential to providing culturally competent care. Vinh-Thomas, Bunch, and Card (2003) highlighted the importance of developing an assessment tool that evaluated the level of cultural competence of practitioners and programs within the HIV field. This tool encompassed an awareness of a provider's personal biases and values, an understanding of the worldviews of the target population, respect for the target population, nonjudgmental attitudes, involvement of community members in service planning, incorporation of traditional beliefs and practices in treatment, and an assessment of cross-cultural skills employed in relationship building and maintenance. Poindexter, Lane, and Boyer (2002) illustrated the significance of the application of empowerment principles to the design and delivery of culturally competent HIV intervention models. Taylor-Brown, Garcia, and Kingson (2001) cautioned HIV health care and service providers against stereotyping members of any cultural or ethnic group, and stressed the importance of understanding individual life perspectives—versus assuming a group perspective blindly—when building treatment relationships. Rowe (2007) advocated building safe, integrated, and supportive communities where human rights (such as women's empowerment, basic human needs such as food, clothing, shelter, employment, and the demarginalization and social inclusion of stigmatized groups) are protected and promoted. He believes that the provision of human rights is essential to addressing the inequities in the HIV arena and reducing the rise in new infections (Rowe, 2007).

Description of the Risk Factors and Sociocultural Contexts of Various Socially and Economically Vulnerable Groups

African Americans

Researchers have highlighted poverty, socioeconomic inequities, traditional mistrust of the medical establishment, and disparities in health care access and utilization as the chief factors driving the disproportionately large increases in HIV infection within African American communities (Brisset-Chapman & Jackson, 1999; Copeland, 2005). Other factors influencing the rise in HIV infections have been identified as religious beliefs, cultural values with respect to intimacy in relationships, and sexual mores that may discourage open dialogue about sexual behavior and harm reduction (Jones, 2000; Potocky, Dodge, & Green, 2007). Current discussions in the media related to the "down-low" phenomenon (men who have sex with men but are not open about it) have unfairly targeted African American gay men, because being closeted is neither new nor unique to African American men. However, men on the "down low" are being scapegoated and blamed for the spread of HIV within the African American community (CDC, 2004). Another critical issue that has made prevention efforts difficult is the occurrence of unprotected sex among incarcerated men due to policies prohibiting condoms in prisons and the lack of HIV testing prior to release into the community, which subsequently fuels the rise in HIV infections among women (Okie, 2007).

Latinos and Latinas

CDC (2007a), Galanti (2003), McQuiston and Flaskerud (2003), and VanOss-Marin (2003) highlighted the impact of factors such as gender inequality in heterosexual relationships, traditional patriarchal hierarchies, religion, immigrant status, and idiosyncrasies of language and sexual norms on high-risk behaviors among Latinos. Moreno (2007), Mutchler and associates (2008), Somerville and colleagues (2006), and Acevedo (2007) illustrated how the specific cultural beliefs of machismo/marianismo within the Latino community negatively affect heterosexual relationships, men who have sex with men but have long-term heterosexual relationships, and homosexual men. Researchers have identified the weakened power of women with respect to negotiating safe sex in heterosexual relationships, the prevalence of domestic abuse and past trauma, as well as a high resistance (among women) to condom use in "monogamous" relationships, as significant hurdles to reducing HIV infections (Moreno, 2007; VanOss-Marin 2003; Zambrana et al., 2004). Moreno (2007) also identified the concept of *"la suerte"* or submission to one's destiny as a life perspective that may hamper proactive decision-making and help-seeking behaviors in traditional Latino communities.

Asian Americans/Pacific Islanders/Native Hawaiians

Operario and associates (2005), Ka'opua and Mueller (2004), and Chin and colleagues (2006) have identified several cultural and socioeconomic barriers to helping Asians and Pacific Islanders, such as language differences, lack of knowledge, lack of access, mistrust of modern medicine, religious and social values regarding homosexuality, belief in traditional healing practices, and the individual belief in fatalism (Chin et al., 2006; Ka'opua & Mueller, 2004; Operario et al., 2005). While Operario and associates (2005) focused their research on HIV prevention efforts among Asian American and Pacific Islander MSM, Ka'opua and Mueller (2004) reviewed treatment adherence among HIV-positive Native Hawaiians. Both found that incorporation of traditional beliefs was helpful in motivating individuals to engage in treatment. There are some cultural issues that are specific to Asian Americans and Pacific Islanders and may influence prevention and intervention efforts. The concept of "saving face"—the desire to protect families from shame or burden—and fear of discrimination play a central role in many families. Another cultural concept is the emphasis on collective well-being rather than individualism. In other words, the needs of the family or community are paramount and take precedence over individual needs and desires. These perspectives are nestled in the elevated values of harmony and avoidance of unpleasant interactions within Asian American communities. These cultural perspectives may prevent openness about sensitive issues, inadvertently propel persons living with HIV into the shadows, and have an impact on an individual's motivation to seek help, disclose one's HIV status to others, or seek treatment (Yoshioka & Schustack, 2001).

Men Who Have Sex with Men

Researchers have identified cultural norms against homosexuality, societal stigma, and specific religious beliefs that depict homosexuality as "deviant" or "unnatural" behavior as the chief factors that inhibit open dialogue and discussion of safer sex or drug practices. It is believed that the fear of discrimination, ridicule, ostracism, and, in some cases, violence prevent the men from seeking HIV-related information or assistance. Furthermore, since the behavior is driven underground by social mores, suspicion and fear cloud perception, making it hard to reach out to many members of this population, build trust, and engage them in harm-reduction efforts (CDC, 2007b; Mutchler et al., 2008; Sandfort & Dodge, 2008; Wheeler et al., 2008).

Injection Drug Users (IDU)

The labeling of injection drug use as criminal activity and antisocial behavior makes it difficult for practitioners to reach out to this population. High-risk behaviors (unprotected sex and sharing of injecting equipment) can increase when a person is under the influence of substances. Furthermore, individuals in the throes of addiction may resort to sex work or other criminal activity to help feed the addiction. In addition, persons infected and affected by HIV may be interested in seeking information or assistance about HIV, but not quite ready to deal with their substance use, which limits their options for help. Access to adequate health care is hindered due to social stigma, the reluctance of injection drug users to self-identify, and their lack of motivation to seek help (Cofrancesco et al., 2008; Lert & Kazatchkine, 2007; Pardasani, 2005b).

Discussion of Successful Individual and Group Models of Prevention or Intervention Aimed At Specific Vulnerable Groups (African Americans, Latinos, Women, Men Having Sex with Men, Injection Drug Users, and Sex Workers)

Practitioners, educators, and researchers have identified several successful prevention and treatment models that have effectively engaged at-risk individuals, families, and communities. Researchers have provided evidence of the usefulness and feasibility of the varied models of practice that incorporate culturally relevant knowledge and skills. The common themes for these culturally competent models are summarized as follows (Acevedo, 2008; Chin et al., 2006; Somerville, Diaz, Davis, Coleman, & Taveras, 2006; Jones, 2005; Ka'opua & Mueller, 2004; Moreno, 2007; Operario et al., 2005; Pardasani, 2005b; Rowe, 2007; VanOss-Marin, 2003; Van Servellen et al., 2003; Zambrana et al., 2004):

- Understanding the relationship between shame and stigma and a reluctance to seek help. Practitioners need to help reduce the stigma of HIV within communities in order to engage individuals, families, and communities in an active conversation.
- Creating safe, welcoming, and nonjudgmental environments to promote help seeking and HIV treatment adherence.
- Promoting harm-reduction behaviors such as testing, safe sex practices, needle-exchange programs, and increased condom use by sex workers, all of which have been found to reduce the occurrence of new HIV infections.
- Understanding the influence of cultural beliefs and societal norms on individuals and groups and their impact on individual decision making.
- Empowering individuals within relationships and in communities so that they can make life-sustaining decisions.
- Consciousness-raising and educating individuals and communities through the utilization of diverse techniques such as audiovisual and print media, opinion makers, peer leaders, and innovative message placements. Providing information and intervention in languages that are relevant and accessible to the target population.
- Incorporating alternative medicine and traditional healing practices into Western medical treatment models.
- Training staff and volunteers to effectively engage individuals, families, and communities. Using bilingual practitioners where needed.
- Advocating for reduced health care disparities—increasing access to prevention and treatment for all individuals (including the poor or undocumented).

CULTURAL COMPETENCE FRAMEWORKS

Cultural competence has been conceptualized into frameworks that can be used to evaluate and enhance the provision of services for people living with and affected by HIV. The Human Resources and Health Administration (HRSA) has formulated a culturally competent model of practice that encompasses nine domains that can be used to evaluate cultural competence in the health care delivery system (HRSA, 2001). The nine domains of this model are:

1. Values and attitudes
2. Cultural sensitivity
3. Communication

4. Policies and procedures
5. Training and staff development
6. Facility characteristics
7. Intervention and treatment model features
8. Family and community participation
9. Monitoring, evaluation, and research

The National Center for Cultural Competence proposes a model that incorporates a multi-systemic approach aimed at changes at the individual, family, organizational, and community levels (National Center for Cultural Competence, 2008). Meleis (1999) proposes that culturally competent care includes a diversity valuing system; the critical access to, and use of knowledge and models of care that are reflective of cultural differences; as well as the individual provider's understanding that the culturally competent use of language is an important factor in shaping the relationship with the person living with HIV.

A Conceptual Model for Cultural Competence in HIV Work

Utilizing the main concepts of the existing models of care, the authors propose a conceptual model of cultural competence specifically for working with individuals and families affected and infected by HIV (see Figure 3.1). The four interlocking systems that practitioners need to address are individual, family, organization, and community/society:

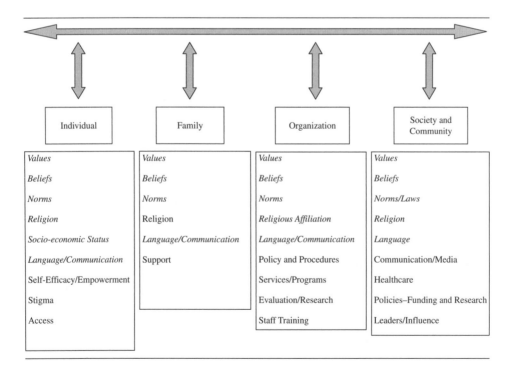

Figure 3.1   Conceptual Model of Cultural Competence in HIV (Adapted by the authors from the models provided by HRSA and the National Center for Cultural Competence)
The factors in italics are common across all the domains of cultural competence, while the rest are specific to a particular domain (as conceptualized by the authors)

Individual

Values/Beliefs   Understanding the values and beliefs of individuals is imperative in working with persons living with HIV. Individuals belonging to minority, oppressed, or at-risk groups hold different worldviews than those from or in the dominant culture. This worldview is shaped by an individual's experiences of discrimination, oppression, sense of powerlessness, lack of access to resources, or shame. On the other hand, individuals from the dominant group may develop a perspective based on their status or privilege. People have different value systems that are rooted not only in their culture but their personal life experiences as well. Thus, values and beliefs vary among individuals within the same cultural group, as well as among individuals belonging to different cultural groups. In other words, level of acculturation (the influence of the values and beliefs of your cultural affiliation on your worldview), hybridity (fusion of values and beliefs from the different cultures one is exposed to), and transnationalism (experiences of immigrants and refugees) are highly personal perspectives. For instance, a person born in the United States whose father is from Trinidad and whose mother is from Puerto Rico will be a fusion of three cultures—and that individual may even differ from a sibling brought up in the same environment.

Cultural values such as race consciousness, allocentrism (the importance of the group), familialism and the importance of the extended family, respect, trust, traditional gender roles, sexuality, collectivism, *simpatia* "good face," *personalismo* (interest in another's personal situation), harmony, and balance are present in different cultures and populations with varying degrees of intensity and conformity. For the practitioner working in the HIV field, understanding an individual's values and belief system and how it influences his or her life choices is critical to engagement and planning for any prevention, social, mental health, or medical service.

Language/Communication   Language represents an essential element that not only guides interpersonal relationships, but also has emotional, historical, and geographic symbolism and meaning. Persons living with HIV may speak the same language, but may have expressions that are unique to a specific region, culture, race, ethnicity, or social class. To engage individuals in a meaningful dialogue or relationship, practitioners must recognize these nuances of language and their significance to the target population. On the other hand, individuals for whom English is a second language may find it difficult to seek information or services. In some environments where bilingual staff is unavailable, an individual's reluctance or hesitation to speak in English may be perceived as resistance, nonadherence, lack of insight, or evidence of illiteracy or a learning disability. The choice of preferred, spoken language is also situational and emotional—you might find someone who speaks fluent English but might prefer services in his or her native language. The use of professional translators is imperative when a practitioner does not speak the person's language. However, care must be taken to assess the comfort level of the individual seeking help with respect to confidentiality and self-disclosure in the presence of another community member (the translator). One must also keep in mind that translation requires not just the transliteration of words but also of their contextual meaning. For example, *guagua* means "child" in Chile, "dog" in Colombia and "bus" in Cuba. Therefore, care must be taken to screen all translated materials and conversations to avoid unintended affronts or insults.

Norms/Power   Norms are culturally sanctioned behavioral patterns specific to groups. Norms set standards for acceptable behavior within groups and are enforced through the use of positive and negative sanctions. Norms are interrelated with power; the dominant group generally defines the norms for all groups and members within a particular community. Due to the power differential between men and women in most patriarchal societies, norms for each gender are separate and disparate. For instance, having many sexual partners may be condoned or even celebrated when men do it, but women who do so may be vilified or condemned for the same behavior. Similarly, boasting about or discussing one's sexual behavior may be considered normal for men but strongly discouraged for women. Thus, women may get the message that they should not be knowledgeable in sexual matters such as condoms, inquiring about their partner's sexual history (including STDs and HIV), negotiating condom use, or revealing one's HIV status to a sexual partner. Societal norms against homosexuality (in the form of ostracism, discrimination, or hostility) may contribute to individuals living secret or dual lives or denying their sexual orientation, thus discouraging self-disclosure and help seeking.

Religion   Religious faith or spirituality can be a powerful source of support for persons living with HIV. Religious observance and membership in religious organizations can provide an individual with a sense of purpose, hope, and fellowship. On the other hand, religious beliefs or teachings may disenfranchise some individuals if their actions, personal beliefs, or identity are at odds with what is sanctioned by that organization. For instance, if homosexuality or premarital sex is not condoned, then individuals who may be gay or sexually active while unmarried may feel discriminated against and may either abandon this vital support system or live in secret and shame. Furthermore, messages such as "married persons are not at risk for HIV" or "people of faith do not engage in high-risk behaviors" can derail the message of prevention or intervention. It is difficult for practitioners to reach out to or engage individuals who are reluctant to disclose their high-risk behaviors or seek information and help for fear of social judgment or ostracism. Another obstacle is the belief among some religious organizations that prayer and penitence is the sole solution to personal issues such as addiction. This may limit the motivation of an individual in seeking treatments/interventions outside the realm of their religious practices.

Socioeconomic Status   Poverty and lack of access to vital health care are inextricably linked. Individuals who are poor or undocumented are most likely to lack the resources (such as health insurance, access to transportation, financial ability) or meet the eligibility requirements for social and health care services. The quality and availability of vital services may also be severely limited in impoverished communities. For instance, in some regions, persons living with HIV may need to travel a long distance to receive services. If they do not have access to public transportation, lack money to pay for travel expenses, cannot get leave from work, do not own a car, or do not have someone who can drive them, they may be less likely to reach out for care. Practitioners need to make sure that resources, services, and access are equitably distributed among all members of our society.

Stigma   Stigma is defined as a "token of disgrace, dishonor, or infamy" (Merriam-Webster dictionary, 2008). Stigma is a powerful deterrent of individual freedom and self-determination. Stigma is experienced as fear, anxiety, shame, disenfranchisement, hostility, ostracism, and a threat to survival. Stigma is influenced by sociocultural experiences and norms that influence disclosure, self-protection, coping behaviors, and acceptance. Stigma is perceived or experienced not only because of a person's HIV status but is further complicated by related issues of accepting one's own self (sexuality, membership in an oppressed group, level of acculturation), feeling guilty about a specific lifestyle (drugs, sex work) and the need to conform for safety and support. For example, among some traditional Latino families, homosexuality is seen negatively, and some Latinos may be more likely to disclose their positive HIV status to sexual partners and friends than to family.

Empowerment/Self-Efficacy   Self-efficacy is the belief in one's own ability to effect change. Individuals who have experienced systematic disenfranchisement, stigma, or trauma may adopt maladaptive coping mechanisms that discourage help-seeking or harm-reduction behaviors. Sustainable and effective change can be achieved only if practitioners empower persons living with HIV within their families, workplaces, and communities. Empowered individuals are more likely to seek help, collaborate on treatment planning, and engage in harm reduction because they have reestablished faith in themselves to be healers. Empowered individuals become influential advocates for their own well-being.

Family

Beliefs/Values/Norms   History, tradition, or current situation may determine the beliefs, values, and norms of families. Families within society are diverse, and each may hold differing characteristics that reflect this diversity. These beliefs, values, and norms can differ for each individual within the family system. Beliefs, values, and norms are held regarding structure of family, expected behavior of individuals within the family, and the role of outside influences on the family. For example, this can potentially cause conflict for a gay male who is living with HIV, for the family member who is HIV-positive due to transmission from illicit injection drug use, or for the HIV-infected individual who wishes to utilize HIV care services that may bring unwanted attention to the family. Understanding that differences may exist within the family system is essential when planning services for the individual and involving family members.

Language/Communication   As language and communication styles differ within society, they can do so within the family system. Communication styles are nested in cultural elements. For instance, cultural norms may require that one family member speak for the entire family. The practitioner should have an awareness and understanding of not only the language that is spoken between family members, spoken words or nuances, but also of what is not said (nonverbal dynamics). When considering HIV, some families' values may promote that HIV be "masked" by utilizing an alternative diagnosis, such as cancer, or by not speaking about it at all. Practitioners should have an awareness of what levels of disclosure individuals living with HIV and their families are comfortable with, and they should understand how HIV and AIDS is verbally and nonverbally communicated.

Religion   Religious belief can provide a strong influence on the family and can guide beliefs, values, and norms and can also affect language and communication. Families often turn to religious faith for support and guidance when faced with a disruption or crisis within the family system. However, religiosity can also differ in belief type and intensity within the family system. For the individual and family faced with HIV, religious organizations may be a source of acceptance and support, a source of anger and rejection, or both. Practitioners should be aware of the level of religiosity of individuals living with HIV and their families. When considering prevention and treatment models, religious belief and organizations can be utilized as a support structure for both individuals and families.

Support   Ideas about social support can differ between and within families and cultures. Whereas in one culture the extended family may supportively encircle a family member in a time of crisis, in other cultures, privacy and individuality are paramount. Support within the family for the individual living with HIV may manifest itself in different ways, be it emotional or financial, temporary or long term. Being diagnosed with HIV disease can redefine a person's role in the family system as family members potentially become caregivers. The practitioner should be aware of the current roles of the family and should identify the types of support that the individual with HIV desires and what the family is willing to offer.

Organizations

Human service organizations are expected to be symbols of a caring society. Organizations are created to meet critical human needs and provide services in a respectful and humane manner. However, many organizations struggle to fulfill their missions while dealing with the realities of fiscal constraints, cultural competence, interpersonal relationships, and so forth. Following are some of the factors that affect the functioning of an organization and, subsequently, the individuals, families, and communities it serves.

Values/Beliefs/Norms   Organizations have ideologies, value systems, and visions of how things should be done. A culturally competent organization should reflect the values and ideology of the population that it serves and engage in a process of working on a vision that incorporates cultural competence. An agency that strives for cultural competence must understand how the norms, values, beliefs, and assumptions that staff, board, and management hold affect the provision of services and the treatment of persons living with HIV. Organizational values and norms that uphold respect for the dignity of all individuals and their right to effective services can be transformative. However, if the values and beliefs of the staff or management lead to judgmental attitudes, disrespect, or lack of empathy, then they could act as barriers to outreach and service delivery.

Language/Communication   Organizations should attend to the linguistic needs of the population that they serve not only by having workers or volunteers who speak their language but also with the dissemination of materials that reflect the needs of the population served. Communication materials should reflect not only the linguistic needs of the population but also incorporate affirming language. For instance, written and verbal communication that includes language that perpetuates homophobia, sexism, ethnocentrism, ageism, racism, or heterosexism may end up alienating the people it hopes to attract. Organizations that only use traditional modes of communication (print and audiovisual media) may fail to transmit their message to the broadest audience possible.

Religion   With the exponential growth in faith-based agencies and organizations providing HIV-related services, it is essential to ensure that a safe, welcoming, and nonjudgmental environment is created. Faith-based agencies are not allowed to proselytize or preach their religious beliefs unless information is specifically requested by individuals. Similarly, individuals cannot be required to participate in any religious rituals or observances, and their nonparticipation in such activities cannot have any negative bearing on their service delivery. On the other hand, faith-based organizations can help connect persons living with HIV with religious institutions that are welcoming and supportive.

Policy/Procedures   Policies and procedures have a direct impact on the treatment of individuals, families, and groups within an agency—they can be supportive and empowering, or they can be alienating and disenfranchising. For instance, if the registration process is cumbersome or requires too much personal information in the initial intake process, it may scare off individuals who are still unsure of their decision to seek help or who fear stigmatization. On the other hand, if the agency policy promotes respect, confidentiality, and participant collaboration in program planning and service delivery, it will enhance constructive behaviors.

Service/Programs Developing culturally competent programs and service delivery systems involves applying relevant knowledge about cultural factors to HIV prevention and treatment. If organizations do not offer holistic services that incorporate traditional belief systems (in non-Western medicine, spirituality, rituals, and healing practices), they may fail to appeal to significant segments of the vulnerable populations. Practitioners should make an effort to involve community leaders and peers in program planning, development, and implementation, while developing their capacity to serve as advocates and as liaisons with the community.

Evaluation/Research Organizations must use culturally competent methods (such as focus groups, community meetings, letters, phone calls, and informal conversations) to evaluate programs, services, and strategies in order to gather feedback and input. When programs are implemented without adequate research or assessments, they may fail to meet the needs of the members of the community they wish to serve. If organizations fail to utilize evidence-based interventions or incorporate current research findings into their practice models, their relevance and effectiveness may be significantly diluted.

Community/Society

Values/Beliefs It is important to understand the values and beliefs systems held by the community. No community or society is monolithic, and there may be many (or few) groups within a community with diverse belief systems and opposing values. However, the values and beliefs of the predominant group take precedence over others. As practitioners, we need to understand these values and belief systems and how they intersect with individual decision making. It is essential to try to incorporate the group values and belief systems into any prevention or treatment models if they are beneficial and empowering to the individuals.

Language If practitioners wish to engage communities, they need to understand not only the overall language preferred by the target population, but also the idiosyncrasies and nuances of the spoken word. Some words or phrases that may be acceptable in one community may be considered offensive in another. If we fail to understand the linguistic diversity within a community, we may end up limiting our access to those who are most in need.

Communication/Media Effective communication that is respectful, engaging, and informative is an essential skill. The methods used to reach out to the communities are critical as well. A thorough assessment of the most common modes of communication within a community is essential to effective outreach. For instance, if an agency creates flyers to publicize HIV testing within a community and leaves them at a grocery store by the cash registers, the lack of privacy may inhibit individuals from picking up those flyers. Or if an agency spends a considerable amount of money on newspaper advertisements to reach out to youth, but they prefer the Internet for their information gathering, then that would defeat the purpose of the task.

Norms/Laws In every community or society, the dominant group leads the way in setting standards for acceptable behavior and promoting consequences for unacceptable or "deviant" behavior. In modern societies, communities enact laws that codify these norms and the punishments to be meted out if there is any deviation from them. As discussed earlier, sex workers, drug users, MSM, and other individuals may be deemed "deviant" and may therefore be stigmatized, discriminated against, or oppressed. This pushes many individuals into the shadows to avoid the negative glare of the community. On the other hand, a community can advocate for policies and legislations that provide more resources for and prevent discrimination of persons living with HIV.

Religion   With the increasing diversity and mobility of the U.S. population, several religions and spiritual beliefs coexist within large communities. Religion plays a central role in the lives of many individuals, families, and groups. The values, beliefs, and teachings of the varied religions may hinder or facilitate prevention and treatment efforts. For instance, if the predominant social religious institution preaches against homosexuality, then individuals within that congregation may be hesitant to self-identify as homosexual. Similarly, if the dominant religious institution labels sex outside of marriage as a sin, then individuals would be less likely to admit to sexual activity. The stronger the base and reach of a religious institution, the greater the pressure felt by individuals within that community to conform to the prevailing teachings and beliefs. Finally, the presence of a dominant religious institution may hinder the provision of prevention and treatment efforts if its members are opposed to it. On the other hand, religious institutions can facilitate the sharing of information, as well as provide referrals to their congregants, thereby acting as conduits to vital HIV-related services for their congregants.

Health Care   The availability of health care services is disparate and depends on several factors, such as the location of the community, the socioeconomic characteristics of that community, the history of services within that community, and the community's ability to advocate for their health care needs. Individuals living in poor rural or urban areas may have limited options for health care services. Similarly, the ability to pay for services (private or public insurance) may restrict the access to specific health care institutions and limit types of available treatment.

IMPLICATIONS FOR PRACTITIONERS

Culturally competent models of prevention and intervention require that the practitioner address the individual within the sociocultural and environment context. Based on our discussion of the conceptual model, we provide practical suggestions for a multisystemic approach.

At the Individual Level

Practitioners must recognize that even though we are all products of our environment and cumulative life experiences, each individual is unique. Rather than make assumptions about an individual because he or she belongs to specific cultural group, it would be helpful to understand the personal worldview of every individual, as well as the impact of their cultural background and affiliation on their individual decision making.

When reaching out to individuals, it is essential that we recognize the fear and stigma they experience or perceive. Comprehensive assessments often include questions about risk behaviors for HIV that are quite personal and may be construed as intrusive. It is important to be sensitive to the fact that it takes time to build a rapport with individuals and gain their trust. Many times you (the practitioner) might be asked personal questions by individuals—they are not trying to be intrusive, but want to assess your level of openness and reciprocity. It is not helpful to always be a blank slate when working with people. Warmth, subtlety, and genuine openness are critical skills.

Special care must be taken when discussing behaviors or activities that are considered illegal (drug use and sex work). Confidentiality, patience, subtlety, respect, and honesty are key tools to transformative relationship building.

The issue of disclosure is critical for many individuals affected by HIV. Thus, care must be taken to ensure confidentiality, privacy, and anonymity (if requested).

It may sound cliché to suggest meeting people where they are, but it is particularly relevant in HIV work. Our role is not to judge people or bring them to the "right" track (whatever that may be). Our responsibility is to increase awareness, provide resources, advocate for justice and respect, and educate individuals. The individual will then make an informed decision about his or her need and capacity for change or harm reduction.

At the Family Level

Families can act as a support as well as a barrier to care. During the assessment stage of treatment, it is important to assess the individual's perception of their family's capacity for support and their potential to be involved in the treatment plan.

A practitioner may have to balance the need for vital information with a person's level of comfort with disclosure within his or her family. It may be helpful to conduct meetings separately at the individual and family levels to facilitate disclosure.

HIV-infected and HIV-affected individuals and families may face guilt, shame, and blame, and these should be mitigated by the practitioner. The practitioner should assess the level of stigma perceived or experienced by the family and address those concerns along with the intervention plan.

Functional coping mechanisms within the family system need to be activated and enhanced to facilitate treatment efforts. Externally, families may be unaware of the support systems and services available within their community. The practitioner should facilitate an awareness of these supports and assist with referrals.

At the Organizational Level

Organizations and agencies must create a safe and welcoming environment where HIV-infected and HIV-affected individuals feel comfortable and embraced.

Training in cultural competence for administrators, staff, and volunteers is essential to increase effectiveness.

Policies and procedures should reflect respect for the dignity of every individual and prevent potential discrimination, oppression, and patronizing. The policies and procedures that guide the agency should evolve systematically and continuously to reflect innovations in research, best practices, demographic changes, and operational planning.

Persons living with HIV, and their families, need to be included as much as possible in program design and implementation efforts, as well as in treatment planning.

Organizations should strive to advocate for and on behalf of the persons living with HIV at all levels of society.

Research is critical and needs to incorporate nontraditional methods, such as qualitative research, action research, feminist methods, and ethnography, as ways of getting to know the context of some issues.

At the Community Level

Assess the traditional power structures and hierarchies within the community. Before you engage in any community-level intervention, an understanding of the community leadership profile is essential. It is critical to learn about the dominant and minority groups within a community and understand the values and belief systems intrinsic to each group.

Create a database of all community organizations, agencies, and institutions—political, business, social, nonprofit, religious, social service, and health care. Collaboration and strategic partnerships with community-based organizations will enhance the outreach efforts. The community partners can serve as potential sources of funding, conduits to reach their constituents, and referral sources.

Identify gaps in services, as well as barriers to service provision and program delivery. Comprehensive community-level needs assessments can help identify gaps and barriers and provide a road map for advocacy efforts.

Practitioners need to educate, inform, and advocate within communities promoting social justice and human rights, reducing stigma related to HIV, and for the equitable distribution of resources for all members of society.

Personal Perspective

HIV and Culture, by Ana, an HIV-Positive Latina: Immigrant, Mother, and Activist

For me, being a Latina who is HIV-positive is hard. It is hard because I can't tell my friends—they don't understand, and I'm afraid they'll run away from me. I can't disclose to my neighbors either because they will not understand. It is like you live in a different world, so you are living a double life. When I meet with women who have the virus, I feel comfortable. In the outside world I have to pretend that I don't have it. I am depressed when I'm around people, I can't tell them what's going on with me because I'm afraid—afraid that they will turn away from me. So it's really hard, I am living two lives. I am a woman from a substance use background and I found out that I was at risk for HIV when I was diagnosed with HIV. As a Latina I have to say honestly that there is not enough information that is educating us about HIV, about protecting ourselves, about our roles and responsibilities as women. We are in the highest-risk category, we are minority women, we are women who are substance users, some of us are homeless. The different issues that impact our lives, even before we get infected, are the issues that actually put us at risk. As a Latina I have realized that the culture we came from gives us a level of oppression and domination; we as minority women are still addressing those issues. But for me personally, I have gotten a level of understanding about my rights and my roles and responsibilities that I have as a woman to protect myself. But now, here I am, infected. I have a tremendous amount of stress, I am a Latina living in the United States and also an immigrant. As an immigrant who is undocumented, I have a limited amount of resources that I have access to. Many Latino immigrants are heads of households, mothers who are caring for children. I have a child who is HIV-positive, and another who is HIV-negative, but she is tremendously affected by this. I have to maintain a level of stability, so I can keep myself healthy so I can give to these two children. My children know about my HIV status because they need to know. I cannot work fully as I would like to because

(Continued)

of health reasons and because of immigration issues. There is financial support and psychological support that I need within my household. I have actually chosen to become empowered. I want to attend meetings, I want to attend conferences, I want as much information as I can learn for me and my children. At times, I cannot attend meetings or doctor's appointments and conferences because of lack of child care. I have noticed that as women we neglect our health care for everyone else because you want to take care of the family, the household. As part of the culture, taking care of the family is what you believe to be the responsibility of a woman. This is something that needs to be embraced and acknowledged. You know, within the Latino culture there is a lot of diversity—my father is Venezuelan, I was born in Trinidad in the West Indies, and I lived in Venezuela up to eight years of age. I have a lot of the Latin culture but also of my Afro-Caribbean culture. It was instilled in me that a man goes out and brings in the food; he is the breadwinner of the family, but you as a woman have to take care and maintain all of it within the household.

CONCLUSIONS

Cultural competence is complex, difficult to contextualize, and even more difficult to realize in practice. This chapter has highlighted the critical role that culture plays in the lives of individuals and families infected with and affected by HIV. How do you now put that understanding into practice? No matter what the context of practice, the essential elements of cultural competence remain the same—values, awareness, knowledge, and skills. No one person holds the definitive knowledge or facts about a particular cultural group. Similarly, no one understands the impact of cultural beliefs, values, and experiences upon a person's worldview better than the individual himself or herself.

Becoming culturally competent is not an event but a journey—a journey of gaining knowledge, opening one's mind to the world, building relationships, and developing greater self-awareness. It is only when we understand our own values, beliefs, biases, and opinions that we can begin to engage others in a meaningful and productive helping relationship. Stigma, shame, oppression, social injustice, and resource inequity are closely related to the experiences of many persons living with HIV and have shaped their worldview. This worldview may make reaching out or engaging difficult. As practitioners in this field, you come across situations where you may become frustrated, hesitant, nervous, or despondent. Sometimes we are so eager to help that when we do not seem to be making any headway, we become disillusioned. We leave you with one important lesson about cultural competence we learned while working in this field: If you are well-informed about HIV-related services and policies, willing to advocate on others' behalf, respectful, patient, nonjudgmental, and resourceful, you will succeed in making a difference.

REFERENCES

Acevedo, V. (2008). Cultural competence in a group intervention designed for Latino patients living with HIV/AIDS. *Health & Social Work, 33*(2), 111–120.

Arcia, E., Skinner, M., Bailey, D., & Correa, V. (2001). Models of acculturation and health behaviors among Latino immigrants to the US. *Social Science & Medicine, 53,* 41–53.

Barbour, R. S., & Kitzinger, J. (1999). *Developing focus group research: Politics, theory and practice.* London, UK: Sage Publishers.

Betancourt, J. R., Green, A. R., & Carrillo, E. (2002). *Cultural competence in health care: Emerging frameworks and practical approaches.* Retrieved October 28, 2008, from http://www.commonwealthfund.org/usr_doc/betancourt_culturalcompetence_576.pdf?section=4039

Berry, J. (2003). Conceptual approaches to acculturation. In K. Chung, P. Balls Organista, & G. Marin., *Acculturation: Advances in theory measurement and applied research* (pp. 17–37). Washington, DC: American Psychological Association.

Boone, L., Mayberry, R., Betancourt, J. R., Coggins, P., & Yancey, E. (2006). Cultural competence in the prevention of sexually transmitted diseases. *American Journal of Health Studies, 21*(3–4), 199–209.

Bowleg, L., Lucas, K., & Tschann, J. (2004). "The ball was always in his court": An exploratory analysis of relationship scripts, sexual scripts, and condom use among African American women. *Psychology of Women Quarterly, 28*(1), 70.

Brisset-Chapman, S., & Jackson, S. (1999). *Serving African American children.* Piscataway, NJ: Transaction Publishers.

Centers for Disease Control and Prevention. (2008). *New estimates of U.S. HIV prevalence.* Retrieved November 15, 2008, from http://www.cdc.gov/HIV/topics/surveillance/resources/factsheets/pdf/prevalence.pdf

Centers for Disease Control and Prevention. (2007a). *HIV/AIDS among Latinos.* Retrieved November 15, 2008, from http://www.cdc.gov/HIV/resources/factsheets/PDF/hispanic.pdf

Centers for Disease Control and Prevention. (2007b). *HIV/AIDS among men who have sex with men.* Retrieved November 15, 2008, from http://www.cdc.gov/HIV/topics/msm/resources/factsheets/pdf/msm.pdf

Centers for Disease Control and Prevention. (2004). *HIV/AIDS surveillance report.* Retrieved November 15, 2008, from http://www.cdc.gov/HIV/topics/aa/resources/qa/downlow.htm

Chin, J., Kang, E., Kim, J., Martinez, J., & Eckholdt, H. (2006). Serving Asians and Pacific Islanders with HIV/AIDS: Challenges and lessons learned. *Journal of Healthcare for the Poor and Underserved, 17,* 910–927.

Cofrancesco J., Scherzer R., Tien P., Gibert C., Southwell H., & Sidney S. (2008). Illicit drug use and HIV treatment outcomes in a US cohort. *AIDS, 22*(3), 357–365.

Copeland, V. (2005). African Americans: Disparities in healthcare access and utilization. *Health & Social Work, 30*(3), 265–270.

Cross, T., Bazron, B., Dennis, K., & Isaacs, M. (1989). *Towards a culturally competent system of care: A monograph on effective services for minority children who are severely emotionally disturbed, Volume I,* Washington, DC: Georgetown University.

Galanti, G. (2003). The Hispanic family and male-female relationships: An overview. *Journal of Transcultural Nursing, 14*(3), 180–185.

Health Resources and Service Administration. (2001, September). *Health resources and services administration study on measuring cultural competence in health care delivery settings.* Washington, DC: U.S. Department of Health and Human Services.

Hunt, L. (2005). Health Research: What's culture got to do with it? *Lancet, 366*(9486), 617–619.

Jones, S. (2005). The Caribbean/West Indies Cultural Competency Program for Florida Nurses: Implications for HIV/AIDS prevention and treatment. *Journal of Multicultural Nursing and Health, 11*(1), 77–83.

Ka'opua, L., & Mueller, C. (2004). Treatment adherence among Native Hawaiins living with HIV. *Social Work, 49*(1), 55–43.

Lert F., & Kazatchkine M. D. (2007). Antiretroviral HIV treatment and care for injecting drug users: An evidence-based overview. *International Journal of Drug Policy, 18*(4), 255–261.

Lum, D. (2003). *Culturally competent practice: A framework for understanding diverse groups and justice isssues.* Pacific Grove, CA: Brooks/Cole-Thomson Learning.

McQuiston, C., & Flaskerud, J. (2003). "If they don't ask about condoms, I just tell them": A descriptive case study of Latino lay health advisers' helping activities. *Health Education and Behavior, 30*(1), 79–96.

Meleis, A. (1999). Culturally competent care. *Journal of Transcultural Nursing, 10*(1), 12.

Moreno, C. (2007). The relationship between culture, gender, structural factors, abuse, trauma, and HIV/AIDS for Latinas. *Qualitative Health Research, 17*(3), 340–352.

Mutchler, M., Bogart, L. M., Elliott, M., & McKay, T. (2008). Psychosocial correlates of unprotected sex without disclosure of HIV-positivity among African-American, Latino, and White men who have sex with men and women. *Archives of Sexual Behavior, 37*(5), 736–747.

National Center for Cultural Competence. (n.d.). *Conceptual frameworks/models, guiding values and principles.* Retrieved November 19, 2008, from http://www11.georgetown.edu/research/gucchd/nccc/foundations/frameworks.html

Okie, S. (2007). Sex, drugs, prisons and HIV. *New England Journal of Medicine, 356*(2), 105–108.

Operario, D., Nemoto, T., Ng, T., Syed, J., & Mazarei, M. (2005). Conducting HIV interventions for Asian Pacific Islander men who have sex with men: Challenges and compromises in community collaborative research. *AIDS Education and Prevention, 17*(4), 334–346.

Pinderhughes, E. (1989). *Understanding race, ethnicity and power: The key to efficacy in clinical practice.* New York: Free Press.

Pardasani, M. (2005a). HIV/AIDS prevention among sex workers in India: An empowerment perspective. *International Journal of Social Welfare, 14*(2), 116–126.

Pardasani, M. (2005b). Supportive housing for the chronically homeless with HIV/AIDS: An effective model. *Journal of HIV/AIDS & Social Services, 4*(1), 23–38.

Poindexter, C., Lane, T., & Boyer, N. C. (2002). Teaching and Learning by example: Empowerment principles applied to development, delivery, and evaluation of community-based training for HIV service providers and supervisors. *AIDS Education and Prevention, 14*(5), 391–401.

Potocky, M., Dodge, K., & Greene, M. (2007). Bridging cultural chasms between providers and HIV-positive Haitians in Palm Beach County, Florida. *Journal of Healthcare for the Poor and Underserved, 18,* 105–117.

Rowe, W. (2007). Cultural competence in HIV prevention and care: Different histories, shared future. *Social Work in Healthcare, 44*(1/2), 45–54.

Sandfort, T., & Dodge, B. (2008). "And then there was the down low": Introduction to Black and Latino male bisexualities. *Archives of Sexual Behavior, 37*(5), 675–682.

Somerville, G., Diaz, S., Davis, S., Coleman, K., & Taveras, S. (2006). Adapting the popular opinion leader intervention for Latino young migrant men who have sex with men. *AIDS Education and Prevention, 18,* 137–148.

Taylor-Brown, S., Garcia, A., & Kingson, E. (2001). Cultural competence versus cultural chauvinism: Implications for social work. *Health & Social Work, 26*(3), 185–187.

VanOss-Martin, B. (2003). HIV prevention in the Hispanic community: Sex, culture and empowerment. *Journal of Transcultural Nursing, 14*(3), 186–192.

Vinh-Thomas, P., Bunch, M., & Card, J. (2003). A research-based tool for identifying and strengthening culturally competent and evaluation-ready HIV/AIDS prevention programs. *AIDS Education and Prevention, 15*(6), 481–499.

Wheeler, D., Lauby, J., Kai-Lih, L. Van Sluytman, L., & Murrill, C. (2008). A comparative analysis of sexual risk characteristics of Black men who have sex with men or with men and women. *Archives of Sexual Behavior, 37*(5), 697–706.

Yoshioka, M. R., & Schustack, A. (2001). Disclosure of HIV status: Cultural issues of Asian patients. *AIDS Patient Care and STDs, 15*(2), 77–82.

Zambrana, R., Cornelius, L., Boykin, S., & Lopez, D. (2004). Latinas and HIV/AIDS risk factors: Implications for harm reduction strategies. *American Journal of Public Health, 94*(7), 1152–1158.

Chapter Four

THE HUMAN RIGHTS FRAMEWORK APPLIED TO HIV SERVICES AND POLICY

Cynthia Cannon Poindexter

INTRODUCTION

HIV has been and remains a worldwide public health crisis, a political crisis, an economic crisis, and a social crisis. For those who are HIV-infected and HIV-affected, the illness is frequently a physical, mental, emotional, social, and spiritual crisis. While not often acknowledged as such, HIV is also a massive human rights crisis. Yet for the most part, in the United States, HIV has *not* been addressed using the human rights framework.

In this chapter I introduce the human rights framework and argue that HIV-related social service, mental health, public health, and medical care systems in the United States have, for the most part, run counter to that framework. The U.S. HIV model has been mostly punitive, moralistic, and restrictive rather than based on the tenets of dignified humanity and universal access (Human Rights Watch, 2006). Persons living with HIV or those most at risk for HIV have been seen as perpetrators or carriers, distrusted, stigmatized, and viewed as needing to be contained. Access to testing, prevention, and treatment has been selective rather than widespread; HIV prevention information has been carefully tailored and often inaccurate; and medical care and medicines are available only for those who have resources. In addition, because U.S. HIV policies are exported globally and the U.S. funds HIV care and prevention programs across the world, our human rights abuses are also transmitted beyond our borders.

HUMAN RIGHTS FORMALIZED AND DECLARED

The modern human rights movement is attributed to the establishment of the United Nations after World War II. The United Nations (UN), formed in 1945, established in 1948 a Human Rights Commission, with former First Lady Eleanor Roosevelt as head, to draft a bill of human rights, with the intention of avoiding the atrocities that characterized

Acknowledgments: I heartily thank Frederica and John for contributing their perspectives on seeking respectful HIV services, and Dr. Manoj Pardasani of Fordham University Graduate School of Social Service for his helpful review of a chapter draft. I dedicate this chapter to the memory of my friend Bill Edens Jr., who died without health insurance while he was suing the state of South Carolina in hopes that others living with HIV might live with insurance.

World War II (the U.S. atomic bombing of Japan, the Nazi genocides, the many horrors on all sides of a worldwide war). A document called the Universal Declaration of Human Rights was the result of that committee's efforts. The Declaration was meant to protect vulnerable and oppressed populations and bind nations in a common commitment to a sacrosanct human family. The Declaration posited the ideas that all humans have worth, are equal in dignity and rights, and are entitled to all fundamental freedoms without discrimination or distinctions. It codified and reaffirmed concepts of self-evident liberties and responsibilities that had existed previously in philosophical, religious, and political documents, such as right to life, safety, and self-determination, and went further to prohibit slavery, persecution, torture, degrading treatment, and arbitrary exile and detention, and to ensure universal suffrage by secret ballot, freedom of movement, right to a nationality, right to marry, right to rest and leisure, right to education, the right to work with equal pay for equal work, and *the right to reasonable standards of living and health care.* These rights and freedoms are accorded without regard to race, ethnicity, color, culture, country, religion, geography, economic environment, gender, language, opinion, origin, property, birth, demographic characteristic, or any other aspect of human diversity or social status (Hunt, 2007; Reichert, 2003; UN, 1948). The Declaration remains, 60 years later, one of the most powerful and frequently published documents in the world (Ife, 2001).

The concept of universal human rights, generated by UN documents and expanded by decades of negotiations and discourse, contains the following three intertwined vital principles: Human rights are inherent, universal, and indivisible (Hunt, 2007). First, human rights are by definition present at birth, natural, and *inherent* by virtue of each of us being human. This birthright principle, that human rights are a given, means that human rights transcend the biases of societies, cultures, religions, governments, and professions (Baxi, 2006). Second, *universality* of rights means that all humans are equally and unconditionally entitled to all of these rights. There are no distinctions among humans. Universality does not mean that all individuals are alike, that all nations or cultures are alike, or that human rights are realized or implemented in the same way in every culture. Rather, it means there should be equal access to equal rights (Ife, 2001; Reichert, 2003). Third, all of these rights are equal to each other, interdependent, *indivisible* from each other, and unable to be placed in a hierarchy. No one right or set of rights is more important or higher than another (Reichert, 2006).

In sum, *all* human rights exist for *every* human unconditionally and are *equally* applicable to *all* humans. The word *universal* really should not have been placed only in front of *declaration*: It might better be called the Universal Declaration of Universal Rights for Humans Universally.

A very important unintended consequence happened in 1966 that forever changed the way people think of these rights, which are not supposed to be divided or ranked in a particular order. In an effort to require nations to enforce human rights principles, the United Nations divided the rights into two documents: (1) the International Covenant on Civil and Political Rights and (2) the International Covenant on Economic, Social, and Cultural Rights. Civil and political rights became known as *first-tier* rights, and those rights that social workers and human services workers might be most intimately concerned with—the economic, social, and cultural rights—became known as *second-tier* rights. The second set of rights addresses survival, quality of life, adequacy of living, and basic safety and well-being: food, clothing, housing, health care, social services, education, employment, and adequate wage (Reichert, 2006). Because human rights discussions usually encompass only the first level of rights, the second set of rights often becomes optional. In the United States, the second layer or set is not considered "rights" at all, but relegated to the realm of charity. While the United States has affirmed the full set of rights in the Universal Declaration and has ratified the Covenant on Civil and Political Rights, the U.S. government has yet to sign off on the Covenant on Economic, Social, and Cultural Rights. The U.S. culture is not one that embraces the idea that lack of medical care, adequate shelter, sufficient education, or subsistence income is problematic (NASW, 2006; Reichert, 2006). Nevertheless, economic, social, and cultural rights are declared in Articles 22 and 25 of the Universal Declaration of Human Rights; therefore, because economic and social justice is the bailiwick of social workers and other human services workers, we *are* by definition human rights workers.

THE HUMAN RIGHTS FRAMEWORK

Assuring equity and universality of human rights involves *raising all humans to a basic level of economic and social justice.* This does not elevate any one group; rather, it strives to make all groups more equitable. In this way, human rights encompass the rights of women, children, elders, gays, transgender persons, sex workers, prisoners, indigenous people, people with disabilities and illnesses, drug users, poor people, dark-skinned people, refugees and immigrants (with or without legal documents), and people of all faiths. The human rights framework demands a commitment that transcends cultural, religious, national, professional, and legal paradigms, as well as personal beliefs and interests (Reichert, 2006).

The universality of rights may seem to infer that no one type of person merits particular attention. Yet it is the most vulnerable groups who are most in need of protection from first-tier rights abuses and the realization of second-tier rights. *The human rights framework demands responsibility to those most oppressed in human societies, because the right to economic and social well-being is denied to the most marginalized.* Taking a human rights approach means that we must confront and deal with any form of oppression, and demands that we fight for an end to all types of discrimination.

Two years before the formal declaration of universal human rights, the United Nations, in a remarkable statement, declared *health as a human right.* In 1946, the United Nations established the World Health Organization (WHO), whose Constitution's preamble states that the highest possible standard of health attainable is one of the fundamental rights of *every* human being, regardless of circumstance, and that health is vital to peace and security:

> Health is a state of complete physical, mental and social wellbeing and not merely the absence of disease or infirmity. The enjoyment of the highest attainable standard of health is one of the fundamental rights of every human being without distinction of race, religion, political belief, economic or social condition. The health of all peoples is fundamental to the attainment of peace and security and is dependent upon the fullest co-operation of individuals and States. Unequal development in different countries in the promotion of health and control of disease, especially communicable disease, is a common danger (UN, 1946, p.1).

The last line bears emphasis: "Unequal development in different countries in the *promotion of health and control of disease, especially communicable disease, is a common danger.*" That was written in 1946. The relevance for the HIV pandemic is obvious.

The United Nations now defines the right to health further, going beyond the right to the highest standards of health to the following: the right to prevention, treatment, and control of diseases; access to essential medicines; access to information and services for sexual and reproductive health; equal and timely access to basic health services; the

provision of health-related education and information; and participation of the population in health-related decision making at the national and community levels. Furthermore,
these rights must be provided to all without any discrimination. Going even further, health
care and facilities must be available, accessible, respectful, gender-sensitive and culturally
competent, sanitary, safe, and provided by trained professionals (UN, 2008b).

Of course, no state or nation can guarantee that any human can be healthy. We are
not biologically or genetically equal and we make different choices. Rather, *the right to
health means equal access to the goods and services that give us an opportunity to be
healthy and to receive basic treatment for illness.*

HUMAN RIGHTS IN RELATIONSHIP TO HIV PRACTICE
AND POLICY

When the human rights framework is applied to HIV practice and policy, it becomes
evident that human rights and HIV intersect in multiple and complicated ways. HIV and
human rights are intertwined in four ways:

1. Persons and groups who have always been vulnerable and marginalized in societies
   are especially susceptible to becoming HIV infected. Oppression, poverty, lack of
   health care, discrimination, stigmas, and human rights violations increase the likelihood that certain persons will become HIV-infected. When one is oppressed, the
   resulting lack of access to information, testing, and services increases the danger
   of HIV transmission. Groups who are more vulnerable to becoming HIV-infected
   include sex workers, prisoners, drug users, poor people, homeless persons, women,
   and men who have sex with men.

2. After people become infected with HIV, regardless of how or whether they were
   marginalized or oppressed previously, they suffer especially from discrimination in
   all societies. They are more likely to lose shelter, employment, social support, and
   insurance.

3. HIV stigma has a negative effect on health by making people unwilling to seek HIV
   testing, counseling, medical care, and social services. Worsening physical and mental health can result, including poorer quality of life and abbreviated life spans.

4. When cultures and societies are punitive and stigmatizing toward persons with HIV,
   or when behaviors associated with the most vulnerable are criminalized [for example, sex work, drug use, same-gender sex], the overall HIV indicators get worse,
   because criminalizing behaviors forces people into the shadows and makes them
   reluctant to seek information or support (UN, 2008b). Lack of access to health care,
   voluntary HIV testing, and anti-HIV medication increases HIV infection rates and
   HIV-related illnesses and deaths.

Conversely, when the human rights framework is used to design and implement policies and services, when people are respected rather than punished or persecuted, when
dignity and privacy are protected and respected, then prevention, social and emotional
care, and treatment improve (Mann, Grushkin, Grodin, & Annas, 1999). The human rights
framework takes the stance that all people have a right to the highest standards of HIV
prevention and treatment regardless of the nature or means of their lives. In June 2001,
a Declaration of Commitment on HIV/AIDS was adopted at the first high-level meeting
on HIV and AIDS at the United Nations. There it was agreed that "Realization of human

rights and fundamental freedoms for all is essential to reduce vulnerability to HIV/AIDS. Respect for the rights of people living with HIV/AIDS drives an effective response" (UN, 2001, paragraph 58). A commitment to human rights permeates that document as the necessary grounding of any response to the HIV pandemic (UN, 2001 & 2008a). It is now a generally accepted principle that human rights must be the framework in HIV practice and policy.

From the beginning of this pandemic, those living with HIV disease immediately felt the need to have their basic human rights protected and to assert their humanity. Two HIV-related documents are touchstones for HIV and human rights: the "Denver Principles" and the "Greater Involvement of People Living with AIDS." The 1983 "Denver Principles," a statement from the advisory committee of people with AIDS in a conference at the beginning of the pandemic, demanded dignity, respect, and full participation, and was a hallmark in the human rights framework for the HIV field. The Denver statement is remarkable in its acknowledgment that people with AIDS (the causal agent HIV had not yet been discovered) have human rights; a list of rights included the rights to medical care and social services without discrimination, the right to choose or refuse types of treatment or research trials and to make informed decisions, the right to confidentiality of records, the right to respect, the right to choose one's own family, the right to sexual and emotional lives as satisfying as anyone else's, and the right to live and die in dignity. The Denver Principles statement recommends that the public support people with HIV in their struggles against oppression, discrimination, stigma, ignorance, blaming, and scapegoating, and recommends that HIV-positive persons become active in advocacy at the agency, community, media, and political levels (Denver Principles, 1983).[1]

The other important guiding document on human rights is "Greater Involvement of People Living with AIDS," or GIPA (UNAIDS, 2007b). GIPA, which puts forth the human rights principles of consumer empowerment, partnership, and participation, was adopted in 1994 at a Paris AIDS summit, where 42 countries declared these principles to be vital to national responses to the pandemic. GIPA posited that the human rights framework was necessary in all HIV responses.

There have been many indisputable and resounding successes in U.S. HIV policy and services, brought about largely by skilled and organized advocacy, community organizing, and legislative efforts. We are fortunate to have the Housing Opportunities for People with AIDS and the Ryan White Comprehensive AIDS Resources Emergency (CARE) Act as two examples. However, generally the U.S. response to people with HIV and to the HIV pandemic has been individualistic, medicalized, judgmental, and stigmatized. Human rights protection has not been the first response. For example, Article 13 of the Universal Declaration, which states: "Everyone has the right to leave any country, including his own, and to return to his country," calls into question the long-standing travel and immigration restrictions for HIV-positive persons to and from the United States.[2] If the human rights standard is science over ideology, then why is marijuana still illegal for control of nausea and wasting in persons with AIDS? If the human rights framework demands that we educate those who are most vulnerable to infection, what are we to do about the abysmal "antiprostitution ban" attached to HIV prevention funding to other countries from the United States? When human rights principles and documents are held up next to many of

---

[1]The Denver statement was also notable for condemning the labels "victims" and "patients," the most popular terms of the time (they could have added "clients"), and demanded that they be called "people" ("We are 'People with AIDS.'").

[2]The U.S. travel and immigration ban for HIV-infected persons began in 1987 and will lift in 2010.

our policies and practices, there is much that can be said and done differently. However, it is never too late to shift organizations and governments toward the human rights framework. In the next sections, I challenge us to imagine what practices and policies might be if we did so.

SOCIAL WORK, SERVICES, AND AGENCIES THROUGH THE HUMAN RIGHTS LENS

The second paragraph of the Universal Declaration states that humanity's "highest aspiration" is "the advent of a world in which human beings shall enjoy freedom of speech and belief and *freedom from fear and want*." The former two freedoms are considered first-tier (that is, those that should be protected) and the latter two are second-tier (that is, social and economic). Freedom from fear and freedom from want are definitely the major concerns of social work, whether micro or macro. Further in the preamble, the peoples of the world's nations "have determined to *promote social progress and better standards of life* in larger freedom" (UN, 1948). "Social progress and better standards of life" could surely be a paraphrase of the purpose of social work. As purveyors of economic and social rights, social workers are furthering human rights through every method and activity in every setting. It does not seem to be a stretch for the social work profession and human services organizations to embrace human rights as a lens. In doing so, the following tenets become guiding principles.

The Rights Approach Supplements the Needs Approach

The "social security" items in the 1948 and 1966 documents (necessary for basic survival) are inherent "rights" that must be realized, not "needs" that can be met or not. Needs are individual and variable. Defining and meeting needs depends on individual assessments, agency rules, funding streams, and cultural norms. In a needs-based approach, basic needs are addressed depending on the availability of resources and the judgments of service providers. In our current system, basic needs such as housing and food are met or not depending on "compliance" of rules or judgments of staff. A human rights framework demands that all humans have the right to have their basic survival needs met, period (Ife, 2001). If we worked from the notion that people with HIV had a right to basic health care and safety, rather than from our current needs perspective where each person must prove his or her eligibility or worth, how might that change our attitudes and behavior? To what extent can we train our staff and volunteers and change organizational cultures to reflect this framework?

Dignity and Respect

The first paragraph of the Declaration affirms the "inherent dignity of all members of the human family" (UN, 1948). Although social work embraces the inherent dignity of each person in principle, service provision mechanisms at times disregard human dignity. Social service, prevention, and health care programs using the human rights lens would be delivered with choice, respect, and dignity, and would not judge, control, punish, blame, or divide based on worthiness. Every volunteer, staff member, and administrator would be required to treat everyone with the utmost dignity and respect and as equal members of humanity. Service applicants would not be asked how they thought they contracted HIV before they were offered services; people would not be treated as if they were subhuman; organizational cultures built around "them versus us" would not be tolerated; and people would not be treated as if they wanted to be sick or in need but would be freely told what services are available and would be offered resources as if they were entitled to them.

Partnership and Participation

Using a framework of universal human rights, any practice or policy response to the HIV pandemic acknowledges our common humanity and links us as partners rather than dividing us into "client" and "provider." Social workers and vulnerable people and populations would all be part of the "us" and not view each other distrustfully from opposite sides of an artificial fence. With a stance that says "we are all in this together," persons with HIV, community members, family members, and caregivers would be genuinely involved from the very beginning in planning, designing, funding, implementing, managing, monitoring, and evaluating any prevention, advocacy, or social service program. This would be true whether the program related to HIV testing and prevention, case management, counseling, medical services and treatment access, mental health support, substance use recovery, practical care (life housing, food, or transportation), or end-of-life care.

Education about Rights

In a rights-based approach, we would be responsible for educating people with HIV about their rights, help them to demand that their rights be met, and aid them in organizing against oppression (Ife, 2001). Copies of the Denver principles and the GIPA principles would be in our agency reception areas. Social workers and other helpers should provide persons with HIV and those at risk for HIV with a tip sheet or fact sheet listing their basic human rights, including legal rights, voting rights, civil rights, appeal processes, and eligibility or entitlement to apply for services. Even something this basic would be a radical change in some case management systems where the mode of operation seems to be keeping service possibilities a secret from those who apply so that staff can dole them out as they see fit. HIV programs should have voter registration forms in their waiting rooms, offer assistance with completing them, and print sample ballots close to election times. This practice does not violate any funding guidelines; voting is a basic civil right. It is useful to let elected officials know that the agency is assisting HIV-infected persons and their social networks with this right as well.

Empowerment

Help would not be "done to" anyone and we would not view ourselves as above anyone requesting help. Coming to us in trauma, crisis, or severe need, recipients of services can become socialized to the language and ways of traditional human services provision and thus see themselves as passive "consumers" of services. The human rights perspective demands that we help people disengage from that stance and become active participants to the extent of their abilities and desires to do so (Ife, 2001). This includes routinely informing service applicants and recipients of their rights and supporting them in claiming these rights (Reichert, 2003). The principle of empowerment does not mean that professionals do not continue to provide such skills as case management, counseling, referrals, crisis intervention, and advocacy; rather, these necessary services are offered with respect, in a participatory person-centered way, actively supporting informed choice and educating persons about their rights.

TESTING AND PREVENTION THROUGH THE HUMAN RIGHTS LENS

HIV Testing

"Know your HIV status" has long been an important HIV prevention and treatment message. Taking an HIV test is the only feasible way to know whether one has HIV disease. HIV stigma makes the decision to test for HIV different from the decision to test for other life-threatening illnesses, even though all medical screening is fraught with emotion. For social and political reasons, a medical model or a public health model alone has not been sufficient to manage the HIV pandemic. The Centers for Disease Control and Prevention (CDC) estimates that a quarter of the people with HIV in the United States still do not know they are infected (Hall et al., 2008).

When people have a choice between testing for HIV with and without giving their name, they tend to choose to test anonymously (Charlebois, 2005; Hertz-Picciotto, Lee, & Hoyo, 1996; Meyer & Jones, 1994), yet the CDC has steadily changed its recommendations toward testing and reporting by name, and testing without written express consent (CDC, 2006). A human rights framework would require antidiscrimination legislation, voluntary testing with counseling and education, and options for testing without giving one's name and identifying information, as has been offered in some states.

Currently, U.S. policies allow for or require mandatory testing for prisoners, immigrants, and military personnel. Article 12 of the Declaration protects us from "arbitrary interference" with privacy. Does that not include mandatory medical procedures? A human rights perspective would set us against HIV testing without consent for anyone, because people have the right to make their own medical screening decisions at a time and place that are best for them. Taking a human rights perspective would compel us to advocate legislatively to repeal mandatory HIV testing in the United States.

Evidence-Based Prevention, Accessible and Funded

A human rights agenda would dictate that a full range of prevention technology and educational messages, based on research rather than philosophy or morality, should be accessible to everyone and funded. As stated previously, the UN definition of health as a human right includes access to sexual and reproductive health education, information, and services (UN, 2008b). From the beginning of the pandemic in the United States, regardless of what political party was in charge, we have hedged on accurate, visible, accessible HIV prevention.

For example, the U.S. government has for almost a decade chosen one option out of a range—the "A" out of "ABCD," which is "abstinence only until marriage" out of "be faithful, use a condom, disclose"—to offer and fund as a prevention strategy in the United States and throughout the world through the President's Emergency Plan for AIDS Relief (PEPFAR). One-third of the PEPFAR prevention budget went to abstinence-only programs, which represented 56% of the sexual transmission budget (Thompson, 2007). This robs people of their right to choose, their right to sexual expression, their right to reproductive freedom, their right to information, their right to health, their right to safety, and their right to technology. Obviously, limiting HIV prevention options to "no sex" was not useful for most women, including married women, the highest-risk group in most developing countries.

Similarly, research has shown over two decades that having access to clean injection equipment prevents HIV transmission without increasing drug use or drug-related crime (Human Rights Watch, 2003; Satcher, 2000). Since sharing injection equipment is a major HIV risk for those who inject, for their sexual partners, and for the children they bear, a human rights perspective would demand that access to sterile injecting equipment would be a major prevention strategy. However, most state laws make possession of sterile injecting equipment a criminal offense, and it is prohibited to use federal funds to provide sterile drug injection equipment. Adopting a human rights framework requires the advocacy for syringe-exchange programs and collaborative agreements with law enforcement officers to leave those programs and their participants alone. We are also compelled to work with federal and state legislators to repeal the restrictions on funding syringe-exchange programs (Elliott, Csete, Wood, & Kerr, 2005; Human Rights Watch, 2003).

Our advocacy efforts should be geared to work toward ensuring access to accurate HIV information for those who are most invisible and vulnerable, for whatever populations we are working with or care about: adolescents, migrant farm workers, Latinas, African American women, gay and bisexual men, elders, prisoners and parolees, homeless persons and families, mentally ill persons, and immigrants and refugees.

MEDICAL CARE AND MEDICINE THROUGH THE HUMAN RIGHTS LENS

Universal Access to Health Care

Obviously, in the United States, health care is not considered to be a human right. The United States maintains a three-tiered health care system: those privately insured (54% insured by employers and 5% by themselves); those partially publicly funded (26% at least partially covered by Medicaid, Medicare, Ryan White CARE Act); and those without insurance (16% with no coverage for health care) (Kaiser Family Foundation, 2008a). For those living with HIV, the figures are as follows: (1) Of persons in the early stages of HIV, 42% have private insurance, whereas only 26% of those who are sicker and less likely to be working have it; (2) half of HIV-infected persons rely on publicly funded programs for their medical expenses; and (3) 20% of HIV-infected persons are completely uninsured (Institute of Medicine, 2004).

In order for a person with HIV in the United States to get medical care if he or she does not have private insurance supplied by an employer, a patchwork of federal and state services must be applied for, with the help of agency-based case managers and advocates, because the eligibility requirements are extremely complicated. Often, appeals must be filed and programs must be fit together like a complex quilt. If we were to design an HIV service system from the perspective of universal human rights, medical care would be available to all, not available based on what resources one can garner. Advocacy toward more accessible health care—as close to universal as possible—as well as advocacy for a National AIDS Strategy (NAS, 2009) is perhaps possible with a change of national administration, and these open windows should be stepped through.

Universal Access to Antiretroviral and Other Necessary Medicines

Pharmaceutical advancements have come far in being able to keep HIV at a manageable level for many years for those who can tolerate the medications and have good nutrition and medical care. Combination antiretroviral therapy has been the standard of care for all HIV-positive adults and children with suppressed immune systems since 1996. A human rights framework, based on Article 3 of the Universal Declaration giving everyone a right to life, would dictate that all persons with HIV have access to anti-HIV medications regardless of their income or insurance status. Remember that the United Nations' definition of health as a human right includes the right to timely access to vital medicines and basic health services (UN, 2008b). The United Nations has called for scaling up to as close as possible to universal access to HIV treatment by 2010 for all those who need it (UN, 2005, 2006; UNAIDS, 2006). While progress is being made, we have fallen far short of the goals for getting anti-HIV medications to people who need them. In addition, as has been said previously, not only do people with HIV who need medicines remain uninsured and therefore without a way to pay for medications, a quarter of people with HIV have not yet learned of their HIV status.

Furthermore, the AIDS Drug Assistance Program (ADAP), often the payer of last resort for uninsured HIV-infected persons, for years has been in trouble. States have capped program enrollment, limited the number of medicines they will cover through ADAP, and maintained waiting lists (Kaiser Family Foundation, 2008b). Even though we have federally funded ways for persons with HIV to get anti-HIV medication, not everyone gets medication, and not everyone gets all the medication prescribed. This is the current U.S. policy for access to HIV medications. Collaborative advocacy efforts should be ongoing to pressure Congress to keep ADAPs funded at adequate levels.[3]

Personal Perspectives

Seeking Respectful Treatment, by Frederica

My name is Frederica. I am an African American woman. I am a social worker. Fifteen years ago I was diagnosed with AIDS and told I had three to six months to live. Since then I have been living with HIV and fighting to stay alive. For the past 13 years I have been clean and sober from a crack cocaine addiction. During those years I have also had to live with being diabetic and having congestive heart failure, both side effects of HIV medications.

I have five children that I have been raising all by myself. My youngest child, who is 15 years old, is also living with HIV and is doing quite well. During the past 15 years I have obtained a BA degree, worked full-time as a case manager and substance use counselor, and obtained my master's degree in social work. I look at the work that I have done as food for my soul.

Within the past six months I have had to accept kidney failure and begin dialysis. Because of my disabilities, I am not presently working, and that fact is

---

[3]There are also advocacy tasks to be done with legislators, drug companies, and embassies regarding trade agreements about medicine patents and generic medicines (UN, 2008b). For more information on the 2001 Doha agreement, compulsory licensing, and Trade-Related Aspects of Intellectual Property Rights (TRIPS), see www.wto.org.

driving me crazy. Each and every day I struggle with not feeling like I am doing anything with my life, not helping others.

I started receiving services back in 1996 in New York City from governmental sources. From the beginning I encountered strong negative viewpoints from the case managers assigned to my family. Most of the case managers seemed to look down upon my single-parent household. It was clear to me that it was going to be a struggle to maintain my pride, dignity, and self-respect. It was very difficult for me to prepare for the monthly home visits because the case managers would come into my home to inspect if I was living up to the program's standards. They would go through my kitchen cabinets and refrigerator, checking to see if I had food. While they were doing this they would remind me of all of the assistance I was receiving from the government and how lucky I was. I can remember one time when a case manager stated that she wished someone would give her the amount of food stamps that I was receiving. I said that I would gladly trade positions with her and she could have all that I had, including HIV disease. I can remember times when my rent was not paid for six months at a time and I had to go down to the office with an eviction notice, waiting all day, receiving no help, only having to come back within a week to receive an emergency rent check.

I remember saying to myself, "They are not enhancing my quality of life and I need to do something that will really enhance my life." So I decided that I could do *their* job while allowing people to maintain their dignity and not feel "less than." I decided to go back to school and obtain my BA. When I started back to school I ran into even more opposition from the case managers. I was not at home to receive my case manager for my monthly home visits and was threatened with being dropped from the program. That meant that I would no longer receive money, food stamps, medical coverage, or rent. My family could become homeless and penniless. I was filled with anxiety and I begun to doubt myself and question my ability to continue with my studies. Due to all the negative energy I was receiving, my health started to fail. My faith in my God and the support and the unconditional positive regard from one case manager is what got me through the rough times. This case manager was not from a governmental agency; she was from a community-based organization. Her unconditional acceptance of me has inspired me to continue with my education and obtain my master's degree in social work.

Weaving my way through the governmental system of services for families and individuals living with HIV has been extremely difficult. I think this is due to society not accepting the devastation that HIV causes. There is a lot of hopelessness and despair associated with HIV, but I feel that things have gotten better. I guess the best advice that I could give to a social worker starting out is:

- Be nonjudgmental.
- Meet the person where the person is.
- Demonstrate unconditional positive regard.
- Listen to what is said and what is not said.
- Help maintain the person's dignity, self-respect, and pride while providing services.
- Be culturally sensitive.
- Check your own points of view and opinions.

Personal Perspectives

The Right to Care, by John

I am a White, gay man who was well educated about HIV and who took tests for HIV routinely every year. I unexpectedly tested HIV-positive in February 1994. Not being at all prepared to deal with this news, I didn't see a doctor until December 1997, at which time I learned that my viral load and T4 tests were at a level that I needed to start antiretrovirals. Once I got through six months of terrible side effects and switching medication protocols, I did fairly well until October 2000, when I was diagnosed with non-Hodgkin's' lymphoma. With chemo treatment over three months, which completely debilitated me, in May 2001 I went into remission. The cancer came back within the next six months and I started chemo again, but my counts became so alarmingly low that they stopped the treatment out of concern for my survival. A third attempt with chemo began in 2002, but I stopped treatment then because *I couldn't afford to continue paying for the treatment.* I had been too sick to work, so I didn't have insurance. In the fall of 2003 I was told that the cancer was beyond help, that there was nothing else the doctors could do, and that I should get my affairs in order and prepare to die.

From early 2001, because of my extremely poor health, I had been unable to work. I had lost my consulting practice due to poor health, so had lost the ability to take care of myself physically and financially. Fortunately I had a place to live, with a mortgage and equity. I don't know what would have happened to me if I had not had a safe place in which to nest during the time in which I was fighting for my life. I had been living off credit cards, small gifts and a large loan from friends, and my partner's income of less than $20,000 a year.

In November 2004 I learned that, without my being in chemotherapy or on ARVs, my cancer had spontaneously gone into remission! As I fought to regain my health after being disabled for years, I felt that I finally had enough strength to deal with social service agencies. In early 2005 I started getting food stamps, Medicaid, SSI, housing assistance, which paid my mortgage, and a $300 monthly stipend. I wanted to go back to work and become independent again after four years of being disabled, and therefore made the difficult decision that I had to sell my home so I could have access to the cash to be financially independent. When I sold my condo, I had to pay back every bit of the housing support I had received when I was on public assistance. Had I been a renter, I would not have had to pay any of it back. Because I owned property, I was not entitled to that benefit without strings attached.

I have experienced a lot of frustration with the social services field. The social workers and case managers were all overworked, with caseloads too large to handle effectively. In addition, all the barriers you have to cross, the hoops you have to jump through, the walls you have to climb to get assistance are frightening and exhausting. You have to talk to a social worker or a psychologist so they can assess your need, and you have to prove your disability. You have to provide tons of personal data. It almost feels like a criminal background check to see if you're telling the truth. When you're sick already and you have to do all this work, often, not always, but often, you're treated like you're trying to cheat the system and you have to prove your need. The waiting period to get disability and other help is six months or more. I found also a general attitude in our society that health care is not a right and that to ask for it or to expect it is preposterous. There has to be a better way, especially for people who are sick and dying.

Taking care of my health had a domino effect: When my health failed, I lost employment, and when I lost employment, I lost insurance. The cost of HIV drugs, medical care, and cancer treatment made my major concerns financial. You're not allowed to have savings; you're not allowed to have property; if you have property, the property has a lien on it. In order to get care, you have to have nothing. The most important thing you have is your health, and access to medicine and treatment should be as basic as food, air, and shelter. To go through the paperwork, the history, the assessment, the interviews, the speculation, the impersonal treatment, especially when you're sick and have lost your job, your health, your pride, your finances, even your sense of purpose, to have to beg for services and money when you are at the lowest point in your life, is almost unforgivable. Especially given the culture of our country, which brags about its health care, brags about how it treats its citizens, and brags about its own wealth. This is something that will always perplex me.

CONCLUSIONS

HIV, a transmissible, life-threatening agent that destroys the human immune system, constitutes a planetwide plague for which we do not yet have a cure or vaccine. Each and every month, approximately the same number of people die from HIV as died in the tsunami of December 26, 2004 (UNAIDS, 2007a). Yet this particular natural disaster does not affect everyone equally: The most marginalized in all cultures and societies are hit the hardest. Why is that? Even before HIV hit, their human rights were not being adequately protected and their basic human survival and safety needs were not being addressed, and HIV has made them even more vulnerable. The HIV tsunami needs to be treated as a human rights crisis.

While social workers tend to be aligned with the human rights perspective, and while the HIV field has been connected to human rights principles from the beginning, there has not been a cohesive or consistent human rights agenda in the U.S. regarding HIV practice or policy at the federal or state levels. If we adopted the human rights framework, we would have these operating principles:

- All persons have the right to accurate information about HIV prevention.
- All persons have the right to be treated with dignity and respect and to be treated as humans equal to all other humans.
- All persons have the right to HIV testing.
- Those who need HIV treatment and care have the right to it. No matter what. No matter what we think. No matter what we think of them.

It is probably not possible to radically and completely change the way a profession, culture, and nation view and deliver services. The definition of social services as optional charity rather than inherent rights is deeply ingrained. Yet it is reasonable and feasible to use elements of the human rights framework in HIV services, advocacy, and policy; indeed, it is imperative. We can move away from those practices and policies that may cast us in the role of gatekeepers and oppressors. Our experience with systems has shown that changing even a small part can have a significant effect. It could be that if each of us introduces the human rights perspective into one agency or program, one university class session or community workshop, one curriculum retreat, one supervision session, one conversation with a community member, one research study, one policy statement, or one legislative testimony, we could begin a change in our small part of the world. As we work for the end of oppression and discrimination for any of the most vulnerable, we are furthering the human rights of persons with HIV and at risk for HIV. As Nelson Mandela (2005) said, simply but clearly: "AIDS is no longer just a disease; it is a human rights issue."

REFERENCES

Baxi, U. (2006). *The Future of Human Rights* (2nd ed.). New Delhi, India: Oxford University Press.

Centers for Disease Control and Prevention. (2006). *Revised recommendations for HIV testing of adults, adolescents, and pregnant women in health-care settings.* September 22, 2006/ 55(RR14); 1–17. Retrieved April 15, 2009, from http://www.cdc.gov/mmwR/preview/ mmwrhtml/rr5514a1.htm

Charlebois, E., Majorana, A., McLaughlin, M., Koester, K., Gaffney, S., & Rutherford, G. W. et al. (2005). Potential deterrent effect of name-based HIV infection surveillance. *Journal of Acquired Immune Deficiency Syndrome, 39*(2), 219–227.

Denver Principles (1983). Retrieved May 9, 2009, from http://www.actupny.org/documents/Denver .html

Elliott, R., Csete, J., Wood, E., & Kerr, T. (2005). Harm Reduction, HIV/AIDS, and the human rights challenge to global drug control policy. *Health and Human Rights, 8*(2), 105–138.

Hall, H. I., Song, R., Rhodes, P., Prejean, J., An, Q., Lee, L. M., et al. (2008). Estimation of HIV incidence in the United States. *Journal of American Medical Association, 300*(5), 520.

Hertz-Picciotto, I., Lee. L. W., & Hoyo, C. (1996). HIV test-seeking before and after the restriction of anonymous testing in North Carolina. *American Journal of Public Health, 86*(10), 1446–1450.

Human Rights Watch. (2003). Injecting reason: Human rights and HIV prevention for injection drug users. *Human Rights Watch Report, 15*(2), 1–56. Retrieved April 15, 2009, from http://www .hrw.org/reports/2003/usa0903/usa0903.pdf

Human Rights Watch. (2006). *Human rights watch world report, United States* (pp. 501–512). New York: Human Rights Watch Report.

Hunt, L. (2007). *Inventing human rights.* New York: Norton and Company.

Ife, J. (2001). *Human rights and social work.* Cambridge, UK: Cambridge University Press.

Institute of Medicine. (2004). *Public financing and delivery of HIV/AIDS care: Securing the legacy of Ryan White.* Washington, DC: Institute of Medicine.

Kaiser Family Foundation. (2008a). *State health facts.* Retrieved April 15, 2009, from http://www .statehealthfacts.org/

Kaiser Family Foundation. (2008b). *National ADAP monitoring project annual report.* Retrieved April 15, 2009, from http://www.kff.org/hivaids/upload/7746ES1.pdf

Mandela, N. (2005). *My son died of AIDS: Mandela* (1/12/05). Retrieved May 15, 2009, from http:// www.southafrica.info/mandela/mandela-son.htm

Mann, J. M., Grushkin, S., Grodin, M. A., & Annas, G. J. (1999). Introduction. In J. M. Mann, S. Grushkin, M. A. Grodin, & G. J. Annas (Eds.), *Health and Human Rights* (pp. 1–3). New York: Routledge.

Meyer, P. A., & Jones, J. L. (1994). Comparison of individuals receiving anonymous and confidential testing for HIV. *Southern Medical Journal, 87*(3), 344–348.

National AIDS Strategy. (2009). Retrieved October 10, 2009, from http://www.nationalaidsstrategy.org/

National Association of Social Workers. (2006). International policy on human rights. In *Social work speaks: National Association of Social Workers policy statements, 2006–2009* (pp. 230–238). Washington, DC: NASW Press.

Reichert, E. (2003). *Social work and human rights: A foundation for policy and practice.* NY: Columbia University Press.

Reichert, E. (2006). *Understanding human rights: An exercise book.* Thousand Oaks, CA: Sage.

Satcher, D. (2000, March 17). *Evidence-based findings on the efficacy of syringe exchange programs: An analysis of the scientific research completed since April 1998.* Press release. Washington, DC: Department of Health and Human Services.

Thompson, H. (2007). *PEPFAR myth busters: Episode two. Reproductive health reality check.* Retrieved March 22, 2007, from http://www.rhrealitycheck.org

United Nations. (1946, July 22). Constitution of the World Health Organization. Retrieved May 9, 2009, from http://flux64.wordpress.com/2006/10/07/constitution-of-the-world-health-organization-july-22-1946/

United Nations. (1948). Universal Declaration of Human Rights. General Assembly resolution 217A (III) of 10 December 1948. New York: General Assembly. Retrieved April 15, 2009, from http://www.un.org/Overview/rights.html

United Nations. (2001, June). Declaration of Commitment on HIV/AIDS, S-26/2 (Agenda item 8). New York: United Nations General Assembly.

United Nations. (2005, April). *Access to medication in the context of pandemics such as HIV/AIDS, tuberculosis and malaria.* New York: United Nations Office of the High Commissioner for Human Rights.

United Nations. (2006, March). *Scaling up access to HIV prevention, treatment, care and support* (A/60/737, Agenda item 45). New York: United Nations General Assembly.

United Nations. (2008a, April). Declaration of Commitment on HIV/AIDS and Political Declaration on HIV/AIDS: Midway to the millennium development goals. Report of the Secretary-General (Agenda item 44). New York: United Nations General Assembly.

United Nations. (2008b, June). The Right to Health: Fact Sheet #31. Geneva: Office of the United Nations High Commissioner for Human Rights and World Health Organization.

UNAIDS. (2006, June). *Setting national targets for moving towards universal access: Operational guidance.* New York: United Nations Office of AIDS.

UNAIDS. (2007a). *AIDS epidemic update.* New York: United Nations Office of AIDS.

UNAIDS. (2007b, March). *The greater involvement of people living with HIV (GIPA).* New York: United Nations Office of AIDS.

PART TWO

SOCIAL WORK PRACTICE

Chapter Five

HIV-RELATED CASE MANAGEMENT
Douglas M. Brooks

INTRODUCTION

Perhaps more than with any other social or public health issue in U.S. history, people living with HIV have been so closely involved in the design, implementation, and advancement of HIV service delivery systems that it is impossible to understand those systems without considering the perspective of those same people. It is appropriate that this chapter, devoted to one of the most vital aspects of HIV services—case management or care management—is authored by a person living with HIV who has been both a provider and receiver of case management services.

When I began working as an HIV case manager in 1992, I was taught that it is an honor to be let into the lives of people living with HIV. "It is an honor and privilege to have people allow us into their lives" said Bill Furdon, now senior case manager at the AIDS Support Group of Cape Cod. At that time the agency was called the Provincetown AIDS Support Group (PASG), and three of us managed a caseload of almost 200 people, mostly men, the majority very ill, many dying. The work at PASG provided me with a rare intensive training ground as a case manager. While currently we are fortunate not to face overwhelming numbers of people very ill and dying from HIV, some of the principles that guided our work at that time are important tools for this book's chapter on case management, principles such as believing that people know what they need for their lives and that our service was to help them access or achieve their goals.

In this chapter I offer a brief overview of HIV case management and put forward as a specific model of case management the services at JRI Health, a division of the 35-year-old Justice Resource Institute (JRI) in Boston. I present the results of interviews with JRI case managers regarding the primary and essential elements, skills, attitudes, and practices of HIV case management.

Acknowledgments: Thank you to Adam Edwards for reviewing drafts and helping with references. My heartfelt thanks to my dear and faithful friend Bruce for writing such a beautiful account of his experiences of HIV case management. I thank the five case managers from JRI Health in Boston, Massachusetts, for their invaluable contributions of time and expertise. This chapter is dedicated to all the people living with HIV who allow those of us at JRI Health the honor of entering their lives. We are truly grateful and humbled to walk with them on their journeys.

HIV CASE MANAGEMENT

HIV case management consists of person-centered services that link people with health care and psychosocial support services in a manner that ensures timely, coordinated access to levels of care appropriate for the person's needs and assets (Boston Public Health Commission, 2001; Massachusetts Department of Public Health, 2003). HIV case management also often includes treatment adherence counseling to ensure readiness for and adherence to complex HIV regimens (Health Resources and Services Administration, 2008). Because testing HIV-positive, receiving a diagnosis, managing stigma and disclosure decisions, living with intermittent illnesses, and negotiating multiple service, legal, and medical systems are all confusing and overwhelming situations, individuals, couples, and families who are facing HIV disease often find they need a case manager and advocate to help guide them through the bewildering maze. For these reasons the Ryan White CARE Act of 1990 mandated HIV case management as part of other services to ensure service coordination and continuity of care (Fleishman, 1998).

Case management is flexible and responsive to the needs of individuals and communities. Nevertheless, all case management systems have these activities in common:

- Assessment of needs, strengths, and personal support systems
- Development of a mutual, comprehensive individual, couple, or family service plan
- Interagency and intra-agency coordination of the services required to implement the plan
- Monitoring of progress to assess the efficacy of the plan
- Periodic reevaluation and revision of the plan as needs and situations change over time

Prevention Case Management (PCM)

Another newer type of service is *prevention case management* (PCM), a behavioral intervention intended for persons having, or likely to have, difficulty initiating and sustaining practices that limit the transmission and acquisition of HIV. Prevention case management presents a blend of HIV risk-avoidance counseling and traditional case management. It provides intensive individualized prevention counseling and support in order to aid the entry into, and sustained participation in, all necessary medical, psychological, and social services (Centers for Disease Control and Prevention, 1997).

Components of PCM include:

- Comprehensive assessment of risks for HIV, hepatitis B virus, hepatitis C virus, and sexually transmitted infections
- Screening and assessment for medical, trauma, mental health, psychosocial, and drug treatment service needs
- Individualized risk-avoidance prevention planning, including goals and strategies to attain and maintain those goals
- Safety planning for people in abusive relationships
- One-to-one counseling and education on prevention strategies
- Counseling regarding previous and current trauma
- Multiple-session risk-avoidance counseling related to HIV or HCV and substance use
- Coordination of all associated referral services, and supportive follow-up

- Transportation to referral providers
- Regular and repeated monitoring and assessment of needs, risks, and progress
- Discharge planning upon attainment and maintenance of goals

A MODEL OF CASE MANAGEMENT: JRI HEALTH

The mission of JRI Health is to "pursue social justice by providing underserved individuals and communities with opportunities to develop the tools and skills essential in creating strength, well-being, and autonomy. We do this through compassionate support, constant innovation and community leadership" (JRI Health, 2001). JRI Health provides HIV prevention and education programming, along with vital health care and social services, to thousands of Boston's most vulnerable and at-risk young people and adults, including homeless and runaway youth; people of all ages actively using drugs; gay, lesbian, bisexual, transgender, and questioning adolescents; people involved in sex work; and youth and adults living with HIV. In all of our work, JRI Health has learned one lesson more clearly than any other: In order to maintain people living with HIV in care and treatment, other life factors—such as homelessness, hunger, substance use, and physical or psychological abuse—must be first addressed. With these basic survival needs unmet, people have little capacity to think about or deal with anything else.

JRI is an organization led by social workers and one that is strongly committed to the underlying theoretical perspective of social work: the biopsychosocial model, derived from systems theory, which submits that all aspects of a person's life influence one another and must be taken into account in order to optimize health outcomes and functioning. Comprehensive, responsive, respectful HIV case management is provided in that context.

CASE MANAGER INTERVIEWS

To get a sense of the day-to-day interactions of JRI Health case managers and the people they serve, I interviewed one former and three current case managers from JRI Health's Assisted Living Program and one case manager from the Sidney Borum Jr. Health Center at JRI Health. Participants were recruited by asking program directors to recommend participants whom they believed would best be able to discuss the practice of case management and advocacy at JRI Health. Each participant had to be an employee of JRI Health who has been engaged in providing HIV case management services for a minimum of three years.

Careful steps were taken to provide informed consent. A form of agreement was used to obtain consent for participation. This consent form was administered to all participants at the beginning of the interview. I explained the purpose and general procedures of the project and exact activities in which the participants would be asked to engage at the outset of data collection. This consent form covered the nature and purpose of the study as well as the participant's rights and privileges. The participants were told clearly that they could decline to participate or answer any questions at any point during the project without affecting their performance reviews, benefits, assignments, or salaries.

In a written questionnaire, I asked the following four questions of each case manager: (1) What are the top five elements of HIV case management? (2) What are the top five skills of an HIV case manager? (3) What are the top five attitudes of an HIV case manager? (4) What are the consistent practices across JRI Health HIV case management service delivery? The consistent practices are included in the answers to the first three questions. After reviewing the responses, I met with each case manager to ask for clarity and to allow the participants an opportunity to expand on their answers.

The data were analyzed by adapting and tailoring methods based on the framework developed by Miles and Huberman (1994): data reduction, data display, conclusion drawing, and verification. As noted earlier, all the participants have worked together for at least three years (and most for much longer), so it was not surprising that many of their responses were similar. I had not asked participants to rank their answers; instead, they listed their top five choices in each domain. In an attempt to make the data more manageable and intelligible in terms of the issues being addressed, I developed categories to capture the broad themes that emerged from the data. For each question, I chose five categories based on the number of times they appeared. There were more than five responses for each question, which led me to collapse responses where it made sense, based on themes. In few instances, I inferred meaning from the data based on their answers, but because I was able to ask clarifying questions, subjective interpretation was mostly unnecessary. The bulk of the data are presented in the rawest form as direct quotations from the participants.

The findings follow. I have assigned each case manager a Greek letter pseudonym to disguise each person's identity.

What Are the Top Five Elements of HIV Case Management?

1. Advocacy

When asked to name the top five elements of HIV case management, JRI Health case managers cited advocacy as one of the most important aspects of service delivery. Gamma said, "We support people in contacting agencies and organizations so that they can receive the services of that organization." There was agreement that advocacy occurs with housing authorities, landlords, medical or mental health providers, substance use agencies, and vocational agencies. Kappa reported working with people living with HIV to ensure that their rights are protected vis-à-vis the legal and social security systems.

Beta offered a sobering challenge to case managers: "While advocating for people to get the assistance they need, the case manager should be explaining what the services are for and how people can access these services and advocate for themselves, always working to make the person with HIV as autonomous and independent as possible."

I think it is worth mentioning that at JRI Health, when we advance the idea of helping the people we serve become more "independent," we mean supporting their sense of agency. It is not to minimize the interrelatedness and interdependence of world community; rather, we believe that one feels a greater sense of belonging when he or she is able to operate from a place of confidence and raise his or her voice within a community.

Sigma noted the importance of modeling appropriate, and thus more effective, techniques of advocacy. Many of the HIV-positive persons with whom we work at JRI Health come from life situations where they have not been taught, or have experienced societal barriers to learning, how to advocate for themselves in a manner that is effective and engaging.

2. Service Delivery and Planning

Another important element of HIV case management is coordination and service delivery, including service planning, resource identification, initial and ongoing evaluation. As Gamma noted, "We must assist people living with HIV by writing out and talking about their plans for the future, building individual service plans [ISPs], conducting needs assessments and behavioral and risk assessments among other person-centered practices." Beta underscored that a person living with HIV is "going to be asked some very personal questions that he or she must feel comfortable answering honestly and completely in order for the case manager to be able to assess where the person is so they [HIV-positive person and case manager] can effectively develop an ISP." Kappa emphasized the importance of building rapport and relationship to assist the person in achieving his or her goals as stated in the ISP and to overcome any barriers to staying in housing.

Lambda emphasized that case management is not "glorified baby-sitting." She shared that she has come "to see the ISP as a tool to work with someone to see what they want for their lives and how they want to get there." She also talked about the importance of using motivational interviewing[1] to encourage the person to talk on a deeper level. She spoke of the necessity of ongoing training and specialization for case managers to assist them with helping persons living with HIV move along the continuum of care, and noted that "the system" can often hinder people from advancing, such that for many of the people who come into "our" system, HIV is not their number one issue. There exists a requirement for people to be HIV-positive to receive our case management services, but often people come to JRI Health's Assisted Living Program because of poverty and lack of adequate housing.

Each person receives a comprehensive assessment that includes physical, psychosocial, cognitive and therapeutic needs. Information is shared at team meetings. With the person's permission, outside caregivers are included in this process. Service plans are developed with the active involvement of persons living with HIV and any other individuals (family, friends, partners) they wish to involve. Program staff continually educate themselves about HIV treatment so that their information remains current and integrated into their supportive work. JRI Health staff members are trained to work collaboratively with any other service providers in order to ensure continuity of services and optimal care (JRI Health, 2007). Program evaluation occurs continually, as does the collection of program participant input.

3. Referrals and Information Provision

Gamma gave concrete examples of what he meant by referrals. "This is not only giving people a name and number of an organization, but might include writing a recommendation for, and with, them, and talking with people at these organizations. For example, I have contacted the Social Security Administration for people and done taxes with people." Sigma noted the importance of "making appropriate and timely referrals for people when required."

Kappa shared that the provision of information and referrals crossed a range of topics, including "medical, nutritional, housing, mental health, legal, job training and placement, to linking people to resources like heat or fuel assistance and substance use treatment. She reminded us that case managers must ensure that "the information is accessible to the person living with HIV" and that case managers should "offer different forms of information such as articles from AIDS Action Committee's HIV library."

4. Follow-Up Care/Continuum of Care/Consistency

Gamma noted that "follow-up care is done to make sure that people have done all that they agreed to do, and needed to do, to access services. Both persons living with HIV and case managers need to check that everything is complete."

---

[1]See Chapter 6 for an explanation of motivational interviewing.

Beta highlighted the significance of the case manager "building a strong relationship with the person with HIV, making it more likely that he or she will return, and thus maintaining the continuum of care."

Kappa explained the essential aspect of consistency: "Often the case manager is the only support or contact person the HIV-positive person has. This makes it extremely important to be there, be available, and be consistent over time, regardless of what the circumstances may be. This can be reinforced by the program's use of a team approach, where colleagues cover for each other, and the persons with whom individual case managers work are known to the whole staff."

5. Skill Building, Teaching, Counseling

While skill building, teaching, and counseling are inherent in the preceding elements, they were specified often enough to rate their own category. Emphasis was placed on case managers having the mastery of several major knowledge groups related to topics in managing HIV: understanding the housing voucher system and its requirements; knowing the basics of counseling skills, harm reduction, motivational interviewing; and being able to provide substance use counseling. Helping people with HIV develop skills to improve or enhance their lives is seen as an essential component to providing services. Sigma said that while the counseling is not therapy, there is an application of clinical theory, based on the social work model, of drawing from various theories and interventions.

What Are the Top Five Skills of an HIV Case Manager?

1. Working from a Person-Centered Perspective

The case managers identified working from the perspective of the people living with HIV as paramount to success in helping them achieve their goals. Over and over again they stressed the importance of empathy: that case managers must be compassionate, and they also must strive to feel what people living with HIV are feeling. In order to be effective, there needs to be genuineness, congruence, and warmth. One case manager said, if he's working with a person "who is dismayed at being homeless," then he "had to examine my own feeling on what it would be like to be homeless."

The respondents emphasized that bonding with people living with HIV—specifically, the ability to create and maintain a trusting relationship and environment—is crucial at the onset of the relationship because it sets the stage for future work. One of the case managers said that when the person living with HIV "first walks in the door, it is essential that the case manager begin building a relationship in which the person feels that he or she can trust the case manager."

Kappa noted that "for a case manager, how you do something is as important as what you do. Using a person-centered approach works well." Sigma asserted that case managers must get to know people with HIV from their frame of reference, "using their words, reframing when helpful, but as a tool for helping the person to realize his or her sense of confidence and knowledge about what is best for her own life, not as a means of control or developing a power imbalance between the person with HIV and the case manager." He went on to connect the importance of developing a mutually respectful relationship with people with HIV for times when the case manager must move into a more directive role, such as when someone has expressed a desire to reach a certain goal and the case manager wants to work with him or her to determine next steps by offering guidance. It is especially important at a time when the case manager must be prescriptive in order to protect the rights of the person, such as in times of preventing evictions. The more there is a sense of mutual respect, the greater the chance for the HIV-positive person and case manager to be in a forward-moving dialogue and relationship. Gamma offered a most powerful statement on working from the person-centered perspective: "We must not only meet the person where they are at—as the expression goes—but also follow the lead of the person wherever *they* want to go."

Within the context of the person-centered approach there was discussion of working within the Stages of Change model (Prochaska & DiClemente, 2002). Gamma offered that persons with HIV might want to learn to lessen the harm that they are creating in their lives in order to better their lives. "This is very connected to the person-centered approach in that case managers must look at every success, no matter how small that success might be."

Lambda shared a story of having to move herself "out of the way" after someone declined to accept a cheaper apartment—which included utilities in the rent—in order to buy school clothes for her teenage child. The person realized that the new apartment would cost less, but the expenses of moving would prevent her from providing new clothes for her child. It would have been easy for Lambda to judge the woman or to be frustrated if she had not placed herself in the position of understanding that it was more important to a mother to provide her teen-age child with nice school clothes than it was to move at that moment. Even if the woman's choice had been frustrating for Lambda, it would have been important for her to accept that the woman made the decision that she thought best for her and her family at that time.

2. Negotiation and Navigation of Systems

Case managers pointed out the value of negotiation skills when working with persons living with HIV, their families, housing agencies, medical or mental health providers, substance use agencies, nutritional programs, transportation or utility companies, the legal/criminal justice system, and other service providers. They drew attention to the need for critical problem-solving and thinking skills and determining when and how it is necessary to intervene with systems, both supporting the person living with HIV to advocate for himself or herself and intervening on behalf of that person.

3. Task Management, Case Load Management, and Paperwork

A case manager must be thorough and consistent in writing reports, case notes, and letters to other providers. Sigma stressed that case managers need to maintain a balance between data collection and relationship building. He was unequivocal in his conviction that developing and maintaining a relationship with the person living with HIV is the most important aspect of the work. At the same time, he stressed that, all too often, case managers view data collection and reporting as tertiary when in fact that work is primary. He expressed his thoughts that the initial intake, and its requisite data collection and assessment, may very well be the most important meeting that a case manager will ever have with a person living with HIV.

Sigma went on to provide an example of how proper note taking and documentation assist the case manager with supporting the person living with HIV. He underscored the need for the case manager to document the specific stage of change that people are expe-riencing. That documentation includes a service plan, with summary notes describing how the stage is being manifested, and the work that the case manager and person living with HIV have determined need to be accomplished and supported.

4. Effective Communication

Sigma accentuated the role of cultural competence and sensitivity in effective communi-cation. "If you don't know how a person feels about a subject or matter, ask! Ask, 'Is this working for you?'" He also shared his concerns about case managers' "discomfort" in traveling to specific geographical areas and the ways in which that is expressed.

5. Modeling

Gamma drew attention to the need for case managers to model for people with HIV how to behave with landlords, with the case manager, with service providers, and with other people living with HIV: "This might include calling a potential landlord with the person present during the call, or going with someone to meet a landlord to allow the person an opportunity to witness how to advocate in an effective manner. It also includes showing the person respect by keeping confidentiality so that they know to keep each other's confidentiality."

What Are the Top Five Attitudes of an HIV Case Manager?

1. An Affirming Attitude

If you believe in the person with HIV, that person will believe in himself or herself. Beta noted that people who have HIV disease are faced with many barriers in their lives; when working with these individuals, it is essential that the case manager remain as affirming as possible.

2. Patience

Case managers suggested that patience goes beyond merely tolerating people with HIV; it means supporting them in their failures and successes. Beta went into great and candid detail about the role of patience and understanding in the context of being person-centered:

> You will often be faced with situations when assisting a person with HIV that are going to involve bureaucratic red tape that will be very frustrating to you, but even more so for the person with HIV. There will often be times when all you can do is wait, and you need to be able to explain this to the person with HIV. They often will not want to hear this, and once again you will need to use your patience to explain the process to them. You may need to simply wait for the person to vent in stressful situations. Just make sure to remember, no matter how frustrating the situation may be for you, it is even more so for them. In order to truly be an effective case manager you need to listen to what people with HIV are telling you. You will be most effective by working on what the person wants to work on. This also fosters a more trusting relationship because it validates what they feel as important and will make it more likely that they will come back to you in the future. Many times a person with HIV will come to you when things have developed into a crisis, such as something that is very time-sensitive; you need to be able to handle the pressure while remaining calm. Also remember, while it may not seem to be a crisis to you (it may be something you've dealt with before for someone else, something that you know how to deal with quickly), if the person with HIV sees it as a crisis you may need to calmly and patiently explain what is going on to them before dealing with the situation itself. You will be dealing with all kinds of people when doing HIV case management, many of whom may have made choices that you do not agree with on a personal level. You need to be able to push your own personal beliefs aside to work with the person. You don't need to agree with their lifestyle to help them get insurance, medical care, or housing.

3. Integrity and Honesty

One case manager drew attention to the need for ethical decision making. He asserted that case managers have an obligation to "do no harm." He stressed the importance of being honest and straightforward.

4. Being Nonjudgmental

Beta expressed the need for case managers to be comfortable talking about any and all subjects. "Being real is important. If the case manager does not agree with the person's decisions, it's okay to be genuine, but not judgmental." Beta noted that he tells people with HIV who come for an initial intake that the "chances are they're not going to say anything I've not already heard, and if you do, it'll be interesting!" He says that it gives people permission to "tell their truth." Kappa highlighted the need to balance a nonjudgmental approach and harm reduction with growth of the person. She expressed the need for "putting the person with HIV in the driver's seat," such as giving a person who is an intravenous drug user a list of providers who work with people who take drugs intravenously so that the person can interview doctors, thus empowering the person with HIV by giving him or her the power of choosing a provider. She also stressed the need to "support the person with HIV where he or she is"—offering opportunities and options, but not forcing, not judging when a person chooses not to avail him- or herself of options. She expressed the need to "frame questions in a manner that provides for the person to think about those options through a lens of empowerment." Kappa also discussed the need to employ a Stages of Change model, which "supports a person by allowing him or her to be where he or she is but also provides a barometer for the case manager to lessen his or her anxiety about moving to the next level."

5. Being Authentic

One person reasoned that case managers must also be realistic, straightforward, and honest so that persons with HIV know exactly what they are dealing with. She said that case managers must remember to be as supportive as possible. "Our clients make many hard decisions in their lives, and we need to be as supportive as possible." Yet sometimes the case manager must be very prescriptive in order to protect the person's rights and benefits or to prevent evictions. Beta suggested that there is a difference between working with kids and adults. He asserted that "kids are often in 'survival mode' and that a history of abuse and/or being preyed upon leads to walls of distrust." He also emphasized the importance of not talking down to young people and working to build a trusting adult relationship with the young person, which may be the first in the person's history.

Personal Profile

Adventures in HIV Case Management, by Bruce

For me, case management has been an adventure in "there and back again." I am someone who: has had no case management, had case management, rejected case management, needed case management and reenrolled, moved to where there was no case management, and now once again has case management. My story has led me to believe that case management is vital to successfully organizing support services and bureaucracies when faced with health problems and the attendant social problems.

From the time of my infection more than 25 years ago, through my HIV diagnosis in 1984, until just before my AIDS diagnosis 1992, I had no knowledge of or experience with case management. I, as most people struggling with the virus then, had been dealing with insurance and medical needs on my own.

(Continued)

My health deteriorated very quickly in 1992 and I moved back home to Massachusetts. I connected with a community health center in New Bedford. The first thing they did was to assign me a case manager. That case manager talked with me about Medicare, Medicaid, and Social Security. I was enrolled and given an appointment with a doctor who had HIV experience. I only understood about half of what I was told and retained even less when my blood test came back, telling me I had a T cell count of fewer than 100. Now I had AIDS. The diagnosis eclipsed my ability to appreciate the help I was being given. At that time I refused to continue taking HIV medications because I was convinced that the years of high-dose AZT had harmed my health as much as HIV had. That team of case managers and health professionals were the first professionals to respect and support my right to make my own health decisions. That respect offered me a renewed sense of value and purpose. It helped me to begin to understand that I could be an advocate for myself—and to advocate for those who, due to circumstances, weren't able to advocate for themselves.

I moved to Provincetown to enroll in an AIDS service organization, mistakenly thinking that it was run by and for volunteers and people with HIV. However, without their paid case management staff I would have been lost. My new case manager guided me through applying for my Social Security disability. He helped me find housing and employment and suggested that I attend a weekly support group. The members of that group were dynamic activists. They were fighting stigma and outdated medical models. And they were working for greater input from persons with HIV, community education, and alternative therapies.

I became a hospice home health aide and learned the HIV field from the ground up. I felt that no one should die of AIDS without having an HIV-infected person as part of their care team. It mattered that they had someone they could talk to who was living through the same difficult experience. This inspired me to get a job at the AIDS support group. I worked there for several years as Volunteer Coordinator, then Client Services Director, and finally as Prevention/Education Director.

During this period I decided that we who were HIV-infected needed to control as much of our care and treatment as possible. So I withdrew from case management services. I did it in the same spirit of independence that had moved me to come off disability and return to the workforce. My intentions were good and my self-empowerment was a result of HIV activism. However, these decisions created serious problems. After returning to work I discovered that I had now had a sizable Social Security overpayment debt due to an internal mistake on their part. As I had done everything on my own and not through a case manager, I had no records of dates, phone calls, or names of the individuals at the Social Security office with whom I had spoken. I tried to straighten it out myself to no avail. I needed help and reenrolled with my previous case manager, whose resources connected me with the necessary legal aid. A paralegal was able to prove that the Social Security Administration had made a mistake. I would not have been able to figure out how, with whom, or what to do without case management.

A couple of years passed and my health took an unexpected dive. I needed to stop working. Case management guided me back onto disability and taught me how to obtain a housing voucher to help pay rent. This was patient, respectful case management, which encouraged me to do most of the work but knew how to guide me through the systems.

For health reasons and to be near some old friends, I moved to California. I was on my own with no case management. I had to move my health care, insurance, and housing assistance. I had to find AIDS organizations, clinics, and resources. My earlier mishaps and experiences made it possible. I was successful. But as I navigated the systems, institutions, applications, and medical and social service organizations, I worried about the newly infected, single moms, or young men still hiding because of stigma in their communities, those who had little or no experience to rely on. With no case management available to them, they often ended up with less care and assistance than they needed and deserved. There were few or no organizations to guide and support them through difficult and complicated decisions.

As my health improved, I decided to move back home to Provincetown. In returning, I needed to reverse all of the connections that I had instituted in California and reestablish them in Massachusetts. My case manager was able to help me make the transition effectively and efficiently. He encouraged and supported me in doing most of the work myself, but his knowledge simplified the confusion. He taught me about changes and systems, which in turn made me more competent and assured in my ongoing adventures as a service recipient.

I've learned that good case management is respectful. It educates and encourages self-empowerment and self-esteem while it connects individuals to services and support. People who have been recently diagnosed or those who, due to health or misfortune, are at risk of being unable to live lives of basic security and assistance need case management services. HIV, cancer, or aging can make us feel isolated and cut off from the rest of the world. Good case management encourages, through its knowledge, care and resources, the new growth each of us must strive for in order to successfully rebuild and stabilize our lives.

CONCLUSIONS

I choose to write about case management because it is my first love in HIV work, not only because it was my first paid work in the field and was a source of great learning and growth, but also because many of my friends and loved ones benefited greatly from relationships with caring informed case managers. It was while working as a case manager that I learned what it means to be a social worker. While I was sitting in on case consultations with professionals from various disciplines, it was the social workers who pressed the importance of considering the whole person, the person in his or her environment, and how all the factors of a person's life affected the way he or she was able to manage HIV disease.

Working as a case manager, I also learned the value of listening with an open mind and heart. It is so easy to judge another, to see another as strange, weird, wrong, or different. It is even easier to see oneself as "better than," to create a false dichotomy between case manager and "client," between the infected and uninfected, between those seeking services and those providing services. The editor insisted that chapter authors adhere to the tenets of the 1984 Denver Principles which require that we always refer to "people living with

HIV" as such, using terms that place humanity in the fore, each and every time. It was such a right and good requirement. Simple really, it is in keeping with the assertion that it is an honor to have people allow us into their lives. If we remember, while providing HIV case management, that we are partners in a process, not experts in charge, then we will have won more than half the battle.

REFERENCES

Boston Public Health Commission, AIDS Services, & Massachusetts Department of Public Health, AIDS Bureau. (2001, March). *HIV case management standards of care* [PDF]. Retrieved May 12, 2008, from http://www.bphc.org/bphc/pdfs/aids_casemgtstandards04.pdf

Centers for Disease Control and Prevention, Department of Health and Human Services, National Center for HIV, STD and TB Prevention. (1997, September). *HIV prevention case management guidance* [PDF]. Retrieved May 12, 2008, from http://www.cdc.gov/hiv/topics/prev_prog/CRCS/resources/PCMG/pdf/hivpcmg.pdf

Fleishman, J. A. (1998, July). Research design issues in evaluating the outcomes of case management for persons with HIV. *Evaluating HIV Case Management: Invited Research & Evaluation Papers,* 25–48.

Health Resources and Services Administration, Department of Health and Human Services, HIV/AIDS Bureau. (2008, November). *HRSA care action: Redefining case management* [PDF]. Retrieved December 30, 2008, from http://hab.hrsa.gov/publications/november2008/November08.pdf

Justice Resource Institute, JRI Health. (2007, June). Ryan Title One Proposal. Boston: Bloom, Buoncuore, et al.

Massachusetts Department of Public Health. (2003, April). Prepared by V. Abuchar, Boston University School of Public Health, Health & Disability Working Group., R. Murphy, S. Rajabiun, C. Tobias. *HIV case management: A review of the literature* [PDF], Boston University. Retrieved May 12, 2008, from http://www.bu.edu/hdwg/pdf/reports/DPH-lit-rev.pdf

Miles, M. B., & Huberman, A. M. (1994). *Qualitative Data Analysis.* Newbury Park, CA: Sage.

Prochaska, J. O., & DiClemente, C. C. (2002). Transtheoretical therapy. In F. W. Kaslow (Ed). *Comprehensive handbook of psychotherapy: Integrative/eclectic, Vol. 4* (pp. 165–183). Hoboken, NJ: John Wiley & Sons, Inc.

Chapter Six

HIV-RELATED CRISIS INTERVENTION AND COUNSELING

Michael P. Melendez

INTRODUCTION

The disease now known as HIV was first documented in the United States in 1981. Over the 25-year-plus history of the pandemic, there have been dramatic changes in the biological, psychosocial, and spiritual needs of people living with HIV. Initially, human services and social work practitioners focused on crisis intervention; contending with HIV-related stigma, discrimination, and rejection; and loss of health insurance, housing, and employment. People living with HIV in the early years required concrete services such as housing, Social Security disability benefits, and companionship. This is equally true for people living with HIV currently. Mental health concerns were depression, thoughts of suicide, grief, death and dying, and bereavement. Beginning in 1996, the introduction of combination medications, known as *highly active antiretroviral therapy* (HAART), caused death rates to decline significantly (Porter, Babkker, Bhaskaran, Deryshire, Pezzozotti, & Walker, 2003; Smit, Lindenburg, Geskus, Brinkman, Coutinho, & Prins, 2006). Those with access to good medical care, payment sources for medicines—such as AIDS Drug Assistance Program (ADAP), which covers the cost for people with low- to-moderate incomes—and the ability to respond to HAART began to recover their health, return to work and social life, live longer, and approach their HIV status not as an imminent death sentence but as learning to live with a protracted chronic illness (Gushue & Brazaitis, 2003; Surg, Grube, & Beckerman, 2002). This is not true for all long-term survivors with HIV. Some lack the necessary skills or resources to live healthily with HIV.

This chapter focuses on the psychosocial/spiritual needs of people living with HIV subsequent to the introduction of life-saving medication (HAART). Given the breadth of the illness and range of people asking for help, it is not possible to address every nuance of direct practice. The intended readers are beginning human services and social work service providers who are engaged in direct practice, casework, crisis intervention, and/or counseling. There is deliberate attention to workers who

(Continued)

Acknowledgments: This chapter is in memory of David Hernandez, Elizabeth Ramos, Libby Santiago, and Bobby Luongo, friends and colleagues who all died of complications due to AIDS. I am grateful to Lena Asmar, Clinical Director of the Cambridge Cares About AIDS, for clarifying comments on a draft of this chapter. I am grateful to Oscar for writing the vignette on getting through the crisis with social work support.

are not necessarily in an HIV-specific program. The chapter is organized around (1) intervention through HIV prevention, both primary and secondary, (2) the decision to be tested for HIV, (3) contending with an HIV-positive test result or AIDS diagnosis and living with HIV, and (4) groups that require special consideration, such as those with co-occurring severe and persistent mental illness and/or addiction.

PREVENTION COUNSELING

Approximately 56,000 individuals are newly infected with HIV every year (Centers for Disease Control [CDC], 2008). While groups such as African American women, young men of color who have sex with men (MSM), and injection drug users (IDU) and their partners have been identified as having a higher risk for being infected with HIV, it is erroneous to assume that if an individual does not fit one of these social identities there is little need to be concerned with addressing the potential for becoming infected with HIV.

Human service professionals and social workers play critical roles in primary prevention using direct practice (also called *micro* or *clinical* skills) in establishing critical relationships with hard-to-reach individuals and in strengthening prevention interventions. There are very specific programs that train social workers to reach out to groups who might be at higher risk for contracting HIV. Prevention programs are generally very specific in the information provided, tailoring the intervention to fit the specific subpopulation (Yep, Merrigan, Martin, Lovaas, & Certon, 2002, 2003; Tolou-Shamus, Paikoff, Mc Kirnan, & Holmbeck, 2007; Lightfoot, Rotheram-Borus, & Tevendale, 2007). As outreach programs are developed for hard-to-reach individuals, a critical skill in outreach work is the attention to developing the professional therapeutic counseling relationship. Prevention is not simply a matter of providing information or referrals or examining research outcomes. Groups requiring outreach often contend with poverty, racism, sexism, homophobia, xenophobia, ageism, and other oppressions. The outreach worker needs to consistently demonstrate regard, nonjudgmental attitudes, warmth, caring, empathy, and sincerity. These attributes are characteristics of good social work practice and are often associated with more advantageous outcomes with many interventions.

Social workers not in organizations specifically providing HIV prevention services may think they are unlikely to encounter someone living with HIV or at risk for HIV infection. However, any individual who is having unprotected anal or vaginal intercourse or using or sharing unsterile injection equipment has some risk of HIV infection. Child welfare settings, elder services, mental health settings, junior high and high schools, and general medical settings present opportunities to do HIV prevention education; these settings require careful consideration of how best to present the information and education. Individuals who are at risk for HIV infection or who are HIV-infected do present in these settings, as do those who have concerns about a parent, sibling, partner, or friend who is living with HIV.

It is common for beginning workers to be anxious or nervous about pursuing certain lines of inquiries such as sexuality and substance use. Sometimes workers consider this irrelevant to the work that they are doing. This is often based on assumptions made about certain kinds of people—for example, the assumption that a single older adult is not sexually active. This reflects a common bias about aging. Current trends in primary prevention look for ways of identifying and intervening with potential risks before an individual develops a disorder. An initial question is: What is the primary service being delivered and how does one integrate HIV prevention messages within the context of the setting? Interventions need to be tailored to the population served, based on age, relational status, culture, ethnicity, sexual orientation, race, and gender.

The critical issue is how to be comfortable with introducing a subject that someone might not identify as relevant. At one level, questions specific to HIV and other STDs and substance use can be embedded in the process of taking a general medical and relational history. Questions should be asked in a straightforward, matter-of-fact manner. Questions at this level normalize certain behaviors, reduce stigma, and create a space for the person to discuss sensitive issues, either at the time or later in your work. The detail of this inquiry will depend on the setting. For example, with a sexually active adolescent, a practitioner can ask what information he or she has on reproductive health and protection from unwanted pregnancy or infection. Considering how one phrases a question helps to create an environment that makes it comfortable for someone to respond to certain questioning. Open-ended questions that invite the story are the preferred manner of exploration. Again, the questions are based on listening deeply and developing a respectful relationship. For example, to begin the exploration, an adolescent in foster care who is sexually active and fairly forthcoming about his or her behavior and who may appear indifferent to the consequences can be asked a direct question: "How worried or concerned are you about being exposed to STDs such as HIV?" or "How are you keeping yourself safe from HIV? For example, how often do you use condoms when you have sex?" "Are you aware of the risk factors associated with sexual and drug using activities, and do you know which ones may be less risky and reduce exposure to potential harm?" Depending on the setting in which you are practicing, having condoms and other safer sex supplies available can be a critical prevention intervention.

Workers develop the ability to critically reflect on who they are as individuals and workers, their comfort or discomfort with certain questions or types of people, and their need for ongoing training and education, and they are vigilant about potential biases and assumptions that may interfere with the work. Good counselors listen carefully and explore and shape their subsequent inquires based on what an individual is telling them. A frequent mistake of beginning practitioners is the desire to communicate an assumption of understanding of the individual's situation and thus to abbreviate their inquiry. Or a worker may minimize a behavior such as binge drinking among teens as normal behavior for that age. Avoid assuming you know what a person you are working with is talking about and ask for clarification, as needed. Additionally, HIV-positive individuals may be in your caseload. Even though their HIV status may not be the focus of your work together, continued information about self-care and avoidance of reinfection are important considerations for secondary prevention with HIV-positive persons.

TO TEST OR NOT TO TEST

There is an ongoing campaign to encourage early HIV testing. The premise is that early detection can lead to early intervention and access to adequate health care. Additionally, promoting universal testing has been argued for as lessening stigma and discrimination associated with the disease (Herek, Capitanio, & Widaman, 2003). The problematic assumption is that everyone, particularly the uninsured or poor, has access to adequate health care. This is not the case. States vary regarding what support and medical services are available, caps on services provided, and at what point in the progression of HIV an individual may access these services. A social worker should understand their state's access to public health care for indigent people and hold this in mind when working with individuals who are thinking about testing. Being given a diagnosis of a life-threatening illness and then not having access to health care can lead to despair, depression, and high-risk behaviors.

In any setting, a person you are working with may raise the question of whether to be tested for HIV. As there are real ramifications for an HIV-positive test result, the worker should explore carefully the "why now" question. There is usually an event prompting the contemplation of testing. Reasons for testing can vary, from someone who is overly anxious with no real risk of exposure to those who are at risk through unprotected sex or syringe use. Every question raised for testing should be addressed respectfully and seriously, even if you believe there is no risk. Remember that people do not tell you everything about their lives. In addition, it is not up to you to determine whether someone should get tested: Everyone should know his or her HIV status, if he or she is prepared to cope with the result.

After the exploration of "why now," the worker should help the person anticipate what he or she might think and feel about the possible results. Both sides should be explored: What it would mean if the individual is HIV-negative is as important as what it might mean to the person's life if he or she is HIV-positive. The goal is to help prepare and anticipate any possible outcome and response to a test result. Besides exploring the emotional and psychological consequence of test results, a critical area to explore is the presence of helpful social supports in the person's life. Social supports include both informal supports (friends, family, colleagues, and faith communities) and formal supports (medical, social, and psychological service providers). With some people, friends and family may be unaware of and/or hostile to certain behaviors of the person, such as drug use or same-gender sex. Thus, important networks may not be available to support the person you are working with. Exploration questions include: "Who in the individual's life is available to support this individual through this time?" "Is there anyone to accompany this person to the testing and be there when the individual learns his or her test results?" "Is this person insured, and does he or she have access to medical care?" "What services are available should the HIV test results be positive?" Answers to these questions should be identified before going for the test. People who live in a small community may not have access to needed services and may face a greater potential for undesired public disclosure of HIV status than a person who lives in a large metropolitan area. These challenges may require the worker to actively identify and broker these services prior to the person going for testing. Many health sites have rapid testing for HIV available. Social workers should be aware of these sites and support services offered.

For those who may not have disclosed to friends and family their sexual or drug behaviors, this may limit the availability of social supports. Locating, seeking support from, and referring to associates/peers, mutual activist/political acquaintances, or therapeutic groups can help the person going for testing feel less alone. The worker will want to consider his or her own availability to the person at the time of testing and when that person is receiving the test results. Scheduling an appointment as soon as possible after the test results are given is critical. Some individuals have suicidal thoughts or plans after learning they are HIV-positive. Suicidality should be monitored regularly, as should other precipitants that tax the individual's ability to cope; rejection by friends and family, noneffectiveness of medication, or severe side effects, among others, can lead to additional crises. Workers will need to be aware of their own desires to avoid the person or the test results. It is not unreasonable for the worker who is uncertain, anxious, or frightened to seek support through supervision and collaboration.

NOW WHAT? COPING AND LIVING WITH HIV

While the availability of life-saving medication is heartening, receiving a diagnosis of HIV is a life-altering event. Common affective responses are anxiety, fear, depression, shame, and rage. Behavioral responses, such as isolation, indifference, passivity, and increased substance use, can vary greatly with the person. Having HIV is a lifelong condition, and psychosocial challenges will change as the individual learns to live with a chronic life-threatening illness. Having a chronic and persistent illness can be a series of crises that stress a person's ability to cope and function.

Crisis Period

A diagnosis of HIV often precipitates a crisis, so interventions should focus on support, fostering and supporting positive coping strategies, and safety. People often experience death anxiety, worry about reactions from family and friends, and fear of stigma and discrimination. Individuals begin with a significant change in their perception of themselves. A young, previously healthy person will have to contend with a new identity as someone with a significant illness that leads to major changes in physical and emotional well-being. This is an ongoing process and not just a one-time event. Living with a chronic illness represents a series of losses, of which identity as a healthy person is just one. Some people may simultaneously deal with feelings of betrayal and rage about being infected by someone else. Some may become hopeless, passive, or self-destructive in the immediate aftermath of positive test results. Social workers may have to take a more active role with people, asking direct questions, exploring areas that a person may be reluctant to answer, and offering active outreach. Shulman (1999) identifies several skills that are useful at this time: tuning in, reaching into silences, being empathic, reaching into feelings, and "partializing and prioritizing" challenges facing the HIV-positive person. Do not assume because the person has not brought these concerns or issues up that he or she is coping well. Workers also need up-to-date factual information about HIV and its progression and available resources. Positive regard, encouragement, empathy, and realistic hopefulness are critical characteristics of the worker at this time. Again, referring the HIV-positive person to a mutual-aid, political/activist, or therapeutic group is an important source of support. Be aware that you may have to serve as the bridge to these resources and to honor the timing in which the HIV-positive person can make use of these referrals. The tendency for the person with HIV may be to withdraw into isolation, and being with others who share the same challenges provides additional support through these times. Additional crises may arise subsequent to receiving a positive diagnosis, such as rejection by family, friends, or a partner.

While most people get through the initial crisis period and cope adequately, as the illness progresses, individuals can and do experience other crises at different time points, and subsequently are sometimes in several layers of crises about multiple losses or changes simultaneously (Poindexter, 1997). Living with HIV involves changes in several major areas of the person's life in addition to the emotional crises that have been discussed. There are (1) changes in medical status, (2) social consequences, (3) changes in sexuality, and (4) the double or triple jeopardy of having additional diagnoses in addition to HIV. As discussed, all of these are affected by the individual's character, perception, coping style, and life experiences. Additionally, poverty, race, ethnicity, sexual orientation, and gender are important factors to consider.

Medical Status

An essential goal in helping is to promote optimal health and well-being, which requires attention to the potential medical changes that will occur. Those who have the resources will have access to medication protocols that suppress the virus replication and maintain the immune system. There is the reality that not all people can benefit from the medications. Additionally, there are significant side effects from these medications that affect the quality of life.

Social workers working with an HIV-positive person should familiarize themselves with the medical treatments and side effects through their own ongoing education. Do not rely on the HIV-infected person to keep you informed about scientific developments. Being knowledgeable will increase the person's sense of trust in your care and services and is an ethical requirement of the professional.

Social Consequences

There are very real social consequences that come with a diagnosis of HIV or AIDS, which workers should be aware of and prepared to assist with. These include rejection by family, friends, and significant others; social isolation; stigma; and economic loss. In spite of the advances made to address discriminatory attitudes and action toward men, women, and children living with HIV, stigma remains a critical component of living with HIV. Stigma is a result of societal attitudes toward behaviors associated with contracting HIV: sexual behaviors and injection drug use. This stigma is further compounded by racism, sexism, classism, ageism, drug phobia, and homophobia, as many who are currently infected represent disadvantaged social groups (Courtney-Quirk, Wolitski, Parsons, & Gomez, 2006; Emlet, 2007; Mamo & Mueller, 2003). An example of racism is the focus on the phenomena labeled "being on the down low." Throughout the course of the pandemic there have been bisexual men or those who identify as "men who have sex with men" of every race and ethnicity who have, for a variety of societal and personal reasons, not been able to tell their female sex partners about their male sex partners. Yet this has received special attention in the African American community, reflecting a racist fascination with Black sexuality as being different than that of the dominant group. Under the guise of care and helpfulness, Black men, sexuality, and danger are subtlety linked, fostering alienation and fear. African American women are further revictimized for not being assertive and self-protective, regardless of the circumstances, such as domestic violence, in which they live (El-Bassel, Gilbert, Wu, Go, & Hill, 2005). Social work practitioners need to be prepared to deconstruct subtle racist, sexist, and homophobic experiences with the people they work with.

Individuals with a life-threatening chronic illness often experience a loss of control over many aspects of their lives. With a stigmatized illness, the issue of disclosure to important people in their lives takes on an added level of stress. The puzzle is that social supports are associated with better prognosis, and yet disclosure of HIV status can result in rejection and further stress, depression, and isolation. Workers need to explore carefully and help the individual anticipate the impact of disclosure to key individuals in the HIV-positive person's life. Control over the timing of disclosure—and the decision of whether to disclose—needs to be at the HIV-positive person's pace. Possible responses from key people in the person's life should be explored carefully and the individual helped to anticipate the range of possible responses. Again, this is a critical time for referral to mutual-aid, activist/political, or therapeutic groups. There is a real possibility, in spite of the antidiscrimination laws, that individuals living with HIV can lose their jobs, housing, or contact with children. Helping HIV-positive people know and understand their legal rights is an important intervention. It may be very reasonable in some circumstances to *not* disclose to certain key individuals in the HIV-positive person's life, and the worker must be prepared to accept and respect the decision of the individual while continually exploring the impact of nondisclosure.

Sexuality

Another issue that surfaces in casework, crisis intervention, and counseling is an HIV-positive person's choice about whether to be sexually active. This can provoke anxiety in the worker, who may be worried about others being placed at risk. Expecting lifelong abstinence for any human is untenable and might result in the departure from services of the individual you are working with or the withholding of critical information needed to work collaboratively with people with HIV. Workers should approach the issue of being sexually active by exploring safer sex practices that reduce the risk of transmission. One could start with an emphasis on self-protection, as it is possible that the individual could be reinfected with different strains of HIV that could be medication-resistant; in addition, the individual could acquire other STDs that could be dangerous for someone with a suppressed immune system. Overly focusing on the possibility of infecting others can leave the HIV person feeling emotionally abandoned and disparaged by the worker.

Many who choose to remain sexually active and who are committed to safer sex practices have contended repeatedly with the issue of disclosure to possible sexual partners that have resulted in rejection. Continual rejection can become a source of despair and depression. Validating the courage it takes to disclose and availability to mourn with the individual one additional loss can lessen the hurt experienced. In states with partner notification programs, individuals may have to contend with public disclosure before they are emotionally able to deal with it. Most people want to disclose to their partners and wrestle with feelings of guilt and shame.

Revealing the HIV status of someone without a signed consent is an ethical and legal violation of confidentiality. This issue becomes anxiety-provoking for the social worker, who may in that very rare case be working with individuals who seem to be indifferent to the consequence of their actions, whether through unsafe sexual practices, sharing drug injection equipment, or other types of drug use that lead to disinhibiting, high-risk sexual activity. These individuals typically represent people with more complex clinical profiles. Workers may feel torn between a perceived duty to warn and honoring confidentiality. Additionally, feelings of anger and disgust can be generated in the worker by the antisocial actions of some people living with HIV. (These types of situations also occur with HIV-negative persons.) When there is not the option to refer, workers should make active use of supervision and consultation for their own emotional support and to control possible destructive negative feelings and actions. An approach to seemingly "resistant" individuals, called *motivational interviewing,* is a technique that has been shown to have effectiveness with individuals who have little readiness to change. This counseling technique will be discussed later.

Remember that the vast majority of conversations about safer sex and drug behavior should and can be handled through the therapeutic relationship. When someone tells a counselor that he or she is not always behaving safely regarding sex or drug use, it is because the person wants to talk about it and get some help with problem solving.

Also remember that behavioral change is an incremental process, which always involves relapse or recycling of old behavior. These discussions provide opportunities to address triggers or obstacles to behavioral change, to normalize the slip in order to not discourage both the worker and the client, and to encourage and strengthen desired behavioral change. With newly sober individuals it is helpful to develop a relapse plan. There is no reason for the counselor to panic. People who have no intention or desire to improve their knowledge and skills around HIV prevention do not broach the topic with social workers and often do not present for counseling. Treat the topic as you would any other disclosure: Explore the person's reasons for raising the concern, validate the person's courage and strengths, normalize that behavioral change takes practice and vigilance, explore options that are personally and culturally feasible, and mutually develop a plan of action and follow-up.

Double or Triple Trouble: Mental Illness and Substance Use

Some groups of individuals at risk for infection or HIV-positive have an added level of complexity. These are people that have what is called a "co-occurring disorder" or are labeled "dually diagnosed" (Odo, 2003) These individuals may have severe and persistent mental illness, active addiction, or both. Typically, these conditions exist prior to infection with HIV, and HIV maybe a direct consequence of living with these two situations. These individuals can be challenging for the worker, as they often are not willing to abstain from substances or sexuality. An abstinence approach has been demonstrated to be ineffective with these groups, as it is with all people, and can lead to worker frustration and compassion fatigue. With these groups of individual, one takes a harm-reduction approach. Two counseling approaches that have been found to be effective with these groups of people are called (1) *harm reduction* and (2) *motivation interviewing* (MI) (Miller & Rollnick, 1991).

Harm reduction is a philosophy that seeks to reduce the harm that can sometimes be caused by addictive behavior or criminal activity (Denning, 2000). This approach, initially developed in England and the Netherlands, was developed early in addictions work and was found to be applicable to the HIV pandemic. Harm reduction has been a significant part of many effective HIV prevention programs, particularly those focused on active drug users. It recognizes that individuals may not be prepared or able to stop using substances or to restrict their sexual activity. The immediate goal is to reduce the severe consequences from active use and unsafe drug or sexual practices and to protect the individual and others. An example of harm reduction is needle or syringe exchange and teaching drug users not share their "works" and how to clean them appropriately. Safer sex practices are another example of harm reduction. The long-term goal is to move the individual toward sobriety or desisting in a harmful behavior. However, some may not desist in using drugs, so the goal is to provide information on the choices available to them for reducing harm to themselves, the family, and friends. It is a process requiring patience, acceptance, and attention to subtle indicators of the desire to change. It is through the quality of the relationship, one that is nonjudgmental and trusting, and its ongoing nature that a helper can take advantage of an individual's readiness to change without undue pressure, which causes people to resent or withdraw from services. It requires a rethinking of how services are delivered to ensure person-centeredness and the removal of potential barriers to services. One of the oldest forms of harm reduction is methadone maintenance. Harm reduction has been incorrectly characterized as enabling addictive behavior or giving permission to continue destructive behavior. Rather, it rests on the understanding of stages of change that a person goes through. Awareness of the stage of change a person is in facilitates the choice of strategies that encourages and supports further change. It recognizes that relapse is a normal part of the process of change and is to be expected. One of harm reduction's ultimate goals is to obtain sobriety. However, it acknowledges that some people may never change. This approach is seen as then protecting the public.

Motivational interviewing (MI) is also predicated on the stages-of-change theory. It begins with the idea that readiness to change is a state that can be influenced by the professional helper. It identifies ambivalence as a normal part of change. This term is preferred to *resistance,* which is viewed as a perspective that obscures the potential to recognize and influence readiness to change and creates a set of expectations about the person. Viewing people we work with as resistant becomes a self-fulfilling phenomenon, with resulting anger, frustration, and hostility. Originally used with people with active addiction, it is a technique that has demonstrated effectiveness with a range of psychosocial problems, such as depression, obesity, smoking cessation, and medical treatment adherence (Arkowitz, Westra, Miller, & Rollnick, 2008; Rollnick, Miller, & Butler, 2008). It is an approach that appears to be especially effective with people who are not voluntarily seeking services and may be coerced or mandated by a legal authority.

The spirit of motivational interviewing is based on collaboration between the individual and worker, the ability to evoke internal resources and strengths, and honoring the autonomy of the individual. The principles and strategies of motivational interviewing are very much in keeping with person-centered approaches to helping and social work values. They include (1) understanding the person's motivation (such as, being interested in the person's concerns, values, and ideas about change); (2) listening actively to the person; (3) empowering the individual to make choices; and (4) resisting the "righting reflex" (the desire to correct another's course of action). Practitioners of MI identify five principles critical to enacting this counseling technique: (1) expressing empathy, (2) developing discrepancy between desired goals and current behavior, (3) avoiding argumentation, (4) rolling with the "resistance," and (5) supporting self-efficacy. Additionally, eight general counseling strategies are identified: (1) giving advice selectively (this is a slightly more directed or structured approach); (2) removing barriers, both emotional and concrete; (3) providing choices even if they are limited in range; (4) decreasing desirability of the targeted behavior; (5) practicing empathy; (6) providing feedback; (7) clarifying achievable goals; and (8) active helping. Most of these techniques and strategies are familiar to most generalist workers and reflect basic social work practices.

As easy as this intervention may sound, the actual implementation of these strategies takes patience, practice, and recognition and appreciation for small changes. The focus of the intervention is on supporting incremental change, and this is done by asking what the individual desires, informing that person of the possible options, and listening actively and respectfully for what he or she wants and is willing to do. A critical aspect for the competent practice of this approach is a concept called "letting go of the outcome," that is, respecting the person's autonomy. Again, it can be very challenging to workers to not intervene more actively, cajoling and confronting when we observe people acting in ways that place them at risk. Good training and supervision helps workers to acquire these skills. An additional benefit is that this style is not meant to replace a worker's preferred style of working; rather, it can be adapted and integrated.

Individuals with a severe and persistent mental illness at risk for HIV infection can also benefit from motivational interviewing. However, it involves careful consideration of the challenges people living with mental illness face and, subsequently, adaptation to them (Marino & Moyers, 2008). Working with this complex set of problems requires attention to people's willingness and ability to address their substance use, their psychiatric difficulty, HIV risk, and the interactions of these issues. Workers need to be aware of the impact of the mental illness on the individuals and, with this understanding, adapt motivational interviewing in several ways. First is to accommodate varying levels of cognitive impairments. This may call for simplifying terms and clarity in reflecting back the individuals' concerns. Many different types of mental illness have a range of symptoms; thus, in using motivational interviewing, the worker will need to consider and accommodate active symptoms such as hallucinations, delusions, disorganized thinking, flashbacks, and impulsivity. There are also passive symptoms, such as isolation, passivity, decreased emotional expression, and dissociation. The worker will have to be more active and interactive with people struggling with these symptoms.

Finally, there are clearly people for whom motivational interviewing is inappropriate. This includes individuals who may not be struggling with a severe and persistent mental illness. Conditions that call for alternative interventions include suicidality, threat of harm to another, and psychiatric decompensation.

Personal Perspective

HIV Social Work, by Oscar

I discovered I had AIDS when I was hospitalized for Pneumocystis carinii pneumonia (PCP) and thrush. I had chosen not to be tested earlier, as there were few treatments available and I was concerned about my becoming depressed and suicidal. I had assumed on some level after seeing partners die from complications from AIDS that I was probably positive. I made decisions to practice safer sex, not use drugs, and take care of my physical well-being more consciously so as to prevent infection, but I assumed that I was already HIV-infected.

During my hospital stay, the medical social worker, Barbara, was very helpful and supportive. This was before the "miracle drugs" came along, and so I assumed that I would be dead in three to four years. My emotional response was all over the place: sometimes tearful, sometimes angry, more often resigned. Barbara was patient with me and would let me speak about what I wanted. Whenever I would make some statement about a decision I had made, she would first affirm my choice and then remind me that this may not be the time to make decisions, as I was still in crisis and reeling from the impact of the diagnosis. I was fearful about dying a painful death and would talk nonstop about wanting no pain in the end. The social worker facilitated a meeting with the HIV specialist doctor and we had a long discussion about possible progression, what I wanted. She, the physician, assured me that I would not be in pain. That relieved my fear tremendously.

I was fortunate to work in a supportive job where people knew I was gay. The medical social worker, at my request, called my boss to inform him of my hospitalization. She did not disclose my diagnosis, just noting that it was serious and encouraged him to visit, which he did. He assured me that I could return to work and that I needed to focus on getting better. This helped a lot. I was in no place to continue to tell people over and over again the story of my illness. Partly, it was because I could not control my emotions, breaking down and crying. At other times it felt like I needed to take care of my friends, as they seemed more overwhelmed and devastated than me. The social worker acted as a mediator and ran interference when I was not up to it.

I quickly recovered and was discharged home. The medical social work continued to provide some follow-up, through telephone contact and the occasional home visit. My primary focus was finding a certain type of therapist. She helped me to locate a clinician that specialized in mind-body, or what is called *behavioral health*. I wanted ways to interrupt my anxiety and fear, to be able to sooth myself and be at peace, and to fully live my life for whatever time I had left. I told the social worker, "I don't want anyone who is going to ask me how I feel. I know how it feels: It sucks." She would laugh and assure me that we would find the right fit. That was another way she helped—she maintained her humor and responded to mine. It wasn't all doom and gloom.

One of our last sessions, which was over the phone, involved her inquiring when I was going to inform my parents of my illness. At first I was not having it. It wasn't that my family did not know I was gay. They had been aware and accepting for years. I initially thought that I didn't want to tell them in order to protect them. I didn't want to cause them pain. Barbara gently explored my reluc-tance to talk with my parents, challenging my reasons, which seem pretty thin in retrospect. What convinced me to tell them was Barbara's reminding me of my closeness with my family and that people who had support from family members tended to do better. I agreed that I would call them (they lived in another state), but I wanted her in my apartment when I made the call, because I was afraid. I wasn't sure what I was afraid of, I was just afraid, and not sure what it would be like for me after the phone call. She agreed to meet with me the next day and I hung up. Just then my mother called to say hi, as she hadn't heard from me in a while. I was evasive and feeling vulnerable. She asked me what was wrong, that she could hear it in my voice. I burst out saying, "Mom, I have AIDS" and started sobbing. My mother said that she had been praying that it would pass me by. She wanted to come immediately to where I was living: "I am not there, I can't even make you a bowl of soup." It was a tremendous relief to tell her. Her response and my father's response could not have been better. My father said to me, "I want you to know you are never alone; we are always with you."

The next day when Barbara showed up I told her the task had been completed. Her talking me through it before my mother's call "primed the engine," and so when the opportunity presented itself I could do it. I don't know what Barbara did for me in that conversation, but it helped me tell my parents. I know I would not have made the call on my own. She helped me to talk about the conversations, what I heard, needed, requested from my parents. She helped me understand that my fear in talking with my parents was fear of acknowledging my vulnerability and impending death. I also knew that I was very fortunate in my family and friends and that I was not alone. That was the last time I saw Barbara officially. I began treatment with a mind-body specialist, whom I saw for two years. Within that time new medications came out, so instead of preparing to die, I needed to get back in the game more fully. I still see Barbara when I go see the HIV specialist; we smile, chat for a minute, tell jokes, and swap gossip, and I'm always uplifted even just seeing her for a moment.

CONCLUSIONS

A diagnosis of HIV begins a process of lifelong accommodation to a stigmatized debili-tating illness. HIV represents a progression of losses, beginning with one's identity as a healthy person. Changes in physical conditions and responses from the person's social world represent crises that must be addressed and worked through. While there are life-saving medications, not all individuals have access to them or benefit from them. At this period of time, we are becoming aware of the long-term debilitating consequences of medication therapy on the individual. Additionally, counselors are seeing people with a range of cognitive impairments and memory loss due to years of living with HIV, continued drug use, and taking HIV medications. People living with HIV represent a range of social and psychological conditions, some of which are more challenging than others. Living with HIV is further complicated by stigma, racism, sexism, classism, ageism, xenophobia, homophobia, addiction, and mental illness. Despite these struggles, many people are able to cope and live full and productive lives. Workers should identify the psychosocial needs of the individuals and provide counseling support and concrete services. As pervasive as the illness may seem in an individual's life, it is important to remember that the person is not the disease, but someone living with a disease.

REFERENCES

Arkowitz, H., Westra, H. A, Miller, W. R., & Rollnick, S. (Eds.). (2008). *Motivational Interviewing in the Treatment of Psychological Problems.* New York: Guildford Press.

Center for Disease Control and Prevention. (2008). HIV prevalence estimates in the U.S. *Morbidity and Morality Weekly Report.* Retrieved October 3, 2008 from http://www.cdc/mmwr/preview/mmwrhtml/mm5739a.htm.

Courtenay Quirk, C., Wolitski, R. J., Parsons, J. T., & Gomez, C. A. (2006). Is HIV/AIDS stigma dividing the gay community? Perceptions of HIV-positive men who have sex with men. *AIDS Education Prevention, 18*(1), 56–67.

Denning, P. (2000). *Practicing Harm Reduction Psychotherapy. An alternative approach to addictions.* New York: Guildford Press.

El-Bassel, N., Gilbert, L., Wu, E., Go, H., & Hill, J. (2005). HIV and intimate partner violence among methadone-maintained women in New York City. *Social Science & Medicine, 61*(1), 171–183.

Emlet, C. A. (2007). Experiences of stigma in older adults living with HIV/AIDS: A mixed-methods analysis. *AIDS Patient Care & STDs, 21*(10), 740–752.

Gushue, G. V., & Brazaitis, S. J. (2003). Lazarus and group psychotherapy: AIDS in the era of protease inhibitors. *Counseling Psychologist, 31*(3), 314–342.

Herek, G. M., Capitanio, J. P., & Widaman, K. F. (2003, September). Stigma, social risk, and health policy: Public attitudes toward HIV surveillance policies and the social construction of illness. *Health Psychology, 22*(5), 533–540

Lightfoot, M., Rotheram-Borus, M. J., & Tevendale, H. (2007, May). An HIV-preventive intervention for youth living with HIV. *Behavior Modification, 31*(3), 345–363.

Mamo, L., & Mueller, M. (2003). Confronting Inequities in HIV/AIDS care in the USA: Suggested lines of investigation. *Critical Public Health, 13*(4), 347–356.

Marino, S., & Moyers, T. R. (2008). Motivational Interviewing with dually diagnosed patients. In H. Arkowitz, H. A. Westra, W. R. Miller, & S. Rollnick (Eds.), *Motivational interviewing in the treatment of psychological problems* (pp. 277–301). New York: Guildford Press.

Miller W. R., & Rollnick, S. (1991). *Motivational interviewing: Preparing people to change addictive behavior.* New York: Guildford Press.

Odo, R. (2003). Hidden epidemic: HIV/AIDS among the seriously and persistently mentally ill. *Social Work in Mental Health, 1*(3), 19–34.

Poindexter, C. (1997). In the aftermath: Serial crisis intervention with persons with HIV. Health and Social Work, 22 (2), 125–132.

Porter, K., Babiker, A., Bhaskaran, K., Derbyshire, J., Pezzotti, P.,& Walker, A. S. (2003). Determinants of survival following HIV-1 seroconversion after the introduction of HAART. *Lancet, 362,* 1267–1274.

Rollnick, S., Miller, W. R., & Butler, C. (2008). *Motivational interviewing in health care: Helping patients change behavior.* New York: Guildford Press.

Smit, C., Lindenburg, K., Geskus, R. B., Brinkman, K., Coutinho, R. A., & Prins, M. (2006, March). Highly active antiretroviral therapy (HAART) among HIV-infected drug users: A prospective cohort study of sexual risk and injecting behaviour. *Addiction, 101*(3), 433–440.

Strug, D. L., Grube, B. A., & Beckerman, N. L. (2002). Challenges and changing roles in HIV/AIDS social work: Implications for training and education. *Social Work in Health Care, 35*(4), 1–19.

Shulman, L. (1999). *The skills of helping individuals, families, groups and communities.* Itasca, IL: F.E. Peacock Publishers.

Tolou Shams, M., Paikoff, R., McKirnan, D. J., & Holmbeck, G. N. (2007). Mental health and HIV risk among African American adolescents. *The Role of Parenting. Social Work in Mental Health, 5,* 27–58.

Yep, G. A., Merrigan, G., M., Martin, J. B., Lovaas, K. E., & Cetron, A. B. (2002–2003) HIV/AIDS in Asian and Pacific Islander communities in the United States: A follow-up review and analysis with recommendations for researchers and practitioners. *International Quarterly of Community Health Education, 21*(3), 199–227.

Chapter Seven

HIV SOCIAL WORK ROLES, TASKS, AND CHALLENGES IN HEALTH CARE SETTINGS

Brian Giddens

INTRODUCTION

As the medical and social service professions are poised to enter the fourth decade assisting with the multiple issues of persons with HIV, it is heartening to see how far treatment and services have come since HIV first appeared. The frightening collection of symptoms that initially provoked anxiety, if not outright panic, in health care providers, is now understood in medical terms (Messeri, 2005). What used to be relegated only to specialists is now seen as a disease that all medical professionals, regardless of whether they are HIV specialists, need to understand. Most significantly, a diagnosis of HIV has changed from a terminal condition to a chronic disease that, for many having access to treatment, can still allow for a longer and healthier life.

Personal Perspective[1]

I have lived with an HIV infection for more than 26 years. I became infected in late 1981 or early 1982, based on evidence from frozen blood samples and other factors. From the beginning, I decided that if I was to become a statistic, I wanted to be one of few who attained long-term survival from this dreadful disease. I have lost two life partners and more friends and acquaintances than I care to count, so I know the toll AIDS has taken over the years and, unfortunately, continues to take today.

With greater understanding of HIV comes the need to adjust the scope and focus of services to complement treatment options. The role of social workers in HIV, like that of physicians and nurses, has changed significantly (Wheeler, 2007). Social work with

Acknowledgments: I thank Susan Reynolds and Brian Myatt for their consultations relating to home health and financial resources and Gary for providing a perspective on living with HIV. This chapter is dedicated to Gary for his advocacy, his humor, and his Big Sky spirit; I thank him for contributing his story.

[1]All personal perspective inserts have been written by Gary.

persons with HIV is no longer seen as the equivalent of hospice work. Instead, the profession looks to other chronic diseases like diabetes for understanding how to work with persons who have lifelong health conditions. HIV, in moving from the acute and terminal to a chronic disease model, requires long-term relationships between persons with HIV and their social service and health care providers.

Personal Perspective

I had almost immediate improvement in my overall health after starting a medical regimen. My medical team worked closely with me to ensure the best combination of drugs. Of course, over a period of years, I had to change medication a couple of times because the virus found a way to get around the drugs I was taking.

The work becomes less of a constant crisis orientation and instead focuses on how to prevent the crises that can occur when individuals in treatment are unable to fully participate in care.

While the enormous gains in the knowledge base have been extremely beneficial for persons with HIV and the social service and health care professionals who work with this population, significant challenges still exist. This chapter addresses the changing scenario of HIV care for social workers in health care settings. In addition to looking at the settings, roles, and functions of social workers in HIV work today, current challenges that health care social workers confront are addressed, such as the increasing emphasis on the economics of care and the continued stereotyping and assumptions that occur, especially regarding HIV-affected persons with co-occurring illnesses such as mental illness and chemical dependency.

THE VALUE OF ANCILLARY SERVICES

In health care, social work is seen as one of several disciplines that engage in the health care assessment, plan, and ongoing care treatment. In some settings, social workers are seen as an ancillary (supplemental or secondary) service—in contrast to the physician, who is seen as the primary provider. A professional hierarchy continues to exist in health care, with the primary medical provider and nurse leading, followed by a range of other supplemental services, such as social work, occupational, speech and physical therapies, nutrition and pharmacy. Outside of health care, the term *ancillary* has a somewhat derogatory definition of "subordinate," "subsidiary," "auxiliary," and "supplementary" (Merriam-Webster, 2008). Fortunately, in most health care settings today, the value of an interdisciplinary team approach that recognizes diverse professional expertise is increasingly favored (Friedland, 2006).

The value of supplemental services has been demonstrated in numerous research studies over the course of the HIV pandemic (Ashman, Conviser, & Pounds, 2002; Messeri, Abramson, Aidala, Lee, & Lee, 2002). Before a person with HIV can engage in treatment, he or she may need assistance obtaining the most basic requirements for survival, such as food and shelter. Social workers are key to connecting people to resources and advocating for services. Whether the resource is housing, mental health care, chemical dependency counseling, in-home supports, or transportation, social work is seen by the interdisciplinary team as being the link to the community resources necessary for an individual to access and maintain treatment.

In addition, the perspective of social work is unique, bringing to the assessment and treatment planning process different strengths (Hall, 2007). For example, it may be the social worker who looks at the larger picture of the person's situation, environment, or context. The doctor may recommend treatment, and the nurse may educate the person and implement the treatment, but the social worker may be the one who thinks to ask the person if he or she believes that the treatment will work and whether the treatment is in accordance with the person's cultural, spiritual, or personal beliefs. This unique perspective brings a layer of depth to the treatment planning that can lead to a healthier outcome.

GENERAL TASKS OF A SOCIAL WORKER IN HEALTH CARE

The role of social workers in health care will vary, depending on the setting in which they work. In general, the social worker assesses for psychosocial issues and tangible needs that could affect the individual's ability to engage in services and manage treatment. Any barriers to care require the social worker to seek solutions. These solutions may include problem-solving sessions with the individual and/or his or her chosen family or support network, mediating in conflicts between support persons and the sick person, providing supportive counseling when the health condition and its effects become overwhelming, assisting in obtaining financial and/or practical assistance for health care services, medications, housing, food, transportation, and/or equipment, and advocating for the sick person to service providers to ensure that the individual's voice is heard. In some settings, the social work role may initially be to help the individual access treatment, and in such cases, the social worker is the first person on the interdisciplinary team to make contact and introduce the person to the health care system.

Given these responsibilities, the following characteristics and skills are essential for good social work practice:

- *Empathy.* An obvious attribute for a social worker, yet sometimes with the pace of health care, providers spend more time doing than listening. Building a long-term relationship may seem impossible in many settings, but a truly empathic worker presents as honest, communicates in a way that makes a person feel heard, and conveys caring. It is the ability to connect and engage with an individual that helps to build trust, even in brief encounters.

Personal Perspective

My advice to a health care provider can be summarized in two words: *Build trust.* Building trust is difficult, especially in the current environment where time is at a premium. But it can be as simple as remembering something personal about someone. One of my favorite providers never fails to ask me about my dog. She knows how important my dog is to me, and having her remember to ask helps establish a connection between us. Of course on my part, I have to respond and nurture that trust by always being as honest with her as possible. So building trust is a very complex matter that both provider and patient must strive to achieve if the goal is to provide and receive the best medical care possible.

- *Knowledge of the disease or conditions affecting the population served.* Obviously, this does not mean knowledge at the level of the physician, but a general understanding of the symptoms, course of the disease and accompanying conditions, and typical treatment interventions and effects. Enough knowledge is needed to know what the individual may expect as he or she participates in care, and how the disease and treatment may alter that person's daily life. In the case of a person newly diagnosed with HIV, common questions may include, "When should I start treatment?" "Will I have treatment side effects?" "How long will I live?" "Should I tell my family?" and/or, "What should I tell my sexual or drug partners?"

- *An ability to work as a member of the interdisciplinary team.* Even if the social worker is an independent case manager, coordination with physicians, nurses, and other professionals is necessary to help the person in care. The team can be a valuable tool to increase adherence and improve the experience of care if the professionals are working together. When the team members are coordinating effectively and communicating with each other, the person in care hears the same plan from all the providers, and interventions and expected outcomes are clear.

- *An ability to work independently.* Working independently may seem to contradict the need to work as a member of a team, but the social worker is often the only spokesperson for the social work profession within a health care team. The social worker has to work with team members to stay informed, communicate, and coordinate, but then also move on to accomplish his or her part of the treatment plan independently. Because the social worker may not have readily accessible peers or because he or she may be the only social worker in a peer group with specific knowledge of the disease or condition, the social worker needs to be comfortable independently setting priorities and seeking consultation.

- *Comfort with crisis.* This may be inherent in most social work roles, but in health care, a medical condition often adds a layer of complexity that makes a person's situation all the more fragile. Acute medical episodes, changes in medication protocols, and hospitalizations are a few of the many factors that can trigger instability and crisis.

- *Organizational management skills.* Proficiency in organizational skills is important for two reasons. First, the health condition has its own requirements, in addition to the needs of the person experiencing the condition. For example, the disease requires ongoing therapeutic interventions (such as medications and equipment, therapies) and appointments with providers for monitoring. Second, at the same time, the person with the condition has the same basic needs as the rest of the population (housing, support, food, money, caregiving), but may need help in managing these needs due to health limitations. Thus the social worker can be required to help manage multiple levels of need.

- *Insight into one's own feelings about illness, disability, death and HIV.* One cannot do health care social work for long without confronting his or her own feelings about illness, particularly HIV. There is no escaping the face of an individual who is in chronic pain, the sobs of a longtime partner who has just lost a mate, or the humiliation that a person may be feeling when the initial assessment is continually interrupted by frequent trips to the bathroom to manage a bout of diarrhea. People who may look healthy one day may be close to dying a month later. Visits may be cut short because the individual is in too much pain to talk. A disability can be disfiguring. These in-your-face situations require a perspective on illness and death that, for many people outside of health care, does not get addressed until much later in life. In addition, HIV carries its own level of intensity and stigma. Issues relating to sexual activities and/or drug use may conflict with a social worker's experience and beliefs. New social workers as well as veterans in the field should always seek supervision to address these issues, and make sure that they have a support network readily available.

It is important to note as well why health care work is so appealing to many social workers. Some people enjoy the adrenaline rush that can be present in a busy inpatient or emergency room setting. Others like working in health care because it is ever-changing, with new opportunities for learning available every day. There can be tremendous personal satisfaction in the degree of intimacy that is generated by being present during life crises. Providing support to persons when they may need it the most leaves no doubt of the value of what social workers can do. To be able to share in life's most significant moments, be it birth, death, or somewhere in between, is unique and life-changing.

THE ROLE OF A SOCIAL WORKER IN ASSISTING PERSONS LIVING WITH HIV

A social worker engaged in serving persons with HIV needs to be able to manage the same general tasks as other health care social workers, but as the pandemic evolves, some additional skills are required in order to be truly effective. Among those skills are adherence counseling, risk-reduction counseling, and assessing barriers or needs that disrupt accessing care.

Adherence counseling was not an issue at the beginning of the HIV pandemic because there was not any substantive treatment to stem the course of the disease, beyond prophylactic therapies designed to fight symptomatic diseases and opportunistic infections. Since the advent of antiretrovirals and highly active antiretroviral treatment (HAART), the importance of adherence has become paramount. In the early years of HAART, when the medication regimen for combination therapy was especially complicated, it was apparent that the development of new HIV drugs was in itself not enough. Adherence to the treatment plan—actually managing the drug regimen consistently and correctly—was a significant challenge. The need for frequent dosing, dosing with or without food or liquids, dosing on time, the requirement for some medicines to be refrigerated, living with noxious side effects, the costs of the drugs, and taking the drugs privately all determined whether individuals could adhere to the treatment regimen.

Personal Perspective

I am proof that living long term with HIV is possible, but it is not a walk in the park. Side effects of medication can range from serious to mere nuisance. Accepting a lifetime of popping pills on a regular and consistent basis can be challenging and tiresome.

Numerous studies have shown the benefits of adherence (Stirrat & Gordon, 2005; Gruber, Sorensen, & Haug, 2007) as well as the factors affecting adherence (Hamilton, Razzano, & Martin, 2007; Scheid, 2007; Kang, Goldstein, & Deren, 2008). In addition, nonadherence has been associated not only with significant health consequences, but also with financial and social effects such as decreased productivity and quality of life and increased health care use and cost (Levensky & O'Donohue, 2006).

While HIV treatments have been simplified over the years, they can still be complicated and expensive enough to deter adherence. Extensive education has been necessary for both service providers and service recipients to recognize barriers to adherence. Historically, the tendency was to blame the "patient" for not being "compliant." Over time, and with the contributions of many HIV-positive persons and service providers both within and external to the HIV field, the role of adherence counselor has been created. This role, often appropriately filled by social workers, recognizes the complex factors that determine a person's ability to participate fully in treatment and provides assistance in lessening barriers to success with treatment. While people are referred to social workers for help with adherence in non-HIV settings, it is much less formalized with other disease conditions than it is currently with HIV.

The issues of adherence to the treatment plan have become so primary that other tasks and services are sometimes seen as secondary. For example, the concept of medical case management has been introduced in several HIV case management programs. Primary activities of medical case management focus on linking a person to primary medical care and medical services (Washington State Department of Health, 2007). Programs such as HIV support groups may not be seen as a direct link to medical care and treatment, and as such, may not be funded.

Risk-reduction counseling is also more formalized in HIV work, though obviously social workers face this issue in other specialty areas as well. Due to the ways HIV is transmitted, it is acknowledged that social workers in HIV need to be comfortable discussing matters pertaining to sex and drug use. Risk reduction involves assessing a person's risk for engaging in behaviors that could further harm his or her health, and then problem-solving with the individual to try to lessen the risk of transmission. As with adherence counseling, risk reduction counseling is a collaboration between the provider and the person learning safer behavior. Attempting behavioral change without involving the individual can be a setup for failure. For example, a social worker may be working with a person who appears depressed and whose caregiver needs respite. The social worker may make a referral to an adult daytime health program specifically for persons with HIV. This seems to be a logical referral in that in gives the caregiver a chance to have time off and it could increase socialization for someone who is isolated. But if the social worker does not assess the person's readiness to act on the referral, how would he or she know that this person is reluctant to be with others because of lipodystrophy—and that the idea of attending a daylong group activity might be terrifying to such a person? Social workers need to make sure that their interventions are as sensible in practice as they appear on paper.

Assessing barriers or needs for a person with HIV, in order to begin a plan to address such needs, is vital for a social worker in a health care setting. Messeri et al. (2002) suggest looking at four types of needs:

1. *Logistical.* Instrumental barriers, such as lack of transportation or child care, that keep an individual from accessing treatment.
2. *Coordinative.* Barriers in finding one's way through the complicated systems of care, securing a provider, or obtaining needed resources.
3. *Individually mediated.* Behaviors or conditions that prevent a person from seeking care, such as mental illness or chemical dependency.
4. *Socially mediated.* Barriers that are policy-based or societal, preventing access and follow-up to care.

In identifying and then striving to meet these categories of need, the social worker takes on several different roles, depending on the scope and setting of their work. Broker, coordinator, planner, collaborator, and coach are just a few of the roles or hats that an HIV social worker might put on in the course of a day (Giddens, Ka'opua, & Tomaszewski, 2002) in order to work to lessen or remove the identified barriers.

THE HEALTH CARE SYSTEM AND SETTINGS FOR HIV SOCIAL WORK

What comprises the health care system? A definition needs to encompass all the points of care along the continuum of health care services (see Figure 7.1). The continuum ranges from community services to acute inpatient care, but due to the unpredictable trajectory of the disease, a person can move back and forth within the continuum, necessitating ongoing review and adjustments to the care plan.

Obviously, each setting is going to require different activities of the social worker if, in fact, the setting even has social work available. See Table 7.1 for an overview of priority tasks in each setting.

Clinics or Outpatient Care

Outpatient social work is much different than its inpatient counterpart. Clinics can be freestanding or affiliated with a medical center complex. There are private clinics, not-for-profit clinics, senior clinics, teen clinics, public health clinics, addictions clinics, methadone clinics, sexually transmitted disease clinics, women's clinics, and disease-specific clinics. Some clinics employ social workers, and many do not. The extent of HIV work in clinics is most likely reflective of the clinic population. If an influx of persons with HIV appears in a community, the clinic responds by strengthening staff HIV education programs, and perhaps hiring staff with experience in HIV. Thus, the needs of the community inform the clinic, though the timing of the necessary ramping up of appropriate services is often delayed or inadequate in most health settings today.

A clinic social worker's potential caseload could consist of any individual accessing the clinic. Depending on the clinic, this could mean thousands of persons in the pool of those needing services. Given such a potentially large caseload, social workers may need

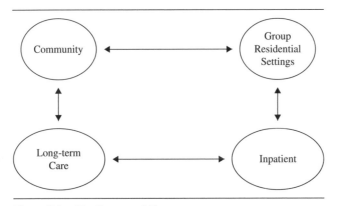

Figure 7.1   Continuum of Care

Table 7.1   Health Care Settings and Social Work Tasks*

1 = Primary task 2 = Possible 3 = Less likely	Community HIV Case Management	Hospital-Based HIV Case Management	Outpatient and Community Clinics	Home Health	Hospice	Adult Family Home, Assisted Living, Retirement Facilities	Long-Term Care	Hospital
Adherence assessment and counseling	1	1	2	2	3	2	3	2
Advocacy	1	1	1	1	1	1	1	1
Bereavement counseling	2	2	3	2	1	2	2	2
Case management	1	1	2	3	3	2	3	3
Discharge planning	3	3	3	3	3	3	1	1
Emotional support	1	1	1	1	1	1	1	1
End-of-life planning	2	2	2	2	1	2	1	1
Information and referral	1	1	1	1	1	1	1	1
Long-term-care planning	1	1	2	1	3	1	3	1
Risk-reduction assessment and counseling	1	1	2	3	3	3	3	3

*Note that the priority ranking of these tasks will vary depending on the characteristics of the setting population, specialty, level of funding, and staffing.

to identify the types of referrals they can accept, based on (1) the needs of the population, (2) the needs of the clinic staff for assistance, and (3) the availability of time for the social worker. Ironically, the more in need the population, the more restrictive the social worker may need to be regarding which issues receive attention. For example, a suburban clinic in a community that attracts a largely insured, socioeconomically stable population would likely see a person with HIV as a natural referral to a social worker, as the disease tends to be associated with a need for support, possible adherence assistance, and, potentially, some behavioral concerns. (A clinic that does not see many persons with HIV may also be at risk for stereotyping an HIV-positive person and making assumptions or asking questions about how the individual acquired the disease.) In contrast, a clinic in a poor urban community may see high numbers of HIV-positive persons who are referred to the social worker only if the practitioner also has concerns about child abuse, lack of resources, or an emerging mental health crisis. In the latter case, HIV is secondary to other, more pressing social and emotional issues, and HIV itself may not be automatically referred to the social worker due to competing demands.

Depending on the demands of the clinic and social work staffing, the level of proactive screening versus reactive crisis management will vary. In some communities, the needs of the population may surpass the resources available to the social worker. Still, the clinic setting can foster a very positive experience for a social worker. Because of the nature of clinic visits being ongoing, there is a greater possibility of building a longer-term relationship with the person seeking care. Progress on goals can be made incrementally, in sessions where the person is not overwhelmed with an acute medical crisis, such as in an inpatient setting. For persons with HIV, the clinic can allow for ongoing monitoring of the treatment plan, and, given the longer-term relationship, adherence issues can be better evaluated over time.

A social worker in a clinic setting would focus on several issues for persons with HIV. Assisting the individual with adjusting to a new diagnosis, helping the person connect to programs that can help with the cost of medications or that provide help in the home, referring the individual to support groups for persons with HIV, and counseling the person about the psychological effects of the disease (though, given clinic caseloads, long-term therapeutic counseling is often referred elsewhere) are examples of the role of a clinic social worker.

There are also models of clinics that have established HIV case management programs. These clinics are specifically for HIV-positive persons, usually with staff expert in the field, who choose to work exclusively with this population. HIV case management has proven to be successful in combining the medical and psychosocial interventions with HIV-positive persons into a comprehensive, coordinated plan (Cunningham, Wong, Hays, 2008; Kushel, Colfax, Heineman, Palacio, & Bangsberg, 2006). While the potential pool of persons needing care in an HIV case management program is likely much less than in a general health care clinic, the caseloads can be just as stressful, in that 100 percent of the service recipients tend to be seen by the social work case manager. This may mean that the person is screened for needs, and at least an initial assessment is the norm. In the past decade, several of the case management programs have created levels of care based on the assessment. In varying degrees of detail, the individual is assessed for *acuity,* a term used in the medical profession to signify severity of a condition. Acuity is based on a number of factors determined by the program and/or the funder, including the number and type of needs, past and present high-risk behaviors, and psychosocial history. Someone who has a new diagnosis but is working, living with a partner, has insurance, and relies on a strong support system would be put at a low acuity level and would only be monitored occasionally by the case manager, perhaps via a phone call. In contrast, someone who has a history of drug use, is low-income, lives alone, and is presenting as depressed would be higher acuity and would be seen face-to-face more regularly.

While the acuity model makes sense for identifying who may require assistance and to what degree, it is also necessary to monitor the situations of the persons who may be initially deemed as less in need. Given how the symptoms of HIV can fluctuate unpredictably, a person's emotional state and resource needs can also shift. In addition, social workers who have an intense caseload with many high-risk, high-need people can take on a crisis mentality and not recognize the more subtle early stages of an impending crisis. For example, if a social worker has been focused on helping several methamphetamine users in constant crisis, other issues may seem relatively minor. Unfortunately, what seems like a minor issue to a busy case manager may be a major concern for a person in crisis. It is important that the social worker continually reviews his or her cases to make sure that reassessments are occurring and that each person's situation is given due consideration.

Home Health

Many HIV-positive persons have received home health care services, and home health agencies employ social workers. The role of a social worker in home health is similar in some ways to a hospital social worker and in other ways to an HIV case manager. Social workers can receive referrals in a situation where there is a medical necessity; for example, an HIV-positive person may need in-home services arranged to help manage a treatment plan, or because mental health issues are acting as a barrier to engagement with care. The focus is on in-home intervention to help the individual and his or her support system with any psychosocial or tangible barriers to treatment. Home health care social work has the advantage of allowing a social worker to see the HIV-positive person in his or her own setting. Such an opportunity to see a person in his or her own environment versus a hospital can shift the balance of power from the provider to the individual in crisis.

Hospice

The philosophy behind hospice is based on *care* rather than aggressively trying to cure a disease or condition that is seen as incurable. It is much more likely that a person with HIV may be enrolled in a hospice program due to another disease, such as cancer. As the population of persons with HIV ages, and as the years of treatment begin to take their toll, persons with HIV become vulnerable to other medical conditions associated with an aging population (discussed in Chapter 16 of this book).

When a social worker in a hospice program works with someone with HIV, it is important to realize that the person with HIV may have a unique perspective on death and dying. Even if the cause of the referral to hospice may be due to another medical condition, a person with HIV may have a long association with the health care system already. How long the people have been living with HIV is a vital question to consider. If they were diagnosed before the advent of HAART, or in the early years of HAART, they likely expected to die early, and may even have gone through some of the rituals that dying people experience. In fact, one of the more difficult psychological issues for some persons with HIV after the advent of HAART was "reversing their plans to die" after having basically come to terms with the possibility. Thus, the natural review with persons new to hospice, which incorporates information and support about the emotional process of facing one's own death, may not be as necessary. Instead, the person with HIV may be angry about the fact that, after all these years of fighting HIV, he or she is now being felled by an entirely different condition. Or the individual may have unrealistic expectations for a last-minute reversal, given how many brushes with death he or she may already have survived. Alternatively, the individual may just be exhausted from years of medications, appointments, being poked by doctors and nurses, counseled by people who "just want to help" and may embrace the idea of being freed from treatment. It is important to realize that a person who has struggled for some time with HIV is truly a survivor, and in that struggle she or he has developed great strengths. Whether those strengths help or hinder a person in a hospice program depends on the level of acceptance about the possibility of death. It is up to the social worker to ensure that the vast knowledge and experience a person with HIV has relating to illness and the dying process is recognized and utilized.

Skilled Nursing Facilities

Social work activities in skilled nursing facilities (SNFs) include providing individual and family support, facilitating resident and family groups, facilitating and participating in care conferences, assisting with compliance and admission activities, and counseling related to end-of-life care and bereavement. The lack of funding for skilled nursing facilities that accept public financing (such as Medicaid and Medicare) can challenge even the most creative social worker. Reimbursement for Medicaid patients in many states has not kept up with the increased cost of medications and staffing. In facilities with especially complex populations, there is often more to do than there is staff available to do it. Additionally, the social worker's time may be consumed with helping the administration of the facility meet regulatory requirements, such as ensuring care conferences are held, initial assessments are done, and complaints are resolved. These tasks can take the social worker away from meeting some of the other psychosocial needs of the residents.

Adult Family Homes, Assisted Living Facilities, and Retirement Homes

These residential categories have been combined because they all may provide some supportive services in a residential group setting. Adult family homes have fewer residents (four to six) and often specialize in working with a specific type of population, such as the chronically mentally ill, developmentally delayed, stroke survivors, or other groups with similar characteristics and needs. There are also models of such homes specifically for persons with HIV. Due to the size of the facility, the funding is likely lacking to have a social worker on-site, but some facilities contract independent services or, more likely, coordinate with existing case managers in the community. Thus, an HIV case manager may work with the adult family home to promote stable housing or to intervene when there are behavior problems.

The majority of assisted living facilities and retirement homes do not have social work services on-site, and it is unknown how many HIV-positive persons access these services. Because there are established in-home services in many communities for persons with HIV, including home health, it is likely that persons who are HIV-positive would stay in their homes, if they have housing, as long as possible, and then move to skilled nursing facilities when they require more extensive care.

Hospital

Social work roles in an inpatient hospital can include discharge planning (ensuring that the person has a safe place to go after hospitalization), crisis intervention, individual and family counseling related to changes in lifestyle due to illness or disability, discovery of new diagnoses or worsening of existing condition, and counseling pertaining to end-of-life decision making and bereavement. A social worker may encounter a person with a primary diagnosis of HIV or, increasingly, another diagnosis necessitating the admission, with HIV being a secondary diagnosis. Depending on the experience of the hospital staff, a social work referral might be made relating to the diagnosis of HIV, as some providers still see a person with HIV as a high-risk situation. Social workers must evaluate whether the individual needs services, or whether they can help coordinate services with existing community providers.

CONSIDERATIONS FOR ALL HEALTH CARE SETTINGS

It is important to also note two additional issues that span all settings: cultural factors and alternative medicine. *Cultural considerations* should be infused throughout the health care continuum, and it will often be up to the social worker to identify and integrate cultural issues into the care planning. Cultural competency is essential to ensure adherence (Rodriguez-Gomez & Salas-Serrano, 2006). This means that the cultural needs and values of the individual are incorporated into the initial assessment interview and in ongoing discussions. While people may share a diagnosis, their perspective on what that diagnosis and subsequent treatment mean to them will be vastly different, depending on their culture. It can be useful to take the big-tent view of culture, considering the variety of factors that affect a person's cultural perspective. These can include cultures of age, gender, sexual orientation, socioeconomics, geography, race, and ethnicity, among other factors. Through practicing social work skills and values in conducting a bio-psycho-social-spiritual-cultural assessment, involving the individual in care planning, and advocating for the individual with the care team, the social worker will elevate the individual and team's efforts to a higher level of care.

Another area that cannot be overlooked, which is also present in all health care settings, is the issue of *complementary and alternative medicine* (CAM). CAM includes nontraditional forms of treatment that include various mind and body interventions, including massage, herbs, nutrition, acupuncture, Reiki, chiropractors, homeopathy, and meditation (Mulkins, Morse, & Best, 2002). A high proportion of persons with HIV look to CAM to help alleviate and/or prevent HIV-related symptoms and reduce side effects from treatment (Littlewood & Venable, 2008). Given this, providers should make it a standard practice to inquire whether an HIV-positive person is participating in CAM. Just as HIV social workers should know about traditional HIV treatments and how they affect the individual, they should also know about any CAM that the person is pursuing because they may affect that person's wellbeing and interact with traditional treatments.

When an individual looks outside of traditional medicine, it may be due to cultural beliefs and/or indicative of a desire on the part of the person to seek out answers independently. Asking questions and seeking alternative approaches should be seen as a positive, empowering act. At the same time, people who ask lots of questions or who participate in care practices that the physician did not approve can also be labeled as "problem patients." These persons take time, engage in debates about efficacy of treatment, and want detailed information from their providers. When a person presents as a problem, a social worker is often called to "fix" the problem. When this occurs, it may be helpful for the social worker to serve as a liaison between the medical team and the person needing care. Educating the medical team to respect alternative beliefs with a long-term goal of building a stronger therapeutic relationship with the person could be one goal. Another may be to coach the individual on how best to focus provider questions and to help that person understand the time constraints of the physician or nurse.

Allowing for an atmosphere in which people feel comfortable disclosing their beliefs and in which the providers show respect for such beliefs will help prevent negative effects, such as contraindicated treatment combinations.

CHALLENGES IN WORKING WITH PERSONS WITH HIV IN TODAY'S HEALTH CARE SYSTEM

There are numerous challenges in the current U.S. health care system in working with persons with HIV. This section focuses on four such challenges: the economics of care; competing demands; limits to accessing care and necessary resources; and stereotyping and assumptions relating to persons with HIV, especially those with co-occurring mental health or chemical dependency issues.

The Economics of Care

Health care is a very expensive and unstable business. The U.S. health care system has a variety of funding sources, all of which are continually tightening up reimbursement to facilities and providers. New technology and medications are costly, but at least for now, no one wants to hold up a new drug or machine that may help improve health outcomes. The institutions providing health care are a mix of government, not-for-profit, and for-profit organizations, each with its own way of operating. Given the variety of institutions and processes, there are organizations such as the Joint Commission that focus solely on ensuring that hospitals and home care agencies are following acceptable practices, and they charge such institutions significant fees to achieve accreditation. Because health care is a business with multiple providers, competition is rampant, with hospitals extensively marketing the latest procedures, programs, and equipment to gain a competitive advantage.

Health care is a staff-intensive operation as well, which creates another layer of complexity. Workforce supply and demand for different health care disciplines often dictates salaries and benefits that otherwise may not seem logical. For example, hospitals may have nursing and social work teams sharing some of the same discharge planning functions. But because the supply of nurses is currently lower than the supply of social workers, the wage differential between social work and nursing is significant.

Each individual payer, whether it is Medicare, Medicaid, Ryan White CARE Act, Native Health, the Veteran's Administration, or one of the multitudes of private insurance companies, has its own contractual requirements of providers and its own procedures for submitting bills, so scores of fiscal experts are hired to manage the contracts and ensure proper billing requirements are in place. As each change in health care practice occurs, or as the accreditation agencies change an interpretation of a standard, institutions have to expend money to provide additional training and monitoring to ensure conformity and safety. When most people think of health care, they think of doctors and nurses. In reality, the medical team is only the preview for a very long double feature of administrators, finance staff, quality improvement experts, medical coders, utilization managers, medical records personnel, compliance officers, and information technologists. In such a bloated and chaotic environment, social workers often are the ones who take on the task of navigating the recipient of services through the system (in fact, a new title of "patient navigator" has been introduced in the oncology arena specifically to help guide people through complex cancer treatment).

In such a costly business, the psychosocial needs of persons with HIV (or other diseases) may be secondary to what is billable. As health care social workers know, it is difficult to have a social work cost center that is revenue-generating. The people social workers tend to see are referred because they do not have resources and cannot afford private counselors or upscale drug rehab centers. While there are some stand-alone services that can be billed, there is also the need for crisis intervention, resource education and referral, and case management—areas of assistance that are not billable.

What has saved many a social work program is illustrating how social work can reduce overall costs of care. For example, if a social worker assists a person with HIV in removing barriers to adherence, there may be fewer visits to the emergency room. Or if the person with HIV is homeless, and the social worker finds housing for the individual, the person may be able to stabilize enough to apply for benefits so that the cost of care can be reimbursed. In hospitals, where the length of stay (the number of days a person occupies a bed) is the hallmark indicator of efficiency and cost savings (the lower the length of stay, the better the reimbursement), the social worker can help to ensure a safe discharge by cobbling together family and resources to allow the person to go home in a timely manner, thus meeting safety and budget goals. In all of these cases, the person in care benefits as well as the providers, and it is due to the systemic view of the social work profession—looking at a situation as a series of interconnected issues that need to be addressed in order to meet a goal.

Unfortunately, the argument for more social workers has to compete with multiple arguments for more nurses, more pharmacists, more MRI machines, more beds, and other demands. Thus, there is often a delay between recognizing the need for more social work, making the case for more staffing, and finally obtaining the needed social work resources. This ongoing process of catching up to meet the need can lead to a high degree of frustration and burnout for social workers in health care.

Competing Demands

There probably is not a social worker around who would say that there is enough time in the day to take care of all the needs that exist. As noted previously, given the cost of health care and competition for resources, there is a constant shortage of social workers to manage the needs. This coincides with a current economic slump and an ongoing high proportion of uninsured or underinsured people, creating a "perfect storm" in medical social work. In addition, the pace of change in health care is increasing for social workers in all settings. Twenty years ago, social workers did handwritten documentation and used the phone to make referrals. Now there are often multiple online charting systems to master (social workers need to access both financial or payer data as well as the clinical data) and e-mail, text messages, phone calls, and faxes to respond to. Some of this change is positive, but much of it adds to the frenzied day of a worker striving for some semblance of organization.

Standards for privacy, safety, compliance, and confidentiality have increased for health care workers, requiring staff to spend more time demonstrating competencies and signing statements that they have been apprised of the standards. The issue of advance directives in hospitals is an example of a good policy that requires more staff time. To meet accreditation, hospitals require that all persons who are admitted be asked whether they have an advance directive. If they do not have one, they must be asked if they want to create one. If they want to create one, the hospital must ensure that staff are available to assist in this process. Obviously, it is important to educate people about advance directives. But for a busy social worker, it is difficult to balance the competing demands of choosing between the "required" work of a person wanting help with an advance directive or spending time with a person who just found out he or she has HIV. The soft tasks, those that are not required by state or federal statute, payer, or credentialing program, are, for the social worker and the sick person, just as important as the other tasks. Yet the health care culture prioritizes differently.

Limits to Accessing Care and Necessary Resources

With 42 percent of U.S. adults being underinsured or uninsured (Schoen, Collins, Kriss, & Doty, 2008), access to care in the United States is a significant concern. While there are programs that have helped the HIV population, such as AIDS Drug Assistance Programs (ADAPs) and Insurance Continuation Programs, eligibility and access vary from state to state, and funding for all medications is not guaranteed (Kaiser Family Foundation, 2008). Medicaid assistance is available for medical care for impoverished persons, but for persons with a mental illness or chemical dependency, applying for assistance and/or maintaining enrollment is often difficult to manage.

Hospitals are required to treat anyone suffering from an emergency medical condition, and public funding is provided to hospitals for undocumented and new immigrants in an acute medical crisis who are not eligible for other Medicaid programs (Sontag, 2008). Yet for undocumented persons, there is no consistent public funding for postacute care, such as home health, medications, or residential care. Some states are providing assistance in limited cases for long-term care, but eligibility is limited to conditions specific to the reason for hospitalization, and for many states, the burdensome application and ongoing reapplication process to obtain the funding deters long-term-care facilities from considering these persons.

For an HIV-positive person with access to health services, hospitalization or long-term care is usually less of a need than medications and proactive monitoring with a primary care physician. Crisis programs, available only for the most sick, without preventive or postacute services, offer very little for undocumented or new immigrants with HIV.

Immigration issues also touch on cultural and ethnic inequalities. It has been noted that, in general, there are disparities in HIV care among racial and ethnic groups (Stirrat & Gordon, 2005), as well as disenfranchised groups such as injection drug users (Barash, Hanson, Buskin, & Teshale, 2007). Given the sexual, societal, cultural, and behavioral issues that already can restrict persons from seeking care, it is imperative that the social worker acts to encourage engagement in care. Ensuring that the atmosphere is welcoming, providing culturally competent assessment, involving the HIV-positive person in designing the treatment plan, educating the other providers about cultural issues, and advocating for the HIV-positive person with internal and external providers of care are all crucial elements to consider in building an ongoing treatment relationship.

Even when an HIV-positive person is engaged in care, the social worker must be creative in finding appropriate resources. Access to drug treatment, mental health services, housing, financial assistance, transportation, and other needs are often compounded by restrictions on eligibility, long waiting lists, or questionable quality. This requires even more of the social work skills of problem-solving creative solutions, brokering services that may be applicable, and monitoring programs to ensure that they truly are meeting the needs of the people being served.

HIV Stereotyping in Health Care

The health care system has come a long way from the early 1980s in terms of attitudes of providers toward persons with HIV. With visibility, public education, and extensive medical education, people with HIV are less likely to be discriminated against due to their HIV status. Yet prejudice and stigma still exist for some marginalized groups that continue to face discrimination, leading to health disparities (Stuber, Meyer, & Link, 2008). Racial and ethnic disparities have been proven to affect initiation of antiretroviral drugs (Stirrat & Gordon, 2005), have been linked to decreased knowledge of HIV testing and treatment in Blacks and Latinos (Ebrahim, Anderson, Weidle, & Purcell, 2004), and could also be a factor in differences in CD4 and viral load testing for injection drug users (IDUs) (Barash et al., 2007).

Of significance is that many persons with HIV belong to multiple marginalized groups that experience stigma and prejudice, further affecting their health (Stuber et al., 2008). For example, a social worker may be empathic to the plight of a person with HIV but nonetheless experience unconscious bias toward drug users, people of color, gay persons, sex workers, transgender persons, or those of low educational status. One stigmatizing condition alone leaves a person vulnerable to discrimination. Several stigmatizing conditions multiply the risk. While the profession of social work holds high value in cultural competence, one cannot assume that the discipline is free of prejudice. Another social work value, supervision/consultation, is key to recognizing conscious and unconscious behaviors that can be perceived as discriminatory. Organizational consultation is also necessary to ensure that structural components of the organization (for example, policies and procedures, forms, language used, hiring practices) are not conveying prejudice as well.

Personal Perspective

Through the years I have become aware that I must be an aggressive advocate for my own health. It is easy to get overwhelmed with the bureaucracy and complexity involved in any medical care environment, but particularly in a huge health maintenance organization. I have learned that, even though most medical providers seem to have an active interest in my well-being, I must be the primary cheerleader for the attention I require. It is not a good idea to be timid about one's need for medical care.

END-OF-LIFE CARE

The benefit of life-sustaining HIV medications is now being challenged by the increased years of survival of the HIV-positive population and the accompanying health concerns. There will be times when even with the best care, the body gives up. It may be from HIV, cancer, heart disease, or one of the other maladies that affect everyone at some point. It is important to follow the medical issues, keeping in contact with the medical team, to be apprised of what is happening physically to the person. At the same time, it is crucial to also follow the person to see how he or she is seeing the situation.

Personal Perspective

A few years ago, I was at another turning point in my treatment. I went in to see an infectious disease specialist at my HMO, who looked at my medical record and said, "Well it looks like you are about out of arrows in your quiver." Instead of depressing me, that made me angry. My experience living with a life-threatening illness is that long-term survival depends a great deal on hope. As far as I am concerned, I will always have a few arrows left in my quiver as long as I have hope for the future. I reported what the doctor had said to my general practitioner, who agreed that it was not the best way to make a point. I knew my choices were narrowing, but was determined that there was hope for improvement in any case.

The medical team and the person with HIV may not reach the same conclusion at the same time, and it will not necessarily be the team who first gives up hope. Given the incidence of depression in long-term survivors, it could be the HIV-positive person who begins to doubt further chances for survival. There is a fine dance of facts and feelings that exists in health care, and sometimes, despite all the facts, feelings of both hope and despair seem to play a part in the eventual outcome. The social worker's role is, as has been the profession's motto, to "start where the person is." Listen, support, serve as the liaison when needed between the medical team and the individual, clarify, problem-solve, and be ready to move to the next level when the individual is ready. This could mean hospice referrals if you are working with an individual at home or in the hospital. It could mean arranging for a skilled nursing facility and/or calling together the family and friends for a last farewell.

Until the individual can no longer speak for himself or herself or is cognitively unable to make decisions, the social worker should do what the person wants done. It sounds simple, but it is very easy to move from advocating for the individual to advocating for the family or the medical team. A social worker can become too enmeshed with a family member who is afraid that the HIV-positive person is unsafe at home and thus may get caught up in recommending a facility placement despite the wishes of the person living with HIV. An HIV-positive person may be wreaking havoc with a medical team by wanting to stay full code (meaning that all attempts to sustain life will be implemented if the individual has a medical crisis) despite a dire medical prognosis, and the social worker may be pressured to help convince the person to allow for a palliative care consultation. It is important to remember who you are advocating for, especially in end-of-life situations.

For social workers in case management or long-term care who have had the advantage of a long-term relationship with an HIV-positive person, being present for the final days can be devastating, wonderful, or likely a bit of both. Knowing the struggles the individual has won, the lessons learned from working with someone who has faced such a difficult illness, even the challenges that an especially difficult personality provided, can remain with a person for a very long time. Supervision and support is essential, as is taking some time to absorb the loss. Without pausing for reflection, a social worker may find the loss reemerging in negative ways at a later date. With a healthy review of one's work with the individual, the social worker can gain perspective on the situation and a renewed respect for the work that was possible.

CONCLUSIONS

This chapter focused on working with HIV-positive persons in health care settings, including a review of the continuum of care, social work tasks and functions, and specific challenges that social workers face when working with HIV-positive persons in health care today. Health care and HIV are two extremely complex arenas and a single chapter can only begin to cover all of the details and insights inherent in this work. The information provided should be a starting point for further exploration of an extremely interesting, rewarding, and dynamic area of social work practice.

REFERENCES

Ashman, J. J., Conviser, R., & Pounds, M. B. (2002). Associations between HIV-positive individuals' receipt of supplemental services and medical care receipt and retention. *AIDS Care, 14,* 109–118.

Barash, E. T., Hanson, D. L., Buskin, S. E., & Teshale, E. (2007). HIV-infected injection drug users: Health care utilization and morbidity. *Journal of Health Care for the Poor and Underserved, 18,* 675–686.

Centers for Disease Control and Prevention. (2005). Persons aged 50 and older. Retrieved August 24, 2008, from http://www.cdc.gov/hiv/topics/over50/index.htm

Cunningham, W. E., Wong, M., & Hays, R. D. (2008). Case management and health-related quality of life outcomes in a national sample of persons with HIV/AIDS. *Journal of the National Medical Association, 100(7),* 840–847.

Ebrahim, S. H., Anderson, J. E., Weidle, P., & Purcell, D. W. (2004). Race/ethnic disparities in HIV testing and knowledge about treatment for HIV/AIDS: United States, 2001. *AIDS Patient Care and STDs, 18,* 27–33.

Friedland, G. H. (2006). HIV medication adherence: The intersection of biomedical, behavioral, and social science research and clinical practice. *Journal of Acquired Immunodeficiency Syndromes, 43,* 3–9.

Giddens, B., Ka'opua, L. S., & Tomaszewski, E. P. (2002). HIV/AIDS case management. In A. R. Roberts & G. J. Greene (Eds.), *Social Workers' Desk Reference* (pp. 506–510). New York: Oxford University Press.

Gruber, V. A., Sorensen, J. L., & Haug, N. A. (2007). Psychosocial predictors of adherence to highly active antiretroviral therapy: Practical implications. *Journal of HIV/AIDS and Social Services, 6*(1/2), 23–37.

Hall, N. (2007). We care don't we? Social workers, the profession and HIV/AIDS. *Social Work and Health Care, 44*(1/2), 55–72.

Hamilton, M. M., Razzano, L. A., Martin, N. B. (2007). The relationship between type and quality of social support and HIV medication adherence. *Journal of HIV/AIDS and Social Services, 6(1/2),* 39–63.

Kaiser Family Foundation. (2008). HIV/AIDS policy fact sheet: AIDS drug assistance programs (ADAPs). Retrieved August 24, 2008, from http://www.kff.org/hivaids/upload/1584_09.pdf

Kang, S. Y., Goldstein, M. F., & Deren, S. (2008). Gender differences in health status and care among HIV-infected minority drug users. *AIDS Care,* 1–6.

Kushel, M. B., Colfax, K. R., Heineman, A., Palacio, H., & Bangsberg, D. R. (2006). Case management is associated with improved antiretroviral adherence and CD4 cell counts in homeless and marginally housed individuals with HIV infection. *Clinical and Infectious Diseases, 43,* 234–242.

Levensky, E. R., & O'Donohue, W. T. (2006). Patient adherence and nonadherence to treatments: An overview for health care providers. In E. R. Levensky & W. T. O'Donohue (Eds.), *Promoting treatment adherence: A practical handbook for health care providers* (pp. 3–14). Thousand Oaks, CA: Sage Publications.

Littlewood, R. A., & Venable, P. A. (2008). Complementary and alternative medicine use among HIV-positive people: Research synthesis and implications for HIV care. *AIDS Care,* 1–17.

Merriam-Webster. (2008). *Merriam-Webster online dictionary.* Retrieved August 24, 2008, from http//www.merriam-webster.com

Messeri, P. A. (2005). Current practices in professional training and technical assistance of HIV providers. *Journal of HIV/AIDS and Social Services, 4/2,* 3–7.

Messeri, P. A., Abramson, D. M., Aidala, A. A., Lee, F., & Lee, G. (2002). The impact of supplemental HIV services on engagement in medical care in New York City. *AIDS Care, 14,* 15–29.

Mulkins, A., Morse, J. M., & Best, A. (2002). Complementary therapy use in HIV/AIDS. *Canadian Journal of Public Health, 93*(4), 308–312.

Rodriguez-Gomez, J. R., & Salas-Serrano, C. C. (2006). Treatment adherence in ethnic minorities: Particularities and alternatives. In E. R. Levensky & W. T. O'Donohue (Eds.), *Promoting treatment adherence: A practical handbook for health care providers* (pp. 393–400). Thousand Oaks, CA: Sage Publications.

Scheid, T. L. (2007). Specialized adherence counselors can improved treatment adherence: Guidelines for specific treatment issues. *Journal of HIV/AIDS and Social Services, 6*(1/2), 121–138.

Schoen, C., Collins, S. R., Kriss, J. L., & Doty, M. M. (2008). How many are underinsured? Trends among U.S. adults, 2003–2007. *Health Affairs, 27*(4), 298–309.

Sontag, D. (2008, August 3). Immigrants facing deportation by U.S. hospitals. *New York Times,* pp. 1–16. Retrieved August 4, 2008, from http://www.nytimes.com/2008/08/03/us/03deport .html

Stirrat, M. J., & Gordon, C. M. (2007). HIV treatment adherence research and intervention: Current advances and future challenges. *Journal of HIV/AIDS and Social Services, 6*(1/2), 9–22.

Stuber, J., Meyer, I., & Link, B. (2008). Introduction: Stigma, prejudice, discrimination and health. *Social Science and Medicine, 67,* 351–357.

Washington State Department of Health. (2007). *Statewide standards for medical HIV case management* (pp. 1–11).

Wheeler, D. P. (2007). HIV and AIDS today: Where is social work going? *Health and Social Work, 32*(2), 155–157.

Chapter Eight

HIV-RELATED GROUP WORK AND FAMILY SUPPORT

Patricia A. Stewart and Valerie Dixson-Anderson

INTRODUCTION

Since the beginning of the pandemic, it has been apparent that as devastating as HIV can be medically, it is at least equally as much a source of psychosocial stress. It has been evident that expert professional care is needed from various sectors of the helping professions. The multiple needs of people living with HIV call for us to be creative, emotionally intact, and present in our approach to the work.

This chapter provides practice wisdom about HIV-related group and family support, with practical details and suggestions, in the hope that readers will be able to use these methods in their work with individuals, families, and/or groups of people who are infected with or affected by HIV.

GROUP WORK

The history of social work with groups dates back to the 1930s and was introduced to the profession in 1935 at the National Conference for Social Workers. In the 1960s and 1970s, with the expansion of the social welfare state due to the Vietnam War, the emergence of the War on Poverty, the Women's Rights Movement, the Black Power Movement, and the Lesbian and Gay Rights Movement, there emerged even more of a need and an appreciation for group work (Balgopal & Vassil, 1983). In the 1980s, group work was employed in work with people living with HIV. Whether we refer to self-help groups, support groups, or group psychotherapy, the intent is to focus on the therapeutic meeting of needs in group work. Here we discuss group dynamics, creative interventions, and effective group leadership in groups that are provided by funded programs rather than those that are self-pay.

Acknowledgments: The authors gratefully acknowledge the efforts of Maria C. Frontera, Director, Division of Children, Youth, and Families, and Danielle Parks, Program Director, Women's Anonymous Test Site, both of the Health Federation of Philadelphia, who provided feedback and shared their insights in the development of this chapter. This chapter is dedicated to the loving memory of Willis Green Jr., HIV advocate, comrade, friend, and to the men and women in our support groups, who contributed their words and wisdom to the chapter and who every day in many ways show us how to celebrate life.

There are advantages and disadvantages to group work for the individual as well as the facilitator, and both have to find the best fit. For the individual, here are a few possible advantages:

- Meeting other people with problems can lend wider perspective to one's own problems.
- Listening to others provides options about how to view and cope with issues.
- There is an opportunity for mutual encouragement and emotional support, a general feeling for the human condition: "We are all in the same boat" (Palme, 2008).

A major disadvantage can exist if one does not like to participate in groups or does not feel comfortable sharing intimate information with others; one may prefer individual work for the individual attention. Scheduling sessions are easier when individual (Palme, 2008).

Each group has its own attributes, personality, ways of functioning, levels of sophistication, and abilities to communicate. Groups are a type of system, so similar principles apply to understanding groups as systems that apply to understanding agencies or families. Each group will have its norms, roles, rules, language, properties, processes, and degrees of functioning (Wagenhals, 2004). Although groups vary, the following are some basic therapeutic factors in group work (Yalom, 1995):

- Instilling hope
- Imitating behaviors of other members and the facilitator
- Altruism (helping other group members)
- Development of socializing techniques
- Universality (feeling that one is not alone)
- Imparting information
- Correction and re-creation of the family group

Clarke (1998) indicates that effective group leaders should have a combination of the following four qualities:

1. *Warmth*
   - Speak well of people.
   - Tend to like and trust rather than fear other people.
   - Establish warm relationship with people.
2. *Indirectness*
   - Allow people to discover things for themselves.
   - Be willing to refrain from telling everything they know, even when it would be "good for people." (Researcher Allan Tough found that learners preferred helpers who offered helpful resources rather than answers to their insightful process.)
3. *Cognitive organization*
   - Have clear behavioral objectives in mind.
   - Divide learning into orderly steps.

- Have knowledge well categorized so that they can offer appropriate data in response to questions.
- Be clear about what one knows; do not pretend when in doubt.
4. *Enthusiasm*
   - Feel enthusiastic about people.
   - Be enthusiastic about the subject matter.

A balanced blending of these qualities makes for an effective group leader. It is especially helpful to have passion about the work and to enjoy the people in the group. Honor their knowledge and experience, share yours, learn from them, and laugh with them (Clarke, 1998). Working with people living with HIV can be intense, because what they face is very serious. An effective group leader who can be with them in that gravity—to give them the space within which their pain can be heard—can then have the privilege of bearing witness to their resilience, of watching them tap into their creativity, their depth, and their humor.

Group Examples

Each of the authors of this chapter facilitates a support group for people living with HIV. One is voluntary for women from the community, some of whom receive case management services; the other is mandatory for men living in a transitional housing program with a single facilitator. Each is described here in detail.

"Celebration of Life," by Valerie, group facilitator (a poem inspired by the voices of the women who participated in the support group when it first began in 2001)

You have infected me
I need to tell you how it has affected me
I'm afraid to date
feeling I will never find a life mate
I harbor feelings of hate
for I have been given a death sentence
and now stand in need of repentance
because I wanted to harm you,
somebody, anybody
for this disease you have given me
but, I think of my children
how I don't want their lives ruined
ruined by the disease that has spread
to my mind
I must give this reality some time
time for the feelings to no longer
cut like a knife
I must choose to celebrate life

The Women's Group

The facilitators often begin the group with a poem to set the mood or generate the topic for that session. The group was started in 2001; by that time there had been a shift in focus from seeing HIV as a death sentence to a more hopeful outlook in which there was more talk about living with HIV and making adjustments. Over time the group has changed format, purpose, co-facilitators, and types of participants several times, but the name has remained.

The Health Federation of Philadelphia, a nonprofit agency in Philadelphia, and its Family Centered Home Visitation Program, a federally funded demonstration program by the Children's Bureau Abandoned Infant Assistance, sponsored the group. In 2001, the group served mothers at high risk: those with substance abuse, domestic violence, mental health issues, and incarceration, and only a few with HIV.

Initially, the facilitators were an African American female and a Latina. The group was new, and the facilitators were new to the field. The group design was psychoeducational and supportive, with a rather traditional structure and approach to group work. Child care, tokens, and refreshments were provided. The group met twice a month, on Thursdays, for two hours. Then referrals dwindled, but one HIV-positive woman began to attend the group and invited other HIV-positive women from her community. With her input, we began to design a specialized support group for women living with HIV and focusing on wellness. We made new flyers and brochures for our group and attracted new participants. We began to use the Wellness Model by the National Wellness Institute (Eberhardt, 1994), *Working with Women's Groups,* Volumes 1 and 2. With these curricula we focused on helping each woman to:

- Explore how she views and feels about herself
- Learn to identify what she is feeling, to express feelings and thoughts freely and openly
- Learn to take care of her body
- Expand her awareness of others
- Discover her strengths, talents, and creativity
- Give and receive feedback about the impact she has on others, and vice versa
- Discover her life goals, desires, and values
- Develop more meaningful and open relationships with other women
- Increase her interpersonal skills
- Experiment with new behaviors

We hoped to help the women better integrate HIV into their lives through self-discovery and learn to or continue to celebrate life. Although we did not have a specific screening process, most of the women were African American (with children) who reported that they acquired HIV through heterosexual relationships. They said that other support groups they had attended were mixed groups that included gay men and people in addictions recovery. Although they were all living with HIV, in mixed groups these women did not feel safe talking about their experiences in heterosexual relationships and without claim to addictions.

The group was open-ended, so occasionally women who were in recovery attended. They were welcomed; however, they did not attend regularly or for as long as the other women. In retrospect, we realized that when membership is open but the group is of long duration, a core group of members is likely to emerge. When this occurs, the core group assumes responsibilities for indoctrinating new members (Schopler & Galinsky, 1995a; Shulman, 1999 and 2006). The core group (and facilitators) apparently unconsciously set up a group dynamic that did not allow the new members in recovery to feel comfortable.

For a year following a funding cut, there was only one facilitator for the women's support group. While single facilitation has its advantages, it also presents challenges. With co-facilitation there is opportunity to capitalize on the strengths of each, add to or clarify what the other facilitator may have overlooked or missed, and share from the perspective of each, all of which can enrich the group process. Each facilitator can bring her skills, talents, and interests to the group. For example, one of the co-facilitators had an interest in women's issues and in reading and writing poetry; she shared some of her writings with the group and encouraged them to write. Not only was it a powerful emotional outlet, but they also had fun in the process. The poems from four women in the support group are on the following page.

Poetry, prose, art, photography, and performance were used in other ways to stimulate creative expression and healing. For example, the writings of other poets and writers prompted the women to write and share their own thoughts and stories:

- Poems by Langston Hughes from "Dream Deferred" were used to prompt the writings, "What were my dreams before being diagnosed with HIV, and what are my dreams now?"
- Lucille Clifton's poem, "Homage to My Hips," inspired the women to pay homage in writing to a body part that they felt alienated from due to HIV.
- Using the provocative script from Eve Ensler's "Vagina Monologue," women responded to the prompt "If my vagina could talk."
- Using poems from a book titled *Soul Talk: Urban Youth Poetry,* the women responded to "Just Because," "Where I'm From," and "Urban Life" with their own experience in poetic and prosaic form.
- Women who struggled with literacy issues had alternative tasks, such as collage work or use of tape recorders to tell their stories.
- A local poet, Gweny Love, assisted women who wanted to do so to perform their writings in a choreographed poem presentation.

The second facilitator had interest in the arts, restaurants, and cultural events. She developed a resource guide that included places for families and adults to visit throughout the city for free or at affordable cost. Over time, core group members assisted periodically by leading group discussions with topics of interest. As a group, the women began providing peer mentoring to other women in the program who were not HIV-infected as they became increasingly comfortable with disclosure; once, they spoke to a teen group in the community about living with HIV, a powerful experience for all.

We began a writing project with another agency serving a group of men and women living with HIV; the purpose was to search for beauty and hope in their everyday lives using photography and journals (written and visual) to express feelings, thoughts, and experiences during the four weeks of discovery. Participants were given disposable cameras, asked to take pictures of the world around them, and to keep a journal about the experience. Each was given writing and photo prompts, a blank journal, and a copy of *Soul Talk*. We met each week to discuss the experience, including health and illness, nature, relationships with the community, isolation, spirituality, recovery, the arts, and street violence. At the end of the series, group participants' photos were exhibited at a special photo gallery exhibit. This is an example of group work and community involvement helping and supporting persons with HIV to improve connections with the community

If My Vagina Could Talk

If my vagina could talk:
It would say you took my
    innocence
Although I gotten use to it
You made me want you
    more and more
You spit out your liquid
    form of destruction in
    me,
Now I live in this world
    of loneliness
Afraid of what I might
    now spit out
Retract back to the days
    of my innocence
Before we met
I reminisce about the days
    of grandeur
And of the fun we use to
    have
But today I am ashamed
    to even open up again.
    —Rose

HIV and Me

HIV is a part of me
But a very small part
I have a great heart
I love to laugh
And make people laugh
I am kind and sweet
I love hugs and kisses
I love to take a walk in
    the park
Or ride on the bus
I love life
I hope you do too
I love the movies and
    theatre
See HIV is a part of me,
But a small part.
    —Lisa

Positive but Positive

Ups or Downs
Wrongs or Rights
Everyone in this world has
    a fight
Good or Bad
Happy or Sad
I can't live my life just
    being mad . . . .
Standing strong being
    proud . . . .
I live my life for the now
Tomorrow isn't promised
    to any of us
So why should I make a
    fuss
OK, I'm living with HIV
Think about how much
    worse it could be?
I have a chance
I have a fight
Everything will be all right!
    —Rachael

HIV Defined

HIV does it define me
Refine me or divide me
It's just something
    inside me
It doesn't make me
I refuse to let it take me
Mentally, emotionally,
Or physically.
Right now, I have
My whole family
Who is my support
A husband
Two sons
And seven daughters
Even though
They are not with me
Everywhere I go
HIV is
So I guess in some
    strange way
HIV has redefined me.
    —Johna

while providing opportunities to use the arts as a therapeutic tool for self-expression and reflection. Participants discovered that learning to see beauty in the streets allowed them to see beauty within themselves since they were diagnosed.

The group described here has changed over time. Today, it is completely made up of women living with HIV, all mothers with a median age of 25 years, predominately African American, who choose to participate in this voluntary community-based group. A once-a-month evening group has been added to the schedule to meet the needs of women who are working or have difficult day schedules. The co-facilitators continue to utilize a psychoeducational group design, integrating expressive arts and narrative process. They also have wellness activities that include yoga, aroma therapy, drumming, meditation, and nutrition and cooking classes.

The Men's Group

The HIV-infected men's group is held in a facility in a residential community; for confidentiality reasons we call it "The House." The House is a transitional housing setting with capacity for 12 HIV-infected men. The home has many programs and services to support the men and to enable them to prepare for self-sufficiency, including case management that allows them to obtain subsidized housing when it becomes available. The average length of stay is 12 months. The support group is one of the many services offered to them. It is important to note, however, that the group is one of a number of services for which attendance is mandatory. The group is open-ended: As men move into and out of the home, the makeup of the group changes. The group began with weekly frequency, which is considered ideal, both clinically and administratively. Due to funding cuts, the frequency was decreased to biweekly. The group meets for 1.5 hours per session in The House.

The fact that the group is mandatory poses some challenges for all involved. The men living with HIV, most of whom are referred from drug and alcohol treatment programs, arrive exhausted from years of wear and tear on their bodies and their psyches from using drugs and from having HIV. They have already begun the process of healing in the treatment facility and arrive at the house with clearer minds, with gratitude for being alive and for being clean and sober. Most of all, they arrive with hope. They talk openly about their lives in the streets, when their lives were at great risk because nothing mattered as much as the next drink or drug. Often, the addictive behavior preceded the HIV diagnosis and may have been the suspected route of exposure to HIV. Some have used the drugs to mask the pain and shame of having HIV. Amazingly open and honest, they have learned the value of being so through the treatment programs and the subsequent 12-step programs and intensive outpatient therapy they are also mandated to attend.

Enter the group facilitator. Experience has shown that it takes a facilitator with a certain skill set to rise to the challenge of managing this mandated group. And it takes something more, it seems. A colleague once said, ". . . AIDS work is soul work. . . ." There is an assertion here that those whose interventions are most successful are those who have a passion for working with people living with HIV. An example of this is found in the recollection of a woman with whom the facilitator worked long ago. She had advanced HIV, as did her husband; one of their two children was also HIV-infected. She gave the providers many lessons, one of which was, ". . . don't waste my time; I am dying here." While not nearly as many are literally dying, thanks to the advances in care and treatment, in the experience of the facilitator, it is safe to say that among people living with chronic, critical illness, which has astounding public health, social, emotional, and relationship implications, the sentiment is very much the same: "Don't waste my time." There can be an urgency and intensity for meaningful experiences of life when living with HIV. The onus is on the social worker to produce quality care.

By the time the men attend the first group, they have had the opportunity to be indoctrinated with house rules, both formally and informally. Respect and congeniality are conveyed at the point of initial contact with each man. The facilitator is sure to do the following:

1. Greet each newcomer enthusiastically, with a smile and a firm handshake, when he enters the House, before group begins.
2. Show genuine interest in him as a human being and a newcomer.
3. Make a point of welcoming him to the group.
4. Ask the group members to share with the newcomer the group's purpose, function, and what they have gotten from it.
5. Invite the newcomer to share, if and when he feels ready, after others have shared and modeled the process for him.

Group Process   Since there is a separate group during the week in which group members discuss HIV treatment concerns, as well as HIV's effect on them, the facilitator's challenge is to engage them primarily around other issues, while, of course, incorporating HIV issues as they arise. The facilitator had for years developed a model of group check-in with feelings, using the following handout (see Figure 8.1).

The preceding checklist is intended as a way to identify how they are feeling. Initially, and periodically throughout, there is a discussion about feelings, and why it is important to identify feelings so that behavior is congruent with those feelings. It is explained that there are only 10 "feeling words" on the chart because these are considered to be "primary feelings." We use many feeling words in society, just as we use many words to describe colors; there are, however, only eight primary colors, and the men are encouraged

Name:_____

HOW DO I FEEL TODAY?

	January _, 2009	January _, 2009	February _, 2009	February _, 2009
HAPPY				
SAD				
ANGRY				
AFRAID				
ASHAMED				
GUILTY				
LONELY				
HURT				
HOPEFUL				
GRATEFUL				

Figure 8.1   House Support Group
Source: Patricia A. Stewart, MSS, LCSW

to think of it in this way. Also, it is felt that these feeling words help to identify specific feelings more readily. Sometimes, though infrequently, a man will say, "What I am feeling is not on here—I am feeling *anxious*." This gives the facilitator the opportunity to then assist the man to "back into" the "primary (bottom-line) feeling." See the example in the sidebar.

Facilitator: Okay, do you know what you are feeling anxious about?

Participant: Yes, I have a growth and they don't know what it is.

Facilitator: Oh, my goodness. What information do you have about it thus far?

Participant: Well, they say it could be okay, but then again, it could be cancer.

Facilitator: I'm really sorry to hear that—are you thinking about what it will mean for you if it is cancer?

Participant: Yeah, man, I don't want that . . .

Facilitator: So, are you feeling somewhat afraid about this?

Participant: Yeah, you could say that.

Facilitator: And of course you know that you can feel more than one of the feelings on the list at a time—it would be understandable if you also feel some sadness and some anger about it—this is a tough situation.

Participant: You know, that's true. But I am hopeful that it will turn out okay. In fact, I know from my [12-step] program that whatever it is, I will get through it.

In this way the facilitator has addressed an individual concern by leading in an exploration of the basic feeling about a situation. The other men witness the process, sitting respectfully while their comrade expresses himself and works through some pretty anguishing thoughts and feelings. This not only gives them an opportunity to hear from another about something he is going through, but also how that is affecting him. The processing of it also models for them what anyone can do to get in touch with feelings beneath the surface.

These men tend, in their addictions, to have spent many years avoiding, denying, or numbing feelings. To think of them sitting in a group with a feelings sheet is rather amazing. The group continues in that way, with each man doing check-in using feeling words. Group rules were established by them at the outset and are reviewed periodically, especially when there is a new member. Among the rules of group behavior is the rule of confidentiality. They pledge to keep each others' confidence, as does the facilitator, with the standard exceptions that protect their safety [that is, if they become so upset that the facilitator feels they may be a danger to themselves or someone else, the facilitator will need to let someone else know to keep them safe.] Those contracts have not been violated over time so that trust develops—trust in each other, in the facilitator, and in the process. In that context, they have been able to refer to their sheet, checking off feelings. In addition, they have moved to the point of sharing, in great detail, not only what they were feeling but also why. The previous example is a process carried out with each man, to the extent that it feels appropriate and helpful to him. The facilitator works strategically with each man, careful to balance the work by probing to express interest and to help the man talk more deeply about the issue without being intrusive. When the facilitator follows up in subsequent groups, inquiring about the status or the outcome of an issue previously shared, it tends to solidify for them that her interest in them and in what they are going through is genuine. It must be noted that they also share encouraging things that are happening for them, and that is applauded by all. There is more than an occasional focus on their strengths. In fact, the facilitator makes it a point to keenly identify and acknowledge their strengths as a way to encourage, support, and model ways to do that for themselves and each other.

Group Conflict   There have been times that conflict arises in a group meeting or that may have been brewing between two or more men outside of the group meeting, resulting in violation of their agreement with each other to be respectful. This requires immediate and skilled intervention: listening to the issues expressed by each, validating their feelings, helping them to see that there is another way to express the feelings, stopping the attack on the other, sometimes with a loud, firm voice. Once things have calmed, the facilitator can then do more to:

- Validate the feelings
- Provide alternative ways of expressing the feelings
- Utilize the opportunity of this process to demonstrate how they can handle conflict in other areas of their lives

In this way, they have learned through experience and by precept and example that conflict, which is inevitable, can be endured and resolved, and that it can be an opportunity for growth. In a group session directly following one in which a heated altercation occurred, the facilitator brought the following handout as a model for safe and healthy confrontation (See Figure 8.2).

We emphasize the **[Period]** element. It is important to end the sentence with the feeling. Further discussion about the issue or the feelings runs the risk of escalating the situation

MODEL FOR A SAFE AND HEALTHY CONFRONTATION

When you _____

[Do or say _____; Don't do or say _____]

[Behavior]

I feel _____. **[Period]**

[Feeling word]

Happy, Sad, Angry, Afraid, Lonely, Hurt, Ashamed, Guilty, Hopeful, Grateful

Figure 8.2   Model for a Safe and Healthy Confrontation
Source: Patricia A. Stewart, MSS, LCSW

and detracts from the power of a simple, direct statement that the other person has a better chance of hearing. And it works. The men have been willing, with coaching from the facilitator, to use this model. Recognizing that it feels awkward and unfamiliar, the point is made that asserting oneself does not have to be attacking when one is in touch with one's own feelings about the offending behavior.

Group Format

- Facilitator arrives—the men are waiting in the living room for the group to begin.
- Each man comes to group with his personalized packet—a two-pocket folder.
- Facilitator distributes the Feelings Sheet at the beginning of the month. (Since the group was reduced to every other week, there are two months of dates on the sheet.)
- Facilitator passes around the group attendance sheet, which is in two columns. Names are in the left column; the men sign beside their name on the right. (They know that this sheet is eventually given to the director of the home.)
- Facilitator, usually voluntarily assisted by one or more of the residents, passes out pens to those who do not have them.
- The men take a few minutes to reflect on how they are feeling, making a checkmark beside the feelings that apply.
- The men talk about their current feelings, one at a time from 2 minutes to 15 minutes (if having a difficult time). The average time is roughly five or six minutes. It should be noted that they may talk about the superficial, (for example, "Today I feel grateful and hopeful") to the very profound (for example: "This is the anniversary of my son's death; I am feeling sad and angry" or "I just found out that I have cancer and I am feeling sad and afraid"). Whatever feelings a man presents are accepted and respected.
- As each man says how he feels, the facilitator may draw him out some, asking for examples, what he may be feeling grateful for; the facilitator will also often follow up on some issue shared in the previous group, asking how that may be going, whether there are new developments, or whether a man enjoyed that special weekend home with his family. Initially, they seemed somewhat pleasantly surprised that there was follow-up, that their information was remembered; they have since become comfortable with it—and actually seem to expect it. The message: "I matter to someone; my story, information, and circumstances are important; I am important."
- At the end of each group, there is an inspirational reading, with a copy for each man. This is read aloud. This has changed over time. Initially, the facilitator read it and the men would listen and comment afterward. Then, without any verbal direction, they began spontaneously reading a paragraph at a time, with each man reading, as comfortable. This has been a very special time for the group. So often, the reading, preselected by the facilitator, speaks very nicely to one or more things that were discussed in the group. The men really like this, often making comments such as, "That's deep" or "That's exactly what we were just talking about" or "You always bring something to us to uplift us." After the group, they place the reading in their personalized packet; they are encouraged to look through it and read when they are feeling low. They also then take the packet, with all the inspirational and educational information, with them when they move into permanent housing.
- For the past few months the facilitator brought something called "Angel cards" in a pouch that is passed around at the beginning of the group. These cards have one word on them—for example, "Freedom," "Transformation," "Patience." The men

readily accepted this, and after they shared their current concerns and without prompting, they spoke to what their word was and what it means to them, or what message they think is in the word for them to reflect upon. Recently, this has shifted to a one- or two-line inspirational message; the effect is the same.

- The group ends with the men expressing gratitude for the meeting; sometimes thanking the facilitator for the meeting or commenting that it was a particularly helpful meeting.

Conclusion

We hope that this detailed description of the group process is helpful to those who may want to create a group. A key reason for success in both groups is their homogeneity. One group consists of HIV-infected women who are not addicted; the other group members are all HIV-infected men, most of them in recovery. Although the commonality of having HIV bonds them, the additional life experiences may deepen their ability to understand and support each other.

FAMILY SUPPORT

Now we turn our attention to family supports for people living with HIV. The good news is that due to advances in treatment, many are living longer, feeling better and more productive than their comrades who came before them. However, lifelong medication regimens, side effects, life changes, disclosure decisions, stigma, and parenting concerns have for some increased emotional and social problems. HIV touches every aspect of one's life. For every issue, there arises another to be addressed for and by people living with HIV. This calls for a comprehensive approach to care, with issues addressed in various intervention modalities—individual, family, group, community, and agency—by the range of providers: social workers, health care providers, mental health workers, home visitors, and the community at large.

There are many constellations and definitions of families; but no matter what configuration, it is felt by some that no family can truly thrive without the help of the community in which it lives. Kalichman and associates (1996) state that support for people living with HIV infection can come from multiple sources, including traditionally defined family, friends, relationship partners, professional caregivers, and others. In short, it is important to view family broadly and to define family in the same way as the person with HIV does. For example, at the Health Federation of Philadelphia Family Centered Home Visitation Program, it is the role of the team (parent or child specialists and family advocates) to support individuals living with HIV, their children, significant others, and traditionally defined family members. The program utilizes a family-centered home visitation and community model. Family-centered service delivery, across disciplines and settings, recognizes the centrality of the family in the lives of individuals. It is guided by fully informed choices made by the family and focuses on the family's strengths and capabilities. It recognizes and supports the cultural values, norms, and child-rearing practices of the family. It also recognizes that the family is the constant stabilizing system in the child's life, whereas the service systems and support personnel within service systems may fluctuate (Allen & Petr, 1998).

One of the goals of the program is to prevent out-of-home placement for children; if an HIV-positive mother is incarcerated and the child is living at home with family, services are provided to that family. When children from birth to three years of age are in foster care, services are provided to the biological and foster parent or parents with the goal of reunification whenever possible. If the father is the primary caretaker of a child and is HIV-infected, he can receive services as well. Through our interventions, we offer child development and support for parent-child relationships, supportive services and counseling and assess when therapy may be beneficial and/or necessary, and make referrals, as indicated. The role of the family is highly valued and critical in supporting individuals living with HIV.

One of the most emotionally laden issues to be addressed is disclosure of HIV diagnosis. Many persons living with HIV have difficulty informing family members of their HIV status, thereby possibly limiting their supports. It is good practice to include the issue of disclosure in the bio-psycho-social-spiritual assessment phase of work with the HIV-infected person. We have found that a question such as, "What is keeping you from disclosing your HIV status?" sometimes yields the response, "You don't know my family." Upon exploring this statement, what is learned is that the person fears rejection by his or her family members. The stigma of HIV looms large for them, tapping into the shame they feel about the diagnosis; often that shame is deep-seated, dating back to childhood. So we start where he or she is by acknowledging those feelings without judgment, criticism, or need to change the feelings. It is clear that once the assessment phase is complete, individuals will need the space within which they can be heard and begin healing their wounded sense of self. Over time, persons with HIV will know when it is time to disclose their diagnosis and to whom. With time and support from the social worker and from their peers, most people with HIV are strengthened and more able to begin the process of disclosure to others.

Often it is the case that, upon disclosing the HIV diagnosis, people learn that family members already knew at some level from some source that their loved one was HIV-infected. Some families are able to be supportive. Others, unfortunately, are not. The negative responses range from outright rejection to subtle shaming. The latter can be expressed in ways that family members convey fear of contagion: bleaching everything used by the HIV-positive person [such as utensils, dishes, toilet seats], not allowing the infected person to touch certain things or people. Here again, the work of the practitioner is to attend to the emotional needs of HIV-infected persons, to be continually supportive, reminding them of their worth. [For example, "You have a disease, you are not the disease, you are so much more."]

In addition to working with HIV-infected individuals, one works with family members, individually and as a unit. They, too, need unconditional regard, regardless of how difficult it is for practitioners to provide when they witness how hurtful their responses are to the person with HIV. Remembering that their response is likely caused by fear can help us to see them as human beings with needs that we can assist in addressing. Again, beginning where they are, the practitioner can acknowledge their feelings, doing what is necessary to help them reframe how they express that fear so they do not continue to hurt another. When they are ready to hear it, we can present to them information about HIV, about routes of transmission, and about the treatment process. We must remember that some of the fear can be that their family member will die. Ways to address families' concerns can range from individual intervention to family meetings to exposure to educational literature to direct education provided by health care providers to community-based workshops for HIV-affected persons.

The practitioner must continually assess the strengths and needs of the entire family. Our supportive relationship with the person living with HIV, no matter how therapeutic, is not a substitute for healthy relationships with family members. Both are needed. When practitioners learn of some of the unbelievable ways that the person before them has been treated by family—abandonment, neglect, abuse of many forms—there may be a natural desire to protect. This is a pitfall to be avoided. If we overidentify with the pain of the HIV-infected person, we may miss an opportunity for facilitating a healing process in a family member and/or between the person living with HIV and a family member. An HIV diagnosis, as serious as it is, can be the catalyst for healing old wounds, individually and in family relationships.

Because the most vulnerable of society are the ones most infected with HIV, the disease serves as yet another psychosocial stressor with which they have to contend. Boyd-Franklin states, "These families are confronted with poverty, racism, discrimination, high school dropout rates, teenage pregnancy, crime, homelessness, HIV, and drug and alcohol abuse. These realities create a level of fear in many of these families that must be addressed" (Boyd-Franklin, 1989). Boyd-Franklin addresses the complexities of these psychosocial stressors for parents, their infants and toddlers, and their extended families. Earlier in the pandemic in this country, there was more talk about those *affected* by HIV, which was a way to view the pervasive effects on the families, friends, and significant others of the person *infected*. The same concept applies when we speak of people *living with* HIV. All are potentially in need and at risk and are worthy of our attention and care.

Often, mothers are socialized to take care of the needs of others; in turn they can neglect their own. When side effects of the medication are particularly noxious, the person may not take them or take them inconsistently. Also, the prospect of taking medication for the rest of one's life can be overwhelming. It is known that inconsistent medication management is problematic in a number of ways. Witness the HIV-infected mother whose status rapidly progresses to AIDS or who has frequent hospitalizations. She must then resort to others who will take care of the children so she can get the medical attention she needs. There are times that mothers do not have enough supports and become so worried about their children that they leave the hospital against medical advice. Often, family members, because of their limited resources, call the hospitalized mother several times a day for money to take care of and feed the children. How can she possibly concentrate on her own care under these circumstances? The agency can assist in these situations by providing supermarket vouchers, tokens for transportation, and information about food cupboards, thus allaying the mother's fears and concerns. In addition, the social worker can facilitate family meetings to develop a plan of action in advance, in the event the mother has to be hospitalized. That plan can include arrangements for child care, home health care, and homemaker services. The social worker can assess the availability of other support persons, such as friends and neighbors, who stand ready to perform specific tasks to support the mother while she is hospitalized and recuperating afterward to allow for optimum focus on her health and wellness.

Permanency planning for children is yet another issue for families. Few things can be as emotionally charged as asking a parent to think about his or her death in this way. In January 1999, the AIDS Law Project of Pennsylvania and other advocates were instrumental in designing a Standby Guardianship Law which was passed by the Pennsylvania legislature, that allows a parent to petition the courts to approve a guardian before he or she is ill, so the guardian will be available on standby if the parent becomes too sick to care for her children (AIDS Law Project, 1999). Though emotionally taxing and calling for highly skilled and sensitive intervention, it has ultimately provided a sense of relief for some who have completed the process.

When the Family of Origin Is Not Available

It has been said that there is only one family to which we belong, and that is the human family. Society dictates that we see as family those to whom we are related by blood: the family of origin. There are many rules by which we as members of family are to live, among them: "Honor thy father and thy mother" and "Blood is thicker than water." Then there are often rules for children: "Children should be seen and not heard"; "Don't talk back to adults"; Throughout the year, there are national holidays that honor some family member or that are seen as "family holidays." There are many advantages to these traditions, especially as family members increasingly live at great distances from each other. Holidays provide a forum for families to come together for fellowship and enjoyment.

Unfortunately, the idea of family is not always helpful for all of its members. Societal ills and human conditions can turn the Waltons or the Cosbys into the Mansons over time; for some people, family contact can be unsafe—emotionally, physically, and psychologically. Much is written about the effects and aftereffects of abuse, addictions, and physical and mental illness on the family system, which negatively affect the well-being of all. Children, especially, can develop a set of behaviors and thought patterns that help them to survive their childhoods. They can construct creative, life-saving coping strategies. Over time, however, the very tools they use to survive can develop into maladaptive coping mechanisms that then outlive their usefulness. For example, the child who lives in so much fear that she learns to suppress her real feelings and puts on a happy face finds that as an adult she is a people pleaser, unaware of what she really wants or feels. Her brother may find solace in the bottle or in the joint, which is initially used to take the edge off but then becomes a compulsion that takes on a life of its own. Their younger sister may lose touch with reality altogether, having mental illness that devastates her life and breaks the heart of those who love her. These escape or coping strategies abound in any family where children have been abused, witnessed domestic violence, or have lived with an addicted parent. Hopelessness, helplessness, or poor self-concept set in. The person is then predisposed to high-risk living, and some acquire HIV.

When people have been abused or abandoned in their homes, they are not likely to turn to traditional family for support. Sometimes they languish, isolated, bitter, and alone, for years. Witness the homeless transgender teenagers who depend on each other because of not belonging anywhere else, or gay men who have formed gay families when they lose the support of traditional families, or those who have been ostracized for trading their bodies for survival and have bonded with each other. These reconstituted "families" become their primary sources of support. Then they encounter a provider of HIV services and can, perhaps for the first time, come into contact with professionals on whom they can depend, who treat them and their families of choice with compassion and respect, who do not judge them. The onus is on us as providers—to understand what we might represent to them. It is important, therefore, for us to do the following:

- Be consistent.
- Be fair and honest.
- Be nonjudgmental.
- Be compassionate.
- Set appropriate boundaries in ways that model consideration and respect.
- Accept their definition of family.

It is noteworthy to mention that in the absence of family, we humans can also encounter people with whom we bond negatively. Examples are gangs, cults, drug buddies, and unhealthy relationships. When we become frustrated when someone with whom we work cannot seem to separate themselves from unhealthy people, places and things, it is important to remember that those relationships might be difficult to leave because they have become, to them, family. This may invoke intense feelings of fear, usually expressed as criticism or judgment. That is how we humans tend to handle difference.

As helpers, we are not immune to having prejudicial feelings. It is essential that we acknowledge these unlovely feelings as they arise and work to deal with them so that they do not negatively affect the therapeutic relationship. It is important to make no assumptions as we learn from people living with HIV whom they consider to be "family." It is our responsibility to deal with any reaction that we may have by (1) talking about our prejudices in supervision, (2) having a life rich and full, and (3) participating in other growth-enhancing activities. In this way, we can then provide optimum quality care to any family.

Conclusion

Family support is a vital concern for HIV-infected children, adolescents, and adults. Even when one is estranged from one's family of origin, perhaps especially so, one carries that family inside, complete with all the hurts, expectations, joys, disappointments, experiences, and judgments of one's upbringing. Social workers and human services workers must take into consideration each person's family of origin and family of choice in order to understand and serve people with HIV.

HIV PREVENTION AND EDUCATION

It is likely that the reader will have an interest in working in social work or related human services and/or with people living with HIV. The reader may have or will one day have a position in which he or she will or will not work exclusively with those living with HIV. It does not matter which path one takes, for the social worker, by very definition, will be presented with people who for one reason or another are challenged by some aspect of their lives. When people face problems, there is often a long period of time before they come for help, after their survival strategies and mechanisms for coping no longer serve them. Some of those ways of surviving and coping may have put them at high risk for HIV. Consider the foster child who has moved from one home to another and has never felt truly loved. She may be vulnerable to someone who says he wants to love her. He may insist on doing that without a condom. Or consider the teen who has already had one baby and her mother "took" her baby from her. The mother may believe that she has given her daughter an opportunity to experience life as she would have before she had the baby. The teen, however, may feel she never had an opportunity to be a mother, so she becomes pregnant again. This time, she will raise her own baby. Or consider the 27-year-old woman who presents with depression and lack of motivation. She has a history of sexual abuse and, as a result, feels she has lost her "voice," and she does not feel she has much value. If she is dating a popular man and he does not like condoms, she is not likely, with her poor self-concept, to enter into condom negotiation. She will tell you that she "doesn't like condoms either." Then there is the young man who has fathered his third child, each child with a different woman. He is at risk for HIV and other STDs. The gay youth may be so battered by years of name-calling about his sexual identity that no one told him that anal intercourse is the highest risk for HIV; the same is true for the girl who agrees to anal sex to avoid pregnancy.

It goes without saying that prevention is an integral part of HIV-specific services as well. A colleague, Danielle Parks, Program Director of Women's Anonymous Test Site at the Health Federation of Philadelphia, recalls the following encounter.

=========== **Personal Perspective** ===========

Story of Shanae

"How could this be happening?" she asked as she spoke with her counselor. "I am smart, I have a degree, and I know so much about HIV! How could I let myself get to a place where I am praying that I am negative?" Her counselor just listened as she continued. "I know I should have used a condom, but at that moment it never crossed my mind . . . condoms . . . it was an afterthought . . . why didn't I make him use a condom!" The tears began to fall, she began to cry, and then Shanae began to weep. "What if I am HIV-positive?" she asked. "What would my family think of me? I am supposed to set a good example. . . . I am supposed to be different. . . . How could I let this happen? I can't have HIV! I just can't!"

It is imperative for the social worker who is doing group work or family work to have an eye always toward HIV prevention and education. Regardless of the primary focus of the work, it is essential to develop a plan of action that places high priority on the safety of the person coming for help, including sexual safety. Just as we screen for suicidal or homicidal ideation, for domestic violence, for child abuse, it is vital that we screen for sexual and drug safety. We must not fail to ask directly, and early in the assessment phase of work with a person, if he or she is safe in all ways. People may respond as though they think it odd or embarrassing to be asked, but the very question and the fact that it is asked as routinely as date of birth sends a message that it is okay to talk about anything with the social worker. As rapport and trust in the helping relationship develops, people may share information that could ultimately protect their health and lives.

If you work in a setting that does not ask the hard-to-ask questions as a matter of routine, consider it your opportunity to suggest that the administration revise the forms. Regardless of the advances in care and treatment, HIV is still a debilitating disease that affects quality of life and relationships. We have none in the community to spare. We cannot be remiss on the issue of prevention and education, including with those who are currently living with the virus. Dating and meeting new people when one is living with HIV poses a serious challenge about disclosure. Is it not easier not to tell the person and hope? Isn't that preferable to risk being rejected? One of the things that can be overwhelming about working with HIV and/or working with HIV consciousness is this: The more we think about it and the possibilities, the more things there are to think about. It is one of the things that leads to providers feeling overwhelmed.

THE ROLE OF TRAUMA IN HIV CARE: THE IMPACT ON THE SOCIAL WORKER

Trauma is a psychologically distressing event that is outside the range of usual human experiences. Trauma often involves a sense of intense fear, terror, and helplessness. Trauma should not be confused with stress. Trauma is an experience that induces an abnormally intense and prolonged stress response (Perry, 2003). Some people living with HIV have histories of trauma. For example, childhood abuse is a pandemic that cuts across all socioeconomic lines, so it stands to reason that some who are living with HIV have abuse histories; their stories also confirm it. Other forms of trauma include living with violence, living with addiction, and serial maladaptive relationships. In fact, learning of one's HIV diagnosis and then managing it on a daily basis can result in a trauma response, as can deciding when and how to disclose to others.

While we value the individuality of each person with whom we work, we find that there are some common themes as people tell their stories. This repeated witness bearing of the social worker to the traumatic lives of those they serve takes its toll. Compassion for the poor and the oppressed is one of the attributes that draws us to the work; constant exposure to trauma can result in what Figley and associates (1995) call "compassion fatigue." It is the high cost of caring. Training on transference and countertransference, while essential, only begin to help us understand ourselves and our reactions to the sheer volume of trauma to which we are exposed as we listen intently to people's life stories. Perry's research found that secondary trauma can occur following the exposure to a single traumatic event. So imagine the impact of working with large numbers of traumatized people. One of the authors has a total caseload of women who live with HIV and who are living within the federal poverty guidelines. In addition to having the arduous task of helping them process the impact of the disease on their lives and on the lives of the children and other loved ones, she must also watch them struggle to make ends meet—to wonder at times where the next meal will come from. Or she will lament that a mother will choose to sign out of the hospital against medical advice because she does not have adequate supports for child care. Although she has good clinical supervision, there may be some restless nights for the social worker until the time for supervision is available. The other author also works in a setting that serves only the economically underserved, some of whom are living with HIV. It is difficult to see how one person might manage to function under such dire circumstances—to witness this in one's entire caseload can generate feelings in the social worker about the unequal and unjust distribution of wealth in this country. Doing this work can feel like the proverbial attempt to patch holes in the dyke, ever mindful that at any time, the dam could break. That can also be a metaphor for what it feels like inside the practitioner to provide services in a system that by design demonstrates that it does not care for those we care about. It can translate into feelings of powerlessness that feel personal. Perry (2003) suggests consideration of the following questions: (1) Have I done the best I can under the circumstances? (2) Do I have realistic expectations of myself and others? It is helpful to ask these questions on a regular basis and to create systems in which there can be peer support to ponder such questions.

Lipsksy (2007) asks the following: How is this (response) working for my deepest, most honest self? How is this really working for those I'm serving? How is this sustainable? Is there a more functional way? In her work, *Becoming Trauma Stewards,* she defines trauma stewardship as the entirety of how we interact with others' suffering, pain, crisis, and trauma; the *trauma exposure response* is the transformation that takes place within us as a result of exposure to another's suffering. Often, practitioners begin to recognize the effect of trauma exposure when they realize they are behaving in a way they never would have when they first started working in their field. There can be the tendency to ruminate about one group member's troubling medical condition or social circumstances. Friends can hear only so much of the work-related stress, however anonymously presented, before they begin to withdraw. Even colleagues who do not work in this field have looked at us askance, wondering, "How do you do that work?" The social worker can, without realizing it, tend to isolate, feeling very alone with the grief. One extreme reaction after a number of deaths some years ago left one of the authors waking up at night, seeing the faces of so many who had succumbed to the illness, crying and rocking as the waves of grief washed over her. We work so intensively with people that, on a human level, we can feel the pain with them. There is nothing wrong with feeling pain. However, it is then up to us to work through those feelings so that we can be emotionally available to those with whom we work and to ourselves and our loved ones in our personal lives.

Other questions to ask oneself: How much of what I am hearing do I need to address directly to be of service to this person in the interest of his or her functioning? How much needs to be addressed now? What can I now make note of that perhaps can be addressed at a later time? Asking and answering these questions for ourselves helps us to set limits for ourselves, to bind the trauma so that it does not overwhelm us. It also can help us to allow the people with whom we work to share what they need to without having an automatic response to "fix it." The concept here is that we all have within us the answers to the questions or concerns in our lives. We don't need someone to fix it; what we need is the space within which to be heard so that we can clear the emotional and psychological debris that blocks us from our answers. Change comes when we decide to change. If we can embrace that, we can hopefully remember that we are change agents; the person sitting before us does the changing in his or her own way, in his or her own time.

To be culturally competent includes being careful not to impose our values and beliefs on others, but rather to hear from them what is important to address, to change, and at what rate in what time frame. It is also very important to know your limits. HIV work is not for everyone. If there is constant turmoil related to one's work, a good question to ask is whether we are suited to the work. Along with considering our personal suitability to the work, we consider also whether we are getting enough of our needs met in the organization in which we are working.

- Is there regularly scheduled administrative supervision?
- Are there regularly scheduled staff meetings?
- Does the agency demonstrate in its policies and practices that people living with HIV are valued?
- Do you have enough guidance from agency policy to do your job?
- Are the agency practices, values, and norms consistent with your own?
- Do you have enough support?
- Are you able to be creative in your work? Is your practice respected and valued?
- Is there regularly scheduled clinical supervision?
- Do you have regular time to sit with someone knowledgeable about the clinical issues in your work?
- Is there time and opportunity to meet with peers in supervision, formal and informal?
- In short, are there enough ways for you to be fed so that you are replenished on a regular basis to continue to find respite and to continue to do work that can be draining?

CONCLUSIONS

Sandra Bloom, a noted psychiatrist in Philadelphia, has done much for the professional helping community by offering training that promotes trauma-informed systems, such as The Health Federation of Philadelphia. Taking the theory of secondary trauma to another level, she recognized that entire organizations and systems display behaviors that indicate that they are suffering the effects of trauma. Maladaptive responses to repeated exposure to the trauma of those we are meant to serve can result in policies and practices that "blame the victim," as it were, with punitive and judgmental treatment. She engages entire programs and agencies; all personnel participate, from the receptionist to the housekeeping staff to the direct care and administrative staff to the executive director. This comprehensive approach affords an opportunity for all to reflect on their values and practices, to understand more about why they may feel and behave as they do toward the people coming for assistance, and to make a commitment to change, as necessary. It is easy to see how trauma theory is applicable to work with people living with HIV. Whether we work with them individually, in groups, with their families of origin or families of choice, we can see that entering their lives at this crucial time is a privilege to us and often pivotal for them at whatever stage of wellness or disease they find themselves.

REFERENCES

Allen, R. & Petr, C. (1998). Rethinking family-centered practice. *American Journal of Orthopsychiatry, 68*(1), 4–15.

Balgopal, P. R., & Vassil, T. V. (1983). *Groups in social work: An ecological perspective.* New York: Macmillian Publishing Company, Inc.

Bloom, Sandra. (1997). *Creating sanctuary: Toward an evolution of sane societies.* New York: Routledge Publishers.

Boyd-Franklin, N. (2003). *Black families in therapy: Understanding the African-American experience.* New York: Guilford Press, Inc.

Boyd-Franklin, N. (1989). *Black families in therapy: A multisystems approach.* New York: Guilford Press, Inc.

Clarke, I. J. (1998). *Who, me lead a group?* Seattle, Washington: Parenting Press, Inc.

Eberhardt, L. (1994). *Working with women's groups* (Vol. 1). Duluth, MN: Whole Person Associations, Inc.

Figley, C. R. (1995). *Compassion fatigue: Coping with secondary traumatic stress disorder in those who treat the traumatized.* New York: Brunner/Mazel.

Hay, Louise. (2002). *Meditations to heal your life.* Carson, California: Hay House, Inc.

Health Federation of Philadelphia. (2004). Previous Abandoned Infants Comprehensive Service Demonstration Project, 2004-ACF-ACYE-CB-0018 [Grant proposal].

Kalichman, S. C., Sikkeman, K. J., & Somlai, A. (1996, October). People living with HIV infection who attend and do not attend support groups: A pilot study of needs, characteristics, and experiences. *AIDS Care, 8*(5), 589–599.

Lipsky, L. (2007). *Trauma stewardship: An everyday guide to caring for self while caring for others.* Seattle, Washington: Las Olas Press.

Palme, (2008). Group Therapy or Individual Therapy. Retrieved on October 13, 2009 from http://web4health.info/en

Perry, B. (2003). *The cost of caring: Secondary traumatic stress and the impact of working with high-risk children and families.* Houston: Child Trauma Academy www.childtrauma.org.

Shulman, L. (1999). The skills of helping: Individuals, families, groups, and communities (4th edition). Itasca, IL: Peacock

Schulman, L. (2006). The skills of helping individuals, families, groups, and communities (Fifth edition). Belmont, CA: Thompson.

Wagenhals, Diane (2004). *Group facilitation.* Philadelphia: Institute for Family Professionals.

Yalom, Irvin. (1995). *The theory and practice of group psychotherapy.* New York: Basic Books, Inc.

Web Sites for Further Information

http://en.wikipedia.org/wiki/social work with groups

http://www.demonline.org/jax-medicine/2002journals/junejuly2001/psychosocial.htm

Chapter Nine

ADMINISTRATION OF HIV SERVICES: PROGRAM DEVELOPMENT, MANAGEMENT, AND FUND DEVELOPMENT

Dana B. Marlowe

INTRODUCTION

The purpose of this chapter is to guide the reader in managing an AIDS service organization (ASO) or HIV-related program. I have had the privilege of doing this since 1995. Here, I share others' experience and knowledge as well as my own. This topic, like the others in this book, could merit an entire book. I have chosen to discuss key points to highlight topics and themes that are priorities in the management of HIV-related services.

Administration, fund-raising, and program development are particularly important topics in the social work profession because social workers are losing their roles as managers. We are seeing other types of professionals, such as graduates of business and public administration programs, taking our places in administering human services agencies (Wuenschel, 2006). Professionals who graduate from programs of business and administration may excel at the business and administration of social programs, but may not know how to deal with the social administration of social issues. I am convinced that it is wiser and easier to teach social workers—who are grounded in social work values and practice skills—the necessary management tasks than to teach business-trained managers the necessary values, passion, and commitment that social workers bring to the work.

Social workers are well suited to be managers of ASOs for a variety of reasons. Social worker managers are especially adept at interpersonal skills, using ethical reasoning, working with professionals outside of one's own agency, advocating for the oppressed, and understanding social justice issues (Patti, 2000). Social work education, which focuses on both micro and macro approaches, prepares social workers to sincerely empathize with individuals while effectively leading the agency. Furthermore, the profession's core values of social justice, dignity and

(Continued)

Acknowledgments: This chapter is dedicated to the HIV-positive children who taught me so much—J., C., K., and A.—and to my friend, Joe. He welcomed me into the field with warmth and caring, and his spirit continues to soar. I thank Robert and Liz for adding their voices and stories. I am grateful to Reedie King and the Fordham University Graduate School of Social Service Writing Group for their assistance on this chapter.

worth of a person, importance of human relationships, integrity, and competence (National Association of Social Workers [NASW], 1999) lay the foundation for effective social worker management skills in an ASO.

As I talked with my peers about the management of HIV-related services, two of the main themes that emerged were loss and hope, which may seem dichotomous. It may be surprising that those are the themes generated from discussions about management, rather than direct practice. Nevertheless, these themes were consistently raised. A manager of an HIV-related program may experience many losses. It is likely that HIV-positive individuals whom your agency is serving will die. HIV-positive staff and volunteers may die. On the administrative end of the spectrum, there may be losses of funding and programs. Whatever the losses that have occurred, there is the constant worry that there will be more. The history of loss over the course of this pandemic has been tremendous. Yet there also must be hope. There is hope that there will be a cure or vaccine and hope that people will continue to live longer with HIV. We hope that these vital programs continue to provide individuals with the services they need.

Both loss and hope are part of the administrative work of an HIV-related program. It is the manager's responsibility to support the staff when they are grieving over losses as well as help them maintain hope. While these themes will not be explicitly discussed further, it is important to acknowledge that loss and hope permeate a manager's decision making, even if he or she is not conscious of that fact.

This chapter discusses what I consider to be the most pertinent issues to a social work manager of an ASO or HIV-related program. These are presented as more of a guide for working in the HIV field. The chapter begins by setting the context of a changing field, and then moves to the specific management skills needed to run an ASO or HIV-related program.

THE CHALLENGE OF A CHANGING FIELD

Social work managers must operate in areas that are both vague and frequently filled with contradiction. They are often forced to balance divergent needs and wants of others. In addition to all of the roles they play, social work managers must be able to regenerate their enthusiasm to face the demands created by differing constituents (Berger, Robbins, Lewis, Mizrahi, & Fleit, 2003; Globerman, White, Mullings, & Davies, 2003; Mizrahi & Berger, 2005). This is especially true in the HIV field.

The HIV field, even though it is only a quarter of a century old, has changed dramatically and repeatedly. First, instead of HIV being the mostly terminal illness it once was, due to advances in treating HIV during the mid- to late 1990s, people with HIV are living longer and healthier lives; there has been a dramatic decrease in the number of individuals dying with AIDS; and HIV has become more of a chronic illness (Centers for Disease Control [CDC], 2008; Chambre, 1997). Over the past decade, the number of AIDS-related deaths decreased by 75% (CDC, 2003; Hergenrather, Rhodes, & Clark, 2006). Second, there have been significant changes in the populations most affected by HIV. In the first few years, HIV service provision and advocacy had been largely the domain of gay men, but today the picture has changed. African Americans and women now constitute 45% and 27%, respectively, of all new diagnoses. Sexual contact still remains the most significant risk factor, however, accounting for nearly 85% of all new cases, 31% due to heterosexual contact and 53% acquired through male-to-male sexual contact (CDC, 2008). Third, more people are living with HIV than ever before. From 1990 to 2003, the number of people living with AIDS increased by 519% (CDC, 2003).

SOCIAL WORK MANAGER SKILLS IN AN ASO

As the field of HIV has changed dramatically since its beginning, so, too, have the agencies established to serve the individuals infected and affected by HIV. The changes in the field have forced social worker managers to adjust their roles, creating many challenges for the social worker who is leading an agency and addressing the needs of individuals who are dealing with ever-shifting issues. This requires ASO managers to be flexible, adaptable, and creative.

A constant balance must be maintained, a difficult task in an ever-changing environment. Each time there is a lull, a new crisis is usually in the offing. Each time a manager readies for a set of issues by writing a grant or setting a new policy, a new crisis will likely occur. In the midst of all of this, a manager may be dealing with discrimination, oppression, and dying.

A program manager of an ASO has to balance many different responsibilities, such as organizational budgets, grant reporting, working with outside agencies, managing staff, and assisting with crises of persons with HIV. According to the National Network for Social Work Managers (2004), one needs to possess a basic set of administrative skills in order to be an effective social work manager. These standards are divided into 14 competencies, which provide a fundamental structure of information necessary to practice social work at the management level. The competencies are the following:

> . . . advocacy, communication and interpersonal relationships, ethics, evaluation, financial development, financial management, governance, human resource management and development, information technology, leadership, planning, program development and organizational management, public/community relations and marketing and public policy (p. 1–2).

It is recommended that social workers who become HIV-related program managers become educated and trained in the preceding management skills listed.

Although ASOs are similar in some ways to other types of service agencies in characteristics and history, there are significant differences, which affect the management of them. Poindexter (2007) states that there are distinct struggles of an ASO, such as "stigma, changing practice contexts, volunteerism, partnership, cultural competence, financial health, professionalism, service integration, job stress, and organizational cohesion" (p. 5). At the outset of the AIDS crisis, there was an immense social stigma associated with the medical condition. Some people living with HIV lost their families, friends, jobs, homes, schools, and churches (Herek & Glunt, 1988). Working with persons who are discriminated against and witnessing these injustices made the work even more difficult. There is also a painful history of the struggle that ASOs have had to go through, with governmental neglect and discrimination from the community. In addition to all of this, many ASOs had little funding.

Volunteers were the first workers in this field. They were HIV-infected and HIV-affected individuals who were able to rally themselves together, advocate, and provide essential services that the government and public were not providing. The organizations that were born out of these efforts were true grassroots organizations, surviving on the dedication and commitment of those volunteers. One example was "buddies," created by the Gay Men's Health Crisis (GMHC), that was a vital service in helping those in crisis (Chambre, 1997) and those who needed companions (Poindexter, 2002). The ASOs had a dual purpose: (1) provide necessary services to people living with HIV and (2) advocate for people living with HIV. When funding finally increased, paid staff was hired and volunteer programs began to diminish. Some agencies did not have the time to train volunteers anymore. Further, some volunteers were infected with HIV, became ill, and were unable to continue the work.

As agencies relied less on volunteers, professional social workers began to become the leaders of the ASOs, using both their administrative and direct social work skills. Some were direct service social workers in the HIV field who became managers, while others were managers in other types of social service agencies who moved into an administrative position serving a different population (Wimpfheimer, 2004). The pandemic created many jobs for social workers. (At a statewide conference I attended, an HIV-positive speaker asked all of the service providers to thank him for creating their jobs!) In New York, where the numbers of people with HIV are highest, between the years of 1982 and 1998, 166 ASOs were established (Chambre, 1999).

Managers who had been direct service social workers empathize with HIV-infected and HIV-affected persons, have excellent interpersonal skills, and are able to apply micro-, mezzo-, and macrolevel understanding to their situations (Nesoff, 2007). We are social workers first, which is our strength. Herein also lies the difficulty. Imagine that you are in the midst of applying for funding and have a grant application deadline to meet. Your staff interrupts you and tells you that an HIV-positive girl to whom your program provides services has just been expelled from school because of her HIV-positive status. This is outrageous. This is a girl you have known for 10 years. You have seen her flourish in school and sports. You are going to feel something. Besides giving your staff guidance on how to proceed, you may feel much sadness and anger at what has occurred. An effective social work administrator will use those feelings, combined with strong administrative skills, to best guide the staff.

Commonly, an effective social work manager in an ASO will be in contact with persons with HIV. This does not mean that the manager will have his or her own caseload or group. It just means that the manager will know who the service recipients are and what their salient issues are. So the work becomes one of balancing grants and funding, working with other agencies, answering to one's own supervisor, managing staff, and putting out management fires. The difference between a manager of an ASO and another type of agency is that, in an ASO, you are still dealing with HIV stigma and discrimination, you are working with people who are chronically ill from an incurable disease, and service recipients and staff have died or are dying from it. As a result of these differences, social work managers of ASOs may have more involvement with those they are serving than do managers in other types of agencies.

It is important that a manager remain aware of the service population and their environments. That can be accomplished in a wide variety of ways. One ASO required its supervisor of all clinical services to deliver groceries (from its grocery delivery program) once a week to constituents' homes. In addition to all of the supervisory responsibilities, whoever held that position delivered groceries to an HIV-positive woman who was living in poverty every Friday afternoon, a task that kept the manager aware of and part of tasks performed by staff and volunteers of the agency. Clinical supervisors in this position consistently reported that this was vital part of their jobs.

There are vital issues that every administrator must deal with in running an ASO that they may not be prepared for. The following skills are discussed in detail because of their importance for ASO administrators to understand for effective discharge of their duties:

working with other organizations, funding, managing the team (including volunteerism, HIV-positive individuals as staff members, veterans versus rookies, staff grief and stress), and flexibility and creativity.

Working with Other Organizations

Establishing and maintaining interorganizational relationships gives the agency power, validity, and resource maximization (Perlmutter et al., 2001). This interaction is key to the survival of an organization because it enables it to work within any constraints of the environment (Hasenfeld, 2000). In the current political climate, no one organization can exist as a lone wolf. It is paramount to maintain good relationships with all interorganizational structures to optimize resources for the individuals and families you serve. Any agency must have a healthy relationship with other organizations and subcontractors (who are beholden to their own organizations), yet have a responsibility for its own survival as well. When working with other agencies, a manager has to consider power sharing, monetary risks, and interpersonal relationships.

Rier and Indyk (2006) suggest that interorganizational linkages must be established in order to formulate a coordinated response to the HIV pandemic. They argue that knowledge disseminated from different areas of expertise, be they medical institutions, community-based organizations, or directly from service recipients, must be harnessed in a way that allows for the most effective use and sharing of information.

Due to the sociomedical nature of this complex disease, people with HIV have needs that are in constant flux and do not follow predictable steps. Often shifting between prevention information, social service needs, and medical and mental health assistance, expertise most often will come from varying areas of function, discipline, and location. If the system of service provision and information delivery remains fragmented, resources and expertise will be squandered and HIV-infected persons may ultimately fail to connect with the system at all, falling victim to communication breakdowns. These linkages may be even more important in rural areas where services are more spread out (Grace, Soons, Kutzko, Alston, & Ramundo, 1999).

ASOs and those whom they serve were alienated from each other for a long time, due to realistic distrust that historically oppressed communities held toward public agencies, especially governmental or faith-based organizations that asked questions about sexual or drug behavior. During this time, people with HIV learned to depend only on themselves or other people with HIV for the care they needed. Due to this history, it is not uncommon for ASOs not to look to other types of service agencies to provide resources to people living with HIV, because traditional agencies could not be trusted to be free of HIV stigma and discrimination. The following vignette offers an example of this situation.

Personal Perspective

By Liz, Consultant, Trainer, Speaker

In 2000 I took over a nonprofit that had been established in the early 1990s when the AIDS pandemic was at its height. This nonprofit was founded by politicians in partnership with individuals who were infected and affected by HIV. It was funded solely by donations and managed to raise enough money and support to bring the "AIDS Quilt" [the Names Project] to my county in 1998. After that, the agency was dormant.

(Continued)

I am an HIV-infected woman diagnosed in 1994. I also have a master's degree in social work. After my diagnosis, I stopped working and was now by circumstance forced to become a "client" rather than the social worker providing services. It was a humbling experience. I was accustomed to aiding others and now felt so helpless having to ask others for assistance. At first I was out of my element, and so devastated by my diagnosis that I relished the thought of having another person take over what I could not do for myself. I learned to rely on others to help me navigate the services I needed but was not familiar with, and for the first few years, it worked fine for me.

Over time, I began to recover my self-esteem and became increasingly active in the HIV community. I started attending seminars and trainings as well as doing outreach. I became frustrated at how little case managers knew about what services existed both for me and for others I met who are HIV-positive. I began to reach out to individuals working in the HIV field. I wanted to make them aware that more education and outreach was needed in order to empower those infected with HIV to have knowledge about services they were entitled to. During this time, I was approached by the last active member of the nonprofit agency [referred to earlier in the vignette] who asked me if I would be interested in taking it over. By doing this, my outreach and education could reach more people while helping me to offset the cost of doing so. Although there was less than $2,000 in the bank account, it was enough to pay for a work phone in my house and to assemble brochures. I jumped at the opportunity and began immediately to recruit board members. In addition to attending more HIV meetings, I became a voting member of the Ryan White Title A Steering Committee.

During one seminar, I had a "lightbulb" moment. At the conclusion of the meeting attended by roughly 40 people and 15 to 20 different agencies, there was a question-and-answer period during which half of us realized how little we actually knew about the services offered by other agencies. Not only were we ignorant about what services the agencies offered, many of us were unaware these agencies even existed. At that moment I decided that the philosophy I wanted to adopt for my nonprofit was to "think outside the box" and to educate both service recipients and staff about different services available in the small county where we lived.

To start, I joined several different collaboratives of agencies who met in various parts of the county working to educate the public about their purpose and to form partnerships for grants and for referrals. After several months of attending meetings, I decided to hold a monthly forum open to the community and invite different agencies to come and speak about the services they offered. I sent mailings to all the HIV agencies and to HIV-positive individuals I knew. I designed fliers and asked both the agencies in the collaboratives and the HIV agencies to post them to make people aware of the free forums. It was both amazing and gratifying to have so many people, both case managers and people with HIV, thank me for educating them about the benefits they could seek out from agencies they didn't even know existed. In one instance, a case manager was attempting to have her client's phone bill paid through the Department of Social Services, and was encountering much red tape. After hearing another case manager from a different agency (not an ASO) explain a monetary benefit they offered for emergency situations, she called them and within two days had her client's phone bill paid and services restored. Afterwards, she called to thank me and said she would have never "in a million years" have thought to call a different type of social service agency. What I was discovering in the HIV community was that case managers were not looking at their "clients" as whole people. They boxed them in, viewing them as just HIV-positive rather than looking at other aspects, like life experiences, which might help to determine appropriate services. Due to this closed-minded attitude, many people with HIV weren't utilizing services to which they were entitled. This concept of boxing in is not relegated to merely the HIV community but exists in many fields. The best way to realize the infinite number of services available to someone is to sit with them to discover who they are outside of why they are coming to see you. If they are an immigrant who is new to this country and struggling financially, perhaps a local club or agency offers free English classes, or offers free seminars on how to find an appropriate job interview. There may be a local church with a food pantry they could access, or free school supplies given to children in need. Although these programs may exist outside of the HIV community, they are services that people may be entitled to receive yet would never be aware of without the assistance to network outside of a single service area. The more knowledgeable you make yourself, the more beneficial you will be. And who knows, like me, you too may need to utilize one of these services for your own benefit one day.

As Liz points out, HIV is the disease, not the person. By providing services based only on the disease, many key options are missed. Working with different agencies and groups can result in much more comprehensive services for individuals living with HIV.

Funding

A basic requirement of a social work manager is to evaluate resources, acquire resources and funding, and then to distribute them (Perlmutter & Crook, 2004). These are skills that can be learned through one's social work education or through training. Although this can be very tedious, it is an essential part of a social work manager's job. It is therefore very important to have a comprehensive understanding of the main funding sources for ASOs.

Initially, there was no government funding for HIV services. All funding came from private donations. When funding did become available for these services, there was strong competition between the already existing agencies and agencies that wanted to expand and service this population (Chambre, 1999).

The Ryan White Comprehensive AIDS Resource Emergency (CARE) Act, passed by Congress in 1990, provided funding for HIV social and medical services (Lewis and Crook, 2001). The CARE act has been reauthorized three times since its passage. In the most recent passage, in 2006, the CARE act was renamed the Ryan White HIV/AIDS Treatment Modernization Act (HRSA, 2008). The Ryan White HIV program is the main federal program expressly intended for people living with HIV. The program provides people affected by HIV with services for support and care. The more involved the manager becomes in the community, the more essential it is to understand what other services are available for people living with HIV. This knowledge includes having an understanding of the various programs offered under the Ryan White program. The Ryan White program is divided into five main parts, called *titles* (see Appendix A).

A combination of private and public funding is essential to provide the necessary services and have a bit more financial security. Depending on only one resource will cause agencies to become too vulnerable (James, 2003). To help ensure lasting financial viability, ASOs need to find nontraditional funding venues to ensure a steady stream of income into their organizations. By not restricting funding services to a single entity, ASOs will help guarantee a stronger influx of funds. Technology has also allowed ASOs greater facility in tapping an even broader base of potential donors in an easier and time-lier fashion. The Internet has allowed ASOs to also tap the non-HIV-infected community as a potential donor source (Poindexter, 2007).

In addition, community projects cannot be minimized as potential resources for the agency. Agencies have had office furniture donated, cases of food donated by summer camps, temples, and churches for food pantries, and holiday gifts for HIV-infected children and their siblings donated by a local hospital staff. These types of projects are beneficial to the recipients, agency, and community. While all of these avenues open up potential revenue streams, it is essential that managers stay involved in all of the accounting practices that are occurring. The manager is the expert on the ASO budget in terms of what is needed. While financial staff can assist with the budgets, the manager must have input.

Managers must understand the political economy of organizations because it will make them more effective. Even though funding exists, it is limited. To exist, an organization needs power, and power is tantamount to funding and resources. When resources in the environment change, the agency must adapt in order to continue to access these resources and to obtain new sources (Hasenfeld, 1992). HIV is the perfect example of how as the environment changes, so do the agencies. Agencies will fight to survive. For example, if an agency is not meeting the goals of its case management grant, then another agency in the county may get that grant instead. Another agency that needs that funding may establish new objectives or change its mission just to become eligible for that grant.

Sometimes we are confronted with having to choose between losing funding and changing the mission. The following example, with which the author is personally familiar, occurred when New York State changed its funding to family-centered HIV programs as opposed to comprehensive pediatric HIV or adult HIV programs.

After the community hospital had a grant for a comprehensive pediatric program for eight years, the state announced that comprehensive pediatric HIV programs had a choice. Either their grant would not be renewed or they could apply to become a Pediatric Center of Excellence or a Family Centered Program. There was really no option because they did not want to lose their funding and they did not have enough pediatric patients to become a Pediatric Center of Excellence. They opted to apply and later become a Family Centered Program. They incorporated their former pediatric program into it and subcontracted with an adult HIV program. One of the rationales behind the change was to have one-stop shopping for families, where all HIV-infected family members could receive medical and support services. There were staff from both programs who were resistant because change can be difficult. However, in the end they had to be flexible enough to change part of the mission and provide people with HIV with the best possible services.

Changes in policies also affect the way in which we offer services. Throughout the pandemic there have been numerous HIV policies that have gone into effect and have even changed over time—for example, the HIV confidentiality law, mandatory counseling and voluntary testing of pregnant mothers, HIV reporting, and partner notification. When policies are put into effect, additional money is not always provided. When money is not available, programmatic changes must be made in order to adapt.

Advancements in the field also provide opportunities for agencies to grow. At the time that rapid HIV testing came into effect, different types of agencies began to offer this service. People could know their HIV test results within 20 minutes (if the assay showed a negative test result) as opposed to having to wait two weeks for results. ASOs such as those providing street outreach, medical services, and even food pantries offered this service as a way to get more people tested for HIV. Many agencies also believed this was a good way to increase the number of people they were reaching with test counseling.

Managing the Team

There are some very distinct aspects of managing staff in an ASO. Skills that are needed are common to all social work administrative positions. There are additional issues that one needs to be sensitive to because of the nature of HIV, its related problems, and how it can affect staff. Here I discuss managing volunteers, HIV-positive employees, merging old and new staff, and helping staff with grief.

Managing Volunteers

Although some may not consider volunteers staff, they are so integral to this field that they will be considered staff in this chapter. Volunteers created the HIV field. They were able to unite and provide services at a time when the government denied assistance. When funding finally increased, paid staff were hired and volunteer programs began to diminish. Some agencies did not have the time to train volunteers anymore. Some volunteers were infected with HIV early on and became sick and died.

Although volunteers do require staff time, they can be a true asset to ASOs. Volunteers can also fill important agency roles: delivering food, doing outreach, providing support, raising funds and supplies for the agency, and filling administrative roles. A manager is ultimately responsible for recruiting, training, and supervising volunteers (Chambre, 1997), even though this can be delegated to a staff person who is in charge of volunteers.

Before taking on volunteers, it is essential to know what needs the agency has that can be fulfilled by a volunteer and the abilities that will be required of the volunteer (Perlmutter & Crook, 2004). It is also important to know what the volunteer's expectations are. I still receive phone calls from interested volunteers stating that they would like to hold the "AIDS babies" in the nursery. I try to explain that there are not any "AIDS babies" in the nurseries anymore because of medical advancements, and I try to steer them in a different direction.

Volunteers can truly assist with agency tasks that staff are unable to take on. Sometimes, it is these tasks which become the most fulfilling for the volunteer and the individual receiving the service. The following example, drawn from the author's experience, illustrates the invaluable service volunteers can provide.

One summer the town camp provided our program with a scholarship for one HIV-positive child to attend a day camp, which included special trips two days each week. We knew exactly which child would benefit from this camp. He came from a resource-poor home. During home visits, staff would comment on the thousands of roaches that were in the house. The only problem was that there was no transportation provided to get him to and from camp. For the five weeks of camp, we needed to find 50 rides for him! Through the use of two very committed volunteers, we were able to accomplish this. When he frequently informed the volunteers that there was no food in the house for him to bring lunch, the volunteers provided it for him. It was the best summer of his life. Without volunteers, this would have never happened.

Having committed volunteers is also a support for paid staff. Staff know that there is someone there to assist them, and knowing that the community is helping can increase morale.

HIV-Positive Individuals as Staff Members

The field of HIV management has always been sensitive to include affected and infected persons in the planning of provided services. The reasoning behind this is that these services were originated by the very people they were meant to serve (Poindexter, 2007; Poindexter & Lane, 2003; Van Roey, 1999). Your funding may require that you include HIV-positive individuals in some aspects of your program. For example, some parts of the Ryan White HIV program require that an HIV-positive individual provide recommendations on agency goals, needs, and planning (Poindexter & Lane, 2003). Whether it is a requirement or not, your agency will benefit from having someone living with HIV on staff. This individual understands the true realities of living with the virus better than any noninfected individuals. His or her input can be extraordinarily useful.

Getting HIV-positive individuals involved in the agency can sometimes be difficult. In the past, HIV-infected people were unable to work and participate in daily activities because there was no or little treatment for the disease. Today, people with HIV are living full lives and do not always have the time to participate in an ASO. Furthermore, for some it is just a reminder that they are HIV-positive, something they may not want to think about now that they are living healthy lives.

A manager of one program was able to obtain a consultant line in the grant budget, which was used to hire an HIV-positive individual to work with other HIV-positive individuals as an advocate. The service recipients became very connected to this person, and she was an excellent liaison with staff. This proves to be a strong example of how an administrator can be creative and flexible in budgeting in order to provide an essential service.

Veterans versus Rookies

If you survived the initial years of the pandemic, your veteran status becomes a part of you. It becomes a piece of the way you deal with staff, outside agencies, and people living with HIV. If you were not a participant or witness, you will learn about it by the very nature of the ability of history to define current practice. You will find long-term ASO workers—staff who started out, possibly as volunteers, years earlier and have continued in the field. You will also find staff who are new to the field. The combination of both types of workers can be beneficial because it brings the important history and knowledge together with renewed energy and ideas.

There may also be conflict between a long-term worker and a new worker because of the difference in what they understand about the pandemic. The long-term worker may resent the new worker who did not experience the first 10 years of the crisis. It is the manager's responsibility to educate all new workers about their job responsibilities as well as to educate them about the history. Sending new staff to trainings is a start to providing them with the necessary education. Even having them view commercial films, such as *Philadelphia, And the Band Played On,* and *Longtime Companion,* can give them an understanding of the beginning context of the pandemic.

When referring to HIV-positive individuals who have died, it is important to take a moment and tell the staff about this important person. Again, it is a balancing act—keep the memory of the individual and what you as a worker gained from that individual alive while moving on in a positive way to help other HIV-infected persons. More-seasoned workers can also help with this process.

The second vignette provides a view of the changes in HIV and the resulting changes in agencies and leadership. It also illustrates the possible tensions involved between those professionals who are trying to help. Robert sums up the division that can occur between different types of professionals who have varying amounts of time in the field. When running an ASO, awareness of this potential conflict and efforts to resolve it are vital in order to have a cohesive staff.

Staff Grief and Stress

It is not uncommon to be confronted with deaths while working in the field of social work (Strom-Gottfried & Mowbray, 2006). Although HIV is seen as more of a chronic illness, there is no cure, and people are still dying as a result of it. People with HIV are still fighting for their lives.

The staff in ASOs are often part of the community in which they are serving. Often, they have come into this field because someone who is important to them has been affected by HIV. Sometimes, they themselves are HIV-positive. Very often, they are experiencing loss with the people whom they are serving. It is because of this that some staff may even seem overcommitted. As the manager, it is important to be aware of this and help the staff member to use it as a strength as opposed to something that will cause added stress and burnout.

It is important to know what you can do for your staff and for yourself in coping with the emotional stress of working in this field. Rituals for the staff can be very significant and can help them in their grieving process. ASOs may choose to encourage staff to participate in the rituals that they feel comfortable with. This may be attending a funeral or participating in a memorial service with staff and service recipients (Strom-Gottfried & Mowbray, 2006).

Having organizational policies and procedures related to deaths may also aid staff in knowing what to do when someone dies. Having condolence cards in the office and a list of bereavement services in order to make referrals can be very helpful. Staff should not have to purchase these or look up these services when someone dies (Ellison & Ptacek, 2002).

As with managing any social work agency, you need to be able to identify staff who are experiencing psychological exhaustion. There is an increased incidence of HIV in lower-income individuals of color, yet often HIV is the least of the person's worries. Individuals living in poverty, some of whom are homeless, and many who struggle to adhere to medical treatments often require services from ASOs. The problems that are often characteristic of HIV necessitate more than one type of service. Encouraging positive relationships with staff and between staff, communicating about traumatic experiences in service provision, and feedback from the administrator can help with the stress that staff may feel (Leon, Altholz, & Dziegielewski, 1999).

Flexibility and Creativity

An effective manager is one who is attentive to detail, provides the necessary services, and fulfills all of the administrative duties. A very effective manager is one who can also provide services in a flexible and creative way.

The programs that I have seen as successful have been so not only because they meet their goals and objectives, but also because they are creative and meet the community members where they are. We have to remember that we are working with individuals who are fighting a chronic illness that has no cure. Many of them thought they would die within a short period of time, and have luckily survived for much longer. Here are some examples of that creativity:

- One social worker in an ASO joined an HIV-positive boy and his adoptive mother to hear Magic Johnson speak and to meet him. They spent the day together, sharing in the excitement of meeting Magic Johnson and processing the feelings surrounding the boy's diagnosis.
- The four main ASOs in one county had an annual holiday party for people living with HIV. For five years, the four agencies worked together to accomplish this. A holiday dinner was donated for all who attended, gifts were given to the children, and there was a sense of community felt by all of the agencies and guests.
- A comprehensive family-centered program accepts donated children's books. The home care nurse brings a book to an HIV-positive child and sibling each time she visits their home.
- Through private donations, two agencies were able to provide amusement park admission tickets and food vouchers to 20 families affected by HIV. Some of the individuals knew each other and some did not. The boys on the trip were all HIV-positive and between the ages of 8 and 10. They all knew that they went to the same doctor in the same clinic. None of them actually knew their true diagnosis, but there was a connection. As the day went on, they seemed to gravitate toward each other and went on the rides together. They related to each other and formed a new support system.
- One food pantry had volunteers deliver turkeys to all of the HIV-infected low-income persons on Christmas Eve.

Personal Perspective

The Professionalism of HIV Community Service Organizations and the Return to Grass Roots, by Robert

While attending college in the early 1980s, I had a professor who canceled his classes on Friday, as he was not feeling well. It was on the following Monday that I received news that he had died on Sunday from some unknown new disease. This was my introduction to the HIV pandemic. I became part of a renewed grass-roots movement, a type of passionate call to rally that had not existed since the peace demonstrations of the 1960s. As HIV was a disease identified among White, middle-class, 30- to 40-year-old gay men, and at the time the country's politics were in a heightened conservative vain, this nonunified, stigmatized, and closeted gay population put aside their differences to force change and demand research and funding for people living with HIV.

Through this grassroots movement, organizations like ACT UP (AIDS Coalition to Unleash Power) and GMHC (Gay Men's Health Crisis) were formed by HIV-infected and HIV-affected gay and straight individuals. People forced to leave their for-profit professions due to failing health from HIV infection founded these pioneer organizations. With little or no experience in running nonprofit organizations, many with no background in public health, social service, or mental health were forced to learn new skills. Due to early grassroots success in securing funding and providing service for people living with HIV disease, these organizations grew to require a broader range of professional employees. Individuals not directly affected by HIV, yet with a certain skill set, found themselves working in the new field of HIV service providers. Within a short time, it became clear that treating HIV was going to be difficult. Recognizing that this disease would linger, people started making career choices to enter and remain in the field of HIV services. This shift in skill and mind-set led to the early professionalism of HIV. Although this change is not uncommon and is seen with other nonprofit causes, the dynamic force that had unified the gay community began to dismantle. In addition, the early founders of these organizations began to find themselves at odds with the new professionals. Unfortunately, some new professionals looked upon the founding HIV-affected leadership and employees as well-intentioned individuals, but not as equals, due to their lack of professional schooling. In some cases, the pressure between founding-organization individuals and "professionals" forced the founders, still in need of services for their own HIV issues, to leave organizations they themselves had created. At the same time, there was a parallel shift in the dynamic between staff members and service recipients. During the early days of the pandemic, HIV-infected persons could feel comfortable that the organization understood important issues of stigma and loss that are part of living with HIV disease because staff members were often affected by HIV disease themselves. Today, many professionals do not fully comprehend the unique conditions under which individuals with HIV must live.

Nonetheless, some professionals have learned that the nondegreed, HIV service veteran can offer crucial knowledge on needs and concerns of HIV-infected persons. Today, it is the intelligent professional who can effect the greatest change by—putting aside biases and prejudices—working with the community to take advantage of all available resources.

The HIV pandemic now has better treatment options yet is having a devastating impact on the disenfranchised and stigmatized communities of color. Several issues that existed in the early 1980s have returned and need to be addressed within these communities. Nevertheless, accessing needed services proves difficult within a population often lacking a strong educational or economic foundation. This problem is then compounded by the separation formed within the relationship in the system of care of "professional to client," an "us versus them" mentality, and is further fueled by pressures from decreased public concern and cuts in federal and state funding.

As these trends continue, "members," as is my preferred term for all people involved with HIV issues, will need to return to greater grassroots participation. The era of professionalism in HIV service delivery may be ending. The infected and affected HIV population must reunite and advocate for themselves if social support organizations are going to survive into the future.

CONCLUSIONS

I believe that it is essential that ASOs and HIV-related programs be managed by social workers due to their unique skill sets and values. Due to the significant increase in the need for social work administrators, the social work profession has not been able to keep up with training social workers for these positions. More traditional schools of management are producing different types of professionals, with degrees in business and public administration to run social service agencies (Wuenschel, 2006). Social workers can often move into middle management roles, but cannot reach the CEO level (Perlmutter, 2006). Management professionals tend to put management goals first, sometimes at the cost of social work skills. This will be especially detrimental to ASOs, where social work skills are so vital.

Social workers are able to wear two hats, one with their generalist knowledge of working with individuals, families, and groups, and the other working on an organizational level. ASOs require this combination of skills because of the changing nature of HIV, the changes in the surrounding environment, and the emotions involved in helping people with HIV.

Social work skills and management skills are necessary to manage an ASO. Additional, unique skills will also be required. These skills are:

- Battling HIV stigma and concurrent oppressions
- Fighting for social justice
- Staying connected to the infected, affected, and at-risk communities
- Helping staff deal with losses and stress
- Maintaining realistic hope in the face of the preceding items

As the HIV pandemic continues to shift, so, too, do the agencies that are serving HIV-positive individuals. Continued future focus in ASOs must include employment counseling in their services roster, because more HIV-positive persons are becoming well enough to return to work (Hergenrather, Rhodes, Clark, 2005; Poindexter, 2007; Timmons & Fesko, 1997) and should include an even stronger emphasis on cultural competency because of the increasing diversity of the pandemic.

REFERENCES

Berger, C. S., Robbins, C., Lewis, M., Mizrahi, T., & Fleit, S. (2003). The impact of organizational change on social work staffing in a hospital setting: A national, longitudinal study of social work in hospitals. *Social Work in Health Care, 37*(1), 1–18.

Centers for Disease Control and Prevention. (2008, August). Estimates of new HIV infections in the United States. Retrieved from http://www.cdc.gov/hiv/topics/surveillance/resources/factsheets/pdf/incidence/pd

Centers for Disease Control and Prevention. (2003). *HIV Surveillance Report, 14*(1), 1–48.

Chambre, S. M. (1997, October–December). New tactics: Volunteer programs adapt to meet changing needs of people with AIDS. *Volunteer Leadership,* 17–19.

Chambre, S. M. (1999). Redundancy, third-party government, and consumer choice: HIV nonprofit organizations in New York City. *Policy Studies Journal, 27*(4), 840–854.

Ellison, N. M., & Ptacek, J. T. (2002). Physician interactions with families and caregivers after a patient's death: Current practices and proposed changes. *Journal of Palliative Medicine, 5*(1), 49–55.

Globerman, J., White, J. J., Mullings, D., & Davies, J. M. (2003). Thriving in program management environments: The case of social work in hospitals. *Social Work in Health Care, 38*(1), 1–18.

Grace, C. J., Soons, K. R., Kutzko, D., Alston, W. K., Ramundo, M. (1999). Service delivery for patients with HIV in a rural state: The Vermont model. *AIDS Patient Care and STDs, 13*(11), 659–666.

Hasenfeld, Y. (1992). Theoretical approaches to human service organizations. In Y. Hasenfeld (Ed.), *Human Services as Complex Organizations*. Thousand Oaks, CA: Sage.

Hasenfeld, Y. (2000). Social welfare administration and organizational theory. In R. J. Patti (Ed.), *The handbook of social welfare management* (pp. 89–112). Thousand Oaks, CA: Sage.

Herek, G. M., & Glunt, E. K. (1988). An epidemic of stigma: Public reaction to AIDS. *American Psychologist, 43*(11), 886–891.

Hergenrather, K. C., Rhodes, S. D., & Clark, G. (2006). Windows to work: Exploring employment-seeking behaviors of persons with HIV through photovoice. *AIDS Education and Prevention, 18*(3), 243–258.

Indyk, D., & Rier, D. A. (2006). Wiring the HIV system: Building interorganizational infrastructure to link people, sites, and networks. *Social Work in Health Care, 42*(3/4), 29–45.

Kaiser Family Foundation. (2008). *HIV policy fact sheet*. The Ryan White Program. Retrieved from http://www.kff.org/hivaids/upload/7582_04.pdf

Leon, A. M., Altholz, J. A., & Dziegielewski, S. F. (1999). Compassion fatigue: Considerations for working with the elderly. *Journal of Gerontological Social Work, 32*(1), 43–62.

Lewis, S., & Crook, W. P. (2001). Shifting sands: An AIDS service organization adapts to a changing environment. *Administration in Social Work, 25*(2), 1–20.

Mizrahi, T., & Berger, C. S. (2005). A longitudinal look at social work leadership in hospitals: The impact of a changing health care system. *Health and Social Work, 30*(2), 155–165.

National Association of Social Workers. (1999). *Code of Ethics*. Washington, DC: NASW Press.

National Network for Social Work Managers. (2004). *Leadership and management practice standards*. Chicago: Jane Addams College of Social Work.

Nesoff, I. (2007). The importance of revitalizing management education for social workers. *Social Work, 52*(3), 283.

Patti, R. J. (2000). The landscape of social work management. In R. J. Patti (Ed.), *The handbook of social welfare management* (pp. 3–25). Thousand Oaks, CA: Sage.

Perlmutter, F. D. (2006). Ensuring social work administration. *Administration in Social Work, 30*(2), 3–10.

Perlmutter, F. D., Bailey, D., & Netting, F. E. (2001). *Managing human resources in the human services: Supervisory challenges*. New York: Oxford University Press.

Perlmutter, F. D., & Crook, W. P. (2004). *Changing hats while managing change: From social work practice to administration*. Washington, DC: National Association of Social Workers.

Poindexter, C. C. (2002). "Be generous of spirit": Organization development of an AIDS service organization. *Journal of Community Practice, 10*(2), 53–70.

Poindexter, C. C. (2007). Management successes and struggles for AIDS service organizations. *Administration in Social Work, 31*(3), 5–28.

Poindexter, C. C., & Lane, T. S. (2003). Choices and voices: Participation of people with HIV in Ryan White Title II Consumer Advisory Boards. *Health and Social Work, 28*(3), 196–205.

Rier, D. A., & Indyk, D. (2006). The rationale of interorganizational linkages to connect multiple sites of expertise, knowledge production, and knowledge transfer: An example from HIV services for the inner city. *Social Work in Health Care, 42*(3/4), 9–27.

Strom-Gottfried, K., & Mowbray, N. D. (2006). Who heals the helper? Facilitating the social worker's grief. *Families in Society: The Journal of Contemporary Social Services, 87*(1), 9–15.

Timmons, J. C., & Fesko, S. L. (1997, May). Employment needs of individuals with HIV: Service providers' viewpoints. *Research to Practice*.

U.S. Department of Health and Human Services. Health Resources and Services Administration (HRSA). (2008). *The HIV programs: Who was Ryan White?* Retrieved August 25, 2008, from http://hab.hrsa.gov/about/ryanwhite.htm

Van Roey, J. (1999). *From principle to practice: Greater involvement of people living with or affected by HIV* (Joint United Nations Programme on HIV). Geneva, Switzerland: UNAIDS.

Wimpfheimer, S. (2004). Leadership and management competencies defined by practicing social work managers: An overview of standards developed by the National Network of Social Work Managers. *Administration in Social Work, 8*(1), 45–56.

Wuenschel, P. C. (2006). The diminishing role of social work administrators in social service agencies: Issues for consideration. *Administration in Social Work, 30*(4), 5–18.

Appendix: Ryan White HIV Program

Part A funds both metropolitan areas that report in excess of 2,000 cases of AIDS and transitional areas where the reported instances of AIDS fall between 1,000 and 1,999 tracked over the most recent five-year period. Additional money is awarded through a competitive grant process based on need. As part of recent reauthorization, 75 percent of Part A funding must be directed toward core medical services.

Part B provides funding to all of the states and various territories in the form of base and supplemental grants, ADAP and ADAP supplemental grants, and Emerging Communities grants. Grantee states either provide direct services or deliver them via a collective group of organizations designed to plan and implement HIV care. Seventy-five percent of funds are required to be spent on core medical services.

Under Part C grants are awarded to public and private organizations to fund Early Intervention Services and Capacity Development and Planning. Seventy-five percent of Part C funding must target core medical services.

Part D funding is targeted to reach families living with HIV through community-based help that focuses on the specific needs of children, youth, and women. Funding is for prevention services, outreach, medical care, and to address psychosocial needs. Support is also given to link this population to new research and clinical trials.

Part F partially funds AIDS Education and Training Centers, community dental programs, and the Minority AIDS Initiative. Special Projects of National Significance Program is a research and development entity to address the developing needs of people with HIV in underserved populations (Kaiser Family Foundation, 2008).

Chapter Ten

HIV-RELATED COMMUNITY ORGANIZING AND GRASSROOTS ADVOCACY

Larry M. Gant

> *However you do it, organizing is the process of finding out what people want as individuals and then helping them find collective ways of getting it.*
> —Bobo, Kendall, and Max, 2003 (p. 10)

INTRODUCTION

This chapter focuses on various methods of HIV-related community organizing—that is, organizing and mobilizing people to engage in social and political action on their own behalf or on behalf of others in order to achieve HIV services and policies that are appropriate, accessible, and adequate. Readers will analyze different approaches to mobilizing people for collective action, challenging oppressive structures and processes, building organizational capacity, implementing action plans, and generating power in the community. The chapter includes content on the analysis of power structures; the formulation of action strategies; the use of tactics involving persuasion, consensus, and conflict; the organization, implementation, and evaluation of community campaigns; the use of political and media advocacy; and the relationship of social and political action to contemporary issues that affect oppressed and disadvantaged communities and community members.

There are scores of books concerning community organizing—what it is, what it is not, and how to do it. This chapter will be far from definitive; that is not its purpose. I hope to provide some basic ideas common to the many perspectives of community organizing and social advocacy. I infuse this discussion with HIV context; it is impossible to do HIV advocacy that does not include community organizing and notions of power, gender, race, and class. The day when social workers stop fighting and advocating for HIV issues is either the day the pandemic is over or the day social work ceases to be the best, most honorable profession in the world. I, of course, hope that the first happens and that the second never happens. Community organizing and social action have been a part of HIV work since the beginning, for direct practice, administrative, and community practice social workers. Of course, those most affected by the pandemic were not sitting on their hands waiting for activist social workers to rescue them; rather, histories of HIV activism document the die-ins, protest marches, and creation of grassroots programs by legendary

(Continued)

Acknowledgments: This chapter is dedicated to Felix Sirls, Paula Sirls, and to the memory of Michael Shernoff, Tracy St. Croix, and Roderick David ("Terry") Thomas (my brother).

HIV-positive activists such as Larry Kramer, Eric Sawyer, Michael Shernoff, Willis Green, and many others who inspired and taught us. These and other HIV-positive advocates set up the classic HIV social service and advocacy programs. The programs were brought into the world kicking and screaming, insisting that society and institutions not ignore them, not imagine them out of reality. Social action was the mouthpiece for those temporarily without a voice, and people did scream!

In this chapter, I provide a brief context for HIV-related community organizing, a conceptual foundation for HIV-related community organizing using social work frameworks, and a case study of grassroots advocacy in action by presenting the practice side of the establishment of legal syringe-exchange programs in Detroit, Michigan.

WHAT IS THE CONTEXT FOR HIV COMMUNITY ORGANIZING?

HIV-related community organizing has evolved with the pandemic and general response in almost a life-cycle fashion. As HIV has moved to the representation of a manageable, if expensive, chronic illness condition, the issues of service access and stigma surge forward. Most of the community organizing efforts now serve to hold ground and not lose resources or funding, as the main component of HIV care—the Ryan White CARE Act—continues to transform along with the HIV pandemic.

Early in the pandemic, activist organizations such as AIDS Coalition to Unleash Power (ACT UP), used social action tactics outlined by community organizer Saul Alinsky (1971) to achieve a profound societal transformation. Different entities forged powerful responses to HIV awareness, responsive funding for care, affordable care, support for care continuum, and development of a wraparound service system. The current context of community advocacy reflects challenges at three levels: individual, social, and structural. The current context of community organizing and grassroots advocacy also takes place within the medicalization of HIV, as discussed here.

Medicalization of HIV

Medicalization is a well-studied phenomenon that describes the process of social response and services as a physical illness becomes better understood and more treatable, with the locus of care shifting from community to institutions. The response shifts from informal, neighborhood-based, and grassroots to more formal, professionalized, institutionalized, and bureaucratic. The interactions move from being characterized by equality and balance to inequity and imbalance, despite medical professional admonitions to encourage active participation in care (Conrad & Schneider, 1992). Medicalization happened with HIV: Funding of HIV care shifted from community-based organizations to medical programs, and formulas for distribution of dollars favored the number of people in care. This resulted in a disconnection from the grassroots advocacy that had given birth to the services in the first place.

Advocacy and the Treatment/Prevention Divide

Consistently, medical treatment of HIV has overwhelmingly been funded at higher levels than prevention of HIV. While the treatment of HIV is currently located in hospitals, prevention of HIV has moved increasingly from paid to volunteer movements at the community level.

The community advisory panels that once provided direct access to the allocation of resources for HIV care under Title I of the Ryan White CARE Act (RWCA) requires far more resources for training and facilitation. Community advisory panels were not immune to contextual politics and preexisting conflicts between city and suburb, gay and heterosexual, rich and poor, and White and people of color. In moves to shift more resources to treatment and fewer resources to structural process that called for community involvement, decisions were eventually made that dismantled community advisory panels as resource allocation became more formulated, more streamlined, and more bureaucratized. With the transformation of RWCA from funder of last resort for comprehensive emergency care to funder for primary medical treatment and medication, fewer dollars were available for services and prevention. As treatment for HIV became more complex and more difficult to follow for all but the most persistent and better-educated community members, the need to expend scarce resources to educate community advisory groups dissipated.

At the same time, many of the early HIV-positive grassroots and community-based advocates have either died or wearied from the frontline battles, while their HIV-negative allies similarly retired or moved to other issues and areas. Ironically, while grassroots advocacy emerges in incredible form in developing countries, in the United States grassroots advocacy is increasingly becoming the primary activity of a few dedicated and typically unpaid individuals. Alternatively, activism appears to be concentrated into a few relentless national organizations—not grassroots or community-based at all. Outside of the epicenters of the pandemic (that is, New York, San Francisco, Miami, Chicago, and Los Angeles), grassroots advocacy is a challenge. This is obvious in rural areas.

The change in allocation of funding also resulted in the closing of many grassroots organizations, which were simply unprepared for the financial realities of running a professional organization. Many of these organizations were run and operated by grassroots community-based individuals; these organizations provided advocacy as well as care. However, with the demise of funding of advocacy programs, these programs also dried up.

Within urban communities, faith-based organizations have begun to address HIV, yet the focus is often purely on heterosexual service recipients and continues to reflect the experience of increasing HIV infections among African American women. The other part of the pandemic among African American communities—among men having sex with men—is often philosophically difficult for these organizations to address, and often advocacy is morphed into community empowerment interventions. There again, the emphasis is more on prevention and less on services.

Medicalization and the Delegitimization of Community Organization

In many ways, medicalization was a benefit to thousands of people living with HIV, because medical treatment is clearly needed. However, the consequences of medicalization included the invisibility of persons living with HIV; it turned them into "patients" rather than citizens and activists. Medicalization also quieted the attention to the social barriers to preventive care, to medical care, and to mental health resources, and to the structural inequities that encouraged the spread of HIV. Medicalization requires the person to ignore context issues (at least some of which could be addressed by comprehensive case management or advocacy) in order to receive care.

At one time, during the early years of the U.S. HIV pandemic, community organizing and grassroots advocacy were strengthened by a general sense of strategy, relationships forged under pressure, community-based resources, and a cohesive analysis of the problems faced. The lack of a comprehensive strategy today leaves organization and advocacy poised, but not ready. The lack of relationships leaves community organization and advocacy fragmented. The lack of resources leaves community-based organizations and grassroots advocacy exhausted. The lack of critical analyses of structural issues results in opportunities for citizen participation that is more of a token than truly participatory. This must change. True change can be accomplished using tried-and-true practices in community practice and community organization.

A CONCEPTUAL FOUNDATION FOR HIV-RELATED COMMUNITY ORGANIZING

> . . . whatever its other goals, [community practice] should be about promoting social justice and changing sources of injustice along the way. Social justice cannot occur without fundamental and continual change because we are clearly far away from having socially just institutions or communities. . . . Second, all forms of community practice ought to promote social participation and human health and well being and work to prevent the development of problems. . . . (Reed, 2005, p. 84).

Community organization and social advocacy compel citizens to experience meaning in their social conditions and experiences. Other macro practice methods, such as popular education or social history, promote discussion of the context of social problems and underscore the importance of historical perspective in the ways in which problems, power, and relationships are constructed over time. These methods also promote questioning of the relations of power and social inequity that shape and maintain current situations. However, community organization is a method for promoting democratization and is a "just practice" for the promotion of social change (Finn & Jacobson, 2008).

Weil and Gamble's (1994) models of community practice roughly organize eight types of community practice in scale from local neighborhood and community organizing to social movements (Table 10.1). Weil and Gamble encourage the use of comparative characteristics—ways of thinking about community practice—as desired outcomes, systems targeted for change, primary constituencies, scope of concern and social work roles. In this model, the forms of community organizing are located within the political/social action, coalition, and social movement models.

The second model—Rothman's (1996) revised "interweaving" community intervention model—proposes the interweaving of three dominant modes of community practice (social action, social planning, and locality development) to derive additional variants (planning/development, development/action, and action/planning). Rothman argues that the reality of community practice reflects ideal types with less frequency and mixed types of practice with greater frequency. Obviously, community organizing falls into Rothman's "social action" model of practice.

The importance and relevance of community organizing is—and has been—so clear in HIV advocacy. AIDS advocates are and were people who are HIV-infected or HIV-affected, and those allies who simply cannot stand by while human beings are left to die for no reason other than they are not considered as people worthy of love, compassion, respect, and help. Although the early AIDS advocates did not know to

Table 10.1. Models of Community Practice for Social Work (Gamble and Weil 1994)

Comparative Characteristics	Neighborhood and Community Organizing	Organizing Functional Communities	Community Social and Economic Development	Social Planning	Program Development and Community Liaison	Political and Social Action	Coalitions	Social Movements
Desired Outcome	Develop capacity of members to organize: change the impact of citywide planning and external development	Action for social justice focused on advocacy and on changing behaviors and attitudes; may also provide service	Initiate development plans from a grassroots perspective; prepare citizens to make use of social and economic investments	Citywide or regional proposals for action by elected body or human services planning councils	Expansion or redirection of agency program to improve community service effectiveness; organize new service	Action for social justice focused on changing policy or policy makers	Build a multi-organizational power base large enough to influence program direction or draw down resources	Action for social justice that provides a new paradigm for a particular population group or issue
System for Change	Municipal government; external developers, community members	General public; government institutions	Banks, foundations; external developers; community citizens	Perspectives of community leaders; perspectives of human services leaders	Funders of agency programs; beneficiaries of agency services	Voting public, elected officials, inactive or potential participants	Elected officials; foundations; government institutions	General public; political systems
Primary Constituency	Residents of neighborhood, parish or rural county	Like-minded people in a community, regions, nation or across the globe	Low-income, marginalized or oppressed population groups in a city or region	Elected officials; social agencies and interagency organizations	Agency board of administrators; community representatives	Citizens in a particularly political jurisdiction	Organizations that have a stake in a particular issue	Leaders and organizations able to create new visions and images

call themselves "human rights activists," that was their framework. HIV is not *only* an illness, but a social and political construct, a creation of powerful people to attack less powerful people.

While community organizing and grassroots advocacy are often used interchangeably (see Table 10.2), the concepts are synonymous only in a few limited situations. Many community organizers and researchers distinguish organizing and advocacy as follows:

HIV advocacy involves both community organizing and grassroots advocacy. Community organizing and grassroots advocacy share much in common. Both are located on a community organizing continuum (Figure 10.1) that tends toward challenging existing power relationships. Sometimes they are used as specific tactics or strategies depending on the situation and the problem.

In the case study on syringe exchange that follows this discussion, a small team of committee members combined a tactical use of grassroots advocacy with community organization. We did this because we found a very simple leverage point in the larger, overarching goal of securing legal syringe exchange. We certainly could have hit the ground with protest marches, public education rallies, and highly visible publicity. Our review and critical analysis of the situation revealed what was potentially a much simpler solution—amendment of a local ordinance—that would obtain the same result, provided we could establish a sense of trust and problem solving among key individuals. We used grassroots advocacy to convene community discussions and dialogue groups, then tactically moved to a more proactive community organizing strategy. Had the community organizing strategy not been effective, we were prepared to return to a more expansive grassroots advocacy model.

Case Study: Creating Legal Syringe-Exchange Programs in Detroit Michigan: Modifying the Detroit City Council Drug Paraphernalia Ordinance, 1994–1996

The need for syringe-exchange programs had been established by national reviews of the efficacy of syringe exchange in reducing HIV infections among injection drug users, their sexual and/or drug partners, and any infants born as a result of sexual encounters between injection drug users and their sexual and drug partners. Not only had the dramatic reductions in HIV infection rates among injection drug users been established, but also there

Table 10.2.   Characteristics of Community Organizing and Grass Roots Advocacy

Community Organizing	Grassroots Advocacy
Builds permanent community organizations that can address systemic and structural issues.	Can change power relationships but does not simultaneously empower poor and disempowered people.
Creates legitimate safe space and power base for organization workers and those whom are represented.	Issues are usually raised on behalf of people affected by policies and practices, but not raised *by* people who are affected.
Provides space and opportunity for disempowered, disenfranchised people to practice skills of citizenship and leadership.	
Leads to individual and collective empowerment and enables consistent challenge to established institutions in power within a given society.	

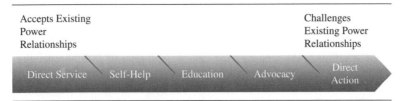

Figure 10.1   The forms of community organizing
Source: From Bobo, Kendall, and Max, 2003, p. 11. Copyrighted material reprinted with permission from the National Association of Social Workers, Inc.

were no indications that new injection drug users were being created by the presence of needle-exchange programs (NEPs) or syringe-exchange programs (SEPs). Ironically, federal funding for needle- or syringe-exchange programs existed very briefly; the funds were effectively extinguished through the efforts of Senator Jessie Helms from North Carolina. Oddly, while funds to *support* NEPs or SEPs were eliminated, federal funds to *study* the efficacy or success of such NEPs or SEPs remained flush and available.

Detroit was among many urban areas where informal and illegal syringe exchange was conducted by individuals who either purchased or received donated syringes, funds to purchase large quantities of syringes, or by anonymous donations from hospitals and clinics. Armed with red "sharps" containers, Tom McNitt (recognized as one of the first needle-exchange providers in Detroit) and other individuals would operate small NEPs or SEPs from the trunks of their cars, usually in neighborhoods or locations historically frequented by injecting drug users. Frequently, but not always, the operators of the exchanges were recovering drug users or living with HIV or both. While most were male, there were a few females involved as well. The need was overwhelming, and resources were always scarce, and the possibility of attack and assault was a possibility. Law enforcement was contextual and discretionary; some officers knew of the NEPs or SEPs and opted to arrest neither injection drug users nor the exchangers (the possession of syringes without prescription was a clear violation of the local municipal ordinance). Other officers would regularly arrest or roust those who had come to exchange syringes and the service providers. Clearly, however, it became evident that only a massive, consistent response and provision of syringes would lead to detectable reductions in HIV consistent with the results in other communities. While an increasing number of individuals operated exchanges, this was not seen as a viable, reasonable, and sustainable response by activists and practitioners in health care.

While professionals in the fields of HIV, sexually transmitted infections, and substance use expressed concerns and some quiet endorsement of NEPs and SEPs, they were expressly prohibited from taking action to remedy the situation. The task of identifying the problems, securing support from grassroots and relevant stakeholder groups, developing the strategy, and providing the resources for presentation and formal proposal of ordinance change were all left to community residents, organizations, and activists.

The efforts to secure modifications in the syringe-exchange ordinance in Detroit, Michigan, provide a case study of grassroots and community organizing approaches that led to substantive change in Michigan. The initial efforts to begin discussions of syringe exchange were initiated by a grassroots ad hoc group of individuals led by Tracy St. Croix, an HIV-positive former injection drug user who believed that she acquired HIV through use of shared needles and syringes. She formed a small grassroots committee called "Point of Exchange," later "Point of Change" (POC). Founding members included David Withers, actively involved in informal syringe exchange as an employee of the Pontiac Lighthouse, Robert "Bob" Beattie, an employee of the state of Michigan department of community health who joined the initiative as an individual, not as a representative of the state of Michigan (at the time, the state of Michigan followed the lead of then governor John Engler, who stated vociferously that he was against any formulation or approval of syringe exchange). Another active member of Point of Change was George Gaines, then the executive director of Detroit Central City Community Mental Health, and a former director of Detroit Department of Health and long-standing health-related community outreach specialist, who in part ushered in the "bleach and teach" needle and works cleaning and disinfecting programs of the 1980s. Another member (this chapter's author) was invited to participate, given his association and relationship with Dr. Peter Lurie, then an acknowledged expert in the national and international evaluation of syringe-exchange programs and author or coauthor of six commissioned evaluations of the effectiveness of syringe-exchange programs. Other members participated, but these were the core members of the ad hoc group. Other critical stakeholders who were involved but not core members of the Point of Change included Shirley McIntyre, long-standing community activist and founder of many community-based responses to HIV and AIDS in the early 1990s, including Community Health Outreach Workers (CHOW), and Harry Simpson, then the executive director of Community Health Awareness Group (C-HAG).

The principal issue preventing the use of formal syringe exchange in the city of Detroit was found not to be a state statute but rather a municipal city of Detroit drug paraphernalia ordinance that identified material like syringes as contraband—leading to arrest and incarceration of the person on whom they were located. The immediate strategy deployed was to develop and propose modifications to the drug paraphernalia ordinance that would permit the legal use of syringe-exchange programs, or at least provide an exception for syringe-exchange programs within the existing ordinance.

Member George Gaines reported the most extensive experience with the process of changing and modifying the ordinance, and he provided extensive and accurate history of how the ordinance was created and generated. He also provided the rough outline of strategy that would need to be followed in order to change or modify the ordinance:

- Ordinance revision modified by common council, based upon recommendation by designated task force
- Identification of appropriate due diligence (for example, monitoring and regulation by designated municipal body, as in the city department of health)
- Generation of relevant policy and procedure
- Review of need for revision by task force
- Presentation of evidence
- Public task force hearing and presentation
- Confirming and resolving tactics for deployment
  - Having council members speak to council members
  - Having political opposition members (for example, Republican White males) explain how and why they came to understand and then endorse syringe-exchange ordinances
  - Including city attorneys from other states (for example, New Haven, Connecticut) who had expertise in writing appropriate legislation for syringe-exchange programs (who would bring examples of ordinance)
  - Bringing in external experts from the United States

- Discussing the issue before city council
- Developing consensus among stakeholder community
- Recruiting allies to address the issue
- Identifying successful experiences elsewhere (for example, New Haven, Connecticut)
- Clarifying need and concern for legal syringe-exchange programs

The initial meetings of POC were to outline the basic points of inquiry and attack. We met initially in the basement of Friends Alliance, an HIV service organization located in Ferndale, Michigan. To secure the active participation of the most experienced and knowledgeable member of the group (Gaines), many of the meetings were held in the boardroom of Detroit Central City Community Mental Health Services, Inc. (DCCCMH). The meetings were held between 1992 and 1994, and the action was deployed between 1995 and 1996.

During the process, it was decided that a data-based presentation needed to be introduced to the city council, raising concern about the increasing rates of HIV and AIDS among injection drug users, stating the multiplier effect of HIV among injection drug users, and providing three brief scenarios for the council's consideration:

1. Scenario A: Make no change to the ordinance, and witness dramatic increases in HIV infection rates in three related risk groups in the city of Detroit.
2. Scenario B: Completely eliminate the ordinance, witness dramatic decreases in HIV infection rates in three related risk groups in the city of Detroit, and encounter massive unforeseen consequences.
3. Scenario C: Provide a modest revision or amendment to the ordinance, decriminalizing possession of syringes without prescription to people who would show ID cards signifying their membership in a licensed NEP or SEP.

The five-minute presentation ended with a request for a public hearing on the matter, which was granted by the chair of the respective committee. Tellingly, support for review of the drug paraphernalia ordinance (scenario C) came from a member of the city council whose father was the author of the paraphernalia ordinance as a former member of the city council. He indicated that he appreciated our understanding of the rationale behind the initial presentation of the ordinance, and indicated that both he and his father supported the need to modify the current ordinance to exempt participants in legal syringe-exchange programs from prosecution and arrest. With this endorsement, common council unanimously agreed to a public hearing on the matter.

The public hearing was scheduled for six months after our presentation. At this point, the committee moved to plan, organize, and orchestrate a one-hour meeting to support a modest change to the ordinance (scenario C). This modest change would leave the wording of the ordinance intact but add a statement of modification exempting participants in licensed syringe-exchange programs from arrest and prosecution if they were in possession of empty syringes.[1] It was the intent of the committee not only to ensure approval of an amended ordinance at that meeting, but to move to implementation of the amended ordinance as quickly as possible. To do this, the committee reviewed instances of effective and ineffective community presentations and public actions in the city of Detroit

---

[1]However, if these same individuals possessed illicit narcotics as well as syringes (including dried drug residue in the syringe) they would be arrested and subject to prosecution.

from 1970 to 1996. We found that so often in the past, public hearings led to approval of changes in concept. However, the lack of follow-through actions led to nothing being done. Movement from approval in concept or in principle required drafting of legally reviewed and vetted language. City council would simply not adopt or approve ordinances that would not survive a legal review. Beyond this, changes in ordinances might also require changes or action in other designated or determined city offices or municipal departments. Our study of past experiences led to the conclusion that without a legally worded, rendered, and vetted ordinance and a clear analysis of actions and procedures required of relevant service systems and sectors, the advocacy effort would fail to yield implementable policy and programs.

The committee determined that the success of the initiative lay in preparing an extraordinary public hearing that would go far beyond the typical public appeals for support and need for change. We determined that our successful presentation would yield several outcomes:

- Support for the initiative from a wide body of affected individuals, stakeholder organizations that supported the initiative, organizations that expressed real concerns about the program but who would support a six-month trial period for enactment of the ordinance
- Presentation and discussion of the model ordinance in New Haven, Connecticut, by New Haven City council members: one initially supportive and one initially nonsupportive of the ordinance
- Research and support of the ordinance by a respected medical professional outside the state of Michigan
- Preparation of wording and language of the modified drug paraphernalia ordinance exempting participants in legal, licensed syringe-exchange programs from prosecution under ordinance, while excluding Council and municipal governments from any possible legal liability or action
- Presentation of an established and approved protocol and procedure for city health department provision of licensed syringe-exchange programs (based upon protocols developed and implemented by New Haven City Health Department)

Thus began six months of exhaustive planning and preparation on the part of the small handful of volunteer committee members as well as courageous allies in the highest levels of Detroit Health Department administration—then director Cynthia Taueg and HIV services coordinator Loretta Davis-Satterla made public pronouncements encouraging the need for syringe-exchange programs. We secured funding—about $9,000—from Earl "Skip" Schipper, then the executive director of the Michigan AIDS Fund, to fly in council members and legal researchers from New Haven, Connecticut. We also flew in John Newmeyer, a physician from San Francisco, California, who was a principal in establishing the Haight Ashbury Health Clinic and the prolific author of *Big City News,* a monthly newsletter that provided in-depth analysis of HIV policies and services, including extensive research on the impact of San Francisco's own well-established syringe-exchange programs. We were fortunate that Peter Lurie, physician researcher and author of the several federally funded studies on syringe exchange was residing in Southeast Michigan during this time and agreed to make a brief presentation of relevant research findings.

Contrary to the advice of many advocates, we decided not to engage or involve the media in any way, due to the inability to control the content, timing, and nature of news reports and analysis. It was decided that media would find out about the situation after the fact and that none of the Point of Change committee members would be identified as a spokesperson; the only spokespersons would be from the administration of the health departments and Detroit City Council.

The order of presentation was extensively reviewed and revised. It was again determined that POC committee members have no speaking role or part, aside from a brief acknowledgment by the city council chairperson of the committee. Instead, the chair read from the agenda, intensely prepared by the POC committee. The speakers list included physicians Lurie and Newmeyer, who first reviewed the literature and research on syringe-exchange programs. They were followed by New Haven City Council members who related their experience—and the impact on HIV infection rates – of the syringe-exchange ordinance in their city. Harry Simpson, from Community Health Awareness Group, made brief comments and presented recovering and active HIV-positive and HIV-negative injection drug users. These individuals provided public testimony on the importance of syringe-exchange programs from those at greatest risk of HIV infection. The brief presentations were practiced and rehearsed several times, and efforts were successful in ensuring that presenters were neatly dressed, easy to find, not actively using during the time of presentation, and spoke from scripts without deviation.

After these presentations, council members agreed the issue was important and agreed that the ordinance needed to be changed, but were concerned that there was neither wording nor external legal counsel for the ordinance. They were also concerned that there appeared to be neither a strategy nor entity that could provide appropriate licensing of syringe-exchange programs.

At this point (as per our planning), the New Haven legal counsel raised his hand, stood up and handed out draft copies of a prospective ordinance revision for the city of Detroit. He agreed to speak then and there with Detroit City Council legal counsel (and city of Detroit corporate council) to assist in immediate development of a legally binding ordinance revision.

This was followed by a comment from an audience participant, none other than the director of the Detroit Health Department who (as per our planning) then provided public support of the city health department for the initiative and also provided to council members a sample legally vetted protocol for recruiting and licensing syringe-exchange programs in the city of Detroit.

By voice vote and acclamation, Detroit City Council passed changes in the ordinance pending incorporation and approval of the new wording, and they agreed to work with the health department to rapidly implement and deploy syringe-exchange licensure. By the end of the meeting, it was clear that the ordinance changes would happen and that the stakeholders—Detroit City Council, New Haven City Council members, and the Detroit Health Department—would ensure enactment and implementation of the policy. The task complete, Point of Change committee members quietly withdrew, and within several months, mission completed, dissolved as an organization. Within one month of the public hearing, the first licensed syringe-exchange programs began. Per our commitment, six months afterward a small community group of stakeholders reviewed the progress and documentation of effort. Not a single syringe was found on the ground in any identified area of Detroit. Over 100,000 syringes had been exchanged. No one could identify new injection drug users created by the exchanges. News coverage of the syringe-exchange programs were limited to a few bylines, then disappeared entirely within several weeks of passage of the new ordinance. Within one year of the establishment of ordinances, HIV infection rates of injection drug users dropped from 11.5 per 100,000 to less than 4 per 100,000. Licensed syringe-exchange programs in the city of Detroit now reflect standard of care without controversy or discussion.

Personal Perspective

1995 Commentary by HIV-positive (and recovering IDU) community activist, Ms. Tracy St. Croix (born 1957, died 1995), compiled from her notes and letters.

"Point of Change" was founded in 1993. Tom McNitt, the founder, saw a need for prevention services for injection drug users (IDUs) that was not being met by any existing agency in Southeastern Michigan. Over the course of the following year he gathered support from people involved in AIDS prevention, substance use, and other interested persons. In October of 1994 Point of Change became a non-profit corporation in the state of Michigan and was registered with the Michigan Attorney General's Office as a charitable trust.

The organizational objectives of Point of Change, as taken from the organization's bylaws, are as follows:

• Support a harm-reduction model of behavior for IDUs.
• Establish and support a Needle Exchange Program (NEP).
• Act as a referral source for IDUs seeking health, mental health, or primary needs services.
• Advocate for and build community acceptance of a harm-reduction model of behavior for IDUs.
• Support and advocate for legislation and/or local ordinances which will further the purposes of Point of Change, and/or support and advocate for the repeal of those laws and/or ordinances which will impair the viability of the aforementioned purposes and objectives.
• Collect meaningful statistical data and general information on the effectiveness of NEPs and harm reduction model of behavior for IDUs.

At this time, 1995, Point of Change is funded solely through private donations. 1994 donations . . . totaled approximately $750.

The first quarter of 1995 brought many changes for Point of Change. Creative differences within the organization led to major changes within our board of directors. This severely impaired both out financial status and our ability to staff our site. While we had been operating for a short time in the city of Pontiac, we felt that we were no longer in a position to provide consistently scheduled syringe exchange and the additional services that we feel are essential for true harm reduction. As a result of these setbacks, we have had to temporarily suspend exchange and have revised our action plan.

Our goal is to be operating on regularly scheduled hours at two locations in the Detroit area beginning June 1, 1995. We have developed a strong base of community support, and are committed to providing consistent service. Our biggest problem seems to be the one which plagues all NEPs—WE DON'T HAVE ENOUGH MONEY! Our board or directors is in the process of implementing fundraising strategies, but a stock of available syringes and additional supplies (cookers, alcohol wipes, etc.) would help immensely. . . . We are anxious to provide this desperately needed service to IDUs in Southeastern Michigan and quickly and effectively as is possible.

CONCLUSIONS

Summing up, community organizing is an important model of community practice and an important tool in social work and human services. There are many paradigms describing the range of approaches within community practice. Two common models of community practice are regularly used in social work community practice texts, and there are many variants of these models. The intent is neither to pit the two models against each other nor provide a critique and review of them. Rather, the models are interesting ways to think deeply and contextually about community practice.

The case study of syringe exchange included in this chapter shows one successful example of community-based grassroots advocacy in the HIV field. The history of HIV prevention and services is peppered with such examples of policy change brought about by consistent and strategic pressure from those who are most affected and most vulnerable, in partnership with allies in agencies and academia.

REFERENCES

Alinsky, S. (1971). *Rules for radicals: A practical primer for realistic radicals*. New York: Vintage Books.

Bobo, K., Kendall, J., & Max, S. (2003). *Organize! Organizing for social change: Midwest academy manual for activists* (3rd ed.). Santa Ana, CA: Seven Locks Press.

Conrad, P. & Schneider, J.W. (1992). *Deviance and medicalization: From badness to sickness* (Expanded ed.). Philadelphia: Temple University Press.

Finn, J., & Jacobson, M. (2008). *Just practice: A social justice approach to social work*. Pesota, IA: Eddie Bowers Publishing, Inc.

Gamble, D., & Weil, M. (1994). Citizen participation. *Encyclopedia of social work* (10th ed., Vol. 1, pp. 483–494). Silver Spring, MD; National Association of Social Workers.

Reed, B. G. (2005). Theorizing in community practice: Essential tools for building community, promoting social justice, and implementing social change. In M. Weil (Ed.), *Handbook of community practice* (pp. 84–102). Thousand Oaks, CA: Sage Publications.

Rothman, J. (1996). The interweaving of community intervention approaches. Published simultaneously in *Journal of Community Practice* 3(3/4), 69–99, and Marie Weil (Ed.), *Community practice: Conceptual models* (pp. 69–99). New York: Haworth Press, Inc.

Chapter Eleven

HIV-RELATED POLITICAL AND LEGISLATIVE INTERVENTION

Gary Bailey

INTRODUCTION
Paulo Freire (2005), the Brazilian educator and social change activist, said in *Therapy for Liberation:* First, we *see* the problem or situation lived in by ourselves and others; second, we *analyze* the factors (the personal, cultural, and institutional) that contribute to the problem; third, we must *act* to change the problems or situations. As the tension in deciding among critical social welfare needs escalates, as a profession and as individuals, we must be at the table where policy decisions are made in order to determine priorities and identify strategies to meet them.

SOCIAL WORKER AS CHANGE AGENT

Staying current with both problems and solutions allows us to advocate for change, provide feedback and guidance to elected and appointed officials, and professionally negotiate the systems in which we practice. This chapter seeks to help individuals who are on the front lines working in the HIV field to:

- Appreciate the role of the social worker as a change agent
- Develop and understand one's own values and strengths as an advocate and social activist within the context of one's work
- Gain an understanding of case-to-cause advocacy and learn how individuals can intervene in systems to create positive social and organizational change
- Recognize the effects of racism, heterosexism, sexism, ageism, ableism, and other forms of oppression
- Develop understanding of social action at various levels: personal, cultural and institutional

---

Acknowledgments: I thank my friends and colleagues at the AIDS Action Committee, Boston, Massachusetts, particularly Executive Director Rebecca Hague, for their hard work and leadership in the HIV field, as evidenced by the vignette that they have provided. I thank my partner, Rick McCarthy, for his willingness to continue to sacrifice as I go about doing my work, and finally, I acknowledge all of those friends and colleagues who are living with HIV.

- Develop knowledge of the role and responsibility of government entities in meeting the basic human needs of individuals and families
- Understand the role of advocacy in influencing policy outcomes
- Understand the role of advocacy in influencing resource allocation decisions within social institutions.

Social workers have worked in direct services and on the policy level since the early days of HIV and AIDS (Aronstein & Thompson, 1998). During the ensuing decades of the pandemic, the social work profession has provided leadership in the response to ever-changing funding, epidemiology, prevention, and treatment options for persons infected and affected by HIV. Given the reality that HIV was initially affecting disenfranchised populations (for example, sex workers, homeless persons, substance users, men who have sex with men (MSM), and people of color), programs serving persons with HIV were helping people manage not only a disease, but also a disease that was significantly stigmatized (Brennan, 1996). For example, certain modes of transmission (for example, intravenous drug use, homosexual sexual contact), was translated into negative views of all persons living within these stigmatized communities. At the societal level, HIV stigma has been manifested in laws, policies, and overall negative public discourse (Junius & Tomaszewski, 2002). For example, as a profession, we have spoken out against:

- Mandatory testing of newborns, because that translates to mandatory testing of women
- Named-based reporting and mandated partner notification, because it challenges the core values and ethics of our profession
- The sole use of abstinence-only education, by stressing the importance and benefit of fact-based sexuality education
- Antigay civil rights regulations, policies, or legislation, because such actions select a group of individuals and treat them as unequal citizens

As social workers, we recognize that persons infected and affected by HIV continue to face discrimination in employment, military service, housing, access to health services, social and community programs, and basic civil and human rights (National Association of Social Workers, 2003). As educators, service providers, and advocates, social workers have been and will continue to be an integral part of prevention and treatment in the HIV pandemic.

Civil society is the social fabric that connects individuals, families, institutions, and businesses to one another. Advocacy is a set of hands-on technical skills and practices needed to effectively press for change. It is also the foundation of active citizenship and helps to create civil society.

Organizations are the primary way through which ordinary people can make their voices heard. We should focus more of our efforts on strengthening organizations' ability to represent and serve their constituents. This is especially true of AIDS service organizations (ASOs).

Advocacy is a process through which ordinary people learn to participate in decision making at all levels. Identifying priorities, crafting a strategy, stepping forward, taking action, and achieving results are critical steps to finding one's voice, making oneself heard, and shaping one's future.

Where advocacy assumes that people have rights, and those rights are enforceable, social action involves a coordinated and sustained effort to achieve institutional change to meet a need, solve a social problem, or correct an injustice to improve and/or enhance the quality of human life and individual well-being (Barker 2003).

At every step, it is important to engage local partners working on local issues and initiatives. These nonprofit organizations address a broad range of issues of their own, advocating on behalf of their constituents, connecting people, or providing services where the government is not able to do so. Social service organizations, think tanks, watchdog groups, and consumer and business associations all play critical roles in helping people make their communities better places to live.

Advocacy works to give nonprofit organizations the tools, skills, and resources they need to get what we call a "seat at the table" alongside government and business in decisions affecting public life. By a *seat at the table,* we mean that the nonprofit sector is seen as a trusted, influential, and permanent partner in public decision making. Many of these efforts occur at the initiative and direction of professional social workers, or it may occur through the efforts of individuals directly affected by the problem or policy change.

One of the most important advocacy tools available to social work is legislative advocacy: that is, working through the local, state, and federal lawmaking and policymaking systems to effect social change and to develop and fund social programs. That can mean supporting proposed bills so that they become laws, but often it means opposing proposals so that they do not become law. Social workers, in their roles as community-based case managers and agency administrators, working in partnership with persons with HIV, are in an excellent position to work in partnership with their constituents to testify to what is needed and workable in the communities. To do so, they need to know the specific techniques of legislative advocacy.

WHAT ARE SOME OF THE KEY ISSUES IN LEGISLATIVE ADVOCACY?

Individuals who are working in the HIV arena should learn the formal legislative process: laws, budgets, and regulations. They must develop an understanding of the informal means by which policy is made, learn to assess how power and influence affects the legislative process, recognize ethical issues in legislative advocacy, and develop their advocacy skills. Also very important is an appreciation for the role that the media plays in shaping policy and policy debate.

Activists advocate for fair and effective HIV policy at the city, state, and federal levels. As advocates, we focus primarily on four major policy areas affecting HIV: prevention, disparities, privacy, and funding.

1. *Prevention, education and science.* Effective prevention and education for HIV are often controversial. In recent years, prevention has become more ideologically driven, even though science-based prevention has been proven effective.

2. *Racial and ethnic disparities in health care.* From the data, it is clear that persons living with and affected by HIV are largely from historically disenfranchised populations. Disparities based on historical discrimination, the stigma of living with HIV, and the slow pace of government response and public financing are found globally. An issue where these merge is seen in access to care. In the United States, people of color are more

likely than Whites to be uninsured and depend on Medicaid and other publicly funded health care programs (Kaiser, 2004). As a group, women's access to health care is limited. Women overall, and low-income women in particular, have lower health insurance coverage and less stable coverage (Kaiser, 2004). And, as we have seen with the access to HIV medications, more people with HIV are living and remain in the workforce, presenting concerns about health care access and provision, disability issues, and private health insurance for employees, employers, the general population, and the government. Health care disparities, access to care, and continuity of care have a direct effect on persons living with HIV.

3. *Privacy and confidentiality.* Privacy and confidentiality are fundamental concerns for everyone with health issues, particularly for people with HIV, in light of the stigma and taboo that continue to surround HIV.

4. *Paying for it.* Although there exists a patchwork of public programs available to help people with HIV pay for their treatment, this is an area where most of the debate and advocacy occur: making sure that the funds are there to do the necessary work. David Harvey (former executive director of AIDS Alliance for Children, Youth, and Families) wrote that federal funding for HIV prevention, intervention, and care services, as well as research, is seemingly a patchwork of policies that are part of other administrative policy, regulatory, and legislative decisions (Harvey, 2002). Social workers understand patchwork; we understand that macro practice calls for looking at the whole picture or the whole person and seeing the strengths, the needs, and the necessary recourse. That is why our work and our response to HIV address all persons and all populations.

HOW DOES THE SYSTEM WORK?

In order for advocates to affect the social service system, they must understand how it works. Many individuals have not thought about some of the terms used to describe government functions since they took social studies or civics classes early in their lives. Questions arise such as: how are state and federal systems different, and how are they similar? What is the difference between state and federal legislative government? Most of the advocacy work of ASOs is done at the state level, but it is a good idea to know who your representatives are on both the state and federal levels and where action is being taken on issues that matter to you. A quick review of these terms is a good place to start. Here is a basic primer that may prove helpful before beginning your own advocacy efforts:

- *State legislative government.* Generally, on the state level, you have a representative and a senator who are working for you in your state legislature, which consists of two branches: the state house of representatives and the state senate. In the state's house of representatives, one of your state representatives represents *you*. In the state senate, one of your state senators represents *you*.

- *Federal legislative government or the U.S. Congress.* On the federal level, you get one representative and two senators on Capitol Hill at the Capitol Building (that's the White dome in Washington, D.C.) The U.S. Congress consists of two branches: the U.S. House of Representatives and the U.S. Senate. In the U.S. House of Representatives, one representative (or congressman/-woman) represents you. (Depending on the population of your state, you may have more than one official in the U.S. House of Representatives.) In the U.S. Senate, two senators represent you (and everyone else in your state).

LEGISLATIVE ADVOCACY

Meeting with a member of Congress or congressional staff is a very effective way to convey a message about a specific legislative issue. Following are some suggestions to consider when planning a visit to a congressional office.

- *Plan your visit carefully*. Be clear about what it is you want to achieve; determine in advance which member or committee staff member you need to meet with to achieve your purpose.
- *Make an appointment*. When attempting to meet with a member, contact the appointment secretary or scheduler. Explain your purpose and who you represent. It is easier for congressional staff to arrange a meeting if they know what you wish to discuss and your relationship to the area or interests represented by the member.
- *Be prompt and patient*. When it is time to meet with a member, be punctual and patient. It is not uncommon for a Congressman or Congresswoman to be late or to have a meeting interrupted due to the member's crowded schedule. If interruptions do occur, be flexible. When the opportunity presents itself, continue your meeting with a member's staff.

TRICKY TERMINOLOGY

Congressman/-woman/-person. At the federal level, both houses together are known as the *Congress,* so it may seem that technically everyone in the Congress is a Congressperson. Not really. Traditionally, when we say "Congressman" or "Congresswoman," we really mean U.S. Representative.

Representative. While the term *representative* may be used in a general way to mean any person representing another in government, as in "the president is a representative of the people," it can also be used to mean something more specific. Officials in the U.S. House of Representatives or in state houses of representatives may all be referred to as "Representative." Accordingly, they should be distinguished from one another by referring to them as "U.S. representatives" or "state representatives," respectively.

Senator. The term *senator* refers to both officials in the U.S. Senate in Washington, D.C. (think Kennedy and Kerry) and to the state senators who represent you in your state capitol. For example, everyone in Massachusetts has three senators: two in Washington, D.C., and one in Boston. No matter how many people are in a state, a state still gets just two senators on Capitol Hill in Washington. U.S. senators are not referred to as "Representative," although we may say something like, "Senator Kerry *represents* the state of Massachusetts in the U.S. Senate."

Legislators are called on to make a variety of difficult decisions regarding the funding of HIV and AIDS surveillance, prevention, treatment, and research programs. These decisions can involve domestic activities or international financial aid. To legislators, voting on these issues requires making tough choices regarding allocation of scarce resources. To persons living with HIV, however, these

(Continued)

legislative choices are deeply important to the quality of their lives, or even to life itself. Traditionally, legislators make decisions on political grounds, and, of course, they are accountable to the electorate in a democracy. Consequently, legislators pay attention to local constituents (who elect the representatives) and sometimes to special-interest groups (who offer financial support). These legislators, of course, understand that they must make difficult judgments with an open mind and without the involvement of conflicts of interest, but are there deeper moral and ethical considerations that ought to influence their decisions? Although there exists no code of ethics, per se, for legislators that dictates taking moral considerations into account, legislators should be motivated by ethical principles. Ethical considerations, moreover, are most important when decisions have powerful effects on the health and lives of people. Voting on HIV and AIDS funding provides a classic illustration of the importance of ethical values in the legislative process for some of the major AIDS funding decisions that legislators face, both domestically and globally; the effects that these legislative choices have on persons living with HIV, their families, and their communities are usually the focus of our individual and organizational advocacy efforts. ASOs also have worked to create a set of ethical guidelines that can help legislators in making the hard choices they face (Legislative Ethics in the HIV/AIDS Pandemic, 2004).

- *Be prepared.* Whenever possible, bring to the meeting information and materials supporting your position or request. Members are required to take positions on many different issues. In some instances, a member may lack important details about the pros and cons of a particular matter. It is therefore helpful to share with the member information and examples that demonstrate clearly the impact or benefits associated with a particular issue or piece of legislation. Remember to also bring paper and a writing implement with you to the meeting(s).
- *Be political.* Members of Congress want to represent the best interests of their district or state. Wherever possible, demonstrate the connection between what you are requesting and the interests of the member's constituency. If possible, describe for the member how you or your group can be of assistance to him or her. Where it is appropriate, remember to ask for a commitment. Remember to not only register to vote and to help register others to vote, but also *to vote.*
- *Be responsive.* Be prepared to answer questions or provide additional information in the event the member expresses interest or asks questions. Follow up the meeting with a brief thank-you letter that outlines the different points covered during the meeting, and send along any additional information and materials requested.
- *Dress for success.* Appearances *do* matter when you are meeting with your elected officials at the city, state, or federal level. In other environments, it may not be as important. However, it does make sense to dress your best for the meeting, regardless of the dress code at your own organization, which may be much more informal. If you are in doubt about how to dress, it is best to err on the side of conservatism. It is much better to be overdressed than underdressed (or undressed). If you are not sure, check with the person who scheduled the meeting. Some basic suggestions are included here in the accompanying box.

Women's Interview Attire

Solid-color, conservative suit, dress, or pantsuit with coordinated blouse.

Moderate shoes. (A lot of walking is required when on the Hill. Comfort is important, but flip-flops or sneakers are not advised. If you wear them, bring shoes to change into.)

Limited, neat jewelry.

Neat, professional hairstyle.

Sparse makeup and perfume.

Conservatively manicured nails.

Portfolio or briefcase.

Men's Interview Attire

Solid-color, conservative suit or jacket.

Long-sleeve shirt and tie.

Dark socks, professional shoes.

Very limited jewelry.

Neat, professional hairstyle.

Limited aftershave.

Neatly trimmed nails.

Portfolio or briefcase.

(Doyle, 2009)

SOCIAL WORK RESPONSE

As social workers, whether we are providing HIV-related services or working in one of the many diverse practice settings, we should be working to ensure safe, confidential, and respectful contact with HIV-infected and HIV-affected persons or those who are vulnerable to HIV. As a profession working on behalf of individuals and community, social work has a long history of advocacy. Social workers organized in the early days of AIDS activism, spoke at the first congressional hearings held in 1983, and joined in the earliest ACT UP demonstrations. As a profession, we have spoken out against exclusionary research protocols and fought with letters, visits, and phone calls for funding and services. Social workers include those who testified at their statehouses and in the halls of Congress—about not only funding the much-needed medications, but also addressing the whole person through funding, counseling, prevention, and early and ongoing intervention services. Some fights were won only to be lost with a new administration or different funding formularies, but we have not backed down. As a profession, we were at the table helping to define the Americans with Disabilities Act, using it to challenge housing, work, and benefits discrimination. In the 1990s, we also worked with volunteers, colleagues, and friends to support Housing Opportunities for Persons with AIDS (HOPWA) and to ensure that female-specific symptoms and AIDS-defining illnesses were recognized. Many social workers worked to help pass the Ryan White CARE Act, the largest federal response to a public health crisis in the history of the United States. Social workers were joined by like-minded activists in allied health and mental health professions in the public efforts to challenge antiquated thinking on needle-exchange programs, in support of condom distribution, and rallying for the right to comprehensive sexuality education. An example of this is the successful Clean Needle Access Campaign in Massachusetts (see accompanying box).

CLEAN NEEDLE ACCESS CAMPAIGN IN MASSACHUSETTS

In 2005, the need for and benefit of increased access to clean needles was clear. The rate of HIV infection related to injection drug use hovered around 40 percent among all people living with HIV in the Commonwealth of Massachusetts, one of only three states in the nation in which it was illegal to purchase a syringe in a pharmacy without a prescription. In order to reduce the rate of new infections, the AIDS Action Committee (AAC) set as its number one priority the passage of legislation to repeal the requirement for a prescription to purchase hypodermic needles and syringes in pharmacies.

Believing that then governor Mitt Romney would veto the plan, the goal was to have the legislation pass both chambers by veto-proof margins. In Massachusetts that means support of two-thirds of the present and voting members in each chamber.

To achieve this goal, AAC formed and chaired the Massachusetts Pharmacy Access Campaign, a coalition of groups committed to removing the prescription requirement for needle sales. Campaign members included representatives from all stakeholder groups: AIDS service organizations, law enforcement, the pharmacy community, the substance use and recovery community, as well as many other public health and community-based organizations.

The campaign produced a briefing packet with fact sheets, copies of supportive editorials, and various supporting documents that outlined the basics about the bill. These packets were distributed to all members of the state legislature. As the campaign progressed, staff developed additional educational materials to address concerns, such as adequate disposal systems for syringes.

AAC maintained and monitored detailed lists of all state legislators to track votes and to ensure that key influential legislators had been contacted or visited by constituents in their district. This required increasing the constituent capacity in each legislative district through phone banks, e-mail, and individual phone calls.

Several bills proposing removing the prescription requirement were filed. In May 2005, the Joint Committee on Public Health held a hearing on these bills. The campaign presented more than five hours of testimony from people living with HIV, people with a history of injection drug use, pharmacists, public health officials, law enforcement officials, substance use and health care providers, academics, and local officials—notably two of the state's district attorneys.

As a result of this successful hearing, several bills were consolidated into one (H4176) and reported out of committee favorably in June. By October 2005, campaign members had visited or communicated with all of the 160 members of the House of Representatives. By November, the House leadership was encouraged by the level of support (90 of 160 members) and agreed to bring the legislation to the floor for a vote and seek a larger majority. The House of Representatives passed the pharmacy access bill by 115 to 37, a veto-proof majority.

The bill then went to the Massachusetts Senate for action. The campaign worked with key senators and staff to outline the benefits of the legislation and to formulate a strategy. In early February 2006, the coalition sponsored a legislative briefing, hosted by the Senate chairperson of the Joint Committee on Public Health, to educate members of the Senate on the issues, and supplemented with individual meetings. The Senate amended the bill to include an expanded disposal-system provision and additional criminal penalties for using a used needle as a weapon. A vote on the bill was delayed due to procedural maneuvers by a single senator. However, because of support from the Senate president's office, the bill was finally passed by the Senate in late June 2006.

Governor Romney vetoed the legislation over the Fourth of July weekend, but on July 14, 2006, the Massachusetts Senate and House of Representatives enacted the legislation over the governor's veto. The decriminalization provision of the law became effective immediately; pharmacies were authorized to begin sales on September 18, 2006. Social workers have continued to respond by coming together at meetings within the state and region to ensure that HIV stays on the radar and in the discussion.

CONCLUSIONS

What challenges do we face today that will continue with us for years to come? What is on the horizon? Health care access, the right to treatment and care, and limited resources for services translates to the social work profession's continued need for advocacy. Clearly, social workers have been and continue to be among the leaders in planning, advocacy, and translating knowledge of HIV and the myriad of related social welfare needs into practice solutions.

REFERENCES

Aronstein, D., & Thompson, B. (Eds.). (1998) *HIV and social work: A practitioner's guide* (p. xxiii). New York: Harrington Park Press.

Barker, R. L. (2003). *The social work dictionary* (5th ed). Washington, DC: NASW Press.

Brennan, J. (1996). Comprehensive case management with HIV clients. In C. D. Austin & R. W. McClelland (Eds.), *Case management practice.* Milwaukee, WI: Families International.

Doyle, A. (2009). *How to dress for an interview.* Retrieved June 8, 2009, from http://jobsearch .about.com/od/interviewattire/a/interviewdress.htm

Freire, P. (2005, Winter). Mental health care after capitalism. *Radical Psychology, 4*(2).

Harvey, D. (2002). Toward empowering social workers and consumers as HIV/AIDS policy makers: An editorial opinion. *Journal of HIV/AIDS and Social Services, 1*(3), 3. New York: Haworth Press.

Junius, J., & Tomaszewski, E. (2002). *HIV/AIDS stigma: Making the connections to discrimination and prejudice* [Factsheet]. Washington, DC: NASW.

Kaiser Family Foundation. (2004, January 9). *Implications of the new Medicare law for dual eligibles: 10 key questions and answers.* Retrieved February 18, 2004, from http://www.kff.org/ medicaid/loader.cfm?url=/commonspot/securtity/getfile.cfm&PageID=28805

Legislative Ethics in the HIV/AIDS Pandemic (2004). *Journal of Timely and Appropriate Care of People with HIV Disease, 1*(1), 4.

National Association of Social Workers. (2003). HIV and AIDS. *Social work speaks: National Association of Social Workers policy statement, 2003–2006* (6th ed., pp. 176–183). Washington, DC: NASW Press.

Chapter Twelve

HIV PREVENTION INNOVATIONS AND CHALLENGES

Peter A. Newman

INTRODUCTION

HIV prevention remains one of the most important areas in the field of HIV, intersecting direct practice, policy, research, and administration. HIV prevention continues to pose some of the most contentious challenges in health and social welfare. Despite increasing recognition of the synergistic goals of prevention and treatment for HIV, prevention often takes a backseat. Paradoxically, dramatic advances in HIV treatment have simultaneously aided prevention—by reducing the transmission of HIV among HIV-infected people who undergo testing and treatment (Castilla et al., 2005; UNAIDS, 2008)—and have further marginalized HIV prevention, as HIV is perceived to be less of a threat and prevention less of an imperative.

HIV INCIDENCE IN THE UNITED STATES UNCHANGED

A renewed focus on prevention is necessary if we are ever to curtail the HIV pandemic. In the United States alone, an estimated 55,000 to 58,500 people are HIV-infected each year (Hall et al., 2008). This estimate from the Centers for Disease Control and Prevention's recently revised statistics acknowledges greater annual HIV incidence for the past two decades than had been reported. The number of people becoming HIV-infected in the United States each year is 40 percent higher than previously thought (Hall et al., 2008). While significant gains have been made in HIV treatment for those who have access to it, there have not been parallel gains in prevention. Overall annual HIV incidence has remained the same in the United States for nearly two decades, but in the past 10 years alone, over half a million people have become HIV-infected.

To put the sobering challenges of HIV prevention in global perspective, for every one or two persons who newly gain access to HIV treatment, another five become infected (Cohen, 2008). This is clearly an unsustainable path if we are ever to stem this pandemic, treatment advances notwithstanding.

Acknowledgments: This chapter is dedicated to the memory of Tyrone, my first "buddy" at AIDS Action Committee in Boston in 1984, and to Steven Carter, 1963–1992 ("now the ears of my ears awake and now the eyes of my eyes are opened," e.e. cummings).

HIV TESTING

HIV testing is one of the cornerstones of HIV prevention. Persons who test positive for HIV largely reduce the sexual and syringe-sharing behaviors that might transmit HIV to others. Recent efforts in the United States have focused on expanding and mainstreaming HIV testing to facilitate increased testing, which is also a gateway to appropriate HIV treatment. Nevertheless, an estimated 233,000 people living with HIV in the United States do not know they are infected (*Morbidity and Mortality Weekly Report* [MMWR], 2008). In other words, more than one in five people living with HIV in the United States have never been diagnosed (MMWR, 2008). Furthermore, in 2005, more than one-third (38 percent) of persons newly diagnosed with HIV progressed to an AIDS diagnosis within one year (MMWR, 2008), which is indicative of a significant delay from HIV infection to detection of HIV. This statistic is particularly striking in a high-income country in which antiretroviral treatment is available—although not universally accessible—with the potential to significantly increase longevity and quality of life of persons living with HIV. Late diagnosis of HIV has a negative effect both on the individual's health and the overall epidemic. If individuals do not know they are HIV-infected, they do not have the opportunity to change their behavior based on knowledge of their diagnosis. Additionally, in the absence of a diagnosis, individuals are not accessing treatment, which has an important impact in reducing infectiousness and, in turn, HIV transmission. In fact, a substantial proportion of new HIV infections, among men who have sex with men (MSM) in particular, might occur in clusters when individuals are newly infected, highly infectious, do not know their status and have unprotected sex with multiple partners (Brenner et al., 2007). Expansion of new, more sensitive testing technologies and targeted, culturally appropriate opportunities for HIV testing and diagnosis remain a vital challenge for HIV prevention (MMWR, 2008; Rotheram-Borus, Newman, & Etzel, 2000).

VAST ETHNIC AND RACIAL DISPARITIES IN HIV

A powerfully important dimension of HIV in North America, particularly for social work, is the pandemic's vastly disproportionate impact on people of color and the poor (Centers for Disease Control and Prevention [CDC], 2008a, 2008b, 2008c; Robles & Stringer, 2006). Extreme disparities exist in U.S. infection rates among ethnic groups. African Americans comprise 13% of the population and the largest proportion (45%) of new HIV infections in 2006, with rates of new HIV infections more then seven times that of Whites (83.7 versus 11.5 new infections per 100,000 population) (CDC, 2008a). Latinos make up 13% of the population and 18% of new HIV infections in 2006; the rate of new HIV infections among Latinos in 2006 was three times the rate of Whites (29.3 versus 11.5 per 100,000) (CDC, 2008b). Furthermore, HIV is the leading cause of death for African American women ages 25 to 34 (CDC, 2008c). The overall rate of AIDS diagnoses for Black women (45.5 per 100,000 women) is more than 20 times the population rate for White women (2.0 per 100,000) (CDC, 2008c). These disparities in HIV infection are truly staggering.

There is nothing about HIV that has any preference for skin color; these stark disparities in HIV infection are due to multiple social and systemic factors for which ethnicity, nationality, race, or color is a stand-in: poverty, oppression, discrimination, lack of access to health care, stigma, and homelessness. In fact, merely citing "race" as an explanation for disparities in HIV infection is irresponsible; it may reinforce the very stigma and discrimination that help to produce these disparities.

GAY, BISEXUAL, AND OTHER MEN WHO HAVE
SEX WITH MEN (MSM)

Gay, bisexual, and other MSM have always accounted for the majority of persons living with HIV in the United States (CDC, 2008a). In the first decade of the pandemic, dramatic behavior change through reductions in unprotected anal intercourse among gay and bisexual men (McKusick, Coates, Morin, Pollack, & Hoff, 1990) resulted in significant declines in new HIV infections (Winkelstein et al., 1987). However, almost no one at that time believed that more than 25 years later HIV would continue to be a threat. The requirements for behavior change in crisis mode, however, are different than for behavior change that must be sustained for a lifetime, including the challenges of reaching new generations of gay and bisexual men in an era in which antiretroviral therapies (ART) have increased the health and survival of people living with HIV.

Increasing rates of HIV infection among MSM in North America, as well as Europe and Australia (Jaffe, Valdisseri, & De Cock, 2007), are serious concerns that demand a renewed focus on prevention and innovative targeted approaches. For one, strategies to facilitate better implementation of existing technologies, (namely condom use and HIV testing), culturally competent drug treatment programs for those MSM who use stimulants (Colfax & Shoptaw, 2005), and accessible clean syringes for injecting drug users would have a significant impact on reducing new HIV infections.

Beyond condom use and HIV testing are broader social and systemic factors that may be at the heart of continued high rates of HIV infection among MSM, and even more pronounced among MSM of color (CDC, 2008a). Sexual prejudice (Herek, 2004), racism (against MSM of color, both within and outside gay communities), stigma, and institutionalized discrimination (such as in health care and lack of legal recognition of same-gender marriage) contribute to social exclusion—alienation and disenfranchisement from the broader society—that operates through a number of pathways (for example, lack of appropriate sex education and HIV prevention messages for MSM, lack of familial social support, high rates of alcohol and drug use, and sexual risk behaviors) to make MSM more vulnerable to becoming infected with HIV (Meyer & Northridge, 2007).

CHAPTER GOALS

Current challenges in HIV prevention cross social, systemic, behavioral, psychological, emotional, spiritual, cultural, and medical realms, all of which demand a sustained social work response. The themes of this chapter are as follows: (1) We must put greater emphasis on prevention of HIV infection than we have been; (2) the future of successful HIV prevention is a combination approach requiring sustained action in advocacy, intervention, research, and policy; and (3) the synergy of social, systemic, behavioral, and medical interventions that form an integrated approach to HIV prevention requires social workers and other social service and health care providers to be well-versed in a bio-psycho-social model as it relates to HIV, adept at interdisciplinary collaboration, and able to marshal responses across individual, group, social, and systems levels. Just as no one HIV prevention method is a universal solution, HIV prevention strategies that operate at only one level of intervention (micro-, mezzo-, or macro-) are unlikely to be effective. Frequently, the microlevel of HIV prevention (individual knowledge, attitudes, skills, and behaviors) has been emphasized to the relative neglect of macrosocial factors (poverty, discrimination, and stigma).

This chapter equips social workers and other social service providers with a working knowledge of current and future HIV prevention technologies and poses an array of challenges that would benefit from a social work response. Harvey Gochros (1992) of the University of Hawaii School of Social Work wrote in 1992 that HIV is quintessential social work, and his words are as applicable now as they were then.

COMBINATION PREVENTION

No single prevention method is capable of reversing the HIV pandemic. A combination approach (Stephenson, 2008), tailored for local circumstances and social and cultural contexts, that builds on the synergistic effects of an array of methods is likely to be most effective in preventing new HIV infections. New technologies present a variety of possibilities for advancing HIV prevention; however, these technologies require much greater focus than is given at present on social, systemic, and behavioral factors. I review several biomedical technologies on the horizon that may constitute components of a combination approach to HIV prevention. Associated with each potential technology are social, systems, and behavioral challenges that ultimately may determine its effectiveness for HIV prevention.

Condoms

More than two decades into the pandemic, the preeminent HIV prevention tool remains the same: the male condom. On one hand, condoms have helped to prevent untold millions of new HIV infections, and they remain the most reliable tool to prevent HIV infection. Nevertheless, condoms are often held up to higher standards than prevention tools for other conditions, and promotion of their widespread, correct, and consistent use has frequently been sabotaged as a result of U.S. HIV policies that favor religious dogma over scientific evidence (Bristol, 2008; SID, 2003). Condoms are highly effective in reducing the risk of HIV transmission (Holmes, Levine, & Weaver, 2004). Condoms surpass the effectiveness of several existing mechanisms for preventing or detecting many other conditions (for example, a dazzling array of dietary regimens, nicotine replacement therapies, PAP smears). In laboratory settings, assuming a 2 percent breakage or slippage rate during actual use, the relative risk of exposure to semen from condom breakage (compared to using no condom) is estimated to be less than 1% (NIAID, 2001). Reviews of studies conducted in real-world settings estimate that condom use reduces HIV transmission risk by around 80% (Weller & Davis, 2004)—a highly effective prevention tool.

The greatest challenges to the effectiveness of condoms in preventing HIV infection are neither mechanical nor technical; they are systemic, social, psychological, and behavioral. On the other hand, the fact that nearly three decades into the most deadly pandemic in modern history we are still reliant on the same technology is regrettable. A significant challenge for condoms as a prevention tool is that they must be used consistently and correctly in every sexual encounter. Second, and of vital importance, is that ultimately male condoms remain under the control of men. This is a grave reality, given gender power imbalances and societal factors such as the feminization of poverty that tend to disempower women—women of color in particular—in sexual relationships with men (Amaro, 1995; Newman, Williams, & Massaquoi, 2008; Wingood & DiClemente, 1998). Third, despite an abundance of evidence supporting the efficacy of condoms in preventing HIV infection (Weller & Davis, 2004) and evidence that debunks the myth of an association between safer sex education and increased sexual activity or earlier sexual debut among youth (Kirby, Laris, & Rolleri, 2007), the U.S. government has been encumbered by an HIV prevention policy that has long been a slave to ideology (Bristol, 2008; SID, 1993). We do not translate what we know to be supported by the weight of scientific evidence into programs and policies.

Implications for practice and policy are that condoms by themselves are not the problem; interventions need to focus on broader social and systemic factors that disadvantage women, ethnic or racial groups, and sexual minorities—and on supporting the broad implementation of evidence-informed interventions into practice. Additionally, although knowledge and positive attitudes toward condoms are important, they are not sufficient: Condoms must be made widely accessible and affordable.

"Cabbages & Condoms" (Population and Community Development Association [PDA], 2008) is the name of a chain of restaurants (adorned with condoms) in Thailand, run by what is now the largest nonprofit organization in the country. What is significant for the North American context is that the name highlights the direct importance of social and systemic factors in preventing HIV. Condoms are an important ingredient, but equally important are the means of earning enough income for subsistence. In many cases, it is not lack of knowledge, will, or intentions that present the greatest obstacles to condom use, but factors such as women's dependence on male partners for financial support, and both women's and men's trading sex for money, housing, or food for subsistence. Cabbages & Condoms, the brainchild of Meechai Viravaidya, a former Thai senator, is a commercial venture (including a restaurant and hotel chain) that in turn supports community health and development projects to provide poor communities with health education and increased options for subsistence. At the same time, it contributes to destigmatizing condoms, sex, and HIV across Thai society. This community development approach to HIV prevention foreshadowed later research and interventions in other parts of the world that have begun to emphasize the importance of systemic (including economic, political, social, and institutional) factors in HIV vulnerability and prevention.

Microbicides

Microbicides include a range of antimicrobial gels, creams, films, or suppositories that have been tested in clinical trials as a possible method for preventing HIV transmission when put into the vagina or rectum. Initially, microbicides were envisioned for women's use in vaginal intercourse. Given the deficits of male condoms from a gendered perspective, microbicides represent the important possibility of a woman-controlled HIV prevention technology. This would be a milestone for HIV prevention. Microbicides also may be a prevention tool for sex between men, as a rectal application, with the potential for a significant impact on HIV prevention in North America.

The primary challenge for microbicides at present is that no product has yet been successful in clinical trials. Recent research includes attempts to use antiretroviral preparations in a microbicide in the hopes of preventing viral replication and use of a vaginal ring as a delivery mechanism (Microbicide Development Programme [MDP], 2008). Nevertheless, it is important to anticipate social and behavioral challenges that may arise in the context of microbicides. These include the need to apply the microbicide consistently and correctly before sex. In this case, some of the same problems that face condoms might continue to present challenges to microbicide effectiveness. Biomedical research also includes attempts to identify a long-acting microbicide (in combination with the use of antiretrovirals as a prevention tool) that wouldn't require application before each and every sexual encounter; this would have a significant impact in addressing challenges to microbicide effectiveness in real-world situations.

It is important to remember that any product in the form of a new technology for HIV prevention requires real human beings to access and use it with some degree of comfort, often in the context of a sexual encounter. From this perspective, additional challenges facing microbicides include basic but important qualities such as smell, texture, color, and mode of application, all of which may affect microbicide acceptability and adherence. Formative research to determine the relative acceptability of different products is an important component of microbicide development (Morrow & Ruiz, 2007), as it is in the development of other new prevention technologies (Newman Duan, Rudy, & Anton, 2004a).

Further challenges that are not unique to microbicides revolve around the fact that they may not be completely effective in preventing HIV transmission. If a woman's or man's use of a partially effective microbicide is accompanied by a reduction in their partner's use of condoms, the latter might actually increase overall risk of HIV infection. Additionally, second-generation microbicides containing antiretrovirals may have the potential to engender drug resistance in women who are HIV-positive, which may in turn result in transmission of drug-resistant HIV—with serious consequences on a population level (Wilson, Coplan, Wainberg, & Blower, 2008). As with the other prevention methods discussed, microbicides would make a significant contribution to combination prevention in the context of culturally competent, evidence-informed, and sustained social and behavioral interventions to support their effectiveness.

Preexposure Prophylaxis (PREP)

Preexposure prophylaxis (PREP) means giving HIV antiretroviral drugs to people who are not HIV-infected in order to try to *prevent* HIV infection. Clinical trials around the world are testing the use of PREP, with a good deal of optimism about its potential effectiveness. Nevertheless, caution is warranted, as similar optimism has been invoked for other technologies that unfortunately have not yet been supported as efficacious, such as microbicides. At the same time as conducting clinical trials to test the efficacy of PREP in preventing HIV, it is vital to address social, structural, and behavioral challenges of PREP. Among these are challenges to adherence, possible side effects, affordability, and access.

Social workers continue to play a role in the area of adherence to existing ART regimens among people living with HIV (Linsk & Bonk, 2000; Rier & Indyk, 2006). Given challenges with adherence to existing regimens among people living with HIV who need the medications to survive, we might reasonably expect even greater challenges when the medication is being used as a preventive measure. People may be more likely to overcome barriers to the correct and consistent use of anti-HIV medications when they need them for their survival, in contrast to using the medications to prevent a disease they might possibly contract in the future. Another challenge with existing medications that requires investigation in current trials is possible side effects from PREP that may pose obstacles to its use.

Beyond physical challenges, social, psychological, emotional, and systemic factors will determine the effectiveness of PREP in preventing HIV infection. Taking HIV medications remains highly stigmatized. Stigma is associated with lack of adherence to HIV medications (Rintamaki, Davis, Skripkauskas, Bennett, & Wolf, 2006). Similarly, stigma may be a deterrent to using PREP. Stigma is amplified into a systemic challenge, such as in the case of immigrants in the United States who face government policies barring entry to persons living with HIV, thus restricting travel and creating legal difficulties. Earlier regimens that required refrigeration were not readily usable by people without stable housing, another example of a systemic obstacle, in this case related to poverty.

An additional and important potential obstacle for PREP is illustrated by the fact that, presently, many people living with HIV in the United States (and more so in low-and middle-income countries) do not have consistent access to (affordable) medications. Accordingly, PREP cannot be presumed to be automatically accessible and acceptable to the vulnerable communities that would most benefit from it. Finally, it is important to consider that adherence to medication or prevention techniques is typically greater in the context of a clinical trial—for which people are often paid and receive reinforcement through regular clinic visits or staff contact—than in real-world situations. Overall, PREP holds much promise; but its effectiveness may be determined by a variety of psychological, social, and systemic factors that must be addressed through evidence-informed programs and policies.

Male Circumcision

Male circumcision is quite different from condoms, microbicides, or PREP as an HIV prevention strategy. For one, circumcision involves a surgical procedure, and one that is laden with powerful religious, cultural, and social meanings. However, several randomized trials conducted in sub-Saharan Africa support male circumcision as an effective measure in reducing men's risk of becoming infected with HIV in penile-vaginal sex (Auvert et al., 2005; Bailey et al., 2007; Gray et al., 2007). Overall, it is estimated that circumcision may reduce men's risk of HIV acquisition in heterosexual sex by 58 percent (Padian, Buvé, Balkus, Serwadda, & Cates, 2008). In 2007, given the weight of evidence, the World Health Organization (2007) endorsed male circumcision as an effective preventive intervention for heterosexual acquisition of HIV in men—to be implemented in tandem with condoms.

The evidence for the effectiveness of circumcision in reducing HIV transmission in the United States and among men who have sex with men is less clear. These two issues are intertwined, as the majority of HIV infections in the United States are among MSM; furthermore, rates of circumcision tend to be higher in the United States than in some high-HIV-prevalence settings. Overall, 79% of men reported being circumcised in a U.S. national survey from 1999 to 2004 (CDC, 2008d). According to a national hospital discharge survey, 65% of newborns were circumcised in 1999 (CDC, 2008d). Some U.S. studies suggest lack of circumcision is associated with a twofold increase in the risk for HIV infection (Buchbinder et al., 2005); however, other U.S. studies have yielded mixed results. The evidence to date about the effectiveness of circumcision in reducing HIV transmission among MSM remains inconclusive (Millet, Flores, Marks, Reed, & Herbert, 2008).

A notably positive feature of male circumcision as an HIV prevention strategy is that it requires only a one-time procedure, in contrast to technologies that require correct and consistent implementation before each and every sexual encounter. However, male circumcision is not completely effective in preventing HIV infection; as a result, it may confront behavioral challenges to its effectiveness. If men who are newly circumcised believe themselves to be completely protected against HIV and reduce condom use or increase their number of sexual partners, the benefits of circumcision may be outweighed. These disadvantages might be more pronounced among men who have sex with men, for whom there is less evidence of the efficacy of circumcision in preventing HIV transmission. Therefore it is essential that the introduction of male circumcision as an HIV prevention strategy be promoted as a component of combination prevention and include sustained education and counseling, tailored to various populations at risk, about the need for consistent use of condoms and other risk-reduction measures.

Beyond challenges due to behavior change (or risk compensation), a variety of social and cultural challenges ensue in the case of male circumcision. Male circumcision is associated with various religious and cultural meanings, and population rates of circumcision vary widely, even within the United States (Xu, Markowitz, Sternberg, & Aral, 2007). Although men in the limited context of research studies may agree to being circumcised, what may be a simple medical procedure may require well-designed education, counseling, and family interventions to succeed—and it may remain unacceptable in some cases. Most important for the United States, the evidence remains inconclusive regarding the effectiveness of circumcision in preventing HIV acquisition in insertive anal sex.

HIV Vaccines

A safe and effective HIV vaccine offers the greatest long-term hope for controlling the pandemic (Butler, Pandrea, Marx, & Apitrei, 2007; Newman et al., 2006). More than 80 clinical trials of test vaccines to prevent HIV infection have been conducted, including three large-scale (Phase III) trials (International AIDS Vaccine Initiative [IAVI], 2008). Collectively these trials have enrolled more than 24,000 volunteers (Newman, Daley, Halpenny, & Loutfy, 2008) although no one vaccine has yet proven effective.

One of the most pressing challenges for HIV vaccines is that HIV has proven vastly more difficult to contain than previous infectious agents; the body's natural immune response is largely inadequate. As a result, traditional methods used in vaccine development that have relied on mimicking the body's natural immune response have not been sufficient in the case of HIV. Some of the major scientific challenges for HIV vaccine development are as follows: (1) HIV integrates itself into the DNA (the genetic material) of some of the body's cells, where it remains largely invisible to the immune system; (2) there is only a very short window period after initial infection in which a vaccine might have an opportunity to eliminate HIV; and (3) HIV mutates rapidly, leading to wide genetic variability, which makes it a very difficult target for a vaccine (Butler et al., 2007; Johnston & Fauci, 2008). Nevertheless, broad scientific (Coordinating Committee of the Global HIV Vaccine Enterprise, 2005) and financial (Cohen, 2006) resources are being marshaled in the face of these obstacles to HIV vaccine development, which is among the highest priorities in AIDS research (Titti et al., 2007).

Beyond these complex biological challenges lie a number of human challenges in HIV vaccine development. These include sustaining a long-term commitment to the financial and human capital required for HIV vaccine research. Competing demands for funding, both within the HIV field and with other important diseases (as well as trillion-dollar wars), pose significant obstacles, as does attracting young scientists to the field of HIV vaccine research. Additionally, tens of thousands of volunteers, most from vulnerable communities, will be needed to participate in clinical trials on the path to HIV vaccine development, which raises a host of social, ethical, logistical, and systemic challenges (Newman et al., 2004a; Newman et al., 2006b; Newman et al., 2008).

Given this powerful array of obstacles, some have questioned the rationale for continuing HIV vaccine research. What might be the response to that concern? For one, historically, vaccine development takes decades. In any scientific enterprise, trials of products that do not work far exceed those that do; the key is to learn from what does not work and move forward. And of paramount importance, a onetime dose of an ideal vaccine with a high degree of efficacy could reverse the most deadly pandemic of our time. It is plausible that an initial vaccine may be of low to moderate effectiveness; but even such a partially effective HIV vaccine would have a tremendous impact on a population level (Gilbert et al., 2003; Stover, Bollinger, Hecht, Williams, & Roca, 2007). Vaccines also may require multiple doses, and if protective effects do not last for 20 years, they will need to be administered to adolescents as well as adults, more challenging than providing vaccinations in infancy. Therefore, social and behavioral challenges will persist even in the case of a safe and effective HIV vaccine, with vaccines playing an important role in combination prevention (Newman, Duan, Rudy, & Roberts, 2004b).

One of the premiere challenges for an eventual HIV vaccine is ensuring it is accessible and affordable for vulnerable communities (Newman et al., 2004a; Newman et al., 2006a). The absence of universal health insurance coverage in the United States will present obstacles to HIV vaccine uptake among people from poor and disenfranchised communities, precisely those who remain most vulnerable to HIV.

An additional challenge to the effectiveness of a future vaccine is whether the public, particularly vulnerable communities, will accept it (Newman et al., 2006b). Although even a moderately effective vaccine could prevent tens of thousands of HIV infections in the United States and millions worldwide, if people are reluctant to accept a 50% efficacy vaccine or fear contracting HIV from the vaccine (although that is impossible), that would seriously constrain its effectiveness. Formative research, which has revealed low levels of acceptability for partial-efficacy HIV vaccines, fears of vaccine-induced HIV infection, and obstacles due to HIV stigma (Newman et al., 2006a), may help to support strategies for increasing understanding and acceptability of imperfect HIV vaccines (Newman et al., 2004a). Building trust among communities who harbor realistic fears about the intentions of the U.S. government regarding health care and medical research (such as the Tuskegee Study of Untreated Syphilis) may be essential to facilitating future HIV vaccine uptake among vulnerable communities (Roberts, Newman, Duan, Rudy, & Swendeman, 2005).

Finally, an important concern is that the advent of HIV vaccines may result in risk compensation: People may increase their risk behavior if they think they are fully protected against HIV infection. Similar changes have been documented in association with belief in the efficacy of ART to reduce HIV transmission and reduced concerns about engaging in unprotected sex since the availability of ART (Crepaz, Hart, & Marks, 2004). Formative research has revealed people's understandable conceptualizations (mental models) of HIV vaccines as providing complete immunity; engaging with these mental models to increase understanding of the role and function of a partial-efficacy vaccine may support vaccine uptake and the imperative of sustained behavioral prevention (Newman, Seiden, Roberts, Kakinami, & Duan, 2007).

Personal Perspective

Taking Part in a Vaccine Trial, from an Interview with a Gay Man Who Participated in the "Step Study" HIV Vaccine Trial

Initially I was motivated to participate in the HIV vaccine trial because I guess I felt a part of the gay community, like it was a way of making a contribution. I have known people who are HIV-positive and I just think it would be such an important step for us to get an HIV vaccine. I know that people aren't participating in studies, so I thought, "Well someone has to, right?" And I thought, "Why not me?" And if it did work, then wouldn't it be awesome to be one of the first people to be vaccinated? So that's why I participated.

(Continued)

The first reaction I had to the study results was it was very disappointing, of course. And then it moved from disappointment to frightening, because they also suggested in the results that I had read that some people who received the vaccine had been put at higher risk for HIV. I mean, it didn't give them HIV, but it put them in a higher risk category, and, of course, in a double-blind study, I had no idea which group I fell into at that point.

I tried to get unblinded unsuccessfully, meaning that I tried to find out which part of the study I had been in. But when the principal researcher got back from a meeting in which they made decisions about how to proceed, she called me directly because I'd had this conversation with her before. She told me that I was in the placebo group, which was very comforting. I had a lot of anxiety related to that phone call. I just felt like since there was a failure to produce a vaccine, I didn't want to be—I hesitate to use the word *punished*—but subjected to a negative outcome that's going to follow me for the rest of my life. So there was a lot of relief for myself that I was in that placebo group.

The other dimension was the simple fact that the vaccine didn't work. As much as I went into it sort of realistically expecting that it wouldn't work because it's very new science, there's always that little part of you that, when you participate in something like this or even when you hear about something like this, you think, oh, wouldn't that be great, wouldn't that be great. And wouldn't it be great if I was one of the people who not only benefited from it but could feel a little bit of pride that I helped make this happen. It would be such a nice feeling to be able to say that. But there was a degree of disappointment in feeling that failure. And you sort of feel like, "I've committed a lot of time to this." I mean every failure does contribute to the overall scientific investigation, but still, it's a much smaller contribution than the one that would have worked. To be completely honest and a little bit selfish, it would have been nice to be like, "Oh my god, I'm vaccinated against HIV; isn't that awesome to not have that worry anymore."

CONCLUSIONS

Exciting biomedical innovations in HIV prevention are on the horizon. No single approach is a universal solution, but a combination prevention approach supported by evidence-informed systemic, sociocultural, and behavioral interventions may yield vast benefits in changing the course of the pandemic.

The main implications of this chapter from a social work perspective are as follows:

1. HIV prevention research does not happen without our help. Sustained advocacy and support for making HIV prevention a priority is crucial. HIV prevention advocacy spans the spectrum, from engaging vulnerable communities in prevention strategies and research, to marshaling public support for biomedical HIV prevention research, to cost-effectiveness studies documenting the worthiness of prevention, to lobbying policymakers to fund and implement programs based on available evidence in the face of ideological opposition.

2. Advances in medicine must be supported by evidence-informed social and behavioral interventions and policies. Ultimately, social, systems, and behavioral factors

will determine the effectiveness of biomedical technologies in preventing HIV infection amidst real-world challenges, outside a laboratory or clinical trial. Furthermore, major challenges and opportunities remain in translating existing interventions that are already supported by scientific evidence (that is, condoms and HIV testing) into practice and policy.

3. There is no vaccine for sexism, racism, classism, xenophobia, ageism, or sexual prejudice. Biological or medical innovations do little if anything to address long-standing social and systemic conditions that fuel immense disparities in the U.S. HIV epidemic and in rates of new HIV infections. HIV in the United States is classified as a concentrated pandemic, given the disproportionate impact of HIV on particular vulnerable communities (for example, MSM, African Americans, Latinos, injecting drug users) in contrast to low prevalence in the general population. A focus on new technology development must be advanced in tandem with approaches that address social, political, economic, legal, and other systemic factors that continue to contribute to vulnerability; otherwise, new biological or medical technologies will likely face the same obstacles as existing prevention measures. As a result, gains in HIV prevention may remain inaccessible and unacceptable to the communities for whom they are most crucial—a potentially grave outcome from social work, public health, and human rights perspectives.

4. It is not time to throw out condoms. Existing prevention tools such as condoms, along with voluntary counseling and testing, will remain an important component of HIV prevention for years to come. In fact, supporting widespread, age-appropriate safer sex education in schools (Kirby, Laris, & Rolleri, 2007), along with condom availability and access, is more important than ever given increases in new HIV diagnoses.

5. A particularly important contribution of social workers to HIV prevention is ensuring that communities most affected by the pandemic are engaged in ethical and participatory ways in ongoing efforts to support prevention, including research and development for new technologies (Newman, 2006). Community engagement in HIV prevention research includes a variety of activities: awareness of and informed participation in clinical trials (Newman et al., 2007), contributions to decision making in clinical trials and to understanding and addressing the potential social and behavioral impact of participation in biomedical HIV prevention research, and ensuring knowledge transfer and exchange regarding information resulting from clinical trials and products currently in testing. Ongoing engagement of vulnerable communities and persons living with HIV in research, practice, and policy—to understand social and behavioral implications of new prevention technologies, and to support culturally competent implementation of combination prevention that is acceptable and accessible to communities most vulnerable to HIV—will remain central to the success of HIV prevention.

In conclusion, the need for integration of biological, medical, behavioral, social, and systemic prevention measures spans the spectrum of individuals and communities most vulnerable to HIV, community advocates, social workers, social service and health care professionals, researchers, and policymakers. A broadly educated, motivated, and committed pool of social workers working at multiple levels of practice—individual, group, community, and systemic—is a key component to the success of a new era of combination HIV prevention.

REFERENCES

Amaro, H. (1995). Love, sex, and power. Considering women's realities in HIV prevention. *American Psychologist, 50*(6), 437–447.

Auvert, B., Taljaard, D., Lagarde, E., Sobngwi-Tambekou, J., Sitta, R., & Puren, A. (2005). Randomized, controlled intervention trial of male circumcision for reduction of HIV infection risk: The ANRS 1265 trial. *PLOS Medicine, 2,* e298.

Bailey, R. C., Moses, S., Parker, C. B., Agot, K., Maclean, I., Krieger, J. N., et al. (2007). Male circumcision for HIV prevention in young men in Kisumu, Kenya: A randomised controlled trial. *Lancet, 369,* 643–656.

Brenner, B. G., Roger, M., Routy, J. P., Moisi, D., Ntemgwa, M., Matte, C., et al. (2007). High rates of forward transmission events after acute/early HIV-1 infection. *Journal of Infectious Diseases, 195*(7), 951–959.

Bristol, N. (2008). US Senate passes new PEPFAR bill. *Lancet, 372,* 277–278.

Buchbinder, S. P., Vittinghoff, E., Heagerty, P. J., Celum, C. L., Seage, G. R., Judson, F. N., et al. (2005). Sexual risk, nitrite inhalant use, and lack of circumcision associated with HIV sero-conversion in men who have sex with men in the United States. *Journal of Acquired Immune Deficiency Syndromes, 39,* 82–89.

Butler, I. F., Pandrea, I., Marx, P. A., & Apetrei, C. (2007). HIV genetic diversity: Biological and public health consequences [Review]. *Current Opinions in HIV Research, 5*(1), 23–45.

Castilla, J., Del Romero, J., Hernando, V., Marincovich, B., Garcia, S., & Rodriguez, C. (2005). Effectiveness of highly active antiretroviral therapy in reducing heterosexual transmission of HIV. *Journal of Acquired Immune Deficiency Syndromes, 40,* 96–101.

Centers for Disease Control and Prevention. (2008a). *Estimates of new HIV infections in the United States.* Retrieved September 7, 2008, from http://www.cdc.gov/hiv/topics/surveillance/resources/factsheets/pdf/incidence.pdf

Centers for Disease Control and Prevention. (2008b). *HIV/AIDS among Hispanics/Latinos.* Retrieved September 7, 2008, from http://www.cdc.gov/hiv/hispanics/resources/factsheets/hispanic.htm

Centers for Disease Control and Prevention. (2008c). *HIV/AIDS among women.* Retrieved September 7, 2008, from http://www.cdc.gov/hiv/topics/women/resources/factsheets/women.htm

Centers for Disease Control and Prevention. (2008d). *Male circumcision and risk for HIV transmission and other health conditions: Implications for the United States.* Retrieved September 7, 2008, from http://www.cdc.gov/hiv/resources/factsheets/circumcision.htm

Cohen, J. (2006). Gates Foundation doubles support for AIDS vaccine research. *Science, 313,* 283.

Cohen, J. (2008). Treatment and prevention exchange vows at international conference. *Science, 321,* 902–903.

Colfax, G., & Shoptaw, S. (2005). The methamphetamine pandemic: Implications for HIV prevention and treatment. *Current HIV/AIDS Reports, 2,* 194–199.

Coordinating Committee of the Global HIV/AIDS Vaccine Enterprise. (2005). The Global HIV/AIDS Vaccine Enterprise: Scientific Strategic Plan. *PLoS Medicine, 2*(2): e25. doi:10.1371/journal.pmed.0020025

Crepaz, N., Hart, T. A., & Marks, G. (2004). Highly active antiretroviral therapy and sexual risk behavior: A meta-analytic review. *Journal of the American Medical Association, 292*(2), 224–236.

Gilbert, P. B., DeGruttola, V. G., Hudgens, M. G., Self, S. G., Hammer, S. M., & Corey, L. (2003). What constitutes efficacy for a human immunodeficiency virus vaccine that ameliorates viremia: Issues involving surrogate end points in phase 3 trials. *Journal of Infectious Diseases, 188*(2), 179–193.

Gochros, H. L. (1992). The sexuality of gay men with HIV infection. *Social Work, 37*(2), 105–109.

Gray, R. H., Kigozi, G., Serwadda, D., Makumbi, F., Watya, S., Nalugoda, F., et al. (2007). Male circumcision for HIV prevention in men in Rakai, Uganda: A randomised trial. *Lancet, 369,* 657–666.

Hall, H. I., Song, R., Rhodes, P., Prejean, J., An, Q., Lee, L. M., et al. (2008). Estimation of HIV incidence in the United States. *Journal of the American Medical Association, 300*(5), 520–529.

Herek, G. M. (2004). Beyond "homophobia": Thinking about sexual stigma and prejudice in the twenty-first century. *Sexuality Research and Social Policy, 1*(2), 6–24.

Holmes, K. K., Levine, R., & Weaver, M. (2004). Effectiveness of condoms in preventing sexually transmitted infections. *Bulletin of the World Health Organization, 82,* 454–461.

International AIDS Vaccine Initiative. (2008*). IAVI Database of AIDS vaccines in human trials.* Special Features. Retrieved May 5, 2008, from http://www.iavireport.org/trialsdb/

Jaffe, H. W., Valdiserri, R. O., & De Cock, K. M. (2007). The reemerging HIV/AIDS pandemic in men who have sex with men. *Journal of the American Medical Association, 298,* 2412–2414.

Johnston, M. I., & Fauci, A. S. (2008). An HIV vaccine—challenges and prospects. *New England Journal of Medicine, 359*(9), 888–890.

Kirby, D., Laris, B., & Rolleri, L. (2007). Sex and HIV education programs: Their impact on sexual behaviors of young people throughout the world. *Journal of Adolescent Health, 40*(3), 206–217.

Linsk, N. L., & Bonk, N. (2000). Adherence to treatment as social work challenges. In. V. Lynch (Ed.), *HIV/AIDS at year 2000: A sourcebook for social workers.* New York: Allyn & Bacon.

McKusick, L., Coates, T. J., Morin, S. F., Pollack, L., & Hoff, C. (1990). Longitudinal predictors of reductions in unprotected anal intercourse among gay men in San Francisco: The AIDS Behavioral Research Project. *American Journal of Public Health, 80,* 978–983.

Meyer, I. H., & Northridge, M. E. (2007). *The health of sexual minorities: Public health perspectives on lesbian, gay, bisexual, and transgender populations.* New York: Springer.

Microbicide Development Programme. (2008). Microbicide Development Programme update June 2008: *IDMC recommend MDP301 Phase III trial to continue.* Retrieved September 1, 2008, from http://www.mdp.mrc.ac.uk/downloads/FINAL_MDP_Announcement_11_June_2008_Statement.pdf

Millet, G. A., Flores, S. A., Marks, G., Reed, B., & Herbst, J. H. (2008). Circumcision status and risk of HIV and sexually transmitted infections among men who have sex with men: A meta-analysis. *Journal of the American Medical Association, 300*(14), 1674–1684.

Morbidity and Mortality Weekly Report. (2008). Persons Tested for HIV—United States, 2006. *MMWR 57*(31), 845–849.

Morrow, K. M., & Ruiz., M. (2008). Assessing microbicide acceptability: A comprehensive and integrated approach. *AIDS and Behavior, 12*(2), 272–283.

National Institute of Allergy and Infectious Diseases. (2001). *Scientific evidence on condom effectiveness for sexually transmitted disease (STD) prevention.* Retrieved November 3, 2008, from http://www3.niaid.nih.gov/about/organization/dmid/PDF/condomReport.pdf

Newman, P. A. (2006). Towards a science of community engagement. *Lancet, 367,* 302.

Newman, P. A., Daley, A., Halpenny, R., & Loutfy, M. (2008). Community heroes or "high-risk" pariahs? Reasons for declining to enroll in an HIV vaccine trial. *Vaccine, 26,* 1091–1097.

Newman, P. A., Duan, N., Lee, S-J., Rudy, E., Seiden, D., Kakinami, L., et al. (2006b). HIV vaccine acceptability among communities at risk: The impact of vaccine characteristics. *Vaccine, 24*(12), 2094–2101.

Newman, P. A., Duan, N., Lee, S-J., Rudy, E. T., Seiden, D., Kakinami, L., et al. (2007). Willingness to participate in HIV vaccine trials among communities at risk: The impact of trial attributes. *Preventive Medicine, 44*(6), 554–557.

Newman, P. A., Duan, N., Roberts, K. J., Seiden, D., Rudy, E. T., Swendeman, D., et al. (2006a). HIV vaccine trial participation among ethnic minority communities. *Journal of Acquired Immune Deficiency Syndromes, 41,* 210–217.

Newman, P. A., Duan, N., Rudy, E. T., & Anton, P. A. (2004a). Challenges for HIV vaccine dissemination and clinical trial recruitment: If we build it, will they come? *AIDS Patient Care & STDs, 18*(12), 691–701.

Newman, P. A., Duan, N., Rudy, E., & Roberts, K. J. (2004b). HIV risk and prevention in a post-vaccine context. *Vaccine, 22*(15–16), 1954–1963.

Newman, P. A., Seiden, D., Roberts, K., Kakinami, L., & Duan, N. (2007). A small dose of HIV? HIV vaccine mental models and risk communication. *Health Education & Behavior.* Prepublished November 21, 2007, DOI:10.1177/1090198107305078.

Newman, P. A., Williams, C. C., Massaquoi, N., Brown, M., & Logie, C. (2008). HIV prevention for Black women: Structural barriers and opportunities. *Journal of Health Care for the Poor and Underserved, 19*(3), 829–841.

Padian, N. S., Buvé, A., Balkus, J., Serwadda, D., & Cates, W., Jr. (2008). Biomedical interventions to prevent HIV infection: Evidence, challenges and way forward. *Lancet, 372,* 585–599.

Population and Community Development Association. (2008). Cabbages & Condoms [Restaurants/resorts]. Retrieved September 8, 2008, from http://www.cabbagesandcondoms.com

Rier, D. A., & Indyk, D. (2006). Flexible rigidity: Supporting HIV treatment adherence in a rapidly changing treatment environment. *Social Work in Health Care, 42*(3/4), 133–150.

Rintamaki, L. S., Davis, T. C., Skripkauskas, S., Bennett, C. L., & Wolf, M. S. (2006). Social stigma concerns and HIV medication adherence. *AIDS Patient Care and STDs, 20*(5), 359–368.

Roberts, K. J., Newman, P. A., Duan, N., Rudy, E. T., & Swendeman, D. (2005). HIV vaccine knowledge and beliefs among communities at elevated risk: Concerns, questions and conspiracies. *Journal of the American Medical Association, 97*(12), 1662–71.

Robles, A. M., & Stringer, H. G. (2006). HIV-AIDS in minorities. *Clinics in Chest Medicine, 27*(3), 511–519.

Rotheram Borus, M. J., Newman, P. A., & Etzel, M. (2000). Effective detection of HIV. *Journal of Acquired Immune Deficiency Syndrome, 25*(Suppl. 2), S105–S114.

Special Investigations Division, Minority Staff of the Committee on Government Reform. (2003). *Politics and science in the Bush administration: Prepared for Rep. Henry A. Waxman.* Washington, DC: U.S. House of Representatives. Retrieved September 7, 2008, from http://oversight.house.gov/features/politics_and_science/pdfs/pdf_politics_and_science_rep.pdf

Stover, J., Bollinger, L., Hecht, R., Williams, C., & Roca, E. (2007). The impact of an AIDS vaccine in developing countries: A new model and initial results. *Health Affairs, 26*(4), 1147–1158.

Titti, F., Cafaro, A., Ferrantelli, F., Tripiciano, A., Moretti, S., Caputo A., et al. (2007). Problems and emerging approaches in HIV/AIDS vaccine development. *Expert Opinion on Emerging Drugs, 12*(1), 23–48.

UNAIDS/WHO. (2008). *Antiretroviral therapy and sexual transmission of HIV.* Retrieved September 7, 2008, from http://data.unaids.org/pub/PressStatement/2008/080201_hivtransmission_en.pdf

Weller, S., & Davis, K. (2004). Condom effectiveness in reducing heterosexual HIV transmission. *Cochrane Database of Systematic Reviews, 1.*

Wilson, D. P., Coplan, P. M., Wainberg, M. A., & Blower, S. M. (2008). The paradoxical effects of using antiretroviral-based microbicides to control HIV epidemics. *Proceedings of the National Academy of Sciences, 105*(28), 9835–9840.

Wingood, G. M., & DiClemente, R. J. (1998). Partner influences and gender-related factors associated with noncondom use among young adult African American women. *American Journal of Community Psychology, 26*(1), 29–51.

Winkelstein, W., Jr., Samuel, M., Padian, N. S., Wiley, J. A., Lang, W., Anderson, R. E., et al. (1987). The San Francisco Men's Health Study: III. Reduction in human immunodeficiency virus transmission among homosexual/bisexual men, 1982–86. *American Journal of Public Health, 77,* 685–689.

World Health Organization. (2007). New data on male circumcision and HIV prevention: Policy and programme implications. Retrieved September 1, 2008, from http://data.unaids.org/pub/Report/2007/mc_recommendations_en.pdf

Xu, F., Markowitz, L. E., Sternberg, M. R., & Aral, S. O. (2007). Prevalence of circumcision and herpes simplex virus type 2 infection in men in the United States: The National Health and Nutrition Examination Survey (NHANES), 1999–2004. *Sexually Transmitted Diseases, 34,* 479–484.

PART THREE

SPECIFIC VULNERABLE POPULATIONS

Chapter Thirteen

WOMEN AND HIV IN THE U. S.: FROM INVISIBLE TO SELF-DETERMINED

Sally Mason

INTRODUCTION

Women have always been *affected* by HIV as partners, sisters, friends, mothers, and professional caregivers of men, women, teens, and children living with HIV. Early in the U.S. epidemic, however, women were not considered at risk for being infected with HIV. Although a woman was diagnosed with AIDS in 1981, the year that marked the recognition of the U.S. epidemic, the vast majority of those infected with HIV early in the epidemic were gay men (Centers for Disease Control [CDC], 2008a). With the focus on risk *groups* (such as "men who have sex with men," "IV drug users") rather than risk *behaviors,* women did not see themselves as at risk, nor did their health care professionals (Schiller, Crystal, & Lewellen, 1994). HIV prevention and services were directed almost exclusively to gay men, partially because the gay male community took leadership in early HIV efforts (CDC, 2007).

In the late 1980s the rising number of infants and children infected perinatally (through birth) and "boarder baby" phenomenon (babies abandoned in hospitals) raised awareness of HIV infection rates in women. Since more babies were being born HIV-positive, it followed that women must be HIV-infected. Still, women were often perceived as "vectors of transmission" to babies or to men rather than recognized as *people,* living with HIV, with specific needs of their own. Women were not likely to get tested for HIV, and, when they did, testing or diagnosis often came too late in the disease process for treatment to be effective. In fact, until the 1993 revision, the Centers for Disease Control's definition of AIDS did not include many of the manifestations of HIV that were commonly seen in women, such as recurrent vaginal yeast infections, severe pelvic inflammatory disease (PID), and an increased risk of precancerous changes in the cervix. With the change in definition, there was a 111% increase in AIDS diagnoses in the United States between 1992 and 1993. The jump in diagnoses was not due to a substantial increase in new infections, but because some people with HIV, especially women, were no longer invisible. They were finally recognized as having HIV because their conditions were now accepted as AIDS-defining by the Social Security Administration and the Centers for Disease Control and Prevention.

Acknowledgments: This chapter is dedicated to the women with HIV with whom I have worked, from Linda in 1987 to Wendy, Tracey, and Deb (to name a few) now, who taught me so much about self-determination. I thank Wendy for writing the perspective on living with HIV and Vickey Sultzman for her valuable feedback during the preparation of this chapter.

A SNAPSHOT OF WOMEN AND HIV RISK

We want to avoid stereotypes because they contribute to misperceptions about risk and increased stigma for those perceived at risk. However, an examination of the shared characteristics of women with HIV can inform our understanding of women's needs within the epidemic, not only those living with HIV, but those at risk for HIV. For years, the Centers for Disease Control and Prevention (CDC) collected data only on people with a diagnosis of AIDS, the advanced stage of HIV infection. With the availability of highly active antiretroviral therapy (HAART), fewer people were progressing to AIDS, so surveillance data collected by the CDC no longer accurately reflected the number of people contracting HIV. As of 2008, all states in the United States collect HIV *and* AIDS data. Although the collection of the HIV data is controversial due to name-based reporting and thus concerns about risks to confidentiality, the HIV infection surveillance data adds to the current picture of the epidemic and describes trends in HIV infection.

In 2005, women represented 26% of all new diagnoses of HIV or AIDS. Of women living with HIV or AIDS, a disproportionate number are African American and Latina. African American women and Latinas account for 24% of all U.S. women but 79% of women with HIV. Although the number of women with HIV who are over 50 years of age is steadily increasing, younger women appear at greatest risk. Women between 15 and 39 years of age represent the largest group of newly diagnosed women. AIDS was the leading cause of death in 2004 of Black women between the ages of 25 and 34. Clearly, the greatest percentages of women with HIV are of reproductive age. Through prenatal counseling, testing, and medical intervention, transmission from mother to child has been greatly reduced in the United States. However, when a baby is born with HIV, he or she is most likely Black, again reflecting the high rate of HIV in African American women. The presence of sexually transmitted infections (STIs) increases the risk for HIV, a grave concern for racial minority women and young women, who have higher rates of STIs than Caucasian women (CDC, 2008b).

Early in the epidemic, injected drug use (IDU) was the main risk factor for women with HIV (CDC, 2008b). In 2005, however, 80 percent of new infections in women were from unprotected sex with a man (CDC, 2008b); transmission from male to female during intercourse is more likely than female-to-male transmission. Historically, women with HIV have been concentrated in large urban areas in the United States, especially the Northeast. Increasingly new infections in women are in the Southern states. The majority of women with HIV (64%) have incomes below $10,000, a much higher percentage than men with HIV (41%) (Kaiser Family Foundation, 2008).

Collectively, these data depict a woman at risk for HIV as most likely African American or Latina, low-income, having a history of substance use, of reproductive age, heterosexually active, and living in the inner city. As we look at this description, a distinction between *risk* and *vulnerability* helps us understand women within the pandemic. Risk is "the probability of an individual becoming infected by HIV, either through his or her own actions, knowingly or not, or via another person's actions" (UNAIDS, 2008, p. 65). Having unprotected sex and using unclean injection equipment are examples of risks. Vulnerability "results from a range of factors outside the control of the individual that reduce the ability of individual and communities to avoid HIV risk." Gender and racial inequality, poverty, and homophobia are some examples of socioeconomic and cultural factors that enhance an individual's vulnerability and thus increase the likelihood that he or she will participate in risky behaviors. Women with HIV have participated in risky behaviors. However, the preceding description of women at risk is also remarkable in the multiple cultural and socioeconomic factors that increase women's vulnerability or likelihood that they will participate in those behaviors.

WOMEN'S SOCIOECONOMIC AND CULTURAL VULNERABILITY TO HIV

There are several factors contributing to women's vulnerability to HIV infection: their roles in society and unequal social status, health disparities, and the intersection of HIV stigma with other forms of oppression. These factors are discussed here.

Roles and Status

Traditionally, women are at the center of family relationships: nurturing emotional connections between members, raising children, and providing care for disabled or ill family members and elderly parents. The roles of caregiver, partner, parent, and provider are rewarding but can take their toll. While caring for others, women may not attend to their own needs or put their needs after those of children and loved ones. This "silencing the self" (Jack, 1991) may prevent women from taking steps to reduce their HIV risk and promote health or, if HIV-positive, can affect their coping with HIV, including accessing health care (DeMarco, Lynch, & Board, 2002).

Like other women, HIV-infected women value the role of parent and the meaning it provides in their lives (Lindau et al., 2006). Women vulnerable to HIV, however, are often low-income, raising children alone, and sole providers for their families—stressors that make the fulfillment of multiple roles even more challenging. Additionally, women with HIV are balancing their own considerable health needs with those of children and other family members. If a child is also HIV-positive, parenting is made even more complex by disclosure of HIV status to the child and the maintenance of the child's health and mental health care. If a mother discloses her child's HIV status to others, she hazards shame and blame because of her role in transmitting HIV to the child. As a result of these multilayered responsibilities and roles, women may not receive the care they need, nor can they care effectively for others; those relationships and people may suffer as the woman's self-esteem erodes (DeMarco et al., 2002).

One of the most studied aspects of HIV self-care has been adherence to complicated medication or highly active antiretroviral therapy (HAART) regimens. HAART adherence is associated with many factors, including side effects, the effects of substance use, and health care provider attitudes. For women specifically, parenting stress, disclosure to children, having small children, and having a partner are factors in HIV medication adherence (Gant & Welch, 2004; Mellins et al., 2002; Murphy, Greenwell, & Hoffman, 2002), affirming that women's family connections and roles can be facilitators and barriers to effective coping.

As women account for a growing percentage of people with HIV, and as people with HIV are living longer, the number of children and adolescents whose mothers have HIV will increase exponentially. A mother may be especially sensitive to her children's responses to learning about her HIV status and to protecting the children from the burden of her illness, as well as from HIV stigma. To protect herself and her children, a mother may choose not to tell anyone about her HIV diagnosis, thus closing herself off from emotional and concrete support. Women are also deeply concerned about preventing their children from making the same mistakes as they themselves did. Mothers tend to teach their children about safer sex and the evils of substance use and the streets, using their own lives as examples. Mothers worry that the neighborhoods where they live offer much temptation for teens and that, despite their best efforts, adolescents may find trouble.

While balancing care for others with care for self, women contend with the constraints of lower social and financial status than men. Although essential, women's roles of nurturance and support are not valued in our culture and, if provided informally as parents or family caregivers, are not reimbursed financially. When formalized into employment, traditional women's positions, such as childcare worker or nurse's aide, are lower paid than male-dominated jobs. Lacking financial resources, women may trade sex for money or shelter, putting themselves at risk. Reliant on and subordinate to men, women remain in unhealthy relationships for their own and their children's safety and protection.

Within sexual relationships with men, women have few methods at their disposal to prevent HIV transmission, except to choose not to be sexual, to negotiate sexual expression that does not involve intercourse, or to ask their partner to use a male or female condom. In the role of taking care of her partner, a woman may not feel comfortable negotiating sexual expression or refusing to have intercourse. An unequal partner, a woman may risk abandonment, violence, or loss of love if she asserts her needs and safety. In fact, the power differential in male/female relationships is often played out in relationship violence or sexual assault.

Women living with HIV are no exception to this power differential: 68% of women with HIV report abuse as adults (Simoni & Ng, 2000) and many perceive the violence to be related to their HIV diagnosis (Zierler et al., 2000). Moreover, HIV-positive women experience higher rates of not only sexual assault and partner violence than HIV-negative women, but also criminal violence such as robbery and being mugged (Axelrod, Myers, Durvasula, Wyatt, & Cheng, 1999; Kimerling, Armistead, & Forehand, 1999). Alarmingly, the path of victimization appears to begin in childhood, with at least 50% of women with HIV reporting being physically and sexually abused as children. Early trauma increases risk for depression, ineffective coping, and may lead to revictimization, including sexual, substance use, and other HIV risks (Wyatt, Myers, & Loeb, 2004). Substance use and mental health problems are also highly associated with low adherence to life-saving HIV medications. These vulnerabilities are compounded by the crime and violence of inner-city communities, where many women with HIV and at risk for HIV live and raise their families.

Health Disparities

In recent years, reports on health disparities in the United States have drawn our attention to how race, ethnicity, gender, or socioeconomic status affect health outcomes. In the United States, racial or ethnic minorities are less likely to have access to medical and mental health care and health insurance and are more likely to receive insufficient or inappropriate care, resulting in poor outcomes (Agency for Healthcare Research Quality, 2007). Additionally, historical suspicion of the medical professional and the stigma associated with mental health affects African Americans' willingness to use health, and especially mental health, services. Many delay seeking services to receive care in emergency rooms after symptoms become more severe. For Latinas, language may pose a barrier to services and unbalance power with a partner who speaks English and thus is the gatekeeper to service access.

In the HIV Costs and Services Utilization Study (HCSUS), a large-scale study of people with HIV, people with HIV who were of low socioeconomic status (SES) and those who were African American or Latino accessed fewer health services, were less likely than other ethnic groups to access HAART, were less likely to have health insurance, and were likely to have higher mortality rates from HIV (Cunningham et al., 2005). As women with HIV are predominantly low SES and racial/ethnic minorities, gender must be considered a major factor in health disparities within the epidemic. In fact, women with HIV are less likely to receive combination therapy and access than men and more likely to postpone care due to lack of transportation or a bout of ill health.

In addition to HIV medical care, women have mental health needs that affect their ability to prevent HIV or receive HIV care. Women with HIV report significantly more depressive symptoms than HIV-negative women, even when researchers take into account income and substance use (Axelrod et al., 1999). Some women may have been depressed prior to learning their HIV status—for example, experiencing depressive symptoms related to previous trauma or abuse. For others, depression may be related to having HIV, or previous depressive symptoms may worsen as the woman copes with HIV-related illnesses and stressors. We do know that depression is associated with lower use of HAART and can reduce life expectancy for women with HIV, even when they are taking HAART (Cook et al., 2002). Conversely, mental health service use greatly increases the likelihood of taking medication and improves life expectancy. We should not ignore the relationship between mental health, especially substance use and the effects of trauma, and HIV medical care for women. Health disparities or inequalities in access, use, and the woman's experience of treatment intensify this relationship, reducing women's quality and length of life.

HIV Stigma and Discrimination

HIV disease is one of the most stigmatized illnesses in modern history (Mahajan et al., 2008; Parker & Aggleton, 2003). This stigma has its roots in fears of contagion, fears of death and dying, and the historical marginalization of people who have been affected by HIV, such as homosexuals and injecting drug users (Herek, 1999; Mahajan et al., 2008). Due to HIV stigma, people with HIV are rejected, excluded, and shunned and consequently feel anger, anxiety, depression, hopelessness, loneliness, and decreased self-esteem (Antle, Wells, Goldie, DeMatteo, & King, 2001; Clark, Lindner, Armistead, & Austin, 2003; Ingram & Hutchinson, 1999; Lee, Kochman, & Sikkema, 2002). Women have the added stigma of being perceived as engaging in "immoral" sexual or drug activity. Sexual mores have traditionally been different for men and women, with sexuality being more accepted and even encouraged in men. In addition, women who use drugs or alcohol to excess are judged more harshly than are men. If a woman has HIV, she is likely to be blamed for that and considered deviant, junkie, or a prostitute and a vector of transmission to children and to men (Sandelowski, Lambe, & Barroso, 2004).

Since women are interdependent with children, parents, and family, stigma has a ripple effect, extending out in waves to loved ones. Family members or friends of people with HIV also report stigma-related concerns, including fear of potential rejection, anger, and shame, and stigma has been associated with depression for family members (Bogart et al., 2008; Joslin, 2000; Poindexter, 2002; Wight, Aneshensel, Murphy, Miller-Martinez, & Beals, 2006). Adolescents, specifically, worry that they may be rejected or considered HIV-infected if others find out their parent's status (Brackis-Cott,

Mellins, & Block, 2003; Murphy, Roberts, & Hoffman, 2002). In fact, children and adolescents may feel stigma as acutely as their HIV-positive parents because of their close connection and because children cannot easily distance themselves from the stigmatized person, as a friend or extended family member might (Cree, Kay, Tisdall, & Wallace, 2004).

Stigma has been cited as a reason for not getting tested, for not accessing HIV care, for not disclosing one's diagnosis, and for lack of adherence to medication regimens (U.S. Department of Health and Human Services, 2003; Vanable, Carey, Blair, & Littlewood, 2006). Stigma also reduces the likelihood of practicing safer sex—using a condom is implicit acknowledgment that one might have HIV—thus sabotaging risk-reduction and prevention efforts. Enacted stigma or direct experiences of stigma may indeed be less virulent than 20 years ago, but felt or perceived stigma persists. In recent research, women still report HIV stigma from health care providers, and some women with HIV cite poor treatment and blame from providers as a barrier to accessing prenatal care and treatment (Lindau et al., 2006).

Women adapt their behavior in order to reduce stigma's impact, keeping the secret to themselves or picking and choosing carefully whom and how to tell. A woman, however, may find herself in a lose-lose situation. If she decides not to disclose to family members, she cuts herself off from support for her diagnosis. If she discloses to friends or family, she risks anger, fear, and isolation due to HIV stigma or the stigma attached to risk behaviors, such as sexuality and substance use.

HIV stigma intersects with racism, classism, and sexism, exacerbating the differential treatment already experienced by African American women and Latinas, who may also be low-income and/or substance using. We have some evidence that there are racial differences in how women experience HIV stigma (Rao, Pryor, Gaddist, & Mayer, 2008) and those differences may be more negative for African American than Caucasian women (Wingood et al., 2007). In any case, many women with HIV lack a supportive community and financial resources to help manage their disease, including stigma (Hudson, Lee, Miramontes, & Portillo, 2001; Buseh & Stevens, 2006). In this context, stigma is not solely an attribute but a social process that "produces and reproduces social inequality," (Parker & Aggleton, 2003), thus compounding the vulnerability of women and their children.

APPROACHES TO HIV PREVENTION AND CARE

Woven together, the preceding socioeconomic and cultural factors add depth to our picture of women at risk for or living with HIV and help us understand them beyond labels of race or age. These women have needs that are silenced by gender roles and stigma; they have less access to and quality of care due to health disparities and stigma; and, although they can draw on the strength and support of others, they are also weighed down by or alienated from those relationships, especially with the stresses of low income and poor health. These are large issues that we have struggled with for decades—poverty, multiple layers of stigma and oppression, inadequate health care systems, cultural norms—and that are not changed easily. However, there are steps we can take to promote HIV prevention with women and, when a woman does become infected, improve her quality of life. In order to address women's vulnerabilities to and with HIV, service plans, program models, and public policies should embrace the following components: a focus on family and relationships; the integration of mental health, substance use, and health services; and the use of empowerment approaches.

Family and Relational Focus

Identify the key people in women's lives and recognize that these relationships have an impact on women's functioning. Women's interdependency can be a strength and a weakness, lending meaning to her life while stretching limited emotional, physical, and financial resources. Use women's relational strengths to build support systems that facilitate healthy behavior. If family and friend support systems have been disrupted because of family history or stigma, help women think through and practice how and with whom they will reconnect. If support and family systems are damaged irreparably or too unhealthy, help women build new networks. Support from other women is especially valued, as evidenced by the extensive use of support and psychoeducational groups in HIV prevention and care.

Develop strong alliances with family-oriented service organizations in order to facilitate referrals but also to build partners in advocating for the needs of families and informal caregivers. Support partners, extended family (as defined by the women), and friends as key to women's health and, due to similar demographic and geographic characteristics, as potentially vulnerable themselves to HIV. Provide not only supportive, woman-friendly services such as child care and transportation—services integral to women's use of services—but also include partners, siblings, parents, friends, and fathers in family sessions or special events. Consider the informal caregivers for women with HIV. The support networks of women with HIV most often comprise other women—mothers, sisters, colleagues, or best friends. These women are informal caregivers when the woman with HIV is sick and when her children need care. Although the women most at risk now for HIV are identified as heterosexual or bisexual, we must not be heterosexist. Women who have sex with women, an overlooked group in the epidemic, have acquired HIV through injected drug use or through unprotected sex with men. Their sexual and drug partners may also be women at risk for and vulnerable to HIV.

Parenting and children are fundamental to many women's sense of purpose, while drawing resources from mother's self-care. Children are also affected by a mother's HIV status and vulnerability. As women with HIV are living longer, parent/child relationships are increasingly key to women's self-esteem and to children's healthy development. Assess children's mental health, mother's parenting needs, and family functioning in order to promote and sustain health as well as reduce intergenerational risk. Be prepared to provide or refer to and work closely with agencies that provide children's mental health services, parenting and parent management training, family therapy, or multiple family groups.

Integrated Mental Health, Substance Use, and Health Services

Mental health, including substance use, and physical health are inextricably linked for women at risk for and living with HIV. We can no longer afford to think of mental and physical health as two separate systems or constructs. Primary health care services will not be used or useful if a woman's mental health does not support active involvement in her health care, including monitoring her health, taking medications, and staying in substance use recovery. Women face a broad array of stressors from the past and in the present. Stigma and gender socialization promote passive and avoidant coping. The effects of trauma and violence are an additional burden on mental health and coping. Cultivate approaches and techniques that develop and encourage active coping and combine mental health and medical outcomes nontraditionally. For example, a group intervention has been developed and proven effective for medication adherence and for addressing trauma (Jones et al., 2007).

When mental health and other health services cannot be provided in the same building or system, develop partnerships between the two. Partnerships take time and are often not considered in funding or reimbursement. However, the time is well spent if women live longer and have better lives as a result. Additionally, if women's lives are improved, then potentially so are their children's lives and other lives within the family circle.

Empowerment Approaches

We must be careful not to reproduce stigma and women's unequal status in our approaches. Rather, we develop and promote women's skills to speak for themselves and those in their care. We can reframe HIV stigma as the ignorance of fear of others (Buseh & Stevens, 2006) and provide information and build skills so women can educate others. Similarly, we can reframe self-advocacy and expression of need as "taking care of yourself so you can take care of your children," thus supporting women's self-care and recognizing that they are as important as the people in their care.

As advocates we must assert the need for prevention methods that women can control, such as the female condom or microbicide gels (not yet available) that women can insert before intercourse in order to kill HIV. We must always work with women *and men* to recognize and develop relationships in which they are equal partners and can negotiate safer sex. Relationship-based HIV prevention strategies with heterosexual couples, for example, are being implemented on a limited basis and are effective. As women are living longer, paid employment or volunteering in order to develop work skills and resumes can increase self-esteem and promote women's financial self-reliance, rather than total reliance on male partners for financial survival.

We should examine our service delivery systems and other formal networks that women use. Offer periodic training and discussions for professionals on service provision to women and on women's experience of stigma and discriminatory behavior. Consider community and traditional organizations for supporting women. Many racial and ethnic minority women find strength in spirituality or religion. Women with HIV have varied experiences with the church, synagogue, temple, or mosque; some have felt rejected by and are estranged from their religion, and others have renewed their faith and found great strength. Faith-based initiatives—approaches incorporating the science of HIV transmission and prevention into community-based religious institutions—can enhance churches' ability to respond to the pandemic while building natural networks of community support for those at risk and living with HIV.

Women with HIV often report finding a new perspective on and meaning to life with an HIV diagnosis. Faced with severe illness, the women reprioritized their goals and found power in taking control (Goggin et al., 2001). These women are powerful role models. Women with HIV are peer educators, group facilitators, health educators, and community activists. In high-risk communities, women—infected or not—are volunteers or paid employees doing street outreach, facilitating groups, and working with community leaders to develop and deliver prevention messages.

The use of participatory methods—the inclusion of women vulnerable to and living with HIV into services and research development—has multiple benefits. The people receiving the message of prevention or care are most likely to change behavior if the person delivering the message is similar: For example, an African American woman living in the neighborhood. The women delivering the message or designing the program find their voices in changing systems and developing knowledge while at the same time developing their networks and skills for future employment and self-care. In addition, we ensure that the services are acceptable to women and thus used.

What Is It Like to Be a Woman Living with HIV? by Wendy

Before I can answer this question I must first give you some background of where I came from—alcoholic, physical abuse, and incest. My mother died when I was six years old. We then moved to Chicago from Detroit. Due to these things going on in my life I became a prostitute, which took me into the drug and alcoholic scene. I began to drink at the age of 11, endeavoring to get rid of the guilt and shame from being molested at home by my brothers. By age 18, I was dropping speed and drinking alcohol. By age 22, I started using heroin intravenously along with cocaine, you name the drug; I tried it to be happy but none of it worked. I got married to my pimp. I was in that relationship for 15 years, where a lot of physical abuse took place. He broke both of my arms at one time, fractured my ribs, broke my elbows, and beat me with wire coat hangers, and he cut me. I could write a book on domestic violence; it was always present in my life in some form or fashion.

At the age of 37, I lost custody of my children to the child welfare system. My life was going downhill at a fast pace. I even ended up homeless at one period of this time. I was living in a building that had been set on fire but was still habitable, so I slept there for about three months without anyone discovering it. While living through all this I thought nothing could get worse. In August of 1990, I gave birth to a beautiful baby girl.

In December of 1990, I was diagnosed with HIV. I wanted to kill myself. I increased my drug and alcohol use to kill myself. Everything bad that had ever happened to me stood up that day! I asked God, why has my life been so miserable? I could not remember anything that had ever gone right. My life never had any productivity in it that I could ever remember. And now this disease that everyone was afraid of and whispering about had become part of my life . . . why? And then again, why not? . . . Everything bad seemed to always find me.

My family rejected me right away after I told them I had HIV. I tried medical treatment, but the medical staff was even afraid of what I had! Ha ha, was that not a laugh? The living in fear and secrecy of keeping people from knowing was truly more than a person could bear. Sometimes I wanted to shout from the highest mountain, "I got HIV," but the majority of the time I lived in fear of someone finding out about me having it. What a life. I finally got my children returned back into my home. I maintained three years of sobriety, but one day the pressure was more than I could bear. For you see, I had a daughter—my baby—whom I did not know whether was HIV-positive or not, and fear kept me from finding out. I was lonely and afraid to tell anyone about this, so it would send me on binges that looked like I would never return to a sober life again.

Then in 1993, I became aware of the Lord Jesus Christ . . . what a wonderful change came over me. I began to learn about why I could not stay sober and that there is nothing that the Power of the Almighty Jehovah God could not deliver me from . . . including the guilt and shame along with pain I had. . . . I must take the time to give flowers to whom they are due, for without Christ in my life I would not be sitting here writing this excerpt about my life. Through this change I was able to get my daughter tested; she tested HIV-negative. I was able

(Continued)

to begin to disclose my HIV status, slowly but surely. I am now a witness that HIV is not a death sentence, and I disclose every opportunity I am given to do so. I can tell other women today that this is not a death sentence but a new lease on life, if you get educated and disclose to your children and siblings and to other women living with your old fears. For there is some woman newly diagnosed every day somewhere in the world.

The hardest thing now is that I have progressed into another step with this illness: I now live with AIDS. The medication is so hard for me to keep in place for my health—God, how I hate that daily ritual of taking them. I struggle even to this day with that, and it is due to a medicine I once took that almost killed me. But I must take them, because I am still parenting my youngest daughter, who is soon to be 18. She needs me now even more than before; she will meet new challenges and roadblocks as she works to achieve the will and strength to mature into whatever field or profession she desires for her life. I must strive to make the right decisions; they will not always be right but at least she will know that I have only her best interest in mind. There are days where I am overprotective because I am HIV-positive and because of my former lifestyle. I also have grandchildren whom I look at as my own children. Rearing children while living with HIV can be very difficult some days. You must deal with days of depression and feeling sorry for yourself and days that you're tired from the virus or just plain age.

Being a woman living with HIV includes my taking care of myself physically and medically, which can be a real chore for me at times. It is worth the fight and struggle at the end when you see the rewarding results. But there is still one fight I have daily and that is being an African American woman. You see, we think that we must be strong unto death when it comes to parenting. We forget that we need time also for ourselves, and that we are human too, not made of steel. The moment I fully accept that challenge then I will be on my way to higher horizons.

CONCLUSIONS

With the introduction of HAART and the shift in the epidemic toward women, we have broadened our understanding of the factors that affect women, whether at risk for or living with HIV—children, partners, mental health, trauma, and substance use. We have also seen a shift in HIV service priorities from planning for children's care in case of mother's death to supporting active parenting, from coping with severe illness to developing skills and resumes for employment. Women with HIV and at risk for HIV may be constrained by vulnerabilities, but they do not have to be determined by them (Buseh & Stevens, 2006). We accept their right to exist and thrive, and support and encourage their ability to be self-determined.

REFERENCES

Agency for Healthcare Research and Quality. (2007). National Healthcare Disparities Report. www .ahrq.gov/qual/qrdr07.htm

Antle, B. J., Wells, L. M., Goldie, R. S., DeMatteo, D., & King, S. M. (2001). Challenges of parenting for families living with HIV/AIDS. *Social Work, 46*(2), 59–169.

Axelrod, J., Myers, H. F., Durvasula, R. S., Wyatt, G. E., & Cheng, M. (1999). The impact of relationship violence, HIV, and ethnicity on adjustment in women. *Cultural Diversity and Ethnic Minority Psychology, 5*(3), 263–275.

Bogart, L. M., Cowgill, B. O., Kennedy, D., Ryan, G., Murphy, D. A., Elijah, J., et al. (2008). HIV-related stigma among people with HIV and their families: A qualitative analysis. *AIDS and Behavior, 12*(2), 244–254.

Brackis-Cott, E., Mellins, C. A., & Block, M. (2003). Current life concerns of early adolescents and their mothers: Influence of maternal HIV. *Journal of Early Adolescence, 23*(1), 51–77.

Buseh, A. G., & Stevens, P. E. (2006). Constrained but not determined by stigma: Resistance by African American women living with HIV. *Women & Health, 44*(3), 1–18.

Centers for Disease Control and Prevention. (2007). *HIV/AIDS and men who have sex with men (MSM).* Retrieved from /www.cdc.gov/hiv/topics/msm/index.htm

Centers for Disease Control and Prevention. (2008a). Updated slide set: *HIV/AIDS surveillance in men who have sex with men (MSM).* Retrieved from www.cdc.gov/hiv/topics/surveillance/index.htm

Centers for Disease Control and Prevention. (2008b). *HIV/AIDS among women.* Retrieved from www.cdc.gov/hiv/topics/women/resources/factsheets/women.htm

Clark, H. J., Lindner, G., Armistead, L., & Austin, B. J. (2003). Stigma, disclosure, and psychological functioning among HIV-infected and non-infected African American women. *Women & Health, 38*(4), 57–71.

Cook, J. A., Cohen, M. H., Burke, J., Grey, D., Anastos, K., Kirstein, L., et al. (2002). Effect of treated and untreated depressive symptoms on highly active antiretroviral therapy use in a US multi-site cohort of HIV-positive women. *AIDS Care, 18*(2), 93–100.

Cree, V. E., Kay, H., Tisdall, K., & Wallace, J. (2004). Stigma and parental HIV. *Qualitative Social Work 3*(1), 7–25.

Cunningham, W. E., Hays, R. D., Duan, N., Andersen, R. M., Nakazono, T. T., Bozzette, S. A., et al. (2005). The effect of socioeconomic status on the survival of people receiving care for HIV infection in the United States. *Journal of Health Care for the Poor and Underserved 16,* 655–676.

DeMarco, R., Lynch, M., & Board, R. (2002). Mothers who silence themselves: A concept with clinical implications for women living with HIV/AIDS and their children. *Journal of Pediatric Nursing, 17*(2), 89–95.

Gant, L. M., & Welch, L. A. (2004). Voice less heard: HIV-positive African American women, medication adherence, sexual abuse, and self care. *Journal of HIV/AIDS & Social Services, 3*(2), 67–91.

Goggin, K., Catley, D., Brisco, S. T., Engelson, E. S., Rabkin, J. G., & Kotler, D. P. (2001). A female perspective on living with HIV disease. *Health & Social Work, 26*(2), 80–89.

Herek, G. M. (1999). AIDS and stigma. *American Behavioral Scientist, 42*(7), 1102–1112.

Hudson, A. L., Lee, K. A., Miramontes, H., & Portillo, C. J. (2001). Social interactions, perceived support, and level of distress in HIV-positive women. *Journal of the Association of Nurses in AIDS Care, 12*(4), 68–76.

Ingram, D., & Hutchinson, S. A. (1999). HIV-positive mothers and stigma. *Health Care for Women International, 20,* 93–103.

Jack, D. C. (1991). *Silencing the self.* Cambridge, MA: Harvard University Press.

Jones, D. L., McPherson-Baker, S., Lydston, D., Camille, J., Brondolo, E., Tobin, J. N., et al. (2007). Efficacy of a group medication adherence intervention among HIV-positive women: The SMART/EST Women's Project. *AIDS Behavior, 11,* 79–86.

Joslin, D. (2000). Emotional well-being among grandparents raising children affected and orphaned by HIV disease. In B. Hayslip Jr. & R. Goldberg-Glen (Eds.), *Grandparent raising grandchildren: Theoretical, empirical, and clinical perspectives.* New York: Springer.

Kaiser Family Foundation. (2008). *HIV/AIDS policy fact sheet—Women and HIV/AIDS in the U.S.* Retrieved from www.kff.org/hivaids/6092.cfm

Kimerling, R., Armistead, L., & Forehand, R. (1999). Victimization experiences and HIV infection in women: Association with serostatus, psychological symptoms, and health status. *Journal of Traumatic Stress, 12*(1), 41–58.

Lee, R. S., Kochman, A., & Sikkema, K. J. (2002). Internalized stigma among people living with HIV-AIDS. *AIDS and Behavior, 6*(4), 309–319.

Lindau, S. T., Jerome, J., Miller, K., Monk, E., Garcia, P., & Cohen, M. (2006). Mothers on the margins: Implications for eradicating perinatal HIV. *Social Science & Medicine, 62*(1), 59–69.

Mahajan, A. P., Sayles, J. N., Patel, V. A., Remien, R. H., Sawires, S. R., Ortiz, D. J., et al. (2008*). Stigma in the HIV/AIDS epidemic: A review of the literature and recommendations for the way forward. AIDS, 22*(Suppl. 2), S67–S79.

Mellins, C. A., Havens, J. F., McCaskill, E. O., Leu, C. S., Brudney, K., & Chesney, M. A. (2002). Mental health, substance use and disclosure are significantly associated with the medical treatment adherence of HIV-infected mothers. *Psychology, Health & Medicine 7*(4), 451–460.

Murphy, D. A., Greenwell, L., & Hoffman, D. (2002). Factors associated with antiretroviral adherence among HIV-infected women with children. *Women & Health, 36*(1), 97–111.

Murphy, D. A., Roberts, K. J., & Hoffman, D. (2002). Stigma and ostracism associated with HIV/AIDS: Children carrying the secret of their mothers' HIV+ serostatus. *Journal of Child and Family Studies, 11*(2), 191–202.

Parker, R., & Aggleton, P. (2003). HIV and AIDS-related stigma and discrimination: A conceptual framework and implications for action. *Social Science & Medicine, 57,* 13–24.

Poindexter, C. C. (2002). "It don't matter what people say as long as I love you": Experiencing stigma when raising an HIV-infected grandchild. *Journal of Mental Health and Aging, 8*(4), 331–347.

Rao, D., Pryor, J. B., Gaddist, B. W., & Mayer, R. (2008). Stigma, secrecy, and discrimination: Ethnic/racial differences in the concerns of people living with HIV/AIDS. *AIDS Behavior, 12*(2), 265–271.

Sandelowski, M., Lambe, C., & Barroso, J. (2004). Stigma in HIV-positive women. *Journal of Nursing Scholarship, 36*(2), 122–128.

Schiller, N., Crystal, S., & Lewellen, D. (1994). Risky business: The cultural construction of AIDS risk groups. *Social Science and Medicine, 38*(10), 1337–1346.

Simoni, J. M., & Ng, M. T. (2000). Trauma, coping, and depression among women with HIV/AIDS in New York City. *AIDS Care, 12*(5), 567–580.

U.S. Department of Health and Human Services, Health Resources and Services Administration, HIV/AIDS Bureau. (2003). *Providing HIV/AIDS care in a changing environment.* Retrieved August 2003, from HRSACareAction http://www.hab.hrsa.gov/publications/august2003.htm

UNAIDS. (2008). Addressing societal causes of HIV risk and vulnerability. *Report on the Global AIDS Epidemic.* Available online at http://data.unaids.org/pub/GlobalReport/2008/jc1510_2008_global_report_pp63_94_en.pdf

Vanable P. A., Carey, M. P., Blair, D. C., & Littlewood, R. A. (2006). Impact of HIV-related stigma on health behaviors and psychological adjustment among HIV-positive men and women. *AIDS and Behavior, 10*(5), 473–482.

Wight, R. G., Aneshensel, C. S., Murphy, D. A., Miller-Martinez, D., & Beals, K. P. (2006). Perceived HIV stigma in AIDS caregiving dyads. *Social Science & Medicine, 62,* 444–456.

Wingood, G. M., DiClemente, R. J., Mikhail, I., McCree, D. H., Davies, S. L., Hardin, J. W., et al. (2007). HIV discrimination and the health of women living with HIV. *Women & Health, 46*(2/3), 99–112.

Wyatt, G. E., Myers, H. F., & Loeb, T. B. (2004). Women, trauma, and HIV: An overview. *AIDS and Behavior, 8*(4), 401–403.

Zierler, S., Cunningham, W. E., Andersen, R. M., Shapiro, M. F., Bozzette, S. A., Nakazono, T. T., et al. (2000). Violence victimization after HIV infection in a U.S. probability sample of adult patients in primary care. *American Journal of Public Health, 90*(2), 208–215.

Chapter Fourteen

HIV PREVENTION AND SERVICES FOR GAY, BISEXUAL, AND OTHER MEN WHO HAVE SEX WITH MEN: NOW IS STILL THE TIME

David J. Brennan and Winston Husbands

INTRODUCTION

This chapter examines some of the key factors involved in contributing to and preventing the spread of HIV among men who have sex with men (MSM),[1] as well as issues related to providing services to MSM. We offer examples of useful programs, policies, and interventions for HIV-infected gay and bisexual men. Additionally, we provide some recommendations to reduce the impact of HIV on the lives of gay and bisexual men.

Gay and bisexual men have been at the forefront of battling HIV and AIDS since the earliest days of the pandemic. Beginning in the early and mid-1980s, gay and bisexual men organized a response to the new, mysterious disease without support from institutions that traditionally assisted people in dealing with health risks. Many government, education, family, and church supports were lacking an urgent and compassionate response to the HIV pandemic early on. During the early days of the HIV pandemic, gay and bisexual men demonstrated one of the most successful grassroots, population-based behavior change efforts ever recorded—a decrease in risky sexual behavior. Gay and bisexual men in the early days of the HIV pandemic created and taught safer sex techniques, including condom use. They created workshops and small private parties to demonstrate the erotic nature of safer sex and the urgency to avoid HIV. They also organized and actively engaged

(Continued)

Acknowledgments: Dr. Brennan dedicates this chapter to the memory of Billy and Eric, whom he still misses, even after 20 years. Dr. Husbands dedicates this chapter to his colleagues and friends in Toronto working on the front lines to halt the spread of HIV.

[1]In North American culture, men who have sex with men often identify as gay (or homosexual, in older terminology). Those who have sexual relations with both men and women may identify as bisexual, though some may consider themselves heterosexual, or straight. In First Nation or Native American communities, the term "two-spirit" is often used, denoting someone who lives between traditional gendered experiences or roles. Men who identify as gay, bisexual, or two-spirit are more likely to be connected to communities of other men who identify as gay or bisexual and to identify as members of the gay or bisexual male culture. For the purposes of this chapter, we primarily use the term *gay and bisexual men*. MSM is a more inclusive term used to identify all men who have sex with other men, regardless of whether they identify as straight, gay, or bisexual.

with the larger institutions of government, medicine, public health, and social services to advocate for massive system changes that allowed for them to access the services required to care for themselves and their friends, families, and loved ones. Gay communities did all of this in the face of death and discrimination, demonstrating enormous resilience.

HIV continues to have an extremely harmful and lasting impact on the health and well-being of gay and bisexual men. In North America, unprotected anal sexual intercourse is the most common cause of HIV transmission among MSM. In the United States, the Centers for Disease Control and Prevention (CDC) reports that the majority of new HIV infections in 2006 were among MSM (53 percent, or 28,720) and that young Black MSM had more new infections than any other age or racial group (CDC, 2008). In the United States, HIV is still likely to occur among gay and bisexual men at a rate 100 times that of the general population (Sullivan & Wolitski, 2008).

It is critical to understand and acknowledge that gay and bisexual men remain at risk for becoming infected with HIV and still experience challenges accessing appropriate prevention education and HIV-related services when they need them. The ongoing pandemic among gay and bisexual men warrants thoughtful critique and analysis of the delivery of prevention and other health and social services. Here we explore the societal, systemic, and individual vulnerability of gay and bisexual men in North America, build on that discussion to present the need for targeted prevention education and culturally competent services, recommend some successful model programs, and make recommendations for practice and advocacy.

MULTIPLE LEVELS OF RISKS FOR GAY AND BISEXUAL MEN

Society-Level Vulnerability Factors

Homophobia—prejudice and discrimination based on sexual orientation—is one of the major issues that affects the health and well-being of gay and bisexual men and other MSM. Though there have been many advances in the rights of gay, lesbian, bisexual, and transgender people over the past 20 years, homophobia is a pervasive factor in our society. Gay and bisexual men may also face rejection from their families, friends, and medical and social service providers. Almost half (48%) of all people in the United States consider homosexual relations morally wrong, with 40% believing that homosexual relations should be illegal (Gallup Organization, 2008). In the most extreme form, this attitude can result in gay and bisexual men being harassed or being physically or verbally assaulted. By some estimates, 11 to 18 percent of all gay and bisexual men report being a victim of a physical or verbal harassment for being gay (Herek & Sims, 2008), though this may be a conservative estimate, as often these forms of harassment go unreported. Discrimination against lesbian, gay, bisexual, and transgender (LGBT) people persists among a wide range of racial and ethnic groups (Fullilove & Fullilove, 1999; Ramirez-Valles, Fergus, Reisen, Poppen, & Zea, 2005) as well as among students in social work (Cramer, 1997) and psychology (Korfhage, 2006). Evidence suggests that systemic factors may increase some men's vulnerability to HIV (Cáceres, Aggleton, & Galea, 2008; Diaz, 2008; Diaz,

Ayala, Bein, Henne, & Marin, 2001; Gardezi, Calzavara, Husbands, Tharao, Lawson et al., 2008; Mays, Cochran, & Zamudio, 2004). Gay and bisexual men who endure poor economic conditions, racism, and homophobia may be unable to realistically assess their risk of becoming infected and less likely to sustain life-enhancing behaviors (for example, adhering to safer sex practices or getting tested for HIV [Huebner, Davis, Nemeroff, & Aiken, 2002]) and may be discouraged from seeking HIV testing and services (Flowers, Knussen, & Church, 2003; Herek & Sims, 2008). Homophobia is associated with greater mental and physical health risks, including alienation, lack of self-acceptance (Stokes & Peterson, 1998), depression, increased alcohol and substance use, and suicide (Gilman, Cochran, Mays, & Hughes, 2001). Gay and bisexual men from racial or ethnic communities may experience stigma that is associated with both racism and homophobia, which may increase the risks to their health (Fullilove & Fullilove, 1999; Ramirez-Valles et al., 2005).

Information about HIV transmission and sexual behavior for gay and bisexual men is not readily available. It is not always taught in schools or by parents and guardians; one may need to seek out this information. Though the Internet has increased access to information for many individuals, one person accessing a Web page may not by itself create a larger cultural behavioral change. Early in the pandemic, frank and explicit information on sexual health was not even allowed under United States federal guidelines. More recently, the United States "abstinence-only until marriage" education and funding has ignored the reality of many people living with and at risk for HIV, including MSM, who are generally not eligible for marriage (Open Society Institute, 2006; Trenholm et al., 2007). If MSM do not have adequate relevant, accurate, nonjudgmental information that is supported by research, they are less likely to have the resources they need to engage in healthy sexual activity.

Much of the research conducted on MSM has focused on men who reside, work, and/or socialize in urban gay enclaves. Why do health disparities exist among men who live in large urban centers, who are generally highly knowledgeable and educated about HIV? Stall, Freidman, and Catania (2008) have recently articulated the notion that each of these health disparities represents a piece of a web of mutually reinforcing pandemics that, when interconnected, negatively affect the health of the community. Stall and his colleagues drew on the findings of the Urban Men's Health Study (for example, see Stall et al., 2003), a large health-focused household-based sample of gay and bisexual men who lived in large U.S. cities. The analyses of these data highlighted the associations between mental health, physical health, alcohol and drug use, and violence with HIV risk. In these findings, it became clear that multiple epidemics were having an impact on the health and well-being of gay and bisexual men who live in urban areas. These epidemics are intertwined into what is referred to as "syndemics." Stall and associates (2008) define *syndemics* as "a set of mutually reinforcing epidemics that together lower the overall health profile of a population more than each epidemic by itself might be expected to do" (p. 251). In other words, the intersection of multiple forces is at play here, and these factors increase the risk and struggles that gay and bisexual men may be experiencing. Though gay and bisexual men may move to urban centers to build community or to find more opportunities for dating and sexual contacts, there are also risks in larger cities, such as more HIV infection and more drug use.

Many gay and bisexual men from outside of urban areas choose to move and live in areas that have a larger gay and bisexual male community, not only out of a desire to connect with a community and socialize and date with other gay and bisexual men, but also to attend to their own health and lessen discrimination and prejudice. However, urban gay communities are undergoing massive changes. Urban gay communities often have political clout to make social policy and changes that address their needs. Rosser, West, & Weinmeyer (2008) report that increased LGBT rights and protections, increased visibility and community organizing, and vibrant social networking online have led to an "overall declining visibility of gay communities" in cities throughout the globe (p. 588). Thus, previous methods of connecting to gay and bisexual men in certain geographical locations may need to be reevaluated, given the changes experienced in these communities.

Additionally, many MSM live in rural areas and are not connected with urban communities, except for the occasional visit to such cities and communities. These men are likely to have specific needs related to accessing HIV-related information and services. Recent research has highlighted issues that gay and bisexual men in rural areas face that may have a negative impact up their health and their ability to access HIV services and prevention. For instance, among a sample of rural gay and bisexual men in Pennsylvania, 52% of the men reported unprotected anal intercourse, thus putting them at high risk for HIV infection (Preston, D'Augelli, Kassab, & Starks, 2007). Additionally, these men reported that homophobia was present in their communities, though not necessarily from health providers and family.

Individual-Level Vulnerability

Though systemic practices and policies are critical factors in HIV risk and sexual health for gay and bisexual men, personal factors are known to be associated with this continuing HIV pandemic among MSM. For instance, many gay and bisexual men lived through the earlier days of the pandemic when they often witnessed their friends, colleagues, and other peers with HIV get sick and die very quickly. Some men may feel that now that better treatments are available, HIV is no longer a particularly urgent health issue. This is sometimes referred to as HIV optimism or HIV treatment optimism. Now that better treatment is available, many people living with HIV experience relatively healthy lives. HIV treatment, however, can have complications and requires consistent medical care and follow-up. Moreover, people are still dying from AIDS. Gay and bisexual men may take more sexual or injection risks if they think that treatment for HIV means that HIV is less severe and that they are less likely to get HIV from someone who is on treatment.

Research highlights a connection between alcohol and drug use and unprotected sex leading to HIV infection (Koblin et al., 2006). Gay and bisexual men who drink excessively or use drugs frequently are more likely to have unprotected sex. One drug, crystal methamphetamine, has been identified as being of particular concern. There has been an increase in crystal methamphetamine use among MSM over the past decade (Semple, Patterson, & Grant, 2000). It is a drug that simultaneously causes heightened sexual energy and impairs judgment. Thus, when people are high they are less likely to make safer sexual decisions.

Other factors that may be associated with HIV risk for gay and bisexual men include the effects of social networks and peers upon sexual risk behavior. Research shows that gay and bisexual men, like others in society, tend to be greatly affected by their friends and social networks. These peers can influence decisions about condom use: The more likely that gay and bisexual men are connected to other gay and bisexual men who do not use condoms consistently, the more likely they are to use condoms inconsistently themselves (Scott-Sheldon, Marsh, Johnson, & Glasford, 2006). Research shows that peer norms have an especially influential impact on condom use among African American MSM as well (Bakeman & Peterson, 2007).

There are also concerns that if gay and bisexual men have not been tested for HIV and are not aware of their HIV status, they may not be aware that they are at risk for

HIV transmission. Recent research in the United Stares has shown that young gay and bisexual men, and in particular young men of color, are frequently unaware of their HIV status. In one study by the CDC, 46% of HIV-infected Black MSM were unaware that they were HIV-infected (CDC, 2005). This is cause for concern because there is also evidence that people who know they are HIV-infected are less likely to engage in risky sexual behavior (Dilley et al., 2002).

The situation of African American MSM challenges us to be creative about HIV prevention. In a comparison of Bhite, Black, and Latino MSM in the United States in 2006, Black men accounted for 35% of new infections among MSM, and almost half (46%) of new infections among MSM 13 to 29 years old (Morbidity and Mortality Weekly Report, 2008; CDC, 2008). Yet it is widely understood that Black MSM are no more likely than White MSM to engage in risky sex (Crosby, Holtgrave, Stall, Peterson, & Shouse, 2007; Harawa et al., 2004; Millett, Flores, Peterson, & Bakeman, 2007; Wilson, Wright, & Isbell, 2008). Instead, their disproportionate rate of HIV infection may be attributed to a greater presence of sexually transmitted infections (STIs), which increases susceptibility to HIV acquisition, and higher rates of unrecognized HIV infection (Millett, Peterson, Wolitski, & Stall, 2006). Clearly, current prevention efforts must focus specifically on these risks for men of color.

HIV PREVENTION FOR GAY AND BISEXUAL MEN

The success of HIV prevention programs depends on, among other factors, how well researchers, public health authorities, and health promotion practitioners understand the pandemic (Wilson & Halperin, 2008). While it is certainly true that anyone who has unprotected sex or shares injecting equipment may become infected, current epidemiological evidence shows that MSM bear the major burden of HIV infection in the United States. This suggests that MSM should be a priority population for HIV prevention efforts, and that preventing the spread of HIV among MSM will contribute substantially to halting the pandemic in the population as a whole. Moreover, as with any other target population, HIV prevention and social service efforts must engage gay and bisexual men, as well as other MSM, in the response to HIV in their communities and must attend to their needs, circumstances, and priorities.

"Safer sex" refers to sexual norms, practices, and behaviors that reduce the transmission or acquisition of HIV. In the early days of the pandemic, gay and bisexual men engaged in a large grassroots effort to educate each other about safer sex and ways to reduce risk of HIV infection. These included developing brochures, workshops and "safer sex parties," where safer sex was eroticized and encouraged in order to reduce HIV transmission. One of the cornerstones of safer sex is correct and consistent use of condoms. Therefore, HIV prevention work among gay and bisexual men almost always includes programs to (1) ensure that condoms are readily available within gay communities, networks, and venues, (2) promote condom use and stress the importance of condoms, (3) educate gay and bisexual men about correct and consistent condom use, and (4) build or reinforce self-efficacy about using condoms.

However, there are still some challenges associated with condom use among MSM. For instance, research has shown that the incidence of condom failure (slippage or breakage) in anal sex among MSM is an issue that deserves more attention (Gross et al., 1999; Stone et al., 1999), particularly among gay and bisexual men who are more inexperienced with using condoms (Thompson, Yager, & Martin, 1993). Moreover, there are situations in which some gay and bisexual men may forgo condom use or exempt themselves from safer sex, despite strong intentions to do otherwise (Adam, Husbands, Murray, & Maxwell, 2005; Williams, Ellwood, & Bowen, 2000). Adherence to consistent condom use may break down among gay and bisexual men who experience erectile difficulties, or in times of personal turmoil and depression, during bouts of intoxication or impairment associated with the use of alcohol or other substances, or in heat-of-the-moment (unplanned) encounters. In addition, some gay and bisexual men may forgo condoms as part of a process of anticipating or building a relationship with a partner, or because of expectations about monogamy with their partner, or based on their intuitions about the HIV status of sex partners.

It is still important to promote condoms as a method for preventing transmission and acquisition of HIV and to educate gay and bisexual men about correct and consistent condom use. However, we cannot simply say, "Use a condom every time." Many gay and bisexual men may not find this message relevant. Some gay and bisexual men practice risk reduction without using condoms. For instance, if partners in a monogamous relationship both have the same HIV status (positive or negative), and neither has a sexually transmitted infection (STI), the partners might safely choose to not use condoms. This situation, of course, happens in heterosexual relationships as well. Similarly, couples may choose to use condoms only with any secondary partners (again, assuming that both primary partners are of the same HIV status and neither has an STI). Gay and bisexual men also sometimes choose to have sex with those who are of the same HIV status, sometimes referred to as "serosorting" (*sero* meaning blood), whether one's blood is HIV-positive or negative. Though this may not protect HIV-positive men from other STIs or from reinfection with HIV, it is often employed as a harm-reduction strategy to reduce the possibility of transmitting HIV to another person.

These forms of negotiated safety still present challenges, however. In serosorting, for example, how would one man actually know the HIV status of another man? Most forms of knowing may rely on unwarranted or unreliable cues or assumptions. Similarly, monogamous relations, whether gay or straight, rely on trust that may or may not be warranted. Additionally, unprotected anal intercourse presents other dangers to HIV-infected persons, such as the transmission of other STIs, a higher viral load, and transmission of drug-resistant HIV. Other forms of safer sex include oral sex without swallowing semen, body rubbing, and mutual masturbation.

MSM may also be at risk for HIV as a result of sharing needles and syringes for any reason, but most commonly for injecting street drugs or steroids. HIV prevention efforts have highlighted the need to avoid sharing used needles or syringes, as HIV can be transmitted through blood that may be on the needles or in the syringes. Efforts have been made to help those who use injecting equipment to access clean equipment. Some local communities have needle-exchange or syringe exchange sites where a person who has a used needle or syringe can exchange it for sterile equipment without fear of being arrested. However, due to the stigma of HIV and injection, many communities, and indeed the U.S. federal government, currently will not support needle-exchange or syringe programs, even though strong evidence exists that these programs do not increase injection drug usage and in fact assist drug users in accessing available treatment (Strathdee et al., 2006).

Prevention Specifically for HIV-Positive Gay and Bisexual Men

Agencies that are funded to implement HIV prevention services for gay and bisexual men should provide accurate information about HIV transmission and sexual risks within the contexts of the lived experiences of HIV-positive people, including the reality that HIV-positive people are sexual beings. Prevention models for HIV-positive gay and bisexual men should be designed in a manner that addresses the factors found to be associated with risk, such as treatment optimism, alcohol use, drug use, mental health needs, and other potential factors, as well as effective community-based and population-specific interventions (Ross & Williams, 2002). It is critical that those living with HIV have a voice in the discussion about what prevention policies would be most beneficial to them.

HIV stigma may have an impact on those who are newly diagnosed. Today, men who test HIV-positive may be alienated because of the notion that one should "know better" and not engage in any risky behavior. It is important to note that we all struggle with various forms of risk (not wearing seat belts, driving faster than the posted speed limit, smoking, being overweight), so we should be careful not to be judgmental about how someone might have been infected with HIV. Just as this was an issue early in the pandemic, it has become an issue again as we continue to see an increase in the number of gay and bisexual men who are becoming infected with HIV. The notion that one should "know better" may not be a helpful response. As noted earlier, many factors influence the lived reality of gay and bisexual men. Some factors and situations may increase some people's exposure to risky sex (such as denial, emotional challenges, drug and alcohol use, racial or socioeconomic power differences, access to health care, social services and prevention efforts, stigma and shame), and some factors (community-based information and services, peer norms) may protect gay and bisexual men. All of these factors influence the ability of individuals and communities to protect themselves from HIV infection.

Treating those who are already infected should ensure that they can experience reasonably healthy and productive lives. Treatment may also have benefits for preventing the spread of HIV, because people with a low viral load are less likely to pass on the virus to their sex partners. However, treatment does not stop HIV from spreading. Efforts to prevent the spread of HIV are as important now as in any earlier phase of the pandemic (Merson, O'Malley, Serwadda, & Apisuk, 2008).

Best Practices for Prevention

Given that gay and bisexual men do not always have the tools, information, and resources required to reduce their transmission risk, what are the best practices to work with gay and bisexual men to improve their sexual health and address health disparities?

Some effective intervention strategies include one-on-one cognitive behavioral counseling that attempts to modify the relationship between what the person is thinking and feeling and the way in which he is behaving (Dilley et al., 2007; Rosser, 1990). These include motivational enhancement techniques that are designed to enhance motivation to have protected sex (Picciano, Roffman, Kalichman, Rutledge, & Berghuis, 2001). Additionally, group-level interventions that emphasize group discussions about HIV risk and safer sexual behavior, role-playing, exercises, skill building, assertiveness training, and motivational enhancement have been shown to be helpful in promoting safer sex (Herbst et al., 2007). Community-level interventions, such as selecting community role models who could encourage others to use condoms during sex (Kelly, St. Lawrence, Diaz, & Stevenson, 1991) and peer-led programs that mobilize the community and offer social groups, educational programming, social marketing campaigns, and community building (Kegeles, Hays, & Coates, 1996), have proven successful in changing community norms and reducing unsafe sexual behavior. Finally, social marketing campaigns are useful tools for the dissemination of information on HIV transmission and the promotion of behaviors to reduce the sexual risk. Campaigns such as the "Condom Country" and "Assumptions" campaigns in Canada were conveyed through outdoor media (such as through billboards and advertisements in the public transit system), gay community media, posters, postcards, informational booklets, and advertisements on television and were shown to be effective (Shea & Co., 2002).

Public education campaigns may also generate greater appreciation of the structural or systemic factors that affect vulnerability to HIV among certain population segments (for example, campaigns to address stigma, homophobia, racism, in relation to HIV). However, preventing the spread of HIV among gay and bisexual men and MSM, as among any target group, requires a combination of approaches tailored to the specific aspects of risk and vulnerability (Coates et al., 2008; Gupta et al., 2008) within a framework that engages and supports communities in their health and well-being.

In general, HIV prevention efforts involve disseminating important information to the target populations, on the assumption that people who are informed and knowledgeable will change the behaviors that put them at risk of becoming infected. However, knowing the facts about risk is not necessarily sufficient to prompt behavior change. For example, individuals or groups whose life situation is affected by social oppression (such as racism, homophobia), unemployment, low incomes, and housing instability, may be unable to sustain behavior change despite their best intentions. In other words, "individuals do not always have the power to put healthy choices into practice" (Campbell, 2003, p. 41).

In North America, gay men are probably more knowledgeable about the basic facts of HIV transmission than any other segment of the population. This is because, based on the epidemiology of HIV and advocacy by communities of gay men, HIV prevention education for gay men has been well resourced compared to other population segments. Still, gay and bisexual men continue to become infected.

This perspective suggests that part of the role of social workers, health providers, researchers, and health promotion practitioners is to engage communities in the development of infrastructures to support behavior change among community members. Community engagement therefore opens possibilities for gay men and other affected population groups to (1) recognize and acknowledge their interest in HIV prevention, (2) understand the social conditions that challenge or support HIV prevention, and (3) devise collective action that supports their practical interest in HIV prevention. Collective action may involve mobilizing community members around the development and implementation of specific initiatives and engaging stakeholders and institutions (such as elected representatives, religious bodies, research organizations) to gain access to needed resources and expertise. In other words, communities create conditions to support and sustain individual commitment to behavior change.

SERVICE PROVISION FOR GAY AND BISEXUAL MEN

Community-based HIV programs and services, delivered though AIDS-related organizations, are common features of the response to HIV and AIDS in many settings. In large urban areas in particular, gay and bisexual men may access HIV prevention, education, outreach, and other social services. Social services generally provided to people living with HIV include counseling, case management, practical assistance, support groups, housing services, and referrals to medical providers who are experienced with HIV. Service users who access case management and counseling programs also receive emotional and practical support and help with building their skills to cope with daily living.

These programs also reinforce or support HIV prevention efforts (Husbands et al., 2007). In rural areas services may be less available. Most public health departments should have accurate information about how to access HIV services.

The Social Service Needs of Gay and Bisexual Men Living with HIV

Services may be offered in an office or clinical setting, in community-based organizations, through gay venues, or through the Internet. Venue-based services include HIV prevention and safer sex initiatives ranging from condom distribution to theory-based interventions offered by AIDS-related organizations through bars and bathhouses (Flowers, Hart, Williamson, Frankis, & Der, 2002). Internet-based health promotion and HIV prevention efforts also cover a range of activities, from banner ads on dating and hook-up sites, to more structured approaches to engaging users, answering questions, and delivering information (McFarlane et al. 2005; Rhodes, 2004).

Gay and bisexual men still experience a number of barriers to accessing services, even in large urban areas with substantial gay communities, where there is a tradition of service provision dating from the early years of the pandemic. These include a lack of access to providers who are aware of the issues and needs of gay and bisexual men. Moreover, as the HIV pandemic has spread or grown among different population segments, other barriers, such as age, language, culture, racism, poverty, and homophobia, may affect the quality of and access to needed services. HIV-positive gay and bisexual men report a desire for health care and social service providers who have qualities such as being nonjudgmental, empathic, respectful, having knowledge about HIV and related resources, and conveying some expertise, while also remaining egalitarian in their approach (Harris & Alderson, 2007). These qualities in a provider have been shown to provide a decreased sense of isolation, significant emotional support, helpful assistance with problem solving, and useful referrals for beneficial services for gay and bisexual men (Harris & Alderson, 2007).

As mentioned earlier, HIV stigma and homophobia are still very prevalent in North American culture (Gallup Organization, 2008). Gay and bisexual men may feel as though it might be easier to avoid coming out to providers as gay or bisexual because they think they are less likely to deal with homophobia. However, for HIV-positive gay and bisexual men who are accessing HIV-related social services, it is much more difficult to avoid coming out because medical and social service providers often assess risk factors associated with being HIV-positive in the process of providing an assessment for services. Therefore, providers are likely to ask whether an HIV-positive male has sex with other men (and therefore may identify as gay or bisexual). Sexual orientation and sexual behavior are private, and, like anyone, HIV-positive gay and bisexual men may feel uncomfortable in a setting if they think that they are being discriminated against or judged based on their sexual behavior. Human service and health care providers should be aware that because of this stigma, gay and bisexual men may not feel welcome in many settings. They may be concerned that the providers in that setting are uncomfortable talking about issues that may be important to address, including sexual behavior, same-sex relationships, and other aspects of gay community and culture. Therefore, they may not be specific or clear about what their needs might be. It would be important for providers to conduct a thorough assessment of needs without assumptions and judgment. For instance, gay or bisexual men who do not feel comfortable with a provider may avoid talking about issues of sexual or romantic relationships because they may feel judged, even though they may have challenges to face in that area of their life and could use the resources and support of the provider.

However, given the critical and personal issues of sex, drugs, health, and mental health that often arise in the lives of those living with HIV, gay and bisexual men need to have places where they can talk about these very personal issues. Being HIV-positive brings up new challenges in dating and other relationships. Issues of disclosure are critical (Driskell, Salomon, Mayer, Capistrant, & Safren, 2008), because there remains stigma associated with an HIV-positive diagnosis (Driskell et al., 2008). Often, disclosing you are HIV-positive to potential sex partners results in rejection. This can lead to feelings of low self-esteem and depression. HIV-positive gay and bisexual men have also developed strategies to decrease the risk of transmitting HIV to sexual partners, which includes serosorting (having sex only with other HIV-positive men) and strategic sexual positioning or activities that decreases the risk of HIV transmission. These are important issues for gay and bisexual men to be able to discuss with health care and social service providers.

HIV-positive gay and bisexual men may also experience rejection from biological family members based on moral or religious beliefs (Godfrey, Haddock, Fisher, & Lund, 2006). Many HIV-positive gay and bisexual men do not identify their biological family as their main source of support. Often, gay and bisexual men have close social connections that they define as their family (Bor, du Plessis, & Russell, 2004). It would be important to assess the ways in which HIV-positive gay and bisexual men define who their family is and the level and type of support they experience. It is also important to assess whether they are experiencing feelings of isolation and disconnection from their biological family, community, religious, and other cultural institutions. Research has shown that those who have supportive family (in whatever way family is defined) and social supports tend to have more positive health status and well-being (Bor et al., 2004).

Gay and bisexual men live in a world where often their primary intimate relationships are not recognized, either legally or culturally. In Canada, same-sex marriage has been federally legalized since 2005 (Canadian Press, 2005), whereas in the United States, currently only Massachusetts, Connecticut, Vermont, and Iowa do not discriminate against same-sex couples in marriage. Many communities and organizations are opposed to same-sex marriage, and recent ballot initiatives against same-sex marriage in many states in the United States have brought this issue into the spotlight. Issues of stigma and discrimination by family, communities, and religious organizations still remain, and those who experience this stigma may choose not to access marriage rights, even if those rights are available to them.

Regardless of legal standing, many gay and bisexual men live in long-term committed relationships, and social service and health care providers must assess for the significance and meaning of any relationship and respect the right of the individuals involved to define their family as they so choose. Additionally, it is imperative that providers work to protect the rights of gay and bisexual men to define the important relationships in their lives. If one or both partners are living with HIV, it is often the case that, in addition to support for coping with living with HIV, one or both may require housing assistance, social services, medical referrals, medication adherence support, caregiving support, and financial and/or legal advice on dealing with various issues (such as power of attorney, living wills and wills, taxes). Additionally, couples may require counseling for emotional support, stress-reduction strategies, and adjustment to living with HIV. As with any other couple, same-sex couples may also require counseling to manage the challenges that come with being in a primary relationship.

Because of HIV advances in treatment, people living with HIV may experience fewer symptoms and bouts of illness than was the experience earlier in the pandemic. However, medication side effects and erratic symptoms can provide challenges to managing day-to-day activities. Providers are essential in assisting those living with HIV in managing their medications. Though medication routines are generally less complicated today, adherence to medication is an important factor in maintaining health and well-being. Evidence suggests that those with HIV who struggle with mental health concerns have more difficulty managing their medications and that these mental health issues of anxiety and depression have a negative impact on health and well-being (Leserman, 2003). Therefore, service providers have an important role in assisting HIV-infected persons with medication adherence.

Gay and bisexual men who are living with HIV may also be struggling to find employment in an environment that can accommodate their needs. Although discrimination against someone who has HIV (or any other medical condition) is illegal in both the United States and Canada, discrimination still exists, and people living with HIV are often underemployed. Those living with HIV fear discrimination, a lack of skills, concerns over any gaps in their resumes, and issues with attending to medical issues while at work (Maguire, McNally, Britton, Werth, & Borges, 2008). Additionally, gay and bisexual men may experience homophobia in their workplace.

HIV-positive gay and bisexual men from racialized communities may also experience multiple forms of stigma, including HIV-related stigma, homophobia, and racism. For instance, in the United States, where HIV has a far greater impact on the Black population than its share of the national population would suggest, the Black AIDS Institute (Wilson et al., 2008) has noted the paucity of HIV prevention interventions designed for Black populations and that current interventions designed for individuals and small groups may have limited potential for Black populations. In terms of access to care and treatment, Wheeler (2005) has reported that researchers, care providers, and health promotion practitioners do not sufficiently appreciate how issues such as race, ethnicity, gender, and sexual identity affect ethno-racial and sexual minorities. Similar issues have been reported for Latino gay and bisexual men as well (Diaz, Ayala, & National Gay and Lesbian Task Force Policy Institute, 2001). Only one randomized, controlled trial has been reported that demonstrated the effectiveness of specific intervention for African American MSM (Wilton et al., 2009).

Gay and bisexual men who are HIV-positive may also be experiencing significant grief. Given the large number of HIV-related deaths among gay and bisexual men early in the pandemic in North America, many gay and bisexual men have experienced individual as well as community grief (Maasen, 1998). Many gay and bisexual men lost numerous friends, colleagues, lovers, and partners. Evidence suggests that gay and bisexual men who have cared for partners who have died from HIV developed coping strategies to manage exhaustion of long-term and chronic care of a partner, as well as the grief that has come along with the loss of a partner, often at an early age (Munro & Edward, 2008). Additionally, gay and bisexual carers of those living with HIV have had to struggle with the stigma associated with having an HIV-positive partner—stigma that came from family friends and professional caregivers alike (Munro & Edward, 2008). It is also important to note that long-term grief can lead to mental and physical health complications as well as sexual risk (Villa & Demmer, 2005). Health care and social service providers can help to assess for grief responses and provide appropriate referrals for counseling or support, as needed.

RECOMMENDATIONS FOR PRACTICE AND ADVOCACY

Here we provide recommendations for social workers, health care providers, people living with HIV, gay and bisexual men, other men who have sex with men, and family and friends. Because this pandemic has not diminished among gay and bisexual men, we now need a new commitment and focused resources to help address the needs of gay and bisexual men. Comprehensive and targeted actions are needed to eliminate the health disparity faced by gay and bisexual men, particularly in the context of HIV.

As social workers and persons and families affected by HIV, we must consider ways to reduce the stigma associated with being gay and bisexual or having HIV. In order to create change that will help gay and bisexual men (as well as lesbians, bisexual women, and transgender people) to avoid the negative effects of this stigma, it is important to work together to build an inclusive and accepting society. Some of the ways that we can do this is to take on leadership roles as helping professionals, family members, and friends. We must work for equal rights for LGBT people by advocating changes in laws to protect against discrimination and work toward making sure that those who provide services to LGBT people also provide them in a way that recognizes the humanity of those they serve. In the United States, there is still no federal law that bars discrimination against someone who is known or perceived to be LGBT.

We must also challenge coworkers or other providers when they make rude or insensitive statements about LGBT people or those living with HIV. We must advocate for open, explicit, and science-based health information that is pertinent and specific to gay and bisexual men, including sexual behavior, mental health, alcohol and drug use, and other risks.

It is important to recognize that for many people HIV is but one of a number of other factors that affect their lives (racism, poverty, and other social oppression can create a great deal of harm as well). It is also important to make sure we advocate for better funding for HIV services and prevention programs.

Social oppression plays a role in the impact of HIV upon disenfranchised communities. We must work to reduce the impact of various forms of social oppression. Throughout this chapter we have highlighted some of the ways that racism has had an impact on HIV services and prevention for gay and bisexual men. It is important to recognize that not all men who have sex with other men identify as gay or bisexual and that those who identify with a racial or ethnic community may feel especially disconnected from that terminology. Therefore, when developing programs and services, it is important to make sure that you either focus on specific communities at risk or use the broadest and most inclusive language, imagery, and venues to be certain that you are able to reach those for whom your message is intended. Again, the use of the Internet to connect with sexual partners and to meet other social needs requires that HIV services and information be made readily accessible to the online communities.

Poverty can affect the health and well-being of gay and bisexual men. Though there exists a stereotype that all gay men are White, well-educated, and have more disposable income, it may be because these are often the most visible gay and bisexual men and that they are most likely to fill out a survey or participate in a study. We know that poverty directly influences health care access, so we need to continue to advocate for an elimination of poverty for everyone, including gay and bisexual men.

HIV has an impact on the mental health needs of those who are infected and affected and those who are at risk. As social workers and others concerned about HIV risk, we must make sure that mental health services are accessible to all who may need them. Our response to the mental health needs of HIV-infected or at-risk gay and bisexual men must include three important tasks. First, we must ensure that we are up-to-date on the mental health needs of those living with HIV and those affected by HIV, as well as the specific mental health needs of gay and bisexual men. Second, we must advocate for more inclusive services throughout the mental health delivery system. This includes services for those who are HIV-positive, those who may be at risk, and the family and friends who support those with HIV and those at risk. Third, it is important to advocate for better services for those living in rural areas, who often lack access to culturally competent services for gay and bisexual men and those living with HIV.

Social workers, family, friends, and those living with and at risk for HIV must educate themselves and others about the specific sexual health needs of gay and bisexual men. Since gay and bisexual men constitute a large proportion of people living with HIV across North America, a substantial amount of funding is required to address their needs and risks. Increased funding to address the sexual health needs of gay and bisexual men and other MSM is a top priority. Additionally, these funds should be targeted to the specific needs of particular populations (such as men of color, those who are HIV-positive, rural men). Instead of fearing that explicit information will "make someone gay" or increase sexual risk, we need to advocate for better access to accurate, research-based information that is relevant to their health needs. Young gay men in particular require access to relevant and appropriate information about HIV transmission and safer sex from reliable and credible sources. Creative approaches must be tried—for example, recent uses of the Internet to deliver potentially helpful interventions to address sexual risk among rural MSM (Bowen, Horvath, & Williams, 2007).

Medical and social service providers must remain up-to-date and educated about current issues in HIV treatment and services needed. HIV treatment is a quickly changing and developing field. People who are living with HIV and those who care for them require access to current and accurate data on the types of medications available and the ways in which HIV treatment impacts HIV transmission. Addressing issues such as treatment optimism can assist people who are living with HIV to protect their health and the health of their partners.

Gay and bisexual men and other men who have sex with men have strengths and resiliencies. As social workers, family, and friends of gay and bisexual men who are living with HIV or at risk for HIV, we must acknowledge and employ these resiliencies to better the lives of gay and bisexual men.

One of the major strengths identified in both research and community practice is that most gay and bisexual men and MSM are strongly influenced by their peers. These networks are critical to the development of health behavior norms within gay communities, and they can be very useful in helping gay and bisexual men connect with adequate health and social services. As social workers, family, friends, and others interested in bettering the health and well-being of gay and bisexual men, we can creatively use these networks to make sure that messages that promote health and access to care and services are fostered. The Internet provides a useful and critical venue for advancing community. Using online social networks provides great opportunities for accessing sexual health, harm-reduction, and HIV prevention and service information.

Encourage and promote HIV testing among gay and bisexual men, providing the necessary resources and services for those who test HIV-positive. HIV testing can reduce the possibility of HIV transmission, because those who know their status are more likely to reduce their sexual risk. HIV testing also allows gay and bisexual men who are HIV-positive to access treatment and care, which can reduce the impact of HIV on their immune systems and can increase their overall health. Being on HIV treatment may reduce the possibility of HIV transmission as well, thus reducing the impact of HIV among gay and bisexual men. Those who test positive can also access a host of community-based services to assist in managing their health and well-being. As providers and family and friends, it is essential that we encourage gay and bisexual men who are at risk for HIV to be tested.

Medical and social service providers must create environments that invite and welcome all people living with HIV, including gay and bisexual men. Service providers must create an atmosphere that is welcoming and supportive. This can be done by having posters, brochures, and staff that reflect images of the gay community. Additionally, providers should stay up-to-date about resources for gay and bisexual men, including web sites and organizations that connect men to each other and to organizations that are working to build a more inclusive society, where gay and bisexual men (and all people living with HIV) are welcomed as engaged and important contributors to their families and communities.

Personal Perspective

Being Gay and Living with HIV, by Tony

I am a gay man living in Toronto. I was born and raised in the Caribbean and moved to Canada several years ago. I knew that I was gay from as long as I can remember. However, when I lived in the Caribbean I experienced homophobia—name-calling, gossip, and threats of abuse—even though I never really "came out" about my sexual orientation. This influenced my decision to leave the Caribbean.

I was required to have my health checked by a doctor as part of the Canadian immigration process. I was tested for HIV and my test was positive. The doctor informed me of the positive HIV test and referred me to a physician specializing in HIV. I was thankful that the doctor also referred me to an AIDS service organization. I was devastated by my HIV-positive test result. At first I thought of returning to the Caribbean. However, I disclosed my HIV status to a relative in Toronto, who urged me to stay in Canada. This relative is still the only member of my family who knows that I'm HIV-positive.

I have received excellent support from my doctor and the organization to which I was referred. When I first tested positive I did not know about AIDS service organizations. But I called the agency and made an appointment with a support worker. I have been accessing services there ever since, and I have also volunteered with the agency. I also access services at several other AIDS service organizations. I attend various churches in Toronto. In the Caribbean I experienced homophobia in a church where I was a member of the congregation. However, this has not stopped me from going to church on a regular basis. Church is part of my self-care.

CONCLUSIONS

HIV continues to have a direct and powerful effect on the health and well-being of gay and bisexual men. Though many individuals and organizations have been working hard to reduce the impact of HIV on gay and bisexual men, there is still much work to be done. Now is still the time to take action and to make strident and bold changes. We can assume that without making drastic and significant changes in the direction of HIV prevention programs, HIV will have an impact on the lives of gay and bisexual men for generations to come. Now is still the time to address the impact of homophobia and ideologies that stigmatize LGBT people. Efforts to mitigate HIV need to come from many sectors and need to be well financed and focused on those who are most marginalized and vulnerable. These efforts must include policy changes as well as continued efforts to provide interpersonal and community-based efforts to reduce HIV transmission among gay and bisexual men.

We argue that HIV is not just about a having a virus, but also about the ways in which we understand power and control in our world. If our health care system or health care practitioners routinely deny honest and explicit information to gay and bisexual men about protecting themselves and their sexual health, if health providers make assumptions about the sexual behavior of the men they see (for example, assume that the person before them is heterosexual), if the language that health providers and social workers use to describe sexual behavior is not language that is recognized by others, then we have a heterosexist system that refuses to value the choices, behaviors, and potential for self-protection among gay and bisexual men.

It is clear that HIV prevention efforts must address the interpersonal, societal, and structural factors that influence vulnerability to HIV. Public education campaigns to address issues like racism, homophobia, stigma, and partner abuse, or that promote a sense of community solidarity, may be helpful in this respect. Similarly, interventions delivered to individuals or small groups may promote efficacious condom use by addressing the various interpersonal barriers to safer sex. These interventions must not be merely one-message interventions but must be directed at the lived experiences of gay and bisexual men.

Now is still the time for HIV prevention work to include advocating to governments and other relevant bodies about policy and programs related to the social determinants of health and about laws or policy that deliberately or inadvertently limit gay men's ability to institute health-enhancing practices. In addition, case management, counseling, and health promotion programs should be designed to help gay and bisexual men overcome or mitigate the conditions that prevent them from maintaining good sexual health.

Now is still the time to garner multiple resources such as social workers and other health care providers, academics, people living with HIV, LGBT people, and family and friends to make sure that we are doing all that we can to reduce the impact of HIV on the lives of gay and bisexual men.

REFERENCES

Adam, B., Husbands, W., Murray, J., & Maxwell, J. (2005). AIDS optimism, condom fatigue, or self-esteem? Explaining unsafe sex among gay and bisexual men. *Journal of Sex Research, 42*(3), 238–248.

Bakeman, R., & Peterson, J. L. (2007). Do risky beliefs about HIV treatments affect peer norms and risky sexual behavior among African American men who have sex with men? *International Journal of STD and AIDS, 18*(2), 105–108.

Bor, R., du Plessis, P., & Russell, M. (2004). The impact of disclosure of HIV on the index patient's self-defined family. *Journal of Family Therapy, 26*(2), 167–192.

Bowen, A. M., Horvath, K., & Williams, M. L. (2007). A randomized control trial of internet-delivered HIV prevention targeting rural MSM. *Health Education Research, 22*(1), 120–127.

Canadian Press. (2005, July 20). Same sex bill approved. *The Globe and Mail,* Retrieved from http://www.theglobeandmail.com/servlet/Page/document/v5/content/subscribe?user_URL=http://www.theglobeandmail.com%2Fservlet%2Fstory%2FRTGAM.20050720.wsamesex0720%2FBNStory%2FNational%2F&ord=65837346&brand=theglobeandmail&redirect_reason=2&denial_reasons=none&force_login=false

Cáceres, C., Aggleton, P., & Galea, J. (2008). Sexual diversity, social inclusion and HIV/AIDS. *AIDS, 22*(Suppl. 2), S45–S55.

Campbell, C. (2003). *"Letting them die": Why HIV/AIDS programmes fail.* Oxford, England: International African Institute and James Currey.

Centers for Disease Control and Prevention. (2005). HIV prevalence, unrecognized infection, and HIV testing among men who have sex with men: Five U.S. cities, June 2004–April 2005. *Morbidity and Mortality Weekly Report, 54*(24), 597–601.

Centers for Disease Control and Prevention. (2008). Subpopulation estimates from the HIV incidence surveillance system—United States, 2006. *Morbidity & Mortality Weekly Report, 57*(36), 985–989. Retrieved September 12, 2008, from http://www.cdc.gov/mmwr/preview/mmwrhtml/mm5736a1.htm

Coates, T., Richter, L., & Cáceres, C. (2008). Behavioural strategies to reduce HIV transmission: How to make them work better [Special issue on HIV prevention]. *Lancet, 372*(9639), 669–684.

Cramer, E. P. (1997). Effects of an educational unit about lesbian identity development and disclosure in a social work methods course. *Journal of Social Work Education, 33(3)*, 461–472.

Crosby, R., Holtgrave, D., Stall, R., Peterson, J., & Shouse, L. (2007). Differences in HIV risk behaviours among Black and White men who have sex with men. *Sexually Transmitted Diseases, 34*(10), 744–748.

Díaz, R. (2008, November). HIV stigmatization among Latino gay men in the U.S. Paper presented at the Ontario Gay Men's Sexual Health Summit, Toronto.

Díaz, R., Ayala, G., Bein, E., Henne, J., & Marin, B. (2001). The impact of homophobia, poverty, and racism on the mental health of gay and bisexual Latino men: Findings from 3 US Cities. *American Journal of Public Health, 91*(6), 927–932.

Diaz, R. M., Ayala, G., & National Gay and Lesbian Task Force Policy Institute. (2001). *Social discrimination and health: The case of Latino gay men and HIV risk.* Washington, DC: National Gay & Lesbian Task Force.

Dilley, J. W., Woods, W. J., Loeb, L., Nelson, K., Sheon, N., Mullan, J., et al. (2007). Brief cognitive counseling with HIV testing to reduce sexual risk among men who have sex with men: Results from a randomized controlled trial using paraprofessional counselors. *JAIDS Journal of Acquired Immune Deficiency Syndromes, 44*(5), 569–577.

Dilley, J. W., Woods, W. J., Sabatino, J., Lihatsh, T., Adler, B., Casey, S., et al. (2002). Changing sexual behavior among gay male repeat testers for HIV: A randomized, controlled trial of a single-session intervention. *Journal of Acquired Immune Deficiency Syndromes, 30*(2), 177.

Driskell, J. R., Salomon, L., Mayer, K. H., Capistrant, B., & Safren, S. A. (2008). Barriers and facilitators of HIV disclosure among sexually risky HIV-infected men who have sex with men. *Journal of HIV/AIDS and Social Services, 7*(2), 135–156.

Flowers, P., Hart, G., Williamson, L., Frankis, J., & Der, G. (2002). Does bar-based, peer-led sexual health promotion have a community-level effect amongst gay men in Scotland? *International Journal of STD and AIDS, 13*(2), 102–108.

Flowers, P., Knussen, C., & Church, S. (2003). Psychosocial factors associated with HIV testing amongst Scottish gay men. *Psychology & Health, 18*(6), 739–752.

Fullilove, M. T., & Fullilove, R. E., III. (1999). Stigma as an obstacle to AIDS action. *American Behavioral Scientist, 42*(7), 1117–1129.

Gallup Organization. (2008, June 18). *Americans evenly divided on morality of homosexuality.* Retrieved August 1, 2008, from http://www.gallup.com/poll/108115/Americans-Evenly-Divided-Morality-Homosexuality.aspx

Gardezi, F., Calzavara, L., Husbands, W., Tharao, W., Lawson, E., Myers, T., et al. (2008). Experiences of and responses to HIV stigma among African and Caribbean communities in Toronto, Canada. *AIDS Care, 20*(6), 718–725.

Gilman, S. E., Cochran, S. D., Mays, V. M., & Hughes, M. (2001). Risk of psychiatric disorders among individuals reporting same-sex sexual partners in the national comorbidity survey. *American Journal of Public Health, 91*(6), 933.

Godfrey, K., Haddock, S. A., Fisher, A., & Lund, L. (2006). Essential components of curricula for preparing therapists to work effectively with lesbian, gay, and bisexual clients: A Delphi study. *Journal of Marital and Family Therapy, 32*(4), 491–504.

Gross, M., Buchbinder, S., Holte, S., Celum, C., Koblin, B., & Douglas, J. (1999). Use of Reality "female condoms" for anal sex by U.S. men who have sex with men. *American Journal of Public Health, 89*(11), 1739–1741.

Gupta, G., Parkhurst, J., Ogden, J., Aggleton, P., & Mahal, A. (2008). Structural approaches to HIV prevention [Special issue on HIV prevention]. *Lancet, 372*(9640), 764–775.

Harawa, N., Greenland, S., Bingham, T., Johnson, D., Cochrane, S., Cunningham, W., et al. (2004). Associations of race/ethnicity with HIV prevalence and HIV-related behaviors among young men who have sex with men in 7 urban centers in the United States. *Journal of Acquired Immune Deficiency Syndrome, 35*(5), 526–536.

Harris, G. E., & Alderson, K. (2007). An investigation of gay men's experiences with HIV counseling and peer support services. *Canadian Journal of Community Mental Health, 26*(1), 129–142.

Herbst, J. H., Beeker, C., Mathew, A., McNally, T., Passin, W. F., Kay, L. S., et al. (2007). The effectiveness of individual-, group-, and community-level HIV behavioral risk-reduction interventions for adult men who have sex with men: A systematic review. *American Journal of Preventive Medicine, 32*(Suppl. 4), S38–S67.

Herek, G. M., & Sims, C. (2008). Sexual orientation and violent crime victimization: Hate crimes and intimate partner violence among gay and bisexual males in the United States. In R. J. Wolitski, R. Stall, & R. O. Valdiserri (Eds.), *Unequal opportunity: Health disparities affecting gay and bisexual men in the United States* (pp. 35–71). New York: Oxford University Press.

Huebner, D. M., Davis, M. C., Nemeroff, C. J., & Aiken, L. S. (2002). The impact of internalized homophobia on HIV preventive interventions. *American Journal of Community Psychology, 30*(3), 327–348.

Husbands, W., Browne, G., Caswell, J., Buck, K., Braybrook, D., Roberts. J., et al. (2007). Case management community care for people living with HIV/AIDS. *AIDS Care, 19*(8), 1065–1072.

Kegeles, S. M., Hays, R. B., & Coates, T. J. (1996). The empowerment project: A community-level HIV prevention intervention for young gay men. *American Journal of Public Health, 86*(8, Pt. 1), 1129–1136.

Kelly, J. A., St. Lawrence, J. S., Diaz, Y. E., & Stevenson, L. Y. (1991). HIV risk behavior reduction following intervention with key opinion leaders of population: An experimental analysis. *American Journal of Public Health, 81*(2), 168–171.

Koblin, B. A., Husnik, M. J., Colfax, G., Huang, Y., Madison, M., Mayer, K., et al. (2006). Risk factors for HIV infection among men who have sex with men. *AIDS, 20*(5), 731–739.

Korfhage, B. A. (2006). Psychology graduate students' attitudes toward lesbians and gay men. *Journal of Homosexuality, 51*(4), 145–159.

Leserman, J. (2003). HIV disease progression: Depression, stress, and possible mechanisms. *Biological Psychiatry, 54*(3), 295–306.

Maasen, T. (1998). Counseling gay men with multiple loss and survival problems: The bereavement group as a transitional object. *AIDS Care, 10*(2, Suppl. 1), 57.

Maguire, C. P., McNally, C. J., Britton, P. J., Werth, J. L., Jr., & Borges, N. J. (2008). Challenges of work: Voices of persons with HIV disease. *Counseling Psychologist, 36*(1), 42–89.

Mays, V., Cochran, S., & Zamudio, A. (2004). HIV prevention research: Are we meeting the needs of African American men who have sex with men? *Journal of Black Psychology, 30*(1), 78–105.

McFarlane, M., Kachur, R., Klausner, J., Roland, E., & Cohen, M. (2005). Internet-based health promotion and disease control in the 8 cities: Successes, barriers, and future plans. *Sexually Transmitted Diseases 32*(10), October Supplement, S60–S64.

Merson, M., O'Malley, J., Serwadda, D., & Apisuk, C. (2008). The history and challenge of HIV prevention. [Special Issue on HIV Prevention]. *Lancet, 372*(9637), 475–488.

Millett, G., Flores, S., Peterson. J., & Bakeman, R. (2007). Explaining disparities in HIV infection among Black and White men who have sex with men: A meta-analysis of HIV risk behaviors. *AIDS, 21*(15), 2083–2091.

Millett, G., Peterson, J., Wolitski, R., & Stall, R., (2006). Greater risk for HIV infection of Black men who have sex with men: A critical literature review. *American Journal of Public Health, 96*(6), 1007–1019.

Morbidity and Mortality Weekly Report. (2008, September 12). Subpopulation estimates from the HIV incidence surveillance system. *57*(36), 985–989.

Munro, I., & Edward, K. (2008). The lived experience of gay men caring for others with HIV & AIDS: Resilient coping skills. *International Journal of Nursing Practice, 14*(2), 122–128.

Open Society Institute. (2006). *HIV/AIDS policy in the United States: Monitoring the UNGASS declaration of commitment on HIV/AIDS.* New York: Open Society Institute.

Picciano, J. F., Roffman, R. A., Kalichman, S. C., Rutledge, S. E., & Berghuis, J. P. (2001). A telephone based brief intervention using motivational enhancement to facilitate HIV risk reduction among MSM: A pilot study. *AIDS & Behavior, 5*(3), 251–262.

Preston, D. B., D'Augelli, A. R., Kassab, C. D., & Starks, M. T. (2007). The relationship of stigma to the sexual risk behavior of rural men who have sex with men. *AIDS Education and Prevention, 19*(3), 218–230.

Ramirez-Valles, J., Fergus, S., Reisen, C. A., Poppen, P. J., & Zea, M. C. (2005). Confronting stigma: Community involvement and psychological well-being among HIV-positive Latino gay men. *Hispanic Journal of Behavioral Sciences, 27*(1), 101–119.

Rhodes, S. (2004). Hookups or health promotion? An exploratory study of a chat room–based HIV prevention intervention for men who have sex with men. *AIDS Education and Prevention, 16*(4), 315–327.

Ross, M. W., & Williams, M. L. (2002). Effective targeted and community HIV/STD prevention programs. *Journal of Sex Research, 39*(1), 58–62.

Rosser, B. R. S. (1990). Evaluation of the efficacy of AIDS education interventions for homosexually active men. *Health Education Research, 5*(3), 299–308.

Rosser, B. R. S., Bockting, W. O., Ross, M. W., Miner, M. H., & Coleman, E. (2008). The relationship between homosexuality, internalized homo-negativity, and mental health in men who have sex with men. *Journal of Homosexuality, 55*(1), 150–168.

Rosser, B. R. S., West, W., & Weinmeyer, R. (2008). Are gay communities dying or just in transition? Results from an international consultation examining possible structural change in gay communities. *AIDS Care, 20*(5), 588–595.

Scott-Sheldon, L. A. J., Marsh, K. L., Johnson, B. T., & Glasford, D. E. (2006). Condoms + pleasure = safer sex? A missing addend in the safer sex message. *AIDS Care, 18*(7), 750–754.

Semple, S. J., Patterson, T. L., & Grant, I. (2000). The sexual negotiation behavior of HIV-positive gay and bisexual men. *Journal of Consulting and Clinical Psychology, 68*(5), 934–937.

Shea & Co. (2002). *Welcome to Condom Country final evaluation report.* Retrieved January 28, 2010, from www.actoronto.org/research.nsf/pages/condomcountryreportfinalpdf/$file/CC%20Final%20Evaluation%20Report-Final.pdf.

Stall, R., Friedman, M., & Catania, J. A. (2008). Interacting epidemics and gay men's health: A theory of syndemic production among urban gay men. In R. J. Wolitski, R. Stall, & R. O. Valdiserri (Eds.), *Unequal opportunity: Health disparities affecting gay and bisexual men in the United States* (pp. 251–274). New York: Oxford University Press.

Stall, R., Mills, T. C., Williamson, J., Hart, T., Greendwood, G., Paul, J. P., et al. (2003). Association of co-occurring psychosocial health problems and increased vulnerability to HIV/AIDS among urban men who have sex with men. *American Journal of Public Health, 93*(6), 939–942.

Stokes, J. P., & Peterson, J. L. (1998). Homophobia, self-esteem, and risk for HIV among African American men who have sex with men. *AIDS Education & Prevention, 10*(3), 278–292.

Stone, E., Heagerty, P., Vittinghoff, E., Douglas, J., Koblin, B., Mayer, K., et al. (1999). Correlates of condom failure in a sexually active cohort of men who have sex with men. *Journal of Acquired Immune Deficiency Syndrome, 20*(5), 495–501.

Strathdee, S. A., Ricketts, E. P., Huettner, S., Cornelius, L., Bishai, D., Havens, J. R., et al. (2006). Facilitating entry into drug treatment among injection drug users referred from a needle exchange program: Results from a community-based behavioral intervention trial. *Drug and Alcohol Dependence, 83*(3), 225–232.

Sullivan, P. S., & Wolitski, R. J. (2008). HIV infection among gay and bisexual men. In R. J. Wolitski, R. D. Stall, & R. O. Valdiserri (Eds.), *Unequal opportunity: Health disparities affecting gay and bisexual men in the United States* (pp. 220–247). New York: Oxford University Press.

Thompson, J., Yager, T., & Martin, J. (1993). Estimated condom failure and frequency of condom use among gay men. *American Journal of Public Health, 83*(10), 1409–1413.

Trenholm, C., Devaney, B., Fortson, K., Quay, L., Wheeler, J., & Clark, M. (2007). *Impacts of Title V, Section 510 abstinence education programs: Final report.* Princeton, NJ: Mathematica Policy Research, Inc.

Villa, D. P., & Demmer, C. (2005). Exploring the link between AIDS-related grief and unsafe sex. *Illness, Crisis, & Loss, 13*(3), 219–233.

Wheeler, D. (2005). Working with positive men: HIV prevention with Black men who have sex with men. *AIDS Education and Prevention, 17*(Suppl. A), 102–115.

Williams, M., Elwood, W., & Bowen, A. M. (2000). Escape from risk: A qualitative exploration of relapse to unprotected anal sex among men who have sex with men. *Journal of Psychology & Human Sexuality, 11*(4), 25–49.

Wilson, D., & Halperin, D. (2008). "Know your epidemic, know your response": A useful approach, if we get it right [Special issue on HIV prevention]. *Lancet, 372*(9637), 423–426.

Wilson, P., Wright, K., & Isbell, M. (2008). *Left behind. Black America: A neglected priority in the global AIDS epidemic.* Los Angeles: Black AIDS Institute.

Wilton, L., Herbst, J., Coury-Doniger, P., Painter, T. M., English, G., Alvarez, M.E., et al. (2009). Efficacy of an STI/STI prevention intervention for Black men who have sex with men: Findings from the Many Men, Many Voices (3MV) project [Published online March 9, 2009]. *AIDS and Behavior.*

Chapter Fifteen

THE IMPACT OF HIV ON CHILDREN AND ADOLESCENTS

Lori Wiener and Susan Taylor-Brown

> ### INTRODUCTION: WHERE WE ARE TODAY
>
> The impact of the HIV pandemic on children, teens, and their families has been and will continue to be devastating. Worldwide, each day, more than 1,100 children under 15 years of age are infected with HIV, most as a result of mother-to-baby transmission of HIV through pregnancy, birth, or breast-feeding. By 2003, AIDS had left 15 million children under the age of 18 without one or both parents, with more than 320,000 parentless HIV-affected children living in the United States (UNAIDS, 2007).
>
> In the first decade of the HIV pandemic, ways to prevent the transmission of HIV from pregnant women to fetus was unknown. Without effective treatment, approximately a quarter of babies born to HIV-infected women became infected. A major clinical study (ACTG 076) led to the discovery that mother-to-child transmission can be reduced from 25 percent to 8 percent by the use of antiretroviral drugs for mother and baby during and following pregnancy (Conner et al., 1994). More recent combinations of antiretroviral medications and the benefit of cesarean section have reduced the transmission rate to between 1 and 2 percent. This, along with the use of voluntary HIV testing, has led to a significant decline of the incidence of children age 13 and under being diagnosed with AIDS (CDC, 2004). Moreover, by the mid-1990s, effective treatments were developed for infected babies and children, and many began to survive past the initial five-year life expectancy. In fact, these children born predominately in the 1980s and early 1990s are now in their late adolescence and early adulthood. Today, many of these youngsters are exploring college or job options. Unfortunately, their survival, while considered miraculous by some, has been plagued with significant medical, psychological, and social consequences.
>
> HIV is a family disease; each family member is HIV-affected regardless of whether or not they are HIV-infected. HIV-affected families are simultaneously confronting a potentially life-threatening condition in one or more family members.
>
> *(Continued)*

Acknowledgments: We dedicate this chapter to the late Elizabeth Glaser, whose courage and perseverance paved the road for the voices and needs of children living with HIV to be recognized throughout the world, and to all those who may remain invisible but will live in our hearts forever. The authors thank and acknowledge Lyn Blackburn, retired director of Community Services, AIDS Community Health Center for commenting on a draft of this chapter. She has regularly volunteered to staff *Family Unity Retreat* and continues to be supportive to families living with HIV, so her input on our manuscript was insightful and relevant.

Siblings, while not HIV-infected, have been deeply affected. They have grown up with the daily reality of HIV and its associated losses. Children and adolescents living with HIV are challenged to live their lives in the context of an uncertain future. It is common for these families to experience multiple deaths related to HIV. Many family units do not remain intact after the death of a parent. A parental death may disrupt the existing family unit, with siblings going to live with various relatives, who may live in other areas of the country. Unfortunately, some siblings lose all contact with each other during this challenging grieving period and are left to cope with parental death in the absence of sibling support. HIV stigma keeps many families isolated from both familial support and community services. Beyond the losses within the immediate family, many children and adolescents experience HIV-related deaths among families from their social networks, compounding the grief and loss issues.

This chapter shares lessons we learned from over 25 years of working with HIV-affected families. The impact of HIV on children and teens and their families is addressed. The chapter offers useful interventions, identifies challenges to the delivery of effective care, calls for quality care for the complete family unit, and encourages all practitioners to advocate for improved services.

THE HIV TRAJECTORY

Adolescent HIV transmission has occurred in three predominant ways: through blood, mother-to-baby, and sexual (Rogers, 2006). During the early 1980s, when the cause of AIDS and the link to the nation's blood supply was unknown, thousands of children and adults who required blood products through transfusions were infected. In this group were babies who were born prematurely and received blood as part of standard acute neonatal care. Conditions such as hemophilia, where missing clotting factors have to be regularly replenished from donor supplies, resulted in a significant percentage of the hemophilia community becoming infected with HIV. Between the years 1978 and 1985 the blood supply, and therefore much of the clotting factor hemophiliacs use to treat bleeding episodes, became infected with HIV; as a result, more than 5 percent of the estimated 20,000 people with hemophilia in the United States were HIV-positive, and as many as 90 percent of people with severe hemophilia were infected with HIV (Blake, 1992). Unfortunately, those who were already transfused with infected blood products often received large amounts of HIV and became ill rapidly. This was also a time when effective treatments were not yet available. The rate of infection peaked during 1982–1983 and declined sharply during 1984–1985. More than half of those HIV-infected persons with hemophilia were children or adolescents (Rosenberg & Goedert, 1998). In 1985, a screening test was approved to identify and exclude infected blood from donation pools. Cases of AIDS in children acquiring HIV from transfusions have declined steadily over the years as a result.

The major route of transmission of HIV to children today is through perinatal (before birth) infection from an HIV-infected mother. Women who are identified as HIV- infected are told to avoid breast-feeding, so transmission caused by breast-feeding has not played a major role in transmission of HIV in the United States. HIV transmission in teenage girls and boys is predominately sexual. The HIV epidemic in the United States is disproportionately borne by oppressed communities of color. Two out of every three newly diagnosed AIDS cases are identified in females. Forty percent of newly diagnosed males between the ages of 13 and 19 are African American and approximately one in every five, Latina (CDC, 2001).

Medical Realities

The medical course of HIV infection in youth differs from that of adults. It has been well documented that children infected with HIV are at risk for developing central nervous system (CNS) disease characterized by impairments in cognitive, language, motor, and behavioral functions (Wolters & Brouwers, 2005). Manifestations range from mild impairments in certain areas of cognitive functioning to the most severe form, referred to as HIV encephalopathy, in which children exhibit debilitating developmental deficits with possible loss of previously acquired skills (Belman, 1994). Neurological changes can impair language, motor, and behavioral functions. When this occurs, children may have problems functioning in school, struggle with social relationships, and consequently have a lower sense of self-competency.

HIV infection may also change the hormonal system, which is involved in the control of growth and pubertal development. Clinical reports have identified a growth lag that appears early and persists throughout later childhood, with HIV-positive boys and girls being shorter and weighing less than their HIV-negative siblings and peers (Buchacz et al., 2001). Delays in sexual maturation compared to the general adolescent population have also been reported (de Martino, Tovo, Galli, Gabiano, Chiarelli, Zappa et al., 2001; Mahoney et al., 1999). Similar to adults, effective antiretroviral medications can have significant physical side effects including diarrhea, nausea, skin rashes, and unusual deposits of body fat. While adolescents must also navigate a similar array of medications as adults, for teens this process can be especially grueling. They often experience conflicts between the need to adhere to a specific plan of care in order to keep their disease in check and other competing demands, such as the need for secrecy about their infection, pressure to keep up with the schedules of their peers, distress around the illness, and the desire to rebel against medical treatment in general (Pao & Wiener, 2008). The side effects of the treatment alone become a significant barrier to adherence to medication and nutrition (Santos et al., 2005).

While the development of effective antiretroviral therapy for HIV has led to significant viral suppression and immune reconstitution, early treatment regimens were unpalatable and required a high pill burden. This has resulted in the emergence of drug-resistant virus in many treated children and adolescents (Day et al., 2008). Some children infected at birth or early in life are able to maintain viral load control with little or no medication, though many others find themselves barely able to keep pace with the development of new therapies (Rogers, 2006). These highly treatment experienced adolescents may have to take combinations of four, five, or six drugs, compared to the simpler (and often more effective) regimens available to newly diagnosed adolescents or adults (Armstrong, 2002; Van Dyke, 2002). When the remaining available treatment options become more limited, these youngsters move from one critical illness to the next (Rogers, 2006). Factors associated with less adherence in adolescents include advanced HIV disease, being out of school, higher alcohol use, and depression (Wiener, Riekert, Ryder, & Wood, 2004; Murphy et al., 2005). High rates of depression, in particular, raise medical concerns because of the strong relationship between depression and HIV anti-HIV treatment non-adherence in HIV-positive adolescents. A social crisis such as a death, a breakup with a girlfriend or boyfriend, a family fight, or a problem in school or on the job, can also lead to a period of nonadherence. Furthermore, HIV infected teenagers in crisis or teenagers who are depressed may stop taking their medications, may no longer eat well, or may be more likely to have unprotected sex (Pao & Wiener, 2008).

Psychological Stress

Levels of stress in coping with HIV appear to increase over time, beginning with the onset of adolescence, when the need for a change in antiretroviral therapy may develop, when dating begins, when future goals are being considered, and when decisions about informing friends or potential romantic partners need to be made (Grubman et al., 1995; Pao & Wiener, 2008). Furthermore, as these adolescents and young adults age, pregnancy may occur or be an area of concern (Centers for Disease Control and Prevention [MMWR], 2002), and social workers have a key role in reviewing safer sexual behaviors and making barrier protection available.

A 2006 review of the scholarly literature found high rates of anxiety, depression, and attention-deficit/hyperactivity disorder in HIV-positive children 4 to 17 years old when compared to rates of these disorders within the general population of children (Scharko, 2006). Another study that examined long-term outcomes among HIV-infected children and HIV-uninfected children born to HIV-infected women found that children with HIV are at an increased risk for psychiatric hospitalization during childhood and early adolescence (Gaughan et al., 2004). Depression, behavior disorders, and suicidal ideation or attempts were the leading cause of hospitalization. In this study, there was also a higher use of psychotropic medical use compared with HIV-negative children. A cross-sectional study at the National Cancer Institute found that over a four-year period, almost half of these youth were prescribed at least one psychotropic medication (often antidepressants or stimulants), a rate much higher than in the general population (Wiener, Battles, Ryder, & Pao, 2006). One of the factors that appear to be related to the high incidence of psychiatric symptoms is the cumulative effect of significant losses that most of these youngsters have suffered.

Multiple Losses

As many HIV-infected youngsters age, they find themselves thinking about, missing, and grieving for parents, siblings, and/or close friends who did not live long enough to benefit from currently available drug treatments. These youth have been shuffled between care providers, households, schools, neighborhoods, and social service agencies following the death of their mother. Often it is not until late adolescence that these losses hit home. This distress tends to peak at times of transition, when other losses are experienced, such as when the older adolescent is required to leave his or her pediatric care providers and move to adult programs or centers (Wiener, Zobel, Battles, & Ryder, 2007). These youth may also experience deaths of peers who were HIV-infected. Unresolved and complicated grief reactions can manifest as difficulty making decisions, feeling lost, guilt surrounding survival, oppositional behavior, depression, and anxiety, each of which can lead to disabling mental health problems. Assessing for grief reactions needs to be a part of the mental health assessment and care provided for each HIV-infected child, adolescent, and surviving young adult.

Disclosure of HIV Diagnosis

One of the greatest areas of psychological stress for parents and caregivers is the question of when and how to disclose the HIV diagnosis to one's child. Furthermore, as HIV-infected children reach adolescence, issues such as maintaining adherence to complex medication regimens and preventing transmission via sexual behavior are of critical concern and are likely influenced by the knowledge of having a chronic, life-threatening, sexually transmissible illness. The potential negative individual and public health risks of nonadherence and risky sexual behavior substantively add a sense of urgency to the issue of disclosure of HIV status (Pao & Wiener, 2008).

Several factors add to the concern about disclosing to a child his or her HIV diagnosis. These include fear that the child will be psychologically harmed by this information, that the child will not be able to keep this information confidential, fear of rejection and ostracism (Wiener, Mellins, Marhefka, & Battles, 2007; Wiener & Lyons, 2006; Wiener, Battles, Heilman, Sigelman, & Pizzo, 1996; Wiener, 1998), and that to tell a child this diagnosis often means disclosing other family secrets, including paternity and history of parental sexual behavior and substance use (Havens, Mellins, & Ryan, 2005). The fact that the majority of children acquired HIV from their mothers and that there is ensuing parental guilt about transmission also distinguishes disclosing this disease from cancer and other life-threatening pediatric illnesses.

The American Academy of Pediatrics (1999) published guidelines that endorse disclosure of HIV to older children and adolescents as beneficial and ethically appropriate. Several reports that reviewed factors associated with a parent's decision to disclose the HIV diagnosis to his or her child followed, and these addressed predictors of disclosure and the psychological impact of disclosure (Nehring et al., 2000; Gerson, 2001; Mellins et al., 2002; Lester et al., 2002; Sherman et al., 2000; Instone, 2000; Wiener, Battles, Heilman, Sigelman, & Pizzo, 1996; Bachanas, 2001; Howland et al., 2000). While some studies suggest positive outcomes associated with disclosure, including the promotion of trust, improved adherence, enhanced support services, open family communication, and better long-term health and emotional well-being (Lipson, 1994; Funck-Brentano et al., 1997; Reikert, Wiener, & Battles, 1999; Mellins et al., 2002), other studies underscore negative outcomes, including increased internalizing behavior problems (Bachanas et al., 2001) and closed and isolating communication patterns (Hardy et al., 1994). Knowledge of HIV status has also been reported to contribute to depression, anxiety, and behavioral problems (Lester et al., 2002; New et al., 2003) and increased risk of psychiatric hospitalizations (Gaughan et al., 2004). While a relationship between timing of disclosure and psychological adjustment, social support, or the adolescent's own decision to disclose his or her HIV status to others has not been found (Wiener & Battles, 2006), a caregiver's intuition must be respected. One report found 65% of children felt the right person told them (in almost all cases, this was a parent), and 86% felt the disclosure was at the right time (Wiener, Battles, Heilman, Sigelman, & Pizzo, 1996). Disclosure of an HIV diagnosis to children is best understood as an individualized and dynamic process. Patterns of disclosure vary from full disclosure (providing the name of the illness, ways to treat the disease, and transmission routes) to partial disclosure (giving the child a description of symptoms and treatment without revealing the exact name of the illness), with patterns of nondisclosure varying from deception (hiding the illness behind another condition) to complete nondisclosure (not communicating about the illness at all) (Funck-Brentano et al., 1997). It has been recommended that disclosure be planned, that it take place in a supportive atmosphere of cooperation between health professionals and parents, and that it be conceived of as a process, occurring over several visits, rather than as a single event (Lipson 1993, 1994).

A clear understanding of the family's cultural background and the factors that might influence responses to an HIV diagnosis or disclosure of the diagnosis to the child is essential for culturally competent care to be provided (Mason et al., 1995). This includes clear and effective language interpretation services when delivering a diagnosis, reviewing treatment options, or talking to a family about disclosure-related issues in a language different than their native tongue (Munet-Vilaro, 2004). Assessment of the child's cognitive impairment must be considered as well. For example, while the adolescent may be able to meet "mature minor" criteria for competence, observations of dementia whose onset begins during adolescence, or impairment of thinking skills and judgment, point to the need for careful consideration of earlier disclosure and development of new models for comprehensive support of HIV-related information as children mature (Armstrong et al., 2002).

While the child's disclosure reaction tends to be consistent with previous responses to a crisis, it is essential for a child's parent to be aware of the scope of emotions that might follow. Postdisclosure reactions can range from no reaction at all to a delayed reaction or acute anxiety. In some children, psychosomatic complaints, nightmares, frequent changes in mood, and regression to behavior more appropriate to a younger developmental stage are common, while other children initially present with an adultlike acceptance (Wiener, Havens, & Ng, 2003). In spite of what appears to be acceptance of the illness, it is important to help parents be sensitive to a profound sense of confusion and shame often worsened by the stigma and the need for secrecy associated with the diagnosis (Hays et al., 1993).

Scheduled postdisclosure counseling is highly recommended. Qualitative reports and artwork often reveal confusion, guilt, or a sense of damage the child may have internalized postdisclosure (Wiener & Battles, 2002). Yet with time and support, most children demonstrate increased knowledge about the illness, reduction of guilt, and the ability to tolerate procedures such as blood draws and pill swallowing (Wiener & Battles, 2002). Inquiring about the inner world of children and helping them put understanding and meaning into their plight can help facilitate psychological movement, growth, and healing (Wiener & Figueroa, 1998).

SERVICES AND SUPPORT FOR CHILDREN AND ADOLESCENTS AND THEIR FAMILIES

Children, adolescents and their families affected by HIV must meet multiple challenges associated with and beyond those of the disease (Pequegnat, 2006). A comprehensive array of services must take into account the strengths and vulnerabilities of the individual and family unit and include psychosocial assessment, safer sex education, transition to adult care, end-of-life support, mental health services, and family interventions, including retreats, planning, and advocacy. All of these interventions are examined in this section.

Psychosocial Assessment

Evidence suggests that the majority of HIV-infected children ages 6 to 11 are psychologically stable (Wiener, Battles, & Riekert, 1999; Bose et al., 1994) despite the stress inherent in living with the disease. With age, however, psychological distress appears to increase on measures of social function, anxiety, depressive symptoms, and behavioral problems, along with a decline in positive social self-concept (Battles & Wiener, 2002; New, et al., 2003). Depression, anxiety, behavior disorders, hyperactivity, and social problems have been described in 12 to 44% of children and adolescents living with HIV infection (Mellins et al., 2003; Wiener & Battles, 2006). Additional investigations have reported that negative life events (Moss et al., 1998), limited social support (Battles & Wiener, 2002), diagnosis disclosure (Battles & Wiener,

2002; Gaughan et al., 2004, Lester et al., 2002), maternal loss (Battles & Wiener, 2002), and clinical neurological abnormalities (Misdrahi et al., 2004) are associated with adverse psychological and behavioral outcomes.

Comparisons of HIV-infected children to HIV-exposed but uninfected children (Havens et al., 1994; Mellins et al., 2003) and/or matched non-HIV-exposed control group (Havens et al., 1994, Bachanas et al., 2001) suggest that some behavior problems are not related to HIV variables (such as severity of CNS disease, length and type of antiretroviral therapy), but rather may be attributed to other causes such as environmental conditions (parent/primary caregiver mental health, substance use, family stability, and the cumulative effects of poverty), biological factors (maternal/paternal mental illness), or other psychosocial difficulties (Wolters & Brouwers, 2005). Whatever the ultimate root of the mental health symptoms, these youth appear to be at high risk for psychological distress and at greater risk for psychiatric symptoms.

How the child or adolescent copes with his or her illness depends on many factors, including age and developmental stage, parental adaptation, social skills, and his or her psychological makeup (Wiener, Havens, & Ng, 2003). When possible, a comprehensive psychosocial assessment should be completed that includes information about the child's ability to trust, to use and/or reach out for help, to tolerate pain or frustration, to make and maintain friendships, to cope with change and separation, and whether or not support from family and others is available (see Table 15.1). The need to assess the child's cognitive abilities, disclosure status, and stage of illness is critical, as these factors determine the meaning the illness carries for the child and the psychological and intellectual resources available to cope with the disease and to meet each challenge (Pao & Wiener, 2008).

Table 15.1   Child and Adolescent Psychosocial Assessment

Family Membership

Biological as well as adoptive/foster/extended family members
Legal status if not living with a biological parent

History of Illness

Route of transmission (if it may pertain to the person's adjustment to having HIV)
Serious hospitalizations (including psychiatric hospitalizations)
History of symptoms including CNS manifestations in both child/parent
Child and family's knowledge and reactions to the disease
Treatment toxicities
Adherence history, issues, or concerns

Child and Adolescent Development and Personality Profile

Birth, medical, developmental, and educational history
Energy level, mood
Behavior at home, school, play
Learning or school difficulties
Attention difficulties/ADHD
Standardized test information including neuropsychological and academic
Coping abilities, strengths, concerns
Ability to adapt to change and separation
Pain tolerance
Frustration tolerance

(Continued)

Table 15.1   (Continued)

Relationship with parents/caregivers, siblings
Ability to make and maintain friendships
Whether disclosed to peers, school
Prior losses
Recent losses
Beliefs, expectations, attitudes toward disease, treatment, and outcome
Use of drugs, alcohol, or other substances
Whether child has been seen by a mental health provider—precipitating event, outcome
If prescribed a stimulant or psychotropic medication—outcome, still prescribed
Sexual history
Knowledge and self-efficacy around HIV transmission/risk reduction

Family History

Family's beliefs, attitudes, and expectations regarding treatment and outcome
Who is aware of the diagnosis
Reactions of family members/friends/neighbors
Health status of all family members
Marital status of caregivers
Ability and willingness to assess care and community resources
Coping abilities during previous crises and with previous health issues
Family communication style and cohesiveness
History of familial mental illness or nonprescribed drug and alcohol use
History of incarceration
Nature and stability of residential and occupational arrangements
Preexisting family conflicts, previous trauma
Financial stresses on the family
Cultural/religious factors that might affect treatment, disclosure, adaptation
History of previous losses
Sources of emotional and financial support; availability of medical insurance
Reported concerns for the child/adolescent

Source: Pizzo, P. A., & Wilfert, C. M. (1998). *Pediatric AIDS: The Challenge of HIV infection in infants, adolescents, and children.* Philadelphia: Lippincott Williams & Wilkins.

Safer Sex Education

Adolescence typically is a time of sexual and lifestyle behavioral experimentation. Adolescents born with HIV infection and those infected early in life are becoming sexually active just as their peers are (Frederick et al., 2000; Wiener, Battles, & Wood, 2007). Even HIV-infected youth who are quite ill with AIDS-related symptoms can be sexually active. Degree of illness does not preclude sexual behavior or necessarily facilitate safer behavior (Brown, 2000). Moreover, a growing number of these adolescents and young adults have conceived or are planning to conceive. For some, this begins the third generation of HIV in their family. Because of highly active antiretroviral treatment (HAART), most of the children born to HIV-positive adolescents will be HIV-negative.

Like their HIV-negative peers, HIV-infected youth perceive that most people their age are having sex and that there is indeed pressure to do so, both by a certain age and by a certain point in a relationship (Hoff et al., 2003). In a study conducted with HIV-infected adolescents and young adults, low HIV transmission knowledge was found (Wiener, Battles, & Wood, 2007). Knowledge was not better for those who were sexually active than for those who were not, though sexual knowledge increased over time. Importantly, overall ability to use condoms was significantly correlated with sexual risk behavior knowledge, establishing an important link between knowledge of HIV sexual transmission risk behaviors and an individual's confidence in his or her ability to use condoms, a critical behavior in preventing HIV transmission. As this knowledge may influence whether individuals engage in risky behaviors, it is important to assess HIV transmission knowledge of HIV-infected adolescents and young adults who are coming to sexual maturity so that appropriate prevention messages and intervention programs can be offered.

HIV-positive youth also appear to have a later onset of sexually risky behavior than a normative sample of U.S. high school students (Wiener, Battles, & Wood, 2007; Ezeanolue et al., 2006). This may be a result of delayed emotional maturity resulting from low expectations of survival early in life (Battles & Wiener, 2002) or a consequence of delayed puberty, a finding associated with HIV disease (Buchacz et al., 2003). These results again highlight the critical need to provide risk-reduction education to adolescents who acquired HIV early in life, regardless of whether or not they are currently sexually active. Routine medical visits are ideal times to pay particular attention to the specific issues relating to behaviors of HIV-infected youth, including sexual risk factors, psychological distress, and drug or alcohol use, which may be associated with sex. These visits allow social workers and other team members the opportunity to (1) assess and maximize knowledge of sexual transmission, (2) improve and reinforce consistency of correct condom use and other safer sex practices, and (3) repeatedly deliver abstinence and prevention messages. As risk-reduction behavior may not always be immediate or sustained, repeated messages surrounding HIV prevention and disclosure are essential. Visual and written material specifically aimed for the HIV-positive adolescent about sexual behavior and practices can be extremely useful (Wiener & Wood, 2006).

For adolescents who are sexually active or considering becoming sexually active, diagnosis disclosure to sexual partners is critical. Most adolescents fear the consequences of disclosure of their diagnosis and therefore wish to avoid such discussions. They often lack the skills and confidence to discuss such sensitive topics with their potential sexual partners. This suggests that interventions designed to reduce the risk of sexually transmitting HIV require developmentally appropriate psychological and social approaches that target perceptions of peer influence and emotional well-being (Brown, 2000). Innovative programs that address the implications of secondary prevention of HIV infection and offer reproductive health education, including reproductive choices and considerations, are clearly needed (Ezeanolue et al., 2006). The critical need for providing consistent and continuous secondary prevention messages cannot be overemphasized, given the troubling public health implications that could result from a failure to do so (Wiener, Battles, & Wood, 2007).

The need to incorporate prevention messages into primary care is challenged by the need for adolescents to make the transition from pediatric to adult health care as they age. Anxiety associated with having to break ties with pediatric health care providers with whom these adolescents have had long-standing relationships can compromise a successful transition. If these youth become disengaged from the health care system, the opportunities to provide prevention messages and to achieve prevention goals are lost (Wiener, Zobel, Battles, & Ryder, 2007).

Transition from Pediatric to Adult Services

Transition is a complex process incorporating all aspects of the adolescent's life (Scal, 2002; Miles, Edwards, & Clapson, 2004; Pinzon, Jacobson, & Reiss, 2004; Por et al., 2004; Reiss, Gibson, & Walker, 2005). There are an estimated 500,000 adolescents with special health care needs who turn 18 each year, for whom there is a sense of urgency for the transition to adult-oriented care to be smooth and uninterrupted to ensure positive health outcomes (Lotstein et al., 2005). Recognizing the priority of helping adolescents with chronic health conditions to make a transition, a consensus conference was held in conjunction with the American Academy of Pediatrics, the American Academy of Family Physicians, and the American College of Physicians–American Society of Internal Medicine with the purpose of crafting a policy statement for adolescent transition that would have widespread support. It specifically outlined "critical first steps" to ensuring successful transition to adult-oriented care, followed by specific recommendations to provide clarity for efforts to implement programs and reduce barriers to successful health care transition (Rosen, 2003). The steps included the following: (1) identifying health care providers for young people with special needs who will assume broad responsibility for the coordination and planning of transition; (2) identifying core competencies needed by health care providers to render appropriate health care for special-needs youth and making sure those skills are integrated into medical education and certification requirements; (3) developing a portable and accessible health care record; (4) developing detailed transition plans by provider, person with HIV, and family; (5) ensuring the same standards for primary care and prevention services for special-needs youth as for the general population; and (6) ensuring affordable, continuous, comprehensive health insurance coverage.

As the pediatric HIV population approaches adulthood, they are faced with the challenges of learning to manage their chronic illness, organize their own health care, fill prescriptions, deal with specialists, negotiate insurance and benefit plans, and adjust to living independently, while also making decisions about initiating sexual relationships (Wiener, Zobel, Battles, & Ryder, 2007). Furthermore, stigmatizing attitudes by health care providers can hinder the success of transition. A recent study found that health care workers rely on the same stereotypes and misinformation about HIV that are commonplace among the general public (Rintamaki, 2007).

In an attempt to examine whether an association existed between transition-readiness, specific barriers to transition, and level of stated anxiety, an HIV program studied 51 pediatric/adolescent youth who needed to transfer from a pediatric program to community-based programs when the program was being phased out (Wiener, Zobel, Battles, & Ryder, 2007). What they learned was that increased stated anxiety levels, greater number of years enrolled in the current treatment program, and lack of confidence in a home provider were associated with poorer readiness scores. Neither readiness nor anxiety was associated with disease severity, suggesting that making a transition from a center where there is a strong emotional attachment is a stronger predictor for poor readiness than the anxiety associated with advanced disease status. The emotional attachment to clinic staff may also be associated with the fact that, owing to the nature of the disease, many children had lost at least one parent to HIV while receiving care at this center, and leaving the center would also be leaving that link behind. Furthermore, some did not have adequate health care insurance. Concerns about having to pay for medications out of pocket, lack of insurance coverage, paucity of HIV community-based providers that understand pediatric issues and the need to transfer out of pediatric care, and lack of a social worker to provide advocacy and support resulted in a high degree of discomfort among the families.

The identification of barriers can guide the development of an individualized transition plan. Social workers are in an ideal role to engage people in assessing individual barriers and to identify appropriate youth-friendly medical care and support services to ensure positive health and psychosocial outcomes. Interventions need to focus on equipping young adults with the skills and knowledge to understand their disease and medications, in addition to the warning signs of illness/infection, how to access a pharmacy and refills, medical insurance coverage, resources that help cover out-of-pocket expenses, and complete tasks involved with managing their health care (Hauser & Dorn, 1999; Betz, 1999; Lewis-Gary, 2001). The development of interventions to help adolescents and their families transfer to adult-centered care is the current call to action by the pediatric medical community. Skills that social workers are uniquely qualified to provide include the assessment of psychosocial needs, emotional barriers, and parental and/or provider resistance; resource acquisition; and the promotion of developmental growth (Wiener, Zobel, Battles, & Ryder, 2007). There are also a growing number of transition tools (workbooks and videos) that are available. Some of these can be found at http://hctransitions.ichp.ufl.edu.

End-of-Life Support

End-of-life issues are sad and unfortunate realities for many adolescents and young adults living with life-threatening illnesses. While AIDS-related death and disease rates have declined in the highly active antiretroviral therapy (HAART) era and remain low, children and adolescents have died and will continue to die from the disease. An estimated 330,000 children died of AIDS-related illnesses in 2007, approximately 15 percent of the total deaths due to AIDS (UNAIDS, 2007).

Unlike cancer or other diseases where there is a clear point when treatment has failed, with HIV, end-of-life usually presents as a result of overwhelming opportunistic infections in the face of severe immune suppression (Pao & Wiener, 2008). Severe wasting, chronic diarrhea, and poor quality of life are common. Meetings with the family to discuss options and to explore palliative or hospice care are often helpful, especially if staff members who have been most intimately involved with the child can be present (Wiener, Fair, & Pizzo, in press). Many of the young adults whose disease progresses to AIDS have recently made the transition from pediatric to adult care. Engaging the support of those health care members who were available during their childhood and early adolescent years can be extremely useful. Most adolescents and young adults want to live as fully a life as they can while they are able and also wish to be involved in the decision making.

In fact, the success of comprehensive care is dependent on open discussions ahead of time that address painful decisions, including withdrawal of medications, home versus hospital care, "do not resuscitate" status, and funeral arrangements. Once these logistics have been discussed, the family can reinvest energy to supporting their child. Open communication, pain control, involvement with friends and family, distractions, and the maintenance of familiar routines all convey a sense of security that is important in supporting the family and dying child (Wiener, Hersh, & Kazak, 2007).

Mental Health Services

There is a general reluctance for HIV-infected youth to seek or use mental health services or to attend traditional support groups despite the potential they have to offer tremendous benefit. This reluctance is associated with the stigma associated with receiving mental health care as well as the fear of disclosure if they were to see someone they know. Support groups in particular can offer a sense of belonging for HIV-infected youth: a place where they can be open about their illness, have their experiences validated, isolation reduced, and trauma understood, and where a deeper connection with other teens living with HIV can be made. Youth are often much more willing to attend overnight camping programs for HIV-positive or HIV-affected youth and/or their family members.

Peer empowerment can be a very important tool in helping HIV-positive youth cope with their infection. Many camps offer summer employment through counselor training programs. Community-based service providers often hire HIV-positive youth to serve as peer leaders. Such programs provide HIV-positive young men and women the opportunity to deliver HIV prevention messages to other youth (Luna & Rotheram-Borus, 1999). Their messages are often perceived as more credible and powerful than those of HIV-negative educators. HIV-positive teens and young adults who are able to keep themselves mentally active, believe their life has purpose, maintain a sense of humor, adapt to loss and change, and who create a backup plan in case they become ill appear to be thriving under the continued uncertainties associated with HIV disease (Wiener, Havens, & Ng, 2003). In fact, despite the many stresses inherent in living with HIV, these young adults should be given the opportunity to develop and pursue individual aspirations and goals. If recognized and nurtured, they have the potential to significantly contribute to society (Wiener, Septimus, & Grady, 1998).

Family Interventions

Today there are two distinct treatment realities for HIV-affected families based on geography. Families in the epicenters (urban areas with high concentrations of people with HIV) may have HIV-specific federally funded services available, whereas the majority of HIV-affected families live in regions where these services are not readily available. Information from the epicenters is highlighted in this section to stimulate family programming for HIV-affected families in the emerging areas. A few programs, such as the Family Center in New York City, stand out in providing comprehensive care for families confronting life-threatening illness (Bernard, 2003) and providing interventions targeted to affected children that strengthen the children's resilience (Stein et al., 2007; Stein et al., 1999). As HIV disease may force children to assume caregiver roles by necessity, services to support these youth are needed, and providers must be creative in securing funding to provide family intervention and support.

HIV-affected families are disproportionately from African American and Latino communities, with the majority of them living in poverty. Additionally, coping with poverty permeates the family's daily life, and HIV is just one of many factors creating further stress. Often, when families are described as not caring or being noncompliant, in reality another pressing issue may have taken precedence; for example, the threat of gas and electric services being shut off can result in a family missing an appointment). All interventions must be aware of the day-to-day concrete needs that many of these families face. Today, many human service programs are fragmented, time-limited, and difficult to access. As a result, many HIV-affected families are wary of human service agencies. It is critical that the family's perspective is understood and individual perspectives are obtained pertaining to what the family needs most. As noted previously, there is a reluctance to engage in services, and practitioners need to be realistic about what can be achieved.

Within these families, the medical teams caring for HIV-positive family members frequently overlook HIV-negative children. Including these children in the family assessment can help identify unmet psychological, social, academic, or spiritual needs and concerns. They may benefit from receiving supportive services and engagement in youth development activities that promote well-being, emotional functioning, and resilience and help to balance the responsibility that a well child may have in a family. Family intervention studies (Stein et al., 2007; Lee et al., 2007; Rotheram-Borus et al., 2001) report that strengthening social supports is effective in reducing negative outcomes among youth affected by HIV. Parentification, the process whereby a child assumes a parental caretaking role, was initially reported to be predictive of more emotional distress, substance use, and behavior problems in adolescents living with a parent with HIV (Silver et al., 1999). A follow-up study of this cohort found parentification predicted better adaptive coping skills and less alcohol and tobacco use six years later (Stein et al., 2007). Masten (2001) noted that resilience is a common phenomenon that arises from the basic ability of humans to adapt and, indeed, that development is robust even in the face of adversity. This section highlights family retreat interventions and future planning needs for HIV-affected children and adolescents and calls for family-centered advocacy efforts to improve services.

Family Retreats

Family retreat opportunities help families cope more effectively with HIV disease and its impact on the whole family unit, similar to the peer empowerment opportunities offered via camp experiences noted earlier. Programs that allow parents to act with integrity and to play an active role in planning for their children to have the best chance of meeting the family's needs in a holistic manner (Gilbert, 1999). Taylor-Brown and associates (1999) called for a community-based developmental approach that would maximize the resiliency of family members confronting this situation. The potential death of a parent poses a major developmental challenge to the surviving children.

One program, Family Unity, is a four-day retreat for HIV-affected families that provides a strengths-oriented, experiential, empowerment-based set of interventions, including recreational activities, adventure-based work, family rituals, and respite. Each activity is designed to facilitate grieving and remembrance and to enhance the youths' connection to their families and the broader Family Unity community (Itin, McFeaters, & Taylor-Brown, 2004). Many HIV-infected children and adults must cope with the possibility of their own death while simultaneously mourning family members who have died (Boyd-Franklin et al., 1995). This "out of season" loss is difficult for HIV-infected parents to address (Taylor-Brown, Teeter, Blackburn, Oinen, & Wedderburn, 1998). Hence, anticipatory loss is an important issue for individuals and families coping with any terminal illness (Wolfelt, 1983). In a group setting, removed from the harsh realities of daily life, families are able to explore these issues and gain new coping skills while strengthening relationships within their own family and among the participating families. The power of a community response to the death of a loved one has been found to support the grieving family members and to provide a forum for remembering other Family Unity participants who have died. Families comfort each other during these challenging times, and the support continues when they return to their community.

Planning

The media and American public policy would lead us to believe that all "AIDS orphans" are in Africa. The reality could not be further from the truth. Presidential policy focuses on the plight of African orphans (Bush, 2008) rather than on our own. Because the "AIDS orphan" issue has been constructed as a problem of developing countries, it is difficult to fund and secure services within this country. Orphans in the United States have had varying access to programs whose funding is based on geographical location. The exact number of AIDS orphans in the United States is unknown, despite concerted and prolonged efforts to address their issues (Mason, 2007; Taylor-Brown, Teeter, Blackburn, Oinen, & Wedderburn, 1998; Levine, 1995; Mason, 1998). Research has shown that a large majority of the children born to mothers who are HIV-positive come from homes headed by a single mother (Coon, Laresen, Manes, & Palmer, 2005), with mothers reporting greatly elevated levels of depression (Silver et al., 2003; Jones et al., 2001). There is no national tracking system to inform us of the outcomes for AIDS orphans.

Carol Levine's pioneering effort captured in the *Report on Orphans* (1995) laid the groundwork for the care and custody of AIDS orphans and community-developed interventions (Taylor-Brown, Blackburn, Oinen, & Wedderburn, 1998). Levine (1995) projected that there would be 72,000 to 125,000 children and adolescents and 60,000 young adults who lost their mothers by 2010. These figures were recently supported in a study that estimated that between 1980 and 1998, 51,473 women with AIDS died, resulting in 97,376 children without mothers (Brackis-Cott, Mellins, Dolezal, & Spiegel, 2007). The death of a parent significantly affects the surviving family members and leaves a gap caused not only by the lack of the dead parent's physical presence, but also by the part this parent played in framing and directing the family's life (Silverman, 2000).

In the early days of the pandemic, the threat of imminent parental death stimulated a call for permanency planning efforts. There was an optimism that we could help families to plan for their children's future. Social work interventions incorporating family-centered care were promoted to best serve the collective family needs in coping with HIV (Anderson et al., 1998; Taylor-Brown, 1999). Custody planning efforts were directed toward developing a formal legal custody plan, yet few families achieved this. The majority of orphans were placed informally in the care of relatives. Adolescents are particularly difficult to place with relatives or in programs. Countless unforeseen barriers combined to limit the successful development of custody plans. As a result, after losing their mother and/or father and their family unit, orphans have been and continue to be frequently divided among relatives (Itin, McFeaters, & Taylor-Brown, 2004).

Family caregivers frequently care for orphaned children without financial or psychosocial supports. They are often living in poverty, and the additional family member(s) can cause a greater financial strain. Grandparents, primarily grandmothers, are the most common primary care for orphans, with one estimate that 2.4 million children in the United States receive primary care from a grandparent (Coon, Laresen, Manes, & Palmer, 2005). Winston (2006) reports that grandmothers become the caregivers because of the value of families taking care of their own. Kinship caregivers may offer more stable placements as well as allow for retention of cultural identity (Cameron, 2000). The contemporary approach to future planning is to help parents and youth examine what might happen in the case of parental incapacity or death. As Mason (2007) notes, everyone may not make a legal plan, but each step toward a legal plan increases the children's chance for stability and may lead to a firmer plan. In families with adolescents, helping the adolescent plan for independence may be the most fruitful approach.

Family-Centered Advocacy

When one member of the family has HIV, the impact radiates through the entire family (Pequegnat et al., 2001). More than ever, the need for advocacy on behalf of and in partnership with affected families is critical. Twenty-five years have passed since AIDS was recognized, and social workers still need to advocate for quality services for HIV-affected families, ranging from an individual case basis to national and international systems change. Today, many think that we are through with AIDS; it is believed that HIV has become a manageable chronic condition. Recent reports indicate that further advocacy is warranted to stem the spread of HIV and its adverse effects on families, particularly on African American and Latino families. At the 2008 International AIDS Conference, the CDC reported that the U.S. infection rate is 40 percent higher than reported earlier (56,500 people versus 40,000), with African American men and women carrying a disproportionate burden. Infection rates among Blacks were found to be seven times as high as for Whites (83.7 per 100,000 people versus 11.5 per 100,000) and almost three times as high as for Latinos (29.3 per 100,000 people), a group that was also disproportionately affected (Altman, 2008).

In the United States, the overall infection rate is declining, but the rate of infections in women is quickly rising (Blumenthal, 2008; CDC, 2007; AMFAR, 2005). In 1990, women accounted for about 115 of all newly reported AIDS cases, and this has increased to over 25% of cases in 2005 (CDC, 2007), with HIV the third leading cause of death for Black women in this age group. These disparities are unacceptable and present a compelling argument for advocacy efforts specifically tailored to communities of color.

HIV-affected families engage with social workers across all settings yet frequently fail to acknowledge the role of HIV disease in their request for services. Being alert to stories of family illness can assist the social worker in developing appropriate care plans. Equally, each social worker should advocate for effective, culturally specific AIDS prevention and treatment efforts.

The Ryan White CARE Act, now the Ryan White HIV program, provides funding for family-centered services for HIV-affected families. This is a vital funding source, as HIV infection continues to disproportionately affect women and youth of color. As the incidence of HIV infection has continued to climb, the flat funding of the act has not kept pace with the demand for family-centered care in the United States. The act was reauthorized in 2006 and sunsets the Ryan White programs at the end of the fiscal year 2009 (AIDS Alliance, 2006). As the pandemic spreads inward, newly affected communities are particularly hard hit and inadequately prepared and underfinanced to provide support to affected families. Federal funding to support affected families through the act is woefully inadequate. The latest reauthorization provides funding to 56 cities, leaving the remaining areas to fund services in alternative ways (Eckholm, 2007) or not at all. Affected communities must create and fund responses that address local needs. With many of the original challenges to providing quality HIV prevention and care persisting into the third decade of the epidemic, social workers must continue to advocate for high-quality, accessible interventions for all.

Personal Perspective

Our Personal Journey, by Bonnie (and Leanna)

I'll never forget the day my doctor came to see me while I, Bonnie, was incarcerated to tell me my three-week-old daughter Leanna was HIV-positive. She told me I needed to be tested as well, and this was how I found out I had HIV. I felt like dying right then. All I knew about HIV is you get it and you die. There was a lot of this going on in 1991. Doctors said my daughter Leanna had two years to live. I started worrying that my other daughter Ashley would be HIV-positive as well. So I had her tested. Thank God it came back negative. My life was already pretty out of control before all this—a traumatic childhood that included sexual molestation led me into a world of alcohol, drugs, and prostitution, and now I was faced with living with HIV.

The first few years were pretty tough. I was so scared my daughter wasn't going to live. My life was beginning to spiral out of control. I couldn't take it anymore. Determined to break the cycle, and to send a clear message I did not want to be a victim anymore, I gave custody of my children to my mother for a year so I could become clean and sober, rather than risk putting the girls in foster care that might separate the girls from one another. This was the hardest thing for me to do, but I knew I had to do it in order to learn how to take care of myself better so I could live healthier with this virus and have my children live healthier lives.

I was on my way to recovery; I was not going to let HIV or drugs take control of my life. I learned a very important tool in recovery, and that was that secrets

(Continued)

can kill you. So I began speaking up about my HIV status. I did not want to keep HIV a secret. It was too much to deal with alone.

Now I have been drug and alcohol free for 15 years. Me and my daughter have been living with the virus for 17 years. I have always kept a very open and honest relationship with both my girls. I believe this is very important. Like I said earlier, secrets can kill you or leave very deep wounds. I've heard so many times "I can't tell my children I'm sick or they're sick." I say, "Why not? Do you think they're stupid? They know something's wrong, trust me." My fear was always if I wasn't honest with them and talked to them and have the resources in place to fall back on if needed, they would be angrier I didn't tell them the truth, or leave them confused, wondering why their mother couldn't tell them something about themselves or their mom that could affect the rest of their lives. Children need to know the truth and need to hear it from someone they can trust. They're stronger then we think.

I am personally very proud of my girls in the choices they made about knowing and sharing the truth. They are two beautiful, strong young ladies, one 17 the other 20. They have both attended many HIV-infected and HIV-affected camps as campers since they've been six years old to be with other children they could relate to. They both went back to these camps when they aged out to be camp counselors or counselors in training. Ashley, my oldest daughter who's not infected, and Leanna, who is infected, both have a very powerful message to be heard. At the age of 13, both started speaking at legislative breakfasts, became peer educators for their community, and have attended many HIV health fairs and other HIV events where they've shared their stories about living with HIV or being HIV-affected. We have also attended the Ryan White CARE Act National Youth Conference and have been on national TV's *Extreme Makeover: Home Edition* season finale, where we went to actually help build a new recreation center at a family camp we attended in Connecticut for families living with HIV. Leanna has been in *Poz* magazine and had a poem published by Children Affected by AIDS Foundation. Ashley has also been in the book published by Children Affected by AIDS Foundation, been to a few different states, spoken at several colleges, and has spoken at the school she attended.

Today my hopes and dreams for my children are like any mother's: for them to be successful in life in whatever they decide to do—most importantly to stay strong, delivering the message that whatever you face in life today you don't have to be a victim. Me and my daughter Leanna have HIV, but it doesn't have us.

CONCLUSIONS

For over a quarter of a century we have worked on the front line of the pandemic to support HIV-affected families. Yet our work is far from complete. As the pandemic is spreading inward and to the southern portion of the United States, efforts are needed to reach out to HIV-affected families in areas where stigma persists and HIV-specific services are limited. Over the decades, much has been learned that will be useful to practitioners in areas that are now experiencing the impact of HIV on families. These lessons need to be adapted to the unique needs of these communities. As confidentiality is difficult to preserve, families may be reluctant to access services. Frequently, families will seek assistance from non-HIV-specific services without identifying HIV as a concern.

HIV is a daunting condition that affects the whole family. No other contemporary disease challenges the integrity of families and results in as many losses as the HIV pandemic. Children who are growing up with HIV after the loss of their biological parent(s) need the support and recognition that will facilitate healthy grieving, promote emotional stability, and foster future growth and healing. Through our clinical expertise, public policy knowledge, and advocacy skills, social workers are uniquely equipped to efficiently and creatively address the ongoing challenges that the HIV pandemic poses in the foreseeable future.

REFERENCES

AIDS Alliance. (2006, February 28). Implementation of Ryan White and the challenges ahead. *AIDS News Alert, 1.*

Altman, L. (2008, August 3). HIV study says rate 40% higher than estimate. *New York Times.* Retrieved August 8, 2008, from http://www.nytimes.com/2008/08/03/health/03aids.html?pagewanted=1&_r=1&ref=todayspaper&adxnnlx=1217858747-ZVeaOdoCm%20o36GrkCDwmoA

American Academy of Pediatrics Committee on Pediatric AIDS. (1999). Disclosure of illness status to children and adolescents with HIV infection. *Pediatrics 103,* 164–166.

AMFAR. (2005). *About HIV/AID. Statistics: United States.* Retrieved November 29, 2006, from http://www.amfar.org/cgi bin/iowa/abouthiv/record.html?record=5

Anderson, G., Ryan, C. Taylor-Brown, S., & White-Gray, M. (Eds.). (1998). HIV/AIDS and children, youth, and families: Lessons learned. Introduction. *Child Welfare, 77,* 101–105.

Armstrong, W., Calabrese, L., & Taege, A. (2002, December). HIV update 2002: Delaying treatment to curb rising resistance. *Cleveland Clinic Journal of Medicine, 69*(12), 995–999.

Armstrong D., Levy, J., Briery, B., Vazquez, E., Jensen, M., Miloslavich, K., et al. (2002). *Merging of neuroscience, psychosocial functioning, and bioethics in pediatric HIV.* Paper presented at the 110th Annual American Psychological Association, Chicago, IL.

Bachanas, P., Kullgren, K., Schwartz, K., Lanier, B., McDaniel, S., Smith, J., et al. (2001). Predictors of psychological adjustment in school-age children infected with HIV. *Journal of Pediatric Psychology, 26,* 343–352.

Battles, H., & Wiener, L. (2002). From adolescence through young adulthood: Psychosocial adjustment associated with long-term survival of HIV. *Journal of Adolescent Health, 30*(3), 161–168.

Belman A. (1994). HIV-1 associated CNS disease in infants and children. In R. Price & S. Perry (Eds.), *HIV, AIDS and the Brain* (p. 289). New York: Raven Press.

Bernard, A. (2003, May 21). The family center is an outstanding and caring community agency. *New York Beacon, 10*(19), 19.

Betz, C. (1999). Adolescents with chronic conditions: Linkages to adult systems. *Pediatric Nursing, 25*(5), 43–56.

Blake, L. (1992, July 19–24). *Hemophilia and HIV—A hidden majority. International Conference on AIDS, 8,* D.480. Abstract no. PoD 5565 retrieved November 11, 2008, from http://gateway.nlm.nih.gov/MeetingAbstracts/ma?f=102200766.html

Blumenthal, S. (2008, March 31) *Women, HIV, and stigma: Results from a national survey.* Retrieved August 39, 2008, from: http://www.amfar.org/binary-data/AMFAR_PDF/pdf/000/000/181-1.pdf

Bose, S., Moss, H., Brouwer, P., Pizzo, P., & Lorion, R. (1994). Psychological adjustment of human immunodeficiency virus-infected school-age children. *Journal of Developmental and Behavioral Pediatrics, 15*(3), S26–S33.

Boyd-Franklin, N., Steiner, G. Boland, M. & Mellins, C. (1995). *Children, families, and HIV/AIDS: Psychosocial and therapeutic issues.* New York: Guilford Press.

Brackis-Cott, E., Mellins, C., Dolezal, C., & Spiegel, D. (2007). HIV. *Journal of Early Adolescence, 27*(1), 67–89.

Brown, L., Schultz, J., Parsons, J., Butler, R., Forsberg, A., Kocik, S., et al. (2000). Sexual behavior change among human immunodeficiency virus-infected adolescents with hemophilia. Adolescent hemophilia behavioral intervention evaluation project study group. *Pediatrics, 106*(2), E22.

Buchacz, K., Cervia, J., Lindsey, J., Hughes, M., Seage, G., Dankner, W., et al. (2001, October). Impact of protease inhibitor-containing combination antiretroviral therapies on height and weight growth in HIV-infected children. *Pediatrics 108*(4), E72.

Buchacz, K., Rogol, A., Lindsey, J., Wilson, C., Hughes, M., Seage, G., et al. (2003, May). Pediatric AIDS Clinical Trials Group 219 Study Team. Delayed onset of pubertal development in children and adolescents with perinatally acquired HIV infection. *Journal of Acquired Immune Deficiency Syndrome, 33*(1), 56–65.

Bush, G. (2008, July 23) President Bush Signs H.R. 5501, the Tom Lantos and Henry J. Hyde United States Global Leadership Against HIV/AIDS, Tuberculosis and Malaria Reauthorization Act of 2008. Retrieved November 19, 2008, from http://www.whitehouse.gov/news/releases/2008/07/20080730-12.html

Cameron, T. (2000). Proposed initiatives for health children orphaned by AIDS. *Journal of Health and Social Policy,* 11(4), 15–39.

Centers for Disease Control and Prevention. (2001*). HIV surveillance report, 13*(2), 16–17.

Centers for Disease Control and Prevention. (2004). *HIV surveillance report, 2003* (Vol. 15, pp. 13). Atlanta, GA: US Department of Health and Human Services.

Centers for Disease Control and Prevention. (2007). *HIV surveillance report, 2005* (Vol. 17, rev. ed.). Atlanta, GA: US Department of Health and Human Services. CDC, 1–46. Retrieved August 15, 2008, from http://www.cdc.gov/hiv/topics/surveillance/resources/reports/2005report/

Centers for Disease Control and Prevention. (2002). Pregnancy in perinatally HIV-infected adolescents and young adults—Puerto Rico. *MMWR, 52*(8), 149–151.

Connor, E., Sperling, R., Gelber, R., Kiselev, P., Scott, G., O'Sullivan, M., et al. (1994, November 3). Reduction of maternal-infant transmission of human immunodeficiency virus type 1 with zidovudine treatment. Pediatric AIDS Clinical Trials Group Protocol 076 Study Group. *New England Journal of Medicine, 331*(18), 1173–1180.

Coon, L., Laresen, J., Manes, C., & Palmer, C. (2005, September). *Guide to future care and custody planning for children.* University of California at Berkeley, CA: National Abandoned Infants Assistance Resource Center.

Day, E., Buckberry, K., Sharland, M., & Chakraborty, R. (2008, February) Novel treatment options for pediatric HIV infection. *Current Opinions: Investigative Drugs, 9*(2), 170–175.

Eckholm, E. (2007, August 1). HIV patients anxious as support programs cut. *New York Times.* Retrieved August 8, 2008, from http://www.nytimes.com/2007/08/01/washington/01aids.html?scp=5&sq=Ryan%20White%20Care%20Act&st=cse

Ezeanolue, E., Wodi, A., Patel, R., Dieudonne, A., & Oleske, J. (2006, June). Sexual behaviors and procreational intentions of adolescents and young adults with perinatally acquired human immunodeficiency virus infection: Experience of an urban tertiary center. *Journal of Adolescent Health, 38*(6), 719–725.

Frederick, T., Thomas, P., Mascola, L., Hsu, H., Rakusan, T., Mapson, C., et al. (2000). Human immunodeficiency virus-infected adolescents: A descriptive study of older children in New York City, Los Angeles County, Massachusetts and Washington, DC. *Pediatric Infectious Diseases Journal, 19,* 551–555.

Funck-Brentano, I., Costagliola, D., Seibel, N., Straub, E., Tardieu, M., & Blanche, S. (1997). Patterns of disclosure and perceptions of the human immunodeficiency virus in infected elementary school-age children. *Archives of Pediatric & Adolescent Medicine, 151,* 978–985.

Gaughan, D., Hughes, M., Oleske, J., Malee, K., Gore, C., & Nachman, S. (2004). For the Pediatric AIDS Clinical Trials Group 219C Team. Psychiatric hospitalizations among children and youths with human immunodeficiency virus infection. *Pediatrics, 113,* e544–e551.

Gerson, A., Joyner, M., Fosarelli, P., Butz, A., Wissow, L., Marks, P., et al. (2001). Disclosure of HIV diagnosis to children: When, where, why, and how. *Journal of Pediatric Health Care, 15,* 161–167.

Gilbert, D. (1999). Introduction. In S. Taylor-Brown & A. Garcia (Eds.), *HIV affected and vulnerable youth: Preventative issues and approaches* (pp. 99–117). Binghamton, NY: Haworth Press.

Grubman, S., Gross, E., Lerner-Weiss, N., Hernandez, M., McSherry, G., Hoyt, L., et al. (1995, May). Older children and adolescents living with perinatally acquired human immunodeficiency virus infection. *Pediatrics, 95*(5), 657–663.

Hardy, M., Armstrong, F., Routh, D., Albrecht, J., Davis, J. (1994). Coping and communication among parents and children with human immunodeficiency virus and cancer. *Journal of Developmental and Behavioral Pediatrics, 15,* S49–S53.

Hauser, E., & Dorn, L. (1999). Transitioning adolescents with sickle cell disease to adult centered care. *Pediatric Nursing, 25*(5), 479–488.

Havens, J., Mellins, C., & Ryan S. (2005). Child psychiatry: Psychiatric sequalae of HIV and AIDS. In B. Sadock & V. Sadock V. (Eds.), *Kaplan & Sadock's comprehensive textbook of psychiatry* (8th ed., pp. 3434–3440). Philadelphia: Williams & Wilkins.

Havens, J., Whitaker, A., Feldman, J., & Ehrhardt, A. (1994). Psychiatric morbidity in school-age children with congenital human immunodeficiency virus infection: A pilot study. *Developmental and Behavioral Pediatrics, 15*(3), S18–S25.

Hays, R., McKusick, L., Pollack, L., Hilliard, R., Hoff, C., & Coates, T. (1993). Disclosing HIV seropositivity to significant others. *AIDS, 7.* 425–431.

Hoff, T., Greene, L., & Davis, J. (2003). *National survey of adolescents and young adults. Sexual health knowledge, attitudes and experiences.* Menlo Park, CA: Henry J. Kaiser Family Foundation.

Howland, L., Gortmaker, S., Mofenson, L., Spino, C., Gardner, J. D, Gorski, H., et al. (2000). Effects of negative life events on immune suppression in children and youth infected with human immunodeficiency virus type 1. *Pediatrics, 106,* 540–546.

Instone, S. (2000). Perceptions of children with HIV infection when not told for so long: Implications for diagnosis disclosure. *Journal of Pediatric Health Care, 14,* 235–243.

Itin, C., McFeaters, S., & Taylor-Brown, S. (2004). Family unity for HIV affected families: Creating a family-centered and community capacity building context for interventions that facilitate coping with HIV related losses. In J. Berzoff & P. Silverman (Eds.), *End of life care for social workers* (pp. 642–660). New York: Columbia University Press.

Jones, D., Beach, S. R. H., & Forehand, R. (2001). The Family Health Research Group. HIV infection and depressive symptoms: An investigation of African American single mothers. *AIDS Care, 13,* 343–350.

Lee, S., Rotheram-Borus, M., & Duan, N. (2007, October). The effect of social support on mental and behavioral outcomes among adolescents with parents with HIV. *American Journal of Public Health, 97*(10), 1820–1826.

Lester, P., Chesney, M., Cooke, M., Weiss, R., Whalley, P., Perez, B., et al. (2002). When the time comes to talk about HIV: Factors associated with diagnostic disclosure and emotional distress in HIV-infected children. *Journal of Acquired Immune Deficiency Syndrome, 31,* 309–317.

Levine, C. (1995). Orphans of the HIV Epidemic: Unmet needs in six US cities. *AIDS Care, 1*(7).

Lewis-Gary, M. (2001). Transitioning to adult health care facilities for young adults with chronic conditions. *Pediatric Nursing, 27*(5), 521–525.

Lipson, M. (1993). What do you say to a child with AIDS? *Hastings Center Report, 23,* 6–12.

Lipson, M. (1994). Disclosure of diagnosis to children with human immunodeficiency virus or acquired immunodeficiency syndrome. *Journal of Developmental and Behavioral Pediatrics, 15,* S61–S65.

Lotstein, D., McPherson, M., Strickland, B., & Newacheck, P. (2005). Transition planning for youth with special health care needs: Results from the national survey of children with special health care needs. *Pediatrics, 115*(6), 1562–1568.

Luna, G., & Rotheram-Borus, M. (1999). Youth living with HIV as peer leaders. *American Journal of Community Psychology, 27*(1), 1–23.

Mahoney, E., Donfield, S., Howard, C., Kaufman, F., & Gertner, J. (1999, August 1). HIV-associated immune dysfunction and delayed pubertal development in a cohort of young hemophiliacs. Hemophilia Growth and Development Study. *Journal of Acquired Immune Deficiency Syndrome, 21*(4), 333–337.

Mason, H., Marks, G., Simoni, J., Ruiz, M., & Richardson J. (1995). Culturally sanctioned secrets: Latino men's nondisclosure of HIV infection to family, friends, and lovers. *Health Psychology, 14,* 6–12.

Mason, S. (2007, May). Custody planning with families affected by HIV. *Health & Social Work, 32*(2), 143–147.

Mason, S. (1998). Custody planning with HIV-affected families: Considerations for child welfare. *Child Welfare, 77,* 161–177.

Masten, A. (2001). Ordinary magic: Resilience processes in development. *American Psychologist, 56,* 227–238.

Mellins, C., Brackis-Cott, E., Dolezal, C., Richards, A., Nicholas, S., & Abrams, E. (2002). Patterns of status disclosure to perinatally HIV-infected children and subsequent mental health outcomes. *Clinical Child Psychology & Psychiatry, 7*(1), 101–114.

Mellins, C., Kang, E., Leu, C., Havens J., & Chesney M. (2003, August). Longitudinal study of mental health and psychosocial predictors of medical treatment adherence in mothers living with HIV disease. *AIDS Patient Care STDS, 17*(8), 407–416.

Mellins, C., Smith, R., O'Driscoll, P., Magder, L., Brouwers, P., Chase, C., et al. (2003, February). High rates of behavioral problems in perinatally HIV-infected children are not linked to HIV disease. *Pediatrics, 111*(2), 384–393.

Miles, K., Edwards, S., & Clapson, M. (2004). Transition from pediatric to adult services: Experiences of HIV-positive adolescents. *AIDS Care, 16*(3), 305–314.

Misdrahi, D., Vila, G., Funk-Brentano, I., Tardieu, M., Blanche, S., & Mouren-Simeoni, M. (2004). DSM-IV mental disorders and neurological complications in children and adolescents with human immunodeficiency virus type 1 infection (HIV-1). *European Psychiatry 19*(3), 182–184.

Moss, H., Bose, S., Wolters, P., & Brouwers, P. (1998). A preliminary study of factors associated with psychological adjustment and disease course in school-age children infected with the human immunodeficiency virus. *Journal of Developmental and Behavioral Pediatrics,19*(1), 18–25.

Munet-Vilaro, F. (2004). Delivery of culturally competent care to children with cancer and their families—The Latino experience. *Journal of Pediatric Oncology Nursing, 21,* 155–159.

Murphy, D., Belzer, M., Durako, S., Sarr, M., Craig, M., Wilson, C., et al. (2005). Longitudinal Antiretroviral Adherence Among Adolescents Infected With Human Immunodeficiency Virus. *Archives of Pediatric & Adolescent Medicine 159,* 764–770.

Nehring, W., Lashley, F., & Malm, K. (2000). Disclosing the diagnosis of pediatric HIV infection: Mother's views. *Journal of Society for Pediatric Nursing, 5,* 5–14.

New, M., Lee, S., & Pao, M. (2003). *Prevalence of mental health in pediatric HIV: A family perspective.* Presented at the NIMH Conference on the Role of Families in Preventing and Adapting to HIV, Washington, DC.

Pao, M., & Wiener, L. (2008). AIDS Psychiatry through the life cycle: Childhood and adolescence. In M. Cohen & J. Gorman (Eds.), *Comprehensive textbook of AIDS psychiatry* (pp. 307–339). New York: Oxford University Press.

Pequegnat, W. (2006). Mental health issues for children infected and affected by HIV and their families. In M. Lyons & L. D'Angelo (Eds.), *Teenagers HIV & AIDS* (pp. 127–142). Westport, CT: Praeger Publishers.

Pequegnat, W., Bauman, L., Bray, J. H., DiClemente, R, DiIorio, C., & Hoppe, S. (2001). Measurement of the role of families in prevention and adaptation to HIV. *AIDS and Behavior, 5*(1), 1–19.

Pinzon, J., Jacobson, K., & Reiss, J. (2004). Say goodbye and say hello: The transition from pediatric to adult gastroenterology. *Canadian Journal of Gastroenterology, 18*(12), 735–742.

Por, J., Golberg, B., Lennox, V., Burr, P., Barrow, J., & Dennard, L. (2004). Transition of care: Health care professionals' view. *Journal of Nursing Management, 12,* 354–361.

Reiss, J., Gibson, R., & Walker, L. (2005). Health care transition: Youth, family and provider perspectives. *Pediatrics, 115*(1), 112–120.

Riekert, K., Wiener, L., & Battles, H. (1999). Prediction of psychological distress in school-age children with HIV. *Children's Health Care, 28*(3), 201–220.

Rintamaki, L., Scott, A., Kosenko, K., & Jensen, R. (2007). Male patient perceptions of HIV stigma in health care contexts. *AIDS Patient Care STDS, 21*(12), 956–969.

Rogers, A. (2006). HIV in Youth: How are they different? In M. Lyons & L. D'Angelo (Eds.), *Teens and HIV* (pp. 3–20). Westport, CT: Praeger Publishers.

Rosen, D. (2003). Transition to adult health care for adolescents and young adults with chronic conditions: Position paper of the Society for Adolescent Medicine. *Journal of Adolescent Health, 33,* 309–311.

Rosenberg, P., & Goedert, J. (1998). Estimating the cumulative incidence of HIV infection among persons with hemophilia in the United States of America. *Statistics in Medicine, 17,* 155–168.

Santos, C., Felipe, Y., Braga, P., Ramos, D., Lima, R., & Segurado, A. (2005). Self-perception of body changes in persons living with HIV: Prevalence and associated factors. *AIDS, 19,* S14–S21.

Scal, P. (2002). Transition for youth with chronic conditions: Primary health physicians' approaches. *Pediatrics, 110*(6), 1315–1321.

Scharko, A. (2006, July). DSM psychiatric disorders in the context of pediatric HIV. *AIDS Care, 18*(5), 441–445.

Sherman, B., Bonanno, G., Wiener, L., & Battles, H. (2000). When children tell their friends they have AIDS: Possible consequences for psychological well-being and disease progression. *Psychosomatic Medicine, 62,* 238–247.

Silver, E., Bauman, L., Camacho, S., & Hudis, J. (2003). Factors associated with psychological distress in urban mothers with late-stage HIV. *AIDS and Behavior, 7*(4), 421–431.

Silverman, P. (2000). *Never too young to know: Death in children's lives.* New York: Oxford Press.

Stein, J., Reidel, M., & Rotheram-Borus, M. (1999). Parentification and its impact among adolescent children of parents with AIDS, *Family Process, 38,* 193–208.

Stein, J., Rotheram-Borus, M., & Lester, P. (2007). Impact of parentification on long-term outcomes among children of parents with HIV. *Family Process, 46*(3), 317–333.

Taylor-Brown, S. (1999). Summer camps for children, adolescents and families. In *Planning children's futures: Meeting the needs of children, adolescents, and families affected by HIV-AIDS-Report of the National Conference* (pp. 51–55). Sheldon, CT: Annie E. Casey Foundation.

Taylor-Brown, S., Teeter, J. A., Blackburn, E., Oinen, L., & Wedderburn, L. (1998). Parental loss due to HIV: Caring for children as a community issue—The Rochester, New York, experience. *Child Welfare, 77*(2), 137–160.

UNAIDS. (2007). AIDS Epidemic Update. Accessed at http://www.unaids.org/en/KnowledgeCentre/HIVData/EpiUpdate/EpiUpdArchive/2007/

Van Dyke, R., Lee, S., Johnson, G., Wiznia, A., Mohan, K., Stanley, K., et al. (2002). Pediatric AIDS Clinical Trials Group Adherence Subcommittee Pediatric AIDS Clinical Trials Group 377 Study Team. Reported adherence as a determinant of response to highly active antiretroviral therapy in children who have human immunodeficiency virus infection. *Pediatrics, 109,* e61.

Wiener L. (1998). Helping a parent with HIV tell his or her children. In D. Aronstein & B. Thompson (Eds.), *HIV and social work: A practitioner's guide* (pp. 327–338). Binghamton, NY: Haworth Press.

Wiener, L. & Battles, H. (2002). Mandalas as a therapeutic technique for HIV infected children and adolescents. *Journal of HIV and Social Work, 1,* 27–39.

Wiener L. & Battles, H. (2006). Untangling the web: A close look at diagnosis disclosure among HIV-infected adolescents. *Journal of Adolescent Health, 38,* 307–309.

Wiener, L., Battles, H., Heilman, N., Sigelman, C., & Pizzo, P. (l996). Factors associated with disclosure of diagnosis to children with HIV. *Pediatric AIDS & HIV Infection: Fetus to Adolescent, 7,* 310–324.

Wiener, L., Battles, H., Riekert, K. (1999). Longitudinal Study of Psychological Disturbances in HIV-Infected, School Aged Children. *Journal of HIV Prevention & Education for Adolescents & Children, 3,* 13–36.

Wiener, L., Battles, H., Ryder, C., & Pao, M (2006). Psychotropic medication use in HIV-infected youth receiving treatment in a single institution. *Journal Child and Adolescent Psychopharmacology, 16*(6), 747–753.

Wiener, L., Battles, H., & Wood, L. (2007). Condom use, risk behavior and sexual knowledge: A longitudinal study of adolescents with perinatally or transfusion acquired HIV infection. *AIDS and Behavior,11*(3), 471–478.

Wiener, L., Fair, C., Pao, M., & Pizzo, P. (in press). Care for the child with HIV infection and AIDS. In A. Armstrong-Dailey & S. Zarbock (Eds.), *Hospice care for children* (3rd ed.). New York: Oxford University Press.

Wiener, L., & Figueroa, V. (l998). Children speaking with children and families about HIV infection. In P. Pizzo & K. Wilfert (Eds.), *Pediatric AIDS: The Challenge of HIV Infection in Infants, Children, and Adolescents* (3rd ed., pp. 729–758). Baltimore, MD: Williams & Wilkins.

Wiener, L., Havens, J., & Ng, W. (2003). Psychosocial problems in pediatric HIV infection. In W. Shearer (Ed.), *Medical management of AIDS in children* (pp. 373–394). Philadelphia: W.B. Saunders Company.

Wiener, L., Hersh, S., & Kazak, A. (2007). Psychiatric and psychosocial support for child and family. In P. Pizzo & D. Poplack (Eds.), *Principles and practices of pediatric oncology* (5th ed., pp. 1410–1414). Philadelphia: Lippincott.

Wiener L., & Lyons, M. (2006). HIV disclosure: Who knows? Who needs to know? Clinical and ethical considerations. In M. Lyons & L. D'Angelo (Eds.), *Teenagers HIV & AIDS* (pp. 197–214). Westport, CT: Praeger Publishers.

Wiener, L., Mellins, C., Marhefka, S., & Battles, H. (2007). Disclosure of an HIV diagnosis to children: History, current research, and future directions, *Journal of Behavioral and Developmental Pediatrics, 28*(2), 155–166.

Wiener, L., Riekert, K., Ryder, C., & Wood, L. (2004). Assessing medication adherence in adolescents with HIV when electronic monitoring is not feasible. *AIDS Patient Care and STDs, 18,* 31–43.

Wiener, L., Septimus, A., & Grady, C. (1998). Psychosocial support and ethical issues for the child and family. In P. Pizzo & K. Wilfert (Eds.), *Pediatric AIDS: The challenge of HIV infection in infants, children, and adolescents* (3rd ed., pp. 703–728). Baltimore, MD: Williams & Wilkins.

Wiener, L., & Wood, L. (2006). Teen Talk: Living with HIV. In M. Lyons & L. D'Angelo (Eds.), *Teenagers HIV & AIDS* (pp. 197–214). Westport, CT: Praeger Publishers.

Wiener, L., Zobel, M., Battles, H., Ryder, C. (2007). Transition from a pediatric intramural clinical research program to adolescent and adult community-based care services: Assessing transition readiness. *Social Work in Health Care, 46*(1), 1–19.

Winston, C. (2006). African American grandmothers parenting AIDS orphans: Grieving and coping. *Qualitative Social Work, 5*(1), 33–43.

Wolfelt, A. (1983). *Helping children cope with grief.* Muncie, Inc.: Accelerated Development Inc.

Wolters, P., & Brouwers, P. (2005). Neurobehavioral function and assessment of children and adolescents with HIV-1 infection. In S. Zeichner & J. Read J. (Eds.), *Textbook of pediatric care* (pp. 269–284). Cambridge, MA: Cambridge University Press.

Chapter Sixteen

HIV-INFECTED AND HIV-AFFECTED MIDLIFE AND OLDER PERSONS

Charles A. Emlet

INTRODUCTION

When members of our society view older adults as a homogeneous group of individuals, they blind themselves to the reality of how diverse older people in the United States really are. Such views create limitations in recognizing that older adults are affected by HIV disease in a variety of ways. In 2005, at the "Expert Workshop on HIV/AIDS and Older People," the International Institute on Aging, United Nations (INIA) acknowledged four distinct groups affected by HIV or AIDS. These groups include: older adults whose behavior places them at risk for HIV or AIDS, older adults newly diagnosed with HIV disease, long-term survivors who are aging with HIV or AIDS, and older HIV-affected caregivers (Fenech, 2006). Each group is differentially affected by HIV, and each group faces its own challenges. They also, however, share increasingly common issues associated with aging and HIV.

This chapter provides an understanding of the physical and psychosocial issues affecting these populations listed above, including demographic and disease-related diversity, and discusses approaches for those who may work with older adults from any of these four distinct groups. As Emlet and Poindexter (2004) have pointed out, aging and HIV are ubiquitous in social work practice, so the likelihood of health and social service providers encountering an older person infected with or affected by HIV is high. Social workers and other human services professionals therefore need to be prepared to skillfully address the needs of this emerging population.

CHANGING DEMOGRAPHICS

Initially HIV was viewed as mostly having an impact on those in young adulthood and early middle age (Riley, 1989). The HIV and AIDS data on older people were primarily focused on the proportion receiving a diagnosis of AIDS after age 50. Everyone over age 50 was considered in one large category. This method of case reporting resulted in what Genke (2000) referred to as the "invisible ten percent," as approximately 10 to 12 percent of

Acknowledgments: I thank Dr. Robert for his perspective on living with HIV. I dedicate this chapter to all the older adults who have lived with HIV/AIDS who have shared their lives and stories with me over the past 20 years.

newly reported cases of AIDS were in adults age 50 and over. The percentage of over-all cases, however, was relatively low and thus "invisible" to many. The success of antiretroviral therapy has created a distinct population of older adults with HIV or AIDS in addition to those being diagnosed in later life. This emerging population consists of individuals—sometimes referred to as long-term survivors—who are now entering late middle age or early old age, having lived with HIV disease for perhaps several decades. Taken together, these populations create a rapidly growing population of people 50 years and older living with HIV or AIDS (Centers for Disease Control and Prevention [CDC], 2008a).

We can better understand just how rapidly this population is growing by examining data from the Centers for Disease Control and Prevention (CDC) annual surveillance reports. The CDC reports the estimated number of persons living with HIV or AIDS by year. By viewing these statistics over time, we can clearly understand the consistent increase in older adults living with HIV or AIDS and why a discussion of this population is no longer unknown. Rather, these statistics suggest the growth in these populations has serious and immediate practice ramifications. As seen in Figure 16.1, in 2001 the CDC estimated that approximately 65,000 adults 50 years and older were living with HIV or AIDS in the United States. By 2006 this number had risen to more than 129,000, a near doubling of cases in a six-year period of time. The CDC data also indicates that in 2005, persons age 50 and over accounted for 15% of all new HIV or AIDS diagnoses and 24% of all people living with HIV or AIDS. This figure is up from 17% in 2001 (CDC, 2008a).

DIVERSITY IN HIV OR AIDS AMONG OLDER ADULTS

It is critical in understanding the impact HIV disease has on older people that professionals in the field of social work and human services recognize the diversity among older people living with HIV or AIDS as well as in those at risk. Like their younger counterparts, older adults diagnosed with HIV or AIDS vary by gender, ethnicity, sexual orientation, and method of infection. Like many other areas of practice, these sociodemographic characteristics play an important role in one's vulnerability, resources, and social support networks.

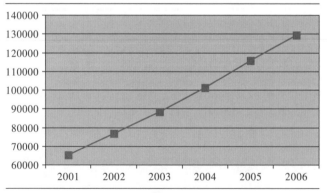

Figure 16.1   Estimated number of persons living with HIV/AIDS age 50+ in the United States, 2001–2006
Source: CDC (2008). *HIV/AIDS Surveillance Report,* Vol. 18, Table 8

Gender

Throughout the pandemic, U.S. men have been disproportionately affected by HIV. According to the surveillance data from the CDC, in 2006 males accounted for approximately 74% of all HIV or AIDS cases in adults and adolescents (CDC, 2008b). We know from empirical evidence that older men continue to be sexually active in later life. Lindau and colleagues (2007) studied a nationally representative sample of 3,005 older adults and found 84% of men age 57 to 64 and 67% of men age 65 to 74 had been sexually active in the past 12 months. Cooperman, Arnsten, and Klein (2007) studied more than 600 men age 50 and older and found more than three-quarters of HIV-negative men and 71.5% of HIV-positive men had engaged in sexual activities with at least one other person in the past six months, with one-quarter of both HIV-positive and HIV-negative men having more than one sexual partner. A major difference, however, was found in the use of condoms. While 57% of HIV-positive older men stated they always used a condom in the past six months, only 18% of HIV-negative men had.

Because of the historically greater impact on men, older women with HIV or AIDS, as well as women at risk for infection, have been overlooked and marginalized. However, older women are now being diagnosed with AIDS at a higher rate than older men and have increased risk of infection per exposure (Hillman, 2007). Older women are less likely than younger women to use condoms correctly and consistently (Zablotsky & Kennedy, 2003), as older women are no longer concerned about pregnancy. In a sample of 160 community-dwelling older adults, Hillman (2007) found older women less likely to have their physician talk to them about HIV or AIDS than are older men, and they themselves believed they maintain less knowledge about the disease than their male counterparts.

Older women face differences in physiology that place them at increased risk for infection. For example, the natural thinning of vaginal walls and decreased vaginal secretions lead to potential microscopic tears during intercourse that place them at increased risk. Older women also face differences in sociodemographic characteristics. Schable, Chu, and Diaz (1996) found older women with HIV or AIDS more likely than their younger female counterparts to be widowed, separated, or divorced and to live alone. Keigher, Stevens, and Plach (2004) suggest that as older women survive with HIV or AIDS, the historical elements of poverty, racism, sexism, and now HIV stigma will continue to have an impact on their lives.

Race and Ethnicity

HIV or AIDS in the United States has heavily affected communities of color, particularly African American and Latino communities. Data from the CDC indicate that while Blacks (including African Americans) account for 13% of the U.S. population, they account for nearly half (49%) of people with HIV or AIDS (CDC, 2007). African Americans also experience shorter survival times and higher rates of death due to HIV disease. While Latinos made up 13% of the U.S. population in 2006, they accounted for 16% of the cases of AIDS since the beginning of the pandemic (CDC, 2008c). These disproportionate patterns hold true for older adults living with HIV or AIDS. Linley and colleagues (2007) found that among persons 50 years and older, rates of HIV or AIDS were 12 times higher among older African Americans and five times higher among older Latinos compared to older Whites.

HIV-infected elders of color may face a variety of issues that may exacerbate their support, care, and treatment. It has been documented that elders of color face greater morbidity and mortality due to chronic health conditions such as diabetes, hypertension, and cardiovascular disease than Whites (Hooyman & Kiyak, 2008). The combination of these chronic diseases, along with HIV or AIDS, may serve to increase functional disabilities.

While it has been well documented that older adults in communities of color value and receive considerable informal social support from numerous sources (Hooyman & Kiyak, 2008), those assumptions may not hold true for older adults diagnosed with HIV or AIDS. Jimenez (2003) found in his study of 110 older men of color who have sex with men that the perception of being labeled gay and having HIV or AIDS was highly stigmatizing. In a mixed methods study of 25 older adults with HIV or AIDS, Emlet (2007a) found older African Americans to experience significantly higher scores on an HIV stigma scale than their White counterparts. Additionally, perceived stigma of using services, institutional racism, and perceptions of experimentation as a result of the continuing changes of standards of care for HIV disease may create additional barriers to care. Social service providers need to be particularly sensitive to concerns of ageism, classism, and racism, as well as perceptions of HIV stigma, when working with HIV-infected older adults.

Sexual Orientation

Older adults, like younger people, vary in sexual orientation. As HIV is a disease that is often sexually transmitted, older adults, service providers, and society must confront ageist views of older persons being either asexual or exclusively heterosexual. Older adults face different and specific challenges regarding HIV disease compared to their younger counterparts, regardless of sexual orientation. Diversity in sexual orientation must also be seen in the context of history, cohort, and belief systems.

Older adults may have decreased sexual communication skills compared to younger adults. The differences may be the result of cohort effects that dictate what is considered proper behavior (University of California, San Francisco, 2000). They may be reluctant to disclose behaviors they view as being socially unacceptable or may lack negotiation skills that promote safer sex. Older gay and bisexual men face unique challenges that are associated with age. Gay men over 50 lived half or more of their lives before the Stonewall Rebellion of 1969 (Grossman, D'Augelli, & O'Connell, 2001). Many of these men felt the need to hide their sexual identities throughout their lives in order to protect themselves from stigma and discrimination. Older sexual minorities came of age when gay-related hate and violence was more pervasive than today and when heterosexism and homophobia remained unchallenged (Grossman, D'Augelli, & O'Connell, 2001).

Social workers and other social service practitioners need to be aware of their own biases and ageist beliefs related to sexuality, aging, and sexual orientation. Our own ageism or homophobia may be among the biggest barriers to working successfully with this population. Anderson (1998) suggests that social service professionals have a responsibility to "create an environment that will encourage older persons to share in the work of surviving HIV/AIDS" (p. 448).

HIV Infection Modes

Older adults become infected with HIV in the same ways as younger persons: primarily unprotected sex or unsafe injecting (Nichols, 2004). Unfortunately, the ageist attitudes in our society often suggest that older people are asexual and that drug users do not live into old age. Such myths serve to contribute to the misinformation about HIV and AIDS among older people. Recent data from the CDC suggest that men who have sex with men and high-risk heterosexual contact accounted for 82% of all cases of HIV and AIDS in the United States diagnosed in 2006 (CDC, 2008d). Persons who inject drugs are also disproportionately affected. The same report indicates that in 2006, 19% of all persons living with HIV or AIDS were classified as injection drug users. In their study of CDC data, Linley et al. (2007) found that compared to younger men, a higher proportion of HIV or AIDS in men over 50 was due to injection drug use (19 versus 11%), while a lower proportion was due to men having sex with men (53 versus 69%). In addition to male-to-male sex and injection drug use, heterosexual exposure continues to emerge as a major risk for transmission. The Research on Older Adults with HIV study (ROAH) (Karpiak, Shippy, & Cantor, 2006) found that 38% of all participants identified vaginal sex as the mode of transmission of HIV. The study concluded that "heterosexual sex is emerging as the current dominant mode of transmission. When comparing ROAH participants who tested HIV-positive in the last five years to those who tested HIV-positive more than 10 years ago, vaginal sex is given as a mode of transmission in 61% of those infected in the last five years as compared to 32% in those who were infected more than ten years ago" (pp. 12–13). These patterns reinforce that older persons engage in the same behaviors as younger adults, placing them at risk for HIV: men having sex with men, injection drug use, and heterosexual sex.

DISTINCT POPULATIONS

When we examine the impact that HIV has on older adults, we must recognize that various and distinct populations exist within what we call older adults. In the following sections, we address four distinct populations: (1) older adults at risk of HIV and other sexually transmitted infections, (2) newly infected older persons, (3) long-term survivors, and (4) HIV-affected caregivers.

Older Adults at Risk of HIV Infection

In the popular text titled *Social Gerontology: An Interdisciplinary Perspective,* Hooyman and Kiyak (2008) point out that in a time when our society is increasingly tolerant of sexuality and safer sex, we continue to hold on to outdated ideas with regard to aging and sexuality. In a largely ageist society, aging and sexuality goes undiscussed or is dealt with inappropriately through jokes and humor. The recent large-scale study on sexuality among older adults examined through a nationally representative sample the sexual practices and problems of more than 3,000 older people (Lindau et al., 2007). While the results of this study found that sexual activity declines with age, three-quarters of those ages 57 to 64 and more than half of those ages 65 to 74 engage in sexual activity. Slightly more than one-quarter of those age 75 and over were sexually active. At the same time, only 38% of men and 22% of women in the sample stated they had discussed sexual matters with their physician since turning 50.

The lack of understanding about what constitutes behavior that places one at risk needs to be shared by older adults as well as health and social service systems that fail them. Nokes and Emlet (2006) point to five myths that exist within society that hinder primary prevention and education efforts related to HIV and older people.

- Older people are no longer interested in sex.
- If they do have sex, it is within a long-term monogamous relationship.

- Older people do not inject drugs.
- Those who were injection drug users have died before reaching old age.
- Older people are all heterosexual (p. 237).

Psychosocial Issues

The overall lack of knowledge about HIV and appropriate preventive behaviors place many older persons at risk. In a qualitative study of 24 older HIV-positive women, Neundorfer and colleagues (2005) found that nearly 40 percent of the informants identified lack of prevention information to be a factor in their infection with HIV. In a larger-scale study in West Central Florida, 62% of older respondents reported having little or no knowledge of HIV or behaviors that place them at risk (Nichols et al., 2002) and in a study of 249 midlife and older adults in central California, Altschuler, Katz, and Tynan (2008) found both older Whites and elders of color to have limited knowledge about HIV, with elders of color consistently showing less knowledge. Now that baby boomers have reached retirement age, a generation raised in a time of relaxed sexual and drug-using mores, the issues of better education and prevention will become more critical.

While we can point to the lack of knowledge regarding HIV and suggest older adults need increased understanding, the health and social service system must be part of the solution. Health and social service agencies and their representatives need to better incorporate appropriate and relevant prevention materials focusing on older people. In a national survey of state health departments, Orel, Wright, and Wagner (2004) found that while all state health departments had HIV prevention materials available, only 30 percent had publications that were specific to older people. In a recent survey of Area Agencies on Aging (AAAs) in Washington state, Emlet, Gerkin and Orel (in press) found that only 16% of AAAs provide any educational programs on HIV for older adults, although more than 91% of agencies felt this charge was consistent with their mission of serving older people. While few education and prevention programs for older people exist, several models are available. The Broward County Health Department in Florida has operated the Seniors HIV Intervention Project for a number of years, providing the community with education and outreach specific to HIV and older adults (Broward County Health Department, 2008). Recently, the AIDS Community Research Initiative of America (ACRIA) has launched a study that aims to educate the senior community about HIV and increase the awareness of service providers about the unique needs of this population. They have developed full- and half-day courses. The educational curriculum is currently being delivered in New York City (Taylor-Akutagawa, 2008).

For service providers who are not directly engaged with prevention activities, improved assessment of sexual health among older adults is a key to education and the prevention of the spread of HIV disease. While this may be an uncomfortable line of questions, one can begin the conversation with questions such as, "I'd like to talk a bit about something that's important for everyone: HIV transmission. Please tell me what you know about HIV." "How have you been keeping yourself safer when you have sex or take drugs?" "What would you like to ask me about HIV testing, HIV treatment, or HIV prevention?" Such simple and straightforward statements or questions can open the door to important and meaningful conversations about HIV knowledge and risk.

The revised recommendations for HIV testing from the CDC recommend that in all health care settings, screening for HIV infection should be performed routinely for all persons ages 13 to 64 years (CDC, 2006). Although this guideline falls short of testing all older persons, which still reflects ageist policies and attitudes, health care professionals can encourage the routine voluntary testing of older adults for HIV.

Practice Suggestions for Working with Older Adults at Risk for HIV

- Educate yourself and your colleagues and do not accept or reinforce ageist attitudes concerning sexual health, injecting, or HIV.
- Integrate sexual and drug-use history questions into standardized assessments and evaluations with all older people. Do not assume an older person, despite advanced age, is asexual or does not engage in potentially risky behavior.
- Work with your local aging network as well as your HIV Coordinating Council to advocate for HIV education and prevention materials for older people.
- Encourage the integration of appropriate HIV and aging concerns into local HIV planning as well as in the area plan for your local Area Agency on Aging.

Newly Diagnosed Older Adults

As previously mentioned, adults age 50 and over accounted for 15% of all new diagnoses of HIV or AIDS in 2005 (CDC, 2008a). In a recent study of the changing trends in HIV or AIDS among older persons, Paul and colleagues (2007) analyzed data from New Jersey, the state with the fifth-largest number of AIDS cases in the nation. They found that the proportion of older men first diagnosed with HIV or AIDS increased significantly from 7.3% in 1992 to 19.2% in 2003. During that same period, cases in older women increased in proportion, from 4.4% to 15.4%.

Because HIV has been typically seen as a disease associated with younger people, it may not be one of the first problems assessed by health care professionals. Health care providers, including social workers, may be reluctant to ask questions regarding sexual or drug use history with older adults. Similarly, older people may be embarrassed to suggest the need for HIV testing because of the stigma associated with the disease. One negative result of lower clinical suspicion and a conspiracy of silence is late diagnosis of HIV disease. An individual is considered to have a late diagnosis of HIV when he or she receives an AIDS diagnosis within 12 months of receiving a diagnosis of HIV infection. Mugavero and associates (2007) outline numerous ways in which late diagnosis is detrimental to the individual and society. For example, there is increased morbidity (illnesses) and mortality (death), a diminished response to antiretroviral treatment, and increased health care expenditure. In additional, a late diagnosis increases the likelihood that HIV-infected persons will pass along the retrovirus to sex or drug partners because of not knowing that they have HIV.

Evidence from the CDC indicates a significant increase in the likelihood of late diagnosis with age. Figure 16.2 shows the percentages of persons receiving an AIDS diagnosis within 12 months of an HIV diagnosis by age group (CDC, 2008b). While 36% of persons ages 30 to 34 years of age fell into the category of late diagnosis, the proportion increased to 56% for those age 65 and over.

Whether the diagnosis of HIV disease is timely or late, once diagnosed, older persons are faced with various facets of care that may be unfamiliar to them. They will need to learn and become familiar with HIV-related terminology, such as monitoring their CD4 counts and understanding viral loads. (See Chapter 1 for information on these tests.) There is evidence that antiretroviral medications are prescribed to older persons in equal proportions as younger individuals with HIV or AIDS and that therapies work equally well for older persons (Wellons et al., 2002). As is the case for people of all ages, longevity with HIV can be partially dependent upon strict adherence to an often complicated regimen of HIV medications. Rintamaki and colleagues (2006), in their study

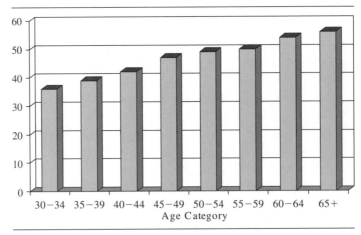

Figure 16.2   Percentage of cases receiving an AIDS diagnosis within 12 months of a diagnosis of HIV infection by age group—2005
Source: CDC (2008). *HIV/AIDS Surveillance Report,* Vol. 18 Table 2

of 204 HIV-infected individuals, found that those with HIV stigma concerns were 2.5 times less likely to define and interpret the meaning of CD4 count correctly and 3.3 times more likely to be nonadherent to their medication regimen than those with low concerns. Therefore, it is important for practitioners to assist newly diagnosed older adults to understand medication adherence and terminology and to assess their perceptions of HIV-related stigma, as well as evaluating their social support networks.

In addition to the complex regimen of antiretroviral medications, midlife and older adults are often taking medications to treat other medical conditions. For example, Shah and associates (2002) found that HIV-positive older adults were taking, on average, 2.7 medications in addition to medications to treat their HIV infection. Medication regimen complexity plays an important role in medication adherence among both older adults (from the general population) and individuals living with HIV disease. Chesney (2003) found that barriers to successful medication adherence among people living with HIV parallels other chronic health conditions and includes regimen complexity. Therefore, the addition of other medical conditions increases the potential of regimen complexity and may threaten medication adherence.

Psychosocial Issues

Psychosocial research on HIV and aging points to several important elements to consider when working with newly diagnosed HIV-positive older persons. In the largest study to date on HIV and older adults, the Research on Older Adults with HIV study (ROAH), Karpiak, Shippy, and Cantor (2006) found 38% of participants ($N = 1,000$) to be moderately depressed and 26% categorized as severely depressed using the Center for Epidemiological Studies Depression Scale (CES-D). In a study of 25 older HIV-positive adults in the Pacific Northwest, Emlet (2007a) found 36% met the CES-D clinical cutoff for depression. Data from the Veterans Aging Cohort Study (VACS) found major depression to be more common in HIV-positive veterans than in their HIV-negative counterparts (Goulet, Fultz, Rimland, Butt, et al., 2007). It is reasonable for social workers and other social service practitioners to routinely screen for depression among older persons with HIV disease, particularly those with a new diagnosis, because learning one is HIV-positive is likely to cause personal, social, financial, and developmental crises.

Practitioners also need to be acutely aware of the serious ramifications of HIV stigma and the parallel issue of disclosure. One theory of disclosure developed by Serovich (2001) is known as consequence theory. This theory posits that the consequences of disclosure are weighed against potential benefits, the end result being a cost/reward analysis on the part of the individual. As was stated in the ROAH study, "They made careful and specific decisions about whom they told" (Karpiak, Shippy, & Cantor, 2006, p. 28). The greater the perception of stigma, the less likely one may be to disclose his or her HIV status to others. Emlet (2008) found that 60% of the older population ($N = 25$) used nondisclosure as a means of self-protection from stigma.

Concerns for substance abuse must be considered when working in older HIV-infected adults. The ROAH study found that a majority of older adults surveyed used cigarettes (84%), alcohol (81%), or illicit drugs (84%) in their lifetime. In addition, the current rate of illicit drug use among respondents was: marijuana (23%), crack (16%), cocaine (15%), and heroin (7%) (Karpiak, Shippy, & Cantor, 2006). These findings run counter to some of the prevailing stereotypes that old people do not use substances.

Dementia is another important consideration in working with older adults with HIV infection. As Valcour and Sacktor (2002) point out, advanced age is a known risk factor for dementia in older HIV-negative individuals. However, the advent of highly active antiretroviral therapy (HAART) and accompanying longevity create the potential for increased risk of HIV-related dementia as well (Valcour & Paul, 2006). Providers need to be aware that the presence of dementia, even in subtle forms, may compromise one's abilities with self-care tasks and medication adherence and can result in increased isolation. While many social service providers are familiar with cognitive screening tests for age-related dementia, such as the Mini Mental State Exam (Folstein, Folstein, & McHugh, 1975), HIV-associated dementia and other HIV cognitive disorders may not be identified through such testing. Knipples and colleagues (2002) have validated a four-question instrument that can provide an initial screening for the presence of HIV-associated dementia. Social workers and other service providers working with HIV-positive elders should uniformly incorporate cognitive screening into their assessments and be sensitive to the potential differences in how age-related and HIV-related dementias many manifest.

Practice Suggestions for Working with Newly Diagnosed Older Adults

- Because of the high potential for a late diagnosis, do not assume that because someone is newly diagnosed with HIV disease that his or her disease is in the early stages.

- Personally assist or provide resources to newly infected individuals for understanding the terminology related to HIV disease, and provide assistance in acknowledging the necessity for very high levels of medication adherence.

- Recognize the potential complexity of having multiple medical conditions and that these conditions may further complicate disease management and medication regimes.

- Routinely screen for depression using a standardized method of assessment. Depending upon the expertise of the practitioner, diagnostic criteria (DSM IV-TR) or screening instruments (such as the Beck Depression Inventory or Center for Epidemiological Studies Depression Scale) are preferred approaches.

- Assess the perceptions of HIV-related stigma. Realize that stigma encompasses multiple dynamics, including intrapersonal and interpersonal elements. Standardized assessment instruments are available (see Berger, Ferrans, & Lashley, 2001; Emlet 2005, 2007b; Sowell et al., 1997).
- Screen for potential issues with HIV-related dementia. (See Knippels, Goodkin, et al. 2002) for suggested alternative screening questions.)
- Assess social support, realizing that a new diagnosis of HIV or AIDS may affect available social support. Be sure their family of choice is included in any evaluation of social networks.

Long-Term Survivors and "Aging In" with HIV or AIDS

One reason for the steep increase in older persons living with HIV or AIDS (as shown in Figure 16.1) is the growth of the population of older persons who were diagnosed earlier in life and are now living into older age with HIV or AIDS. This is a relatively new phenomenon, as longevity was rare prior to the advent of effective HAART in the 1990s.

In a recent study focusing on the cost of HIV care, Schackman and colleagues (2006) estimated the life expectancy at the time of entering HIV care to be 24 years. Longevity with HIV contributes substantially to the prevalence of older adults living with HIV. According to the CDC, persons age 50 and over accounted for 24% of the total number of persons living with HIV in 2005. This is up from 17% in 2001 (CDC, 2008a). While older long-term survivors and newly diagnosed older adults are often seen as a single population (older adults living with HIV), long-term survivors also have unique concerns that can set them apart from newly diagnosed older persons.

Like their newly diagnosed counterparts, those aging with HIV face a multitude of health and psychosocial problems. Having other chronic health conditions is likely, as most chronic health conditions increase in prevalence with age (Hooyman & Kiyak, 2008). The ROAH study found that more than 9 in 10 older persons interviewed had at least one other health condition, and 77% listed two or more (Karpiak, Shippy, & Cantor, 2006). In addition to the chronic health conditions typically associated with aging, some evidence suggests an increased risk for additional disorders associated with HIV disease. For example, Kohli and colleagues (2006) found that "the progression of metabolic and hormonal disorders may accelerate due to the aging process and chronic exposure to HIV and antiretroviral agents" (p. 34). Some research suggests that HIV-positive women experience menopause at a significantly earlier age that their HIV-negative counterparts (Schoenbaum et al., 2005). Some conditions, such as cardiovascular disease, particularly increases in total cholesterol, triglycerides, and low-density lipoprotein (LDL), have been associated with protease-inhibitor-based HAART regimens, as has diabetes mellitus (Kohli et al., 2006). Analysis from Veterans Aging Cohort Study found older, HIV-infected veterans to have increased risk for liver and kidney disease, substance abuse disorders, and multiple illnesses than their HIV-negative counterparts (Goulet et al., 2007). Thus, long-term survivors may experience an increased likelihood of managing multiple conditions through aging itself, as well as HIV-related or HIV-induced issues, including HIV treatment.

Another related issue that may have an impact on long-term survivors is the complexity and duration of medication adherence. In a recent review of the literature, Ingersoll and Cohen (2008) reported that regimen complexity, including dosages per day, significantly affects medication adherence in HIV-positive populations. Konkle-Parker and colleagues

(2008) found that pill burden was a barrier to adherence in a sample of 20 HIV-positive persons of color in the southern United States. We cannot assume that longevity of time on antiretroviral therapy is always a benefit to adherence. While newly diagnosed older persons face issues of understanding medications and the importance of adherence, long-term survivors face problems of medication burden, the potential for regimen complexity, and problems with side effects.

Older adults living with HIV are at increased risk of cognitive impairments (Valcour & Paul, 2006). Cognitive deficits in both HIV-infected and older non-HIV-infected individuals can affect everyday functioning as well as impact the quality of life of those affected (Vance & Burrage, 2006). Older adults "aging in" with HIV may be at increased risk for HIV-related cognitive impairment, including HIV associated dementia (HAD) and mild cognitive/motor disorder (MCMD). Valcour and colleagues (2004) studied 106 adults 50 years and over diagnosed with HIV infection from the Hawaii Aging with HIV Cohort Study and compared them to 96 adults ages 20 to 39 years. An 80-minute neuropsychological battery was used to assess multiple cognitive domains. The results found a significant increase in the number of older persons (25.2% versus 13.7%) who met diagnostic criteria for dementia. The odds of meeting criteria for HAD were 2.13 times greater than in the younger group. Vance and Burrage (2006) have suggested that prevention and intervention activities can be used to augment cognition. Promoting good health habits (nutrition and exercise), reducing the negative effects of substance abuse or depression, and encouraging social and mental stimulation are all strategies for assisting with improved cognition.

Psychosocial Issues

Like their newly diagnosed counterparts, individuals "aging in" with HIV may face significant psychosocial issues, including depression, issues of stigma and disclosure, and changes in social support. We know from the gerontological literature that depressive symptoms are among the most prevalent forms of late-life psychopathology (Hooyman & Kiyak, 2008). Considering the high rates of depression among older HIV-positive adults discussed earlier, the potential exists for long-term survivors to be at increased risk for depression.

The repeated loss of family and friends from HIV and/or aging can complicate depression for older survivors. These losses can result in one's social network becoming smaller over time. As noted by Sikkema and colleagues (2006), HIV-related loss is unique, whereby "the bereaved individual faces threat of death from the same illness as the deceased" (p. 563). Losses may remind the bereaved individual of his or her own mortality, creating the potential for substantial psychological distress. It is common for individuals who are diagnosed with HIV or AIDS to experience multiple HIV-related losses (Sikkema et al., 2006). Practitioners, particularly in cases of long-term survivors, should routinely discuss grief and bereavement and assess the potential impact on the psychological distress, grief reactions, loss of social support networks, and depression. Karpiak, Shippy, and Cantor (2006), found feelings of loneliness to be significantly higher among HIV-positive older adults than older HIV-negative individuals, concluding that loneliness is a significant problem.

It is unclear how the trajectory of HIV-related stigma is affected by time. For some, longevity and a more comfortable sense of self may serve as protective factors against stigma. On the other hand, as one ages with HIV disease, the potential for layering of multiple stigmatizing conditions increases. Emlet (2006) found 68% of the older adults in a study on aging and HIV stigma experienced both HIV-associated stigma and ageism.

Like newly infected older persons, an assessment of stigma and discrimination and the impact of these phenomena should be included in the assessment and evaluation process.

Practice Suggestions for Working with Long-Term Survivors
"Aging In" with HIV

- While long-term survivors may be skilled at the management of their HIV disease, having multiple medical conditions may develop new challenges. HIV treatment in and of itself may cause someone to develop additional side effects or medical conditions.
- Fear of stigma and anxiety of disclosure may still be an issue even after years of living with HIV. The assessment of HIV-related stigma and careful understanding of the individual's process of disclosure is critical to understand.
- Time as well as HIV disease may have eroded the social networks of these individuals. Assessment of social networks and sources of support is critical.
- Assessment of depression is as relevant to these individuals as it is to newly diagnosed older adults.
- Assessment of cognitive impairment, which may include neuropsychological testing, should be considered. Prevention and intervention strategies such as the ones mentioned earlier may be important to implement.
- Include a risk assessment for substance use, even if injection drug use is not a risk factor. While substance use declines with age, the ROAH study found as many as one-quarter of adults surveyed currently engage in some form of illicit drug use.

HIV-Affected Older Adults

A growing number of older adults are HIV-affected. This term refers to "those family members who have responsibilities for caregiving for an adult or child who has HIV disease" (Poindexter, 2001, p. 525). It is common for older family members to serve as caregivers for their adult children and/or their grandchildren living with HIV (Poindexter, 2006; Knodel, 2006). When children (whether HIV-negative or HIV-positive) are orphaned by HIV, their care often falls to grandparents or great-grandparents (Poindexter, 2006). While there is no certainty regarding the number of HIV-positive adults being cared for by older adults, it has been estimated that as many as one-third of persons with AIDS are being cared for by older relatives for financial, emotional, and physical support (Allers, 1990).

Psychosocial Issues

Older HIV-affected caregivers face numerous challenges and rewards for accepting their caregiving role. These issues include the caregiver's own health and aging-related issues, unexpected role change, more social isolation from age peers (Hayslip & Kaminski, 2005), and the stigma and disclosure issues that emerge from HIV disease (Poindexter & Boyer, 2003). They also find rewards and positive life experiences from these relationships (Poindexter, 2001).

Older caregivers often report poorer health than their noncaregiving counterparts and have higher incidences of depression (Fuller-Thomson & Minkler, 2000). Like older adults infected with HIV, older caregivers must also confront issues of stigma, discrimination, and the potential detriments and benefits of disclosure. (For additional information see Chapter 19, "HIV-Affected Caregivers".)

Practice Suggestions for Working with Older HIV-Affected Caregivers

- Recognize and be sensitive to aging-related health issues with older caregivers.
- Understand that stigma and feelings of discrimination may be very real for older affected caregivers.
- Older caregivers may need considerable assistance understanding and navigating multiple systems of services, including the child welfare system, HIV care and services, and the aging network.
- Many older adults maintain a stance of fierce independence and can be reluctant to ask for help and assistance. If help is offered in a sincere, sensitive, and authentic way, without judgment, it is often accepted.

Personal Perspective

Aging with AIDS, by Dr. Robert

I'm between my 65th and 66th birthdays, an age I thought some years ago I'd never reach, since I had tested positive for HIV in 1985. But I am still very much alive, relatively well, and when I retired from my public health role in 2009, I entered a new phase of my life and career.

As one of the first Seattle physicians to care for people with AIDS, and as a researcher seeing this epidemic unfold, in the mid-80s when I learned of my infection I estimated that I probably had at most 10 to 12 years from the time my new partner, Dave, and I likely became infected (in early 1983 when we both had a bad case of what looked like the flu) to make my contribution before becoming disabled and in need of my own terminal care.

Luckily, we survived until the new highly active antiretroviral treatments (HAART) for HIV came along in 1996; but by then Dave's T cell count had dropped below 200 and he had acquired cryptosporidiosis (a parasitic disease of the intestines which I'd already seen take several of my patients from this world). These facts qualified him as a case of AIDS a couple years earlier. I held out better, delaying my own fall to AIDS until 2001, when several of the antiretrovirals themselves nearly killed me from treatment-induced lactic acidosis and hepatitis, and a T cell count of 160, qualifying me also as having AIDS. Unfortunately, just as Dave's T cells started to recover from HAART in 2004, his improving immune system attacked his liver, which was also afflicted with hepatitis C virus, and within six months he died of liver failure, 22 years after our relationship began.

I was just turning 40 when we both acquired HIV, together with so many other gay men at the peak of new infections on the West Coast. While most people perceive that gay men are most likely to get infected in their 20s, in Seattle at least the highest rates of new infection in gay men still occur in their early to mid-30s. But those of us still living with HIV are getting older thanks to HAART, and as the meds are allowing us to feel physically better and to both feel and act upon those sexual urges that I'd been told are still present in your late 60s, 70s, 80s, and even beyond, and as the mean age of people living with HIV is increasing—the average age of HIV acquisition is also going to gradually increase, and like me, more and more people with HIV and AIDS will add to their HIV problem other chronic diseases that come with age.

(Continued)

For example, in 1998 after years of heartburn, an inadequately chewed pickle spear I swallowed stuck in and tore my lower esophagus, requiring a transfusion of five pints of blood, emergency surgery, and a weeklong stay in a local intensive care unit. Before I could surgically fix that problem incidental to having HIV, I suddenly had a need to get my gall bladder removed. Then, shortly after Dave died I decided to medically investigate episodes of weakness I'd experienced associated with exercise only to find an almost totally obstructed anterior coronary artery, needing a stent. My friends, who, like me, expected that I would succumb long ago now think of me as the Energizer Bunny who takes a medical licking yet keeps on ticking. But to me it's been an extraordinary roller-coaster ride—expecting to die as I watched my T cells gradually decline, then riding the upswing as those cells responded to HAART and returned almost to normal levels, then developing treatment complications, then developing other medical problems not much related to HIV as I've been aging. Now, who knows, will I live a normal life span, or will I die early of HIV complications or some other totally unrelated condition? In the meantime I'm having a longer time than I would have imagined to do something of merit, and I try to keep looking forward to whatever comes next.

CONCLUSIONS

HIV disease has great impact on older adults through new infections, complications of long-term survivorship, being at risk for infection, and requiring them to serve as caregivers for other HIV-infected individuals. Each of the four distinct groups discussed in this chapter have their own unique needs, yet all share the potential bias of ageism, stigma, and other forms of discrimination levied against them by society.

As service providers and practitioners, it is incumbent upon us to first acknowledge the existence and needs of these individuals and then to provide them with sensitive and humane care. But that in itself is not enough. Many of these individuals are without voices and need advocates: social workers and human service providers to assist them in standing up for their rights and to demand that they receive age-sensitive and disease-appropriate care. As the numbers of older adults living with HIV continue to increase, new methods of providing services will need to be engineered. Social workers with training in ecological and systems theory are in a wonderful position to be the architects of new and innovative programs. Whether we work to replicate models of service delivery for older HIV-infected and affected adults, or draw upon our own creativity to develop new programs, we can make a difference. It is our professional responsibility.

REFERENCES

Allers, C. T. (1990). AIDS and the older adult. *Gerontologist, 30,* 405–407.

Altschuler, J., Katz, A. D., & Tynan, M. A. (2008). Implications for HIV/AIDS research and education among ethnic minority older adults. *Journal of HIV/AIDS and Social Services, 7*(3), 209–228.

Anderson, G. (1998). Providing services to elderly people with HIV. In D. M. Arostein & B. J. Thompson (Eds.), *HIV and social work: A practitioner's guide* (pp. 443–450). New York: Herrington Park Press.

Berger, B. E., Ferrans, C. E., & Lashley, F. (2001). Measuring stigma in people with HIV: Psychometric assessment of the HIV stigma scale. *Research in Nursing and Health, 24*: 518–529.

Broward County Health Department. (2008). *AIDS/HIV Program: S.H.I.P.: Senior HIV Intervention Program.* Retrieved December 1, 2008, from www.browardchd.org/services/AIDS/ship.htm

Centers for Disease Control and Prevention. (2006). Revised recommendations for HIV testing of adults, adolescents, and pregnant women in health-care settings. *Morbidity and Mortality Weekly Review, 55*(RR14), 1–17.

Centers for Disease Control and Prevention. (2007). *HIV/AIDS and African Americans.* Available at http://www.cdc.gov/hiv/topics/aa/index.htm

Centers for Disease Control and Prevention. (2008a). *Persons age 50 and over.* Available at http://www.cdc.gov/hiv/topics/over50/index.htm

Centers for Disease Control and Prevention. (2008b). *HIV/AIDS Surveillance report,* Vol. 18. Atlanta: Author. Available from http://www.cdc.gov/hiv/topics/surveillance/index.htm

Centers for Disease Control and Prevention. (2008c). *Hispanics/Latinos.* Available from http://www.cdc.gov/hiv/hispanics/index.htm

Centers for Disease Control and Prevention. (2008d). *2006 Disease profile: National Center for HIV/AIDS, viral hepatitis, STD and TB Prevention.* Available from http://www.cdc.gov/NCHHSTP/Publications/docs/2006_Disease_Profile_508_FINAL.pdf

Chesney, M. (2003). Adherence to HAART regimens. *AIDS Patient Care and STDs, 17*(4), 169–177.

Cooperman, N. A., Arnsten, J. H., & Klein, R. S. (2007). Current sexual activity and risky sexual behavior in older men with or at risk for HIV infection. *AIDS Education and Prevention, 19,* 321–333.

Emlet, C. A. (2005). Measuring stigma in older and younger adults with HIV/AIDS: An analysis of an HIV stigma scale and initial exploration of subscales. *Research on Social Work Practice, 15,* 291–300.

Emlet, C. A. (2006). "You're awfully old to have *this* disease": Experiences of stigma and ageism in adults 50 years and older living with HIV/AIDS. *Gerontologist, 46,* 781–790.

Emlet, C. A. (2007a). Experiences of stigma in older adults living with HIV/AIDS: A mixed-methods analysis. *AIDS Patient Care and STDs, 21,* 740–752.

Emlet, C. A. (2007b). Extending the use of the 40-item HIV stigma scale to older adults. An examination of reliability and validity. *Journal of HIV/AIDS and Social Services, 6*(3), 43–54.

Emlet, C. A. (2008). Truth and consequences: A qualitative exploration of HIV disclosure in older adults. *AIDS Care, 20,* 710–717.

Emlet, C. A., Gerkin A., & Orel, N. (in press). The Graying of HIV/AIDS: Preparedness and Needs of the Aging Network in a Changing Epidemic. Journal of Gerontological Social Work.

Emlet, C. A., & Poindexter, C. C. (2004). The unserved, unseen and unheard: Integrating program for HIV-infected and affected elders. *Health and Social Work, 29*(2), 86–96.

Fenech, F. (2006). HIV/AIDS and older people: The Valletta Declaration. *International Institute on Aging Bold, 16*(2), 2–7.

Folstein, M. F., Folstein, S. E., & McHugh, P. R. (1975). "Mini Mental State": A practical method for grading the cognitive state of patients for the clinician. *Journal of Psychiatric Research, 12,* 189–198.

Fuller-Thomson, E., & Minkler, M. (2000). The mental and physical health of grandmothers who are raising their grandchildren. *Journal of Mental Health and Aging, 6,* 311–323.

Genke, J. (2000). HIV/AIDS and older adults: The invisible ten percent. *Care Management Journals, 2*(3), 196–205.

Goulet, J. L., Fultz, S. L., Rimland, D., Butt, A., et al. (2007). Do patterns of comorbidity vary by HIV status, age and HIV severity? *Clinical Infectious Diseases, 45,* 1593–1601.

Grossman, A. H., D'Augelli, A. R., & O'Connell, T. S. (2001). Being lesbian, gay, bisexual and 60 or older in North America. *Journal of Gay and Lesbian Social Services, 13*(4), 23–40.

Hayslip, B., & Kaminski, P. L. (2005). Grandparents raising their grandchildren: A review of the literature and suggestions for practice. *The Gerontologist, 45,* 262–269.

Hillman, J. (2007). Knowledge and attitudes about HIV/AIDS among community-living older women: Reexamining issues of age and gender. *Journal of Women and Aging, 19*(3/4), 53–67.

Hooyman, N. R., & Kiyak, H. A. (2008). *Social gerontology: A multidisciplinary perspective* (8th edition). Boston: Allyn & Bacon.

Ingersoll, K. S., & Cohen, J. (2008). The impact of medication regimen factors in adherence to chronic treatment: A review of the literature. *Journal of Behavioral Medicine, 31,* 213–224.

Jimenez, A. D. (2003). Triple jeopardy: Targeting older men of color who have sex with men. *Journal of Acquired Immune Deficiency Syndrome, 33*(Suppl. 2), S222–S225.

Karpiak, S. E., Shippy, R. A., & Cantor, M. H. (2006). *Research on Older Adults with HIV.* New York: AIDS Community Research Initiative of America.

Keigher, S. M., Stevens, P. E., & Plach, S. K. (2004). Midlife and older women and HIV: Health, social and economic factors shaping their future. *Journal of HIV/AIDS and Social Services, 3*(1), 43–58.

Knipples, H. M. A., Goodkin, K., Weiss, J. J., Wilkie, F. L., & Antoni, M. H. (2002). The importance of cognitive self-report in early HIV-1 infection: Validation of a cognitive functional status subscale. *AIDS, 16,* 259–267.

Knodel, J. (2006). Parents of persons with AIDS: Unrecognized contributions and unmet needs. *Global Ageing, 4*(2), 46–55.

Kohli, R., Klein, R. S., Schoenbaum, E. E., Asastos, K., Minkoff, H., & Sacks, H. S. (2006). Aging and HIV infection. *Journal of Urban Health, Bulletin of the New York Academy of Medicine, 83*(1), 31–42.

Konkle-Parker, D. J., Erlen, J. A., & Dubbert, P. M. (2008). Barriers and facilitators to medication adherence in a Southern minority population with HIV disease. *Journal of the Association of Nurses in AIDS Care, 19*(2), 28–104.

Lindau, S. T., Schumm, L. P., Laumann, E. O., Levinson, W., O'Muircheartaigh, C. A., & Waite, L. J. (2007). A study of sexuality and health among older adults in the United States. *New England Journal of Medicine, 357,* 762–774.

Linley, L., Hall, H. I., An, Q., et al. (2007). *HIV/AIDS diagnoses among persons fifty years and older in 33 states, 2001–2005.* Presented at the National HIV Prevention Conference, December 2007, Atlanta. Abstract B08–1. Accessed September 25, 2008.

Mugavero, M. J., Castellano, C., Edelman, D., & Hicks, C. (2007). Late diagnosis of HIV infection: The role of age and sex. *American Journal of Medicine, 120,* 370–373.

Neundorfer, M. M., Harris, P. B., Britton, P. J., & Lynch, D. A. (2005). HIV-risk factors for midlife and older women. *Gerontologist, 45,* 617–625.

Nichols, J. (2004). Prevention of HIV disease in older adults. In C. Emlet (Ed.), *HIV/AIDS and older adults: Challenges for individuals, families and communities* (pp. 21–35). New York: Springer.

Nichols, J., Speer, D. C., Watson, B. J., Watson, M. R., Vergon, T. L., Vallee, C. M., & Meah, J. M. (2002). *Aging with HIV: Psychological, social and health issues.* San Diego: Academic Press.

Nokes, K. M., & Emlet, C. A. (2006). Health care strategies for older adults with HIV/AIDS. In P. M. Burbank (Ed.), *Vulnerable Older Adults: Health Care Needs and Interventions* (pp. 235–250). New York: Springer.

Orel, N. A., Wright, J. M., & Wagner, J. (2004). Scarcity of HIV/AIDS risk-reduction materials targeting the needs of older adults among state departments of public health. *Gerontologist, 44,* 693–696.

Paul, S. M., Martin, R. M., Lu, S.-E., & Lin, Y. (2007). Changing trends in human immunodeficiency virus and acquired immunodeficiency syndrome in the population aged 50 and older. *Journal of American Geriatric Society, 55,* 1393–1397.

Poindexter, C. C. (2001). "I'm still blessed": The assets and needs of HIV-affected caregivers over fifty. *Families in Society, 82*(5), 525–536.

Poindexter, C. C. (2006). Grandparents raising HIV-infected and affected grandchildren. *Global Ageing, 4*(2), 86–93.

Poindexter, C. C., & Boyer, N. C. (2003). Strains and gains of grandmothers raising children in the HIV pandemic. In B. Berkman & L. Harootyan (Eds.), *Social work and health care in an aging society: Education, policy, practice and research.* New York: Springer.

Riley, M. W. (1989). AIDS and older people: The overlooked segment of the population. In M. W. Riley, M. G. Ory, & D. Zablotsky (Eds.), *AIDS in an aging society: What we need to know* (pp. 3–26). New York: Springer.

Rintamaki, L. S., Davis, T. C., Skripkauskas, S., Bennett, C. L., & Wolf, M. S. (2006). Social stigma concerns and HIV medication adherence. *AIDS Patient Care and STDs, 20,* 359–368.

Schable, B., Chu, S., & Diaz, T. (1996). Characteristics of women 50 years of age and older with heterosexually acquired AIDS. *American Journal of Public Health, 86,* 1616–1618.

Schackman, B. R., Gebo, K. A., Walensky, R. P., Losina, E., et al. (2006). The lifetime costs of current human immunodeficiency virus care in the United States. *Medical Care, 44,* 990–997.

Schoenbaum, E. E., Hartel, D., Lo, Y., et al. (2005). HIV infection, drug use and onset of natural menopause. *Clinical Infectious Diseases, 41,*1517–1524.

Serovich, J. (2001). A test of two disclosure theories. *AIDS Education and Prevention, 13,* 355–364.

Shah, S., McGowan, J., Smith, C., Blum, S., & Klein, R. (2002). Comorbid conditions, treatment and health maintenance in older persons with HIV infection in NYC. *Clinical Infectious Diseases, 35,* 1238–1243.

Sikkema, K. J., Hansen, N. B., Ghebremichael, M., Kochman, A., et al. (2006). A randomized controlled trial of a coping group intervention for adults with HIV who are AIDS bereaved: Longitudinal effects on grief. *Health Psychology, 25,* 563–570.

Sowell, R., Lowenstein, A., Moneyham, L., Demi, A., Mizuno, Y., & Seals, B. (1997). Resources, stigma and patterns of disclosure in rural women with HIV infection. *Public health nursing, 14*(5), 302–312.

Taylor-Akutagawa, V. E. (2008). *HIV/AIDS and older adults curriculum overview.* New York: AIDS Community Research Initiative of America.

University of California, San Francisco. (2000). HIV and older adults. *HIV Counselor Perspectives, 9*(5), 1–7.

Valcour, V. G., & Sacktor, N. (2002). HIV-associated dementia and aging. *Journal of Mental Health and Aging, 8*(4), 295–306.

Valcour, V. G., Shikuma, C., Shiramizu, B., Watters, M., et al. (2004). Higher frequency of dementia in older HIV-1 individuals: The Hawaii Aging with HIV-1 Cohort. *Neurology, 63,* 822–827.

Valcour, V. G., & Paul, R. (2006). HIV infection and dementia in older adults. *Clinical Infectious Diseases, 42,* 1449–1454.

Vance, D. E., & Burrage, J. W. (2006, November). Promoting successful cognitive aging in adults with HIV: Strategies for intervention. *Journal of Gerontological Nursing,* 34–41.

Wellons, M. F., Sanders, L., Edwards, L. J., Bartless, J. A., Heald, A. E., & Schmader, K. E. (2002). HIV infection: Treatment outcomes in older and younger adults. *Journal of the American Geriatrics Society, 50,* 603–607.

Zablotsky, D., & Kennedy, M. (2003). Risk factors and HIV transmission to midlife and older women: Knowledge, options and the initiation of safer sexual practices. *Journal of Acquired Immune Deficiency Syndrome, 33*(Suppl. 2), S122–130.

Chapter Seventeen

HIV AND BLACK AND AFRICAN AMERICAN COMMUNITIES IN THE TWENTY-FIRST CENTURY

Darrell P. Wheeler, Bernadette R. Hadden, Michael Lewis, Laurens G. Van Sluytman, and Tyrone M. Parchment

INTRODUCTION

No human services professional interested in the HIV field can be unaffected by the overwhelming burden that the U.S. HIV pandemic has placed on African American communities. In this chapter we challenge traditional approaches and views, which ignore the historical and societal realities of racism and poverty, and offer alternative perspectives to understanding African Americans and HIV.

Despite seemingly rapid scientific and educational developments over the first two decades of the pandemic, political, religious, cultural, and social forces continue to hamper the U.S. response to the HIV pandemic. HIV disease is still widely treated as a direct result of individual stigmatized behaviors and "lifestyle" choices, such as homosexuality, substance use, and sexual "promiscuity." This individualistic way of viewing the pandemic distorts our policies and services.

In 1988, Selik, Castro, and Pappaioanou suggested that prevention strategies must consider racial or ethnic differences in acquiring HIV infection, yet it was not until 1999 that the Minority AIDS Initiative (MAI) was established by the Centers for Disease Control and Prevention (CDC). MAI aimed at reducing the disparity in HIV and AIDS diagnoses nationally among African American and other Black men having sex with men (MSM). Through capacity building and research, MAI assisted and assists community-based organizations (CBOs) serving communities of color to initiate HIV prevention programs and culturally relevant HIV interventions (Minority AIDS Prevention, 2005). Funds are distributed by the Health Resources and Services Administration (HRSA). Also, in 1999 the Divisions for HIV/AIDS Prevention at the CDC published the "Compendium of HIV Prevention Interventions with Evidence of Effectiveness" (CDC, 2006a). MAI and HRSA were precursors to what we now term *diffusion of effective behavioral interventions* (DEBIs), which have standardized the implementation of science-based

(Continued)

Acknowledgments: We dedicate this chapter to all those men, women, adolescents, and children who have lived with or now live with HIV in body, mind, or spirit, and to all those who may never have to because of the efforts of social workers and other service providers around the world. We thank Julian for the eloquent vignette.

interventions and distributed them in a packaged set at community and group levels in hopes of reducing the spread of HIV and other sexually transmitted infections (STIs) and to promote healthy behaviors.[1]

HIV AND AIDS IN THE U.S. AFRICAN DIASPORA

Despite attempts to specifically address African American vulnerabilities to HIV, entering the third decade of the U.S. HIV pandemic, African Americans and Blacks account for 49% of new HIV diagnoses and 50% of new diagnoses of AIDS (*Morbidity and Mortality Weekly Report* [MMWR], 2008), despite being only 12% of the U.S. population (National Center for Health Statistics, 2006). Of persons living with HIV in the United States at the end of 2006, an estimated 46.1% were Black (MMWR, 2008). Among men who have sex with men (MSM), although numbers of cases are highest for White men, HIV prevalence rates are highest for Black MSM (BMSM) (Easterbrook et al., 1993; Samuel & Winkelstein, 1987; Valleroy et al., 2000). Hall and colleagues (2009) estimate the lifetime risk of becoming infected with HIV is 1 in 16 for Black males and 1 in 30 for Black females. In contrast, for White males the lifetime risk of becoming infected with HIV is 1 in 104 and for White females 1 in 588. Blacks and African Americans continue to experience a disproportionate impact from HIV infection. For instance, the CDC in 2005, almost 30 years since 1983, reported that Blacks have accounted for 397,548 (42%) of the estimated 952,629 AIDS cases diagnosed since the beginning of the pandemic. The rate of AIDS diagnoses for Black adults and adolescents was 10 times the rate for Whites. For Black women, the rate was nearly 23 times and for Black men 8 times the rate of their White counterparts (CDC, 2005). Further, Blacks accounted for a smaller proportion of those who were alive nine years after an AIDS diagnoses (CDC, 2005).

Current epidemiological findings reveal that for Black men living with HIV or AIDS, the primary transmission category was sexual contact with other men, followed by injection drug use and high-risk heterosexual contact. For Black women living with HIV or AIDS, the primary transmission category was high-risk heterosexual contact, followed by injection drug use (CDC, 2007). Over the course of the HIV pandemic, several areas of vulnerability have been identified. These areas included sexual risk factors (CDC, 2007); injection drug use (Hader, Smith, Moore, & Holmberg, 2001); substance use (CDC, 2007; Leigh & Stall, 1993; Sharpe, Lee, Nakashima, Elam-Evans, Fleming, 2004); lack of awareness of HIV status (CDC, 2005); histories of sexually transmitted diseases (Fleming & Wasserheit, 1999; Millett, Peterson, Wolitski, & Stall, 2006); homophobia and concealment of homosexual behavior (CDC, 2003; Hart & Peterson, 2004); and poverty (Diaz, 1994). The latter three, homophobia, concealment of homosexual behavior,

---

[1]The U.S. Centers for Disease Control and Prevention's web site provides the most up-to-date list of recognized DEBIs (www.cdc.gov). Presently, 21 DEBIs are the focus of the DEBI Project, including Healthy Relationships, Many Men, Many Voices, MPowerment, Popular Opinion Leader, and Sisters Informing Sisters on Topics about AIDS (SISTA). Of these interventions, only two target Black MSM: (1) Many Men, Many Voices (3MV), a group-level STI/HIV prevention/intervention for MSM of color and (2) d-UP, an adaptation of Popular Opinion Leader (POL), an intervention to identify, enlist, and train key opinion leaders to encourage safe behaviors in their social networks.

and poverty, in conjunction with other social factors, remain underexplored in deference to research that reduces risk of infection to solely individual behaviors. Both research and the interventions that emerge from these assumptions take out of context the individuals and their communities, stripping them of their agency and effectiveness (Wallace, Thompson-Fullilove, & Flisher, 1996). Increasingly, researchers state that health disparities are deeply embedded in social institutions (Williams, 1997).

THE PROBLEM WITH PREVENTION STUDIES: AN INDIVIDUAL FOCUS

Semaan and colleagues (2002) conducted a review of HIV prevention studies conducted from 1988 to 1996 using data complied by the HIV/AIDS Prevention Research Synthesis (PRS) project. PRS was initiated in 1996 by the CDC to identify interventions that were effective at reducing HIV risk. Studies that are part of the PRS cumulative dataset must meet specific criteria. First, that specific data concerning behavioral outcomes were part of the dataset, and, second, studies were either experimental or quasi-experimental, which made use of a control or comparison group, respectively. In both cases, studies made use of unbiased assignment to research conditions. Thus, strong evidence regarding the impact of the intervention could be determined. Semaan et al. (2002) indicated that there were as many as 209 behavioral and social HIV risk intervention studies, 47 of which did not collect evaluation data on behavioral and biological outcomes. Of the remaining 162 studies, only 99 used an experimental or quasi-experimental design. Of these, 10 focused on MSM. Missing data concerning the racial distribution as well as other demographic variables such as socioeconomic status limits the generalizability of these findings to the population at large and to Black MSM specifically. In their review, Semaan and associates concluded that prevention studies need to focus on specific subgroups, given the disproportionate HIV prevalence in specific communities.

More recently, Lyles and colleagues (2007) conducted a similar review of HIV prevention studies conducted between 2000 and 2004 compiled by PRS. These authors employed the same methodological criteria for inclusion for review. Of the 18 interventions in this more recent review of HIV intervention studies, three focused on MSM. These interventions were Personalized Cognitive Risk-Reduction Counseling (Dilley, 2002), EXPLORE (Koblin, 2004; Chesney et al. 2003; Koblin, et al., 2003) and SUMIT Enhanced Peer-led (Wolitski et al., 2005). These studies focused on interventions targeting behavioral change among men who have sex with men (MSM) and included both gay-identified and non-gay-identified; however, the participants were predominantly older White men. As with the review conducted by Semaan and associates (2002), Lyles and colleagues (2007) concluded that the several populations heavily affected by the HIV pandemic are not adequately represented in the intervention studies, particularly Black MSM.

Notwithstanding these apparent omissions, Semaan et al. (2002) found that interventions designed to reduce rates of seroconversion among MSM rely heavily on theories oriented toward *individual* behavior change. Sociocognitive theory or derivatives, most notably in the form of the *theory of planned behavior* (TPB) predominate. TPB, pioneered by Fishbein and Ajzen (1975) and Ajzen (1991) is an extension of the *theory of reasoned action* (TRA), which posits that the best prediction of any voluntary behavior is the intention or decision to perform the behavior (such as, "I intend to use condoms during my next sexual encounter"). Questions concerning the parameters within which intentions to act do in fact predict behavior have been raised (Sheppard, Hartwick, & Warshaw, 1988). For example, the individual may not be able to predict all the elements of the environment within which the behavior will occur.

Due to this critique, the theory of planned behavior modified the theory of reasoned action by including the individual's perceived control over behavior. Perceived control over behavior involves the individual's belief that he or she possesses the required resources and opportunity to perform a behavior (Madden, Scholder, & Ajzen, 1992). Boily, Godin, Hognben, Sherr, and Bastos (2005) commented that the social structure has the capacity to affect the individual's belief that he or she has the resources and opportunity. Social structural factors refer to the social context within which the individual is located. Given the multiple positions occupied by Black MSM and other marginalized groups (for example, transgender persons, substance users, and non-White ethnic group members), explication of the resources relative to these positions are imperative.

While achieving some success in White gay social networks, intervention effects are limited within the context of Black MSM and other communities of color (Wallace, Thompson-Fullilove, & Flisher, 1996). Wallace and associates assert that successful intervention effects within White gay communities are associated with affluence and stability. These factors have been historically uneven in racially marginalized communities and institutions. Additionally, inequities are deeply embedded in social institutions and are leading predictors of health disparity, such as high HIV prevalence among Black MSM (Williams, 1997).

Despite 30 years of mobilization, institution building, and state-of-the-art medical advances, Black men remain overwhelmingly and disproportionately affected by HIV. Prescribing abstinence, behavioral monogamy, and consistent condom use (the so-called ABCs) does not adequately account for the multiple forces that place individuals and groups at risk for living under "syndemic" conditions. The CDC defines *syndemic* as two or more afflictions, interacting synergistically, contributing to excess burden of disease in a population. Singer (1994, 1996) further stated that the afflictions that comprise syndemics are mutually reinforcing conditions that disproportionately affect those living in poverty. In order to disrupt the devastation associated with syndemics, we must address not only the basic problems but also the forces that tie those problems together. Accordingly, reducing incidence of HIV transmission and infection among Black MSM and other marginalized and vulnerable groups must go beyond safer sex guidelines, DEBIs, and self-management techniques to incorporate mental wellness and substance use issues. Interventions must also challenge stigma and discrimination as well as deeply rooted structural and systemic causes of disproportionate rates of incarceration, unemployment, and limited academic achievement among historically marginalized groups. Models of intervention must redirect the focus to examine the sources, not just the victims of oppression in our social systems. Building effective evidence-based interventions with and for marginalized and vulnerable groups starts with substantive engagement with the community. The community must be present from the beginning in acquiring, interpreting, and disseminating knowledge. Furthermore, social work may have to return to its grassroots and community origins in order to address the root causes of HIV.

SOCIAL STRUCTURE, SOCIAL CONSTRAINTS, AND HIV DISPARITIES

Earlier in the chapter we spoke of the relationship of social structure to HIV among marginalized and vulnerable groups such as African Americans. Here we elaborate on that connection.

One of the perennial issues in the social sciences is what forces influence human behavior. Although geneticists might argue for consideration of genes as part of an answer to this question, social scientists, with a few exceptions (Udry, 1995; Zak & Park, 2000), have not focused much on the influence of genes. Social scientists' main concerns have been with the role of individual choice in human behavior and the role of social structures or social constraints. This will be our main concern as well.[2] Although there is a tendency for some analysts to emphasize the role of choice and for others to emphasize the role of structures, we think it is fair to say that social scientists typically understand that both play a role, and the question becomes how choice and structures interact to shape behavior.

Not only have other social science disciplines been concerned with the role of choice and structures in influencing human behavior, but social workers have been as well. When one considers the job of social workers, it should be obvious why we have such a concern. Social work facilitates people's access to the resources they need to meet the obligations and enjoy the benefits associated with the positions or statuses they occupy in society. Sometimes social workers facilitate such access by helping people make better choices. At other times, they do so by focusing on how social constraints—such as racism, sexism, ageism, classism, and homophobia—affect people's choices, and they seek ways to curtail the adverse effects of such constraints.

Given all this attention to social structures in social work and the social sciences, one would think that it would be easy to find a precise definition of social structure in the social work or social science literature. This, however, is not the case. Although one finds examples of what particular analysts regard as constraints—things such as income, poverty, unemployment, and social norms—one rarely finds a precise definition of social constraints. Given this shortcoming in the literature and the fact that we are interested in discussing the relationship between social structures or social constraints and HIV among Blacks, we begin by offering our definition of this concept: *Social constraint refers to the prevention or restriction of a given individual's actions or thoughts that originates from the behaviors or expected behaviors of at least one other individual.*

Two conditions must exist to fully constitute a social constraint. Condition 1 is that the constraint must originate from outside of the person whose behavior is being constrained. Thus, a given individual's own choice is not a constraint with respect to her or his behavior, but the choices or expected choices of others could be. Condition 2 is that social constraints result from the behaviors or expected behaviors of human beings. These may be intended or unintended, equitable or inequitable, oppressive or liberating. The key is that they are consequences of the behaviors or expected behaviors of at least one other person—and often of a collection of persons.

How do social constraints constrain the behavior of an individual? Explaining this requires a brief discussion of beliefs, choices, wants, and resources, and how these interact to influence behavior.

Human beings are typically faced with a set of alternative outcomes that might result from their behaviors.[3] They will want or desire some outcomes more than others, or they may be indifferent between or among some of them. Human beings also have alternative behaviors they can engage in and beliefs about the outcomes that will result from these

---

[2]This does not mean that we deny the influence of genes on human behavior; rather, we believe that such a discussion would be beyond the scope of the social work focus in this chapter.

[3]This concept is important, because in instances where there is no choice (for example, breathing), alternative behaviors and outcomes become moot topics.

behaviors. Humans seek to access resources at their disposal, such as income and wealth, which can be brought to bear to engage in certain behaviors. Given this, people will use the resources available to them to engage in those behaviors they believe will result in their getting as much as possible of what they most want. Social constraints enter in the following ways. First, constraints affect the amount of resources people have available to them. Second, constraints affect people's beliefs about what behaviors are available for them to choose from. Third, constraints affect people's beliefs about what consequences will result from their behaviors. Fourth, constraints affect the set of possible outcomes that might result from different courses of action. Some examples should make all of this clearer.

First, consider how constraints can affect one's income or budget. Certainly people's incomes are affected, to some extent, by the choices they have made. But, in a capitalist system like ours, a given person's income also results, in part, from how one's choices have interacted with those of others. This is so because one's income typically depends on the demand for one's skills. In our complex social structure, such demand is not something a single individual can control through her or his choices. The effect of constraints on one's budget may be related to the fact that some women tend not to take advantage of the female condom even though it may decrease HIV risk. The cost of this device may mean that some women choose not to purchase it but, instead, to purchase goods that meet more immediate (to them) wants or needs.

Now consider how constraints can affect one's beliefs about the behaviors from which he or she can choose. Women socialized in certain cultures where there are certain types of social norms might not even consider that disputing a man is a choice available to them. Or women who have experienced male intimate partner violence, or who are quite familiar with such violence experienced by other women, may decide not to challenge male partners' preferences regarding sexual relations because of fear that they may be subjected to violence for doing so. This type of constraint may be especially significant in explaining why some women may not use condoms when having sex with men even though they realize the HIV-related risk of that choice. They may have simply decided that the risk of HIV in the long run is lower than the risk of experiencing intimate partner violence immediately.

As an example of the third effect of constraints, consider the following. Discrimination against Black males in the labor market, resulting in their not being hired at rates comparable to Whites or members of other ethnic groups, may lead them to believe that hard work will not pay off, so they may choose not to engage in such work.

Finally, consider how constraints can affect the set of possible outcomes that might result from certain courses of action. There are laws that specify that if people engage in certain actions and are caught and convicted, they may go to prison. As another example, people may choose to work hard to "make it in life," but because of their gender, race, sexuality, or perceived sexuality, they are discriminated against in ways that result in their hard work not paying off.

Having explained the concept of social constraint, we turn now to how all this relates to marginalized and vulnerable groups and HIV. The discussion focuses on three major areas: incarceration, income support policies, and the labor market.

INCARCERATION, INCOME SUPPORT POLICIES, AND THE LABOR MARKET

The United States, compared to other nations, is unique when it comes to the proportion of its residents who are incarcerated. In mid-2006, 750 per 100,000 U.S. residents were in prison—the biggest such proportion in the world at that time (*The World Almanac,*

2008). Even though people from all races fill U.S. prisons, there is a stark racial dispar-ity when it comes to imprisonment in this country. In the year 2003, the likelihood of a Black person being in jail was five times that of a White person (Blankenship et al., 2005). For Whites, 465 per 100,000 residents were in state and federal correctional facili-ties. For Blacks, 3,405 per 100,000 residents were in such facilities—a sevenfold differ-ence (Blankenship et al., 2005). By 1997, a White male had about a 4% chance of going to prison in his lifetime. The chance for a Black male was about 25%. In 2003, Black females were more likely to be in prison than White females by a factor of 5 (Blankenship et al., 2005).

According to some analysts, a key social structural factor that helps to explain this disparity is criminal justice policy regarding the possession of illegal drugs (Blankenship et al., 2005). Currently, federal law applies the so-called 100:1 quantity ratio rule when it comes to punishing possession of crack cocaine versus powder cocaine. To understand this rule, consider the following hypothetical example. Suppose someone is arrested for possessing 500 grams of powder cocaine, convicted, and given a five-year sentence. Under the 100:1 quantity ratio, someone else convicted of possessing 0.01 (500 grams) = 5 grams of crack cocaine would receive the same five-year sentence. Thus, someone convicted of possessing only 400 grams of powder cocaine could receive a shorter sen-tence than someone possessing 5 grams of crack cocaine. Since those who possess crack cocaine tend to be poorer and Black, while those who possess powder cocaine tend to be of other racial and ethnic groups, this 100:1 quantity rule is part of the reason for the Black/White incarceration disparity (The Sentencing Project, 2008).

Another part of the explanation for this Black/White incarceration disparity may have to do with an association between unemployment and crime. According to some research-ers (Lee & Holoviak, 2006), higher unemployment rates are associated with higher crime rates. It is also perennially the case that Blacks are more likely to be unemployed than Whites. For example, in the years 1992, 2000, and 2006 the Black unemployment rate was about double that of Whites (*The Statistical Abstract of the United States*, 2008). Thus, it seems that Blacks are more likely than Whites to be encountering a situation that may be associated with participation in crime.

There are two crucial things to note about this discussion of incarceration. First, laws regarding the treatment of crack cocaine versus powder cocaine meet the preceding defi-nition of social constraint. Such laws stipulate the consequences of engaging in certain courses of action, and this is how they constrain the behavior of those who would con-sider partaking in those actions. Second, unemployment has to do with the demand for labor. From the point of view of a single person, he or she cannot do anything to affect the demand for labor. Instead, this demand results from the behaviors of thousands, or perhaps millions, of others. Thus, the choices made by others affect the ability of one to obtain work, and this is how the constraint notion fits in.

How does all this relate to Blacks and HIV?

First, prison environments may be settings within which high-risk behaviors are more likely to occur. That is, men may be more likely to have unprotected sex with men in this environment. This may happen either voluntarily or involuntarily. It appears that a good deal of drug use also occurs in prisons, much of it by way of injecting with shared needles and syringes. Both unprotected anal sex and sharing of needles are efficient mechanisms for contracting and transmitting HIV (Blankenship et al., 2005). The Black/White disparity in imprisonment means that there is a Black/White disparity in exposure to HIV risks.

Second, having been to prison is associated with outcomes that may threaten former inmates' labor market prospects. Those who have been to prison may be less likely to have acquaintances who could connect them to job opportunities. Such acquaintances are what sociologists call "weak ties," and strong ties are important sources of job information for many people (Granovetter, 1973). Those who have been to prison, simply because they have a criminal record, are also more likely than those without such a record to face reluctance, on the part of employers, when it comes to being hired. In fact, there is some evidence that, due to the relatively high incarceration rate of Black males, employers are reluctant to hire them, even those who have never been to prison. That is, employers seem to engage in what economists call "statistical discrimination," using Black race alone is an indication that one might be a criminal and making hiring decisions on this basis (Holzer, Raphael, & Stoll, 2006). Of course, this statistical discrimination is in addition to the plain old "we don't like Black people" variety that Blacks, no doubt, face in the labor market.

The aforementioned effects of incarceration on job prospects mean that imprisonment can result in increased likelihood of a third outcome: poverty or near poverty. Since the United States is a welfare state, one might think that income-support policies might address this problem. But the welfare state has, in some ways, gotten tougher on crime as well. For example, the welfare reform law of 1996 stipulates that convicted felons are not allowed to receive cash assistance (Allard, 2002). Public housing policies and federal laws also deny housing to persons convicted of drug felonies (Travis, Solomon, & Waul, 2001).

We draw the reader's attention to the connections between one's network acquaintances, the hiring decisions of prospective employers, income-support policy rules, and how these fit the preceding social constraint scenario. The Black/White incarceration disparity means that there will also be a disparity regarding who faces these constraints. Now consider how these constraints relate to Black/White HIV disparities.

As stated previously, the nature of one's acquaintances and social networks, the hiring decisions of employers, and policy rules that proscribe offering benefits to convicted felons can affect one's job prospects in such a way that one faces an increased chance of being poor or near poor. This in turn can result in two outcomes related to HIV risk. First, persons facing dire economic circumstances may be more inclined to choose to self-medicate or escape by using illegal drugs, including the use of shared equipment to inject such drugs (Brook & Pahl, 2004). Second, those less economically secure may be more likely to decide to engage in moneymaking ventures that put them at greater risk of contracting HIV as well as infecting others (Waterman, 2008).

So far, we have focused on social constraints, the Black/White incarceration disparity, and how this disparity might be related to HIV. But within the Black community there is a group whose vulnerability to the constraints we discussed is increased by other constraints as well: the group of men who have sex with men (MSM). Whether or not these men identify as gay or bisexual, they face the homophobia that is still very much a part of our society. Not only do they face this from strangers, but also from family members and friends. Even though not all Black MSM are open about having sex with men, Black MSM with a criminal record, in addition to not having acquaintances to tie them to jobs and facing employers who will not hire them because they are Black or have a criminal record, may have to contend with employers who will not hire them because they are gay or bisexual, or perceived to be so. These added constraints faced by Black MSM may render the economic problems they face more severe than those faced by Blacks who are not MSM. These added constraints may be a factor in accounting for the 2005 finding of an HIV prevalence rate among Black MSM of 46 percent (CDC, 2008).

BLACK AND AFRICAN AMERICAN WOMEN AND HIV AND AIDS

Among all women infected with HIV in the United States, HIV infection is highest among Black and African American women. The reasons for this disproportionate distribution are not entirely clear, and social work students, practitioners, administrators, educators, researchers, and policymakers remain challenged in their efforts to prevent HIV infection among Black and African American women. Without an honest, frank, and critical appraisal of the circumstances that facilitate HIV infection among Black and African American women, social workers will respond to the pandemic with well-intentioned but muddled reactive HIV prevention and intervention strategies. Without a proactive, asset-based HIV prevention and intervention approach that meaningfully involves Black and African American women, social workers will continue to develop and employ prevention and intervention strategies that present, at best, false ideas of Black and African American women's HIV experiences. The HIV acquisition behaviors that put Black and African American women at risk need to be understood within the context of these women's lives—a context that includes racial discrimination, stereotypes about Black women's sexuality, and gender-power relations, to name a few.

HIV Prevalence Rates among Black and African American Women

While more men than women are infected with HIV in the United States, HIV infection rates among women are rising, with Black and African American women being infected at disproportionately higher rates than all other women. Furthermore, while injection drug use is still a major risk factor for HIV acquisition and transmission, the HIV pandemic is largely a sexually transmitted infection.[4] The major transmission category for HIV acquisition among women is "high-risk heterosexual contact," with the majority of infections occurring through "unprotected sex with an HIV-infected person" (*Morbidity and Mortality Weekly Report,* 2008).

The more than a quarter (27.6%) HIV infections acquired through "high-risk heterosexual contact" in 2006—with Black and African American women accounting for almost two-thirds (60%) of all HIV infection cases among women—indicate that the pandemic is now firmly rooted among heterosexuals and women. HIV is no longer the heterosexual myth that Fumento (1990) referred to as he decried the attention given to AIDS and women by the media and partisan politics in the first decade of the HIV pandemic as an exaggerated liberal "AIDS does not discriminate" and conservative "retribution for immorality" response (p. 150). This latter response, then driven predominantly by an ill-conceived

---

[4]In order to facilitate a coherent discourse about the HIV pandemic, and to situate Black and African American women in this discourse, the Centers for Disease Control and Prevention (CDC) HIV surveillance naming system for HIV transmission categories (HIV/AIDS Surveillance Reports, 2008) will be used here. This system of naming has its drawbacks, one of them being that it is value-laden and can have a harmful impact on the development and conduct of culturally sensitive HIV prevention and intervention strategies among Black and African American women. Nevertheless, the CDC system has the following seven transmission categories: (1) male-to-male sexual contact; (2) injection drug use; (3) male-to-male sexual contact and injection drug use; (4) hemophilia/coagulation disorder; (5) high-risk heterosexual contact; (6) receipt of blood transfusion, blood components, or tissue; and (7) other/risk factor not reported or identified. The "high-risk heterosexual contact" transmission category is further subdivided into the following five components: (1) sex with injection drug user; (2) sex with bisexual male; (3) sex with persons with hemophilia; (4) sex with HIV-infected transfusion recipient; and (5) sex with HIV-infected person, risk not specified.

alarmist theoretical orientation, proposed that "because HIV is blood-borne, it will continue to be spread through anal sex and shared needles, but will pose far less of a threat to the general heterosexual population" (Fumento, 1990, p. 179). Apparently, the "evils" that HIV infection was extracting retribution for were homosexuality, anal sex, and injection drug use. For some reason, anal sex and sharing injection equipment was seen as something that men did with men, but not with women, and subsequently, HIV prevention and intervention strategies have historically neglected addressing anal sex or injection as risk factors for HIV acquisition among women.

Barriers to HIV Prevention among Black and African American Women

With the burgeoning HIV prevalence rates among women, and among Black and African American women in particular, with the primary HIV transmission category being "high-risk heterosexual contact," studies (Gorbach et al., 2009; Lescano et al., 2009; Hall, Song, et al., 2008) have increasingly focused on anal intercourse as a significant risk factor in the attempt to understand the reasons for this phenomenon. The findings from these studies are important in terms of their contribution to knowledge development. Since it is known that unprotected anal intercourse is an efficient transmission route for HIV infection, we needed empirical evidence that anal sex was occurring in heterosexual relationships. These study findings provide the evidence that anal sex occurs in heterosexual relationships, and the findings will be used to guide future HIV prevention and intervention strategies.

It has long been established that although penile-vaginal sexual intercourse is the major mode of heterosexual HIV transmission, HIV infection risk was increased among heterosexuals if anal intercourse was practiced (Lazzarin, Saracco, Musicco, & Nicolosi, 1991; Padian, Shiboski, & Jewell, 1990; European Study Group, 1989; Padian, Marquis, et al., 1987). In fact, the latter study found that females who engaged in anal intercourse were 2.3 times more likely to acquire HIV infection than women who did not engage in anal intercourse. We also know that male-to-female transmission of HIV per coital episode is higher than female-to-male transmission of HIV per coital episode (Peterman, Stoneburner, Allen, Jaffe, & Curran, 1988; Padian, Marquis, et al., 1987; Anderson & May, 1988). In addition, it is also known that the number of unprotected sex episodes with an HIV-infected partner is associated with HIV transmission in heterosexuals (Lazzarin et al., 1991; Padian, Marquis, et al., 1987). Finally, it is known that correct and consistent use of the male and female condom protects against HIV infection.

With all that is known, our focus should be on the barriers to male and female condom use in the context of Black and African Americans' sexual relationships. As stated by Wyatt, Williams, and Meyers (2008), an increased understanding of African American sexuality within a culturally congruent and ethnocentric approach is critical to decreasing the HIV infection and transmission rates for African Americans. To the extent that the recent studies on anal sex serve these purposes, then we are on the right path. However, this current focus on anal sex within the context of the disproportionately high rates of HIV infection among Blacks and African Americans may, unfortunately, fuel negative stereotypes about Black and African American sexuality. At worst, anal sex may be seen as something that Blacks and African Americans do more than their counterparts, despite the fact that studies (Erikson et al., 1995; Jaffe, Seehaus, Wagner, & Leadbeater, 1998; Friedman, Flom, et al., 2001) have found no significant correlation between race and anal intercourse as risk factors in HIV transmission.

More attention is also being paid to the diversity of Blacks and African Americans in an attempt to develop HIV prevention and intervention strategies that are culturally appropriate and that take the heterogeneity of Blacks and African Americans into account. The increased attention being paid to Africans and immigrants is therefore necessary, and if the end product of initiatives such as those mounted by the National African HIV Initiative and the Multicultural AIDS Coalition, among others, is an increase in access to HIV prevention, testing, and intervention services among Blacks and African Americans, then such attention serves a laudable goal. However, if the heightened focus on Africans and immigrants is misconstrued as evidence of a hypothesis that supports an African immigrant origin for the disproportionately high HIV prevalence rates among Blacks and African Americans, this attention may hinder rather than facilitate HIV prevention in the Black and African American community. The focus on African immigrants has the potential to scapegoat rather than facilitate ethical HIV prevention and intervention strategies. As stated by Chirimuuta and Chirimuuta (1987) in their book *AIDS, Africa and Racism,* "Given the stereotyping of Black people as dirty, disease carrying and sexually promiscuous" (p. 128) the temptation may be, as it was in the initial stages of the HIV epidemic, to attribute the origin of the pandemic to Africa and Africans. Faced with the conundrum of the inexplicable HIV prevalence rates among Blacks and African Americans, and among Black and African women in particular, there may be the temptation to look at Africans and immigrants as the source of the high HIV infection rates.

Rather than being hindered by an appraisal of the HIV epidemic in the Black and African American community as retribution for "immoral" behavior (anal sex) and racist ideology that associates Black people with sexual promiscuity, HIV prevention and intervention strategies among Black and African American women should continue to be guided by existing scientific knowledge obtained from nearly three decades of the HIV pandemic. In addition, the confusion about race-based stereotypes, which negatively influence the understanding of African American sexuality, needs to be cleared up through increased research in this area. As noted by Wyatt and colleagues (2008), conducting research to better understand African American sexuality will facilitate the development of behavioral interventions that address health promotion and HIV risk reduction within the context of African American life.

Women and Condom Use: Negotiation, Intimate Partner Violence, and Microbicides

While the barriers to consistent and correct male and female condom use have been established and addressed in evidence-based HIV prevention interventions (EBIs), an increased understanding of Black and African American sexuality and the cultural and structural constraints that exist as barriers to HIV protective behavior will facilitate our understanding of the barriers to condom use within this community. This increased understanding will also facilitate the development of behavioral interventions that more adequately address health promotion and HIV risk reduction within the context of African-American life. Among the many barriers to condom use is women's lack of power to negotiate both male and female condom use. Although the female condom was initially heralded as a female-controlled physical barrier method that gave women the power to protect themselves, they still have to negotiate its use, even when they choose to use it. The visibility of the device mitigates the power that it was supposed to confer upon women, and its prohibitive cost has made it inaccessible to many low-income women.

For many women, the larger societal and cultural context of discrepant gender power and the threat of violence make condom negotiation by women difficult, if not impossible. The very act of communicating about condom use exposes many women to intimate partner violence (Heise, Pitanguy, & Germain, 1994). Efforts to increase women's control of sexually transmitted HIV infection have increasingly focused on the role of microbicides—nonvisible to the sexual partner—in preventing HIV transmission. Hillier (2006) and Moore (2006) have reviewed the application of antiretroviral therapy (ART)-based gels and intravaginal rings that can be inserted monthly and that slowly release molecules with high levels of potency against HIV. Long-term studies will be needed, however, to ensure that microbicide usage does not lead to migration from condom use and condom underutilization and that microbicide products do not weaken the male or female barrier methods. Studies and discussions about lack of condom use, migration from condom use, and condom underutilization should not, however, occur in a vacuum. They have to simultaneously address the structural factors that create and sustain unequal gender power relations and violence against women (Myers et al., 2006; Wyatt, Carmona, Loeb, & Williams, 2005; Wyatt, Myers, et al., 2002).

EVIDENCE-BASED HIV PREVENTION INTERVENTIONS AND HETEROSEXUAL BLACKS AND AFRICAN AMERICANS

Many existing evidence-based HIV prevention interventions (EBIs) focus on male and female condom use, negotiation, and intimate partner violence, and they are conveniently listed in the CDC's 2008 *Compendium of Evidence-Based HIV Prevention Interventions* (CDC, 2009). Of the 63 EBIs identified by the HIV/AIDS Prevention Research Synthesis (PRS) Project through its efficacy review process, 37 have been identified as "Best-Evidence" and 26 have been identified as "Promising-Evidence" behavioral interventions. The "Best-Evidence" behavioral interventions have been rigorously evaluated in randomized controlled trials and have shown significant effects in eliminating or reducing sex- or drug-related risk behaviors, reducing the rate of new HIV/STD infections, or increasing HIV-protective behaviors. Of the 37 "Best-Evidence" interventions, 24 target or include a majority of participants who are African American, and 19 of them target heterosexual adults and women.

Many of these HIV EBIs, however, contain contrived scenarios that do not accurately reflect the realities of the HIV risk experiences of Black and African American women. Prevention planners and providers implementing these EBIs in Black and African American communities may, as a result, not conduct the interventions with fidelity, thereby reducing the probability of obtaining outcomes similar to those in the original study. Further compromising fidelity in the implementation of these EBIs is the lack of resources—both human and financial—experienced by many agencies and organizations in Black and African American communities functioning under tight financial constraints.

The CDC has responded to this resource deficiency by developing the capacity of organizations to operate optimally and to provide EBIs and public health strategies that can help reduce the burden of HIV infection among high-risk and/or racial or ethnic populations within the United States and its Territories through the provision of financial assistance to nongovernmental HIV prevention organizations (NGOs). These NGOs provide capacity-building assistance services to (1) CBOs, including faith-based organizations; (2) community stakeholders providing HIV prevention services targeting high-risk and/or racial or ethnic populations; and (3) health departments and community planning groups. More recently, the CDC has developed a three-phase process in which materials about HIV EBIs are identified by NGOs, and this will be packaged in a user-friendly format and disseminated nationally to HIV prevention providers. The packaged EBIs may be user friendly once the scientific research jargon has been translated into everyday language that providers can understand and use, but the real test will be whether or not the interventions are accepted by service recipients.

Finally, all the "Best-Evidence" HIV prevention interventions are at the individual or group level. While individual- and group-level interventions have utility, community-level interventions are being advocated as the way forward in HIV prevention in general. Only five community-level HIV prevention interventions, however, have passed the PRS review standards and have been accepted as "Promising-Evidence" rather than "Best-Evidence" interventions. Whether CBOs have the capacity to conduct such community-level interventions remains to be seen.

Personal Perspective

Being African American, Poor, Homeless, and at Risk, by Julian

What do you want to know about me and HIV? Man, I don't wake up thinking about HIV every day. When I get up in the morning the first thing on my mind is where am I sleeping tonight. If I got that taken care of, I am okay for the day. The next thing I need is to know where my bread is coming from for the day; that ain't just food to eat, but also money in my pockets. Sometimes I just want to give up. But you know, somehow I'm just not able to stop. Even when I want to give up the fight I just cannot. I think I keep hearing my grandmother's voice in my head telling me that I am her wonderful baby boy.

What you want to know about me and HIV? Of course I been tested before; what good does that do? They told me I wasn't infected and keep doing whatever I've been doing. They gave me some condoms and some papers about stuff that I don't really care that much about. They didn't give me any services—no help to get an apartment, no help to get a job, not even a job interview. I looked around me and my buddies who were poz, they got job supports, they got a place to go every night, they got somebody to help them with their problems. I don't know why I keep trying to stay HIV-negative. It's like, what difference does it really make? I told my old lady that we just stuck in a rut right now and I'm going to get out of this sooner or later. She just smiles and tries to act like everything is okay too. I bet she knows the deal like I do. . . if it's going to be all right it better happen soon or else.

In the past two years I've really tried to get on the right track and try to put all my past behind me and not to focus on the things that have gone wrong in my life . . . I keep coming back to where has life taken me. I don't know, do you? I really wish someone would give me an idea. I look for places to go to get support and to look for people who really understand the situation that I am in, man. I'm trying to make it. I don't want to give up. I don't want just handouts. I want a good place in this world. Can you help me do that? You know what I need? Can you really support me when I need it, when I'm feeling down? Can you be there to celebrate with me when I'm having a great day? Or will you also leave me when you got what you want from me? I tell you, it ain't easy, and I just don't know sometimes.

CONCLUSIONS

In providing adequate and culturally competent HIV interventions—prevention and care—for Black and African American communities, one must understand their lived experiences. According to Friedman, Cooper, and Osborne (2009), public health intervention must be able to understand the cultural traditions of the Black and African American communities and how they operate to increase or decrease risk or to support or oppose public policies or programs to prevent HIV infection. To be culturally competent does not mean that the worker needs to study or memorize specific cultural traits or attributes, but rather to listen to each individual's own history and not the perceived history from the worker's viewpoint. The acceptance and respect of cultural differences, self-analysis of one's own cultural identity and biases, awareness of the dynamics of difference in people of different ethnic groups, and the need for additional knowledge, research, and resources to work with individuals is part of the work toward cultural competence (Lu, Lum, & Chen, 2001, in Acevedo, 2008).

Successful HIV prevention strategies and social service interventions will need to look beyond the individual, group, and community to societal forces. The National Research Council reported in 1990 that effective interventions and high-quality research had been compromised by difficulties in identifying and reaching those most in need. Public health strategies designed to prevent the further spread of HIV infection among Blacks and African Americans have been impeded by fears of disclosure and stigma, yet it is known that persons generally reduce their sexual risk behaviors after being diagnosed with HIV (Weinhardt, Carey, Johnson, & Bickham, 1999). Increasing the percentage of HIV-infected persons who are diagnosed and linked with effective care and prevention services, therefore, has the potential to reduce new HIV infections over time. To help achieve this goal, the CDC has focused resources on increasing testing for HIV, for example, through the creation of the Heightened National Response to the HIV Crisis in the African American Community Program, and allocating funds in 2007 to expand routine HIV testing primarily among Blacks, as part of the president's domestic HIV initiative.

Many interventions designed to address this pandemic rightfully focus on trying to change the degree to which people engage in high-risk behaviors. But this approach needs to be balanced against more sociocultural and macrolevel interventions, including reform of drug laws, income-support policies, housing policies, and interventions to curb labor market discrimination. Curbing high-risk behaviors is fine, but we need to try to curb the "high-risk social structure" as well. Social work interventions to alter HIV vulnerability must build on our professional knowledge of the person-in-environment and the relationships that exist between and among the multiple systems affecting the lives of those most vulnerable. The introduction of evidence-based approaches to HIV prevention and interventions has yielded significant scientific fodder, but far less community impact. Social workers must develop the capacity to engage in intervention development that employs the most rigorous scientific methods *and* (not *but*) contextualizes the intervention in the lived circumstances of the individuals being served. Without more attention to the role of social networks, social constraints, and interventions to redress the oppressive social policies facing vulnerable individuals and communities, interventions will continue to offer dim hopes of far-reaching impacts.

In this chapter, we have underscored the many ways in which HIV risk behaviors interact with and are influenced by social forces affecting the lives of Blacks and African-Americans. Our emphasis has been on the situation of Black MSM and women because of their dire situation in the current HIV pandemic. We want to underscore our awareness of the many groups disproportionately affected by the HIV pandemic, and this is why we emphasize again the role of social constrains and sociocultural factors as a necessary next focus in HIV prevention and intervention for all marginalized and vulnerable groups. It is our view that without such a focus, many more lives will be jeopardized and lost in this pandemic.

REFERENCES

Allard, P. (2002). *Life sentences: Denying welfare benefits to women convicted of drug offenses.* Washington, DC: The Sentencing Project.

Ajzen, I. (1991). The theory of planned behavior. *Organizational Behavior and Human Decision Processes, 50*(2), 179–211.

Anderson, R.M., & May, R.M. (1988). Epidemiological parameters of HIV transmission. *Nature, 333,* 514–519.

Blakenship, K. M., Smoyer, A. B., Bray, S. J., & Mattocks, K. (2005). Black-White disparities in HIV/AIDS: The role of drug policy and the corrections system. *Journal of Health Care for the Poor and Underserved, 16,* 140–156.

Brook, Judith S., & Pahl, Tine. (2004). Predictors of drug use among South African adolescents. *Journal of Adolescent Health, 38*(1), 26–34.

Boily, M. C., Godin, G., Hogben, M., Sherr, L., & Bastos, F. (2005) The impact of the transmission dynamics of the HIV/AIDS epidemic on sexual behaviour: A new hypothesis to explain recent increases in risk taking-behaviour among men who have sex with men. *Medical Hypotheses, 65*(2) 215–226.

Centers for Disease Control and Prevention. (1981). Follow-up on Kaposi's sarcoma and Pneumocycstis pneumonia, *MMWR, 30,* 409–410.

Centers for Disease Control and Prevention. (1982a). Unexplained immunodeficiency and opportunistic infections in infants—New York, New Jersey, California, *MMWR, 31*(49), 665–667.

Centers for Disease Control and Prevention. (1982b). Update on acquired immune deficiency syndrome (AIDS) among patients with hemophilia A, *MMWR, 31,* 644–652.

Centers for Disease Control and Prevention. (2003). HIV/STD risks in young men who have sex with men who do not disclose their sexual orientation—six U.S. cities, 1994–2000. *MMWR, 52,* 81–85.

Centers for Disease Control and Prevention. (2005). HIV prevalence, unrecognized infection, and HIV testing among men who have sex with men—five U.S. cities, June 2004–April 2005. *MMWR, 54,* 597–601.

Centers for Disease Control and Prevention. (2006a, February). Advancing HIV Prevention Progress Summary, April 2003–September 2005. Retrieved June 26, 2009, from http://www.cdc.gov/hiv/topics/prev_prog/AHP/resources/factsheets/Progress_2005.pdf

Centers for Disease Control and Prevention. (2006b). Racial/ethnic disparities in diagnoses of HIV/AIDS—33 states, 2001–2004. *MMWR, 55,* 121–125.

Centers for Disease Control and Prevention. (2007). *HIV/AIDS Surveillance Report, 2005* (Rev. ed.), *17,* 1–46.

Centers for Disease Control and Prevention. (2008). Notice to readers: National Black HIV/AIDS awareness day—February 7, 2008. *MMWR, 57*(04), 98.

Centers for Disease Control and Prevention. HIV/AIDS and men who have sex with men (MSM). Retrieved July 13, 2009 from www.cdc.gov/hiv/topics/msm.

Chesney, M. A. Koblin, B. A., Barresi, P. J., Husnik, M. J., Celum, C. L., Colfax, G., et. al. (2003). An individually tailored intervention for HIV prevention: baseline data from the EXPLORE Study. *American Journal of Public Health, 93,* 933–938.

Chirimuuta, R. C., & Chirimuuta, R. J. (1987). *AIDS, Africa and racism.* Derbyshire, UK: London : Free Association Books.

Diaz, T., Chu, S. Y., Buehler, J. W., Boyd, D., Checko, P. J., Conti, L., et al. (1994). Socioeconomic difference among people with AIDS: Results from a multi-state surveillance project. *American Journal of Preventive Medicine, 10,* 217–222.

Dilley, J., Woods, W., Loeb, L., Nelson, K., Sheon, N., Mullan, J., et al. (2007). Brief cognitive counseling with HIV testing to reduce sexual risk among men who have sex with men: Results from a randomized controlled trial using paraprofessional counselors. *Journal of Acquired Immune Deficiency Syndromes (1999), 44*(5), 569–577.

Easterbrook, P. J., Chmiel, J. S., Hoover, D. R., Saah, A.J., Kaslow, R.A., Kingsley, L.A., & Detels, R. (1993). Racial and ethnic differences in human immunodeficiency virus type 1 (HIV-1) seroprevalence among homosexual and bisexual men. *American Journal of Epidemiology, 138,* 415–429.

Erikson, P. I., Bastani, R., Maxwell, A. E., Marcus, A. C., Capell, F. J., & Yan, K. X. (1995). Prevalence of anal sex among heterosexuals in California and its relationship to other AIDS risk behavior. *AIDS Education Prevention, 7,* 477–493.

European Study Group. (1989). Risk factors for male to female transmission of HIV. *British Medical Journal, 298,* 411–415.

Fishbein, M., & Ajzen, I. (1976). Misconceptions about the Fishbein model: Reflections on a study by Songer-Nocks. *Journal of Experimental Social Psychology 12,* 579–584.

Fleming, D. T., & Wasserheit, J. N. (1999). From epidemiological synergy to public health policy and practice: The contribution of other sexually transmitted diseases to sexual transmission of HIV infection. *Sexually Transmitted Infections, 75,* 3–17.

Friedman, S. R., Cooper, H. L. F., & Osborne, A. H. (2009). Structural and social contexts of HIV risk among African Americans. *American Journal of Public Health, 99*(6), 1002–1009.

Friedman, S. R., Flom, P. L., Kottiri, B. J., Neaigus, A., Sandoval, M., Curtis, R., et al. (2001). Prevalence and correlates of anal sex with men among young adult women in an inner-city neighborhood. *AIDS, 15,* 2057–2060.

Fumento, M. (1990). *The myth of heterosexual AIDS: How a tragedy has been distorted by the media and partisan politics.* New York: Basic Books, Inc.

Gorbach, P. M., Manhart, L. E., Hess, K. L., Stoner, B. P., Martin, D. H., & Holmes, K. K. (2009). Anal intercourse among young heterosexuals in three sexually transmitted disease clinics in the United States. *Sexually Transmitted Disease, 36* (4), 193–198.

Granovetter, Mark. (1973, May). The strength of weak ties. *American Journal of Sociology, 78*(6), 1360–1380.

Hader, S. L., Smith, D. K., Moore, J. S., & Holmberg, S. D. (2001). HIV infection in women in the United States: Status at the millennium. *JAMA, 285,* 1186–1192.

Hall, H. I., An, Q., Hutchinson, A. B., & Sansom, S. (2009). Estimating the lifetime risk of a diagnosis of the HIV infection in 33 states, 2004–2005. *Journal of Acquired Immune Deficiency Syndromes, 49*(3), 294–297.

Hall, H. I., Song, R., Rhodes, P., Prejean, J., An, Q., Lee, L. M., et al. (2008). Estimation of HIV incidence in the United States. *Journal of the American Medical Association, 300*(5) 520–529.

Heise, L. L., Pitanguy, J., & Germain, A. (1994). Violence against women. The hidden health burden. Washington, DC: World Bank.

Hillier, S. (2006, February 5–8). *Beyond condoms: Chemical and physical barriers to protect women from HIV.* Program and abstracts of the 13th Conference on Retroviruses and Opportunistic Infections, Abstract No. 55. Denver, CO.

Hart, T., & Peterson, J. (2004). Predictors of risky sexual behavior among young African American men who have sex with men. *American Journal of Public Health, 94,* 1122–1123.

HIV/AIDS Surveillance Report. (2008). *Technical Notes.* Retrieved June 19, 2009, from http://www.cdc.gov/hiv/topics/surveillance/resources/reports/2006report/technicalnotes.htm

Holzer, H. J., Raphael, S. & Stoll, M., A. (2006). How do employer perceptions of crime and incarceration affect the employment prospects of less-educated young Black men. In Ronald B. Mincy (Ed.), *Black males left behind.* Washington, DC: Urban Institute Press.

Jaffe, L. R., Seehaus, M., Wagner, C., & Leadbeater, B. J. (1998). Anal intercourse and knowledge of acquired immunodeficiency syndrome among minority-group female adolescents. *Journal of Pediatrics, 112*(6), 1005–1007.

Koblin, B., (2004). Effects of a behavioural intervention to reduce acquisition of HIV infection among men who have sex with men: The EXPLORE randomized controlled study. *Lancet, 364,* 41–50.

Koblin, B. A., Chesney, M. A. Husnik, M. J., Bozeman, S., Celum, C. L., Buchbinder, S., et al. (2003). High risk behaviors among men who have sex with men in 6 US cities: Baseline data from the EXPLORE Study. *American Journal of Public Health, 93,* 926–932.

Lazzarin, A., Saracco, A., Musicco, M., & Nicolosi, A. (1991). Man-to-woman sexual transmission of the human immunodeficiency virus. Risk factors related to sexual behavior, man's infectiousness, and woman's susceptibility. *Archives of Internal Medicine, 151,* 2411–2416.

Lee, D. Y., & Holoviak, S. J. (2006, October). Unemployment and crime: An empirical investigation. *Applied Economics Letters, (13)*12, 805–810.

Leigh, B. C., & Stall, R. (1993). Substance use and risky sexual behavior for exposure to HIV: Issues in methodology, interpretation, and prevention. *American Psychologist, 48,* 1035–1045.

Lescano, C. M., Houck, C. D., Brown, L. K., Doherty, G., DiClemente, R. J., Fernandez, M. I., et al. (2009). Correlates of heterosexual anal intercourse among at-risk adolescents and young adults. *American Journal of Public Health, 99*(1), 1–7.

Lu, Y. E., Lum, D., & Chen, S. (2001). Cultural competency and achieving styles in clinical social work practice: A conceptual and empirical exploration. In V. Acevedo (2008), Cultural competence in a group intervention designed for Latino patients living with HIV/AIDS. *Health & Social Work, 33*(2), 111–120.

Lyles, C. M., Kay, L. S., Crepaz, N., Herbst, J. H., Passin, W. F., Kim, A. S., et al. (2007). Best-evidence interventions: Findings from a systematic review of HIV behavioral interventions for U.S. populations at high risk, 2000–2004. *American Journal of Public Health, 97,* 133–143.

Madden, T. J., Scholder, P., & Ajzen, I. (1992). A comparison of the theory of planned behavior and the theory of reasoned action. *Personality and Social Psychology Bulletin, 18*(1), 3–9.

Millett, G. A., Peterson, J. L., Wolitski, R. J., & Stall, R. (2006). Greater risk for HIV infection of Black men who have sex with men: A critical literature review. *American Journal of Public Health, 96,* 1007–1019.

Minority AIDS Prevention. (2005). Program in brief. Retrieved June 26, 2009, from http://www.cdc.gov/programs/hiv08.htm

Moore, J. (2006, February 5–8). *Preventing HIV transmission by topical microbicides.* Program and abstracts of the 13th Conference on Retroviruses and Opportunistic Infections, Abstract No. 121. Denver, CO.

Morbidity and Mortality Weekly Report (2008, October 3). HIV Prevalence Estimates-United States, 2006, *57*(39), 1073–1076.

Multicultural AIDS Coalition. (n.d.). *One message, many voices.* Retrieved June 23, 2009, from http://www.mac-boston.org/ViewMainCategory.aspx?ID=17

Myers, H. F., Wyatt, G. E., Loeb, T. B., Vargas, C. J., Umme, W., Longshore, D., et al. (2006). Severity of child sexual abuse, post-traumatic stress and risky sexual behaviors among HIV-positive women. *AIDS and Behavior, 10*(2), 191–199.

National Center for Health Statistics. (2006). Postcensal estimates of the resident population of the United States for July 1, 2000–July 1, 2006, by year, county, bridged-race, Latino origin, and sex (Vintage 2006). Prepared under a collaborative arrangement with the U.S. Census Bureau. Retrieved June 20, 2009, from http://www.cdc.gov/nchs/about/major/dvs/popbridge/popbridge.htm

National Research Council. (1990). *AIDS. The second decade.* H. G. Miller, C. F. Turner, & L. E. Moses, (Eds.), Committee on AIDS Research and the Behavioral, Social, and Statistical Sciences, Commission on the Behavioral and Social Sciences and Education.

Padian, N. S., Marquis, L., Francis, D. P., Anderson, R. M., Rutherford, G. W., O'Malley, P. M., et al. (1987). Male-to-female transmission of human immunodeficiency virus. *Journal of the American Medical Association, 258*(6), 788–790.

Padian, N. S., Shiboski, S. C., & Jewell, N. P. (1990). The effect of number of exposures on the risk of heterosexual HIV transmission. *Journal of Infectious Diseases, 161*(5), 883–887.

Padian, N. S., Shiboski, S. C., & Jewell, N. P. (1991). Female-to-male transmission of human immunodeficiency virus. *Journal of the American Medical Association, 266,* 1164–1167.

Peterman, T. A., Stoneburner, R. L., Allen, J. R., Jaffe, H. W., & Curran, J. W. (1988). Risk of human immunodeficiency virus transmission from heterosexual adults with transfusion-associated infections. *Journal of the American Medical Association, 259,* 55–58.

Samuel M, & Winkelstein W. Jr. (1987). Prevalence of human immunodeficiency virus infection in ethnic minority homosexual/ bisexual men. *Journal of the American Medical Association, 257,* 1901–1902.

Selik, R. M., Castro, K., & Pappaioanou, M. (1988). Racial/ethnic differences in the risk of AIDS in the United States. *American Journal of Public Health, 78*(12), 1539–1545.

Semaan, S., Kay, L., Strouse, D., Sogolow, E., Mullen, P., Neumann, M., et al. (2002). A profile of U.S.-based trials of behavioral and social interventions for HIV risk reduction [Synthesis of HIV Prevention Research and the HIV/AIDS Prevention Research Project]. *Journal of Acquired Immune Deficiency Syndromes, 30* (Suppl 1), S30-S50.

The Sentencing Project. *Crack cocaine sentencing policy: Unjustified and unreasonable.* Retrieved April 20, 2008 from www.sentencingproject.org/Admin?Documents?publications/dp_cc_ sentencingproject.pdf.

Sharpe, T. T., Lee, L. M., Nakashima, A. K., Elam-Evans, L. D., & Fleming, P. (2004). Crack cocaine use and adherence to antiretroviral treatment among HIV-infected Black women. *Journal of Community Health, 29,* 117–127.

Sheppard, B. H., Hartwick, J., & Warshaw, P. R. (1988). The theory of reasoned action: A meta-analysis of past research with recommendations for modifications and future research. *The Journal of Consumer Research, 15*(3), 325–343.

Singer, M. (1994). A dose of drugs, a touch of violence, a case of AIDS: Conceptualizing the SAVA Syndemic. *Free Inquiry in Creative Sociology, 24*(2), 99–110.

Singer, M. (1996). AIDS and the health crisis of the U.S. urban poor. The perspective of critical medical anthropology. *Social Science & Medicine, 39*(7), 931–948.

The Statistical Abstract of the United States (2008). Washington, D.C.: U.S. Bureau of the Census.

Travis, J., Solomon, A. L., & Waul, M. (2001). From prison to home: The dimensions and consequences of prisoner reentry. Washington, DC: Urban Institute.

Udry, J. R. (1995, June). Sociology and biology: What biology do sociologists need to know? *Social Forces, 73*(4), 1267–1278.

Valleroy, L. A., et al. (2000). HIV prevalence and associated risks in young men who have sex with men. *Journal of the American Medical Association, 284*(2), 198–205.

Wallace, R., Thompson-Fullilove, M., & Flisher, A. J. (1996). AIDS, violence and behavioral coding: Information theory, risk behavior and dynamic process on core-group sociogeographic networks. *Social Science & Medicine, 43*(3), 339–352.

Waterman, N. *Commercial sex workers: Adult education and pathways out of poverty.* Retrieved April 20, 2008 from www.gla.ac.uk/centres/cradall/docs/Botwana-papers/Watermanfinal_89.pdf.

Weinhardt, L. S., Carey, M. P., Johnson, B. T., & Bickham, N. L. (1999). Effects of HIV counseling and testing on sexual risk behavior: A meta-analytic review of published research, 1985–1997. *American Journal of Public Health, 89,* 1397–1405.

Williams, D. R. (1997). Race and health: Basic questions, emerging directions. *Annals of Epidemiology, 7*(5), 322–333.

Wolitski, R. J., Gomez, C. A., Parsons J. T., & The SUMIT Study Group. (2005). Effects of a peer-led behavioral intervention to reduce HIV transmission and promote serostatus disclosure among HIV-seropositive gay and bisexual men. *AIDS, 19*(Suppl. 1), S99–S109.

The World Almanac. (2008). Accessed from www.worldalmanac.com/blog/crime

Wyatt, G. E., Williams, J. K., & Myers, H. F. (2008). African-American sexuality and HIV/AIDS: Recommendations for future research. *Journal of the National Medical Association, 100*(1), 44–48, 50–51.

Wyatt, G. E., Carmona, J. V., Loeb, T. B., & Williams, J. K. (2005). HIV-positive Black women with histories of childhood sexual abuse: Patterns of substance use and barriers to health care. *Journal of Health Care for the Poor and Underserved, 16*(4, Suppl. B), 9–23.

Wyatt, G. E., Myers, H. F., Williams, J. K., Kitchen, C. R., Loeb, T., Carmona, J. V., et al. (2002). Does a history of trauma contribute to HIV risk for women of color? Implications for prevention and policy. *American Journal of Public Health, 92*(4), 660–665.

Zak, P. J., & Park, K. W. (2000). *Population genetics and economic growth.* Retrieved from www .claremontmckena.edu/econ/papers/2000_20.pdf

Chapter Eighteen

LATINOS AND HIV: A FRAMEWORK TO DEVELOP EVIDENCE-BASED STRATEGIES

Vincent Guilamo-Ramos, Alida Bouris, and Susan M. Gallego

INTRODUCTION

Social workers and other human services professionals working with Latinos are in a unique position to provide effective prevention, treatment, and support services to those infected with and affected by HIV, as well as those at risk for infection. Since the beginning of the HIV pandemic, social workers have played a key role in the design and delivery of effective services. In addition, social workers have been at the forefront of social action movements undertaken to secure basic rights and services for vulnerable populations affected by HIV.

In this chapter we provide an overview of important factors that will help social workers select and deliver effective services for Latinos infected with and affected by HIV. Recent data from the Centers for Disease Control and Prevention (CDC) and the Joint United Nations Programme on HIV/AIDS (UNAIDS) show that Latinos, both domestically and globally, continue to be disproportionately infected with and affected by HIV (Campsmith, Rhodes, Hall, & Green, 2008; Hall et al., 2008; UNAIDS, 2008).

Unfortunately, a full discussion of HIV among all Latino populations is outside the scope of the chapter. Rather, our goal is to influence how social workers think about and design evidence-based social service and prevention programs for Latinos. In doing so, we draw upon diverse structural, scientific, and practice perspectives. In addition, we have chosen to highlight understudied Latino populations and emerging areas that warrant additional attention with respect to research, practice, and advocacy. It is our hope that social workers and other practitioners will draw upon the information presented here not only to reaffirm their commitment to this work but also to develop innovative programs and practice approaches that can help to alleviate HIV among Latinos.

Throughout this chapter, we use the umbrella term *Latinos* to refer to all people of Latin and Latin-American descent. We recognize that Latinos are a diverse group of individuals consisting of numerous distinct countries and cultural identities and that the use of a single term can obscure potentially important differences between and within different Latino subgroups. In using the term Latino, we do not mean to imply that there is a universal Latino experience or that all Latino communities experience HIV in the same way. Thus, while we discuss broader frameworks that may generalize across diverse groups of Latinos, social workers and human service professionals should be aware that context plays a critical role.

Acknowledgments: We tip our hats to Fernanda for contributing her story.

HIV AND AIDS AMONG LATINOS

The most recent data on the incidence and prevalence of HIV and AIDS in the United States suggests that Latinos are disproportionately affected relative to their White peers. In 2008, the CDC released new estimates of the incidence and prevalence of HIV infection in the United States (Hall et al., 2008; Campsmith et al., 2008). According to the CDC, an estimated 56,300 people in the United States were newly infected with HIV in 2006 (Hall et al.). Notably, the HIV incidence rate among Latinos was almost three times higher than the rate observed for Whites (29.3 per 100,000 for Latinos compared to 11.5 per 100,000 for Whites) (Hall et al.). Currently, there are an estimated 194,000 Latino adolescents and adults living with HIV in the United States (Campsmith et al.). Nationwide, the prevalence of HIV among Latino men is more than twice the rate than for White men, and the prevalence among Latina women is more than four times that of White women (Campsmith et al.). This becomes even more noteworthy when we take into account that Latinos are the fastest-growing group in the United States, and that Latinas have the highest fertility rate in the United States (Hamilton, Martin, & Ventura, 2009).

Although these data paint an alarming picture of HIV among Latinos in the United States, there are two important caveats. First, the new incidence data do not include estimates of HIV infection from Puerto Rico. As a result, the Latino Commission on AIDS estimates that Latinos may actually comprise as much as 22% of the nation's new HIV infections (Kaiser Daily HIV/AIDS Report, 2008). In addition, the elevated rates of HIV infection should not be interpreted to mean that Latinos are engaging in higher-risk behaviors than their White peers. As social workers know, many social problems, including HIV, can result from interactions between persons and their environments. A number of studies have documented how systemic, cultural, and environmental factors can increase vulnerability to HIV infection (Organista, 2007; Ortiz-Torres, Serrano-Garcia, & Torres-Burgos, 2000; Rhodes et al., 2005). These dynamics are especially important when considering key subpopulations within the global Latino community who are experiencing higher rates of HIV and AIDS.

In the following subsections, we discuss some of the relevant systemic and societal factors underlying the disproportionate rates of infection both within and across Latino communities. Although readers will be familiar with some of the populations on which we focus, we have opted to discuss key groups and emerging areas that are understudied in the social work research and practice literature. Specifically, the populations and emerging areas on which we focus are as follows: (1) Latino immigrants in the United States and patterns of transnational migration in the global Latino community; (2) young Latino men who have sex with men; (3) individuals who inject drugs and the role of substance use in the Latino HIV pandemic; (4) incarcerated Latino men and women in the United States and the role of incarceration in shaping HIV at the family and community levels; and (5) Latinos residing in the southern United States.

Immigrants

Immigration and migration processes shape vulnerability to HIV and AIDS for Latinos in the United States and abroad. Between 1990 and 2000, the foreign-born population in the United States increased from 19.8 to 31.1 million (Malone, Baluja, Costanzo, & Davis, 2003). According to the 2000 Census, 51.7% of the foreign-born population in the United States consists of immigrants from Latin American countries (Malone et al., 2003). Latino immigrants experience increased vulnerability to HIV and AIDS for several reasons. First, many Latino immigrants in the United States do not have access to regular health care or to health promotion programs that could offer the types of education and preventive services that reduce the risk of HIV infection. In addition, lack of access to health services also means that many Latinos are not diagnosed with HIV until the later stages of the disease (Nakashima, Campsmith, Wolfe, Nakamura, & Begley, 2003). As a result, Latinos are more likely than Whites to be diagnosed with AIDS within a year of learning that they are HIV-positive (CDC, 2008).

Many Latinos migrate to the United States in search of economic and educational opportunities not available in their countries of origin. A number of studies have noted that Latinos may view immigration to the United States as a temporary relocation rather than a permanent move, and it is not uncommon for many Latino families to be separated by periods of migration to and from the United States. Separation from families and loved ones can decrease social support and increase stress (Organista, 2007). In addition, anti-immigrant sentiment and laws in the United States elevate stress for many undocumented immigrants, who must worry about possible arrest and deportation. Social work researchers have cited the connection between lack of social support, increased stress, and elevated rates of alcohol and substance use among some Latino migrants as critical factors that shape vulnerability to HIV infection (Organista, 2007).

Latino immigrants who become infected with HIV while in the United States may be unaware of their HIV status when they return home to visit their families. As a result, they may unknowingly expose their sexual or drug partners to HIV. The circular migration pattern between the United States and one's country of origin has been observed among numerous Latino populations in the United States, including Mexicans, Dominicans, and Puerto Ricans, and is commonly referred to as an "air bridge," through which both people and infectious diseases can move. A growing body of research has documented the increased risk of HIV infection among rural, married women in Mexico whose husbands work in the United States (Hirsch et al., 2007; Hirsch, Bentley, Higgins, & Nathanson, 2002). In addition, the connection between the "air bridge" and HIV has been documented among Dominicans and Puerto Ricans in New York City (HTC, 2003; Deren, Kang, Colón, & Robles, 2007) since the beginning of the pandemic. Taken together, these studies indicate that more services and programs targeting the unique needs of Latino immigrants are necessary.[1]

Young Men Who Have Sex with Men

Since the beginning of the HIV pandemic in the United States, men who have sex with men (MSM) have experienced disproportionately high rates of HIV infection (Campsmith et al., 2008; Hall et al., 2008). In 2006, 53% of new HIV infections in the United States occurred among MSM (Hall et al., 2008), and sexual intercourse between men remains a leading cause of infection for many Latinos. A number of researchers have expressed concern about a resurgence of HIV infection among U.S. MSM (Wolitski, Valdiserri, Denning, & Levine, 2001). Young MSM of color are especially vulnerable to HIV. Analyzing trends in HIV diagnoses from 1999 to 2003, Rangel, Gavin, Reed, Fowler, and Lee (2006) found that the number of HIV diagnoses among Latino males ages 16 to 24 increased steadily from 260 in 1999 to 412 in 2003. In contrast, the estimated number of diagnoses among young Latinas ranged from 142 diagnoses in 1999 to 146 diagnoses

[1]For a review of potential research opportunities and interventions with Latino immigrants and migrants, see Organista (2007) and the HIV Prevention Services for Immigrant and Migrant Communities report by the Latino Commission on AIDS (available at http://www.latinoaids.org/misc/HIV_Prevention_Immigrant _Migrants.pdf).

in 2003 (Rangel et al., 2006). Next to African American MSM, Latino MSM bear the second-highest burden of HIV and AIDS diagnoses among young people in the United States. Whereas White MSM are more likely to be infected during adulthood, both Latino and African American MSM are more likely to be infected during adolescence and the transition to early adulthood (Valleroy et al., 2000).

A number of factors influence vulnerability to HIV infection among Latino MSM. A number of studies have identified stigma and discrimination as key risk factors for Latino MSM in both the United States and abroad (amfAR, 2008; Diaz & Ayala, 2001; Padilla et al., 2008). This is especially true for Latino men who reside in countries where same-sex sexual behavior is criminalized (amfAR). Research indicates that Latino MSM's experiences with discrimination and homophobia are associated social isolation and low feelings of self-worth, especially for immigrant Latino MSM (Diaz & Ayala; Diaz, Ayala, Bein, Henne, & Marín, 2001). Structural factors such as homophobia, stigma, and discrimination related to sexual orientation can isolate many Latino MSM from their families and from other existing support systems. For example, consider the case of school-aged lesbian, gay, bisexual, or transgender (LGBT) Latino adolescents. Schools are charged with the primary responsibility of educating young people and providing them with the knowledge and skills necessary to succeed as young adults. In addition to education, schools are tasked with providing students with a safe learning environment. However, numerous studies have documented high rates of verbal and physical harassment among LGBT youth in U.S. schools. In a recent national study by the Gay, Lesbian and Straight Education Network (GLSEN, 2009), 86% of LGBT Latino youth reported that they were verbally harassed and 45% reported that they had been physically assaulted at school because of their sexual orientation (GLSEN, 2009). Verbal and physical harassment were associated with a clear pattern of absenteeism among LGBT students, who often skipped school (GLSEN, 2009).

Given the important role that schools play in keeping young people connected to social institutions and forming supportive relationships with peers and caring adults, these findings underscore the importance of addressing how structural factors influence LGBT adolescents. This is especially important given that research has found that high levels of social support operate as a protective factor against depression among LGBT Latinos (Zea, Reisen, & Poppen, 1999). In the absence of supportive services and institutions, experiences with stigma, discrimination, and social isolation can result in maladaptive coping behaviors among Latino LGBT populations. For example, studies have observed elevated rates of alcohol use, substance use, and unprotected sex among Latino MSM (Diaz, Morales, Bein, Dilan, & Rodriguez, 1999; Diaz, Heckert, & Sanchez, 2005; Ramirez-Valles, Garcia, Campbell, Diaz, & Heckathorn, 2008). Across the United States, many MSM are unaware that they are HIV-infected, with the highest levels of unawareness occurring among ethnic men under age 30 (Sifakis et al., 2005). In addition, Latino MSM are more likely than White men to learn of their HIV status when they are in the later stages of HIV disease (Nakashima et al., 2003).

Despite elevated rates of HIV incidence, a number of organizations have noted the absence of prevention programs for Latino MSM. For example, although research on parental and family influences on adolescent sexual behavior has grown considerably in recent years, very little research has focused on how the family context shapes the sexual behavior of young, ethnically diverse MSM (Garofalo, Mustanski, & Donenberg, 2008). However, emerging research indicates that parents are concerned about how to help their child avoid HIV (LaSala, 2007) and can have an important influence on the sexual behavior of their adolescent and young adult children (Garofalo et al., 2008; LaSala; Ryan et al., 2009). In addition, a recent study by Ryan and colleagues (2009) found that negative parental reactions during adolescence were associated with an increased likelihood of unprotected sex during early adulthood among Latino MSM. Taken together, these studies suggest that there are important social work practice and research opportunities to be conducted with Latino MSM.

Injection Drug Use

After sexual behavior, one of the leading causes of HIV infection among Latinos in the United States is injection drug use (IDU). Among Latinos born in Puerto Rico, IDU is leading cause of HIV infection (Espinoza et al., 2008). It also accounts for high rates of HIV infections among other Latinos in the United States (Espinoza et al., 2007). A number of studies have examined how drug use and HIV are affected by drug trade through neighborhoods and communities. In general, routes of drug transport experience higher rates of drug use and associated problems all along the transportation route (Adelekan & Stimson, 1997; Kuo & Strathdee, 2005), including HIV infection (Parfitt, 2003). In addition, many drug trafficking corridors in the United States are located in areas with large Latino communities, including New York City, south Florida, Arizona, Texas, and other states bordering Mexico. This has important implications for social workers practicing in areas of the world affected by high rates of drug trafficking (for additional information on how Latinos living along the U.S.-Mexico border are affected by drug trafficking and other issues see Flores & Kaplan, 2009).

The illegal nature of injection drug use adds a level of complexity for developing effective prevention programs. Although syringe exchange is one of the few evidence-based strategies for prevention of HIV infection among individuals who inject drugs, there is often little public or political support for such programs in the United States. As a result, many Latinos who inject drugs do not have access to clean needles and syringes or to services that could reduce their risk of HIV infection. For example, in addition to providing clean injecting equipment, many syringe-exchange programs also provide information on safer sex, drug treatment programs, health care services, and how to use drugs in ways that reduce the risk of HIV infection. Although some syringe-exchange programs in the United States are operated with the consent of local and state public health departments (for example, San Francisco and New York City), individuals visiting syringe-exchange sites may still be arrested for possessing needles, syringes, drugs, and other paraphernalia associated with drug use. Syringe-exchange sites may not always offer bilingual services, and many Latinos may not access such services because of fear of arrest or deportation (Center for AIDS Prevention Studies, 2002). Service providers who wish to offer syringe-exchange sites should carefully consider location and access to sites. There is a clear need for social workers to develop culturally competent programs that address the prevention and treatment needs surrounding drug use, particularly injection drug use, among Latinos.

Incarcerated Populations

The United States has the highest rate of incarceration of any comparatively industrialized nation (Sentencing Project, 2008), and numerous advocates and practitioners have called upon the U.S. government to address the problem of HIV in U.S. prisons (Arriola, 2006; Braithwaite & Arriola, 2003; Spaulding et al., 2002). Since 1991, studies have consistently shown that the HIV infection rate among incarcerated populations is higher than in the general population (Maruschak, 2004). In addition, formerly incarcerated men are more likely to die from HIV than are men in the general population (Rosen, Schoenbach, & Wohl, 2008).

Latinos are overrepresented in the criminal justice system in the United States (Rios, 2006). Despite accounting for only 15% of the total U.S. population (U.S. Census Bureau, 2007), Latino men and women comprise 19% of inmates incarcerated in federal and state prisons (Sabol & Couture, 2008). In addition, studies show that Latinos in prison experience high rates of HIV infection. In 1997, the most recent year for which data are available, 2.5% of Latino inmates were estimated to be HIV-infected, compared with 2.8% of African American inmates and 1.4% of White inmates (Maruschak, 2004).

Incarceration is related to HIV infection in complex ways. First, incarceration can be a sign of elevated vulnerability to HIV infection in that some Latino inmates have been incarcerated for committing offenses involving HIV-related risk behaviors, such as drug use and commercial sex work. In addition, a high percentage of inmates in the United States suffer from mental illness, a known risk factor for HIV infection (Cournos & McKinnon, 1997). According to the U.S. Bureau of Justice statistics, approximately 16% of all U.S. inmates meet the criteria for at least one major mental illness (Ditton, 1999). Some research also has suggested that some inmates are exposed to HIV, hepatitis B and C, and other STIs during incarceration, through sexual behavior and drug use (Arriola, 2006).

Incarceration also affects HIV vulnerability at the family and community levels, as former Latino inmates return to environments that lack access to the types of health and social services and supports that could reduce vulnerability to HIV infection. Both during incarceration and after release from prison, formerly incarcerated men often look to family members for support and assistance (Comfort, 2008). At the same time, formerly incarcerated Latinos also experience low levels of employment (Bourgois, 2003), high levels of social isolation (Freudenberg, 2002), and high rates of drug and alcohol use (Grinstead, Zack, & Faigeles, 2001; Grinstead, Zack, Faigeles, Grossman, & Blea, 1999) that elevate their vulnerability to HIV infection. In many cases, families may be ill-prepared to deal with these problems and may need additional support to keep their loved one safe. Unfortunately, very few HIV-prevention programs have been developed to address the complex needs of Latinos returning home from prison in a culturally appropriate manner. In one of the few studies examining the poor results of an HIV-prevention intervention with formerly incarcerated Latino males, researchers found that (1) intervention materials were not culturally appropriate; (2) the intervention did not address how issues related to incarceration affect families or how Latinos can discuss health issues with their family members; and (3) the program did not address how Latinos should communicate with their sexual partners (Bryan, Robbins, Ruiz, & O'Neill, 2006). Given the high rates of incarceration among Latinos in the United States, comprehensive HIV-prevention programs focused on helping incarcerated and formerly incarcerated Latinos reduce the risk of HIV infection are necessary. Social workers are well positioned to provide comprehensive interventions to Latino populations affected by incarceration. For example, social workers are often involved with the families of incarcerated or formerly incarcerated men due to issues related to juvenile justice, jail diversion programs, or child protection services, and they have developed *confianza* with the people they serve. The rapport and respect that has been developed in these relationships can be built upon in order to provide comprehensive services to families, including work that is focused on the prevention and treatment of HIV.

Latinos in the Southern United States

Throughout the HIV pandemic in the United States, the majority of cases have been centered in major metropolitan areas, including New York, Los Angeles, San Francisco, Baltimore, and Washington, D.C. In addition, Puerto Rico has experienced high rates of HIV.

In recent years, the incidence and prevalence of HIV and AIDS has risen steeply in the Southern United States. Although African Americans continue to bear the highest burden of HIV both nationwide and in the South, a recent report from the Latino Commission on AIDS (LCA) (2008) shows that Latinos in the South, especially Latino immigrants, are increasingly vulnerable. Examining HIV and AIDS data from North Carolina, South Carolina, Tennessee, Louisiana, Alabama, Georgia, and Mississippi, the LCA report (2008) reveals that Latinos in each state are often twice as likely to be living with HIV as are Whites.

The LCA report is the result of a two-year fact-finding study on HIV among Latinos in the South. To date, it is one of the most exhaustive reports on the emerging HIV pandemic among Latinos in the South, synthesizing information from key informant interviews, state health departments, and Latinos serving organizations throughout the region. According to the report, a number of factors are driving the epidemic among Latinos in the South, including immigration and migration processes, anti-immigrant sentiment, legal difficulties associated with migration status, a lack of access to health care services, a lack of Spanish-speaking health professionals, and a lack of HIV-preventive programs targeting the unique needs of Latinos (LCA, 2008). In addition, the report also suggests that Latino immigrant men are targeted by commercial sex rings that seek to capitalize on the separation from loved ones and the lack of social support experienced by many immigrants (LCA). Taken as a whole, the report indicates that there are a number of opportunities to help Latinos in the South reduce their risk of HIV infection. At the local and state levels, there is a critical shortage of bilingual professionals and services tailored to the unique needs of Latino immigrants. In addition, social workers with proficiency in behavior change counseling and community-based service provision can provide support in developing successful and accessible services. Overall, social workers are well positioned to address many of the systemic and interpersonal issues identified in the LCA report and to deliver the types of culturally, linguistically, and developmentally appropriate evidence-based prevention programs that are critical to stem the HIV epidemic among Latinos in the U.S. South.

These emerging areas are understudied in the research and practice literature with respect to Latinos and HIV. Social workers and other human service professionals interested in working with Latinos infected and affected by HIV are encouraged to consider how these areas can be integrated into their practice and research, as information in these domains would make an important contribution to the field. In the next section, we focus on the prevention and treatment of HIV among Latinos.

PLANNING EFFECTIVE PREVENTION AND TREATMENT PROGRAMS

In August 2008, the International AIDS Conference was held in Mexico City, Mexico. The 2008 Conference was a watershed event for several reasons. First, this was the first time that the conference had been held in the Latin American and Caribbean region, which helped to draw global attention to HIV among Latinos throughout the world. Second, the conference was noteworthy for its emphasis on HIV prevention. Although the global push to scale up access to treatment for HIV-positive people has meant improved health and quality of life for many people living with HIV and AIDS, UNAIDS (2008) estimates that for every two new persons in the world who access treatment, five persons are newly infected with HIV.

In an effort to refocus attention on the important role of prevention, UNAIDS began a campaign titled "Know Your Epidemic, Know Your Response." The campaign recognizes that effective prevention and treatment of HIV requires a contextual approach that enables practitioners to respond at the right time, for the right people and with the right group of programs and services. For example, one of the first steps in designing HIV programs for Latinos should be to use epidemiological data to classify the epidemic as a low-level, concentrated, or generalized epidemic. A low-level epidemic occurs when the prevalence of HIV infection is less than 5% in certain vulnerable groups, such as commercial sex workers, injection drug users, and men who have sex with men, and less than 1% in the general population (Jamison et al., 2006). In contrast, concentrated epidemics are characterized by HIV prevalence rates of 5% or more in one or more key vulnerable groups and a prevalence rate lower than 1% in the general population. Finally, generalized epidemics are distinguished from both low-level and concentrated epidemics in that they are characterized by high rates of HIV infection in both vulnerable groups and the general population. In a low-level generalized epidemic, HIV prevalence is again 5% or more in one or more vulnerable groups, but is only between 1% and 10% in the general population (Jamison et al., 2006). In a high-level generalized epidemic, the prevalence of HIV is 10% or greater in the general population and 5% or more in one or more of the key vulnerable groups. In addition, both low- and high-level generalized epidemics are driven by high rates of HIV transmission through both heterosexual behavior and from mother-to-child.

Distinguishing between concentrated and generalized epidemics is of vital importance and has direct implications for the development of effective prevention and treatment programs for Latinos. For example, concentrated epidemics in the Latino community would indicate that social workers need to design targeted programs focused on the key groups most affected by HIV, such as Latino MSM and Latinos who inject drugs. In contrast, a generalized epidemic in the Latino community would suggest that planners must design *universal* programs that target key vulnerable populations *and* the general Latino population. Programs would target Latino MSM, Latinos who inject drugs, as well as adolescents, heterosexual adults, and pregnant women. Currently, data on the prevalence of HIV in the United States indicates that there is a concentrated epidemic, with key populations such as Latino MSM and injection drug users experiencing higher rates of HIV infection compared to the larger Latino population. Given this, what types of prevention and treatment approaches should social workers offer U.S. Latinos?

Developing Evidence-Based Comprehensive Prevention and Treatment Programs for U.S. Latinos

Social workers are tasked with providing interventions and services based on scientific evidence (Rosen & Proctor, 2003). This is especially imperative when working with Latinos infected and affected by HIV, where access to evidence-based prevention and treatment programs can have profound effects on individual, family, and community well-being. Research on effective HIV prevention and treatment strategies are growing at a rapid pace. In August 2008, the journal *Lancet* published a special issue dedicated solely to the topic of HIV prevention. Although Latinos were not the focus of the issue, the articles in the special issue provide social workers with state-of-the-art summaries of evidence-based approaches to preventing HIV infection.

As of 2009, there is no single method that will prevent HIV among Latinos or any other group vulnerable to HIV infection. In the absence of a vaccine or a cure for HIV, evidence-based prevention and treatment remain the best approach for social workers practicing with Latinos. The current approach to prevention necessitates that social workers provide comprehensive prevention packages based on scientific evidence and tailored to individual needs (Merson, O'Malley, Serwadda, & Apisuk, 2008). This approach is consistent with the growing movement surrounding evidence-based practice that emphasizes the integration of best evidence and cultural values into the provision of social work services.

The concept of providing comprehensive prevention and treatment services is reflected in the concept of highly active HIV prevention (Holmes, as cited by Coates, Richter, & Caceres, 2008), which parallels the concept of highly active antiretroviral therapy (HAART). HAART refers to the combination of three or more different antiretroviral (ARV) medications to manage HIV-disease (Porco et al., 2004) and acknowledges that HIV is a complex disease that requires multiple medications to block HIV and to address the numerous health issues associated with the retrovirus. Similarly, highly active HIV prevention recognizes that no single prevention approach is sufficient to prevent HIV infection and that people need a combination of science-based approaches that are tailored to their unique contexts and needs (Coates et al., 2008). The concept of highly active HIV prevention is depicted in Figure 18.1 and discussed in greater detail by Coates et al. (2008) in the special issue of *The Lancet.*

Highly active HIV prevention focuses on providing individuals with a comprehensive array of evidence-based prevention strategies, including (1) behavioral interventions, (2) biomedical interventions, (3) structural (system) interventions, and (4) antiretroviral treatment of HIV and other sexually transmitted infections (STIs). As shown in Figure 18.1, the approach is grounded in a human rights and social justice framework that also integrates community involvement and political leadership. In addition, the approach integrates prevention of HIV with treatment of HIV. This is particularly important, as the two aspects must go hand in hand. Although the overall approach is consistent with the values and principles of social work, many social workers may be unfamiliar with the key components of each prevention strategy and how they relate to social work with Latino populations. We now briefly review each prevention strategy and discuss the role of social work in developing highly active HIV prevention packages for Latinos.

Behavioral Interventions

Changing individual behavior is one aspect of highly active HIV prevention. Behavioral interventions and strategies for Latinos promote individual risk reduction and include approaches such as voluntary HIV testing and counseling, interventions focused on improving correct and consistent condom use, promoting abstinence or delaying sexual debut among young people, encouraging safer injecting practices among people who inject drugs, and reducing the number of concurrent sexual partners among sexually

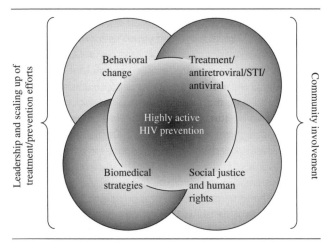

Figure 18.1   Highly active HIV prevention.
Source: Reprinted from *The Lancet,* 372, Coates et al. (2008), with permission from Elsevier.

active individuals. For Latinos living with HIV, behavioral strategies may also include counseling on correct and consistent condom use, adherence to anti-HIV medications, cessation or lessening of alcohol and other drugs, or substituting formula for breast milk to prevent mother-to-child transmission. In each strategy, the focus is on encouraging individual Latinos to adopt behaviors that reduce the risk of HIV transmission.

While effective behavioral interventions for preventing HIV have been developed and evaluated, the observed effects on behavior have tended to be modest or have diminished over time (Coates et al., 2008). This finding is not unique to the field of HIV-prevention; as many social workers know, changing behavior is neither simple nor simplistic (Coates et al.). In part, this is because behavioral interventions often lack the components necessary to change behaviors over time. Developing effective behavioral interventions requires that social workers concentrate on four key areas: (1) Make the program practical, feasible, and economical; (2) reach a broad base of target individuals; (3) ensure that the intervention is sustainable for future generations; and (4) use a strong conceptual framework in order to increase likelihood of the intervention affecting the target behavior (Guilamo-Ramos, Jaccard, & Casillas, 2004).

In addition, there are two other critical areas. First, behavioral interventions need to target the risk factors that are most closely associated with HIV infection. This necessitates careful research to identify the risk factors that shape vulnerability to HIV infection among Latinos. Social workers need to conduct strong behavioral research that identifies the vulnerabilities for HIV infection among diverse Latino subgroups. In addition, behavioral interventions need to be coupled with other evidence-based prevention strategies, such as biomedical interventions or structural interventions (Coates et al., 2008; Organista, 2007).

Finally, a recent review of 20 behavioral interventions focused on reducing HIV-related risk behaviors among Latinos identified several promising approaches (Herbst et al., 2007). Interventions effective at reducing sexual risk behavior (that is, reducing unprotected sex and the number of sexual partners and increasing condom use) among Latinos included information on condom-use skill building, abstaining from sexual behavior, barriers to condom use, problem-solving skills, peer norms, and the cultural value of machismo (Herbst et al.). In addition, successful sexual risk-reduction interventions were facilitated by trained professionals, such as health care providers or counselors rather than peer facilitators (Herbst et al., 2007).

Structural (Systems) Interventions

Social work has a long history of addressing problems in the environment (Kemp, Whittaker, & Tracey, 1997). The person-in-environment approach and the systems perspective acknowledge that environmental factors such as poverty, inequality, social welfare and economic policies, and access to health care all can shape individual, family, and community well-being. Similarly, system-level approaches to HIV prevention seek to modify economic, political, social, and environmental factors that shape the contexts that influence vulnerability to HIV infection at the individual, family, and community levels (Gupta, Parkhurst, Ogden, Aggleton, & Mahal, 2008). An underlying principle of this approach is that individuals often live in environments of heightened vulnerability that require multiple levels of intervention in order to effectively reduce the risk of HIV infection (Padilla, Guilamo-Ramos, Bouris, & Matiz Reyes, 2010).

Designing effective structural interventions for Latinos is complex, as it requires a careful understanding of how different environmental and societal factors shape individual vulnerability to HIV infection. In doing so, social workers must be able to identify the multiple factors that influence vulnerability to HIV infection. Only when the specific factors and pathways of influence are identified can appropriate interventions be designed and delivered. For example, Organista (2007) discusses how superstructural, structural, and environmental factors shape individual vulnerability to HIV infection among Latino migrants who are day laborers. According to Organista (2007), superstructural factors refer to political and macrosocial arrangements that result in unequal access to resources and power, such as poverty, sexism, economic underdevelopment, xenophobia (fear of foreigners), and homophobia. These superstructural factors are reinforced at the structural level, where policies, treaties, and laws, such as human rights, housing regulations, and immigration laws, often codify existing inequalities (Organista, 2007). In turn, superstructural and structural factors create an elevated risk environment for individuals character-ized by environmental factors such as stigma and discrimination, economic vulnerability, social isolation, and inadequate housing (Organista, 2007). Environmental factors are embedded in specific social and interpersonal contexts. Finally, individual factors reflect the ways in which individuals respond to and cope with the risk environment. This can include problem drinking, sexual behavior, mental health, perceptions of environmental and structural factors, and self-efficacy. Organista's (2007) work illustrates the complex-ity of the relationship between superstructural factors and individual vulnerability, and it highlights the need for human service professionals to use a contextual app.   h in their work with Latinos, as the pathways of influence may vary as a function of Latino subgroup and geographical location. Despite this complexity, structural or systemic inter-ventions for Latinos are a promising approach and are consistent with social work's com-mitment to social justice and human rights.

Social Justice and Human Rights

According to the National Association of Social Worker's Code of Ethics, social justice is one of the core values of the profession, and "Social workers promote social justice and social change with and on behalf of clients" (NASW, 2008). In recent years, a growing body of social work scholarship has discussed the importance of integrating both social justice and human rights frameworks into practice with individuals, families, and com-munities. Working to achieve human rights and social justice are central to addressing disparities in the HIV epidemic among Latinos and require that social workers advocate in conjunction with, and on behalf of, vulnerable groups of Latinos.

These efforts should not be understated, as they can have profound and far-reaching effects. For example, a recent amfAR (2008) report on stigma and discrimination among MSM noted the criminalization of same-sex sexual behavior was associated with HIV infection in several countries. The report included a call to action to "Decriminalize same-sex sexual behavior and take the legislative steps necessary to eliminate stigma and dis-crimination against MSM" (amfAR, p. 7). Prior to the International AIDS Conference, activists planned the world's first international march against homophobia in Mexico City. Prior to the march, activists informed the government of Panama that the protest would draw international attention to the country's criminalization of homosexuality. In 2008, Panama was the only Latin American country with active legislation criminalizing same-sex sexual behavior. As a direct result of the intense international focus accompanying the protest, the government of Panama repealed the law two days before the march was to occur. The repeal highlights the success and importance of social justice and human rights in the fight against HIV.

Biomedical Interventions

Unlike behavioral and structural interventions, biomedical interventions and preventions strategies rely on medical technologies to reduce the risk of HIV infection. Currently, a limited number of biomedical prevention strategies have been shown to reduce the risk of HIV infection. These include (1) the use of male condoms to reduce the risk of HIV infection for males and females, (2) male circumcision to reduce the risk of HIV transmission for males engaging in vaginal sexual intercourse, (3) prenatal and antenatal use of antiretroviral medications to prevent mother-to-child transmission of HIV, and (4) the use of contraceptive medicines to prevent unwanted pregnancies among HIV-positive females (Padian, Buvé, Balkus, Serwadda, & Cates, 2008). Other biomedical prevention strategies that have been shown to reduce the risk of HIV infection include syringe exchange and opioid substation therapy (that is, the use of bupenophrine or methadone) for injection drug users (Mattick, Kimber, Breen, & Davoli, 2008; Schottenfeld, Chawarski, & Mazlan, 2008), performing cesarean sections for pregnant women who are HIV-positive (International Perinatal HIV Group, 1999), and substituting formula for breast milk for infants of HIV-positive mothers (Public Health Service Task Force, 2008). Finally, studies also have shown that individuals exposed to HIV by occupational exposure (usually needle sticks) or sexual assault can reduce the risk of HIV infection by taking a focused round of antiretroviral medications, which is more commonly known as *postexposure prophylaxis* (PEP) (Panlilo, Cardo, Grohskopf, Heneine, & Ross, 2005).

Other biomedical prevention strategies that are being evaluated for efficacy include HIV vaccines, the use of vaginal and rectal microbicides, female condoms, and the testing and treatment of STIs such as chlamydia, chanchroid syphilis, herpes simplex virus 2, gonorrhea, and trichomoniasis that are thought to increase vulnerability to HIV (Padian et al., 2008). Finally, a number of studies are currently ongoing to examine the role of *preexposure prophylaxis* (PrEP). Unlike PEP, PrEP is an experimental HIV-prevention strategy in which HIV-negative individuals take ARVs *before* they are exposed to HIV, in hopes that it will lower the risk of infection. Results of several randomized control trials evaluating the efficacy of PrEP are expected to be released in 2009 and 2010. Social workers interested in learning more about biomedical prevention strategies should review the 2008 article by Padian and associates in *The Lancet*.

Conclusion

Together, the four components of highly active HIV prevention represent a comprehensive approach to addressing HIV among Latinos. Typically, social work research and practice has tended to focus on behavioral interventions, structural interventions, and on social justice and human rights. Considerably less effort has focused on biomedical interventions. In part, this reflects the relatively new science behind biomedical interventions. However, social workers need to be clear in their role in using each strategy with Latinos and do so in a way that optimizes the unique skill set of social workers. For example, while condoms are a biomedical intervention, studies show that interventions to promote correct and consistent condom use are most effective when combined with individualized counseling sessions that assist people to address psychosocial barriers and knowledge that may otherwise hamper condom use.

THE ROLE OF SOCIAL WORKERS IN PROMOTING HIGHLY ACTIVE HIV PREVENTION FOR LATINOS

Social workers and other human services professionals are in a unique position to build comprehensive, evidence-based prevention and treatment packages that reflect and respond to the needs of Latino individuals, families, and communities. Helpers must be dedicated to knowing the epidemic and to responding appropriately with culturally appropriate evidence-based approaches in our work with Latinos. The global field of

HIV prevention and treatment has been criticized for targeting the wrong populations with the wrong combination of prevention approaches (Wilson & Halperin, 2008). This is true in the United States, too, where local, state, and national approaches to HIV prevention have often failed to consider the type of epidemic affecting Latinos and target prevention approaches accordingly. As a result, we have seen climbing rates of HIV infection among Latinos and other vulnerable populations throughout the world at a time when we have sufficient knowledge to prevent the spread of HIV.

Social workers and other human service professionals working with Latinos should stay informed about current research, immigration and migration patterns, and best practices on HIV prevention and care. This is challenging, as practitioners are often faced with time constraints and limited access to resources. However, there are a number of easily accessible resources available for social workers that will assist in these efforts. In many cases, resources are available online or can be accessed in digest form via e-mail. A list is available at the end of this chapter.

Personal Perspective

Living with Many Hats, by Fernanda

I like to wear different hats, sometimes according to the mood that I'm in, other times it's what life brings me to deal with, and occasionally I feel obligated to wear certain hats. "Wearing hats" is a figure of speech I use to talk about what and how I react to my experiences in the journey of life. I am proud to say that I'm an immigrant from Ecuador and a Latina. I am a woman living with HIV, a wife of a man with HIV, a mother of a child with HIV, and a helping professional in the HIV field.

I strongly recall when I was told of my HIV diagnosis, while I was pregnant with my daughter in 1993. Since then HIV has been part of my daily life. I have always tried to be in control when I can and learn when I can't be. So right there my first hat came to be part of my life—the hat of being HIV-positive. But in that case my hat was like a helmet for me, because I needed to be strong. I needed to arm myself with everything that I can get a hold of to educate myself and my family. It was hard at the beginning because I was not sure what I was doing, but I knew then that something needed to be done. Then I had to wear the hat of a mother of a child who was living with HIV, and I remember the impact of that. I had to learn to advocate for myself and my family. After struggling with that, I was ready to wear the service provider's hat, to help others, working with children and adults with HIV. At the same time, I was still wearing the hat of having to take care of my husband, my daughter, and myself as we all lived with HIV. I had to learn to define the invisible line that divides those two different worlds.

As hard as it was to wear all those hats on one head, I had many happy years like that. I still do, because I like what I do as I work with other HIV-affected families. I always enjoyed sharing time with my family; very happy moments with my family come to my mind; we were always together, having fun, and when things were tough we had the ties that always kept us standing tall. I had a lot of support from my husband to enhance my professional life.

Unfortunately, recently I am learning to wear another hat—that of widow. My husband died of AIDS a year ago. Everything changed; since then my kids and I have learned to live without a father, best friend, and confidant.

(Continued)

Today I have a beautiful 15-year-old daughter who is well and full of energy. My HIV-negative 19-year-old son is a good support for the family, building his own path in life.

I'm sure the future will bring me a lot of other hats to wear, like a hat of happiness to see my two children successful in life. Soon I will be wearing a student hat, as I have decided to return to school. Perhaps I will wear the hat of a grandmother (no rush on that!), and who knows other surprise hats that life brings.

In reality I have four actual hats: one Black beret, one straw hat for the summer gardening, one ball cap, and of course a Panama hat. I am never afraid to wear any of them, even if they don't look good on me, because they make me feel good, and that's what matters.

CONCLUSIONS

Although the HIV pandemic continues to affect Latinos, there is much to be hopeful about. First, advances in both prevention and treatment have furthered our ability to provide HIV-infected and HIV-affected Latinos with a range of lifesaving and supportive services. Awareness of HIV among Latinos has grown considerably, supported in part by the recent International AIDS Conference and organizations like the Latino Commission on AIDS and the National Minority AIDS Council. In the United States, President Barack Obama announced that he would develop and implement a comprehensive National AIDS Strategy (2008). Thirty years into the HIV pandemic, the United States has yet to develop a national strategy for addressing the serious problem of HIV. The president's plan is expected to be coordinated across all federal agencies and is expected to end the federal ban on needle exchange, support age-appropriate, comprehensive sex education, address HIV among prisoners, and confront stigma and homophobia. For social workers, there is a clear opportunity to utilize our knowledge and skills at the local, state, and federal levels to advocate for a National AIDS Strategy that addresses the needs of Latinos in the United States and abroad.

In sum, the chapter has highlighted several important areas where social workers and other human services workers can make important contributions to HIV prevention and treatment efforts targeting the Latino community. We encourage social workers to consider these emerging issues as critical areas that warrant additional social work practice, research, and advocacy. In addition, we hope that more social workers will become involved in developing comprehensive prevention and treatment packages for Latinos that are both evidence-based and culturally competent. Social workers have a unique role to play in addressing HIV among Latinos, and the profession is positioned well to make an important and lasting contribution to both domestic and international efforts to assist Latinos infected with and affected by HIV.

REFERENCES

Adelekan, M. L., & Stimson, G. V. (1997). Problems and prospects of implementing harm reduction for HIV and injecting drug use in high risk Sub-Saharan African countries. *Journal of Drug Issues, 27,* 97–116.

amfAR. (2008). MSM, HIV and the road to universal access—how far have we come? [Special report]. Available from http://www.amfar.org/binary-data/AMFAR_PUBLICATION/download_file/000/000/54-1.pdf

Arriola, K. R. J. (2006). Debunking the myth of the safe haven: Toward a better understanding of intraprison HIV transmission. *Criminology and Public Policy, 5*(1), 137–148.

Bourgois, P. (2003). *In search of respect: Selling crack in El Barrio,* Cambridge and New York: Cambridge University Press.

Braithwaite, R. L., & Arriola, K. R. J. (2003). Male prisoners and HIV prevention: A call for action ignored. *American Journal of Public Health, 93,* 759–763.

Bryan, A., Robbins, R. N., Ruiz, M.S., & O'Neill, D. (2006). Effectiveness of an HIV prevention intervention in prison among African Americans, Hispanics, and Caucasians. *Health Education & Behavior, 33*(2), 154–177.

Campsmith, M. L., Rhodes, P., Hall, H. I., & Green, T. (2008). HIV Prevalence Estimates—United States, 2006. *Morbidity and Mortality Weekly Reports, 57*(39), 1073–1076.

Center for AIDS Prevention Studies. (2002). *What are U.S. Latinos' HIV prevention needs?* Retrieved December 18, 2007, from: http://www.caps.ucsf.edu/pubs/FS/Latinorev.php

Centers for Disease Control and Prevention. (2008). *HIV/AIDS surveillance report, 18,* 1–55. Retrieved from http://www.cdc.gov/hiv/topics/surveillance/resources/reports

Coates, T. J., Richter, L., & Caceres, C. (2008). Behavioural strategies to reduce HIV transmission: how to make them work better. *Lancet, 372,* 669—684.

Comfort, M. (2008). Doing time together: Love and family in the shadow of the prison. Chicago: University of Chicago Press.

Cournos, F., & McKinnon, K. (1997). HIV seroprevalence among people with severe mental illness in the United States: A critical review. *Clinical Psychology Review, 17,* 159–169.

Deren, S., Kang, S. Y., Colón, H. M., & Robles, R. R. (2007). The Puerto Rico-New York airbridge for drug users: Description and relationship to HIV risk behaviors. *Journal of Urban Health, 84*(2), 243–254.

Diaz, R. M., & Ayala, G. (2001). *Social discrimination and health: The case of Latino gay men and HIV risk.* Washington, DC: Policy Institute, National Gay and Lesbian Task Force.

Diaz, R. M., Ayala, G., Bein, E., Henne, J., & Marín, B. V. (2001). The impact of homophobia, poverty, and racism on the mental health of gay and bisexual Latino men: Findings from 3 U.S. cities. *American Journal of Public Health, 91,* 927–932.

Diaz, R. M., Heckert, A. L., & Sanchez, J. (2005). Reasons for stimulant use among Latino gay men in San Francisco: A comparison between methamphetamine and cocaine users. *Journal of Urban Health, 82*(S1), i71–i78.

Diaz, R. M., Morales, E. S., Bein, E., Dilan, E., & Rodriguez, R. A. (1999). Predictors of sexual risk in Latino gay/bisexual men: The role of demographic, developmental, social cognitive, and behavioral variables. *Hispanic Journal of Behavioral Sciences*, 21, 480–501.

Ditton, P. M. (1999). Mental health and treatment of inmates and probationers. US Department of Justice Special Report. (No. NCJ-174463). Washington, DC: U.S. Department of Justice Office of Justice Programs.

Espinoza, L., Dominguez, K. L., Romaguera, R. A., Hu, X., Valleroy, L. A., & Hall, H. I. (2007). HIV/AIDS among Hispanics - United States, 2001-2005. *Morbidity and Mortality Weekly Report, 56,* 1052–1057.

Flores, L., & Kaplan, A. (2009). *Addressing the mental health problems of border and immigrant youth.* Los Angeles, CA, and Durham, NC: National Center for Child Traumatic Stress.

Freudenberg, N. (2002). Adverse effects of US jail and prison policies on the health and well-being of women of color. *American Journal of Public Health, 92*(12), 1895–1899.

Garofalo, R., Mustanski, B., & Donenberg, G. (2008). Parents know and parents matter; is it time to develop family-based HIV prevention programs for young men who have sex with men? *Journal of Adolescent Health, 43*(2), 201–204.

Gay, Lesbian and Straight Education Network (GLSEN). (2009). *Shared differences: The experiences of lesbian, gay, bisexual and transgender students of color in our nation's schools.*

Grinstead, O., Zack, B., & Faigeles, B. (2001). Reducing postrelease risk behavior among HIV seropositive prison inmates: The health promotion program. *AIDS Education and Prevention, 3*(2), 109–119.

Grinstead, O., Zack, B., Faigeles, B., Grossman, N., & Glea, L. (1999). Reducing postrelease HIV risk among male prison inmates: A peer-led intervention. *Criminal Justice and Behavior, 26*(4), 453–465.

Guilamo-Ramos, V., Jaccard, J., & Casillas, E. (2004). The Parents Matter! program: Practical, theoretical, and methodological perspectives. *Journal of Child and Family Studies, 13*(1), 113–123.

Gupta, G. R., Parkhurst, J. O., Ogden, J. A., Aggleton, P., & Mahal, A. (2008). Structural approaches to HIV prevention. *Lancet, 372,* 764–775.

Hall, H. I., Song, R., Rhodes, P., Prejean, J., An, Q., Lee, L. M., et al. (2008). Estimation of HIV incidence in the United States. *Journal of the American Medical Association, 300,* 520–529.

Hamilton, B. E., Martin, J. A., & Ventura, S. J. (2009). Births: Preliminary data for 2007. *National Vital Statistics Reports, 57*(12), 1–23.

Herbst, J. H., Kay, L. S., Passin, W. F., Lyles, C. M., Crepaz, N., Marín, B. V., for the HIV/AIDS Prevention Research Synthesis (PRS) Team. (2007). A systematic review and meta-analysis of behavioral interventions to reduce HIV risk behaviors of Hispanic/Latinos in the United States and Puerto Rico. *AIDS and Behavior, 11,* 25–47.

Hirsch, J. S., Higgins, J., Bentley, M. E., & Nathanson, C. A. (2002). The social constructions of sexuality: Marital infidelity and sexually transmitted diseases-HIV risk in a Mexican migrant community. *American Journal of Public Health, 92,* 1227–1237.

Hirsch, J. S., Meneses, S., Thompson, B., Negroni, M., Pelcastre, B., & del Rio, C. (2007). The inevitability of infidelity: Sexual reputation, social geographies, and marital HIV risk in rural Mexico. *American Journal of Public Health, 97*(6), 986–996.

HIV/AIDS Transnational Collaborative (HTC). (2003). *Transnational Applied Research and Service Collaborative to Address the HIV/AIDS Needs of the Dominican Community in Santo Domingo and New York City.* Discussion Document, New York, NY.

International Perinatal HIV Group. (1999). The mode of delivery and the risk of vertical transmission of human immunodeficiency virus type 1—a meta-analysis of 15 prospective cohort studies. *New England Journal of Medicine, 340*(13), 977–987.

Joint United Nations Programme on HIV/AIDS (UNAIDS). (2008). 2008 Report on the Global AIDS epidemic. Available at http://www.unaids.org/en/KnowledgeCentre/HIVData/GlobalReport/2008/

Kaiser Daily HIV/AIDS Report. (2008). CDC report on new HIV infections in U.S. did not include data from Puerto Rico; Omission has widespread consequences, advocates say. Available at http://www.kaisernetwork.org/daily_reports/rep_index.cfm?hint=1&DR_ID=54226

Kemp, S. P., Whittaker, J. K., & Tracy, E. M. (1997). Person-environment practice: The social ecology of interpersonal helping. New York: Aldine.

Kuo, I., & Strathdee, S. A. (2005). After the flowers are gone, what happens next? *International Journal of Drug Policy, 16,* 112–114.

Jamison, D. T., Breman, J. G., Measham, A. R., Alleyne, G., Claeson, M., Evans, D. B., et al. (Eds.). (2006). *Disease Control Priorities in Developing Countries* (2nd ed.). Geneva: World Health Organization.

La Sala, M. C. (2007). Parental influence, gay youths, and safer sex. *Health and Social Work, 32*(1), 49–55.

Latino Commission on AIDS (LCA). (2008). Shaping the new response: HIV/AIDS and Latinos in the deep south. Author: Latino Commission on AIDS.

Malone, N., Baluja, K. F., Costanzo, J. M., Davis, C. J. (2003). *The foreign-born population: 2000* (Census 2000 Brief C2KBR-34). Washington, DC: U.S. Government Printing Office.

Maruschak, L. M. (2004). HIV in prisons, 2001. *Bureau of Justice statistics bulletin.* NCJ 202293.

Mattick, R. P., Kimber, J., Breen, C., & Davoli, M. (2008). Buprenorphine maintenance versus placebo or methadone maintenance for opioid dependence. *Cochrane Database of Systematic Reviews,* Issue 2.

Merson, M. H., O'Malley, J., Serwadda, D., & Apisuk, C. (2008). The history and challenge of HIV prevention. *Lancet, 372*(9637), 475–488.

Nakashima, A. K., Campsmith, M. L., Wolfe, M. I., Nakamura, G., & Begley, E. B. (2003). Late versus early testing of HIV: 16 sites, United States, 2000–2003. *Morbidity and Mortality Weekly Reports, 52,* 581–586.

National AIDS Strategy. (2008). Retrieved April 23, 2009, from http://www.nationalaidsstrategy.org/

National Association of Social Workers. (2008). NASW Code of Ethics. Available at http://www .socialworkers.org/pubs/code/code.asp

National Minority AIDS Council. (2007). Monograph on the HIV/AIDS crisis in Puerto Rico. Retrieved January 12, 2009, from http://www.nmac.org/index/grpp-publications

O'Donnell, C. R., O'Donnell, L., San Doval, A., Duran, R., & Labes, K. (1998). Reductions in STD infections subsequent to an STD clinic visit: Using video-based patient education to supplement provider interactions. *Sexually Transmitted Diseases, 25*(3), 161–168.

Organista, K. C. (2007). Towards a structural-environmental model of risk for HIV and problem drinking in Latino labor migrants: The case of day laborers. *Journal of Ethnic and Cultural Diversity in Social Work, 16*(1/2), 95–125.

Ortíz-Torres B., Serrano-García I., & Torres-Burgos N. (2000). Subverting culture: Promoting HIV/AIDS prevention among Spanish Caribbean women. *American Journal of Community Psychology, 28,* 859–881.

Padian, N., Buvé, A., Balkus, J., Serwadda, D., & Cates, W. (2008). Biomedical interventions to prevent HIV infection: Evidence, challenges, and way forward. *Lancet, 372*(9638), 585–599.

Padilla, M. B., Castellanos, D., Guilamo-Ramos, V., Reyes, A. M., Marte, L. E. S., & Soriano, M. A. (2008). Stigma, social inequality, and HIV risk disclosure among Dominican male sex workers. *Social Science and Medicine, 67*(3), 380–388.

Padilla, M. B., Guilamo-Ramos, V., Bouris, A., & Matiz Reyes, A. (2010). HIV/AIDS and tourism in the Caribbean: An ecological systems perspective. *American Journal of Public Health, 100*(1), 70–77.

Panlilo, A. L., Cardo, D. M., Grohskopf, L. A., Heneine, W., & Ross, C. S. (2005). Updated U.S. public health service guidelines for the management of occupational exposures to HIV and recommendations for postexposure prophylaxis. *Morbidity and Mortality Weekly Reports,* 54, 1–17.

Parfitt, T. (2003). Drug addiction and HIV infection on rise in Tajikistan. *Lancet, 362,* 1206.

Porco, T. C., Martin, J. N., Page-Shafer, K. A., Cheng, A., Charlebois, E., Grant, R. M., et al. (2004). Decline in HIV infectivity following the introduction of highly active antiretroviral therapy. *AIDS, 18*(1), 81–88.

Public Health Service Task Force. (2008). *Perinatal guidelines: Public Health Service Task Force recommendations for use of antiretroviral drugs in pregnant HIV-infected women for maternal health and interventions to reduce perinatal HIV transmission in the United States—July 8, 2008.* Available from http://www.aidsinfo.nih.gov/Guidelines/GuidelineDetail.aspx?GuidelineID=9

Ramirez-Valles, J., Garcia, D., Campbell, R. T., Diaz, R., & Heckathorn, D. (2008). Infection, sexual risk behavior, and substance use among Latino gay and bisexual men and transgender persons. *American Journal of Public Health, 98*(6), 1036–1042.

Rangel, M., Gavin, L., Reed, C., Fowler, M., & Lee, L. (2006). Epidemiology of HIV and AIDS among adolescents and young adults in the United States. *Journal of Adolescent Health, 39,* 156–163.

Rhodes, T., Singer, M., Bourgois, P., Friedman, S. R., & Strathdee, S. A. (2005). The social structural production of HIV risk among injecting drug users. *Social Science and Medicine, 61,* 1026–1044.

Rios, V. M. (2006). The hyper-criminalization of Black and Latino male youth in the era of mass incarceration. *Souls, 8*(2), 40–54.

Robles, R., Reyes, J., Colon, H., Sahai, H., Marrero, A., Matos, T., et al. (2004). Effects of combined counseling and case management to reduce HIV risk behaviors among Hispanic drug injectors in Puerto Rico: A randomized controlled study. *Journal of Substance Use Treatment, 27,* 145–152.

Rosen, A., & Proctor, E. K. (Eds.). (2003). *Developing practice guidelines for social work intervention.* New York: Columbia University Press.

Rosen, D. L., Schoenbach, V. J., & Wohl, D. A. (2008). All-cause and cause-specific mortality among men released from state prison, 1980–2005. *American Journal of Public Health, 98*(12), 2278–2284.

Ryan, C., Huebner, D., Diaz, R. M., & Sanchez, J. (2009). Family rejection as a predictor of negative health outcomes in White and Latino lesbian, gay, and bisexual young adults. *Pediatrics, 123*(1), 346–352.

Sabol, W. J., & Couture, H. (2008). *Prison inmates at midyear 2007.* Washington, DC: Bureau of Justice Statistics.

Schottenfeld, R. S., Chawarski, M. C., & Mazlan, M. (2008). Maintenance treatment with buprenorphine and naltrexone for heroin dependence in Malaysia: A randomised, double-blind, placebo-controlled trial. *Lancet, 371*(9631), 2192–2200.

Sentencing Project. (2008). Incarceration. Available at http://www.sentencingproject.org/IssueAreaHome .aspx?IssueID=2

Sifakis, F., Flynn, C. P., Metsch, L., LaLota, M., Murrill, C., Koblin, B. A., et al. (2005). HIV prevalence, unrecognized infection, and HIV testing among men who have sex with men—five U.S. cities, June 2004–April 2005. *Morbidity and Mortality Weekly Report, 54,* 597–601.

Spaulding, A., Stephenson, B., Macalino, G., Ruby, W., Clarke, J. G., & Flanigan, T. P. (2002). Human immunodeficiency virus in correctional facilities: A review. *Clinical Infectious Diseases, 35,* 305–312.

U.S. Census Bureau. (2007). *2006 American Community Survey.* Available online at http://www.census .gov/acs/www/index.html

Valleroy, L. A., MacKellar, D. A., Karon, J. M., Rosen, D. H., McFarland, W., Shehan, D., et al. (2000). HIV prevalence and associated risks in young men who have sex with men. *Journal of the American Medical Association, 284,* 198–204.

Villarruel, A. M., Jemmott, J. B., & Jemmott, L. S. (2006). A randomized controlled trial testing an HIV prevention intervention for Latino youth. *Archives of Pediatric and Adolescent Medicine, 160,* 772–777.

Wilson, D., & Halperin, D. T. (2008). "Know your epidemic, know your response": A useful approach, if we get it right. *Lancet, 372*(9637), 423–426.

Wolitski, R. J., Valdiserri, R. O., Denning, P. H., and Levine, W. C. (2001). Are we headed for a resurgence in HIV infections among men who have sex with men? *American Journal of Public Health, 91,* 883–888.

Zea, M. C., Reisen, C. A., & Poppen, P. J. (1999). Psychological well-being among Latino lesbians and gay men. *Cultural Diversity and Ethnic Minority Psychology, 5,* 371–379.

RESOURCES FOR SOCIAL WORKERS AND HUMAN SERVICES PROFESSIONALS

Kaiser Family Foundation offers the Kaiser Daily HIV/AIDS Report: A free e-mail subscription service that provides daily summaries of domestic and global HIV research, practice and policy issues. Accessible at http://www.kaisernetwork.org/ daily_reports/rep_hiv.cfm

U.S. Department of Health and Human Services operates AIDS INFO/INFO SIDA, a web site in English and Spanish that covers the latest federally approved information on HIV and AIDS clinical research, treatment and prevention, and medical practice guidelines for people living with HIV, their families and friends:

English web site: http://www.aidsinfo.nih.gov/default.aspx

Spanish web site: http://aidsinfo.nih.gov/infoSIDA/

CDC maintains the Diffusion of Effective Behavioral Interventions Project (DEBI), a clearinghouse of HIV and STD interventions that have been found to be effective in rigorous clinical trials. Accessible at http://www.effectiveinterventions.org/

A number of effective interventions are currently available for Latinos, including Voices / Voces (O'Donnell, O'Donnell, San Doval, Duran, & Labes 1998) and Modelo de Intervención Psychomédica / Psycho-Medical Intervention Model (Robles et al., 2004) and Cuidate (Villarruel, Jemmott, & Jemmott, 2006). In addition to providing overviews of effective interventions, DEBI also lists trainings where organizations can receive technical assistance on how to implement effective interventions in their own setting.

Other online resources for social workers include the Latino Commission on AIDS (LCA), a national, nonprofit membership organization focused solely on responding to HIV/ AIDS in the Latino community. The LCA, a strong advocate for prevention and treatment for Latinos, regularly publishes monographs on issues critical to the fight against HIV in the Latino community. Accessible at http://www.latinoaids.org/about.htm

National Minority AIDS Council (NMAC) is an internationally known organization dedicated to responding to HIV among ethnic communities in the United States, including Latinos. NMAC also offers numerous publications for free and has an online database of links related to HIV prevention, treatment, and services. Accessible at http://www.nmac.org/index

National Latino/Hispanic AIDS Agenda is a nationwide organization addressing the HIV crisis in the Latino community (accessible at http://www.latinoaidsagenda. org/). The organization produces a number of important reports and documents on HIV among Latinos and has advanced a national agenda to address prevention, treatment, and advocacy efforts for Latinos.

The Cochrane Collaboration and the Cochrane Reviews publish meta-analyses and systematic reviews on a wide range of health care topics, including HIV. Available at http://www.cochrane.org/

The National Association of Social Workers operates the HIV/AIDS Spectrum project, which seeks to provide the necessary HIV and mental health practice skills for people working in social work, mental health, and substance use fields to enhance and promote culturally competent practice with individuals, families, and communities affected by HIV. The project offers specialized training to social workers around the country on how discrimination, stigma, and other structural inequalities interact to create health disparities in vulnerability to HIV infection and in access to HIV treatment and services. Although the project is not an evidence-based intervention, the NASW Spectrum project addresses many of the issues discussed in our chapter and is a welcome addition to the profession's ability to respond to HIV in the Latino community. Information on the project and upcoming training opportunities are available at http://www.naswdc.org/ practice/hiv_aids/default.asp

Chapter Nineteen

HIV-AFFECTED CAREGIVERS

Helen Land

> *Today was the twentieth anniversary of Keith's death. Can you believe it? In 1989 I couldn't even imagine being alive today. Today I can't imagine what the world will be like in 2029.*
>
> *—Gay man in Los Angeles, 2009*

INTRODUCTION

Since the 1980s, when an unknown, perplexing, and virulent life-threatening virus appeared in gay men residing in New York and California, HIV caregivers have stepped up to assume the roles of support giver, nurse, psychotherapist, spiritual provider, and advocate. At the dawn of the new disease on the U.S. scene, caregivers were there to help, yet unless they were biologically related to the person with HIV, they were often denied access to hospital rooms and doctor visits and to other direct services needed for ongoing HIV care. Caregivers stood as a protective bulwark providing both direct and indirect support. They advocated for access to dental care, nurse visits, health insurance, job security, and medical clinical trials. On an emotional and physical roller coaster across days and weeks, they administered manifold doses of pills such as AZT, diapered and bathed the care recipient, changed soiled sheets, wiped raging fevers, shopped, kept house, and fed their loved ones. Providing hope, humor, distraction, information, and conversation amidst the ups and downs, the final outcome nearly always resulted in dire illness or death. Often, these caregivers were gay or bisexual men who were infected themselves but were at an earlier stage in the life of the disease, and as they took care of their loved ones with HIV, they saw as in a mirror the outcome of what they might soon evidence: extreme fatigue, yeast infections, vomiting, wasting syndrome, purple blotches all over the body, and ultimately death. The illness was called the twentieth-century plague. Frequently in their early adult lives, these caregivers were providing care for significant others who would die. HIV caregiving at that time was one of the most potent and unexpected stressful life events (Pearlin, Mullan, Aneshensel, Wardlaw, & Harrington, 1994). They were the partners, friends, siblings, neighbors, mothers, fathers, grandparents, cousins, aunts, and uncles of children and adults with HIV.

(Continued)

Acknowledgments: I gratefully acknowledge the contributions of Lee Klosinki, for his editorial assistance, and Doris Radford, for her openness and welcoming demeanor. This chapter is dedicated to the countless numbers of caregivers of people with HIV whose commitment to care is vast and enduring.

The funerals, memorial services, and burials were many. Yet routinely, if these caregivers were gay or lesbian, their contributions were not even mentioned in the service—if they were allowed to attend. Also curiously omitted from mourning services was the mention of HIV. The taboos associated with homosexuality, injecting drug use, and ultimate death resulted in tremendous stigma surrounding HIV. It was cancer, leukemia, or some other wasting disease that took its place when death announcements appeared. For their troubles, most caregivers received none of society's gratitude, no days off work, no death benefits, and few sympathy cards. Yet they persisted. They mourned their losses, formed support groups for caregivers, such as Mother's Voices, organized their own memorial services, sewed quilt patches so others could remember their loved ones in the days ahead, and many a time they garnered their strengths and went on to provide care for yet another person who was sick with HIV, until they themselves needed care.

However, over the course of a decade changes began to occur. HIV spread from the mostly gay enclaves in New York and California across the country to the Midwest and from large urban areas to smaller cities and towns. Poorer minority communities began to gain attention, as women, children, and teens were especially affected. The face of HIV has changed, but stigma and shame continue. With lack of English proficiency for those born in other countries, less education, lower income, and fewer connections to power escalators than their White counterparts, access to services was and is limited, their disempowerment great. HIV knows no boundary for age, ethnicity or race, gender, or sexual orientation. Over the course of the past two decades, HIV has become more and more a disease of the poor and a disease of people of color.

WHY CARE ABOUT CAREGIVERS?

Despite differences in caregiver groups, commitment unites them in a common bond. Importantly, as HIV has become a chronic health problem the significance of informal systems of care becomes greater. Caregiving for a chronically ill loved one remains an often emotionally intense and physically demanding experience, characterized by persistent, stressful demands. Unlike professional caregivers, informal caregivers are involved 24 hours a day. They are not protected by limits of a workday or the distance gained by being a professional caregiver. Many caregivers have never before cared for a seriously ill person, yet they must learn new skills—such as how to give shots or insert catheters—under circumstances fraught with stress and sadness. Because HIV is increasingly defined as a chronic disease, it is important to learn how the lengthy and complicated processes of providing care affect various populations of caregivers. In many communities, fear and stigma still surround HIV. What is common to nearly all HIV caregivers is that they are often already stigmatized or disempowered: gay men, injection drug users, the aging, women, African Americans, and Latinas and Latinos. Hence they may conceal their caregiving status to friends, family, and places of employment for fear of social rejection, loss of job, or loss of housing. Others may directly confront the stigma in an effort to stem it (Poindexter, 2005).

Many caregivers report experiencing a sense of burden or compassion fatigue. Whether it is defined solely as a physical burden, a psychological burden, or both depends on the caregiver group (Land & Hudson, 2004). Studies of HIV caregiver stress suggest that stress can proliferate over time so that a direct problem in providing care may result in the secondary stress resulting from conflict between work, caregiving, financial strain, or family conflict. Hence, stressful conditions escalate (Pearlin, Aneshensel, & LeBlanc, 1997). Furthermore, substantial variability exists across caregiver groups with respect to race, gender, educational level, and class. Knowledge of service systems and higher education and income often predict the amount of professional care a caregiver receives. In addition, the type of psychological burden experienced may differ with caregiver group and needs to be explored by those providing services to caregivers. For example, what kinds of stressors or burden does the caregiver experience as stress escalates? Many caregivers have a sense of being out of control of the situation as stress escalates. Some may seek services when they have difficulty managing the multiple roles and responsibilities of providing care for their loved one and yet carrying on with their own lives. Caregivers report frustrations over medications and concerns over treatment failure. Caregivers may feel frustrated, overloaded with caregiving work and responsibilities, and/or trapped in the role of caregiving. In addition, roles change as a result of becoming a caregiver. Partners or spouses may begin to feel more like nurse and patient to each other. Such role loss may result in caregivers experiencing anticipatory bereavement over the loss of their loved one and the life they once shared. Cumulative stress and role changes culminate in the sense of being out of control of one's life. While some caregivers report anger or anxiety over these conditions, many report depression (Pirraglia et al., 2005).

What seems to help depressive symptoms and restore a sense of well-being differs across caregiver groups (Land & Hudson, 2004). For example, how caregivers cope with stress informs us about their levels of resilience. The types and frequency of coping methods may differ, as may the effectiveness that coping strategies have on reducing depression. Moreover, the amount and type of support that caregivers receive from others may also differ. While some caregivers receive considerable emotional support, other groups experience isolation from friends and family members.

Another important domain of concern is the caregiver's health status. Caregivers who experience health concerns in addition to caring for a sick loved one have a greater burden to shoulder and are more likely to feel depleted than their counterparts. In addition, an impaired health status may greatly affect the resilience of the caregiver as lines between sickness and wellness become blurred (LeBlanc & Wight, 2000). Clearly, although certain commonalities exist in the caregiving experience, not everyone has a similar life experience. Not everyone defines stress similarly, reacts to challenges similarly, or requires similar services. If service providers have limited knowledge of what makes caregiving groups unique, they will be less able to design service programs to meet their needs effectively.

A CLOSER LOOK AT HIV CAREGIVERS: WHO THEY ARE

Caregivers of people with HIV are represented by many groups. In fact, with the exception of children, nearly anyone who has been infected with HIV may also be a caregiver. Because covering all groups of caregivers is beyond the scope of this chapter, I have included those groups that are most likely to be providing care and thus need services themselves.

Gay Men

More information exists on gay men than any other group of caregivers, most likely because they were the first to evidence the effects of HIV, and they have been studied longest. Gay men were among the first to take combination anti-HIV medications. With the advent of and access to this treatment, many gay men with HIV moved from the hospital room to home-based care and required help in daily living. Rising health care costs and the preference to receive home health care have driven this trend. Gay male caregivers are in the majority represented by gay partners and friends of other gay men with HIV.

Highly active antiretroviral therapy (HAART), another name for combination therapy, has substantially reduced viral load and given new life for many who take it. Others living with HIV continue to experience decline. While countless numbers have gained years of life, this good news is coupled with other outcomes. The ailments of aging are showing up earlier than expected in many with HIV receiving HAART for lengthy periods of time. Gay men are unmistakably among this group. As they are growing older faster, some require ongoing care, and medication side effects are common.[1] As one gay man of 60 caring for his partner states, "We're seeing things that my mother is experiencing and she's 86" (Engel, 2008). These are people who often require ongoing care. As with the elderly, they are frequently represented by couples caring for one another.

What predicts level of psychological well-being for gay male caregivers? Gay men who are HIV-positive consistently report more depression than those who are HIV-negative, as well as other stressors that provoke depressive episodes (Land, Hudson, & Stiefel, 2003). Findings note that performing caregiving tasks, such as activities of daily living (ADLs) (for example, bathing, toileting, managing external affairs), and managing problematic behavior and cognitive impairment result in more severe depression in gay male caregivers. In addition, men appear to be more vulnerable than women to feelings of being overloaded in their caregiving roles, perhaps because they are less frequently socialized to perform such tasks than are women; thus, they begin to feel overwhelmed and become depressed quicker (Land & Hudson, 2004). In addition, depression for gay male caregivers is often related to internalized homophobia, perceptions of HIV alienation and related stigma, and conflict within their social network (Wight, 2000; Wight, Aneshensel, & LeBlanc, 2003). Vulnerability to depression occurs as ecological risk factors increase, such as younger age, lower income, lower education, and related unemployment (Wight, Aneshensel, & LeBlanc, 2003). Finally, the experience of having endured multiple HIV-related bereavements culminates in a powerful blueprint for depression (Fredriksen-Goldsen, 2007). Clearly, this group of gay caregivers is emotionally susceptible to depression.

Gay men were among the first to organize and empower themselves in the fight against HIV, and it is not surprising to find that self-empowerment is a protective factor in the struggle with depression. Other conditions that seem to buffer stress include strong self-esteem, feelings of being empowered and in control of life, and beneficial coping styles such dispositional optimism. Focusing on the favorable things in life and trying to stay in the present seem to reduce the association between stress and depression in gay male caregivers (Land, Hudson, & Stiefel, 2003; Land & Hudson, 2004; Fredricksen-Goldsen, 2007). Moreover, study findings reveal that older partners with a higher income, who see life as a gift, seem to be more resilient. As one man said, "You can only solve the problem in front of you" (Engel, 2008, p. A15). And, especially for HIV-positive caregivers, a supportive family is associated with lower levels of distress (Wight, Aneshensel, & LeBlanc, 2003).

---

[1]Liprodystrophy is a condition that rearranges fat in the body and can lead to insulin resistance and elevated triglyceride levels in the blood. Heart attack may result despite regular exercise and a controlled diet. In addition, some have developed a bone disease called avascular necrosis, which may be linked to the use of corticosteroids, a drug that decreases chances of contracting often fatal opportunistic infections such as pneumocystis pneumonia. Bone fractures may result and hip replacement may be required. Others aging with HIV are developing symptoms of aging such as memory deficits, liver, and kidney diseases.

Women

In many communities, female HIV caregivers constitute the backbone of family attendant care. In addition to providing care for HIV-infected children, partners, or other loved ones, they often assume a caregiving role for other family members. In fact, many female caregivers dedicate a substantial portion of their lives to the caregiving role. This group of HIV caregivers is composed mostly of ethnic and racial minorities of color. How do these groups of female caregivers differ in background, and what predicts stress and its outcomes?

The stressors experienced and the needs of White women are quite different from those of their sisters of color. The majority of White female caregivers are better educated, have medical insurance, are HIV-negative, and are caring for a partner or adult offspring with HIV (Centers for Disease Control and Prevention [CDC], 2006). These women generally have fewer non-HIV-related chronic illnesses than other groups of caregivers, lower education, and lower income than their White, gay, male counterparts, and more years of providing care. Major stressors that impact and reflect elevated depression include feelings of role captivity in caregiving and loss of self-identity to the caregiving role. However, the presence of strong self-esteem tends to lower the toxic effects of these stressors. In addition, study findings indicate that White women seek services more than any other group of caregivers, indicating their heightened knowledge of available resources and strong potential for reaching out for help. These conditions bode well and should be seen as a resource for this group of caregivers. Service plans may include a support group for caregivers, individual counseling, and in-home services to stem feelings of captivity and loss of self to caregiving.

Women of Color

The majority of women caring for a person with HIV are of Latina or African American heritage. While Asians and Pacific Islanders with HIV are increasing in number, their rates of infection and the total number of documented cases is still extremely low compared with African Americans and Latinos (CDC, 2006). In light of these findings, this section explores circumstances and discusses practice and policy implications for these two groups of women of color caring for a person with HIV.

Latinas With the rise of diversity in the United States, recent attention has turned to family caregiving across cultures, and particularly in the Latino community, where family values are very strong and where women constitute the great majority of caregivers (Magana, 2007; Oliveros, 2008). Especially for those who are newly emigrated, caregiving is allocated to women because of strong cultural role expectations. Female caregivers in the Latino community dedicate an enormous portion of their lives to caregiving by providing substantial assistance to the ill, the orphaned, and the elderly (Choppelas & Wilson, 2006). This group of caregivers is not uniform but is rather composed of many subcultures, including Mexican Americans, Central and South Americans, and those from the Caribbean islands.

For a variety of reasons, caregiving may be more burdensome for some Latino groups, especially those who are poorer and recently emigrated to the United States. Frequently, these women are coping with the stress of acculturation and accompanying isolation. Many of these HIV caregivers have completed only an eighth-grade education, which is the end of compulsory education in Latin America. Moreover, many come from rural areas where highly bureaucratic service systems involving multiple layers of care do not exist (Flaskerud & Nymanthi, 1990). The complexities of a chronic illness such as HIV often require multiple services to promote disease management. To meet the needs of a sick relative, caregivers must understand the illness, facilitate the required services, and likewise become familiar with the services systems and individuals involved in the care plan of the person with HIV. Further, research findings suggest that Latinos are often reluctant to seek outside help or early care for their illness (Land, & Hudson, 2002). This situation may exist because of poverty, HIV stigma, or fear of being deported as undocumented. Importantly, there are few services available that understand and meet the needs of Spanish-speaking people, whose beliefs and cultural values include the preference for a warm personal relationship with medical staff (personalism), the value of familism, and the acceptance of life suffering (Magana, 2007). Most Mexican and Central American female caregivers reside in very poor communities where services are quite limited (Land & Hudson, 2004). Moreover, where outside resources do exist, the family may view them as unnecessary, insensitive to family needs, or intrusive, or they may not know of their existence or understand what they involve (Land & Hudson, 2002). In addition, many are caring for other family members in addition to the person with HIV. Studies reveal that about half of Latina caregivers are HIV-positive themselves (CDC, 2006). HIV transmission for these women most likely occurred through heterosexual contact with an injecting drug user, through unsterile injecting equipment, or through sexual contact with a male partner who had unsafe sex with another man.

Being HIV-positive may leave the caregiver depleted and vulnerable to other chronic illnesses that compound an already aggravated health scene. Yet it is common for Latina HIV caregivers to put the needs of others ahead of their own due to the cultural value of *sympathia* and the value of *marianismo,* being strong and long-suffering in imitation of the Virgin Mary (Neff, Amodei, Valescu, & Pomeroy, 2003). Thus it is anticipated that role strain would be reported (Land & Hudson, 2004).

Given these circumstances, it is not surprising that these women face a powerful stress process that pushes the bounds of physical and emotional capabilities (Demi, Bakeman, Moneyham, Sowell, & Seals, 1997; Magana, Ramirez-Garcia, Hernandez, & Cortez, 2007). Literature reveals that, in contrast to other caregiver groups, predictors of the stress process differ for Latina caregivers. For example, these women report experiencing more non-HIV-related chronic illnesses, including asthma, hypertension, and diabetes. In fact, in one study, fully 80 percent of Latina HIV caregivers reported these illnesses (Land & Hudson, 2004). Moreover, about half of these caregivers were also HIV-positive. In addition, major life events, such as being forced to move from one's home, also occur at greater frequency for this group than for other groups of HIV caregivers. Of interest, in spite of heavy involvement in multiple caregiving roles, reports of stress due to performing the activities of daily living (ADLs) were notably absent for this group of caregivers, in contrast to their male counterparts. Of note, nearly all respondents in one study of Latina caregivers did not disclose to direct family members that they were caring for a loved one with HIV (Land & Hudson, 2004). Thus, social constriction is common and social support is reduced.

Latinas are more likely to have greater anxiety over medication adherence of their loved one than are other caregivers. This finding may indicate that while caregivers often remind people with HIV to take medications, these reminders are not significantly associated with adherence. Study results suggest that these caregivers may be more aware of low adherence behavior in their loved one with HIV, and, as a result, they may become anxious (Beals, Wight, Aneshensel, Murphy, & Miller-Martinez, 2006). Hence, what predicts stress for this group is quite different than that for their gay male counterparts or other groups of women. Findings suggest that poorer health conditions, life events (particularly loss events such as loss of housing), managing cognitive difficulties of the person with HIV, feelings of being trapped and isolated in the caregiving role, and poor self-esteem predict poorer mental well-being for Latina HIV caregivers (Land & Hudson, 2002). Moreover, it is disturbing that no factors cited in the literature appear to lower the relationship between stress and depression for this caregiver group.

Implications for services call for meeting physical as well as mental health needs within a culturally sensitive framework for Latina caregivers. Clearly, stress and burden for this group stem from environmental factors that influence the experience of burden. In particular, being poor and undocumented tends to greatly increase and escalate stress. In turn, poorer overall health is likely to result. Finally, cultural attitudes toward HIV may influence family conflict, lack of support, and the psychological beliefs about the inevitability of suffering and depression.

Adequately addressing services needs may prove to be a challenge, as low use of health and social services has been noted in the literature (Talamantes, Lawler, & Espino, 1995). Further, low utilization of services among this group may persist due to lack of knowledge or access to services, lack of availability of Spanish-speaking providers, and insensitivity to Latino cultural values and community customs. Improvements for service use call for the use of health promoters (promatoras) from within the community. These *promatoras* may be able to provide direct support and reduce isolation. Further, because they are indigenous to the community, *promatoras* may succeed in influencing belief systems that affect stigma, guilt, and other psychological burdens (Ortiz, 2005). Moreover, these health service promoters can educate about disease transmission and day-to-day caregiving for adults and children with HIV.

African American Women   African American female caregivers are a diverse group. They are young women caring for children with HIV, women caring for HIV-infected male partners, older women caring for daughters with HIV or for their orphaned grandchildren, and women with nonkin ties to the person with HIV. Often they are HIV-infected themselves. African American women have been providing care for others for multiple generations in this country, both professionally and informally. They are a strong resource of support in their communities and often live lives of self-sacrifice and dedication to the needs of others.

In the late twentieth and early twenty-first centuries, drug use and increased incarceration of drug offenders in the African American community have fueled HIV infection rates. Currently, prevalence of HIV among African American men who have sex with men is staggering. In many poor African American communities, those who are HIV-negative may harbor homophobic reactions, thus stigmatizing such HIV-positive men. In addition, the African American church has come to play less of a central role in addressing social welfare needs of urban African American communities affected by HIV, in large part due to the stigma around methods of HIV transmission (Poindexter, Linsk, & Warner, 1999). These recent trends have exacerbated the needs of low-income communities for provision of informal caregiving while at the same time reducing their social and economic resources (Knowlton, 2003). For decades in many poor African American communities, HIV has lived underground, claiming the lives of its residents. The culmination of these factors appears to work together to compound the complexity of caregiving for African American female HIV caregivers.

Literature suggests that informal caregiving is more culturally normative among African Americans compared to other U.S. born populations. These are women who provide the labor-intensive HIV care. They are often of lower socioeconomic status, have greater disease burden, and have lower life expectancies than other caregivers of people with HIV. African American women are at very high risk for disease transmission, primarily as a result of injection drug use and secondarily as a result of unprotected sexual activity with an HIV-infected partner (Land & Hudson, 2002). Distressingly, disproportionate drug use and competing subsistence needs among African Americans contribute to their lower access to HIV treatment (Wyatt, Carmona, Loeb, & Williams, 2005). Of note, economic costs of HIV medical care for injection drug users are greater due to their greater use of hospital services. Many female injection drug users have a history of being sexually or physically abused and became homeless at a young age to escape this abuse, often turning to survival sex (Wyatt et al., 2005). Drug and alcohol use may follow to escape the realities of the psychological pain associated with this history and their current methods of employment. It is not surprising that the abuse of drugs and alcohol have been found to be physically self-injurious for HIV-positive groups (Billings, Folkman, Acree, & Moskowitz, 2000).

These factors set a background against which HIV caregiving plays out. In the context of little access to formal medical care, informal care may be especially great. Distressingly, lack of basic resources such as food and money as well as prior care commitments have been found to contribute to the refusal of some basic kinship systems to provide needed informal care for those with HIV; hence, other females' friends and extended family may take up the role of caregiving. As one woman related when visiting a sick girlfriend and her baby, "A lot of people stay away from them. I feel I have lost my identity to what I wanted out of life because I just always give. . . . My son, my grandsons, my husband, my aunt who is sick; it's a constant" (Knowlton, 2003, p. 1308). This is the expression of role loss.

The majority of HIV-positive African American women are likely to be low-income single parents who are unemployed and/or receive public assistance (Wohl et al., 1998). These women are often economically impoverished and residing in stigmatized communities affected by HIV. The need to provide care to others presents an overwhelming demand on scarce resources. Unfortunately, they are at very high risk for a number of reasons. They are more likely than other HIV-positive women to engage in substance use, especially crack cocaine use (Wyatt et al., 2005) and subsistence sex work (Wohl et al., 1998). Of great concern, these women often experience late diagnosis and treatment of their HIV illness (Wohl et al., 1998). They are disproportionately affected by histories of abuse, including childhood sexual abuse (Wyatt et al., 2005) and both verbal and physical abuse in their adult intimate relationships (Jones, Beach, Forehand, & The Family Health Project Research Group, 2001). Depression often results (Devine et al., 2000; Jones et al., 2001).

Other sources suggest that alcohol is misused as a method for self-medication among African American women, especially in those caregivers who have access to fewer resources and great child-care and family responsibilities. Moreover, these women are more likely than men with alcohol problems to experience depression and anxiety (Redgrave, Swartz, & Romanoski, 2003).

Considerable evidence documents that rates of heavy drinking and drug use are higher among people living with HIV and their caregivers (Knowlton, 2003) and specifically higher among African American HIV-positive women with lower incomes and lower levels of education who are caregiving than among other HIV-infected caregivers (Knowlton, 2003). In fact, study findings report that of African American female caregivers who provide primary support for people with AIDS, 26 percent were current drug users, 6 percent reported drinking daily, a majority were living below the poverty line (54 percent), and nearly a quarter of these women were HIV-positive (Knowlton, 2003).

It is a great misfortune that alcohol use among people with HIV is associated with behavioral issues related to the treatment and management of HIV disease; hence, these caregivers have diminished chances of being prescribed antiretroviral treatment (HAART)

(Flexner et al., 2001). For those who do receive HAART, heavy alcohol use is associated with higher HIV levels and lower CD4 counts (Samet et al., 2003), indicating reduced efficacy of treatments. In addition to affecting the effectiveness of medications, heavy drinking has been shown to amplify the toxicity of HIV medications (Fein et al., 1998). These findings sound an alarm for many African American HIV-infected female caregivers and the persons for whom they provide care.

Implications for practice and policy are great. African American caregivers need economic and structural supports such as financial help, housing, and child care. In addition, there is the clear need for advocacy in the area of medical treatment for HIV and substance use, as applicable. These services should be gender-sensitive and focus on the needs of the African American female experience. Finally, the need for emotional support is beyond question. The history of caregiving among women of African American heritage is long and strong. Programs must be designed to be relevant to these women who have cared for others across the generations.

Male Primary Caregivers of HIV-Infected Children

It is a little known fact that the number of male primary caregivers of children with HIV is substantial in the United States. Fathers, uncles, and grandfathers have taken up where mothers and other female relatives have left off in the primary care of these children. Only about half have some support of a female caregiver.

The majority (75%) are biological fathers and adoptive fathers of the child with HIV. It is estimated that about 10 percent of these men are caring for more than one HIV-infected child and about half have other children in the home for whom they provide care. One study reveals that a large percentage of these invisible caregivers are African American (58%) and Latino (23%) men caring for children with HIV between the ages of 5 and 12 years (Strug, Rabb, and Nanton, 2002). These men of color suffer from particular issues that are absent in other caregiving groups. For example, African American men are the bearers of many harmful stereotypes, most commonly that of the absent father (McAdoo, 1993). As a result, medical and service providers may believe that these fathers lack role models for setting limits with children and that they cannot care for or communicate with a sick child. Fathers may face challenges regarding custodial rights to their children, thus complicating their fathering responsibilities. Social service agencies may scrutinize these fathers in a way that mothers do not have to endure. Plans for foster care placement for these children may surface without adequate assessment of the family situation. Interrogations by medical and service providers and school personnel involved in the life of the child may be experienced as shaming and emotionally exhausting for fathers. About a quarter of all male primary caregivers are estimated to be HIV-infected themselves and thus may have diminished energy for these external demands.

Caring for an HIV-infected child is no easy task for male primary caregivers who have little experience in being a single parent and the primary caregiver. The emotional and physical needs of caring for children may task even the most experienced caregivers. Some children are orphaned due to HIV, while others continue to see their mothers in a state of increasing decline. Orphaned children, some of whom are HIV-infected, grow up with significant physical, developmental, and emotional problems. Hence, parenting these children poses a significant challenge (Anderson, 1998). Most male primary caregivers live alone with one or more children and have only sporadic instrumental or emotional support from friends and relatives on which to rely. To complicate the scenario, both child and father are likely to be actively grieving from the loss of the female relationship presence in the home. Because the bereavement process itself is often experienced as depressing and debilitating, caregiving resilience is likely to be inhibited for this group. In addition, because children of different ages grieve differently, the father must have a repertoire of varying responses to the emotional needs of his children during this most difficult time.

Social services providers for these caregivers report that these men often feel left alone and without emotional support when their female partners die. Anxiety is provoked by concerns of how they will raise their children in the absence of their spouses (Strug et al., 2002). Those men with jobs face particular challenges with conflicting roles of caregiver versus wage earner, as they must decide whether to go to work or stay home with a sick child, whether to reduce their workload hours or quit their jobs all together. Reduced hours and unemployment inevitably have repercussions, as anxiety about financial obligations mounts, especially during economically challenging times.

Given both internal and external stress, it is not difficult to understand why fathers are reluctant to access services and may be hesitant to give information about their needs to service providers. Such conditions result in a cycle of growing needs and little support to meet them.

In providing a comprehensive case plan, service providers often need to know about the father's knowledge of child development, the family dynamics in the home, and the father's coping style, including his drug and alcohol history. In addition, it is helpful to know what social supports are available and how the father runs the household. Often it is helpful for providers to understand the fathers' fears and concerns about raising an HIV-infected child.

To resolve this quandary and ascertain appropriate information, it is essential for service providers to take time to build a strong working alliance with a father who requests help. One method to accomplish this goal is to inquire what the father's perception of need involves as information is gathered for the assessment. For example, one study found that fathers have reported feeling overwhelmed with child-care responsibilities and requested a parenting class. As one man put it, "I thought women had it good 'cause they were home with the kids. That's false. Kids are very demanding. They are repetitive. I love my kids but I can't stand them sometimes. . . . This is about children, and AIDS, and HIV, and of being the parents of these kids" (Strug et al., 2002, p. 310). This is a man with good capacity for self-reflection who knows what is needed to keep his family together. Service providers succeed when a strengths-based model is used. An alliance between an HIV-positive person and service provider is sustained when the service recipient's own words can be accessed and repeated for strength to continue on as head of the household. Concurrently, service providers may assist in coaching and supporting fathers in this multilayered, complex situation.

Grandparents and Other Older Relatives

Grandparents have been caregivers of their grandchildren for generations before the HIV pandemic. Especially in African American and Latino communities, grandmothers have played a central role in the family system, backing up parents who worked several jobs or assuming complete responsibility for child rearing when parents were unable to do so.

With the advent of HIV, grandparents have become a mainstay for many children orphaned by HIV. Here, the domestic picture involves a family system that may be stretched to the maximum as aging grandparents care for multiple young children when they themselves may require care.

Stress for these caregivers begins to proliferate, as reduced energies of this aging group of caregivers inevitably confronts the needs of children who are often sick due to HIV infection or who have been affected by the disease as a result of loss of a parent. The manifold needs of children who may be HIV-infected and bereaved, along with the needs of the caregiver, must be taken into account. If the child is HIV-positive, the grandparent may become anxious about medication regimen and overall health maintenance issues (Linsk & Mason, 2004). Such ongoing stress can be extremely depleting.

One of the major stressors for this group of caregivers involves emotional and behavioral issues of grandchildren. The grandparent often must care for both daughter and grandchild. For children, seeing a parent who is debilitated undoubtedly may cause anxiety and depression. Children who have been orphaned by HIV present a challenging set of circumstances even under the best conditions. Most probably, they have had to endure several moves in their residence, have changed schools, have lost an attachment with their primary caregiver, and sometimes they are sick themselves. Disruption in stability for these children culminates in many behavioral problems. Grandparents have described externalizing behaviors as major caregiving concerns. When stealing and lying occur, schools may complain, thus involving the grandparent in a system that requires further energy to monitor. Moreover, internalizing behaviors such as overeating, nightmares, night wandering, and talk of suicide may be present. Children may exhibit quite a bit of unresolved anger toward their parents for dying, for past neglect, or for being victimized at school (Linsk & Mason, 2004). Under such circumstances, child counseling is indicated. As one grandmother eloquently states, "You have to spend a lot of time with these children to make them know they have self-worth and that they are loved . . . and whatever happened to them is not their fault" (Linsk & Mason, 2004, p. 131).

Other children may exhibit problems that have little to do directly with being affected by HIV, but have more to do with the frequency of the status of many children living in the twenty-first century. These difficulties involve sexual, physical, and emotional abuse. Children may call upon aging grandparents for protection from victimizers in their lives. Other problems of these children may include normative adolescent independence and autonomy issues, school performance issues, and problems with completing daily household responsibilities.

All of these problems play out against a scenario where the grandparent may be working and thus experiencing the secondary strain of caregiver/work conflict. Health concerns also play a role should the grandparents need to go to the hospital or become ill themselves.

Such a complex care situation presents challenges for the social service provider. The needs of this vulnerable group of caregivers include both physical and psychological care related to their stressors. As with other caregivers, depression is a common occurrence and needs to be addressed. Moreover, given the tendency of these caregivers, who are mostly women, to put the needs of their grandchildren ahead of their own, service providers must make a special effort to inquire about caregiver well-being and needed services. A psychoeducational approach, which encompasses sensitivity and knowledge of their unique situation coupled with education about available community services, is a starting place. More specifically, these grandparents would benefit from telephone support groups, stress management training, and case management for the multiple needs of all family members.

Personal Perspective

Caring for My Daughter, by Edna, Age 72

My daughter, Ellen, was about 41 when I started taking care of her, and I was 60. She died last fall. It all started in 1996 when she was rushed to the hospital and told she had full-blown AIDS and pneumonia. She had been infected for about 10 to 12 years before that. My husband and I moved her into our house when she was discharged and from that point on it was doctor's appointments almost every day, sometimes even two or three times a day. I swear she had 12 to 14 different doctors, including her primary, which is a lot to remember.

Ellen seemed to have every possible infection you could get from having AIDS. She went to the hospital a lot, and we'd bring her home from the hospital and have to take her right back. We'd have to call 911. One time she said, "Mamma, I'm scared to ride in the ambulance, will you ride with me?" and I said, "I'm going to ride with you." I got through it, I don't know how. It was nothing to be woke up at two and three in the morning and run her to the emergency room. We'd sit there day and night. I didn't mind taking care of her at all. I didn't care, I loved her so much. She was my buddy and we'd go everywhere together. One time I was trying to get her to the bathroom during the night when her blood pressure dropped and I ended up on the bathroom floor. Then she had seizures and that was awful. Toward the end it was bad watching her get worse and worse. She just melted away. We had nurses coming in and out 24 hours a day. I said one time, "What am I going to do if I can't take care of you?" And she said, "I've been thinking about that and I'll go to a hospice." When the cancer came on top of the AIDS, it was pretty bad. We took her to radiation. She finally had to move into a hospice. She didn't want to die at home. She lasted three days. My last words to her were, "Ellen, I love you so much and I miss you." And she said, "I love you too, Mamma." I gave her a beautiful memorial service and I bought the biggest flower arrangement I could find. The chapel was packed with flowers and people from APLA [AIDS Project Los Angeles]. One man said, "Ellen has taught me so much about how to die." I left before they took her away to cremate her. Sometimes I think I should have stayed. She was one of the bravest people I've ever met.

I didn't mind telling people she had the AIDS, but some people can be so ignorant. One neighbor said, "Don't let her into your house because you might get it." But I spoke with her son and asked him if he knew much about AIDS and how you get it and he said yes. I told him what his mother said, and he said, "Don't pay any attention to her."

We've had some family fighting as well along the way. One of Ellen's sisters who was in the army and out of town was jealous that we moved Ellen into her room, even though she was really sick. And Ellen's daughter wasn't any help, being into the drugs and all even though she's in her twenties. She took all her mother's coats after the funeral. Since Ellen died, my husband's been very grouchy and snaps at me. He spends a lot of money. I guess that's how he copes. He ended up in the psych ward once for depression right around the time Ellen got sick. He was in there for two months. I was trying to hide his guns one day and I got knocked around my own kitchen by one of my daughters. We mailed them out of state. I don't go out much these days. I guess I grieve in the house by myself and just try to pass the time. I will never get over losing her.

CONCLUSIONS

The storied lives of HIV caregivers are at once similar and varied. These are people who are united in their efforts to provide comfort and solace for loved ones living with a disease that has an uncertain course, an uncertain future and ending. HIV has evolved from an acute terminal illness to a long, chronic, life-threatening one with significant potential medical complications. Questions remain whether HIV caregiving has substantially changed and whether it is any easier than it once was. Clearly, because of the length of time spent in caregiving and the ups and downs of the disease, caregiving presents new challenges for the caregiver. Moreover, the likelihood of the person with HIV contracting other serious diseases in addition to HIV, such as leukemia, lymphoma, and other cancers, presents new and perhaps more complex scenarios with a new set of implications for the caregiving role. Issues of the aging caregiver now take the center stage. As HIV has a chronic trajectory, so, too, has HIV caregiving.

In their daily lives, many caregivers endure continuous fatigue, chronic substantial stress and illness, and lasting depression, and they rely on few resources. Many face poverty; nearly all face HIV stigma. Despite these conditions, countless HIV caregivers report a sense of gain or satisfaction from HIV caregiving, more so than do caregivers coping with other illnesses (Stetz & Brown, 2004). Those who fare better seem to adopt an attitude of having control over the emphasis that HIV has in life, thus putting HIV in perspective. Getting involved in HIV work outside the immediate caregiving relationship seems to increase feelings of empowerment and altruism for some groups (Carlisle, 2000). Others describe augmented intimacy within the caregiving relationship. For example, one mother of an adult son with HIV states, "I am so thankful to God today that we had those two years. It was like it was set aside for us" (Nelms, 2002, p. 290). Another reveals, "My time with him was very, very important to me. It was very, very enjoyable . . . " (Nelms, p. 290). Several caregivers reflect giving and receiving strength, love, closeness, and connectedness from the person with HIV. "It was the most wonderful, tragic experience of my life," one caregiver states (Nelms, p. 290).

Sense of gain and purpose may take different expressions for varying caregiver groups. Some especially relate to the importance of music, and others reveal that play is a meaningful method of communicating the expression of love and witness to the unique experience between caregiver and the person with HIV (Nelms, 2002). Other beneficial themes evident in the caregiving literature involve personal growth and constructive personality changes, increased understanding of others and their illnesses, a sense of satisfaction and achievement, and gained perspective in life (McCausland & Pakenham, 2003).

The American Association of Retired Persons (AARP) recommends that caregivers be offered supportive counseling; training on caregiving; information about benefits, resources, and HIV; respite care and help with home care; regular assessment of their own health and needs; flexible time in their employment; and legislation guaranteeing caregiving leave (AARP, 2009). Each group of caregivers presents a somewhat distinctive set of circumstances, which requires service providers to, in a sense, know all major groups affected by HIV disease, because caregivers are representatives from these groups. They are gay men, women, single fathers, the aging, and grandparents. They are White, Latino or Latina, African American, and many other ethnic groups. Some are better off economically, but most face poverty and the enormous odds of living in neighborhoods ravaged by drugs, violence, and stigma. Some have better capacities to access resources; others have very few resources available to meet their own needs, let alone the needs of the HIV-infected. Some caregivers are addicted, and some fear leaving children or partners behind. There are many uncertainties in the lives of HIV caregivers, but one thing is definite: They are a group exceptional in their commitment to those for whom they provide care.

REFERENCES

AARP. (2009, March 2–13). Statement at the Commission on the Status of Women, 53rd Session, United Nations. New York: United Nations.

Anderson, V. M. (1998). HIV infection in children: A medical overview. *Journal of the Child Welfare League of America, 57*, 107–114.

Beals, K. P., Wight, R. G., Aneshensel, C. S., Murphy, D., & Miller-Martinez, D. (2006). The role of family caregivers in HIV medication adherence. *AIDS Care, 18*(6), 589–596.

Billings, D. W., Folkman, S., Acree, M., & Moskowitz, J. T. (2000). Coping and physical health during caregiving: The roles of positive and negative affect. *Journal of Personality and Social Psychology, 79*(1), 131–142.

Carlisle, C. (2000). The search for meaning in HIV and AIDS: The carers' experience. *Qualitative Health Research, 10*(6), 750–765.

Centers for Disease Control and Prevention. (2006). *CDC HIV/AIDS fact sheet: HIV/AIDS among women*. Atlanta, GA: CDC, National Center for HIV, STD and TB Prevention, Division of HIV/AIDS.

Choppelas, J., & Wilson, C. (2006). Caregiver burden and stress in African American, Asian, Hispanic and White American caregivers of older family members. *Dissertation Abstracts, 66*(9-B), 508.

Demi, A., Bakeman, R., Moneyham, I., Sowell, R., & Seals, B. (1997). Effects of resources and stressors on burden and depression of family members who provide care to an HIV infected woman. *Journal of Family Psychology, 11*(1), 35–48.

Devine, D., Forehand, R., Morse, E., Simon, P., Clark, L., & Kernis, M. (2000). HIV infection in inner-city African-American women: The role of optimism in predicting depressive symptomatology. *International Journal of Rehabilitation & Health, 5*, 141–156.

Engel, M. (2008, February 5). With HIV, growing older faster. *Los Angeles Times,* pp. 14–15.

Fein, G., Fletcher, D. J., & Di Sclafani, V. (1998). Effect of chronic alcohol abuse on the CNS morbidity of HIV disease. *Alcoholism: Clinical and Experimental Research, 22*, 196S–200S.

Flaskerud, J. & Nymanthi, A. (1990). Effects of AIDS among education programs on the knowledge, attitudes, and practices of low-income Black and Latina women. *Journal of Community Health, 15*(6), 343–355.

Flexner, C. W., Cargill, V. A., Sinclair, J., Kresina, T. F., & Cheever, L. (2001). Alcohol use can result in enhanced drug metabolism in HIV pharmacotherapy. *AIDS Patient Care and STDs, 15*, 57–58.

Fredriksen-Goldsen, K. I. (2007). HIV/AIDS caregiving predictors of well-being and distress. *Journal of Gay and Lesbian Social Services, 18*(34), 53–73.

Jones, D. J., Beach, S. R. H., Forehand, R., & The Family Health Project Research Group. (2001). Disease status in African American single mothers with HIV: The role of depressive symptoms. *Health Psychology, 20*, 417–423.

Knowlton, A.R. (2003). Informal HIV caregiving in a vulnerable population: Toward a network resource framework. *Social Science & Medicine, 56*(6), 1307–1320.

Land, H., & Hudson, S. (2002). HIV serostatus and factors related to physical and mental well-being in Latina family AIDS caregivers. *Social Science and Medicine, 54*(1), 147–159.

Land, H., & Hudson, S. (2004). Stress, coping, and depressive symptomatology in Latina and Anglo AIDS caregivers. *Psychology and Health, 19*(5), 643–666.

Land, H., Hudson, S., & Stiefel, B. (2003). Stress and depression among HIV-positive and HIV-negative gay and bisexual AIDS caregivers. *AIDS and Behavior, 7*(1), 41–53.

Le Blanc, A. J., & Wight, R. G. (2000). Reciprocity and depression in AIDS caregiving. *Sociological Perspectives, 43*(4), 631–649.

Linsk, N., & Mason, S. (2004). Stresses on grandparents and other relatives caring for children affected by HIV/AIDS. *Health and Social Work, 29*(2), 127–136.

Magana, S. (2007). Psychological distress among Latino family caregivers of adults with schizophrenia: The roles of burden and stigma. *Psychiatric Services, 58*(3), 378–384.

Magana, S. M., Ramirez-Garcia, J. I., Hernandez, M. G., & Cortez, R. (2007). Psychological distress among Latino family caregivers of adults with schizophrenia: The roles of burden and stigma. *Psychiatric Services, 58*(3), 378–384.

McAdoo, J. L. (1993). The roles of African-American fathers: An ecological perspective. *Families in Society, 74*, 28–35.

McCausland, J., & Pakenham, K. I. (2003). Investigation of the benefits of HIV/AIDS caregiving and relations among caregiving adjustment, benefit finding, and stress and coping variables. *AIDS Care, 15*(6), 853–869.

Neff, J. A., Amodei, N., Valescu, S., & Pomeroy, E. C. (2003). Psychological adaptation and distress among HIV+ Latina women: Adaptation to HIV in a Mexican American cultural context. *Social Work in Health Care, 37*, 55–74.

Nelms, T. P. (2002). A most wonderful, tragic experience: The phenomenon of mothering in caregiving an adult son with AIDS. *Journal of Family Nursing, 8*(3), 282–300.

Oliveros, C. (2008). The Latino caregiver experience among dementia and non-dementia caregivers: Can community based care management improve caregiver health? *Dissertation Abstracts, 69*(4-B), 2275.

Ortiz, C. (2005). Disclosing concerns of Latinas living with HIV/AIDS. *Journal of Transcultural Nursing, 16*, 210–217.

Pearlin, L.I., Aneshensel, C.S. & LeBlanc, A. J. (1997). The forms and mechanisms of stress proliferation: The case of AIDS caregivers. *Journal of Health and Social Behavior, 38*(3), 223–236.

Pearlin, L. I., Mullan, J. T. Aneshensel, C. S., Wardlaw, L., & Harrington, C. (1994). The structure and function of AIDS caregiving relationships. *Psychosocial Rehabilitation Journal, 17*, 51–67.

Pirraglia, P. A., Bishop, E., Herman, D., Trisvan, E. T., Lopez, R.A., Targersen, C. S., et al. (2005). Caregiver burden and depression among informal caregivers of HIV-infected individuals. *Journal of General Internal Medicine, 20*(6), 510–514.

Poindexter, C. C. (2005). The Lion at the gate: An HIV-affected caregiver resists stigma. *Health and Social Work, 30*(1), 64–74.

Poindexter, C., Linsk, N., & Warner, S. (1999). "He listens . . . and never gossips:" Spiritual coping without church support among older, predominantly African-American caregivers of persons with HIV. *Review of Religious Research, 40*(3), 230–243.

Redgrave, G., Swartz, A., & Romanoski, A. (2003). Alcohol misuse by women. *International Review of Psychiatry, 15*, 256–268.

Samet, J. H., Horton, N. J., Traphagen, E. T., Lyon, S. M., & Freedberg, K. A. (2003). Alcohol consumption and HIV disease progression: Are they related? *Alcoholism: Clinical and Experimental Research, 27*, 862–867.

Stetz, K. M., & Brown, M. A. (2004). Physical and psychosocial health in family caregiving: A comparison of AIDS and cancer caregivers. *Public Health Nursing, 21*(6), 533–540.

Strug, D., Rabb, L., & Nanton, R. (2002). Provider views of the support service needs of male primary caretakers of HIV/AIDS-infected and affected children: A needs assessment. *Families in Society, 83*(3), 303–313.

Talamantes, M. A., Lawler, W. R., & Espino, D. V. (1995). Hispanic elders, caregiving norms surrounding dying and the use of hospice service. *Hospice Journal, 10*, 35–49.

Wight, R. G. (2000). Precursive depression among HIV infected AIDS caregivers over time. *Social Science and Medicine, 51*, 759–770.

Wight, R. G., Aneshensel, C. S., & LeBlanc, Q. J. (2003). Stress buffering effects of family support in AIDS caregiving. *AIDS Care, 15*(5), 595–613.

Wohl, A. R., Lu, S., Odem, S., Sorvillo, F., Pegues, C. F., & Kerndt, P. R. (1998). Sociodemographic and behavioral characteristics of African-American women with HIV and AIDS in Los Angeles County, 1990–1997, *Journal of Acquired Immune Deficiency Syndromes and Human Retrovirology, 19*, 412–420.

Wyatt, G., Carmona, J., Loeb, T., & Williams, J. (2005). HIV-positive Black women with histories of childhood sexual abuse: Patterns of substance use and barriers to health care. *Journal of Health Care for the Poor and Underse*rved, *16*, 9–23.

Chapter Twenty

AFTERWORD: LOOKING BACK, LOOKING FORWARD IN HIV SOCIAL WORK

Cynthia Cannon Poindexter and Nathan L. Linsk

It is possible that the contents of this handbook have overwhelmed you with the enormity of the HIV pandemic, the amount of knowledge and skill required to do effective HIV prevention and care, and the sheer level and depth of need. Indeed, it is realistic to be respectful of the demands that HIV makes on the world, on those who are infected and affected, and on helpers. However, the major lesson of this book is twofold. One, social workers have had the commitment, values, knowledge, and skills to make a difference in the first three decades of the pandemic, and two, social work will continue to be needed in the changing and increasing demands of the future. Social work's competencies have already proved invaluable, despite the huge challenges, and they will continue to be adaptable to new trials as the pandemic increases and changes.

LOOKING BACK

As was made clear in Chapter 1, when HIV surfaced in 1981 as a new, mysterious, stigmatized, deadly syndrome, no one was prepared. Social workers, like everyone else, were taken aback, fearful, and had to approach these events through the lenses of their own experiences in other fields of direct practice (such as oncology and gerontology) and a wide array of other professional activities (such as administration and advocacy). People with AIDS were asking for help in homeless shelters, addictions and methadone programs, prisons, schools, mental health clinics, migrant health centers, and hospitals, and social workers were already in all of those settings, already being called on to work with the most difficult situations. Those social workers who first responded were dedicated, flexible, and innovative—often making things up as they went along—and found ways to work with other disciplines.

Principles

As seen in the discussion of underlying principles in Chapters 2 through 4, as social workers began to respond to HIV, we found that the traditional domains, skills, and values of social work fit perfectly with the needs of the HIV field. What the social work profession has always known about human rights, social justice, empowerment, anti-oppression, strengths, and cultural competence was immediately brought to bear on the

Acknowledgments: We dedicate this chapter to Gary Lloyd, PhD, retired from the faculty of the Tulane University School of Social Work, who was a pioneer in bringing HIV to the attention of social workers and who brought us both inspiration and aspiration.

HIV pandemic. When HIV stigma divided people into worthy and unworthy, we were ready for it. When the complexities of HIV disease called for interdisciplinary, cross-cultural, multiple-setting, interagency, multiple methods, social workers were already trained.

Practice

As can be seen in Chapters 5 through 8, when people living with HIV needed case management, discharge planning, crisis intervention, and individual, group, and family counseling across all types of settings, social workers knew exactly what to do. In addition, people needed coordination of services and family conferences, and social workers were the ones to convene the care teams. Likewise, as discussed in Chapters 9 through 11, when situations called for program development, agency and program leadership, grant writing, policy crafting, community organizing, and legislative advocacy, social workers were the logical practitioners and partners with affected communities. As shown in Chapter 12, social workers, along with infected persons and those most vulnerable, developed, implemented, and evaluated innovative prevention strategies to address an unprecedented crisis.

Populations

In addition, as is illuminated in Part 3, because HIV affects so many types of people with so many diverse needs, social work's expertise in human development and in diverse populations was needed in the HIV field. No matter the race, ethnicity, sexual orientation, age, or gender of the person infected, affected, or vulnerable to infection, we had knowledge and skills to offer.

LOOKING FORWARD

It is clear from all the chapters that even almost three decades after the advent of the disease, there is still nothing quite like getting a diagnosis of HIV and facing the social, emotional, financial, and spiritual results of that traumatic news. There are some things that have not changed, even though they have lessened somewhat: HIV stigma is still problematic; diagnosis disclosure is still a series of difficult decisions, including in help seeking; and HIV still causes multiple complex crises. People in this situation *still need* a good HIV social worker, a specialist in the field. Appropriate, sensitive, skilled direct-care social work is vital for children, teens, men, and women who are living with HIV. It is lifesaving and spirit saving to have accurate benefits information, skilled crisis intervention, supportive counseling, medication adherence support, prevention education, and comprehensive case management offered in an ethical, professional, confidential, respectful way by people who see themselves as partners in a relationship. People living with HIV may want a social worker to help them reflect on the past, deal with the present, and plan for the future, and to do that all at once.

Activism, legislative advocacy, and community organizing in the early years of the pandemic and the social services that were established by the affected communities had a tremendous effect and impact on whether testing, treatment, and care were available. The strengths of the past will also be needed in the future. The following activities, extracted from the chapters, provide an agenda for the future.

Principles

Obviously, HIV continues to be a global plague, and U.S.-based social workers frequently assist in the international arena, whether in other countries or working with immigrants and refugees in the United States. As seen in Chapter 3 and throughout the book, increasingly, *cultural competence* and community development skills and a commitment to grassroots participation are required.

We should continue to work toward the understanding that everyone living with HIV deserves services, health care, and the highest possible quality of life. To do so we will need to sustain our system responses, advocate for access to treatment and health care, and use whatever policy and advocacy windows open to us. The *human rights* framework is vital in these efforts. Fortunately, the human rights framework is playing an increasingly larger part in HIV policy discussions, especially at the United Nations and international AIDS conferences, partially due to the insistence and influence of persons living with HIV. As proposed in Chapter 4, human rights must be seen as integral to the purpose of social work.

Practice

As articulated in Chapter 12 and elsewhere, social workers must take more responsibility for *HIV prevention,* and better HIV prevention must be consistently designed, funded, and implemented at multiple levels. The piecemeal approaches of the past are failing. No one prevention approach can work for anyone anywhere, just as no one antiretroviral treatment should be offered. We must shift to comprehensive combination prevention. Every social worker, regardless of setting or specialty, should be able to do HIV prevention education. We are beginning to accept the climbing rates of HIV as a way of life as inevitable. Passivity is not acceptable. Evidence-based prevention methods must prevail over all political and philosophical dogma. In addition, as medical and pharmaceutical treatments become increasingly merged with prevention, social workers must understand, teach, and advocate for access to new technologies. Likewise, as is introduced in Chapter 1, every social worker should know how to do *HIV test counseling* and advocate for everyone to know his or her HIV status. Social workers have always been able to reach those most vulnerable and difficult to reach, and we should be educating everyone about the options for HIV testing.

As discussed throughout Part 2, *direct psychosocial services* should also be evidence-based, with a mature set of proven techniques to ensure quality of care and quality of life. Social workers must contribute to this through applied, participatory, culturally competent action research to show that psychosocial interventions are valuable and effective and can be used successfully with specific populations.

As is shown in Chapter 9, the *administrators and supervisors* of HIV program managers must continue to balance seemingly opposing forces. They must provide direct services and still be advocates, which often requires that they make waves against the very bureaucracies that fund them. They must balance traditional social work and public health approaches (those usually funded) with human rights. They must balance the needs of many widely diverse cultural groups without losing their focus on HIV. They must be innovative and daring, which appeases the conservative constituencies that govern and fund them, so that they can survive.

As Chapters 10 and 11 espouse, social work must not abandon *activism and advocacy.* HIV is being fueled by inequity. Activism against racial, gender, sexual minority, class, and other disparities and oppressions must be on the social work agenda.

Activism for access to social services, health care, information, funding, and scientific advancement must continue. Pressure must continue on pharmaceutical corporations, governmental bureaucracies, and for-profit health care entities so that the needs and rights of persons living with HIV do not get sacrificed to other agendas.

Advocacy for programs and funding will likely remain vital. HIV-specific federal programs, as well as federal entitlement and insurance programs on which persons with

HIV depend, will probably have ongoing importance as people with HIV live into their older years and as more people acquire HIV. There will always be economic and political stressors and competing forces. It is important to honestly assess the role of these programs as the landscape changes and to advocate for the best scenario for persons living with HIV.

As all authors have confirmed, *HIV stigma* still plays an important role in the pandemic and must continue to be fought and reduced at the individual, family, organizational, community, and national levels.

Populations

As the epidemic in the United States becomes weighted even more heavily toward women and people of color, vigilance against apathy becomes even more imperative. The first wave of this epidemic in the United States devastated a generation of gay and bisexual men; three decades later, it is once again men having sex with men who are overwhelmingly the casualties. As stated in Chapters 14, 17, and 18, at this time African American and Latino men are falling through the societal cracks of racism and homophobia. Social work must take a stand in this fight.

The *nature of programs and services* may change for persons living with HIV in the United States, depending on the widely varying needs of our constituencies. For example, HIV programs founded solely for those who were disabled may need to help people living with HIV decide whether to go back to work. As Chapter 13 states, programs founded by and for men may need to confront the fact that women of color comprise the fastest-growing segment of people with HIV in their area.

Social work supervisors and administrators must know how to "walk the walk" and ensure that organizations are *person-centered, respectful, and participatory,* that persons with HIV do not encounter stigma and neglect in our social service systems. All social service systems must be welcoming of persons with HIV, meaning all types of persons with HIV, including transgender persons, gay men and women, and people of all religions, cultures, nationalities, ethnicities, races, and ages.

It is probably as difficult to recall the world before HIV as it is to imagine a future world without HIV. Both scientists and politicians have given up setting deadlines about when the HIV pandemic will be over. We must *plan for future generations* who have HIV. Yet how can we go on without hope? However, the future may look different from the past, especially if vaccines and microbicides become viable and treatment becomes even more long term and effective. We must continue to advocate for those eventualities.

THE PROFESSION

We must *train social workers* and other human services workers specifically to work in the HIV field, where the needs are specific, growing, and dire. The HIV workforce has been changing, as the veteran HIV workers leave and those coming to the workforce may not have had the same experiences. While some schools of social work teach HIV-related courses, all schools will need to encompass HIV information, as the HIV systems continue to be overwhelmed by social and resource issues and this may need to be reflected in accreditation. As is obvious from the first chapter, practitioners and administrators must more than ever keep up with medical, technical, pharmaceutical, and prevention developments so that we can help persons with HIV and persons at risk for HIV access the information and resources they need to stay safe and healthy.

The HIV social work field is a roller coaster: a world of joy, satisfaction, dedication, and pride in accomplishment, on one hand, and on the other hand a world of underre-sourcing, sadness, frustration, overwork, and stress. *Self-care* gets talked about a lot but less often done. As the authors of Chapter 8 remind us, we need to care for ourselves consistently. The alternative is burnout, compassion fatigue, and disengagement from the workforce.

CONCLUDING REMARKS

A close reading of this handbook shows that HIV-related social work is full of contradictions. (1) HIV is an equal opportunity infector, and clearly the biological agent cannot tell the difference between us, yet the statistics make it look as if only the most oppressed and vulnerable among us are susceptible. (2) HIV is preventable yet continues to worsen. We have worked very hard for a long time and know a great deal, yet on many levels we are failing. (3) HIV throws individuals, couples, families, and groups into crisis, and keeps cultures and nations in turmoil and trauma, yet it is a long-term problem. How is it possible for HIV to be both acute and chronic? (4) HIV is a medical and biological phenomenon that cannot be explained or addressed purely through a traditional preven-tion or public health lens; it requires a framework of social justice and human rights. (5) As social workers and human services workers, we know that certain universal human responses are likely when a life-threatening, stigmatized illness is faced, yet testing, pre-vention, and care programs are not effective unless they take specific cultural beliefs and behaviors into careful account. The balance between all these elements is essential, and it is what makes HIV work special.

HIV social work—service provision, administration, and policy advocacy—consists of all of the challenges, competencies, and satisfaction entailed throughout the social work profession. From the beginning of the pandemic, we had the opportunity to engage all of our knowledge and skills in depth. Along with those opportunities were extraordinary challenges: a new and unknown illness, pervasive stigma, a rapidly evolving pandemic, and novel responses in treatment emerging almost every year. Like the individuals, fami-lies, organizations, and communities with whom we work, social workers interfacing with HIV issues have learned to become resilient, to thrive on challenges, to surmount obstacles, to learn from our experiences, and to embrace life in new ways. Meeting the challenges while developing better interventions will continue to be our tasks.

Author Index

Italic page numbers refer to citations from the reference sections

A

AARP, 323, *324*

Abramson, D. M., 104, *120*

Abramson, P. R., 24, *30*

Acevedo, V., 44, 46, *56*

Acree, M., 318, *324*

Adam, B., 216, *225*

Addams, J., 32, *38*

Adelekan, M. L., 295, *304*

Adler, B., *226*

Agency for Healthcare Research
    and Quality, 202, *208*

Aggleton, P., 203, 204, *210*, 212,
    225, 227, 300, *306*

Agot, K., *194*

Aidala, A. A., 104, *120*

AIDS Alliance, 245, *247*

AIDS Law Project, 1999, 136

Aiken, L. S., 213, *227*

Ajzen, I., 273, 274, *285–287*

Albrecht, J., *249*

Alderson, K., 219, *227*

Aledort, L. M., *29*

Alinsky, S., 160, *171*

Allard, P., 278, *285*

Allen, J. R., 280, *288*

Allen, R., 134, *142*

Allen, S., 24, *27*

Allers, C. T., 264, *266*

Alleyne, G., *306*

Alston, W. K., 147, *156*

Altholz, J. A., 153, *157*

Altman, L., 244, *247*

Altschuler, J., 258, *266*

Alvarez, M. E., *229*

Amaro, H., 186, *194*

American Academy of Pediatrics
    Committee on Pediatrics
    AIDS, 235, *247*

amfAR, 244, *247*, 294, 301, *304*

Ammassari, A., 20, *27*

Amodei, N., 316, *325*

An, Q., *29*, 72, *195*, 268, *286*, *306*

Anastos, K., *209*

Andersen, R. M., *209, 210*

Anderson, G., 244, *247*, 256, *267*

Anderson, H., 37, *38*

Anderson, J. E., 117, *120*

Anderson, R. E., *196*

Anderson, R. M., 280, *285, 287*

Anderson, V. M., 319, *324*

Andrews, J., 32, *39*

Aneshensel, C. S., 203, *210*, 311,
    313, 314, 316, *324–326*

Angarano, G., *30*

Annas, G. J., 62, *72*

Antle, B. J., 203, *208*

Anton, P. A., 188, *195*

Antoni, M. H., *268*

Apetrei, C., *194*

Apisuk, C., 217, *228*, 298, *306*

Aral, S. O., 190, *196*

Arcia, E., *56*

Arici, C., 24, *29, 30*

Arkowitz, H., 97, *100*

Armistead, L., 202, 203, *209, 210*

Armstrong, D., *247*

Armstrong, F., *249*

Armstrong, W., *247*

Arnsten, J. H., 255, *267*

Aronstein, D., 174, *181*

Arriola, K. R. J., 295, 296, *305*

Asastos, K., *268*

Ashman, J. J., 104, *119*

Assmann, S. F., *29*

Athey, T. W., *28*

Austin, B. J., 203, *209*

Auvert, B., 14, *27*, 189, *194*

Axelrod, J., 202, 203, *209*

Ayala, G., 213, 221, *226*, 294, *305*

B

Babiker, A., 8, *28*

Bachanas, P., 235, 237, *247*

Baggaley, R. F., 14, *28*

Bailey, D., *56, 157*

Bailey, R. C., 189, *194*

Bakeman, R., *209*, 214, 215, *225*,
    228, 316, *324*

Balgopal, P. R., 123, *142*

Balkus, J., 189, *196*, 302, *307*

Baluja, K. F., 292, *306*

Bangsberg, D. R., 111, *120*

Barash, E. T., 117, 118, *119*

Barbour, R. S., 43, *57*

Barker, R. L., 175, *181*

Barresi, P. J., *285*

Barroso, J., 203, *210*

Barrow, J., *251*

Bartless, J. A., *269*

Bascones, A., *28*

Bastani, R., *286*

Bastos, F., 274, *285*

Battles, H., 234–241, *247*,
    251, 252

333

Bauman, L., *251*

Baxi, U., 60, *72*

Bazron, B., 34, *38*, 42, *57*

Beach, S. R. H., *249*, 318, *324*

Beals, K. P., 203, *210*, 316, *324*

Beckerman, N. L., 89, *101*

Beeker, C., *227*

Begley, E. B., 293, *307*

Behel, S., *29*

Bein, E., 213, *226*, 294, *305*

Belman, A., 233, *247*

Belzer, M., *250*

Bennett, C. L., 188, *196*, *269*

Bentley, M. E., 293, *306*

Berger, B. E., 262, *267*

Berger, C. S., 144, *156*, *157*

Berghuis, J. P., 217, *228*

Bernard, A., 242, *247*

Berry, J., *57*

Best, A., 114, *120*

Betancourt, J. R., 41, 42, *57*

Betz, C., 241, *247*

Bickham, N. L., 284, *288*

Billings, D. W., 318, *324*

Bingham, T., *29*, *227*

Bishai, D., *229*

Bishop, E., *325*

Blackburn, E., 243, *251*

Blair, D. C., 204, *210*

Blake, L., 232, *247*

Blakenship, K. M., 277, *285*

Blanche, S., *248*, *250*

Blea, L., *306*

Block, M., 204, *209*

Bloom, S., *142*

Blower, S. M., 188, *196*

Blum, S., *269*

Blumenthal, S., 244, *247*

Board, R., 201, *209*

Bobo, K., 159, 165, *171*

Bockting, W. O., *228*

Bogart, L. M., *58*, 203, *209*

Boily, M. C., 14, *28*, 274, *275*

Boland, M., *247*

Bollinger, L., 191, *196*

Bonanno, G., *251*

Bonk, N., 188, *195*

Boone, L., 42, 43, *57*

Bor, R., 220, *225*

Borges, N. J., 221, *227*

Boschi-Pinto, C., 24, *29*

Bose, S., 236, *247*, *250*

Boston Public Health
  Commission, AIDS Services,
  78, *88*

Bourgois, P., 296, *305*, *307*

Bouris, A., 300, *307*

Bowen, A. M., 216, 223, *225*, *229*

Bowleg, L., 43, *57*

Boyd, D., *285*

Boyd-Franklin, N., 136, *142*,
  243, *247*

Boyer, N. C., 43, 44, *58*, 264, *269*

Boykin, S., *58*

Bozeman, S., *287*

Bozzette, S. A., *209*, *210*

Brackis-Cott, E., 203, *209*, 244,
  248, *250*

Braga, P., *251*

Braithwaite, R. L., 295, *305*

Bray, J. H., *251*

Bray, S. J., *285*

Braybrook, D., *227*

Brazaitis, S. J., 89, *100*

Breen, C., 302, *306*

Breman, J. G., *306*

Brennan, J., 174, *181*

Brenner, B. G., 184, *194*

Brester, M., *30*

Briery, B., *247*

Brinkman, K., 89, *101*

Brisco, S. T., *209*

Brisset-Chapman, S., 44, *57*

Bristol, N., 186, 187, *194*

Britton, P. J., 221, *227*, *268*

Brondolo, E., *209*

Brook, J. S., 278, *285*

Brouwer, P., *247*, *250*

Brouwers, P., 233, 237, *250*, *252*

Broward County Health
  Department, 258, *267*

Brown, L., 238, 239, *248*

Brown, L. K., *287*

Brown, M., *196*

Brown, M. A., 323, *325*

Browne, G., *227*

Brudney, K., *210*

Bryan, A., 296, *305*

Buchacz, K., 233, 239, *248*

Buchbinder, S., *227*, *287*

Buchbinder, S. P., 189, *194*

Buck, K., *227*

Buckberry, K., *248*

Buehler, J. W., *285*

Bunch, M., 43, *58*

Burger, D. M., *29*

Burke, J., *209*

Burr, P., *251*

Burrage, J. W., 263, *269*

Buseh, A. G., 204, 206, 208, *209*

Bush, G., 243, *248*

Buskin, S. E., 117, *119*

Butler, C., 97, *101*

Butler, I. F., 190, *194*

Butler, R., *248*

Butt, A., 260, *268*

Butz, A., *249*

Buvé, A., 27, 189, *196*, 302, *307*

C

Caceres, C., 299, *305*

Cáceres, C., 212, *225*, *226*

Cadman, E. C., 23, *29*

Cafaro, A., *196*

Calabrese, L., *247*

Calzavara, L., 213, *226*

Camacho, S., *251*

Camille, J., *209*

Campbell, C., 218, *225*

Campbell, R. T., 294, *307*

Campo, J., 14, *28*

Campsmith, M. L., 291–293,
  305, *307*

Canadian Press, 220, *225*

Cano, J., *28*

Cantor, M. H., 257, 260–263, *268*

Capell, F. J., *286*

Capistrant, B., 220, *226*

Capitanio, J. P., 91, *100*

Caputo, A., *196*

Caputo, R. K., 34, *38*

Card, J., 43, *58*

Carey, M. P., 204, *210*, 284, *288*

Carey, R. F., 24, *28*

Cargill, V. A., *324*

Carlisle, C., 323, *324*

Carmona, J., 318, *326*

Carmona, J. V., 282, *289*

Carrillo, E., 41, *57*

Casey, S., *226*

Casillas, E., 300, *306*

Castellano, C., *268*

Castellanos, D., *307*

Castelli, F., *27*

Castilho, E. A., 24, *29*

Castilla, J., 28, 183, *194*

Castro, K., *288*

Castro, K. G., 5, 6, *28*

Caswell, J., *227*

Catania, J. A., 213, *228*

Cates, W., 302, *307*

Cates, W., Jr., 189, *196*

Catley, D., *209*

Celentano, D. D., *29*

Celum, C., *227*

Celum, C. L., *194*, *285*, *287*

Center for AIDS Prevention
    Studies, 295, *305*

Centers for Disease Control and
    Prevention, 4, 6, 7, 15, *28*,
    42–45, *57*, 66, *72*, 78, *88*, 90,
    100, *120*, 144, 145, *156*, 184,
    185, 189, *194*, 199, *209*, 212,
    215, *226*, 231, 233, 234, 244,
    245, *248*, 254, 255, 257–260,
    262, *267*, 271, 272, 278, 282,
    285, 293, 302, *305*, 315,
    316, *324*

Cervia, J., *248*

Cetron, A. B., 90, *101*

Chakraborty, R., *248*

Chambre, S. M., 144, 146, 149,
    151, *156*

Chang, B., 20, *30*

Charlebois, E., 66, *72*, *307*

Charurat, M., *28*

Chase, C., *250*

Chawarski, M. C., 302, *308*

Chazin, R., 35, *38*

Checko, P. J., *285*

Cheever, L., *324*

Chege, J., *27*

Chen, S., 284, *287*

Cheng, A., *307*

Cheng, M., 202, *209*

Chesney, M., *249*, 260, *267*

Chesney, M. A., *28*, *210*, 273,
    285, *287*

Chin, J., 45, 46, *57*

Chirimuuta, R. C., 281, *285*

Chirimuuta, R. J., 281, *285*

Chmiel, J. S., *286*

Choppelas, J., 315, *324*

Chu, S., 255, *269*

Chu, S. Y., *285*

Church, S., 213, *226*

Claeson, M., *306*

Clapson, M., 239, *250*

Clark, G., 144, 156, *157*

Clark, H. J., 203, *209*

Clark, L., *324*

Clark, M., *229*

Clarke, I. J., 125, *142*

Clarke, J. G., *308*

Coates, T., 218, *226*, *249*

Coates, T. J., 185, *195*, 217, *227*,
    299, 300, *305*

Cochran, S., 213, *227*

Cochran, S. D., 213, *226*

Cofrancesco, J., 45, *57*

Coggins, P., 42, *57*

Cohen, J., 183, *194*, 262, *268*

Cohen, M., *210*, *227*

Cohen, M. H., *209*

Coleman, E., *228*

Coleman, K., 46, *58*

Colfax, G., 185, *194*, *227*, *285*

Colfax, K. R., 111, *120*

Collier, A. C., *29*

Collins, S. R., 117, *121*

Colon, H. M., 293, *305*, *307*

Comfort, M., 296, *305*

Connor, E., 231, *248*

Conrad, P., 160, *171*

Conti, L., *285*

Conviser, R., 104, *119*

Cook, J. A., 203, *209*

Cooke, M., *249*

Coon, L., 243, 244, *248*

Cooper, E. R., 18, *28*

Cooper, H. L. F., 284, *286*

Cooperman, N. A., 255, *267*

Coordinating Committee of the
    Global HIV/AIDS Vaccine
    Enterprise, 190, *194*

Copeland, V., 44, *57*

Coplan, P. M., 188, *196*

Corey, L., *194*

Cornelius, L., *58*, *229*

Correa, V., *56*

Cortez, R., 316, *325*

Costagliola, D., *248*

Costanzo, J. M., 292, *306*

Cournos, F., 296, *305*

Courtney, M. E., 32, *39*

Coury-Doniger, P., *229*

Coutinho, R. A., 89, *101*

Couture, H., 296, *308*

Cowgill, B. O., *209*

Craig, M., *250*

Cramer, E. P., 212, *226*

Cree, V. E., 204, *209*

Crepaz, N., 11, *29*, 191, *194*,
    287, *306*

Crook, W. P., 149, 151, *157*

Crosby, R., 215, *226*

Cross, T., 34, *38*, 42, *57*

Crystal, S., 199, *210*

Csete, J., 67, *72*

Cunningham, W., *227*

Cunningham, W. E., 111, *120*,
    203, *209*, *210*

Curran, J. W., 280, *288*

Curtis, R., *286*

D

Daley, A., 190, *195*

Danker, W., *248*

Danner, S. A., *29*

Darby, S. C., 8, *28*

D'Augelli, A. R., 214, *228*,
    256, *268*

Davies, J. M., 144, *156*

Davies, S. L., *210*

Davis, C. J., 292, *306*

Davis, J., *249*

Davis, K., 24, *30*, 186, *196*

Davis, M. C., 213, *227*

Davis, S., 46, *58*

Davis, T. C., 188, *196*, *269*

Davoli, M., 302, *306*

Day, E., 233, *248*

De Angelis, D., 8, *28*

Dearing, J. W., 35, *38*

De Cock, K. M., 185, *195*

DeGruttola, V. G., *194*

del Rio, C., *306*

del Romero, J., 15, *28*, *194*

DeMarco, R., 201, *209*

DeMatteo, D., 203, *208*

Demi, A., *269*, 316, *324*

Demmer, C., 221, *229*

Dennard, L., *251*

Denning, P., 96, *100*

Denning, P. H., 293, *308*

Dennis, K., 34, *38*, 42, *57*

Denver Principles, 63, *72*

Department of Health and Human
Services, 78, *88*

Der, G., 219, *226*

Deren, S., 107, *120*, 293, *305*

Detels, R., *286*

Devaney, B., *229*

De Vincenzi, I., 24, *28*

Devine, D., 318, *324*

Diaz, C., *28*

Diaz, R., 294, *308*

Díaz, R., 212, *226*

Diaz, R. M., 221, *226*, 294,
305, 307

Diaz, S., 46, *58*

Diaz, T., 255, *269*, 272, *285*

Diaz, Y. E., 217, *227*

Dickinson, G. M., *28*

DiClemente, C. C., 83, *88*

DiClemente, R. J., 186, *196*, 210,
251, 287

Dietrich, S. L., *29*

Dieudonne, A., *248*

Dilan, E., 294, *305*

Dilley, J. W., *30*, 215, 217, *226*

Dillon, B., 14, *28*

Dilorio, C., *251*

Di Sclafani, V., *324*

Ditton, P. M., 296, *305*

Dodge, B., 44, 45, *58*

Doherty, G., *287*

Dolezal, C., 244, *247, 250*

Dominguez, K. L., *305*

Donenberg, G., 294, *305*

Donfield, S., *250*

Dorn, L., 241, *249*

Doty, M. M., 117, *121*

Douglas, J., *227, 229*

Doyle, A., 179, *181*

Driskell, J. R., 220, *226*

Duan, N., 188, 191, *195, 196,
209, 249*

Dubbert, P. M., *268*

du Plessis, P., 220, *225*

Durako, S., *250*

Duran, R., *307*

Durvasula, R. S., 202, *209*

Dziegielewski, S. F., 153, *157*

E

Easterbrook, P. J., 272, *286*

Eberhardt, L., 126, *142*

Ebrahim, S. H., 117, *120*

Eckholdt, H., *57*

Eckholm, E., 245, *248*

Edelman, D., *268*

Edward, K., 221, *228*

Edwards, L. J., *269*

Edwards, S., 239, *250*

Ehrhardt, A., *249*

Elam-Evans, L. D., 272, *288*

El-Bassel, N., 94, *100*

Elijah, J., *209*

Elliott, M., *58*

Elliott, R., 67, *72*

Ellison, N. M., 153, *156*

Elwood, W., 216, *229*

Emerson, C., 36, *38*

Emeson, E. E., *29*

Emlet, C. A., 94, *100*, 253,
256–258, 260–263, *267, 268*

Engel, M., 314, *324*

Engelson, E. S., *209*

English, G., *229*

Epston, D., 36, 37, *38*, *39*

Erikson, P. I., 280, *286*

Erlen, J. A., *268*

Espino, D. V., 317, *325*

Espinoza, L., 295, *305*

Etzel, M., 184, *196*

European Study Group, 280, *286*

Evans, D. B., *306*

Ewart, D., 8, *28*

Ezeanolue, E., 239, *248*

F

Faigeles, B., 296, *305, 306*

Fair, C., 241, *252*

Family Health Project Research
Group, 318, *324*

Fauci, A. S., *195*

Fein, G., 319, *324*

Feldman, J., *249*

Felipe, Y., *251*

Fenech, F., 253, *267*

Fergus, S., 212, *228*

Fernandez, M. I., *287*

Ferrans, C. E., 262, *267*

Ferrantelli, F., *196*

Fesko, S. L., 156, *157*

Figley, C. R., 140, *142*

Figueroa, V., 236, *252*

Finn, J., 162, *171*

Fischl, M. A., 16, *28*

Fishbein, M., 273, *286*

Fisher, A., 220, *227*

Flanigan, T. P., *29, 308*

Flaskerud, J., 44, *58*, 315, *324*

Fleishman, J. A., 78, *88*

Fleit, S., 144, *156*

Fleming, D. T., 14, *28*, 272, *286*

Fleming, P., 272, *288*

Fletcher, D. J., *324*

Fletcher, M. A., *28*

Flexner, C. W., 319, *324*

Flisher, A. J., 273, 274, *288*

Flom, P. L., 280, *286*

Flores, L., 295, *305*

Flores, S., *228*

Flores, S. A., *195*

Flowers, P., 213, 219, *226*

Flynn, C. P., *308*

Folkman, S., 318, *324*

Folstein, M. F., 261, *267*

Folstein, S. E., 261, *267*

Forehand, R., 202, *210*, 249,
318, *324*

Forsberg, A., *248*

Fortson, K., *229*

Fosarelli, P., *249*

Fowler, M., 293, *307*

Francis, D. P., *287*

Frankis, J., 219, *226*

Frederick, T., 238, *248*

Fredriksen-Golden, K. I., 314, *324*

Freedberg, K. A., *325*

Freire, P., 35, 36, *38*, 173, *181*

Freudenberg, N., *305*

Friedland, G. H., 16, *28, 29*,
104, *120*

Friedman, M., 213, *228*

Friedman, S. R., 280, 284, *286,
307*

Fuller-Thomas, E., 264, *267*

Fullilove, M. T., 212, 213, *226*

Fullilove, R. E., III, 212, 213, *226*
Fultz, S. L., 260, *268*
Fumento, M., 279, 280, *286*
Funck-Brentano, I., 235, *248*
Funk-Brentano, I., *250*

G

Gaddist, B. W., 204, *210*
Gaffney, S., *72*
Gagnon, J. H., 4, *29*
Galanti, G., 44, *57*
Galea, J., 212, *225*
Gallup Organization, 212, 219, *226*
Gamble, D., 162, *171*
Gant, L. M., 201, *209*
Garcia, A., 43, 44, *58*
Garcia, D., 294, *307*
Garcia, L., 20, *30*
Garcia, P., *210*
Garcia, S., *194*
García, S., *28*
Garcia-Lerma, J., 25, *29*
Gardezi, F., 213, *226*
Gardner, J. D., *249*
Garofalo, R., 294, *305*
Gaughan, D., 234, 235, 237, *248*
Gavazzeni, G., *29, 30*
Gavin, L., 293, *307*
Gay, Lesbian and Straight Education Network (GLSEN), 294, *305*
Gebo, K. A., *269*
Gelber, R., *248*
Genke, J., 253, *267*
George, J., 34, *38*
Gerkin, A., 258, *267*
Germain, A., 282, *286*
Gerson, A., 235, *249*
Gertner, J., *250*
Geskus, R. B., 89, *101*
Getz, W. M., *30*
Ghebremichael, M., *269*
Gibert, C., *57*
Gibson, R., 239, *251*
Giddens, B., 109, *120*
Gil, D. G., 32, *38*
Gilbert, D., 243, *249*
Gilbert, L., 94, *100*

Gilbert, P. B., 190, *194*
Gilman, S. E., 213, *226*
Gjerset, G. F., *29*
Glasford, D. E., 214, *228*
Glass, S. O., 14, *29*
Globerman, J., 144, *156*
Glunt, E. K., 145, *157*
Glynn, M., 6, *29*
Go, H., 94, *100*
Gochros, H. L., 186, *194*
Godfrey, K., 220, *227*
Godin, G., 274, *285*
Goedert, J., 232, *251*
Goggin, K., 206, *209*
Golberg, B., *251*
Goldie, R. S., 203, *208*
Goldstein, M. F., 107, *120*
Gomez, C. A., *288*
Goodkin, K., 262, *268*
Gorbach, P. M., 280, *286*
Gordon, C. M., 107, 117, *121*
Gore, C., *248*
Gorski, H., *249*
Gortmaker, S., *249*
Goulet, J. L., 260, 262, *268*
Goupil-Sormany, I., *28*
Gouws, E., *30*
Grace, C. J., 147, *156*
Grady, C., 242, *252*
Granovetter, M., 278, *286*
Grant, I., 214, *228*
Grant, R. M., *28, 307*
Gray, R. H., 189, *194*
Green, A. R., 41, 44, *57*
Green, T., 291, *305*
Greendwood, G., *228*
Greene, L., *249*
Greenland, S., *227*
Greenwell, L., 201, *210*
Grey, D., *209*
Griffith, J. L., 37, *38*
Griffith, M. E., 37, *38*
Grinstead, O., 296, *305, 306*
Grodin, M. A., 62, *72*
Groseclose, S. L., *30*
Gross, E., *249*
Gross, M., 215, *227*
Grossman, A. H., 256, *268*
Grossman, N., 296, *306*
Grube, B. A., 89, *101*

Gruber, V. A., 107, *120*
Grubman, S., 234, *249*
Grushkin, S., 62, *72*
Guilamo-Ramos, V., 300, *306, 307*
Guimarães, M. D. C., 24, *29*
Gupta, G., 218, *227*
Gupta, G. R., 300, *306*
Gushue, G. V., 89, *100*

H

Haddock, S. A., 220, *227*
Hader, S. L., 272, *286*
Hall, H. I., 6, 7, 15, *29*, 66, *72*, 183, *195*, 268, 272, 280, *286*, 291–293, *305, 306*
Hall, N., 105, *120*
Halpenny, R., 190, *195*
Halperin, D. T., 215, *229*, 303, *308*
Hamilton, B. E., 292, *306*
Hamilton, M. M., 107, *120*
Hammer, S. M., *194*
Hankins, C., *30*
Hansen, N. B., *269*
Hanson, D. L., 117, *119*
Hanson, I. C., *28*
Harawa, N., *227*
Hardin, J. W., *210*
Hardy, M., 235, *249*
Hargrove, J., *30*
Harrington, C., 311, *325*
Harris, C., 4, *29*
Harris, G. E., 219, *227*
Harris, P. B., *268*
Hart, G., 219, *226*
Hart, T., 228, 272, *286*
Hart, T. A., 191, *194*
Hartel, D., *269*
Hartwick, J., 273, *288*
Harvey, D., 176, *181*
Hasenfeld, Y., 147, 150, *157*
Haug, N. A., 107, *120*
Hauser, E., 241, *249*
Havens, J., 235–237, 242, *249, 250, 252*
Havens, J. F., *210*
Havens, J. R., *229*
Hay, L., *142*
Hays, R., 236, *249*
Hays, R. B., 217, *227*

Hays, R. D., 111, *120, 209*
Hayslip, B., 264, *268*
Heagerty, P., *229*
Heagerty, P. J., *194*
Heald, A. E., *269*
Health Federation of Philadelphia, 142
Health Resources and Services Administration, Department of Health and Human Services, HIV/AIDS Bureau, 78, *88*
Health Resources and Sevice Administration, 46, *57*
Hecht, F. M., *28*
Hecht, R., 191, *196*
Heckathorn, D., 294, *307*
Heckert, A. L., 294, *305*
Heilman, N., 235, *252*
Heimer, R., 23, *29*
Heineman, A., 111, *120*
Heise, L. L., 282, *286*
Henne, J., 213, *226*, 294, *305*
Herbst, J., *229*
Herbst, J. H., *195*, 217, *227, 287*, 300, *306*
Herek, G. M., 91, *100*, 145, *157*, 185, *195*, 203, *209*, 212, 213, *227*
Hergenrather, K. C., 144, 156, *157*
Herman, B. A., *28*
Herman, D., *325*
Herman, W. A., *28*
Hernandez, M., *249*
Hernandez, M. G., 316, *325*
Hernando, V., *28, 194*
Hersh, S., 241, *252*
Hertz-Picciotto, I., 66, *72*
Hess, K. L., *286*
Hicks, C., *268*
Higgins, J., 293, *306*
Hilgartner, M. W., *29*
Hill, J., 94, *100*
Hilliard, R., *249*
Hillier, S., 282, *286*
Hillman, J., 255, *268*
Hirsch, J. S., 293, *306*
HIV/AIDS Prevention Research Synthesis (PRS) Team, *306*
HIV/AIDS Surveillance Report, 283n.4, *286*
Hoetelmans, R. M. W., *29*

Hoff, C., 185, *195, 249*
Hoff, T., 238, *249*
Hoffman, D., 201, 204, *210*
Hogan, J. W., *30*
Hogben, M., 274, *285*
Holmbeck, G. N., 90, *101*
Holmberg, S. D., 272, *286*
Holmes, K. K., 186, *195, 286*
Holoviak, S. J., 277, *287*
Holte, S., *227*
Holtgrave, D., 215, *226*
Holzer, H. J., 278, *286*
Hoover, D. R., *286*
Hooyman, N. R., 256, 257, 262, 263, *268*
Hoppe, S., *251*
Horton, N. J., *325*
Horvath, K., 223, *225*
Houck, C. D., *287*
Howard, A. A., *30*
Howard, C., *250*
Howland, L., 235, *249*
Hoyo, C., 66, *72*
Hoyt, L., *249*
Hsu, H., *248*
Hu, X., *305*
Huang, Y., *227*
Huberman, A. M., 80, *88*
Hudgens, M. G., *194*
Hudges, E., *27*
Hudis, J., *251*
Hudson, A. L., 204, *209*
Hudson, S., 313, 314, 316–318, *324, 325*
Huebner, D., *308*
Huebner, D. M., 213, *227*
Huettner, S., *229*
Hugen, P. W. H., *29*
Hughes, M., 213, *226*, 248,
Human Rights Watch, 59, 67, *72*
Hunt, L., 43, *57*, 60, *72*
Husbands, W., 213, 216, 219, *225–227*
Husnik, M. J., *227, 285, 287*
Hutchinson, S. A., 203, *209*

I

Ife, J., 60, 64, 65, *72*
Indyk, D., 147, *157*, 188, *196*

Ingersoll, K. S., 262, *268*
Ingram, D., 203, *209*
Institute of Medicine, 67, *72*
Instone, S., 235, *249*
International AIDS Vaccine Initiative, 190, *195*
The International Perinatal HIV Group, 302, *306*
Isaacs, M., 34, *38*, 42, *57*
Isbell, M., 215, *229*
Itin, C., 243, 244, *249*

J

Jaccard, J., 300, *306*
Jack, D. C., 201, *209*
Jackson, E., *29*
Jackson, S., 44, *57*
Jacobson, K., 239, *251*
Jacobson, M., 162, *171*
Jaffe, H. W., 185, *195*, 280, *288*
Jaffe, L. R., 280, *286*
Jamison, D. T., 298, *306*
Janssen, R. S., 11, *29*
Jariwala, B., 23, *29*
Jemmott, J. B., *308*
Jemmott, L. S., *308*
Jensen, M., *247*
Jensen, R., *251*
Jerome, J., *210*
Jewell, N. P., 280, *287, 288*
Jimenez, A. D., 256, *268*
Johnson, B. T., 214, *228*, 284, *288*
Johnson, D., *227*
Johnson, G., *251*
Johnston, M. I., *195*
Joint United Nations Programme on HIV/AIDS (UNAIDS), 291, 297, *306*
Jones, D., 243, *249*
Jones, D. J., 318, *324*
Jones, D. L., 205, *209*
Jones, J. L., 66, *73*
Jones, S., 44, 46, *57*
Jones, T. S., *30*
Joslin, D., 203, *209*
Journal of the American Medical Association, 13
Joyner, M., *249*
Judson, F. N., *194*

Junge, B., 23, *30*

Junius, J., 174, *181*

Justice Resource Institute, JRI Health, 79, 81, *88*

K

Kachur, R., *227*

Kahindo, M., *27*

Kahl, P. A., *28*

Kai-Lih, L., *58*

Kaiser Daily, HIV/AIDS Report, 292, *306*

Kaiser Family Foundation, 67, 68, *72*, 117, *120*, *157*, 176, *181*, 199, *209*

Kakinami, L., 191, *195*, *196*

Kalichman, S. C., 134, *142*, 217, *228*

Kalish, L. A., *29*

Kaminski, P. L., 264, *268*

Kamya, H., 36, *38*

Kang, E., *57*, *250*

Kang, S. Y., 107, *120*, 293, *305*

Ka'opua, L. S., 45, 46, *57*, 109, *120*

Kaplan, A., 295, *305*

Kaplan, E. H., 23, *29*

Kaplan, S., 35, *38*

Karon, J. M., *308*

Karpiak, S. E., 257, 260–263, *268*

Kaslow, R. A., *286*

Kassab, C. D., 214, *228*

Kassler, W. J., *30*

Katz, A. D., 258, *266*

Kaufman, F., *250*

Kay, H., 204, *209*

Kay, L. S., *227*, *287*, *288*, *306*

Kazak, A., 241, *252*

Kazatchkine, M. D., 45, *57*

Kegeles, S. M., 217, *227*

Keigher, S. M., 255, *268*

Kelly, J. A., 217, *227*

Kemp, S. P., 300, *306*

Kendall, J., 159, 165, *171*

Kennedy, D., *209*

Kennedy, M., 255, *269*

Kerndt, P. R., *326*

Kernis, M., *324*

Kerr, T., 67, *72*

Khoshnood, K., 23, *29*

Kigozi, G., *194*

Kim, A. S., *287*

Kim, J., *57*

Kimber, J., 302, *306*

Kimerling, R., 202, *210*

King, S. M., 203, *208*

Kingsley, L. A., *286*

Kingson, E., 43, *58*

Kirby, D., 187, 193, *195*

Kirstein, L., *209*

Kiselev, P., *248*

Kitchen, C. R., *289*

Kitzinger, J., 43, *57*

Kiyak, H. A., 256, 257, 262, 263, *268*

Klausner, J., *227*

Klein, R., *269*

Klein, R. S., *29*, 255, *267*, *268*

Klimas, N., *28*

Knipples, H. M. A., 261, 262, *268*

Knodel, J., 264, *268*

Knowlton, A. R., 317, 318, *324*

Knussen, C., 213, *226*

Koblin, B. A., 214, *227*, *229*, 273, 285, *287*, *308*

Kochman, A., 203, *210*, *269*

Kocik, S., *248*

Koester, K., *72*

Kohli, R., 262, *268*

Konkle-Parker, D. J., 262, *268*

Korfhage, B. A., 212, *227*

Korkontzelou, C., *30*

Kosenko, K., *251*

Kotler, D. P., *209*

Kottiri, B. J., *286*

Kresina, T. F., *324*

Krieger, J. N., *194*

Kriss, J. L., 117, *121*

Kullgren, K., *247*

Kuo, I., 295, *306*

Kushel, M. B., 111, *120*

Kutzko, D., 147, *156*

L

Labes, K., *307*

Lagarde, E., *27*, *194*

LaLota, M., *308*

Lambe, C., 203, *210*

Land, H., 313, 314, 316–318, *324*, *325*

Lane, T. S., 35, *38*, 43, 44, *58*, 152, *157*

Lang, W., *196*

Lanier, B., *247*

Laresen, J., 243, 244, *248*

Laris, B., 187, 193, *195*

Larson, S., 35, *38*

La Sala, M. C., 294, *306*

Lashley, F., *250*, 262, *267*

Latino Commission on AIDS (LCA), 297, 303, *306*

Lauby, J., *58*

Laumann, E. O., *268*

Laurian, Y., 24, *29*

Lawler, W. R., 317, *325*

Lawson, E., 213, *226*

Lazzarin, A., *29*, 280, *287*

Leadbeater, B. J., 280, *286*

LeBlanc, A. J., 313, *325*

LeBlanc, Q. J., 314, *326*

Lee, D. Y., 277, *287*

Lee, F., 104, *120*

Lee, G., 104, *120*

Lee, K. A., 204, *209*

Lee, L., *307*

Lee, L. M., *29*, *72*, *195*, 272, *286*, *288*, *306*

Lee, L. W., 66, *72*

Lee, R. S., 203, *210*

Lee, S., 242, *249*, *250*, *251*

Lee, S.-J., *195*

Legislative Ethics in the HIV/SIDS Pandemic, 178, *181*

Leigh, B. C., 272, *287*

Leite, M. L. C., 24, *29*

Lennox, V., *251*

Leon, A. M., 153, *157*

Lerner-Weiss, N., *249*

Lert, F., 45, *57*

Lescano, C. M., 280, *287*

Leserman, J., 221, *227*

Lesser, M. L., *28*

Lester, P., 235, 237, *249*, ,*251*

Leu, C. S., *210*, *250*

Levensky, E. R., 108, *120*

Levine, C., 243, *249*

Levine, M. P., 4, *29*

Levine, R., 186, *195*

Levine, W. C., 293, *308*

Levinson, W., *268*

Levy, J., *247*

Levy, J. A., 13, *29*

Lewellen, D., 199, *210*

Lewis, M., 144, *156*

Lewis, S., 149, *157*

Lewis-Gary, M., 241, *249*

Lightfoot, M., 90, *100*

Lihatsh, T., *226*

Lima, R., *251*

Lin, Y., *269*

Lindau, S. T., 201, 204, *210*, 255, 257, *268*

Lindenberg, K., 89, *101*

Lindner, G., 203, *209*

Lindsey, J., *248*

Link, B., 117, *121*

Linley, L., 255, 257, *268*

Linsk, N. L., 188, *195*, 317, 321, *325*

Lipsky, L., 140, *142*

Lipson, M., 235, *249*

Littlewood, R. A., 114, *120*, 204, *210*

Lloyd-Smith, J. O., *30*

Lo, Y., *269*

Loeb, L., *226*

Loeb, T., *289*, 318, *326*

Loeb, T. B., 202, *210*, 282, *287*, *288*

Logie, C., *196*

Lombardi, E., 20, *30*

Longshore, D., *287*

Lopez, D., *58*

Lopez, R. A., *325*

Lorion, R., *247*

Losina, E., *269*

Lotstein, D., 239, *250*

Loutfy, M., 190, *195*

Lovaas, K. E., 90, *101*

Lowenstein, A., *269*

Lu, S. E., *269*, *326*

Lu, Y. E., 284, *287*

Lucas, K., *57*

Lum, D., 41, *57*, 284, *287*

Luna, G., 242, *250*

Lund, L., 220, *227*

Luo, W., *29*

Lusher, J. M., 16, *29*

Lydston, D., *209*

Lyles, C. M., 273, *287*, *306*

Lynch, D. A., *268*

Lynch, M., 201, *209*

Lyon, S. M., *325*

Lyons, M., 235, *252*

M

Maasen, T., 221, *227*

McAdoo, J. L., 319, *325*

Macalino, G., *308*

McCaskill, E. O., *210*

McCausland, J., 323, *325*

McCree, D. H., *210*

McDaniel, S., *247*

McFarland, W., *30*, *308*

McFarlane, M., 219, *227*

McFeaters, S., 243, 244, *249*

McGowan, J., *269*

McHugh, P. R., 261, *267*

McKay, T., *58*

MacKellar, D. A., 11, *29*, *308*

McKinnon, K., 296, *305*

McKirnan, D. J., 90, *101*

McKusick, L., 185, *195*, *249*

McLaughlin, M., *72*

Maclean, I., *194*

McNally, C. J., 221, *227*

McNally, T., *227*

McPherson, M., *250*

McPherson-Baker, S., *209*

McQuiston, C., 44, *58*

McSherry, G., *249*

Madden, T. J., 274, *287*

Madison, M., *227*

Madsen, W., 37, *38*

Magana, S. M., 315, 316, *325*

Magder, L., *250*

Maguire, C. P., 221, *227*

Mahajan, A. P., 203, *210*

Mahal, A., *227*, 300, *306*

Mahoney, E., 233, *250*

Maj, M., *307*

Majorana, A., *72*

Makumbi, F., *194*

Malee, K., *248*

Malm, K., *250*

Malone, N., 292, *306*

Mamo, L., 94, *100*

Mandela, N., *72*, *72*

Manes, C., 243, 244, *248*

Manhart, L. E., *286*

Mann, J. M., 62, *72*

Mapson, C., *248*

Marcus, A. C., *286*

Marhefka, S., 235, *252*

Marin, B., 213, *226*

Marín, B. V., 294, *305*, *306*

Marincovich, B., 28, *194*

Marino, S., 97, *100*

Markowitz, L. E., 190, *196*

Marks, G., 11, *29*, 191, *194*, *195*, *250*

Marks, P., *249*

Marquis, L., 280, *287*

Marrero, A., *307*

Marsh, K. L., 214, *228*

Marte, L. E. S., *307*

Martin, D. H., *286*

Martin, J., 215, *229*

Martin, J. A., 292, *306*

Martin, J. B., 90, *101*

Martin, J. N., *307*

Martin, N. B., 107, *120*

Martin, R. M., *269*

Martinez, J., *57*

Maruschak, L. M., 295, 296, *306*

Marx, P. A., 190, *194*

Mascola, L., *248*

Maselko, J., *307*

Mason, H., 235, *250*

Mason, S., 243, 244, *250*, 321, *325*

Massachusetts Department of Public Health, 78, *88*

Massaquoi, N., 186, *196*

Masten, A., 243, *250*

Mathew, A., *227*

Matiz Reyes, A., 300, *307*

Matos, T., *307*

Matte, C., *194*

Mattick, R. P., 302, *306*

Mattocks, K., *285*

Max, S., 159, 165, *171*

Maxwell, A. E., *286*

Maxwell, J., 216, *225*

May, R. M., 280, *285*

Mayberry, R., 42, *57*

Mayer, K. H., 220, *226*, *227*, *229*

Mayer, R., 204, *210*

Mayers, M. M., *28*

Mays, V. M., 213, *226*, *227*

Mazarei, M., *58*

Mazlan, M., 302, *308*

Meah, J. M., *268*

Measham, A. R., *306*

Meleis, A., 43, 47, *58*

Mellins, C., *247*

Mellins, C. A., 201, 204, *209, 210*, 235–237, 244, *247, 250, 252*

Meneses, S., *306*

Merriam-Webster, 104, *120*

Merrigan, G. M., 90, *101*

Merson, M., 217, *228*

Merson, M. H., 298, *306*

Messeri, P. A., 103, 104, 108, *120*

Metsch, L., *308*

Meyer, I. H., 117, *121*, 185, *195*

Meyer, P. A., 66, *73*

Microbicide Development Programme, 187, *195*

Mikhail, I., *210*

Miles, K., 239, *250*

Miles, M. B., 80, *88*

Miller, D., 34, *38*

Miller, K., *210*

Miller, W. R., 96, 97, *100, 101*

Miller-Martinez, D., 203, *210*, 316, *324*

Millett, G. A., 189, *195*, 215, *228*, 272, *287*

Mills, T. C., *228*

Miloslavich, K., *247*

Miner, M. H., *228*

Minkler, M., 264, *267*

Minkoff, H., *268*

Minority AIDS Prevention, 271, *287*

Miramontes, H., 204, *209*

Misdrahi, D., 237, *250*

Mizrahi, T., 144, *156, 157*

Mizuno, Y., *269*

Mofenson, L., *28, 249*

Mohan, K., *251*

Mohr, J., *30*

Moisi, D., *194*

Moll, B., *29*

Moneyham, I., 316, *324*

Moneyham, L., *209, 269*

Monk, E., *210*

Monsour, M., *29*

Montgomery, P., 23, *30*

Moore, J. S., 272, *286, 287*

Morales, E. S., 294, *305*

Morbidity and Mortality Weekly Report, 184, *195*, 215, *228*, 272, 279, *287*

Moreno, C., 44, 46, *58*

Moretti, S., *196*

Morin, S. F., 185, *195*

Morrow, K. M., 188, *195*

Morse, E., *324*

Morse, J. M., 114, *120*

Morson, G. S., 36, *38*

Moses, S., *194*

Moskowitz, J. T., 318, *324*

Moss, H., 236, *247, 250*

Mouren-Simeoni, M., *250*

Mowbray, N. D., 153, *157*

Moyers, T. R., 97, *100*

Mueller, C., 45, 46, *57*

Mueller, M., 94, *100*

Mugavero, M. J., 259, *268*

Mulkins, A., 114, *120*

Mullan, J., *226*

Mullan, J. T., 311, *325*

Mullen, P., *288*

Mullings, D., 144, *156*

Multicultural AIDS Coalition, *287*

Munet-Varo, F., 236, *250*

Muñoz, A., 24, *29*

Munro, I., 221, *228*

Murphy, D., 233, *250*, 316, *324*

Murphy, D. A., 201, 203, 204, *209–210*

Murphy, E. L., 20, *29*

Murray, J., 216, *225*

Murri, R., *27*

Murrill, C., *58, 308*

Musicco, M., 24, *29, 30*, 280, *287*

Mustanski, B., 294, *305*

Mutchler, M., 44, 45, *58*

Myers, H. F., 202, *209, 210*, 280, 282, *287, 289*

Myers, T., *226*

Nalugoda, F., *194*

Nanton, R., 319, *325*

Narciso, P., *27*

Nardi, P. M., 4, *29*

Nathanson, C. A., 293, *306*

National AIDS Strategy, 67, 73, *307*

National Association of Social Workers, 32, *38*, 61, *73*, 144, 157, 174, *181*, 301, *307*

National Center for Cultural Competence, 47, *58*

National Center for Health Statistics, 272, *287*

National Center for HIV, STD and TB Prevention, 78, *88*

National Gay and Lesbian Task Force Policy Institute, 221, *226*

National Institute of Allergy and Infectious Diseases (NIAID), 186, *195*

National Minority AIDS Council, *287, 307*

National Network for Social Work Managers, 145, *157*

National Research Council, *287*

Neaigus, A., *286*

Neff, J. A., 316, *325*

Negroni, M., *306*

Nehring, W., 235, *250*

Nelms, T. P., 323, *325*

Nelson, K., *226*

Nemeroff, C. J., 213, *227*

Nemoto, T., *58*

Nesoff, I., 146, *157*

Netting, F. E., *157*

Neumann, M., *288*

Neundorfer, M. M., 258, *268*

New, M., 235, 236, *250*

Newacheck, P., *250*

Newman, P. A., 184, 186, 188, 190, 191, 193, *195, 196*

Ng, M. T., 202, *210*

Ng, T., *58*

Ng, W., 236, 237, 242, *252*

Nicholas, S., *250*

Nichols, J., 256, 258, *268*

Nicolosi, A., 24, *29, 30*, 280, *287*

Nieuwkerk, P. T., 20, *29*

Nokes, K. M., 257, *268*

Northridge, M. E., 185, *195*

N

Nachman, S., *248*

Nakamura, G., 293, *307*

Nakashima, A. K., 272, *288*, 293, 294, *307*

Nakazono, T. T., *209, 210*

Noto, P., *27*

Nsengumuremyi, F., *27*

Ntemgwa, M., *194*

Nymanthi, A., 315, *324*

O

O'Connell, T. S., 256, *268*

Odem, S., *326*

Odo, R., 96, *100*

O'Donnell, C. R., *307*

O'Donnell, L., *307*

O'Donohue, W. T., 108, *120*

O'Driscoll, P., *250*

Ogden, J., *227*

Ogden, J. A., 300, *306*

Oinen, L., 243, *251*

Okie, S., 44, *58*

Oleske, J., *248,*

Oliveros, C., 315, *325*

O'Malley, J., 217, *228*, 298, *306*

O'Malley, P. M., *287*

O'Muircheartaigh, C. A., *268*

O'Neill, D., 296, *305*

Open Society Institute, 213, *228*

Operario, D., 23, *30*, 45, 46, *58*

Operskalski, E. A., *29*

Orel, N., 258, *267*

Orel, N. A., 258, *267, 268*

Organista, K. C., 292, 293, 300, 301, *307*

Ortiz, C., 317, *325*

Ortiz, D. J., *210*

Ortíz-Torres, B., 292, *307*

Osborne, A. H., 284, *286*

Osmond, D. H., *30*

O'Sullivan, M., *248*

Otten, R., *29*

P

Padian, N., 302, *307*

Padian, N. S., 14, *29*, 189, *196*, 280, *287, 288*

Padilla, M. B., 300, *307*

Page-Shafer, K., 15, *30*

Page-Shafer, K. A., *307*

Pahl, T., 278, *285*

Paikoff, R., 90, *101*

Painter, T. M., *229*

Pakenham, K. I., 323, *325*

Palacio, H., 111, *120*

Palmer, C., 243, 244, *248*

Pandrea, I., 190, *194*

Pao, M., 233–235, 237, 241, *250, 252*

Pappaioanou, M., *288*

Para, M. F., *29*

Pardasani, M., 43, 45, 46, *58*

Parfitt, T., 295, *307*

Park, K. W., 275, *289*

Parker, C. B., *194*

Parker, R., 203, 204, *210*

Parkhurst, J. O., 227, 300, *306*

Parks, W., *28*

Parsons, J., *248*

Parsons, J. T., *288*

Passin, W. F., 227, *287, 306*

Patel, R., *248*

Patel, V., *307*

Patel, V. A., *210*

Paterson, D. L., 20, *30*

Patterson, T. L., 214, *228*

Patti, R. J., 143, *157*

Paul, J. P., *228*

Paul, R., 261, 263, *269*

Paul, S. M., 259, *269*

Pearlin, L. I., 311, 313, *325*

Pegues, C. F., *326*

Pelcastre, B., *306*

Pequegnat, W., 236, 244, *250, 251*

Perea, M. A., *28*

Perez, B., *249*

Perlmutter, F. D., 147, 149, 151, 156, *157*

Perry, B., 139, 140, *142*

Peterman, T. A., 280, *288*

Peterson, J., 214, 215, *226, 228*, 272, *286*

Peterson, J. L., 213, *225, 229*, 272, *287*

Petr, C., 134, *142*

Peynet, J., 24, *29*

Phillips, M., *307*

Picciano, J. F., 217, *228*

Pinderhughes, E., 34, *38*, 41, *58*

Pinkerton, S. D., 14, 24, *30*

Pinzon, J., 239, *251*

Piot, P., xiii, *xvi*

Pirraglia, P. A., 313, *325*

Pitanguy, J., 282, *286*

Pitt, J., *28*

Pizzo, P., 235, 241, *247, 252*

Plach, S. K., 255, *268*

Poindexter, C. C., 35, *38*, 43, 44, 58, *93, 100*, 145, 146, 150, 152, 156, *157*, 203, *210*, 253, 264, *267, 269*, 312, *325*

Pollack, L., 185, *195, 249*

Pomeroy, E. C., 316, *325*

Pope, R., 35, *38*

Poppen, P. J., 212, *228*, 294, *308*

Population and Community Development Association, 187, *196*

Por, J., 239, *251*

Porco, T. C., 299, *307*

Porter, K., 8, *28*

Portillo, C. J., 204, *209*

Potocky, M., 44, *58*

Pounds, M. B., 104, *119*

Prejean, J., *29*, 72, *195, 286, 306*

Preston, D. B., 214, *228*

Prince, M., *307*

Prins, M., 89, *101*

Prochaska, J. O., 83, *88*

Proctor, E. K., 298, *307*

Pryor, J. B., 204, *210*

Ptacek, J. T., 153, *156*

Public Health Service Taskforce, 302, *307*

Purcell, D. W., 117, *120*

Puren, A., *27, 194*

Q

Qari, S., *29*

Quay, L., *229*

R

Rabb, L., 319, *325*

Rabkin, J. G., *209*

Rakusan, T., *248*

Ramirez-Garcia, J. I., 316, *325*

Ramirez-Valles, J., 212, 213, *228*, 294, *307*

Ramos, D., *251*

Ramundo, M., 147, *156*

Randall, L. M., 35, *38*

Rangel, M., 293, 294, *307*
Rao, D., 204, *210*
Raphael, S., 278, *286*
Rappaport, J., 35, *38*
Razzano, L. A., 107, *120*
Redgrave, G., 318, *325*
Reed, B., *195*
Reed, B. G., 162, *171*
Reed, C., 293, *307*
Reichert, E., 34, *39*, 60, 61, 65, *73*
Reid, P. N., 31, *39*
Reidel, M., *251*
Reisch, M., 32, *39*
Reisen, C. A., 212, *228*, 294, *308*
Reiss, J., 239, *251*
Remien, R. H., *210*
Retta, S. M., *28*
Reyes, A. M., *307*
Reyes, J., *307*
Rhodes, P., 6, *29*, *72*, *195*, *286*, 291, *305*, *306*
Rhodes, S., 219, *228*
Rhodes, S. D., 144, 156, *157*
Rhodes, T., 292, *307*
Richards, A., *250*
Richardson, J., *250*
Richter, L., *226*, 299, *305*
Ricketts, E. P., *229*
Riekert, K., 233, 236, *251*, *252*
Rier, D. A., 147, *157*, 188, *196*
Riley, M. W., 253, *269*
Rimland, D., 260, *268*
Rinaldi, J. E., *28*
Rintamaki, L., 240, *251*
Rintamaki, L. S., 188, *196*, 259, *269*
Rios, V. M., 296, *307*
Robbins, C., 144, *156*
Robbins, R. N., 296, *305*
Roberts, J., *227*
Roberts, K., 191, *196*
Roberts, K. J., 191, *195*, *196*, 204, *210*
Robles, A. M., 184, *196*
Robles, R., *307*
Robles, R. R., 293, *305*
Roca, E., 191, *196*
Rodriguez, C., *194*
Rodriguez, R. A., 294, *305*
Rodriguez-Gomez, J. R., 114, *120*

Roffman, R. A., 217, *228*
Roger, M., *194*
Rogers, A., 232, 233, *251*
Rogers, M. F., *28*
Rogol, A., *248*
Roland, E., *227*
Rolfs, R. T., *30*
Rolleri, L., 187, 193, *195*
Rollnick, S., 96, 97, *100*, *101*
Romaguera, R. A., *305*
Romanoski, A., 318, *325*
Rompalo, A. M., *30*
Rosen, A., 298, *307*
Rosen, D., 240, *251*
Rosen, D. H., *308*
Rosen, D. L., 295, *308*
Rosenberg, P., 232, *251*
Ross, M. W., 217, *228*
Rosser, B. R. S., 214, 217, *228*
Rotheram-Borus, M., 242, 249–251
Rotheram-Borus, M. J., 90, *100*, 184, *196*
Rothman, J., 162, *171*
Routh, D., *249*
Routy, J. P., *194*
Rowe, W., 42–44, 46, *58*
Ruby, W., *308*
Rudy, E., 191, *195*
Rudy, E. T., 188, 191, *195*, *196*
Ruiz, M., 188, *195*, *250*
Ruiz, M. S., 296, *305*
Russell, M., 220, *225*
Rutenberg, N., *27*
Rutherford, *72*
Rutherford, G. W., *287*
Rutledge, S. E., 217, *228*
Ryan, C., 235, *247*, 294, *308*
Ryan, G., *209*
Ryder, C., 233, 234, 239–241, *252*,

S

Saah, A. J., *286*
Sabatino, J., *226*
Sabol, W. J., 296, *308*
Sacks, H. S., *268*
Sacktor, N., 261, *269*
Safren, S. A., 220, *226*

Sahai, H., *307*
Salas-Serrano, C. C., 114, *120*
Salomon, L., 220, *226*
Saltzman, B. R., *28*
Samet, J. H., 319, *325*
Samuel, M., *196*, 272, *288*
Sanchez, J., 294, *305*, *308*
Sandelowski, M., 203, *210*
Sanders, L., *269*
Sandfort, T., 45, *58*
San Doval, A., *307*
Sandoval, M., *286*
Santos, C., 233, *251*
Saracco, A., 24, *30*, 280, *287*
Sarr, M., *250*
Satcher, D., 67, *73*
Sawires, S. R., *210*
Saxena, S., *307*
Sayles, J. N., *210*
Scal, P., *251*
Schable, B., 255, *269*
Schackman, B. R., 262, *269*
Scharko, A., 234, *251*
Scheid, T. L., 107, *120*
Schiller, N., 199, *210*
Schmader, K. E., *269*
Schneider, J. W., 160, *171*
Schoen, C., 117, *121*
Schoenbach, V. J., 295, *308*
Schoenbaum, E. E., 262, *268*, *269*
Scholder, P., 274, *287*
Schottenfeld, R. S., 302, *308*
Schulman, L., *142*
Schuman, P., *30*
Schumm, L. P., *268*
Schüssler-Fiorenza, E., 36, *39*
Schustack, A., 45, *58*
Schwartz, K., *247*
Scott, A., *251*
Scott, G. B., *28*, *248*
Scott-Sheldon, L. A. J., 214, *228*
Seage, G., *248*
Seage, G. R., *194*, *248*
Seals, B., *209*, *269*, 316, *324*
Secura, G. M., *29*
Seehaus, M., 280, *286*
Segurado, A., *251*
Seibel, N., *248*
Seiden, D., 191, *195*, *196*
Self, S. G., *194*

Selik, R. M., *288*

Semaan, S., 273, *288*

Semple, S. J., 214, *228*

Sentencing Project, 295, *308*

The Sentencing Project, 277, *288*

Senterfitt, J. W., 11, *29*

Septimus, A., 242, *252*

Serovich, J., 261, *269*

Serrano-García, I., 292, *307*

Serufilira, A., *27*

Serwadda, D., 189, *194*, *196*, 217, *228*, 298, 302, *306*, *307*

Shah, S., 260, *269*

Shapiro, M. F., *210*

Sharland, M., *248*

Sharpe, T. T., 272, *288*

Shea & Co, 218, *228*

Shehan, D., *308*

Sheon, N., *226*

Sheppard, B. H., 273, *288*

Sherman, B., 235, *251*

Shernoff, M., *xvi*

Sherr, L., 274, *285*

Sherzer, R., *57*

Shiboski, C. H., *30*

Shiboski, S. C., 14, *29*, *30*, 280, *287*, *288*

Shikuma, C., *269*

Shippy, R. A., 257, 260–263, *268*

Shiramizu, B., *269*

Shoptaw, S., 185, *194*

Shouse, L., *226*

Shulman, L., 93, *101*, 127, *142*

Shultz, J., *248*

Sidney, S., *57*

Sifakis, F., 294, *308*

Sigelman, C., 235, *252*

Sikkema, K. J., 203, *210*, 263, *269*

Sikkeman, K. J., *142*

Silver, E., 242, 243, *251*

Silverman, P., 244, *251*

Simon, P., *324*

Simoni, J. M., 202, *210*, *250*

Sims, C., 212, 213, *227*

Sinclair, J., *324*

Singer, M., *307*

Sitta, R., *27*, *194*

Skinner, M., *56*

Skripkauskas, S., 188, *196*, *269*

Slutsker, L., 5, *28*

Small, C. B., *29*

Smit, C., 89, *101*

Smith, C., *269*

Smith, D. K., 272, *286*

Smith, J., *247*

Smith, R., *250*

Smoyer, A. B., *285*

Sobngwi-Tambekou, J., *27*, *194*

Sogolow, E., *288*

Solomon, A. L., 278, *288*

Somerville, G., 44, 46, *58*

Somlai, A., *142*

Song, R., *29*, *72*, *195*, 280, *286*, *306*

Sontag, D., 117, *121*

Soons, K. R., 147, *156*

Sorensen, J. L., 107, *120*

Soriano, M. A., *307*

Sorvillo, F., *326*

Southwell, H., *57*

Sowell, R., *209*, 262, *269*, 316, *324*

Spaulding, A., 295, *308*

Specht, H., 32, *39*

Special Investigations Division, Minority Staff of the Committee on Government Reform, 186, 187, *196*

Speer, D. C., *268*

Sperling, R., *248*

Spiegel, D., 244, *247*

Spino, C., *249*

Sprangers, M. A. G., *29*

Squier, C., *30*

St. Lawrence, J. S., 217, *227*

Stainton, T., 34, *39*

Stall, R., 213, 215, *226*, *228*, 272, *287*

Stanley, K., *251*

Starks, M. T., 214, *228*

Stein, J., 242, 243, *251*,

Steiner, G., *247*

Stephenson, B., *308*

Sternberg, M. R., 190, *196*

Stetz, K. M., 323, *325*

Stevens, P. E., 204, 206, 208, *209*, 255, *268*

Stevenson, L. Y., 217, *227*

Stewart, Patricia A., 130, 132

Stiefel, B., 314, *325*

Stimson, G. V., 295, *304*

Stirrat, M. J., 107, 117, *121*

Stokes, J. P., 213, *229*

Stoll, M. A., 278, *286*

Stone, E., 215, *229*

Stone, V. E., 20, *30*

Stoneburner, R. L., 280, *288*

Stoner, B. P., *286*

Stover, J., 191, *196*

Strathdee, S. A., 216, *229*, 295, *306*, *307*

Straub, E., *248*

Strickland, B., *250*

Stringer, H. G., 184, *196*

Strom-Gottfried, K., 153, *157*

Strouse, D., *288*

Strug, D., 319, 320, *325*

Strug, D. L., 89, *101*

Stuber, J., 117, 118, *121*

Sullivan, A., 6, *30*

Sullivan, P. S., 212, *229*

SUMIT Study Group, *288*

Swanson, M., *28*

Swartz, A., 318, *325*

Swendeman, D., 191, *195*, *196*

Swindells, S., *30*

Syed, J., *58*

T

Taege, A., *247*

Talamantes, M. A., 317, *325*

Taljaard, D., *27*, *194*

Tardieu, M., *248*, *250*

Targersen, C. S., *325*

Taveras, S., 46, *58*

Taylor-Akutagawa, V. E., 258, *269*

Taylor-Brown, S., 43, 44, *58*, 243, 244, *247*, *249*, *251*

Teeter, J. A., 243, *251*

Terio, S., 35, *38*

Teshale, E., 117, *119*

Tevendale, H., 90, *100*

Tharao, W., 213, *226*

Thomas, P., *248*

Thompson, B., 174, *181*, *306*

Thompson, H., 66, *73*

Thompson, J., 215, *229*

Thompson-Fullilove, M., 273, 274, *288*

Tice, J., *27*

Tien, P., *57*

Timmons, J. C., 156, *157*

Tisdall, K., 204, *209*

Titti, F., 190, *196*

Tobin, J. N., *209*

Tolou Shams, M., 90, *101*

Tomaszewski, E., 174, *181*

Tomaszewski, E. P., 109, *120*

Torres-Burgos, N., 292, *307*

Tracy, E. M., 300, *306*

Traphagen, E. T., *325*

Travis, J., 278, *288*

Trenholm, C., 213, *229*

Trimble, D., 36, *38*

Tripiciano, A., *196*

Trisvan, E. T., *325*

Trotta, M. P., *27*

Tschann, J., *57*

Tynan, M. A., 258, *266*

U

Udry, J. R., 275, *288*

Umme, W., *287*

UNAIDS, 7, 63, 68, 71, 73, 183, 199, *210*, 231, 241, *251*. *See also* Joint United Nations Programme on HIV/AIDS

UNAIDS/UNIFEM, 35, *39*

UNAIDS/WHO, *196*

Underhill, K., 23, *30*

United Nations, 60–64, 66, 68, *73*

U.S. Census Bureau, 296, *308*

U.S. Department of Health and Human Services, Health Resources and Services Administration, *157*

U.S. Department of Health and Human Services, Health Resources and Services Administration HIV/AIDS Bureau, 204, *210*

University of California, San Francisco, 256, *269*

V

Valcour, V. G., 261, 263, *269*

Valdiserri, R. O., 185, *195*, 293, *308*

Valescu, S., 316, *325*

Vallarruel, A. M., *308*

Vallee, C. M., *268*

Valleroy, L. A., 23, *29*, *30*, 272, *288*, 294, *305*, *308*

Vanable, P. A., 204, *210*

Vance, D. E., 263, *269*

Van de Perre, P., *27*

Van Dyke, R., 233, *251*

VanOss-Martin, B., 44, 46, *58*

Van Roey, J., 152, *157*

van Servellen, G., 20, *30*

Van Sluytman, L., *58*

Vargas, C. J., *287*

Vassil, T. V., 123, *142*

Vazquez, E., *247*

Venable, P. A., 114, *120*

Ventura, S. J., 292, *306*

Vergis, E. N., *30*

Vergon, T. L., *268*

Verroust, F., 24, *29*

Vila, G., *250*

Villa, D. P., 221, *229*

Vinh-Thomas, P., 43, *58*

Vittinghoff, E., 14, *29*, *194*, *229*

Vlahov, D., 23, *30*

W

Wagenhals, D., 124, *142*

Wagner, C., 280, *286*

Wagner, J., 258, *268*

Wainberg, M. A., 188, *196*

Waite, L. J., *268*

Walensky, R. P., *269*

Walker, L., 239, *251*

Wallace, J., 204, *209*

Wallace, R., 273, 274, *288*

Ward, J. W., 5, *28*

Wardlaw, L., 311, *325*

Warner, S., 317, *325*

Warshaw, P. R., 273, *288*

Washington State Department of Health, 108, *121*

Wasserheit, J. N., 272, *286*

Waterman, N., 278, *288*

Watson, B. J., *268*

Watson, M. R., *268*

Watters, M., *269*

Watya, S., *194*

Waul, M., 278, *288*

Weaver, M., 186, *195*

Wedderburn, L., 243, *251*

Weidle, P., 117, *120*

Weil, M., 162, *171*

Weingarten, K., 36, 37, *39*

Weinhardt, L. S., 284, *288*

Weinmeyer, R., 214, *228*

Weinstein, B., *30*

Weiss, J. J., *268*

Weiss, R., *250*

Welch, L. A., 201, *209*

Weller, S., 24, *30*, 186, *196*

Wellons, M. F., 259, *269*

Wells, L. M., 203, *208*

Werth, J. L., Jr., 221, *227*

West, W., 214, *228*

Westra, H. A., 97, *100*

Whalley, P., *249*

Wheeler, D., 45, *58*, 221, *229*

Wheeler, D. P., 103, *121*

Wheeler, J., *229*

Whitaker, A., *249*

White, J. J., 144, *156*

White, M., 36, 37, *38*, *39*

White, R. G., 14, *28*

White-Gray, M., *247*

Whittaker, J. K., 300, *306*

Widaman, K. F., 91, *100*

Wiener, L., 233–242, *247*, *250–252*

Wight, R. G., 203, *210*

Wight, R. G., 313, 314, 316, *324–326*

Wiley, J. A., *196*

Wilkie, F. L., *268*

Williams, B. G., 14, *30*

Williams, C., 191, *196*

Williams, C. C., 186, *196*

Williams, D. R., 273, 274, *289*

Williams, J., 318, *326*

Williams, J. K., 280, 282, *289*

Williams, M., 216, *229*

Williams, M. L., 217, 223, *225*, *228*

Williamson, J., *228*

Williamson, L., 219, *226*

Wilson, C., 248, *250*, 315, *324*

Wilson, D., 215, *229*, 303, *308*

Wilson, D. P., 188, *196*

Wilson, P., 215, 221, *229*
Wilton, L., 221, *229*
Wimpfheimer, S., 146, *158*
Wingood, G. M., 186, *196*, 204, *210*
Winkelstein, W., Jr., 185, *196*, 272, *288*
Winston, C., 244, *252*
Wissow, L., *249*
Wiznia, A., *251*
Wodi, A., *248*
Wohl, A. R., 318, *326*
Wohl, D. A., 295, *308*
Wolf, M. S., 188, *196*, *269*
Wolfe, M. I., 293, *307*
Wolitski, R., 215, *228*
Wolitski, R. J., 212, *229*, 272, 273, *287*, *288*, 293, *308*
Wolters, P., 233, 237, *250*, *252*

Wong, M., 111, *120*
Wood, E., 67, *72*
Wood, L., 233, 238, 239, *252*,
Woods, W. J., *226*
The World Almanac, 276, *288*
World Health Organization, 189, *196*
Wright, J. M., 258, *268*
Wright, K., 215, *229*
Wu, E., 94, *100*
Wuenschel, P. C., 143, 156, *158*
Wyatt, G., 318, *326*
Wyatt, G. E., 202, *209*, *210*, 280–282, *287*, *288*, *289*

X

Xu, F., 190, *196*

Y

Yager, T., 215, *229*
Yalom, I., 124, *142*
Yan, K. X., *286*
Yancey, E., 42, *57*
Yep, G. A., 90, *101*
Yoshioka, M. R., 45, *58*

Z

Zablotsky, D., 255, *269*
Zack, B., 296, *305*, *306*
Zak, P. J., 275, *289*
Zambrana, R., 44, 46, *58*
Zamudio, A., 213, *227*
Zea, M. C., 212, *228*, 294, *308*
Zierler, S., 202, *210*
Zobel, M., 234, 239–241, *252*

Subject Index

A

AAC (AIDS Action Committee), 180

AARP (American Association of Retired Persons), 323

Abstinence, 22, 66, 95, 174, 213

ACRIA (AIDS Community Research Initiative of America), 258

Activism, 328

ACT UP, *see* AIDS Coalition to Unleash Power

Acuity, 111–112

Acute infection, 9–10

Acute retroviral syndrome (ARS), 10

ADAP, *see* AIDS Drug Assistance Program

Adherence counseling, 107–108

Adolescents, *see* Children and adolescents

Adult family homes, 113

Advocacy:
  in case management, 80
  family-centered, 244–245
  for gay, bisexual, and other MSM, 221–224
  grassroots, 160–165
  for health care access, 67
  legislative, *see* Legislative advocacy
  for prevention, 192

African American/black -communities, 271–284
  caregivers in, 317–319
  health care access in, 202
  and incarceration, 276–278

incidence rates in, 7, 42, 144, 244, 272, 279–280

men who have sex with men in, 215, 272–274, 278

older persons in, 255

prevention for, 184, 273–274, 280–283

risk factors for, 44

and social structure, 274–276

women in, 200, 279–282

Ageism, 256, 263

AIDS Action Committee (AAC), 180

AIDS Coalition to Unleash Power (ACT UP), 4–5, 160

AIDS Community Research Initiative of America (ACRIA), 258

AIDS Drug Assistance Program (ADAP), 68, 89, 117

AIDS Law Project of Pennsylvania, 136

AIDS Project Los Angeles (APLA), 4

AIDS service organizations (ASOs), 143–156
  distinct features of, 145
  ethical guidelines of, 178
  flexibility and creativity in, 153–154
  funding for, 149–151
  leadership in, 146
  managing staff in, 151–153
  and working with other organizations, 147–149

Alcohol use, 318–319

Alternative medicine, 46, 114

American Academy of Pediatrics, 235

American Association of Retired Persons (AARP), 323

Americans with Disabilities Act, 179

AmfAR, 301

Ancillary services, 104–105

Antibody testing, 11

Antiretroviral treatment (ART), 10, 17–20, 68, 231

Anxiety, 234, 239

APLA (AIDS Project Los Angeles), 4

ARS (acute retroviral syndrome), 10

ART, *see* Antiretroviral treatment

Art, 127

Asian American communities, 45

ASOs, *see* AIDS service organizations

Assessments, 53–54
  in prevention case management, 78
  psychosocial, 236–238

Assisted living facilities, 113

Assumptions campaign, 218

Asymptomatic stage, 10

Attention-deficit/hyperactivity disorder, 234

B

Becoming Trauma Stewards (L. Lipsky), 140

Behavioral interventions, 299–300

Biomedical interventions, 301–302

Biopsychosocial model, 79

Birthright principle, 60

347

Bisexual men, *see* Gay, bisexual, and other men who have sex with men
Black AIDS Institute, 221
Black communities, *see* African American/black communities
Blood transmission, 15
Boarder baby phenomenon, 199
Bone loss, 19
Boyd-Franklin, N., 136
Breast-feeding, 232

C

Cabbages & Condoms, 187
CAM (complementary and -alternative medicine), 114
Canada, 220
Cantor, M. H., 263
Caregivers, 311–324
   and children/adolescents, 244, 264
   gay men as, 313–314
   grandparents/older relatives as, 320–321
   importance of, 312–313
   male primary, 319–320
   women as, 315–319
Care providers, 43
Case load management, 83
Case management, 77–88
   attitudes of managers in, 84–85
   elements of, 80–82
   prevention case management, 78–79
   skills of managers in, 82–84
CD4 counts, 5–6
   for diagnosis, 8–9
   in older adults, 259
CDC, *see* Centers for Disease Control and Prevention
Centers for Disease Control and Prevention (CDC), 4, 6, 15, 66, 183, 199, 200, 212, 244, 254, 257, 274, 282, 283, 291,292
Central nervous system (CNS) disease, 233
Children and adolescents, 231–247
   end-of-life support for, 241

and family interventions, 242–245
means of transmission to, 199, 232–233
medical treatment for, 233
mental health services for, 241–242
and mothers with HIV, 201–202
and multiple losses, 234
out-of-home placement for, 134–135
parental disclosure of diagnosis to, 234–236
psychology stress of, 234
psychosocial assessment of, 236–238
safer sex education for, 238–239
and stigma, 204
and transition to adult services, 239–241
Cholesterol, 19
Circumcision, 14, 189–190
Civil society, 174
Clinics, 109, 111–112
CNS (central nervous system) disease, 233
Code of Ethics (NASW), 32, 33
Cognitive behavioral counseling, 217
Cognitive organization, 124–125
Combination prevention, 186–191
Combination therapy, 6, 17–18, 314
Communication:
   in case management, 83
   and cultural competence, 48, 50–52
Communities, 52–53, 55
Community advisory panels, 161
Community organizing, 159–171
   conceptual foundation for, 162–164
   and medicalization of HIV, 160–162
   syringe-exchange program case study, 164–170
Community practice, 162
Community projects, 150
Compassion, 36, 140
Complementary and alternative medicine (CAM), 114
Conceptual model for cultural competence, 47–53

Condoms:
   prevention with use of, 23–25, 186–187, 193
   usage by MSM, 215–216
   usage in Latino communities, 300
   and women, 281–282
Condom Country campaign, 218
Confianza, 296
Confidentiality, 54, 95, 176, 246
Connecticut, 23
Consequence theory, 261
Consistency, 82
Co-occurring disorders, 96–98
Cooperman, N. A., 255
Counseling. *See also* Crisis intervention and counseling
   adherence, 107–108
   in case management, 82
   cognitive behavioral, 217
   prevention, 90–91
   in prevention case management, 78
   risk-reduction, 108–109
Countertransference, 140
Creativity, 153–154
Crisis intervention and counseling, 89–100
   and medical status, 94
   for mental illness, 96–98
   prevention counseling, 90–91
   and sexuality, 95–96
   and social consequences of HIV, 94–95
   and testing, 91–93
Critical consciousness, 35
Cross-resistance, 20
Crystal methamphetamine, 214
Cultural competence, 41–56
   in case management, 83
   defined, 41–42
   frameworks of, 46–53
   in group work/family support, 141
   in health care settings, 114
   and practitioners, 53–55
   in prevention and treatment, 42–43
   as principle of helping, 34
   research on, 43–46
Custody planning, 244

D

Death, 144
  and hospice, 112
  of staff members, 152–153
DEBIs (diffusion of effective
    behavioral interventions),
    271–272
Declaration of Commitment on
    HIV/AIDS, 62–63
Dementia, 261
Denver Principles statement, 63,
    87–88
Depression:
  in adolescents, 233, 234
  as medication side effect, 19
  in older adults with HIV,
    260, 261
  in women with HIV, 203
Detroit City Council, 164–169
Diabetes, 19
Diffusion of effective behavioral
    interventions (DEBIs),
    271–272
Dignity, 33, 64–65
Disclosure of diagnosis:
  to children and adolescents,
    234–236
  to family, 135
  by MSM, 220
  by older adults, 261
  to sexual partners, 239
  and stigma, 204
  timing of, 94
Discrimination, 62
  in health care settings, 117–118
  and human rights, 34
  and legal rights, 95
  toward women with HIV,
    203–204
Diversity, 43, 254–257
Donations, 154
"Down-low" phenomenon,
    44, 94
Drug trafficking, 295
Drug users, injection, see Injection
    drug users

E

Education:
  about adherence, 108

about rights, 65
  importance of, 138–139
  in legislative advocacy, 175
  public education campaigns, 218
Elizabethan Poor Law, 31–32
Empathy, 105
Employment, 221
Empowerment, 35
  and cultural competence, 44,
    46, 50
  of gay men, 314
  in human rights framework,
    65–66
  peer, 241
  of women with HIV, 206
End-of-life care, 118, 119, 241
Enthusiasm, 125
Enzyme immunoassay tests, 11
Ethic of care, 37
Ethnicity:
  and health care disparities,
    175–176, 202
  of older adults with HIV,
    255–256
  and prevention, 184
Evaluation, 52
Evidence-based prevention,
    66–67, 282, 298–302
EXPLORE interventions, 273

F

Faith-based initiatives, 206
Family:
  and cultural competence,
    50–51, 54
  and women with HIV, 205
Family Center, 242
Family-centered advocacy,
    244–245
Family interventions, 242–245
Family retreats, 243
Family support, 134–138
Family Unity, 243
Fat redistribution, 19
Federal legislative government, 176
Female condoms, 24, 281
First-tier rights, 60
Flexibility, 153–154
Follow-up care, 81–82
Funding:

for AIDS service organizations,
    145, 149–151
  and medicalization, 160

G

Gay, bisexual, and other men who
    have sex with men (MSM),
    12–13, 211–225
  advocacy for, 221–224
  in African American/black com-
    munities, 272–274, 278
  as caregivers, 313–314
  and cultural competence, 45
  and down-low phenomenon,
    9, 44
  and emergence of HIV, 4
  incidence rates of, 42, 144
  in Latino communities,
    293–295
  levels of risk for, 6–7, 212–215
  prevention for, 185, 215–218
  service provision for, 218–221
Gay, Lesbian and Straight
    Education Network
    (GLSEN), 294
Gay Men's Health Crisis
    (GMHC), 4, 146
Gender, 255. See also Women
GLSEN (Gay, Lesbian and Straight
    Education Network), 294
GMHC, see Gay Men's Health
    Crisis
Government funding, 149, 165, 176
Grandparents, 320–321
Grassroots advocacy, 160–165.
    See also Community
    organizing
"Greater Involvement of
    People Living with AIDS"
    (GIPA), 63
Grief, 153
Group work, 123–134
  advantages of, 124
  history of, 123
  men's groups, 129–134
  women's groups, 126–129

H

HAART, see Highly active antiret-
    roviral therapy

Harm reduction, 96–97

HCSUS (HIV Costs and Services Utilization Study), 203

Health care access, 62
  challenges in, 115–117
  and crisis intervention, 92
  as human right, 61–62
  and Latino communities, 293
  universal, 67–68
  and vaccinations, 191

Health care system and settings, 103–119
  ancillary services in, 104–105
  availability of services in, 53
  challenges in, 115–118
  cultural considerations for, 114–115
  end-of-life care in, 118, 119
  role of social worker in, 105–109
  setting types, 109–114

Health Federation of Philadelphia, 126, 134

Health Resources and Services Administration (HRSA), 46, 271

Hemophilia, 232

Heterosexual transmission, 6, 12–13, 42
  in black/African American communities, 279–280
  in Latino communities, 44
  and women, 200

Highly active antiretroviral therapy (HAART):
  adherence to, 107, 201
  and death, 112
  and dementia, 261
  and depression, 203
  and evidence-based practice, 299
  and home health, 314
  introduction of, 89

HIV, 3–27. See also specific headings
  biological aspects of, 7–11
  emergence of, 4–6
  prevention of, 22–26
  statistics on, 6–7
  strains of, 7–8
  testing for, 11–12
  transmission of, 12–16

treatment of, 16–22

HIV/AIDS Prevention Research Synthesis (PRS), 273

HIV Costs and Services Utilization Study (HCSUS), 203

Home health, 112, 314

Homophobia, 4, 212–213, 219, 256, 294, 301

Homosexuality, 49, 50

Honesty, 84

Hope, 36

HOPWA (Housing Opportunities for Persons with AIDS), 179

Hospice, 112–113

Hospitals, 113–114, 117

Housing Opportunities for Persons with AIDS (HOPWA), 179

HRSA (Health Resources and Services Administration), 46, 271

Human relationships, 33

Human rights framework, 33–34, 59–72
  components of, 64–66
  in evidence-based practice, 301
  history of, 59–60
  HIV practice/policy in, 62–64
  medical care in, 67–68
  testing/prevention in, 66–67

I

IDUs, see Injection drug users

Illegal activities, 54

Immigrants, 292–293

Immigration, 117

Immune system, 8

Incarceration:
  and African American/black communities, 276–278
  and Latino communities, 295–296
  and prevention efforts, 44

Indirectness, 124

Information provision, 81

Injection drug users (IDUs):
  in black/African American communities, 318
  and cultural competence, 45
  as high risk population, 6
  incidence rates of, 42

in Latino communities, 295

and prevention, 23

syringe-exchange program case study, 164–170

transmission amongst, 12–13, 15

and women, 200

Insight, 106–107

Insurance, 117

Insurance Continuation Program, 117

Integrity, 84

International AIDS Conference, 297

International Institute on Ageing, 253

Internet, 223

Intervention, crisis, see Crisis intervention and counseling

Interweaving community intervention model, 162

J

Joint Committee on Public Health, 180

Joint United Nations Programme on HIV/AIDS (UNAIDS), 7, 291, 297

Justice Resource Institute (JRI), 77, 79–85

K

Kaposi's sarcoma, 4

Kidney damage, 19

L

Laboratory analysis, 22

Lancet, 298

Language:
  as barrier to health care access, 202
  and cultural competence, 48, 50–52, 235–236

"La suerte" concept, 44

Late-stage disease, 10

Latino communities, 291–304
  caregivers in, 315–317
  evidence-based prevention and treatment for, 298–302

health care access in, 202
immigrants in, 292–293
and incarceration, 295–296
incidence rates in, 7, 42, 244,
    292–297
injection drug use in, 295
men who have sex with men in,
    293–295
older persons in, 255
prevention for, 184
risk factors for, 44–45
and social workers, 302–303
in Southern U.S., 296–297
women in, 200
Law, 52–53
Lazarus syndrome, 6
Leadership, 146
Legislative advocacy, 175–181
    key issues in, 175–176
    meeting with members of
        Congress for, 177–179
    and social work, 179–181
    and system fundamentals, 176
    terminology, 177
Liver damage, 19
Loneliness, 263
Long-term survivors, 262–264

M

MAI (Minority AIDS Initiative),
    271
Male circumcision, 14, 189–190
Male condoms, 23, 186
Male primary caregivers caregiv-
    ers, 319–320
Managers, social work, *see* Social
    work managers
Marianismo, 316
Marriage, 220
Masking effect, 12–13
Massachusetts, 180–181
Media, 52
Medicaid, 113, 117
Medical care, 67–68
Medicalization of HIV, 160–162
Medical status, 94
Medication:
    access to, 68, 176
    adherence to, 20, 220

advances in, 6, 16–18
preexposure prophylaxis, 188
side effects of, 19–20, 233
for treatment of older adults,
    260, 263
viral suppression with, 7
Menopause, 262
Men's groups, 129–134
Mental health and illness:
    and crisis intervention/counsel-
        ing, 96–98
    of incarcerated Latinos, 296
    of women with HIV, 205
Mental health services, 241–242
Men who have sex with men
    (MSM), *see* Gay, bisexual,
    and other men who have sex
    with men
Methadone maintenance, 96
Microbicides, 26, 187–188, 282
Mini Mental State Exam, 261
Minority AIDS Initiative (MAI),
    271
Modeling, 84
Monotherapy, 18
Motivational interviewing:
    in case management, 81
    in crisis intervention, 95,
        97–98

N

Named-based reporting, 174
National Association of Social
    Workers (NASW), 32,
    33, 301
National Center for Cultural
    Competence, 47
National Network for Social Work
    Managers, 145
National Research Council, 284
Native Hawaiians, 45
Needle-exchange programs
    (NEPs), *see* Syringe-
    exchange programs
Needs, 64
Negotiation skills, 83
New Haven City Council,
    168–169
New York State, 150
NGOs, *see* Nongovernmental
    organizations

Nongovernmental organizations
    (NGOs), 282–283
Non-nucleoside reverse transcrip-
    tase inhibitors (NNRTIs), 18
Norms, 48–53
Nucleoside/nucleotide reverse
    transcriptase inhibitors
    (NRTIs), 18

O

Occupational exposure, 15, 302
Older adults, 253–266
    assumptions made about,
        90–91
    diversity in HIV among,
        254–257
    HIV-affected, 264–265
    incidence rates of, 253–254
    long-term survivors, 262–264
    newly diagnosed, 259–262
    at risk of HIV infection,
        257–259
Oral sex, 14
Organizational management skills,
    106
Organizations, 51–52, 54. *See also*
    AIDS service organizations
Orphans, 243–244
Outpatient care, 109, 111–112
Outreach programs, 90

P

Pacific Islanders, 45
Panama, 301
Paperwork, 83
Pappaionou, M., 271
Parentification, 242
Participation, 65
Partnership, 65
Patience, 84
PCM, *see* Prevention case
    management
Peer empowerment, 241
PEP, *see* Postexposure prophylaxis
PEPFAR (President's Emergency
    Plan for AIDS Relief), 66
Perinatal transmission, 15–16,
    199, 232

Permanency planning, 136

Personalized Cognitive Risk-Reduction Counseling, 273

Photography, 127

PIs, *see* Protease inhibitors

Pneumocystis carinii pneumonia, 4

POC, *see* Point of Change

Poetry, 127

Point of Change (POC), 165–170

Policy:
  and cultural competence, 51–52
  effects of changes to, 150–151
  in human rights framework, 62–64
  and prevention, 187

Postexposure prophylaxis (PEP), 25, 302

Poverty:
  and cultural competence, 42, 49
  of gay and bisexual men, 222
  as vulnerability, 200

Power, 48–49

Preexposure prophylaxis (PrEP), 25, 188–189, 302

PrEP, *see* Preexposure prophylaxis

President's Emergency Plan for AIDS Relief (PEPFAR), 66

Prevention, 22–26, 183–193
  for African American/black communities, 273–274, 280–283
  and community organizing, 160–161
  with condom usage, 186–187, 193
  cultural competence in, 42–43
  and ethnic/racial disparities, 184
  for gay, bisexual, and other MSM, 215–218
  in human rights framework, 66–67
  importance of, 138–139
  and incidence rates, 183
  for Latino communities, 298–302
  in legislative advocacy, 175
  with male circumcision, 189–190

with microbicides, 187–188

with preexposure prophylaxis, 188–189

and sexuality, 185

testing as cornerstone of, 184

vaccines for, 190–191

for women, 204–206

Prevention case management (PCM), 78–79

Prevention counseling, 90–91

Primary infection, 9–10

Privacy, 176

Procedures, 51–52

Programs, 52

Prophylactic treatments, 10

Protease inhibitors (PIs), 6, 17–18

PRS (HIV/AIDS Prevention Research Synthesis), 273

Psychosocial assessments, 236–238

Public education campaigns, 218

Puerto Rico, 296

R

Race:
  and health care disparities, 175–176, 202
  and incarceration, 277
  of older adults with HIV, 255–256
  and prevention, 184

Racism, 94

Referrals, 81, 93

Relationships, 33, 147

Religion, 49–51, 53

Report on Orphans (Carol Levine), 243–244

Research, 52

Research on Older Adults with HIV (ROAH) study, 257, 260–262

Resistance to medication, 20

Respect, 64–65

Retirement homes, 113

Risk behaviors, 199–201

Risk-reduction counseling, 108–109

ROAH, *see* Research on Older Adults with HIV study

Ryan White Comprehensive AIDS Resources Emergency (CARE) Act, 5, 78, 149, 160, 161, 179

Ryan White HIV/AIDS Treatment Modernization Act, 5, 149, 158, 245

S

Safer sex education:
  for children and adolescents, 238–239
  and evidence-based prevention, 66–67
  for men who have sex with men, 215
  myth of increased sexual activity and, 186
  as prevention method, 22–24

Same-sex marriage, 220

"Saving face" concept, 45

Science, 175

Secondary trauma, 141

Second-tier rights, 60

Seeman, S., 273

Self-efficacy, 50

SEPs, *see* Syringe-exchange programs

Seroconversion, 10

Service delivery and planning, 80–81

Service provision, 218–221

Services, 52

Settlement house movement, 32

Sex education, *see* Safer sex education

Sexually transmitted infections (STIs), 200, 215, 302

Sexual orientation, 219, 256. *See also* Gay, bisexual, and other men who have sex with men
  and crisis intervention/counseling, 95–96
  and emergence of HIV, 4
  and prevention, 185

Sexual transmission, 12–15, 144–145
  among adolescents, 232
  testing for prevention of, 184

Sex workers, 43, 297

Shame, 46

Skill building, 82

Skilled nursing facilities (SNFs), 113

SNFs (skilled nursing facilities), 113

Social action tactics, 160

Social activism, 34

Social constraints, 275–276

Social Gerontology (N. R. Hooyman and H. A. Kiyak), 257

Social justice, 32–33, 301

Social marketing campaigns, 217–218

Social oppression, 222

Social structure, 274–276

Social support, 92, 220

Social transformation, 35–36

Social welfare, 31

Social workers, 105–109

  and assisting persons with HIV, 107–109

  general tasks of, 105–107

Social work managers, 143–147, 149–154

Societies, 52–53

Sociocognitive theory, 273

Soul Talk: Urban Youth Poetry, 127

Staff management, 151–153

Standby Guardianship Law, 136

State legislative government, 176

Stigma:

  and cultural competence, 49–50

  in health care settings, 117–118

  of Latino MSM, 294

  of MSM with HIV, 217, 219, 222

  and negative effect on health, 62

  of older adults with HIV, 260–264

  and shame, 46

  and social consequences of diagnoses, 94

  of women with HIV, 204–206

STIs, *see* Sexually transmitted infections

Strengths perspective, 35

Stress, 153, 234

Structural interventions, 300–301

Substance use:

  in black/African American communities, 318

  as co-occurring disorder, 96–98

  by older adults, 261

  in prisons, 277–278

Sumit Enhanced Peer-led interventions, 273

Support, 50–51

Sustiva, 19

Sympathia, 316

Symptomatic stage, 10

Syndemics, 213, 274

Syringe-exchange programs (SEPs):

  Detroit case study, 164–170

  as evidence-based prevention, 67

  as harm reduction technique, 96

  lack of government support for, 216, 295

  Massachusetts case study, 180–181

  and prevention, 23

T

Task management, 83

Testing:

  as cornerstone of prevention, 184

  and crisis intervention/ counseling, 91–93

  in human rights framework, 66–67

  methods of, 11–12

  of newborns, 174

Theory of planned behavior (TPB), 273–274

Theory of reasoned action (TRA), 273

Transference, 140

Transmission, 12–16. *See also specific headings*

Transportation, 79

Trauma, 139–142, 205

Treatment, 16–22

  for children and adolescents, 233

and community organizing, 160–161

cultural competence in, 42–43

for Latino communities, 298–302

U

UNAIDS, *see* Joint United Nations Programme on HIV/AIDS

Unemployment, 277–278

United Nations, 59–63, 68

U.S. Congress, 176–179

U.S. Department of Health and Human Services, 21

Universal Declaration of Human Rights, 34, 60–61, 63, 64, 66

Universality of rights, 60, 61

Urban Men's Health Study, 213

V

Vaccines, 26, 190–191

VACS (Veterans Aging Cohort Study), 260

Values, 48, 50–52

Value system, 31

Vertical transmission, 15–16

Veterans Aging Cohort Study (VACS), 260

Volunteers, 146, 151–152, 190

Voting, 178

W

Warmth, 124

Welfare, 278

Welness Model, 126

Western blot test, 11

WHO, *see* World Health Organization

Window period, 11

Witness, 36–37

Women, 199–208

  in African American/black communities, 279–282

Women (*Continued*)
  as caregivers, 315–319
  and case definition revisions, 6
  and condom use, 186, 276,
    281–282
  health care disparities of, 176,
    202–203

in history of epidemic, 199
incidence rates of, 7, 42–43,
    144, 200, 244–245
prevention and care for,
    204–206
roles and status of, 201–202
and sexual behavior norms, 49

social constraints of, 276
and stigma, 203–204
Women's groups, 126–129
World Health Organization
  (WHO), 61, 189
Worth of the person, 33